INDIA & IDENTITY
SOME REFLECTIONS

DR. FIROJ HIGH SARWAR
BISWARUP GANGULY

BLUEROSE PUBLISHERS
India | U.K.

Copyright © Dr Firoj High Sarwar & Biswarup Ganguly 2023

All rights reserved by author. No part of this publication may be reproduced, stored in a retrieval system or transmitted in any form or by any means, electronic, mechanical, photocopying, recording or otherwise, without the prior permission of the author. Although every precaution has been taken to verify the accuracy of the information contained herein, the publisher assumes no responsibility for any errors or omissions. No liability is assumed for damages that may result from the use of information contained within.

BlueRose Publishers takes no responsibility for any damages, losses, or liabilities that may arise from the use or misuse of the information, products, or services provided in this publication.

For permissions requests or inquiries regarding this publication, please contact:

BLUEROSE PUBLISHERS
www.BlueRoseONE.com
info@bluerosepublishers.com
+91 8882 898 898
+4407342408967

ISBN: 978-93-5989-833-9

Cover design: Muskan Sachdeva
Typesetting: Rohit

First Edition: December 2023

*For all those noble historians who have laid the foundation
of writing true & unbiased history of India*

Acknowledgements

Over the year this book has conceptualized, developed and culminated with the help and active support of many people. Mainly the national seminar which was held on 22nd March 2023 at our institute, Murshidabad Adarsha Mahavidyalaya (University of Kalyani), on the theme of *India and Identity in the context of History, Polity, Society and Economy* splurged us to edit this book. During this academic journey, we have received support and solidarity from many scholars and well-wishers and we presume that they know who they are. It is impossible to acknowledge them individually as the list of names is quite long. However, it will be morally injustice if we not mention the name of few who really helped a lot in this journey. I would like to begin by thanking Sri Basob Ghosh, the first person, who evoked us to edit this book. We are very grateful to our Principal Dr. Indra Kumar Mistri who continue provided us the enthusiasm and encouragement to complete this huge task. We are deeply thankful to Professor Alok Kumar Ghosh to foreword this book with his valuable thoughts and remarks. Besides we are also very grateful to Professor Md. S. N. Rahman and Dr. Kunal Debnath for providing the ideas and concepts of this book during the time of seminar. We are also thankful to our fellow colleague and college staff who have extended continuous support and advice to edit the articles. Finally, but most importantly, we are highly grateful to all the authors who have contributed a lot by providing their scholarly writings and continuous moral supports.

Foreword

Nation in India is traditionally imagined as a collection of people bound as one by the common factors such as racial ancestry of the *Aryavarta*, root language sanctified as the *devabhasha*, admission of social plurality but belief in confederation of diverse cultures and a territory historically identified as *bharatbarsha*. The colonial rulers rejected this notion of nationhood, defining it only in geo-political terms with absolute denial of popular emotions. They asserted their domination over fragmented power structure and monopolized intellectuality of the land by imposing Katherine Mayo's concept of Indian backwardness, theorized later by Edward Said as de-orientalization. The powerful center, i.e., the colonial 'we,' exploited the colonized periphery and categorized it according to their own need. Of course, the periphery obstructed with its inherited identity but the political deconstruction continued and the nationhood was polarized from the above.

At the end of the Second World War partitioned India was decolonized but by this time the concept of nationality had a sea change. In pre-colonial period *bharat* had a social notion upheld in a huge number of political states but now the social integrity was in question and politics centered round the concept of 'nation state,' a construct of the industrial Europe.

In postcolonial India the colonial 'we' were nationalized, the colonial 'they' being more peripherizd and made to believe that they were destined to be tuned with their new nation state with self-distanced societies. Social unity was now conditional with political and economic standardization and for this the theory of developmental nationalism was popularized. Developmental nationalism meant imitation of western technology and values thereof but with two rejections, one of western individuality in cultural terms and the other of the ancestral tradition.

It was, no doubt, a crisis for the national identity. The crisis was intensified in the last decades of the twentieth century by what is known as globalization through which the people were forced to interconnect their nationality with the 'others' of the global village. The obvious result was denationalization which posed the greatest threat to our citizenry. The process had a profound political and economic impact especially in its current form of uncontrolled global consumerism by which nationalism had been forcefully made consistent with the principles of neo-liberalism. The traditional socio-cultural vision of universalism (*Vasudhaevakutumbakam*) was transformed into the technical view of a single unit of the world.

Apart from structural changes in the economy and polity, life of an Indian in the globalized world has already experienced massive involution by way of living in a post-truth age when reality is created out of the unreal in the new information order. It makes us highly concerned about the future of the most important pillar of our civility – national identity. The ongoing contested process derecognizes the heredity of the territorially bound people and hence the sense of nationality may fade away in the minds of new generations, more so when state borders lose their historical sanctity in diasporic search of a global village.

The re-search for national identity, not only in macro but also in micro level, is therefore the need of the time. The present book, emerging from a national seminar and encapsuling varieties of well-written essays, searching national heredity in socio-religious psyche, scientific inquisition and even in interdependent man-woman relations, is a precious publication. It demands a wide readership.

Alok Kumar Ghosh
Head
Department of History
University of Kalyani

Preface

The term Identity is often used to understand the qualities, beliefs, personality traits, appearance or expressions that characterize a person or a group or a community or a nation. Identity formation has to do with the complex manner in which human beings establish a unique view of self and is characterized by continuity and inner unity. It is therefore highly related to terms such as the self, self-concept, values, and personality development.[1] In general, there are lot of discussions and debates on either the individual identity or collective identity of human beings in the arena of social sciences.[2] This mainly encompasses various aspects such as occupational, religious, national, ethnic or racial, gender, educational, generational, and political identities, among others.[3] Hence, this book is an effort to highlight this kind of identity issues that has been affecting and influencing India since long age.

Identity signifies how we understand and define ourselves. Our sense of identity shows our values and gives us a sense of direction and coherence. Similarly, the identity of a nation defines its people, history, culture, politics, society, economy and so on, and demonstrates its strength and the degree of unity to the world.[4] India, that is our country, is one of the oldest civilizations of the world, and it time and again has reflected its multi-cultural character. With a wide variety of regions, languages, religions, castes, classes India has travelled since remote ancient time, and crossed the border of twentieth century and entered into today's twenty-first century. All these diversified components of Indian's Identity largely help to foster a sense of oneness among the county's inhabitant.[5] In the same way, a sense of oneness may gradually emerge among groups of people who have common interest either on particular region, language, religion, caste, class or gender. All these become another kind of component of India's identity that we may call as 'Internal Identity'.[6] Apart from the national identity, the interest-based identity (viz. gender right, culture, society, politics, economy and history of races), since ancient age to till now remained a great challenge for India & Indians to be established. In terms of management of the proper distribution of economy, sustainable development, social inequalities, management of ethnic and religious diversity, India still is somehow unable to compete with the developed nations of the world. This is the main crux of the discourse of this book.

So, an Indian's identity is multifaceted, and how he or she defines himself or herself is a result of his/her ethnicity, religion, caste and social, educational, economic status. India is a diverse country with a glorious heritage.[7] One can find a beautiful amalgamation of various cultures, traditions, beliefs, and intellectual achievements here. India is a continent masquerading as a country.[8] However, it is the crux of the matter that often Indians relate more to their regional or local identity. The existence of multifarious identity like gender, linguistic, religious, regional and caste etc. often create space for conflicts and movements. The idea of oneness within the territory of India or within the framework of Indian Nationhood, therefore is in vain. For example, if you try to establish your national identity, it's a forced new thing where you cannot acknowledge your geographic and cultural roots as a proud part of India, apparently it has to be India or nothing else. Which is a total opposite of what India stands for. Hence, this book will provide us some reflections of India and diversified identities to comprehend the complexity of the subject.

The book is comprising of more than fifty articles containing the various identity issues of India. From individual identity to political, educational, economic, social, regional, national identities of various personalities, communities, gender, tribes have properly been investigated and highlighted by the reputed scholars across the country and from abroad. The book not only tells us about the issues and aspects of identities but also the historical chain of occurrences of diverse identity movements from ancient to recent days. The articles of this book can be broadly categorised into some sections. The first section comprising of the gender identity issues like the emergence of feminist personalities and the subsequent feminist writings in India. Second category comprising of struggles or movements for establishing identity, like the women in national movement, women in post independent political movement, women in Indian party politics etc. Third section comprising of the status and identities of Muslims in Mediaeval and Modern India. Next section includes those articles which talked about various known and unknown personalities of India who have influenced the history of different localities of our country. There are many articles which tried to highlight the tribal cultures of India and their distinct identities. There are some articles on the theme of Indian educational and political system which have affected the specific strata of the Indian society. The book is also providing some important writings on regional art, cultures, science and language. Besides, the linguistic, community, religious based identities, many articles talked about the international identities like political, economic and cultural variation and relationship of India with the outside world.

In recent days the struggles or conflicts for 'Identities' became the burning issues in India though these conflicts are inseparable part of Indian past. The most recent upheavals like Naxalite/Maoist movement in central India,[9] Ethnic violence in Manipur,[10] anti CAA and NRC protest among the Muslims,[11] Burkhs (veils) issues in Karnataka,[12] Barbri Masjid and the communal eviction issue in

UP,[13] the mob-lynching in north India,[14] the issues of Love-jehad,[15] the Kashmir settlement issue,[16] the tribal identity issues in Chot Nagpur platue, the ongoing feminist movements, the linguistic collision in the states, the state-central (federal) collision and the refugee issues in Assam and others areas,[17] Dalit persecution in north India etc.[18] raised the anxieties and apprehensions among the citizens of India. It is quite clear that these issues became very acute since the RSS controlled BJP led government took the central charge of India in 2014. The issues of identities became very prominent due to the concept of *Hinduttava* or *Hindu Rashtra*, which means a nation of only for upper caste Hindus, leaving all communities and caste behind as second-class citizen.[19] RSS chief Mohan Bhagwat has reportedly said that Hindutva is India's identity. We wonder what he means by the term "Hindutva" and how it is different from the religion of the Upanishads, as interpreted by Swami Vivekananda and Swami Aurobindo, both of whom the RSS projects as its icons. Swami Vivekananda said: "I shall go to the mosque of the Mohammedan; I shall enter the Christian church and kneel before the crucifix; I shall enter the Buddhist temple where I shall take refuge in Buddha and in his law; I shall go into the forest and sit down in meditation with the Hindu who is trying to see the light which enlightens the heart of everyone." It is to be noted that neither Vivekananda nor Aurobindo spoke the "them and us" language.[20] So, to check these conflicts we have to control the encroachment of *Hinduttava* ideology. This is the one way to preserve the Indian identity of *Unity in Diversity*. This would be possible if we the people like scholars try to create awareness among the mass through unbiased writings and debates. So, we should opt this situation as a great opportunity for the intellectual discourses either on national identity or on multilayered identities that many Indians desires for. Therefore, we hope that, this book will provide a scope for greater intellectual debate and discussion on India and Identities.

References

1. Schwartz, Seth J., Luyckx, Koen, Vignoles, Vivian L., eds. *Handbook of Identity Theory and Research.* Springer, New York 2011; Herman, William E. "Identity Formation", *Encyclopedia of Child Behavior and Development*, Springer US, Boston, MA, 2011, pp. 779–781.
2. Franco-Zamudio, J., Dorton, Harold. "Collective Identity", *Encyclopedia of Critical Psychology,* Springer, New York, 2014, pp. 256–259; Identity offers a way of thinking about the links between the personal and the social, that is, how the psychological and social aspects of the self are tied together to create a self-concept (Woodward, 2002)
3. Weinreich, Peter. "14: The operationalization of identity theory in racial and ethnic relations", in Rex, John; Mason, David (eds.). *Theories of Race and Ethnic Relations; Comparative Ethnic and Race Relations,* Cambridge University Press, Cambridge, 1988, pp. 299ff.
4. "The term identity comes from the Latin noun Definition", Law Insider, 2023, pp.5-30.; "Identity: Definition, Types, & Examples", The Berkeley Well-Being Institute, pp. 06-21
5. India – Unity in Cultural Diversity, NCERT, 2018
6. Parekh, Bhikhu. "Defining India's Identity," *India International Centre Quarterly*, vol. 33, no. 1, 2006, pp. 1–15
7. Burke, Peter Kivisto, Peter (ed.), "Identity", *The Cambridge Handbook of Social Theory*, Volume 2, Cambridge University Press, 2020, pp. 63–78,
8. "How to run a continent", *The Economist*, May 21, 2015
9. Gupta, Dipak K. "The Naxalites and the Maoist Movement in India: Birth, Demise, and Reincarnation." *Democracy and Security*, vol. 3, no. 2, 2007, pp. 157–88
10. Kaushik, Krishn, & Rajesh, Y. P., "Manipur: ethnic violence in the Indian state explained", *Reuters,* July 21, 2023
11. Mahmudabad, Ali Khan. "Indian Muslims and the Anti-CAA Protests: From Marginalization Towards Exclusion", *South Asia Multidisciplinary Academic Journal*, 24/25, 2020 [The Hindutva Turn: Authoritarianism and Resistance in India Open Edition Journals, Winter 2019-20]
12. "Hijab controversy: HC said that Karnataka's dress code guideline is violative of fundamental rights", *The Hindu*, February 8, 2022
13. Report "Forced Evictions in India 2021", prepared by Deepak Kumar, Anagha Jaipal, Aishwarya Ayushmaan, and Mohd Yawar, Housing and Land Rights Network, New Delhi, 2022
14. Kohli, Ishita. "Mob Lynching in India: Is the Government Doing Enough?", *Indian Journal of Law and Legal Research,* Vol. IV,

Issue. VI; Gupta, Ishan. "Mob Violence and Vigilantism in India," *World Affairs: The Journal of International Issues*, vol. 23, no. 4, 2019, pp. 152–72

15. Apoorvanand, "India's 'love jihad' laws: Another attempt to subjugate Muslims", *ALJAZEERA,* 15 January, 2021
16. "Kashmir issue one of Modi govt's biggest failures: Congress", *Times of India*, June 17, 2018; "Has India's Kashmir policy under Modi failed?", *ALJAZEERA*, 15 June 2022
17. Dutta, Antara, "Bordering Assam Through Affective Closure: 1971 And the Road to The Citizenship Amendment Act Of 2019", *Asian Affairs*, Volume 53, 2022; Das, Bhargabi. "NRC, 'Jatiyotabaad' and Citizenship Crisis in Assam", *South Asia Multidisciplinary Academic Journal:* 30, 2023; Ghoshal, Anindita. "The journey from "migration certificate" to "citizenship card": Livelihood, demography and changing identities in post-1947 Assam", *South Asia Multidisciplinary Academic Journal:* 36, 2020, pp. 73-90
18. Hanchinamani, Bina B., "Human Rights Abuses of Dalits in India", *Human Rights Brief,* Vol. 8, Issue. 2, 2001, pp. 15-29
19. Varshney, Ashutosh. "Contested Meanings: India's National Identity, Hindu Nationalism, and the Politics of Anxiety," *Daedalus*, vol. 122, no. 3, 1993, pp. 227–61
20. *The Hindu,* August 18, 2014

Contents

Acknowledgements ....*iv*
Foreword .... *v*
Preface ....*vii*

1. **Emergence of Indian Diaspora: A Historical Review** 1
   Dr. Indra Kumar Mistri

2. **Muslim Women in India: Political Participation and Challenges** 10
   Md Jamirul Islam

3. **Gender Identity in Contemporary India: A Case Study of Transgender** 20
   Benazir Rahaman

4. **Religion and Society in India: A Historical Perspective** 32
   Alampik Debbarma

5. **Anti-CAA and NRC Movement in India: A Means of Making Identity of Muslim Women** 45
   Jisan Sarowar & Dr. Sawpna Khatun

6. **Ethnography of Brass Casting Technology of Koitara in Burdwan District: A Traditional Metal Casting Identity of Bengal** 60
   Milan Chandra Roy

7. **Women Empowerment: Perspective of Political Participation in India (1950-2019)** 79
   Dr. Bikash Das

8. **Function of Political Parties in Modern Democracy: A Study of India** 91
   Animesh Chowdhury & Sujoy Pal

9. Indigenous Scientist and the Struggle for Identity in Colonial India 105
   Mohiuddin Shaikh

10. Western Sciences in Colonial India: An identity of Modernity... 120
    Ersad Ali

11. Sir Mohammad Azizul Huque: A Charismatic Muslim Man of Bengal 128
    Dr. Kutubuddin Biswas

12. Islam and the Quest for National Identity: A Critical Study... 141
    Kamal Hasan

13. Bodo Language: A Case of Fading Identity 150
    Anusree Kundu

14. The Local Dialects of Murshidabad: A Study of Distinct Linguistic Identities............................ 172
    Tawsif Ahmed

15. Queer Liberation and Assimilation in India: Navigating Historical Contexts and Contemporary Challenges 181
    Swakshadip Sarkar

16. Forest and Tribal Life of Central India: Interpreting Manoranjan Byapari's Novel Annya Bhuban 194
    Ismail Sarkar

17. Social Philosophy of Indigenous Kurmi (Kudmi) Community of India 205
    Dr. Dhananjoy Mahato

18. Status of Women and The Women's Liberation Movement in Nineteenth Century India: A Historical Analysis 216
    Manas Kumar Das

19. Sir Syed Ahmad: Plural Identity of India with its Relevance in Modern Times 226
Md Sohel Mondal

20. Hindutva in the Post-Truth Era: Electoral and Non-Electoral Narratives 237
Reshmi Biswas & Suranjana Mitra

21. Negative Identity of Indian Party Politics: A Study 251
Biplab Mondal

22. Amavati Ritual: A Mass Cultural Identity of Chotonagpur Region 261
Santosh Mahato

23. Exploring the Role of Women's Print Media in the Indian Nationalist Movement: A Study of Select Women's Magazines in Colonial India................... 267
Obaidul Hoque

24. Politics of Identity and Recognition of the Adivasis of North Bengal.. 280
Raja Lohar

25. Gopalchandra Chakraborty in the Light of Aurobindo Ghosh's Spirituality: A New Direction to the Ushagram Development Center............................ 290
Tonmoy Dey

26. Female Characters of Vyasa's Mahabharata: A Study on Motherhood in Ancient Indian History 303
Shantanu Das

27. Contemporary Communal and Identity Politics in India: An Evaluation from Historical Perspective.... 312
Nandita Das

28. Exploring the Secularism of India: A Historical and Contemporary Analysis 324
Md Hashim Saikh & Ibrahim Sk

29. The Pioneer of Duars' Education System Sri Satyendra Prasad Roy: A Review 337
Soumyadipta Sinha

30. Democratic Decentralization & Good Governance in India: A Comparative Study 345
Prasanta Adhikary

31. India-Myanmar Bilateral Relations: A Historical Analysis and Future Prospects 358
Md Rajibul Islam

32. The Role of Internet and Mass-Media in the Transformation of Bengali Culture: An Overview ... 373
Papia Biswas

33. Women from the Pit of Subjugation to the Sunrise of Freedom: Rokeya Begum Shakhawat Hossain, B. Amma and Khairunnesha 382
Arindam Mandal

34. Post-Modern Feminist Authors of Indian and Their Feminism Conscience of Composing: A Study 395
Md Manzar Reza

35. The Covid-19 Pandemic: Impact on Accredited Social Health Activist (Asha) Workers in Darjeeling District 404
Yangji Tamang

36. Physical Features and Settlement of Coochbehar: A Distinct Geographical Identity of West Bengal 411
Md Ajijur Rahaman

37. Identity Formation of Women in Ancient India: A Review 422
Pipasa Kundu

38. Bengal to the Outside World: The Role of Sultan
    Ghiyas Uddin Azam Shah 432
    Md Sk Maruf Azam

39. Basanti Devi: A Woman Activist of Manbhum's
    Quit India Movement 441
    Tapas Mahato

40. Challenges Towards Muslims Political Identity
    in India in 21st Century 448
    Dr. Md Zaharul Hoque

41. The Story of Anurupa Devi: Woman's Struggle
    for Self-Identity Through the Idea of Creation 456
    Mousumi Singha

42. Murshidabad During Anti-Partition & Swadeshi
    Movement: A Study 472
    Prosenjit Das

43. Feminism - Voice of 'Others' in Indian Perspectives 482
    Ramkrishna Das

44. Indian Public Library: A Gateway Towards
    Women Empowerment 490
    Chinmoy Ghosh

45. Computer and Teacher of Higher Secondary
    Education: A Study of New India 501
    Dr. Tafajul Hoque

46. Lifelong Learning and Rapid Social Change:
    A New Identity of India 509
    Saidul Islam & Md Kawsar Hossain

47. Role of Educational Technology in Shaping
    Indian Society 525
    Binita Bhakat

48. Development of Education and Knowledge System in
    Medieval Bengal: A Survey of 13th to 16th Century 532
    Gopal Singha

49. Three Distinguished Women of British Indian:
    Kadambini Ganguli, Sarala Devi Chowdhury &
    Matangini Hazra 548
    Namrata Dutta

50. Limitation of Women's Participation in Indian
    Politics: A Political Survey 559
    Priya Dutta

51. Feminism and Intersectionality in India:
    Challenges and Opportunities 569
    Rajarshi Maity

52. Mahasweta Devi's Draupadi: A Historical
    Perspective and the Role of the State 582
    Sukanta Barman

Authors' Identity *596*

Emergence of Indian Diaspora: A Historical Review

Dr. Indra Kumar Mistri

The term Diaspora has Greek origin and is used to refer to the mass movement of Jews away from the homeland. Now we understand that Diaspora refers to the people living away from their homeland due to various reasons, which in turn, directly or indirectly, brought the issues of identities. Hence the 'Indian Diaspora' refer to the people or group of people who are living outside India and those who can trace their origin to India. Indians have been migrating out of India for centuries, but the settlement of Indians abroad started taking place rather concretely only during the colonial period. Thus, migration out of India can be seen in four phases: ancient, medieval, colonial and postcolonial period. The ancient and medieval Indian monarchs and traders from the East and West coast of India who tried to reach out and establish contacts with the Middle-East, eastern and northern Africa and with southeast Asia. The ancient Indian emigration can also be traced back to the time of Emperor Ashoka when he attacked Kalinga. It was further followed by the progressive steps of Samudragupta towards Southeast Asia, when a large number of Brahmins migrated to the Southeast Asia for their willing purposes of the cultural growth. They were called as Cholas.[1] During the medieval period, the Indian diaspora was mainly connected with trade and employment. From the beginning of the 16th century to the middle of the 20th century the lively Caravan trade which had previously defined much of India's commercial relationship with its neighbors to the North and West, was augmented by the commercial activities of thousands of Indian diaspora merchants. The Mughal emperor Babur wrote in his

Baburnama that 10 to 20000 Indian merchants annually travelled in caravans to Kabul where they met with other caravans coming from Kashgar, Farghana Turkistan Bukhara Balkh Hisar and Badakhshan.[2] In 1584 Hafiz Tanish wrote his *Sharafnama-i-Shahi* that the presence of several caravans in Peshawar which had originated in the Deccan, Gujarat, Multan and regions of India.[3] In the 19th century immigration occurred of the labouring population to plantation territories of the colonial world. This immigration from India is also included traders and white-collar workers to the British Dutch and French colonies. In this period the Indian merchant communities migrated to South Africa, America, Sri Lanka, Australia England, Burma et cetera countries, who had originated in Deccan, Gujarat, Bengal, Punjab and other regions of India.

The term diaspora is derived from a Greek word meaning dispersion. It was used by the Jewish people after the fall of Jerusalem in the 6th century BCE. It denoted their worldwide dispersion out of their homeland, the land of Israel. In Hebrew it was called Golah or Galut, meaning exile. Since, the Jewish people refused to assimilate and were confronted with repression, they moved out of Israel.[4] The Jewish survived due to migration, adaptation to the new countries and clung to their fate and traditions. Migration also extended the boundaries of the Jewish diaspora. The model of Jewish diaspora was followed by the Armenian, Chinese, African slavery and Indian communities. The difference with the Jewish diaspora is that Indian communities have been dispersed owing to their chosen countries of migration. The origin of the Indian diaspora has always been the regional social structures of the immigrants and migrants. On the basis of regional cultures and languages of Europe, Indians created their Bengali, Punjabi and Telugu diaspora. The Indian diaspora is closely linked to India's trade links and can be stretched back nearly 4 millionaires when the Indus valley civilization traded with ancient Mesopotamians and Egyptians. From 500 to 1600 AD, trade again was the foundation on which a sizable Indian diaspora developed across the Indian Ocean, rises from Zanzibar and Egypt in the west to Yemen and Oman in the Arabian Peninsula to the Arakan and Malacca in the far East.[5]

At present time the term diaspora has been frequently used to characterize people existing away from their homeland. Now we shall try to understand the contemporary meaning of the term diaspora. Many scholars believe that the term diaspora once described the Jewish Greek and Armenian dispersion, now shares meaning with a larger semantic domain that includes words like immigrant expatriate, refugee, guest workers, exiled community, overseas community and ethnic community. Walker Connor has more broadly defined in his essay "the impact of homelands upon diaspora", that segment of people living outside the homeland.[6] Also, we define that any group of people living beyond the boundary of its perceived homeland has enhanced the terms utility for the emerging discipline of transnational studies by facilitating comparative studies and providing new topics of enquiry and a model for understanding such phenomena.

The original signification of the word diaspora can be traced from the Greek diaspora derived from the combination of dia - meaning over and speiro- to sow, as in scattering or planting. The term was probably first used in the third century BCE by the Greek speaking Jews in reference to their exile from the holy land and dispersion among the Gentiles in the 16th century BCE.[7] In this context the term refers to a situation in which a number of communities sharing a common national religious or ethnic identity exist apart from a common homeland. The term also implies that overtime, the communities maintain their district identity despite their existence as a minority living in a host society. A diaspora community may avoid assimilation through continued identification with a socio religious system other than that of the host society. The maintenance of residence in a communal settlement separates from the host society, economical specialization and the pursuit of bilateral relations with similar geographically dispersed diaspora communities. The diaspora can most generally be divided into the categories of provocation and attraction. Briefly, factors which would provoke the formation of a diaspora include society, economy or political coercion which motivate groups of people to leave their homeland in search of improved opportunities elsewhere, need to be discussed here. They are called victim diaspora. All those, who have migrated to a region promising greater recompense for their labour they are called labour diaspora, and where they may be in a position to pursue lucrative commercial endeavors involving the mediation of cross-cultural trade, they are called merchant diaspora. From the beginning of the 16 century to the middle of the 19th century the lively Caravan trade which had previously defined much of India's continuous relationship with its neighbors to the north and West augmented by the commercial activities of thousands of Indian diaspora merchants.[8] During the reign of Mughals, thousands of Indian merchant annually travelled in Caravan to Kabul where they meet with other caravans coming from Kasgarh, Fargana, Turkistan, Samarkand, Bukhara, Balkh, Hisar and Badakhshan. Besides, several Caravan in Peshawar which had originated in the Deccan Gujarat Multan and other region of India and where transporting goods designed for Khurasan and Turkistan. Weather these merchants travelled in Turan themselves or exchanged their commodities in the Frontier markets of Afghanistan and returned to India these accounts suggest a strong Indo Turanian commercial relation. The Indian community in 19th century in Central Asia, the Indian merchants would generally stay in Turan for 2 or 3 years to conduct the trade. Thirty merchants were operating in concordance with the standard diaspora technique of latter years. The emergence and development of the Indian merchant diaspora in Turan in the years following the establishment of the Mughal Empire.[9]

In the 19th century the British traveler G T Vigne reported that the Lohania Powindar, (an Afghan nomadic community, who were involved in Indo Turanian trade) had participated in India's northwestern trance regional trade by incorporating commercial venture and the transportation of bulk commodities in their annual migration between North India and Turan.[10] As Lohaniya tradition they had been active in the transit trade between Hindustan and Kabul since Gajnavids granted them the territory of Derabandh in the 11th century and that since the time of Babar Lohaniya Caravan had been engaged in the transportation of various commodities between Bukhara, the major Afghan commercial centers and Hyderabad, Kolkata, Banaras, Delhi, Jaipur and other large cities of India.[11] In the decade of 1830 a Kashmiri born British intelligence agent named Mohan Lal and his companion a British explorer and agent, Alexander Burnes came across a merchant involved in India's northwestern trans regional trade also identified as Darya Khan Lohani. Mohanlal reported that Lohani and Shikurpuri merchants dominated the mediatory trade between Bukhara and Multan and that, were it not for these merchants, Multan would not become the rival of the markets of Hindustan, Punjab and Khorasan. A huge number of the diaspora was composed of Hindu merchants who belong to a number of mercantile oriented castes engaged in trans-regional trade, brokering or money lending and who in some accounts are collectively referred to as 'Baniyas' or Baniyans, which means the people of Indian origin. There are twelve countries which host over 1 million Indians each, with four of them being home to over 2 million Indians each.[12]

In the beginning of the 17th century, Indian merchants spread northward from Iran into the Caucasus and neighboring Russia where they established a rather significant diaspora community in Astrakhan port which is the Caspian Sea port on the mouth of the Volga and a Russian possession since 1556. Although in some 19th century literature, the term Bania refers to a specific caste affiliation.[13] In earlier literature it is used more generally and referred to an individual or group of individuals whose economic activities focused on commerce only. The Bania communities operated the trading networks from several commercial centers throughout Gujarat, Sindh, Punjab, Rajasthan and the Indus basin, but Multan was the primary focal point on their northwestern trade. In 1976 Tavernier similarly reported that Multan is the place from where all the Banyas migrated who come to trade in Persia where they follow the same occupation as the Jews.[14] One of the most important merchant communities of early modern India was Hindu Khatri caste. The Khatris played an increasingly important role in India's trance-regional trade under the Mughal Empire.

In the 19th century, when the European powers consolidated their claims across Asia, a bright May summer morning in 1879 witnessed the first Indians setting foot in Fiji, destined for work in the sugarcane plantation. A large scale of cash crop plantation in Guyana, Suriname and Trinidad and Tobago -much like Fiji became profitable on the backs of indentured Indian labours. People of Indian origin now constitute 42% of Fiji's population. Similarly, Indian contribution workers from the Punjab laid the East African Railway railway across modern Kenya, Uganda and Tanzania. In the 20th century, Indian independence brought to the fore a new generation of Indians living and working abroad. Large number of Indians moved to Western Europe to fill post war labour shortages in the decades of 1940s and the decade of 1950s. The oil rush in the Middle East around the same decades saw thousands of Indians from the southern states moving to take up maid and low-level jobs in the petroleum sector. In the decade of 1960s too saw the immigration of a new class of Indians especially to the United States. Indian engineers and entrepreneurs, finding the Indian socialist government stifling and with not enough jobs for their qualification, made their way to the US which was then welcoming academic talents and offering a better lifestyle. Now in the 21st century Indians live in over 140 countries across the globe.[15] While some identify themselves as the first-generation non-resident Indians, others, whose forefathers had emigrated are making it easy for the Indian diaspora to return to India is the first step, making them feel at home is next with thousands of Indians. Now returning annually addressing concerns specific to their community in an urgent requirement as author Salman Rushdi said about his diaspora status "sometimes we feel we straddle two cultures at other times that we fall between stools". The Indian diaspora developed gradually during the 19th and 20th century when immigration of indenture and contract labourers, traders and professional, students took place to the British French Dutch and Portuguese colonies in Asia Africa Caribbean and the far eastern countries. At present times the government has laid a strong foundation by making diplomacy people centric with governments constant interaction with the bridge between their nation and India where they can grow simultaneously for betterment of their citizens.

This chapter can be concluded that to become a part of the Indian diaspora in their respective countries, Indians have gone through the process of migration, settlement and formation of organized associations to guard their identity and to fight against discrimination and using the force of diasporic Identity and ethnicity to realize their demands. Having achieved their goals to protect and maintain their identity they are integrated into the system of the European host societies with the help of the Government of India and the global Indian association of the GOPIO (Global Organization of People of Indian Origin).[16] They have become a part of the Indian diaspora and have extended their cultural boundaries. having lived in the European countries in the ethnic multi-cultural society and given their direct integration with the host society, their awareness of Identity has become distinct and very much visible. It is noticed that the Indian diaspora are mainly two groups: intellectuals or businessmen and skilled or semi-skilled workers. The businessmen have been closely connected to the Indian missions, and the workers have been ignored by both groups. They have received moral support from the PIOs (People of Indian Origin). India is their cultural, religious and spiritual home and has a seminal influence in sustaining their identity. The Ugandan and Afghani Indians have lost their home and they want to have a link with India but they are not invited by the Indian Mission. Patriotism, loyalty and belongingness have become fluid emotional terms of 'apon lok' 'apon Sanskriti' and 'apon mulk' in reality express Indianness.[17] The Indian diaspora identity has been advocated by the associations, religious centers and friends. It is an imaginary identity but has become visible with the use of the force of ethnicity. This migration sometimes led towards the issues of identity crisis.

References

1. Dwivedi, Sunil Kumar. "A Conceptual Framework of Indian Diaspora", The Creative Launcher, vol. 7, no. 6, 2022, pp. 66-74
2. Babur, *Baburnama* (Memories of Babur), translated by A. S. Beverage from Turky to English, Vol. I, 1921-22, pp. 20-22
3. Goutam, M.K., *Indian Diaspora: Ethnicity and Diasporic Identity*, CARIM-India Research Report 2013/29, ICM, Unit II, 2013, pp 5-6
4. Ibid. p.15
5. Brahmachari, Akash, *Indian Council of Global Relation*, Gateway House, 2011. pp 20-22
6. Levi, Scott C., *The Indian Diaspora in Central Asia and it's Trade*, Boston, 2002, p86
7. Ibid., p.94
8. Op. cit., Baburnama, pp. 20-22
9. Habib, Irfan, *An Atlas of the Mughal Empire*, Oxford University Press, Delhi, 1986, p. 3
10. See for details: Vigne, G. T. "Outline of a Route Through the Panjáb, Kábul, Kashmír, and into Little Tibet, in the Years 1834-8". *Journal of the Royal Geographical Society of London*, Volume 9, 1 January 1839
11. Op. cit., Habib, I. p 68
12. Op. cit., Brahmachari A., pp 61-65
13. Bania (also spelled Baniya, Banija, Banya, Vaniya, Vani, Vania and Vanya) is a Vaishya caste mainly from the Indian states of Gujarat and Rajasthan, with strong diasporic communities in Uttar Pradesh, Madhya Pradesh, West Bengal, Maharashtra (mainly Mumbai) and other northern states. Traditionally, the main occupations of the community are merchants, bankers, money-lenders, and (in modern times) owners of commercial enterprises.
14. Op. Cit., Goutam M.K., p 31
15. Jain, R. K., *South Indians on the Plantation Frontiers in Malaya*, New Haven, Yale University Press, 1970, p. 48
16. Morris, H.S., *The Indians in Uganda: Caste and Sect in a Plural Society*, Anthony C. Hall, Bookseller, UK, 1968, p.38
17. Op. Cit., Goutam M.K., p 38

Muslim Women in India: Political Participation and Challenges

Md Jamirul Islam

India is the largest democracy in the world with the largest population. A democratic political system refers to a system of government where citizens from all backgrounds can participate and exercise power by voting. A democratic political system can be stronger and healthier if there is an effective participation of people from all sections of society irrespective of caste, gender, and religion. In Indian politics, it is found that the participation of women is lower and limited as compared to men. Historically in India, women are treated as weaker, politically, socially, and economically and they have very limited opportunities to participate in politics. Political Participation of Muslim Women in India is a matter of concern. This chapter is an attempt to study the participation of Muslim women in Indian politics. Muslim women in India can be found as one of the disadvantaged and weaker sections of society. Muslim women are victims and discriminated against both as women and as a member of minority communities. Muslims are the largest minority community in India. Muslim women need to have more participation in politics through their representatives in the parliament not only to address some specific issues related to women but also to mark their own identity in Indian politics.

Women's roles have been historically been confined to the homes in Islamic Countries which has restricted and posed challenges for female leaders. Muslim women in India have lagged in socioeconomic, political and educational attainment and consequently in the process of modernization as compared to women of other communities. They are the most disadvantaged, impoverished and marginalized in the political field. Unlike other women, they face triple discrimination and oppression as women, as members of minority communities. Muslim women have to face crossfire at various levels. Tragedy and dilemma are the two main issues of their existence. At times they become subject to people who wish to protect them and at other times they face oppression from those who wish to liberate them. They are told that politics is a dirty field. It is not meant for women. It is also said women should be confined to their homes in veils. Participation of Muslim women in the Parliament has always been an issue. Only 16 Muslim women could make it to the Parliament in 70 years. In this male-dominated society, women have the upbringing and the way she brought up with a sense that she is not meant for politics. Women from Muslim Community are not allowed to go out. They are restrained a lot for everything. If few Muslim women can contest elections or participate in politics they will lose because no one would vote for them. Representation of Muslim women in the Parliament is as low as 0.7%. Our country has always been male-dominated. Despite having reserved seats for women in our country men take all the benefits and control women from behind. Women have no say nor do they take any decision. Today in India, contesting elections is difficult for minorities, especially for Muslim women. As of 2019, 24 out of 29 states have no Muslim women representation in the parliament. The presence of Muslim women in the parliament will be a big help to Muslim women. Their generations will gain and the entire community atmosphere will improve.

The holy book Quran places a strong emphasis on gender equality and Muslim women are expected to fulfil a variety of duties and responsibilities in society: *"And [as for] the believers, both men and women - they are friends and protectors of one another: they enjoin the doing of what is right and forbid the doing of what is wrong, and are constant in prayer, and render the purifying dues, and pay heed unto God and His apostle. It is they upon whom God will bestow His grace: verily, God is almighty, wise." (Holly Quran, Verse No. 9:71)*. This verse demonstrates that women and men should be equal and women are expected to enjoy the rights and play active roles in society rather than only a passive one. They have collective responsibilities to their social, political, and educational spheres as well and they are also equal in religious practices. The Quran addresses the issue of women giving the *bai'ah* to Prophet Muhammad and God tells Muhammad (PBUH) to accept the pledge of the women: *"O Prophet! Whenever believing women come unto thee to pledge their allegiance to thee...then accept their pledge of allegiance." (Holly Quran, Surah al Mumtahana: 12 verse)*

In Islam, women are permitted to occupy political office. There are no verses in the Quran that forbid women from taking leadership roles. As long as they are not doing so at the expense of their greater obligations of raising and caring for their families, there is nothing in the authentic sources of Islam that prohibits women from running for political offices if they are confident in their knowledge and credentials to make a difference. Islam regards a woman's function as a mother as the highest obligation she can ever carry out; nothing else can take its place. This must always be emphasized. There is nothing in Islam, however, that would prevent women from playing this important function provided her involvement in politics did not get in the way of it.

The parliamentary system of government is established by the Indian Constitution. It protects citizens' rights to vote, free expression, the right to gather and join organizations, and the right to be elected. The Indian constitution prohibits discrimination based on sex and class to address gender disparity. Every citizen in the country, including men and women from all castes, faiths, tribes, educational backgrounds, and economic circumstances, is recognized as equal under the Indian Constitution. Some of the following clauses in the constitution are included in this recognition of equality. First, everyone is treated equally by the law. Everyone is required to abide by the same laws, even the President of the nation and domestic workers. Second, no one is allowed to be treated unfairly because of their gender, race, caste, place of birth, or religion. Third, all public spaces, playgrounds, and hotels are open to everyone. All persons are welcome to use the public roads, Ghats, and wells.

It is widely believed that Muslim women's status is often perceived to be extremely weak in both Indian society and polity. Muslim women's political status is insufficient even though they live in a "Sovereign Socialist Secular Democratic Republic" with equality of opportunity and status as its stated goal. However, they are hardly ever represented in governance throughout the country. There are some disturbing statistics about the political participation of Muslim women in India while looking at past data:

1. Around 612 women have been elected to 16 Lok Sabha since independence; of these, about 21 are Muslim women. Only four out of the 543 current Lok Sabha members, or 0.7%, are Muslim women, even though 6.9% of the general population is Muslim. In the upper house of the parliament in 2020, women held more than 10% of the seats.

2. There are 13 constituencies in India where Muslims make up more than 40% of the population, in addition, there are 14 Lok Sabha seats where Muslims constitute the majority. Muslims account for more than 20% of the population in 101 seats in total.

3. India's 2019 elections saw a record number of women politicians in the lower house of the parliament. 78 were elected, or 14% of the Legislative body. But it didn't progress across the board. The lower house representation of Muslim women went way down, from four to just one.

4. The picture is not much different at the state level. Less than 8% of women are represented in the state Assemblies all over Indian state. So far as states are concerned, of 29 states and 7 Union Territories only three states are headed by women as chief Ministers, but none of them is a Muslim woman. Out of the Governors and Lt. Governors/ Administrators of 29 states and seven Union Territories, only two are women, but there is no Muslim Woman.

5. Of the approximately 36 Lok Sabha Committees currently in existence, only three are led by women, and none of them are led by Muslim women. Similarly, none of the 12 Standing Committees in Rajya Sabha are now led by a Muslim woman.

6. Of the 16 Lok Sabha We never saw a Muslim woman as the speaker and in Rajya Sabha, no Muslim woman occupied the post of Chairman. Of the eighteen times deputy chairman's posts in Rajya Sabha saw four occasions when a Muslim woman was the incumbent.

Muslim women experience suffering on three different levels: as Muslims, as members of a backward minority, and as citizens of a community without leaders. Muslim women need to be informed of the fundamental freedoms and legal protections offered by the Indian constitution.

To understand the reasons for the low political participation of Muslim Women in India it very essential to examine the causes of the backwardness of Muslim women compared to the women of other religious communities in social, economic, cultural, and political fields. The fact that Muslims are a minority in India further deters them from embracing modern culture and ideals. They were wary of adopting a democratic culture out of concern about identity loss and, with the support of their religious leaders, they preserved old practices and traditions. This mentality hurt the advancement of Muslim women. Their overall standing and contribution to social and economic domains like banking, public services, education, politics and other public sector enterprises are terrible. The backwardness of the Muslim community hinders the advancement of its women, who have a much bigger impact on the political socialization of their offspring.

In India, Muslim women are among the most vulnerable groups. Most of them are uneducated, unskilled, and constrained by cultural and religious norms. The much-discussed Sachar Committee Report (2005) cited several signs of the backward state of Muslims in India. According to this analysis, Muslims' socioeconomic laggardness is to blame for Muslim women's regressive status and the primary factor contributing to the low participation in politics of Muslim women. This is primarily due to socioeconomic rather than theological causes, such as poverty, low wages, low rates of literacy, and insufficient employment opportunities. This article claims that Muslims are not just the victims of poverty but also appear to have adopted a fatalistic outlook and silently accepted inequity and discrimination as a part of life.

In a study by Sabiha Hussain titled "The Changing Half: A Study of Indian Muslims," it was discovered that other structural and institutional paradigms, such as customs, traditions, moral systems, patriarchy, the misunderstanding of Islamic principles, a lack of self-initiative or inspiration, and a lack of support, outweighed religious factors as being alone responsible for low participation in politics. The other finding of this study reveals that Muslim men in India are also responsible for Muslim women's poor participation in politics.

According to Azim (1997), Muslim women's levels of modernism and backwardness are on par with those of their counterparts in other civilizations' various income brackets. As the two issues cannot be separated, it is necessary to examine the many economic and sociological issues faced by Muslims about the issues posed by the general underdevelopment and poverty of the Indian population. Furthermore, it has been claimed that Muslim women's backwardness is due to the lack of a sophisticated culture in the community as a whole, clearly implying that Islam has not intervened to help them. However, it can be misleading to generalize about the overall condition of women by ignoring the underlying issue of class difference.

Acute poverty and economic dependence of Muslim women in India affect their political participation. Lack of proper educational facilities and unemployment alienate them from modern education, and for this very reason, they are very much unaware of governance, politics and the decision-making process. In India, the educational marginalization of Muslim women makes them isolated from modern education and that affects their political participation.

Muslim women suffer more because of the patriarchal nature of Indian society and because of the conservative and orthodox attitude of their religion toward them which does not give sufficient freedom and chances to access politics. The practice of the purdah system among Indian Muslim women and the lack of separate educational institutions, especially for women with all requirements in the locality, are the key factors for their political backwardness. Another important factor is the unawareness of Muslim men about the importance of the political participation of women for their upliftment in society.

Indian Patriarchal societies and their people believe that women's real place is to remain at home i.e., to serve the family and to give birth to children. Many Muslim women are religiously conservative and that makes them alienated from politics than other women of different religious groups because of this gender inequality and discrimination arise. Many Muslim women are no longer allowed to practice their political rights. The poor position in politics of Indian Muslim women cannot improve unless special cognizance aids and schemes are provided. Although many special schemes have been adopted by the government of India for women in general, i.e., reservation in local self-government for women, they do not cover all women from every religion and the overall result falls short of expectations for Muslim women.

Due to their low political participation, Muslim women still have a long way to go before they can be guaranteed political empowerment. Although Muslims have their own political parties and pressure groups, Muslim men hold positions of authority far more frequently than Muslim women. There are several obstacles, such as illiteracy, cultural standards, economic reliance, misogyny, a feudal system, poverty, Islamic laws, etc. Even if they are prepared to engage in politics, cultural and religious taboos prevent them from speaking for themselves in that arena. Only Muslim women who have a solid economic foundation and significant public exposure represent themselves in politics. The patriarchal nature of society is the primary cause of Muslim women's poor political participation. Our customs and society perceive women's involvement in politics as a challenge to the traditional roles of wife, domestic worker, etc. for women. Muslim women have been subjugated and depowered by patriarchal values. The majority of Muslim women are seen as housewives who take care of the family, and their male counterparts share this opinion. They prefer that their ladies be subordinate to them and stay out of politics. There are various approaches to encourage Muslim women to get involved in politics, including raising political knowledge and awareness, developing leadership skills, using affirmative action, educating Muslim women, changing one's values, etc. and lastly the most important is to preserve the identity and culture Muslim women need active participation in politics. Women should learn about politics; they should not only be used as voters but as agents of social change.

References

1. Government of India, Towards Equality; Report of the Committee on the Status of Women in India, 1974
2. Husain, Sabiha, *The Changing Half: A Study of Indian Muslim Women*. Classical Publishers, New Delhi, 1998
3. Ahmad Wani, S. & Aaqib Qadri, S., "*Perspectives on the Status of Muslim Women in India: Prospects and Challenges*," *Cape Comorin: An International Multidisciplinary Double-Blind Peer-reviewed Research Journal*, Special Issue, Volume II, Issue VI, November 2020
4. Azam, S., *Muslim women: Emerging Identity,* Rawat Publication, Jaipur, 1997
5. Basant, R., "Social, economic and educational conditions of Indian Muslims", *Economic and Political Weekly*, March 2007
6. Hasan, Z., & Menon, R., *Unequal citizens: A study of Muslim women.* Oxford University Press, New Delhi, 2004
7. Mohammad, A., *Indian Muslim issues and perceptions.* Brown Book Publication, New Delhi, 2015
8. Siddiqui. M., *Muslims in India issues & challenges.* Abadi Publication, New Delhi, 2011
9. Udin, N., "Muslim minority exclusion and development issues: Need for inclusive policy", *International Journal of Multidisciplinary Research*, Vol. 2, Issue. 1, 2012
10. Charles, Rhea, "Muslim Women in Indian Politics." *Indian School of Democracy*, June 15, 2021
11. Rahman, F. N., "An Islamic Perspective on Women in the Political System", *Islamic Research Foundation International,* 2012

12. Kutty. A., in a response to a query can a Muslim women run for political office? 2004
13. George Dimitrov, B.E., and Nongkynrih, N. "A study on Muslim Women Political Participation in India", *International Journal of Research,* Vol.4, Issue. 9, August 2017, pp.41-54
14. Lateef, Shahida. *Muslim women in India: Political and private realities*, Kali for Women, 1990

Gender Identity in Contemporary India: A Case Study of Transgender

Benazir Rahaman

Violence and discrimination on the basis of gender have a long-aged roots in India. Violence and discrimination against transgender people are two important issues. A person who identifies as transgender is one whose gender identity differs from their sex at birth. From the moment of their birth, their gender behaviour or identity do not correspond with their biological sex. They experience more prejudice and violence than people of other genders since they have been the most forgotten, neglected, and marginalized groups in Indian society. This essay offers a thorough analysis of the gender identity-related problems in India. It looks at the complex interactions between cultural practices, societal expectations, and legal frameworks that affect how people of all gender identities, particularly those who identify as transgender and non-binary, experience the world. The writing goes into more detail about the difficulties these communities confront and makes some potential solutions for achieving greater inclusivity and equality.

With its diverse sociocultural fabric, India offers a special environment for the investigation of gender identities. *Hijras* or other way the third-gender communities serve as historical examples of the nation's acceptance of non-binary identities, which contrasts sharply with the current reality of prejudice, marginalization, and violence these people must contend with.[1] This essay focuses on the difficulties and potential solutions in an effort to comprehend the complexities of gender identities in India. The Supreme Court of India issued a landmark decision on April 15, 2014. The third sex, a visible category outside of the biologically polarized characteristics of male and female, was officially recognized by India's top court. The Indian Supreme Court made the following observations as a required corrective step toward securing social justice for all,

...recognizing transgenders as third gender, this Court is not only upholding the rule of law but also advancing justice to the class, so far deprived of their legitimate natural and constitutional rights. It is, therefore, the only just solution which ensures justice not only to transgenders but also justice to the society as well.[2]

The transgender community applauds the decision as a significant step toward their acknowledgment as citizens and members of modern India. But one of the things that distinguishes this ruling as "historic" is the fact that it not only acknowledges the third sex but also the diversity of modern India. The move from a monolithic idea of the nation to an increasingly plural nationhood is obvious as India is still "imagined" and national identities are still being created in the twenty-first century. The Supreme Court of India's decision is the first significant institutional step towards the acceptance of a variety of sexual identities and has dealt a severe blow to the heteronormative sexual binary of the male and female. Regarding their sexual identity, transgender individuals (hijras) are a minority in India. They are excluded from society and have little to no access to citizenship rights. It is a fallacy and a misconception that they possess the ability to bestow blessings on joyous occasions; this may be the only interaction they have with 'regular' people on a social level. On other times, they can be observed robbing train cars while maintaining a strong performative edge. All of these have led to a relatively unfavourable perception of hijras in everyday speech, and despite the Supreme Court's decision, social acceptance of transgender people is still a long way off.

The National Legal Services Authority consistently emphasizes social and constitutional recognition in its writ petition to the Supreme Court -

Seldom, our society realizes or cares to realize the trauma, agony and pain which the members of Transgender community undergo, nor appreciates the innate feelings of the members of the Transgender community, especially of those whose mind and body disown their biological sex. Our society often ridicules and abuses the Transgender community and in public places like railway stations, bus stands, schools, workplaces, malls, theatres, hospitals, they are sidelined and treated as untouchables, forgetting the fact that the moral failure lies in the society's unwillingness to contain or embrace different gender identities and expressions, a mindset which we have to change.[3]

The petition requests "a legal declaration of their gender identity than the one assigned to them, male or female, at the time of birth," while anticipating that attitudes toward transgender people will improve. Every member of that community "has a legal right to decide their sex orientation and to espouse and determine their identity," according to petitions 2 and 3, respectively. Again, the petition makes an effort to explain gender identity by stating as- "Gender identity refers to each person's deeply felt internal and individual experience of gender, which may or may not correspond with the sex assigned at birth, including the personal sense of the body which may involve a freely chosen, modification of bodily appearance or functions by medical, surgical or other means and other expressions of gender, including dress, speech and mannerisms. Gender identity, therefore, refers to an individual's self-identification as a man, woman, transgender or other identified category".[4]

In Indian culture, accepting people who identify with many genders is strongly ingrained. Since ancient times, the Hijras have been a part of Indian culture and are acknowledged as a third gender. Despite being prominent historically and culturally, they have experienced significant marginalization and persecution in contemporary society. Although the purpose of this essay is not to analyses the writ petition's dynamics, it is noteworthy to observe that in a number of the sentences from the preceding quotations, the emphasis is placed on personal choice rather than social constructs in relation to sexual orientation and gender identity. This is radical in that it emphasizes human agency when it comes to determining one's gender and dispels predetermined sexual identity. Following the lead of pioneering work by luminaries like Simone de Beauvoir and Judith Butler, theoretical viewpoints on gender had been positioned on distinctions between a biologically determined sex and a culturally conditioned gender.[5] Joan Scott, for instance, agrees with Simone de Beauvoir that "one is not born a woman, but rather, one becomes one" by defining gender as "a social category imposed on a sexed body."[6] Intriguingly, Scott's claim would be questioned if we consider the growth of LGBTI (Lesbian, Gay, Bisexual, Transgender, Intersex) rights and studies, the dichotomous nature of several biological markers, including the comments in the petition cited above. This is because, in modern society, gender often determines sex rather than the other way around. Through sex re-assignment surgery, one can affix a gender to their body without changing the naturally determined "sexed body," thanks to modern medical technology. As a result, the definition of gender has recently been sufficiently expanded, raising doubts regarding gender identity.

The Protection of Rights Bill, which was passed in 2016, recognized the rights of the transgender population in India and sought to protect them from discrimination. Despite this, the community still has trouble gaining access to jobs, healthcare, education, and fundamental human rights.[7] These difficulties are made more difficult by the prejudice and social stigma associated with gender non-conformity. Because they do not conform to societal expectations on gender, transgender people experience discrimination in every aspect of their lives. Every transgender person has undoubtedly experienced sexual, physical, and verbal abuse at least once in their lifetime. The main cause of this prejudice and violence towards these people is likewise transphobia. Transphobia is the expression of hatred, disbelief, dread, fear, or mistrust against transgender individuals or those whose gender expression deviates from the norm. They consequently experience constant uneasiness and stress. They worry about being scrutinized all the time.

Finding acceptable occupations and the type of work that they want to do is extremely challenging for transgender people. Due to social discrimination in the workplace, they are forced to perform sex work, beg, and dance in bars, among other things. They lose their social, political, and economic authority in society in addition to having low levels of literacy. Many transgender people were unable to even apply for these positions because the majority of forms only have two gender categories, male and female. Here are a few examples where people's once-bright futures were ruined. A young athlete from Tamil Nadu who had been chosen for the police force was later fired once it was discovered that she was transgender, despite the fact that she possessed other qualifications. Similar to this, a young woman in Maharashtra was fired from her job even though she had been qualified since police forms did not recognize transgender as a gender. Another young woman from Tamil Nadu was denied the opportunity to take the UPSC test because she was transgender, and once again, the UPSC only recognizes male or female gender classifications. She submitted an RTI and an appeal, but she was denied permission to take the exam. Since the NALSA ruling, which recognized transgender as a third gender, the situation has changed. According to an NHRC poll, 89 percent of transgender people do not have access to employment prospects despite possessing the qualifications and skills needed for the position. being partially to blame for having to perform sex work to support oneself. These transwomen had greater difficulty finding employment during the Covid-19 epidemic shutdown since the majority of them rely on sex work, begging, or blessing as a means of subsistence, which was prohibited.[8]

The literacy rate for transgender people in India in 2011 was 46%, compared to 74% for the general population. 56 percent of transgender people in Coimbatore, India, have completed elementary and middle school, according to a study of 120 trans people. After noticing the changes in them, some of them were hesitant to enroll in school, and 64% of them belonged to the low-income group. 52 percent of transgender students dropped out of school due to harassment from peers, and 12 percent did so due to harassment from teachers, according to an NHRC report.[9] For some whose entire lives are judged by their gender identity, formal education was a distant fantasy. Transgender people are underrepresented in higher education and colleges due to a fear of discrimination. Because of cultural expectations, transgender people frequently experience discrimination and violence. As a result, trans children are frequently punished, held accountable, and criticized by their families. The National Institute of Epidemiology discovered that a significant portion of the 60,000 transgender people it studied—who lived in 17 states, including Tamil Nadu—had little support from their biological parents. Because they believe it would bring shame and humiliation to the family and frequently have an impact on other children, parents may disown and evict their child. Additionally, transgender people encounter obstacles when trying to inherit or claim the property that is rightfully theirs. Sometimes a teen or child decides to leave their home because they can no longer stand the abuse and prejudice they are subjected to from their family. Only 2% of transgender people, according to a survey done by Kerala Development Society on behalf of the National Human Rights Commission, live with their families.

The government's top priorities do not include transgender people's health issues. Globally, there are significant health disparities and hurdles for transgender persons to get quality medical care. Compared to the general population, transgender people are more likely to experience sexual assault and harassment. Gradually, there is an increased chance of mental health problems, which frequently lead to depression and suicide attempts. Healthcare professionals frequently treated transgender patients unfairly, and many health insurance providers refused to pay for their services. 8.82% was the second-highest rate of HIV prevalence among high-risk categories reported by the National AIDS Control Organization (NACO) in 2015–16. An estimated 8.2 percent of transgender people are HIV positive. These persons have a higher risk of contracting HIV due to a variety of social, economic, and legal issues. To improve transgender people's access to health, social, and legal services, the Pehchan project works with them in 18 Indian states.[10]

Transgender people frequently experience prejudice when trying to access housing, including excessive rents, refusal of housing facilities, and harassment from neighbours and landlords even if they do manage to get housing. Housing is a major issue for transgender persons, and lack of identity verification is another reason that these people are not allowed to use accommodations. In Kochi, 21 transgender people were hired for jobs with Metro Services, but after one week, eight of those individuals had resigned since no one would rent them a house or a room. Because of who they are, transgender people frequently experience violence such as sexual assault, physical abuse, and other forms of assault. As many acts of violence against these people go unreported, the number of incidents is far higher. Most of the violence they have experienced has come from their own families, friends, and romantic partners.[11] The government compiles NCRB data each year that reveals crimes against people that have been committed, but there is no particular reference to crimes against transgender people in this data. Bhavitha, a transgender person from Telangana, was discovered dead next to a trash can on December 2, 2017. Since only blood relatives and parents can make such claims, the police did not permit her sisters and other hijra people to do so. Karan Tripathi requested separate information on transgender convicts in the NCRB reports in a PIL he filed. The National Records Bureau's Prison Statistics Report would henceforth list transgender people as a different gender, the Central Government informed the Delhi High Court.

Transgender people are recognized as "Third Gender" by Indian courts. However, we still have discriminatory legislation in place, such as the prohibition of transsexual people from getting married, having spouses, and starting families. The Surrogacy (Regulation) measure, 2020, which permits surrogacy for divorcees, widows, heterosexual couples, and single women, was recently approved by the government. However, the measure makes no mention whatsoever of transgender people's parental rights. Even the adoption rules prohibit transgender people from adopting children lawfully. To support children who have been run away from or abandoned by their families, they may use illegal means. Gauri Sawant, a self-described hijra, assumes the role of mother to her adopted daughter in real life.[12] Being a mother is frequently viewed through the lens of a gender norm that demands it to meet the requirements of womanhood. The concepts of motherhood and adoption must be reviewed immediately. Beyond marriage and kinship outside of the binary gender sex system, we must look. The Indian Penal Code, 1860, section 377, which decriminalized same-sex relationships between homosexuals and was discriminatory in nature, was repealed. Additionally, the new Transgender Persons (Protection of Rights) Act, 2019, is discriminatory in character and imposes a lesser sentence—between 6 months and 2 years—for sexual offenses committed against transgender people than against women.[13]

People who don't fit in with our society's norms have been reviled and rejected since ancient times. One such group that has experienced prejudice, exclusion, maltreatment, and neglect in practically every known society is the transgender population. They are unnoticed by society. Any events, marriages, or other social gatherings are not extended an invitation to them. In a poll conducted by the National Human Rights Commission, 99 percent of transgender respondents acknowledged that they had experienced multiple societal rejections in the past. These people experience social isolation throughout every stage of their lives and are frequently shunned by families and other social groups. Prior to the Transgender Persons (Protection of Rights) Act of 2019, the rights of transgender people were not specifically addressed.[14] The rights of transgender people to live in dignity and without suffering from many forms of abuse, such as sexual and physical violence, are violated. They are physically beaten, gang raped, unlawfully detained, and many other things. Transgender persons have less access to justice and are not supported and assisted by the police when they seek justice. Instead, they met intimidation from police officers, who demanded bribes in order to hear their case. As a result, people are discouraged from approaching the police. The lack of basic legal recognition for transgender individuals prevents them from seeking redress for crimes perpetrated against them.

Gender expressions in India only incorporate masculine and feminine components, which is why transgender people there face extreme persecution. Every aspect of a person's life, including name, clothing, looks, behaviour, career, mobility, etc., is typically influenced by gender. Every identification document, including a passport, driver's license, mark sheet, Aadhar card, and pan card, carries a gender indicator. In India, public amenities like restrooms in malls and airports, changing rooms, and security checks at airports and other public locations are also gender-specific. India is a country where gender is strictly defined, hence transgender people are not allowed to have their own identities. Lack of knowledge exists on the subtleties of the transgender community's gender identity and biological sex. People who identify as non-binary genders frequently experience pervasive prejudice, which results in exclusion from social, economic, and political realms. A worrisome problem is violence, particularly against transsexual women. In India, the transgender minority frequently encounters difficulties getting access to high-quality healthcare and education. These sectors' marginalization is made worse by discriminatory actions. Although the legal acknowledgment of the transgender population is a big step, there are many difficulties in putting these laws into practice. The efficient execution of laws is hampered by erroneous interpretation and application of the law, as well as ignorance.[15]

It is essential to raise public knowledge of various gender identities and to make them aware of the problems these communities face. Curriculums in schools, media portrayal, and public debate can all help with this. Inclusion should be considered while drafting laws and regulations. It is crucial to make sure that these laws are properly applied and enforced. To address their unique requirements, the government should include transgender community members in policymaking. Strong support networks that include counselling services, hotlines, and shelter houses can considerably lessen the difficulties these community's encounter. Although numerous gender identities are acknowledged in India's cultural history, the reality on the ground paints a different picture. Individuals who identify outside of the gender binary suffer significant and varied difficulties. A multi-pronged strategy comprising legal reforms, more awareness, and the provision of social support systems is required to address these concerns. In order to genuinely celebrate its rich cultural past, India has to promote a more inclusive society.

References

1. *Hijras* or Eunuchs are not the only people labelled as transgenders. For a detailed introduction of transgender persons, see Article 11 in Petition.
2. Article 126, Petition 106, April 15, 2014, Supreme Court of India
3. Petition No. 1-2
4. Petition No.15-16
5. Beauvoir, Simone de. *The Second Sex*. 1949. Trans. H M Parshley. Jonathan Cape, London, 1953. p. 273; Butler, Judith. *Gender Trouble*, Routledge, London and New York, 2007
6. Scott, Joan Wallach, "Gender and the Politics of History," *Gender and Culture Series*, Columbia University Press, 2018
7. India Today, Jan 27, 2020, New Delhi
8. Acharya, Arun Kumar & Clark, Jennifer Bryson. "COVID-19 pandemic and transgender migrant women in India: Socio-economic vulnerability and vaccine hesitancy", *Journal of Migration and Health*, Vol. 8, 2023, 100204; Barik, Rajesh & Others. "How the COVID-19 Pandemic has Affected Transgender Community People: Findings from a Telephonic Survey in Odisha", *Contemporary Voice of Dalit*, online published, June 13, 2022

9. The National Human Rights Commission, study on Human Rights of Transgender as Third Gender, 2017
10. Annual Report, Department of Health and Family Welfare, Ministry of Health and Family Welfare, Government of India (2015-2016)
11. Revathi, A., *The Truth about Me: A Hijra Life Story*, Penguin India, New Delhi, 2010.
12. See for details: Sawant, Gauri. *The inspiring tale of the Transgender Mom*, DD News, 07.06.2017
13. The Transgender Persons (Protection of Rights) Bill, 2019, Ministry: Social Justice and Welfare, India
14. The Transgender Persons (Protection of Rights) Bill, 2019 was introduced in Lok Sabha on July 19, 2019 by the Minister for Social Justice and Empowerment, Mr. Thaawarchand Gehlot.
15. Michelraj, M., "Historical Evolution of Transgender Community in India", *Asian Review of Social Sciences*, Vol. 4 No. 1, 2015, pp. 17-19

Religion and Society in India: A Historical Perspective

Alampik Debbarma

Religion has been a crucial component of Indian society for centuries and has played a significant role in shaping its culture and evolution. This chapter provides a historical perspective on the relationship between religion and society in India. The literature review explores the impact of religion on the caste system, gender roles, social institutions, and communalism. The caste system has been a dominant feature of Indian society for centuries and is closely linked to religion. The literature review examines the influence of religion on gender roles and how it has contributed to the marginalization of women in Indian society. Religion has also played a significant role in shaping social institutions such as marriage and family, education, and politics. The review emphasizes the potential role of religion in addressing contemporary challenges facing Indian society, such as poverty, education, and health care. The discussion section synthesizes the findings of the literature review and highlights the complex relationship between religion and society in India. The discussion emphasizes the impact of religion on the caste system, gender roles, and communalism. The potential role of religion in addressing contemporary challenges facing Indian society is also discussed. The chapter concludes by summarizing the key findings of the literature review and the discussion. The relationship between religion and society in India is complex and has played a significant role in shaping Indian society throughout history. In addition, the writing highlights the importance of understanding this relationship to gain a deeper understanding of the evolution of Indian society over time. The potential role of religion in addressing contemporary challenges facing Indian society is also emphasized.

For centuries religion has played a critical role in shaping India's culture and society. It has influenced Indians' lives in a variety of ways, ranging from the caste system to gender roles, social institutions, and communalism. Religion has long been an important part of Indian society and culture, giving individuals a feeling of identity, community, and purpose. Hinduism, Islam, Christianity, Sikhism, Buddhism, Jainism, and Zoroastrianism are all practised in India. Religion influences millions of Indians' daily lives, from how they dress to the food they consume and the events they attend. Temples, Mosques, Churches and Gurudwaras are vital aspects of Indian cities and towns attracting millions of followers each year. India has a complicated and nuanced relationship between religion and society. The caste system, gender roles, and societal institutions have all been influenced by religion over the years in India. For example, India's caste system, which is intimately related to religion, has long been a defining aspect of Indian society. Religion has had a huge impact on gender roles as well. Religious writings frequently impose rigid gender rules that have pushed women further to the margins of Indian society. Institutions of society like marriage and the family, education, and politics have all been significantly influenced by religion.

The aim of this chapter is to furnish a scholarly historical standpoint concerning the interconnection between religion and society in India. The present study endeavours to acquire a comprehensive comprehension of how the religion has influenced diverse aspects of the Indian society by scrutinizing its impact, thus elucidating its role in shaping the course of Indian society throughout history. The present study aims to investigate the potential influence of religion in tackling contemporaneous challenges existing in the Indian society; specifically, poverty, education, and health care.

The caste system is a hierarchical social structure that has been entrenched as a cornerstone of Indian society for an extended period of time. The concept of "caste" pertains to a particular social assembly that is assigned based on one's birth and frequently correlated with distinct career paths and societal rank. The lineage of the caste system remains uncertain, nonetheless, it is widely speculated that it evolved from the historical varna system. The latter bifurcated society into four generalized categories based on an individual's profession and societal positioning. Hinduism has had a huge impact on India's caste structure. The caste system is mentioned in Hindu scriptures such as the Vedas and the Puranas, and it is typically described as a divine creation. According to Hindu teachings, each caste is assigned a distinct role and obligation based on their birth. For example, the Brahmins are the highest caste and are in charge of religious and intellectual activities, whilst the Shudras, the lowest caste, are assigned to menial labour.

The caste system has exerted a profound influence on the social hierarchy of India. The formation of a rigid social hierarchy predicated solely upon one's birth has resulted in significant obstacles for upward mobility, constraining individuals from traversing the social ladder. The occurrence has given rise to noteworthy social and economic disparity within the Indian society, causing lower-caste individuals to face discrimination and marginalization. Furthermore, the caste system engenders a sense of individual and communal identity, fostering the emergence of discrete social entities distinguished by their exclusive practices, customs, and ceremonial observances. Despite concerted efforts aimed at the elimination of the caste system, it remains a prevalent feature of Indian society albeit manifesting itself in a less overt manner. The

Indian government has adopted various measures to conscientiously tackle the matter of caste-based discrimination and has instituted affirmative action schemes with the objective of enabling individuals who are members of lower castes to gain improved access to opportunities. Nonetheless, notwithstanding persistent efforts, the caste system in India remains a significant impediment to realizing social and economic equality.

For centuries, Indian society has been characterized by the dominance of men in positions of power and authority, which is commonly known as patriarchy. The participation of religion has been crucial in the continuation of male dominance in India. Several religious texts and practices in India promote the concept of male supremacy and mandate subservient positions for women. In Hinduism, the notion of purdah, which involves keeping women secluded from public life, stems from the belief that women need to be sheltered from the male gaze. Likewise, the act of covering oneself in Islam is frequently interpreted as a means of safeguarding women's decency.

Religion has played a noteworthy role in influencing the development of women's rights in India. Religious texts and cultural practices often contain prescribed gender roles that manifest in the subordination of women and restriction of their opportunities in education, employment, and political participation. The Hinduism faith highlights the *Manusmriti* as a fundamental document which delineates the expected codes of social and moral conduct for its adherents. Within this text, it is deemed that women are to be reliant on men for the duration of their lives. Likewise, in Islamic tradition, women are frequently subject to limitations on their involvement in communal affairs and are precluded from assuming prominent roles as prayer leaders or religious figures.

It is widely acknowledged among scholars that religion has played a significant role in perpetuating the marginalization of women in the Indian societal context. Gender inequality is a pervasive issue that affects women, who are frequently viewed as subordinate to men. They are faced with a multitude of discriminatory experiences, such as domestic violence, sexual harassment, and gender-based violence. The perpetuation of marginalization is exacerbated by the hierarchical caste system, as women belonging to lower castes are subjected to heightened levels of unfair treatment and exclusion. Additionally, religion has been utilized to legitimize inequitable customs such as the payment of dowry, the engagement of minors in matrimony, and the killing of newborn females.

Despite the inherent obstacles, concerted endeavours have been undertaken to advance the cause of gender parity and the protection of women's entitlements in India. The active participation of women's movements and feminist organizations has been instrumental in creating a heightened level of consciousness regarding the challenges that women face while advocating for an elevated status of gender equity. The Indian government has enacted numerous legislations and regulations with a view to fostering gender equality and safeguarding women's entitlements. These include, for instance, the Protection of Women from Domestic Violence Act, 2005, and the Criminal Law (Amendment) Act, 2013.

1. Marriage and family

Religion has exerted a profound influence on the configuration of matrimony and kinship systems in India. Historically, the prevalent custom in India has been that of arranged marriages, wherein families regard religion as a key factor determining the choice of a spouse. Religion constitutes a pivotal determinant of the familial roles and obligations assumed by members thereof. In the context of Hinduism, there exists the expectation that the wife shall assume the role of a virtuous wife and mother, whereas the husband is anticipated to undertake the obligation of supporting the family and fulfilling his duties as a father and husband.

2. Education

The impact of religion on education in India has been deemed significant. A number of the most venerable educational institutions in the nation were founded by religious organizations. One illustrative instance is the University of Calcutta, which was founded in 1857 by the British East India Company, however, its administration was mostly overseen by Christian missionaries. Furthermore, in India, a number of private schools and colleges are managed and operated by religious establishments. Religious instruction constitutes a crucial aspect of the Indian educational paradigm, with pupils frequently mandated to undertake religious-cultural classes within their prescribed syllabus.

3. Politics

The significance of religion in Indian politics has been notable since the nation achieved independence. India, being a secular state, has nevertheless been greatly influenced by religion in regard to shaping political discourse and organizing voter participation. The political landscape in India is characterized by the tendency of political parties to associate themselves with particular religious communities, accentuating upon religious symbols and language in order to garner the support of the electorate. One illustration of the interrelation between politics and religion is observable in the present ruling party of India, the Bharatiya Janata Party, which is closely affiliated with the Hindu nationalist movement and has faced allegations of advocating for a Hindu supremacist program. In parallel fashion, the Indian National Congress, a leading opposition party in India, has historically formed an association with the nation's Muslim population.

Religious tensions and the issue of communalism have emerged as significant challenges in the realm of Indian politics. India has witnessed multiple incidents of communal violence, chiefly involving Hindus and Muslims, resulting in major casualties and damage to property. In contemporary times, the escalation of religious intolerance and hate crimes in India has generated significant apprehension.

Communalism is an ideological perspective that upholds the favouring of one specific religious or ethnic community above others. This phenomenon is frequently distinguished by a pronounced collective identification and a conviction of the innate superiority of individuals belonging to a particular cohort over those of another. The existence of communalism in India has posed a noteworthy challenge since the attainment of independence, manifested by numerous occurrences of communal aggression and discord among divergent religious communities.

India boasts a heterogeneous religious topography, comprising an extensive gamut of faiths, including, yet not limited to, Hinduism, Islam, Christianity, Sikhism, Buddhism, and Jainism that hold eminence in the region. Religious discord and hostilities have posed a significant impediment to societal harmony within the nation. The past decades have witnessed a preponderance of communal conflicts between the adherents of Hinduism and Islam, characterized by fierce bouts of violence and riots which have led to significant losses in human lives and property. Other marginalized communities including Sikhs, Christians, and Dalits have been subjected to discrimination and violence.

Religion has frequently been employed as a means of propagating communal tendencies in India. In the realm of politics, it is not uncommon for political leaders and parties to resort to leveraging religious symbols and rhetoric with the intention of appealing to potential constituents and galvanizing their backing. In contemporary times, the idea of Hindutva, a form of Hindu nationalism that propagates the notion of India being a Hindu state, has garnered considerable momentum. The preceding has prompted apprehension regarding the marginalization of religious minority groups and the deterioration of India's foundational concept of secularism. Furthermore, it is noteworthy that the caste system, an intricately intertwined social structure with religion, has played a significant role in fostering communalism within Indian society. The phenomenon of discrimination and marginalization based on caste has given rise to the development of distinctive communities and identities, oftentimes resulting in inter-group discordance.

1. Poverty

India is recognized as one of the countries with the most extensive populace globally, and notable numbers of individuals in the region live in impoverished conditions. The issues of poverty and inequality are pervasive, affecting numerous individuals who struggle to obtain fundamental necessities, including sustenance, housing, and medical care. Religious practices have the potential to substantially contribute to tackling various societal obstacles through the promotion of altruistic contributions, communal support services, and initiatives centered on the local populace. Several religious organizations in India operate social welfare programs that offer critical services to individuals who require them. Various initiatives have been implemented, such as the establishment of food banks, homeless shelters, and healthcare clinics. Religious leaders possess a distinct opportunity to promote policy measures that aid in mitigating poverty and inequality. These measures may encompass progressive taxation, amplified social expenditures, and equitable labor practices.

2. Education

The indispensable role of education resides in its ability to engender social mobility and foster economic progress. The educational landscape of India exhibits a marked heterogeneity with substantial gaps prevalent in terms of caste, gender, and economic strata. Religion may serve as a catalyst for advancing education through the establishment of schools, the allocation of scholarships, and the championship of policies that foster equal opportunities for education. Numerous religious institutions operating in India administer schools and educational initiatives that facilitate the provision of high-quality education to marginalized communities. The aforementioned initiatives are centered on the provision of education for young girls, socially disadvantaged communities, and inhabitants residing in geographically isolated locations. In the realm of policy making, religious leaders possess the capacity to endorse measures that facilitate the attainment of education by all individuals and mitigate prevalent constraints, including economic deprivation, gender bias, and inadequate infrastructure.

3. Health care

India faces a considerable obstacle in attaining access to healthcare, as a substantial proportion of its population lacks access to rudimentary medical facilities. The involvement of religion in healthcare is demonstrated through the establishment of medical facilities, provision of medical services to underprivileged communities, as well as the championing of policies that foster comprehensive access to healthcare. In India, many religious groups operate healthcare clinics and hospitals to provide medical aid to underprivileged communities, especially those in remote areas or with long-term illnesses. Religious leaders can push for policies that ensure equal health care access, with increased government spending and infrastructure investment.

This chapter has undertaken an examination of the historical context concerning the correlation between religion and society in India. The present review elucidates the noteworthy influence of religion on diverse spheres of Indian society, namely the caste hierarchy, gender constructs, social establishments, and communalistic tendencies. The impact of religion on the transformation of Indian society throughout the ages has been substantial. For centuries, the caste system has been a dominant feature of Indian society, closely intertwined with religion, specifically Hinduism. Religion has exerted a noteworthy impact on established societal gender roles, thereby contributing to the systemic subjugation and inadequacy of women in Indian communities. Religion has played a pivotal role in shaping social institutions including but not limited to marriage, education, and politics. The present chapter has undertaken an analysis of the influence of religion on enhancing communalism within India, while also assessing its capacity to tackle existing issues in Indian society, such as inadequate access to education, healthcare, and poverty.

The aforementioned section of discourse has drawn attention to the intricate interplay between religion and society within the context of India. The influence of religion on the caste system, gender roles, and communalism has been considerably noteworthy in academic discourse. The caste system has served as a mechanism for social stratification within Indian society, with its persistence being shaped by religious factors. The perpetuation of gender roles has been attributed to patriarchy, a system of social organization in which men hold primary authority and power. Religion has been identified as a contributing factor in the perpetuation of patriarchy and subsequently gender roles. The phenomenon of communalism has been a substantive source of societal conflict within the Indian context, with religious dynamics serving as a catalyst in its perpetuation. Discussions have been held on the prospective utilization of religion in addressing the current challenges that confront Indian society. Religion possesses the capacity to tackle problems like poverty, education, and healthcare by furnishing a moral and ethical structure for addressing these issues. The realization of such potential is contingent upon the constructive and positive use of religion, as opposed to its deployment as a cause of discord and fragmentation.

Religion has exerted a noteworthy impact upon the Indian society, with particular emphasis upon the caste system, gender roles, and communalism. The caste system holds a preeminent position in the Indian society for an extended period, and its connection to religion is intimately intertwined. In India, religious practices have been instrumental in perpetuating a patriarchal social structure, ultimately contributing to the systemic marginalization of women. The chapter under consideration delved into the influence of religion upon various social institutions, including but not limited to marriage and family, education, and politics. The discourse regarding the prospective impact of religion in confronting present-day predicaments that beset Indian society, such as indigence, education, and medical services, was likewise the subject of examination. Religion could potentially assume a pivotal position in ameliorating these difficulties through its promotion of equitable social circumstances and parity, its facilitation of education and healthcare infrastructures, as well as its empowerment of communities who have been subject to marginalization.

This chapter has proffered a comprehensive historical account of the intersection between religion and society in

India. Nonetheless, there is still considerable potential for additional exploration and analysis on this subject matter. Prospective investigations may delve into the influence of religion on various facets of Indian society, including but not limited to art, literature, and language. The inquiry could also potentially delve into the influence of religion in moulding the concept of Indian identity and fostering nationalism. Empirical investigation may explore religion's potential in addressing Indian societal issues. Further research on religious collaboration for fairness, equitability, and human liberties could advance knowledge. To promote fairness, we must address negative aspects of religion and use its positives to advance equality. Religious leaders and organizations must collaborate with government and civil society to address India's pressing issues.

References

1. Ambedkar, B. R. *Annihilation of Caste: The Annotated Critical Edition*, edited by S. Anand, Navayana Publishing, 2014.
2. Beteille, Andre. "Caste and Politics", *Economic and Political Weekly*, vol. 31, no. 16, 1996, pp. 995-1002.
3. Bhardwaj, Surinder Mohan. *Hindu Places of Pilgrimage in India: A Study in Cultural Geography,* University of California Press, 1973
4. Bose, Sugata. "Towards the Indian Ocean World: An Historiography", *The Indian Economic & Social History Review*, vol. 41, no. 2, 2004, pp. 181-212
5. Chakrabarty, Bidyut. "Political Violence and the Indian State: The 2002 Gujarat Riots", *Asian Survey*, vol. 43, no. 4, 2003, pp. 637-656
6. Chakrabarty, Dipesh. "The Climate of History: Four Theses", *Critical Inquiry,* vol. 35, no. 2, 2009, pp. 197-222.
7. Chatterjee, Partha. *The Politics of the Governed: Reflections on Popular Politics in Most of the World,* Columbia University Press, 2004
8. Gandhi, Mohandas K. "My Religion" in *The Essential Gandhi: An Anthology of His Writings on His Life, Work, and Ideas,* edited by Louis Fischer, Vintage Books, 2002, pp. 28-33

9. Hasan, Mushirul. *India's Partition: Process, Strategy and Mobilization*, Oxford University Press, 1993
10. Jalal, Ayesha. *The Sole Spokesman: Jinnah, the Muslim League, and the Demand for Pakistan*, Cambridge University Press, London, 1994
11. Menon, Dilip M. "The Women's Movement in India: Issues and Perspectives", *The Economic and Political Weekly*, vol. 26, no. 49, 1991, pp. WS117-WS123.
12. Narayanan, Vasudha. "Hinduism and Ecology: The Intersection of Earth, Sky, and Water", *Daedalus*, vol. 130, no. 4, 2001, pp. 191-215.
13. Roy, Arundhati. *The God of Small Things,* Random House, Delhi, 1997
14. Sangari, Kumkum. "Politics of the Possible: Gender and the Indian State", *Economic and Political Weekly*, vol. 33, no. 6, 1998, pp. WS9-WS19.
15. Sen, Amartya. *The Argumentative Indian: Writings on Indian History, Culture, and Identity.* Farrar, Straus and Giroux, 2005
16. Basu, Subho. "Land Reforms in India: Achievements, Failures, and Challenges Ahead", *Journal of Developing Societies*, vol. 21, no. 1-2, 2005, pp. 49-66.
17. Bose, Sugata. *A Hundred Horizons: The Indian Ocean in the Age of Global Empire*, Harvard University Press, USA, 2006
18. Kaviraj, Sudipta. "Modernity and Politics in India", *Daedalus*, vol. 129, no. 2, 2000, pp. 61-76
19. Thapar, Romila. *The Penguin History of Early India: From the Origins to AD 1300*, Penguin Books, Delhi, 2003
20. Rai, Mridu. *Hindu Rulers, Muslim Subjects: Islam, Rights, and the History of Kashmir,* Hurst & Co., Delhi, 2004
21. Rao, Anupama. "Gender, Caste, and Nation: Reconsidering the Debate on Caste Politics in India", *International Feminist Journal of Politics*, vol. 10, no. 4, 2008, pp. 538-555.
22. Thapar Bjorkert, Suruchi. "The Historical Construction of Gender in India: A Feminist Analysis", *The Journal of Developing Areas*, vol. 31, no. 1, 1997, pp. 33-50.
23. Rajagopal, Arvind. *Politics after Television: Hindu Nationalism and the Reshaping of the Public in India,* Cambridge University Press, 2001
24. Sarkar, Sumit. *Modern India: 1885-1947*, Palgrave Macmillan, 1989.

Anti-CAA and NRC Movement in India: A Means of Making Identity of Muslim Women

Jisan Sarowar & Dr. Sawpna Khatun

Women are now slowly being acknowledged as significant, competent and relevant participants in the socio-political realm. As we have seen, since several decades, that mainly the Muslim women in India lag-behind the women of other communities in all kind of engagements whether in the political or economic or cultural aspects. However, interestingly, the engagement of Muslim women during the Anti- CAA & NRC movement (2019) surprised the male dominated notion of India. The people of India felt a different kind of experiences that had never ever seen before. Thus, the present study intends to investigate the sentiments and perspectives of Muslim women in India on their pivotal role in Anti- CAA & NRC movement. The chapter confirms an understanding the scope and magnitude of women participation in the movement throughout the India. The chapter has been written on the basis of primary and secondary date by using analytical and historical method of research. If we talk about the study related to this subject, we will have very few references, and all most all writings revolve around the epicenter of the movement 'Shaheen Bagh', a small sector of Delhi. Some of these important writings are viz., Yash Sharma & Shatakshi Singh's "Shaheen Bagh and the Politics of Protest in the Anti – CAA & NRC movement in India",[1] Syed Mohammed Faisal's "Shaheen Bagh and the hermeneutics of Muslim identity in South Asia",[2] Pratishtha Singh's The Micropolitics of an Adda for Women in India: Shaheen Bagh,[3] Adrija Ghosh's Art as Resistance in Shaheen Bagh,[4] Ziya

Us Salam & Uzma Ausaf's Shaheen Bagh-From a Protest to a Movement,[5] and Seema Mustafa's Shaheen Bagh and the Idea of India.[6]

Before talking about the women participation in the movement we should know what actually CAA and NRC and how it affected the Indian Muslim in particular. The Citizenship Amendment Act 2019 passed to provide Indian citizenship to the illegal migrants of six communities (Hindu, Sikh, Buddhist, Jain, Parsis and Christian of Afghanistan, Bangladesh and Pakistan) except Muslim, who entered India on or before 31st December 2014. This was an obvious communal legal instrument, devised by the BJP lead government, to jeopardize communal harmony and integrity of the country. NRC (National Register of Citizens) is another instrument of eliminating Muslims from the list of Indian citizenship and led them into identity crisis. After all, the CAA-NPR-NRC combination does infuse fear among Indian Muslims. On the surface it appears as if the NRC will check illegal migration and the CAA will provide citizenship to those Sikhs, Hindus, Christians, Parsis and Buddhists from Pakistan, Afghanistan and Bangladesh who had fled persecution before 2014. This makes them seem safe and legit. However, the last experiences of Assam with NRC depict reverse pictures. In which many legal citizens both Hindu and Muslims were ousted and sent to detention centres, while many illegal migrants were counted as citizens. And it is believed by the common that the Muslims are being cornered by such tactics. Because of this comprehension, the Indian Muslims led into protest and then gradually into a country wide movement. But the most overwhelming thing is that the women section of the Muslim society particularly, for the first time, became active and lead the movement. A secular section of Indian citizens both male and female were also very active and supportive to this Anti-CAA & NRC, NPR movement.[7]

As all we know that the protest starts from the Shaheen Bagh, Delhi, as a 24x7 sit-in peaceful non-violent resistance by the Muslim women in response to the passage of the draconian Citizenship Amendment Act on 11th December 2019.[8] By the passing of time, the intensity of the protest got larger and deeper. One by one all mega and metro cities engulfed with anti-CAA march, rallies, candle march and dharnas. Within a month this protest transformed into a countrywide movement. People of almost all the towns of India began to copy the modus-operandi of Shaheen Bagh protest. At various protests against the CAA all over India, pride of place was given to the "father" of the constitution, B. R. Ambedkar. Protestors organized mass readings of the preamble, and placards and memes derived from articles of the constitution were raised in public and on social media posts. Most importantly the anti-CAA movement was styled as a protest to protect the constitution. "Save the Constitution" was perhaps the slogan that began heard most often, whether in Delhi, Aligarh, Lucknow, Mumbai, Kolkata, Hyderabad, Kerala or elsewhere.[9] As according to the Sachar Committee Report of 2006, that Muslims of India in every field are marginalized. Since, not even a single awakening movement or mobilization for upliftment had visualized throughout the country among the Muslims. However, this time shake the community from the state of slag-ness. The Sachar Committee Report had underscored various kinds of marginalization, but the threat posed by the CAA was fundamentally linked to exclusion from that most basic recognition and right granted by a state citizenship.[10]

"The CAA obviously goes against the secular code of the country, by excluding Muslims. To top it is the NRC, which asks for documents to prove citizenship. While the nature of these documents has still not been stated, it can lead to conditions where, with effect of the CAA, even legal Muslims citizens would be on the verge of losing citizenship," Shaheen says. The fear that one could lose one's home is what triggered the anti-CAA protests. The women who participated in them revealed their shared consciousness. "Home, after all is what we all need," says Shaheen. "How can anybody illegally remove us from the homes we have built with so much pain and effort," she says. That is why even the most home-bound women literally left their homes to protect their homes.[11] On the other way it has been described that the CAA threatens women in a larger way than men. "If they win this fight, it would mean a secure future for their children, families and themselves", a women said Images and reports of detention camps in Assam have given demonstration to that effect. And women – not only from minorities, but across sections – have started to feel the fear of being disenfranchised. Thus, the implementation of CAA and National Register of Citizenship (NRC) are introducing a new order, a new 'definition of margin' and a new hegemony, which is posing a grave threat to women across communities, caste and class.[12]

As anti-CAA protests multiplied and intensified, the BJP-RSS led government resorted to the use of violence and strict anti-terror laws to try and stifle dissent. Police either used brutal violence or used anti-terror sedition laws to stifle protests.[13] Where the police were unable to do anything, groups affiliated to the BJP attacked protestors and sought to browbeat them into withdrawal. However, this only added momentum to the anti-CAA protests. The iconic Shaheen Bagh protest was started on the December 15 and by January 2020 the protests had spread all over India and notably the template of a sit-in in a public area, led mostly by Muslim women, was followed across the country.[14]Anti-CAA movement that spread across India, starting from 11 December and lasting until the lockdown was imposed on 24 March. This movement was unique for it was spearheaded by young Muslim women. It surprised many Indians, who had never expected the biggest and most important of recent pro-Constitution movements to be led by women, Muslim at that. Earlier, community leaders and the ulema or religious scholars would force Muslim women to participate in the occasional protest, but that was mostly to strengthen their own negotiating power with the government on issues like, say, the uniform civil code or triple talaq. In these protests, women generally remained silent spectators. However, in the anti-CAA movements they were the planners and executors as well, though many had never protested before.[15] This prove that Indian Muslims women now are not the sleepy community they once were. "Change has come about through internal processes, mostly from growing conscientisation and self-awareness of women. Women are looking at the world outside from a forward-looking perspective."[16]Despite intimidation and threats from the police and right-wing organisations. Not even the Uttar Pradesh government, which browbeat them using a variety of means, could stop these women from raising their voice. That is how Shaheen Bagh, a poor neighbourhood in South Delhi, became a symbol of their defiance, as did hundreds of other protest sites. Mainly the Literate women section of the Muslim society lead the movement.[17]

The campaign, which saw women take to the streets at night to protest, spread quickly across women's colleges in India. Campaigns were successfully led at Jamia Millia Islamia University, Delhi University, Aligarh Muslim University, Hyderabad University, Punjab University, Banaras Hindu University, Jadavpur University, and many more.[18] In the wake of countrywide protests against CAA-NRC-NPR, India is witnessing a watershed massive movement led by women. From organizing to mobilizing to leading – women are at the forefront, often gaining stronghold over their male counterparts. Never in history we have seen such a political scenario where women leaders are emerging from every nook and corner, every village and metro city of the country. A number of women are maintaining the hidden infrastructure of the continuing CAA protests across university campuses. Apart from running errands like organising snacks, warm clothes, and mics for protesters and making posters, women students are compiling contact details of doctors, lawyers and police stations for emergency help. "The protest may have been led by men in many parts but how did they spread so quickly across the country? Because women students have been quietly working round the clock from their homes in an organised manner to circulate messages regarding protest venues and subsequent police action," says Swati, a under graduate student.

When a number of students were beaten up by the police on December 15 at Jamia University, students at the on-campus hostel for girls from the state of Jammu and Kashmir provided first aid to some 150 female and male students. Bushra Khanum, 21, a second-year postgraduate student who lives at the hostel, says: "We have grown up with police and army brutality all our lives. We know how to treat tear gas itches; skin burns and baton injuries." Sarika Chaudhary, 23, a master's in philosophy student at Jawaharlal Nehru University and protester, sees women demonstrating as a mark of solidarity with those affected by the NRC. 20-year-old Salma Khan, a postgraduate student at Jamia Millia Islamia University in the Indian capital. It is about 2pm on December 16, and Salma is holding a heavy box with water bottles and pamphlets for protesters at a demonstration on the university campus. On December 19, Nargis Saifi, 33, a stay-at-home mother with a six-year-old daughter was arrested by the police at the protests against the CAA and NRC. Later, she received several calls from her extended family members reprimanding her for being an irresponsible mother. "I told them that I am protesting for her rights too," she says. "And for the rights of homeless people, my domestic worker and anyone who has no documents because they are too caught up in their struggles to stay alive every day." She said her parents that "Women are not just protesting for their rights," she says, "but for the rights of everyone, in the hope that others will stand up for our rights too."[19]

A 19-year-old Akhtarista Ansari a Hons. student of Jamia, participated in a march led by women against Citizenship (Amendment) Act and the proposed National Register of Citizens on December 12. "It was the first protest led by the girl's hostel, which was later joined by all," she says. Akhtarista is one of the four women students, along with Chanda Yadav, Ladeeda Farsana and Ayesha Renna, who can be seen protecting a male student from police beating on December 15. As the police, including a man in plainclothes, rain blows on the male student, the women encircle him, shouting at the police, "Go back, go back." When her parents asked to come back home (Jharkhand) she relied as "the way the police attacked us and ransacked our library has only made us stronger." "We've organised protests before, but nothing on this scale," says Hina Kausar, a research scholar. "Muslim women don't come out on the street easily," says Sakina Parveen, a social worker who lives near Shaheen Bagh. "But they understand this issue and this is why they are here in such large numbers." At that time women were in no mood to back off. Mothers with babies, domestic workers and school girls among them were all the streets.[20] Shabnam Parveen, PhD holder in English literature from JNU, says, "the decision to leave the home turf was not easy for the anti-CAA protesters". A number of women were arrested, several under the draconian UAPA, such as Safoora Zargar, the student of Jamia Millia Islamia. A pregnant women student, she spent weeks in Tihar Jail in Delhi before she was released on bail on humanitarian grounds late last week. Gulfisha, a 25-year-old who participated in the anti-CAA protests at Jaffarabad, Delhi, is still behind bars.[21]

The Dadis of Shaheen Bagh (mainly Asma Khatoon, Bilkish Banu, & Sarwari) stood their ground for a hundred-and-one days, from December 2019 to March 2020, defying cold and hunger, bearing their responsibilities at home yet abstaining from its comforts.[22] A sign board in Shaheen Bagh covered with posters of prominent leaders, including Mahatma Gandhi, freedom fighter Bhagat Singh, and Dalit leader Dr B. R. Ambedkar. 2019. At Shaheen Bagh women have been chanting slogan of Azadi (freedom), patiently listening to various speakers talking to them about the Indian constitution and human rights. The protests have been devoid of violence, and visitors are welcomed with a kind smile, a cup of tea, and sometimes a sweet or savoury treat from the community kitchen.[23] The Fatima Sheikh Savitri Bai Phule library that emerged at Shaheen Bagh was one such social centre at the protest to read literature, engage critically with political ideas, and raise questions.[24]

Some of these courageous inspiring women those who have led the anti-CAA-NRC movement across India without any fear from state machinery are as follows: Sadiya, a seventeen-year-old girl student of B.A at Rizvi college, Mumbai, has visited several states to address anti-CAA-NRC rallies to create awareness about NRC-CAA, she has shared the stage with the country's foremost youth leaders like Kanhaiya Kumar, Umar Khalid Shahela Rashid and many other activists. "I thought if we choose to be silent now then distorting the constitution and atrocities on students will become a norm," she said on the incident of brutality of state sponsored violence on the students of Jamia in Delhi.[25] Ayesha Renna is a 22 years old student from Jamia Millia Islamia, coming from a small town of Malappuram district of Kerala, she became famous after her photo went viral a day after the 15th December police brutality on Jamia students. In the photo see can be seen warning the policeman against their brutal behaviour.[26] Ayesha became the icon of Women in Hijab breaking the stereotypes and struggling for her rights. She says "My identity was always a subject of liberal saviours, the immediate possibility of a *hijabi* is limited into the immediate binaries of oppressed."[27] Ladeeda Farzana, a 22 years old student of Jamia Millia Islamia who hails from Mallapuram District of Kerela emerged as a face of resistance from the Anti CAA-NRC protests. She was seen as the one amongst the four girls protecting a male student from the police lathi-charge. Later, she has been to different states to convince people regarding CAA-NRC protests. Khalida Parveen, a 64-year-old social activist from Hyderabad, has been actively engaged in educating women about the impact of NRC and CAA by guiding them how to maintain peaceful protests, was detained by the police while protesting. She said that "Muslim women have always been targeted for being inside their houses and not standing up for their right, this movement has shown that, when necessary, they can do every possible thing to safeguard their rights,"[28] Aman Mohammadi, 27-years-old artist from Saharanpur and research scholar of JNU, protests through performance theatre. She organised performance musical protest at several protest sites including Shaheen Bagh, Shahi Eidgah, Azad market, Inderlok and many more. Her creative slogan of protest was-

*"Ayazanana Ka Zamana, Haizanana Ka Zamana,
Khub pa kay aghar maikhana, Inquilab Ko Haipakana"*[29]

Shiba Minai, originally a 33-years-old journalist from Hyderabad, known as the Lady Flash protester of Hyderabad. She says that by bringing the CAA into force, we have wasted our democracy and now women must fight to save India one more time by setting an example for women throughout the world. She was detained for her firing speech. Rehna Sultana, a research scholar from Guwahati University, and also an academician turned full-time activist owing to the social circumstances at her place. She is the eye witness of the dangerous impact of NRC process in Assam.[30] In the wake of CAA, she started to work to help the people across Assam through awareness drives. Rehna says women and children have been worst affected as they are unable to produce the needed documents to prove Indian citizen.[31] Dr. Shagufta Yasmeen of Ranchi became was very active in NRC-CAA protests and initiated the awareness drive to clear the misconceptions about CAA-NRC among the people. Shagufta was very confident in saying that "Our protest is a peaceful protest; it might take time but definitely it will be fruitful".[32] Baba Noushin Khan, A scholar of Jadavpur University of Kolkata continued her protest against CAA and NRC throughout the year of Lockdown through social media. Andy Ghosh, advertising and marketing professional saw the protest as a reaction of ruthless measures taken by BJP government made her active support to the protest.[33]

Muslim women not only meet just at the capital's Shaheen Bagh but also at Patna's Sabzibagh and Kolkata's Park Circus, what is primarily a youth and women-led women has not shown signs of letting up. There was in issue of not getting permission for peaceful protest from police in Ahmedabad, Gujarat. The petitioners said they had applied for permission on January 5 to stage a protest on January 19 in Jamalpur area.[34] Hundreds of Muslim women, with donning *burkhas* and *hijabs*, came out on the streets of Hapur on 21st December to register their protest against the CAA& NRC. These women, claiming to be a part of no group or organisation, marched through the old city area with placards and raised slogans.[35] They submitted their memorandum to the district magistrate and one among them said that "There are no leaders leading our procession. We women ourselves prepared these placards,".[36] Several hundred students including girls, teachers and researchers of the Educational Institutes across India have issued a statement in condemnation of the violence that took place, as right-wing members attacked JNU students and teachers on January 5has also been subsumed in the anti-CAA protests.[37]

Indian women have transformed more than Indian men have, with Muslim women now expressing their need for change and being more articulate, self-aware, and open to speaking out on matters concerning them and the community.[38] The perception of Muslim women has completely changed following the protests against the divisive CAA and NRC. Nabeela Habib, a postgraduate in Journalism and Mass Communication from Aligarh Muslim University, explains that the strength and determination shown by the Burqa-clad mass has changed the fabric of society. The violent retaliation of the government in Jamia Millia triggered the protective instinct of the community, as mothers who had cared for their children at home saw them being attacked. "This sense of insecurity for their wards and future soon transformed into a political consciousness" [39] Habib says. According to activist Shabnam Hashmi "The anti-CAA movement has served as a learning platform for many Muslim women, allowing them to interact with liberal and progressive circles and fight for citizenship rights". The movement has had a lasting impact on the psyche of Muslim women, revealing their inherent strengths and revealing their inherent strengths and standing up to police intimidation during the Ghanta Ghar Protest at Lucknow or Shaheen Bagh. Intimidation no longer scares them, as they have realized their inherent strengths through the demonstrating of their determination and fearlessness.[40] "The time has passed to get documents in my name now," said Sumaira Khan, a 49-year-old homemaker protesting in Patna, in Bihar. "But at least I can ensure that my daughters' are in place and whether my husband has got them done. If he hasn't, I'll run from pillar to post to get them made." Rafiya Naushad, a 42-year-old homemaker from Gaya, in Bihar. "Women are constantly made to feel that they belong at home, but seeing so many women out, I'm certain that, had we studied, we'd be doing so much more with our lives."[41]

Female students in university campuses across India are out to show that the future of politics is shifting rapidly; that 21st century politics is not going to be handled by the rhetoric of masculinity anymore[42]; that the time has come to deal in politics with care and concern for gender discourses. The increasing number of vocal girls is saying that gender-justice is not alms, but a systemic intervention into the nature and logic of politics itself.[43] The polite rejection of the advice of the Vice-Chancellor of Darul Uloom Deoband by women protesting against the Citizenship (Amendment) Act and the National Register of Citizens in the Idgah ground for the last 14 days has revealed how Muslim women are not only fighting to save the Constitution, they are also grappling with a social battle within the community.[44] Muslim women occupied centre stage, both in the spatial optics of protest sites and in the political discourse to advocate for their rights as citizens.[45]

References

1. Sharma, Yash & Singh, S., "Shaheen Bagh and the Politics of Protest in the Anti – CAA movement in India", *Feminist Encounters: A journal of critical studies in Culture and Politics,* 7 (1), 10, March 2023
2. Faisal, S. M., "Shaheen Bagh and the hermeneutics of Muslim identity in South Asia", *Journal of Ethnographic Theory,* 10 (3), 2020, pp. 767-775
3. Singh P., "The Micropolitics of an Adda for Women in India: Shaheen Bagh", *Astragalo,* 27, 2020
4. Ghosh A., "Art as Resistance in Shaheen Bagh", *Forum: University of Edinburgh Postgraduate Journal of Culture and the Arts,* Issue 30, Spring 2020
5. Salam Z. U. & Ausaf U., *Shaheen Bagh-From a Protest to a Movement,* Bloomsbury India, 2020
6. Mustafa, S., (ed.) *Shaheenbagh and the Idea of India,* Speaking Tiger Books LLP, New Delhi, 2020
7. Chopra, D., "The resistance strikes back: women's protest strategies against backlash in India", *Taylor and Francis Online,* 07 Dec 2021, pp. 467-491
8. "Shaheen Bagh: The Women occupying Delhi Street against citizenship law – "I don't want to die proving I am Indian", *BBC,* 4 January 2020
9. Mahmudabad, A. K., "Indian Muslims and the Anti-CAA Protests: From Marginalization Towards Exclusion" & "The Hindutva Turn: Authoritarianism and Resistance in India, Winter 2019-2020", *Awakening to India's New Face,* 24/25, 2020
10. Ibid.; By December 2019, in Lucknow, a group of citizens from various professions, backgrounds and affiliations had gathered to discuss how to articulate and plan protests against the controversial Citizenship Amendment Act (CAA). One of the speakers stood up and began with the customary nod to the Sachar Committee Report but before he could finish, another participant interrupted and said "but Sir, forget about the Sachar Report and talk about the Constitution."
11. Rahman, Syed U., "Anti-CAA Movement Changed Muslim Women Forever", *News Click,* 30 June 2020
12. Lahiri, S., "We Are Seeing, for the First Time, a Sustained Countrywide Movement Led by Women", this article was originally published on January 13, 2020 and is being republished by *The Wire,* March 8, 2020

13. Ahmad, Salik. "AMU: Student's Hand Amputated, 'Police Violence worse than in Jamia," *Outlook*, December 18, 2019, Retrieved September 5, 2020
14. Ibid.,
15. Rahman, Syed U., Op. cit.
16. See Ahmad, Imtiaz., the author of *Caste and Social Stratification Among Muslims in India*
17. Rahman, Syed U. Op. cit.,
18. Dixit N., "The women at the front lines of India's citizenship law protests: Having battled everyday sexism, female students come out in full force against bill excluding Muslims". *Aljazeera*, 23 Dec 2019
19. Bhandare, Namita, "Anti-CAA protests have shown women can lead", *Hindustan Times*, Dec 27, 2019
20. Ibid.,
21. Rahman, Syed U., Op. cit.,
22. Faisal. S. M., Op. cit.,
23. Kapur, M., "At a women-led protest site in India, Muslims navigate identity, hope, and despair", *Quartz*, January 3, 2020
24. Sharma Y & Sing S. Op. cit., p.10
25. Hussain N. & Ashraf M., "Meet 10 women who are spearheading movement against CAA-NRC in India", *Twocircles.net*, March 8, 2020
26. Arun Kumar and New Indian Express.
27. Hussain N. & Ashraf M., Op. cit.
28. Ibid.,
29. Ibid.,
30. Kalita K. & Dutta R., "Thousands of Assam women hit the streets to voice opposition to CAA", *The Times of India*, Guwahati, TNN, Dec 22, 2019
31. Hussain N. & Ashraf M; Dutta R., "Thousands of Assam women hit the streets to voice opposition to CAA", *The Times of India*, Guwahati, TNN, Dec 22, 2019
32. Ibid.,
33. Chattopadhyay, Suhrid Sankar, "People's march against CAA & NRC: A different tune in West Bengal", *Frontline*, Kolkata, Jan 03, 2020
34. The Wire, 15/JAN/2020
35. Intensity of the protest was as much as that to demining the movement the Prime Minster Modi, an election rally in Dumka (Jharkhand), went so far as to declare that those who spread violence were "recognisable through their clothes" (Kumar 2019). This was

mainly a reference to the niqābs and hijābs worn by the Muslim women who had taken a lead in organizing anti-CAA protests across the country. See for detail: Mahmudabad, A. K., Op. cit.

36. Raju, B. S., "Muslim women protest against CAA and NRC in Hapur, apprise DM of their worries, Meerut", *Hindustan Time*, December 22, 2019
37. The Wire, 15/JAN/2020
38. Rahman, Syed U., Op. cit.,
39. Ibid.,
40. Ibid.,
41. Matta, A., "Anti-NRC-CAA Protests Have Left Women More Empowered, Confident at Home", *The swaddle*, 15, 2020
42. Kadiwal, L., "Feminists against Fascism: The Indian Female Muslim Protest in India, Institute of Education", University College London, London WC1E 6BT, UK, Educ. Sci. 2021, 11(12), p.793
43. Lahiri, S., Op. cit.,
44. Kumar, Anuj. "Women playing prominent role in anti-CAA, NRC protests", *The Hindu*, Gaziabad, February 09, 2020
45. Khurana, A., "Three years after Shaheen Bagh: Why the anti-CAA protests were an inflection point in Indian feminism", *The Indian Express*, December 21, 2022

Ethnography of Brass Casting Technology of Koitara in Burdwan District: A Traditional Metal Casting Identity of Bengal

Milan Chandra Roy

Tradition of brass and bell metal work is still persisting in different parts of eastern India. *Rarh* Bengal is one of the most important traditional brass and bell-metal crafts region. These are non-industrial mode of technology and production, which is practice by a number of groups by hereditary. The examples are *Kangsbanik, Karmakar, Kansari* and *Dhokra* Kamar etc.[1] Koitara is one important traditional center of cast metal technology of brass of *Rarh* Bengal of Golsi block -II in Burdwan District. In this chapter an attempt has been made to discuss the technological aspect of contemporary brass work, which is practiced by artisans of Koitara of Golsi Block-II. It may also highlight the sources of raw material, different tools, processing, finishing of objects etc. Objective of the present research is to understand the casting and forging technology of brass in Rarh Bengal as well as in Eastern India. We have very little idea of manufacturing techniques of brass and bell metal images, house hold and religious utensils of ancient to modern India. So, an in-depth study of technology of making and shaping and finishing of the crafts of everyday use home hold utensils to be also highlighted through ethnographic route. An ethnographic study of communities who are still producing these objects will be studied. Raw materials, clay, fuel, different equipment etc are also taken into account.

The major publications and studies on this line are scanty in number. To understand the ancient crafts, technology and its implication on human cultures, an ethnographic study and survey was conducted among the present day *Kansaris* and *Karmakar* of West Bengal. Several researchers and authors have also focused on the *Kansari* and their manufacturing technology. Examples may be cited of Bhattasali (1929), Barapanda (2002 a), Basu (2002), T. N. Mukharjee (1885), Chattopadhyay, P. K. and G. Sengupta (2011), Chattopadhyay (2005), Mukherjee (1977,1978,1984), Ray (1953), Roy Choudhury (1998), Santra (2002,1998), Sarkar (1998), Spooner (1911-12) and Mondal (2017). All those scholars have thrown light on the different aspects of traditional brass and bell metal crafts of this part of the country.

For the present study field survey, direct observation and interview methodology was followed. Observation, interview, case study methods have been used for collection of data from the field. Making of mould and crucible, polished the mould, casting and finishing all are studied by direct observation method. For present study data have been collected in interviewed with the artisans. Different tools for this craft are also study in detail by direct observation method. I used to make field survey to this crafts villages on 30.06.2018. The making process was observed step by step from starting to finish and also interviewed with artisans. Occupational and technological changes was also taken in account.

Copper is perhaps the most important metal discovered by human beings. From metallographic and chemical observation, it is not always possible to identify the manufacturing technology of any protohistoric metal object. Because of corrosion, natural decay and paucity of enough materials, the remnants of evidences of the manufacturing technology become impossible to be evaluated properly. The only alternative is to search seriously whether the manufacturing techniques are still continuing in the present or not.[2] Thompson (1991) suggested that while studying a particular craft from the archaeological point of view, the entire culture with full context ought to be observed to draw any archaeological inference.[3] In eastern India, the bronze technology was first introduced in the last phase of the Chalcolithic period.[4] So far, basic elements known to the people are copper, gold, iron, lead, silver, tin and zinc etc. Before the advent of the concept of element, unknowingly they had the practical idea about it and alloying with little tin is also noted in Eastern India from very beginning of human habitation that is between from the Chalcolithic to Iron ages. The evidence of use of pure metal has so far been discovered in Dhuliapur, Kushadwip, Narhan and Agiabir only. Agiabir is the only reported site about the high-tin bronze dating back to the 5th century BC.[5] In Eastern India the natural resources on minerals and woods are very much helpful to begin with the metallurgy. The ancient mining or smelting activities have been noticed in several places in Bihar, Jharkhand and West Bengal. Copper extraction in Singhbum, iron smelting near Birbhum and gold searching on the banks of Subarnarekha have continued for several thousands of years.[6]

Tradition of brass and bell metal work is still persisting in different parts of eastern India. *Rarh* Bengal is one of the most important traditional brass and bell-metal crafts region. These are non-industrial mode of technology and production, which is Practice by a number of hereditary groups. As example *Kangsbanik, Karmakar,Kansari* and *Dhokra* Kamar etc. Koitara (23º20'14"N, 87º41'33"E) is one important traditional center of cast metal technology of brass of *Rarh* Bengal of Golsi block -II in Burdwan District.[7] Artisans of Koitara, Golsi block-II are experts in making different type of utensil like big and small lota (water pot) named *Balaramghati, Batuaghati, Samsaighati, glass, oil bhar* (oil pot) and religious utensil. They are using the cast metal technique for making these crafts. They are familiar with Brass (an alloy of copper and zinc) and German silver (an alloy of copper, zinc and nickel) for making the jobs. But at present the artisans are mostly used brass scrap for making the new objects. Koitara, a small village of Golsi block-II, located at 23°20'14" N Latitude and at 87°41'33" E Longitude, is a central plain area of the Purba Burdwan District. It is situated Western part of Purba Burdwan District. The area is surrounded by the river Bhagirathi on the east, the Ajay River on the north-west and the Damodar River on the west and south.

One generation or near about three or four decades before so many families were engaged there to the traditional crafts production, says the old artisans of this village, aged 75 years, name is Madhusudhan Das (interview with Madhusudhan Das, dated 30.06.2018). He told that at that time Koitara was a famous traditional crafts center of Burdwan District and produce large variety of brass and bell metal utensils both of religious and house hold. But at present few families, probably 10(ten) to 12(twelve) families are engaged to this traditional craft production. They learn these crafts from their parents and grandparents. They are all Hindu by religion and belong to OBC-B category. Economically all the families are very poor and could not get any facility from the Government.

In metal history it is most important question that how the alloy is made? Copper is the mother element. The addition of other elements to it gives birth to several alloys. Chalcolithic people of Eastern India, knowingly or unknowingly were used ores and prepared bronze or brass alloys. The copper ore was mixed with the ores of tin as cassiterite, zinc as sphalerite or lead as galena.[8] The brass or *pital* is the alloy of copper with zinc. Brass bangle, reported from Kanjipani area of Keonjhor Diostrict (21°30' N, 83°28' E) in Orissa is the earliest evidence of brass in Eastern India.[9] Bronze or *kansa* is the alloy of copper with tin. It is also known as bell metal since it is the common alloy to make bells throughout Asia. According to the tin contents, the bronze or bell metal are classified in three categories. In first category, the percentage of tin is less than ten. Metallurgists call it 'alpha bronze'. In the second category, the percentage of tin is around 10 to 20. It is called beta bronze. In the third category, tin is above 20 percent. It is called high tin-bronze. High tin-bronze is most popular among others two category and golden in colour and mostly used for making house hold utensils.[10]*Bharan* is the alloy of copper, tin and zinc. It is lower bronze or *kansa* and reddish in colour. The technique of manufacture of this alloy is not share to someone, because the artisans maintain their trade secret.[11] From early 20th century in Eastern India, relatively a new alloy is used by the artisans for metal craft named German silver. This alloy is the combination of nickel, zinc and lead with copper. In Rarh Bengal, the artisans of Bishnupur of Bankura district and Bali Dewanganj and Manikpat of Hooghly district are used to make pitcher from this alloy.[12]

Most important information about copper and its alloy is available from Kuruspal in Chhattisgarh. Mahajan has used to make an in-depth study on this matter. He cited in his book about an undated Kuruspal stone inscription of Nagavamshi king Somesvar includes a word *Kansaravado*.[13] The scholar has pointed out that the word '*Kansaravado*' is closely connected with the hamlet inhabited by the workers of copper, bell metal or brass. The place was perhaps situated near *Kuruspal*. From the concerned period two names are also known from this region. These are *Tamanaladesa* and *Kansaravado* denoted the location of metal industry including high Tin-Bronze. These two names also may be suggestive of the place where copper and bell metal workers lived.[14] In 5th century CE, the Chinese traveler Fa-haien visited Bengal and mentioned that he has observed many musical instruments and called the country- the land of music and dance. During the ancient period a highly developed musical culture prevailed in Bengal. Various musical instruments are excavated from Paharpur, Mainamati, Jagjibanpur and so on. So, we can say that the music was an integral part of the Bengal culture. So, it is truth that from very ancient time, the metal craftsmen of Bengal produced musical instruments from *Kansa* (high-tin-bronze or bell metal, an alloy of copper and tin) or *Pital* (brass, an alloy of copper and zinc). The name of the musical instruments is *Kartal* (a small cymbal), *Jhanjar* (large cymbals), *Kansar*, mandira etc. *Kansar*, a musical instrument indicates that it is made of high tin-bronze. The *Kartal* and *Jhanjar* are made of the brass and bronze.[15]

The most illuminating evidence for the popularity of bronze come in the form of the rise of the *Kangsakara* caste in Early Mediaeval literature. The *Kangsa* or *Kansa* is bronze and the generic name *Kangsakara* (the copper-bronze worker) given to a social group indicates the popularity of their occupation, i.e., copper-bronze worker.[16] The copper-bronze producing class in Bengal was mentioned in the two 10th and 11th century's Puran, namely the Brahmavaivarta Puran and the Brihaddharma Puran. This Puran also mentioned that the *Karmakar* (iron smith) and the *Kangsakar* (bell-metal worker or bronze smith) are belonged to the highest category of the shudra.[17] These references in the Puran actually indicate expansion of the fourfold caste-based society by bringing the non-caste occupational or artisan communities into the caste system as *Shudras*. Although the term *Kansa* for bronze was already known from the early literature sources of the Middle Ganga valley, yet the *Kangsakar* occupational group is first reported in the Puran of the 10th -11th century in the context of Lower Ganga plain.[18]

In ancient period the discovery of large number of copperplates directly reflects that the copper smithy provided employment to a large number of artisans of India as well as Bengal and Orissa. The Nagari copper plate of Anangabhimadeva III refers to the term *tāmrākaras* (coppersmiths) who were the makers of copper plate.[19]Apart from the archaeological records much have been known about the metals and metallurgy of Eastern India from the classical texts Silparatna, Manasara, Manasollasa.[20]The metal cast crafts and industry has been reached in the high level of excellence in ancient Bengal.[21] Various kinds of metal works, like weapons of war (arrow-heads, spear-heads etc),[22] images of bronze or octo-alloy[23] have developed in early Bengal. Archaeological records as well as literary works testify the existence of these precious metal crafts. In Deopārā inscription of Vijaya-sena, there is engraved one description about RānakaŚūlapānī (chief artisan) as "Varendra-Śilpigoshthī-Chūdāmani". Sondhakarnandi's Ramacharit also informed us about the metal craft of eastern India. [24]

The Archaeological department of states (W.B). Archaeological Survey of India and the History and Archeology department of various Universities have excavated a large number of sites in Eastern India. All the excavated remains and finding objects reports have been published in Indian Archaeology – A Review (I.A.R.) and other journals. In Eastern India, a large number of Archaeological sites were excavated and a large number of metallurgical objects including copper and bronze objects were reported right from Chalcolithic to Medieval period. Most of the archaeological remans are preserved in different State Museum and Indian museum. Most important excavated Archaeological sites of Rarh Bengal as well as Bengal, which yielded metallic objects including copper and bronze artifacts, are known from Bahiri[25],

Baneswardanga,[26] Bangarh,[27] Bharatpur, Dhuliapur, Dihar,[28] Hatikra,[29] Jagjibanpur, Kankrajhor, Laljal, Mahisdal, Mangalkot,[30] Pakhanna, Pandur Rajar Dhibi,[31] Tamluk, Chandraketugarh,[32] Rajbadidanga,[33] etc. A large number of metallurgical objects were reported right from Chalcolithic to Medieval period.

Village Koitara is one of the most important traditional craft metal centers of Rarh Bengal. It is non-industrial mode of production and technology. The artisans of Koitara village are specialized in making different sizes brass utensil like big and small lota (water pot) named *Balaramghati, Batuaghati, Samsaighati, glass, oil bhar* (oil pot) and religious utensil. They are using here the cast metal technique for making these crafts. They are familiar with Brass (an alloy of copper and zinc) and German silver (an alloy of copper, zinc and nickel) for making the jobs.[34] But at present the artisans are mostly used brass scrap for making the new objects. We can discuss the hole traditional brass craft through ethnographic study among the present ethnic traditional brass craft communities under the following segment: -

Raw Materials:

The artisans of Koitara (Kamarpara) are manufactured brass items by casting technique. In the casting technique melted metal is casted in a mould. Primary raw materials used for the crafts are brass and German silver and different type of clays. Most of the artisans at present use the scrap metals as raw metal for the jobs, which are supplied by middleman as well as shopkeepers of nearby market (e.g., Durgapur, Burdwan and Dubrajpur etc.). Wooden piece and charcoal are used as fuel for furnace.

Equipment:

Different types of equipment are used by the artisans of Koitara. Most of the tools are necessary for after heating the mould and finishing the jobs. The tools are as follows:

i) Hammer (*Haturi*):

Mainly two type of iron hammer are used for these craft. One is comparatively big and other is small. Length and width of big hammer is 5 to 6 inches and 2 to 2.5 inches. On the one head of the hammer is round and flat and other head is tapering. The small hammer is round headed working edge with 4 to 5 inches length and 1 to 1.5 inches width. Another site of the hammer is tapering headed. Both hammers are used for broken the mould after casting. Sometimes the artisans are used small hammer for leveling the articles. Wooden shaft length of hammer is varying from 10 to 12 inches.

ii) Pincers (*Sharasi*):

Two types of pincers are used here. One is small and other is large. Small pincers are 12 to 14 inches in length and used for breaking the casting mould aftercooling. The long pincer is 40to 45 inches in length. It is called in local language "KHABLA". This pincer is used for bring out the mould from furnace and shake it and inverting it.

iii) Iron stick:

Two type of iron stick is necessary to this work. One is small and other is big. A 1.5 to 2 feet iron stick with pointed end is used for moving and pushing the charcoal in the small furnace and a big (also known as *Goj)* as 4 to 5 feet pointes head iron rod also used in big furnace for pushing the charcoal and for taking out the mould out from furnace.

iv) Lathe (*Kunda or Kund*):

Two types of lathes are found here. One is traditional wooden lathe and other is modern machine operated lathe. Indigenous traditional wooden lathe is also known as *KUNDA* or *KUND*. Except one cottage center, most of the workshops are used traditional wooden lathe. It is look like a wooden axle of 20 inches in length, turned manually with a comparatively big wheel. Both wheel and wooden axle are fixed with wooden frame. The big wheel is turned by a man with the help of the crank handle. It is connected to the wooden axle with a belt. When big wheel is turned, the wooden axle is also turned at a very fast speed. One face of wooden axle is covered with shellac. The product is mounted on this face and turned with the lathe. One artisan puts the finish on the job with an iron scraper. Modern machine lathe is operated by electric.

v) Furnace (*Bhati or Shal*):

Two kinds of furnace are used here. The local name of furnace is Bhati or Shal. A furnace where bakes the mould of jobs for casting, is comparatively wider. Other furnace is small and use for finishing the cast articles. The big furnaces are 2 feet to 3 feet high from the ground level. The surface top of the furnace is circular, with a diameter of 35 inches to 40 inches. The working mouth place of furnace is 12 x18 inches. The furnace hole continues down to the ground level, where the grating is located. It continued further underground, for another 2 to 3 feet. There is a slanting passage, which connected to the underground level of the furnace. This passage is the air duct. No bellows are used in this furnace. A small furnace is used for heating the jobs, located on the ground of workshop. This furnace is circular bowl shaped and oven is located at the middle of the furnace. It is used for warming up the bottom portion of the jobs. Hand operated blower machine is used in the furnace.

vi) Blower:

There is used hand operated blower machine in the small furnace, which is used for warming up the bottom portion of the jobs during scraping.

vii) Iron Scraper (*Lohali*):

It is made of iron with bamboo and wooden handle. Lengths of these scrapers are 8 inches to 10 inches including handle. These are used for scraping the jobs. The working end of these scrapers is slightly bent.

viii) Iron files (*Reth*):

Different sizes of iron files are used here for rubbing the extra projection of the objects. The size ranges from 10 inches to 12 inches in length with wooden shaft. Width of the file is 1' inches and tapering end.

ix) Water pot:

One water pot is kept near the small furnace and lathe. Before scraping, the iron scraper is rubbing up on a stone slave mixed with water.

x) Stone slap:

The artisans used one stone slap for scrap the working face of scraper. As the scraping is done very first.

xi) Electronic rubbing machine:

Here one workshop has been used the modern electronic rubbing machine for scraping and polishing the articles.

Fig. Hammer

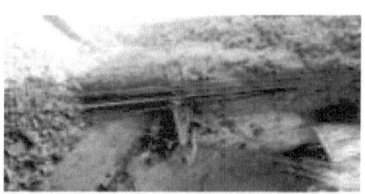
Fig. Big Pincers (*Khabla*)

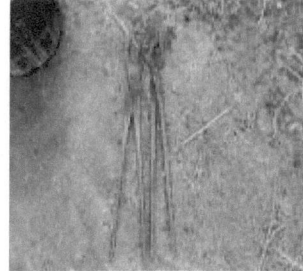
Fig. Small Pincers

Fig. Furnace and Iron Stick

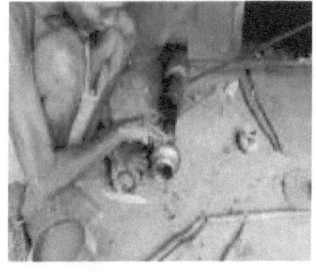
Fig. Scraper

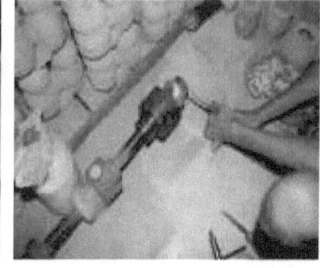
Fig. Electric operate lathe

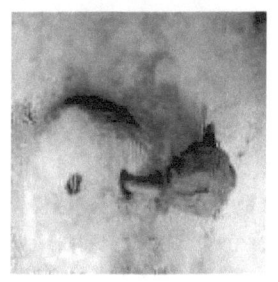
Fig. Blower

Fig. Hand operate wooden lathe

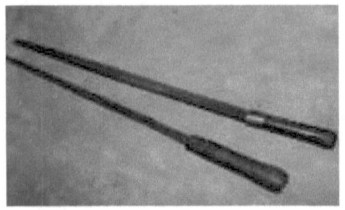 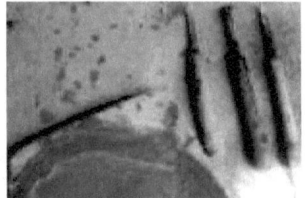

Fig- Iron files (*Reth*)   **Fig- Stone slap and scraper**

Making Process:

Generally, workshops are located adjacent to the house. Here except one workshop, the entire workshop's ground floors are earthen and mud-built house with tiled and straw roof. Except one side, other three sides of the workshops are closed. Big furnace is set at the corner of the workshop and rest area is generally used for breaking mould and finishing the jobs. All the products are made here by casting method. There is long process for making the whole crafts. The whole working establishment is divided into different section. E.g., the crucible and mould making, dry up these, scraping or polishing the mould, the mould set up with *muchi* or crucible (a container filled with metal), heating the mould in a big furnace for casting, bring out the heated mould from furnace with the help of big pincer and shake it and inverting it, breaking the mould and scraping etc.

At first the artisans of Koitara made mould and crucible. Huge quantity of different type clay is used for making of mould and *muchi* or crucible. Generally, three types clay are used for these crafts. These are sticky red soil, used for making of crucible or *muchi* and sandy and alluvial soil, used for making mould. Generally, these soils are collected from local field and nearby Domodar River. They made crucible with sticky red soil mixed with jut and cow dung for tempering. Then it left to dry in the sunshine. After, they use to make a mixture of soil with sandy soil, alluvial soil, rice husk and jut for making the mould.

These are applied for retention of heat and to prevent damage. The artisans are made it with the hands, generally women are engaged to this work. After dried, all these artifacts are also bran. The crucibles are made different size according to the desired sizes of jobs. A crucible may be used only one time for casting. The crucibles are filled up with brass scraps for smelting and casting. Making of mould is an elaborate process. The oil pot mould is made with the help of standard patterns. There are different stages of making of mould. Here the mould is mainly two parts. One is outer part and other is inner part. Outer portion has four parts, such as two outer site body parts, one mouth and other is bottom part. The outer and inner, both parts are used to make separately and joined together after drying.

The inner parts are made with the mixture of cow dung, sandy soil and alluvial soil by hand. It is locally called *core*. This part of mould is very soft and easily broken able. It is look like a round earthen ball with desired size. In case of making outer part of mould, the artisans at first prepare the clay. They mixed jute fabric, rice husk and sand soil with the alluvial soil. After proper mixing, they are used to make the mould. They made it with the help of standard pattern of jobs. This pattern is called *FARMA* in local language.

At first, the outer parts of patterns are smeared with automobile engine oil. Then fine mixture clay is covering the outer surface of the standard patterns and pressed with finger for proper thickness. Then it is left to dry for a moment. After proper dry, the mould is cut vertically into two halves and then left for dry two or three days. When the moulds are proper dried then it is separated from the pattern and all parts are also separated. Then inner part surface and inner site of outer part are polished by sand paper and small piece of white stone. At that time the artisans are also coated all parts by sieved alluvial soil and left these for dry. After drying all parts are put together including the core and tied with a string and coated all body of mould with mixture of alluvial soil and cow dang. A thin space is left between the core and inner portion of the outer mould. A narrow hole or channel is kept one site of the mouth of every mould for running of molten metal. Then crucible is filled up with brass scraps as require and two mould are joined with the crucible and coated the join with red *chetamati* and left to dry for few hours.

After proper dry, the casting is done in a big round furnace. The bottom portion of the furnace is filling up at first with coal and wooden piece. Over the coal, the moulds are arranged in the furnace in an upright position, but the crucibles are placed at the bottom site. At a time 30 or 40 mould and crucible are casting and needed 15to 20 kg coal. During casting the furnace is covered with pieces of earthenware for quick heating. It takes generally 3 hours to 3.30 hours for smelting the metal and the artisans can understand from the colour of crucible and mould. After complete melting, seeing the greenish yellow colour, the artisans bring out the crucibles from the furnace with the help of big pincer (artisans are called it KHABLA) and hold it upright position and also shake gently and inverting it on the mud floor, so that the molten metal can flow from the crucible through the narrow hole and cover the inner gaps of mould. After cooling 30 minutes, the mould including crucibles are broken and the small lota or oil bhar or jobs are taken out. After taken out the jobs, polishing is done by hand operated lathe with different types of iron file and iron scraper and scraping is done both the inner and outer side of the jobs. Before the scraping, the bottom of the job is heated in the small furnace with the help of hand operated blower.

 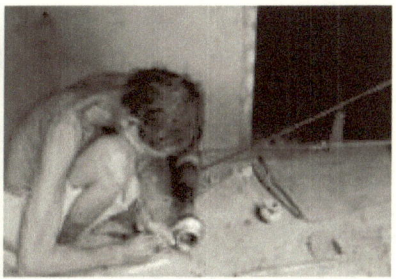

Fig. Pattern, mould and crucible **Fig. Scraping**

It has been found from the present study that the brass craft and the artisans are facing a number of problems. According to Madhusudhan Das, one generation or near about five decades before so many families were engaged their traditional crafts production. He told that at that time Koitara was a famous traditional crafts center of Burdwan District and were produce large variety of brass and bell metal utensils both of religious and house hold. But at present few families, probably 10(ten) to 12(twelve) families are engaged to this traditional craft production. So, day by day the picture of brass craft and craftsman has been changed. Cheap availability of aluminums and stainless steel is the one most important cause for the declining of this traditional craft. Not only that there are also a number of problems related to the traditional brass metal craft like scarcity and high price of raw materials, decreasing of demand due to high price of brass products and available cheaper aluminums and stainless-steel utensils, traditional time-consuming technology, low profit and intervention of meddle men or shopkeepers, scarcity of labour, no interest of next generation to this craft, hard laborious, insufficient capital for investment in the craft etc. In spite of these problems the brass craft is being sustained at present among the market competition of cheaper various utensils. Governmental help and modernizations of technology may improve this traditional craft and development. So, the present traditional knowledge is helpful for reconstructing the past technology. An ethnographic study is helpful and needed for the study of present traditional technology and reconstructing the past technology as well as different aspect of past metal technology.

References

1. Sarkar, S., "Indian craft: Technology static or changing-A case study of the *Kansari's* craft in Bengal, 16th to 18th centuries", *Indian Journal of history of Science,* No.*33* (2), 1998, pp. 131-42
2. Chattopadhyay, P. K., "Kansaris of Bengal: Ethnoarchaeological Studies at Bishnupur*",* in *Past and Present: Ethnoarchaeology in India,* 2006; G. Sengupta. S. Roychoudhury and S. Som (Eds), Pragati Publication, New Delhi, 2006, pp. 347-357
3. Thompson, R. H., "The archaeological purpose of ethnoarchaeology", in W. A. Longacre (Eds), *Ceramic Ethnoarchaeology,* University of Arizona Press, Tuescon, 1991, pp. 231-45
4. Chattopadhyay, P. K. and G. Sengupta. *History of Metals in Eastern India and Bangladesh.* Pentagon Press in association with Infinity Foundation, New Delhi, 2011
5. Singh, A. K. and Chattopadhyay P. K., "In search of high-tin bronze in Eastern India", *Puratattva,* No. 32, 2001-2002, pp. 101-05 & 227-28; Singh, A. K. and Chattopadhyay P. K., "Carinated and knobbed copper vessels from the Narhan Culture", *Iams India,* 23, 2003, pp. 23-27.
6. Chattopadhyay, P. K., *Metalcrafts of Eastern India and Bangladesh,* Publication Scheme, Jaipur, 2005
7. Mukherjee, M., "Metal craftsmen, their work and environment", *Journal of Indian Anthropological Society,* No. 19 (1), 1984, pp. 66-79; Mukherjee, M., *Metalcraftsmen of India*, Anthropological Survey of India, Calcutta, 1978; Mukherjee, M., *Folk metalcraft of Eastern India.* All India Handi-crafts Board, New Delhi,1977
8. Chakrabarti, D. K. and Hasan S. J., "The sequence at Bahiri (Chandra Hajrar Danga), district Birbhum, West Bengal", *Man and Environment,* No. 6, 1982, pp.111-149; Chakrabarti, D. K. 1996, Chakrabarti, D. K. 1993
9. Chattopadhyay, P. K. and G. Sengupta. 2011 & Chakrabarti, D. K. 1993, op. cit.
10. Ibid.; Barapanda, D. K., "Kansa O Petaler Prakarbhed (in Bengali)", *Lokashruti, No.* 20, 2002, pp. 140-53
11. Chattopadhyay, P. K., 2006, Op. cit.,
12. Ibid.,

13. Mahajan, M., *Chhattisgarh: A study in the culture and Historical Geography*, Sharada Publishing House, Delhi, 2000
14. Chattopadhyay, P. K. and G. Sengupta. 2011, Op. cit.,
15. Ibid.,
16. Basu, T., "Pachimbanger Dhatushilpa (in Bengali)", *Lokashruti*, No.20, 2002, pp.154-69
17. Dasgupta, N. and Chattopadhyay, P. K., "Copper Craft Tradition in the Lower Ganga Valley: Early Historic to Early Medieval periods" in Shahnaj Husne Jahan (Ed.) *Abhijnan: Studies in South Asian Archaeology and Art History of Artefacts*, British Archaeological Reports, International Series S1974, 2009, Oxford, pp.78-85; Majumdar, R. C., History of Ancient Bengal, Tulshi Prakashani, Kolata, 1971, p.542
18. Chattopadhyay, P. K. and G. Sengupta. 2011, Op. cit.,
19. Epigraphia Indica, vol. XXVIII, pp. 235-258 & Chattopadhyay, P. K., 2005, op. cit.,
20. Ibid.,
21. Santra, Tarapada, "Banglar Dhatushilpa (in Bengali)", *Kaushiki* 1998, pp.192-220; Santra, T., "Bangar Taijashpatra: Dainandinatar Dhatushilpa (in Bengali)", *Kaushiki*, 2002, pp. 94-151
22. According to statements of Agni-Purāna (245,21ff.) that Vaṅga was an important centre of sword manufacture.
23. Octo-alloy (ashtadhātu) means eight metals, namely copper, tin, lead, antimony, zinc, iron, gold and silver.
24. Majumdar, R. C. 1971, Op. cit.,
25. Chakrabarti and Hasan S. J., 1982, Op. cit.,
26. Mukherjee, S. C., "Excavation at Baneswardanga, District Barddhaman, West Bengal, 1960-1990", *Pratna Samiksha*, No. 2 & 3, 1993-94, pp.1-26
27. Goswami, K. G., *Excavations at Bangarh*, University of Calcutta, Calcutta, 1938-41
28. Pal, A. C., "Dihar: A Chalcolithic site", *Pratna Samiksha*, No. 1, 1992, pp.101-106
29. Ghosh, N. C., Nag A. K. and Chattopadhyay P. K., "The Archaeological background and iron sample from Hatigra," *Puratattva*, No. 18, 1987-88, pp. 21-27
30. Roy, A., "Mangalkot: an ancient township- its history and Archaeology, in Nalinikanta Satavarsiki-Studies" in *Art archaeology of Bihar and Bengal*, edited by D. Mitra and G. Bhattacharya, Sri Satguru Publication, Delhi, 1989, pp. 285-291; Ray, A., "Archaeology of Mangalkot, in Historical Archaeology of India", in *A dialogue between archaeologists and historians*, ed. A. Roy and S.

Mukherjee, Books and Books, New Delhi, 1990, pp. 131-140; Ray, A., "Chalcolithic culture of West Bengal", in *Studies in Archaeology*, ed. A. Dutta, Books and Books, New Delhi, 1991, pp. 109-133; Ray, A. and Mukherjee S. K., "Excavation at Mangalkot", *Pratna Samiksha*, No.1, 1992, pp. 107-225; Roy, Sudhangshu K., "The artisan castes of West Bengal and their craft", in A. Mitra (ed.), *The Tribes and Castes of West Bengal*, West Bengal Government Press,1953; Roy Choudhury, Suchira, "Cire Perdue casting in Bengal: A living tradition among the Dhokra Kamar-A socio-religious case study". *Unpublished post-graduation Dissertation.* Deccan College, Pune,1998

31. Dasgupta, P. C., *Excavation at Pandu Rajar Dhibi*, Directorate of Archaeology, Calcutta, 1965
32. Chattopadhyay, P. K., "Metal finds from Chandraketugar, West Bengal: Archaeotechnical studies", in G. Sengupta and S. Panja ed. *Archaeology of Eastern India: New Perspectives*, CASTEL, Kolkata, 2002
33. Das, S. R., "Rajbadidanga*"*, *Asiatic Society*, Calcutta,1968; Das, S. R., "Archaeological discoveries from Murshidabad district (West Bengal)", *Asiatic Society*, Calcutta, 1971
34. Mondal, D. K., *A study among the brass working communities in Eastern India, Department of Anthropology*, University of Calcutta, Calcutta, 2017

Women Empowerment: Perspective of Political Participation in India (1950-2019)

Dr. Bikash Das

Empowerment has become a fashionable and buzz word. It essentially means decentralization of authority and power. It aims and getting participation of deprived sections of people in decision making process. In other words, giving voice to voiceless. Activists want government to empower poor people including women by legislative measures and welfare programmes. Unless capacity is built in these sections in reality, the power is used by others rather than the section for which they are meant. Empowerment may mean equal status to women, opportunity and freedom to develop herself. The focus of empowerment is equipping women to be economically independent, self-reliant, have a positive self-esteem to enable them to face any difficult situation and they should be able to participate in the process of decision-making. Empowerment is the process by which the disempowered or powerless people can change their circumstances and begin to have control over their lives. Empowerment results in a change in the balance of power, in the living conditions and in the relationships.

The women, world over, are struggling to break the shackles that bind them and challenging the unequal distribution of power in society. Transforming the existing in egalitarian pattern of gender relationships necessitates leadership in the state, markets and civil society – the key centres of power in the present globalizing economy. It is, therefore, imperative for women to be in the corridors of power and have the power to negotiate a better deal for themselves, if they are to influence policy decisions which have an impact upon them. Empowerment of women in all spheres, in particular the political sphere is crucial for their advancement and the foundation of a gender-equal society. Women's political empowerment is premised on "three fundamental and non-negotiable principles: a0) the equality between women and men. B) Women's right to the full development of their potentials, and c) women's right to self-representation and self-determination". In empowerment, the key indeed is 'TOWER". It is power to 'access' 'control' and make 'informed choices'. To use an Indian expression, it is 'SHAKTI', which is manifested through the use of a mix of power, effectiveness, capability, force and influence to challenge and transform the structures and institutions of patriarchal ideology and existing power relations. According to Jakarta declaration, 'Empowerment of women is not only an equity consideration; it was also a necessary precondition for sustainable economic and social development. Involvement of women in the political arena and decisions-making roles is an important tool for empowerment as well as monitoring standards of political performance'. The application of the philosophical underpinnings of the Jakarta declaration are necessary, because in the countries where women have gained near equal representation such as in the Scandinavian countries, they have begun to alter the very nature of politics.

In India numerous steps have been undertaken to provide constitutional safe guards and institutional framework for activities for women welfare. The development of women has been the central focus in developmental planning since independence. There have been various shifts in policy approaches during the last 25 years from the concept of 'welfare' in the 70s to 'development' in the '80s' and now to 'empowerment' in the '90s'. Now the emphasis is on the inclusion of women in decision-making and their participation at the policy formulation levels. The Government of Indian has declared the year 2001 as year for the empowerment of women, but the struggle to reach this stage has been long and arduous. The concern for women's political equality in India first emerged as a political issue during the national movement in which women were active participants. As early as 1917, Indian women raised the issue of representation in politics, which at a time meant a demand for universal adult franchise. By 1929 woman had the right to vote on the basis of wifehood, property and education. Under the Government of India Act, 1935, all women over 21 could vote provided they fulfilled the conditions of property and education. Post independence, women continued to play a significant role in less conventional political activities such as environmental movement, anti-alcohol agitation, peace movement and even revolutionary activities, which equally affect power relationships as they have the capacity to influence the state. Yet, politics proved to be a very inhospitable terrain for women and continuous to be the male bastion into which the entry of women is severely restricted.

Women continue to remain invisible and marginalized in decision-making bodies, leading to lack of a feminist perspective in political decision-making. It was only with the setting up of the Committee on the Status of Women in India (CSWI) September, 1971 that the demand for greater representation of women in political institutions in India was taken up in a systematic way. Earlier the focus of the growing women's movement had been on improving women's socio-economic position. The CSWI Report "Towards Equality" (1974) reveals that political parties have "tended to see the women voters and citizens as appendages of the males ....". It also refers to the 'tokenism' involved in having a few women in the legislature and executive, who are unable to act as spokespersons for women's rights on account of their dependent and minority status. Recognising the 'tokenism' inherent in associating women representatives through election, co-option or nomination in local bodies, the report suggests a more meaningful association of women in the structure of local administration.

The question of reservation of seats was left to the National Perspective Plan for women to take up. It recognised that political participation of women is severely restricted and suggested that a 30 per cent quota for women be introduced at all levels of elective bodies. The process of reservation was initiated during Rajiv Gandhi's Prime-Mini-starship. The entire issue took on a political hue as it became a moot point whether the introduction of reservation at the level of Panchayats and urban local bodies was really meant to give increased representation to women or was a populist measure aiming to create a women's constituency at a time when the Congress Party needed to resurrect its image. These doubts notwithstanding, the 73rd and 74th amendments to the Indian Constitution in 1993, which provided for 33 percent reservation for women in Panchayats and Urban Local Bodies. These amendments, as a strategy of affirmative action, served as a major breakthrough towards ensuring women's equal access and increased participation in political power structures.

Thus, women are making significant gains in the political sphere where increased participation is rapidly empowering women, boosting their confidence, changing perceptions regarding their contribution, and improving their status and position in society. For instance, political participation and grassroot democracy have been strengthened considerably by the 73rd and 74th Constitutional Amendments that have created new democratic institutions for local governance. By 1999, under the provisions of said Amendments 2,27,698 Gram Panchayats at the village level, 5,906 Panchayat Samitis at the Block level and 474 Zilla Parishads at the district level had been created. In addition, some 3,586 urban local bodies had been created. So far, 2.5 million members have been elected to Gram Panchayats, 1,29,871 members have been elected at the Block level to Panchayat Samitis, and another 12,671 members have been elected at the district level as Zilla Parishad members. Reservation of one-third of all seats for women has been constitutionally ensured in local bodies. The impact of this has been phenomenal. By 1999, as many as 7,68,582 women had been elected to Gram Panchayats, and 38,582 women to Panchayat Samitis. Another 4,030 women were elected as Zilla Parishad representatives.

Table:1

Women's Presence in the Lok Sabha

Year	Total Seats	Women MPs	% Women MPs
1952	499	22	4.41
1957	500	27	5.40
1962	503	34	6.76
1967	523	31	5.93
1971	521	22	4.22
1977	544	19	3.29
1980	544	28	5.15
1984	544	44	8.9
1989	517	27	5.22
1991	544	39	7.17

1996	543	39	7.18
1998	543	43	7.92
1999	543	49	9.02
2004	543	45	8.03
2009	543	59	10.86
2014	543	62	11.41
2019	543	78	14.36

[Source: Election Commission of India)

Women have, however, not found adequate representation in the Lok Sabha. The percentage of elected women Lok Sabha members has never exceeded 12. Table 1 shows representation of women in. Lok Sab-has since 1952. Average representation of women in Lok Sabha works out to only 7. The presence of women in the Upper House has been only slightly higher overall, probably due to indirect elections and nomination of some women members. It was highest in 1990 at 15.5 per cent and shows a declining trend thereafter. Nonetheless, this representation does not even come close to the 33 per cent mark (See Table 2). It is significant to note that the Deputy Chairperson of the Rajya Sabha in all for more than 25 years has been women, yet women face increasing competition from male politicians for nomination.

Table:2

Representation of Women Members in the Rajya Sabha

Year	Total Seats	Number of Women	% Women
1952	219	16	7.3
1957	237	18	7.6

1962	238	18	7.6
1967	240	20	8.3
1971	243	17	7.0
1977	244	25	10.2
1980	244	24	9.8
1985	244	28	11.4
1990	245	38	15.5
1996	223	20	9.0
1998	223	19	8.6
2006	245	25	10.20
2009	245	22	8.97
2014	245	29	11.83
2019	245	24	9.79

[Source: Election Commission of India)

The number of women contesting election has always been low, as may be seen from Table 3. The highest number of women contestants has been merely 636 in 2014, while the number of male contestants has always been in thousands, the highest being 13,353 in 1996. Yet it is encouraging to note that the percentage of winners among women has consistently been more than that of the men, notwithstanding the fact that more often than not, the losing seats are offered to women candidates by the respective political parties. For example, in 1996, only 3.8 per cent of male candidates won, in comparison to 6.7 per cent of female candidates. Likewise, the percentage of winners was 11.2 per cent for men and 15.7 per cent for women in 1998 and 12.3 per cent and 17.3 per cent respectively in 1999.

Table:3

Women As Contestants in Lok Sabha:

Year	Males	Females	Total	% Male Winning	% Female Winning
1952	1831	43	1874	26.05	51.16
1957	1473	45	1518	31.7	60
1962	1915	70	1985	24.0	50
1967	2302	67	2369	21.3	44.8
1971	2698	86	2784	18.5	24.4
1977	2369	70	2439	22.1	27.1
1980	4478	142	4620	11.5	19.7
1984	5406	164	5574	9.2	25.6
1989	5962	198	6160	8.5	13.6
1991	8374	325	8699	5.9	12
1996	13353	599	13952	3.8	6.7
1998	4476	274	4750	11.2	15.7
1999	3976	278	4254	12.3	17.3
2004	5080	355	5435	9.8	12.3
2009	2514	556	8070	6.44	10.61
2014	7615	636	8251	6.31	9.74
2019	7316	724	8040	6.35	10.77

[Source: PIB, Ministry of Information and Broadcasting]

This scenario is also typical of the State level. There are only a few instances of women holding portfolios of finance, industry, etc., and are mainly relegated to what are considered 'women specific' departments. The source reveals that the highest percentage of women in the State Legislative Assemblies has been 10.8 per cent in 1957 in Madhya Pradesh. Haryana has had the highest average of women in the Assembly at 6.1 per cent and Manipur, the lowest at 0.3 per cent. The period average varies between a mere 2 per cent and 6 per cent. Significantly, there seems to be slight or no correlation between literacy and female representation. Kerala, with its high literacy rate, has a low state average of 3.6 per cent. Even Rajasthan and Bihar have higher averages at 4.7 per cent and 4.5 per cent respectively.

Reservation for Women in Parliament and State Legislatures: Taking this whole question to its logical conclusion, the demand gathered momentum and the question of quotas came up again in 1995. This time the focus was on women in Parliament. Initially, most political parties agreed to introduce 33 percent reservation for women in Parliament and State Legislatures and in order to attract women voters, the 1996 election manifestoes of almost all the political parties echoed this demand. But soon doubts surfaced. When the Bill addressing this issue was introduced in the Eleventh Lok Sabha in 1997, several parties and groups raised objections. The objections focused around two main issues: first, the issue of overlapping quotas for women in general and those for women of the lower castes; second, the issue of elitism. The Bill was first introduced by Dev Gowda led United Front Government. But persistent demands for a sub-quota for other Backward classes and minorities resulted in its being referred to a Parliamentary Committee headed by Gita Mukherjee, which recommended its passage, rejecting the demand for sub-quotas, despite differences among members on the various issues involved. The demand for sub-quotas for OBCs and minorities is seen, again to be merely a way of stalling reservation for women; there are no instances of political parties having such quotas in their own cadres. The Bill has already been introduced four times, but is stalled each time. The ugly scenes witnessed in Parliament at the time seem to indicate a devaluation of the agenda of women's empowerment.

However, the Rajya Sabha on March 9, 2010, took a historic and giant step' by voting (191 for and 1 against) to amend the Constitution, providing one-third reservation of seats in Parliament and State Assemblies for women. The Bill has to be passed by the Lok Sabha and ratified by one-half of the States before it comes into effect. Assuming that the Women's Reservation Bill gets signed into law, how will it work on the ground? If women gain control of one-third of the seats in the Lok Sabha and the State Legislative Assemblies, what will be its effect on their male counterparts? How will rotation of seats work in practice? Who decides which seats go to women? And what happens to pocket-borough constituencies such as Amethi, Rae Bareli and Chhindwara?

First, the key features of the Bill: One-third of all seats in the Lok Sabha and the Assemblies (including Delhi) will be reserved for women. In the case of the Scheduled Castes and Scheduled Tribes, the reservation will work as a quota within quota–A third of the seats currently reserved for the two categories will be sub-reserved for SC/ST women. Reservation of seats for women will be in rotation and will cease 15 years after the commencement of the Act. Seat allocation will be done in a manner determined by Parliament through enactment of a law. Now is the time of implications of the legislation. Since one-third of the seats will be reserved during each general election, each seat in the Lok Sabha and each seat in each of the Assemblies will have one reserved term and two free terms in the course of three elections. In a 15-year time limit, this will translate as each seat getting reserved for women just once—provided, of course, that governments complete their terms and elections are held once every five years. If there are six instead of three elections in this period, each seat will get reserved twice. After 15 years, each seat will have been reserved at least once, the idea being that women representatives should have reach and spread across the country.

It can be conclusively stated that there has been a radical change in the movement for empowerment of women. Recognition is dawning that women are indeed becoming a political force, both nationally and internationally. In this context it would be noteworthy to recall the observations of Nobel Laureate Amartya Sen in his book, "India: Economic Development and Social Opportunity", "Women's empowerment can positively influence the lives not only of women themselves but also of men, and of course, those of children."

References

1. Gupta, N.L., *Women's Education through Ages,* Concept Publications Co., New Delhi, 2003

2. Agarwal, Bina, "Land Rights for Women: Making the Case, in a Field of One's Own", *Gender and Land Rights in South Asia*, Cambridge Univ. Press, 1994, pp.1-50

3. Agarwal, S. P., *Women's Education in India*, Vol-III, Concept publications Co. New Delhi, 2001

4. Parihar, Lalita, *Women & Law-From Impoverishment to Empowerment- A Critique*, Eastern Book Company, 2011

5. Rao, R.K., *Women and Education*, Kalpaz Publications, Delhi. 2001

6. Gordon, L.P., *Violence against Women,* NY Nara Science Publishers, 2002

7. Rao, M.K., *Empowerment of Women in India*, Discovery Publishing House, New Delhi, 2005

8. Bhuyan, D., Panigrahi R.L., *Women Empowerment,* Discovery Publishing House, New Delhi, 2006

9. "Constitutional Law: Constitutional and Charter Provisions: Right of Women to Vote", *Michigan Law Review*, vol. 16, No. 2, 1917, p. 125

10. Agrawal, Meenu. "Women Towards Political Mobilization in Panchayati Raj Institution", in J.L Singh (ed.), *Women and Panchayati Raj*, Sunnrise Publications, New Delhi, 2005, p. 41.

11. Palanithurai, *Dynamics of New Panchayati Raj System in India,* Vol. IV, Concept Publishing Company, New Delhi, 2005, pp. 7-8

12. Archana Srivastava, "Political Participation of Women through Panchayati Raj Institutions in India", *Indian Journal of Political Science*, No.3, 2008, p. 214

13. Praveen, Rai. "Electoral Participation of Women in India: Key Determinants and Barriers", *Economic and Political Weekly*, Vol. XVLI (3), January 2011, pp. 47–55

14. Rukmini, S. "Rising female voter turnout, the big story of 50 years", The Hindu, 7 November 2013

15. Rout, Akshay. "Women's Participation in the Electoral Process", Election Commission of India, March 2014

16. Guha, Phulrenu; et al. (December 1974). "Towards Equality: Report of the Committee on the Status of Women in India" Government of India. Ministry of Education and Social Welfare, March 2014

17. Kaul, Shashi; Shradha Sahni. "Study on the Participation of Women in Panchayati Raj Institution". Studies on Home and Community Science, Vol. 3 (1), 2009. pp. 29–38

Function of Political Parties in Modern Democracy:
A Study of India

Animesh Chowdhury & Sujoy Pal

The political party system has become an essential feature of the modern social system and the process of modernization. In the current social system, political parties are playing an important role as institutions protecting people's needs and interests. Therefore, in a representative parliamentary democracy, political parties are essential. The existence of the first political party is usually traced back to the British period. In the 19th and 20th centuries, the issue of party system began to gain importance. Today, party system is the lifeblood of democracy. The science that discusses political parties is called "Stasiology" and this term is derived from "stasis" which means the attitude of opposition. Political parties are maintaining political stability in the modern state system by performing various functions.

According to Edmund Burke, a group of people who believe in a particular ideology and want to serve the national interest is called a political party. Joseph Schumpeter again thinks that a group of people who believe in certain ideologies are interested in capturing political power. Professor Alan Ball defines a political party as the acquisition of political power and the groupings that form on the basis of that power. There are some basic features of political Party, viz. A political party is a group of people who believe in the same political ideology; Members belonging to a political party believe in the same political ideology and are guided by this belief; Political parties participate in elections with the objective of forming the government; Political parties have to build party organization and campaign in every constituency to win elections; Political parties have to garner massive public opinion to win elections; All the political parties may not be able to win the elections and capture the power so those who cannot win play the role of opposition parties; Political parties adopt programs of public interest and national interest to win elections and form government; Political parties openly express their party policies and objectives to the public; Political parties form alliances or coalitions among themselves to gain government power and Political parties keep the people politically alert, aware and educated. The survival and operation of contemporary political society are now dependent on political parties. In this section, we look at the definitions, histories, traits, roles, and purposes of political parties in various international political systems. After finishing this lesson, you ought to be able to describe the features of a political party, the origin of political parties, functions performed by a political party under different types of political systems and will be identify the challenges faced by political parties in contemporary times.

Merits of political parties: Political parties play a crucial role in a democratic system of government. Professor Barker contends that if democracy is acknowledged, then the party system must also be accepted. Without the party system, it is difficult to create and maintain a representative democratic democracy. Political parties' significance is being established by expanding their roles in the contemporary state structure.

a) Election of representatives is easy

In the political system, citizens may easily elect their representatives. It is impossible to assess the unique credentials of each candidate for office on behalf of the electorate. As a result, if the political party arranges the matter, it will be simple for the electors to choose representatives in line with the party's philosophy and platform.

b) Emergence of best policies and practices

Political parties select the subjects that are more crucial to society. As a result, during the election campaign, the critical debates about the nation's numerous challenges and their remedies are where the best tactics and policies are produced. wherein the state's quick development is made possible.

c) Building solidarity among representatives

The party system in representative governance creates consensus among the elected officials, allowing the efficient and focused operation of the government.

d) Duration of Government:

In a democratic system of government, the majority party received credit for forming the government when elections were held. The result is that the government is always supported by the majority of the parliamentarians. So, there is no worry about durability.

e) Cooperation between the Executive and the Legislature:

As a result of a majority party in the legislature constituting the government, cooperation is fostered in both categories, which improves administrative excellence for the growth of the democratic state.

f) To preserve a form of democracy:

The Democracy Public opinion is seen as a form of governance. Democracy is based on what people think. During election season, the majority party is in power. Therefore, the party system aids in forming and expressing public opinion and upholds democracy.

Demerits of political parties: there are some demerits of existence of multy political parties as follows

a) Against national unity:

If in a nation several-party system if there is national harmony disruption possibility never absent. Party members' rigid party loyalty Be motivated. They are just concerned with what is best for their own party. How many political parties are at odds with one another nationwide undermines the nation's cohesiveness.

b) Damage to national interest:

A political party National interest is disregarded as a result of constant preoccupation with narrow party objectives. This is frequently seen as placing party interests ahead of national interests.

c) The morality of society has declined:

Political parties utilize a variety of dishonest tactics to fulfill their own goals, including making false assertions. As a result, there is more corruption in society. As a result, moral standards are lowered and the political climate of the nation is corrupted.

d) The person qualified in governance can't participate:

Regarding the party system Many intelligent and competent citizens are denying opportunities to participate in governance. Due to the corruption and ugliness of the party structure, a highly intelligent and efficient individual does not want to be involved. Therefore, their expertise and wisdom are not being contributed to the nation's administrative sector.

e) Government Party Bias:

Party to the agreement Instead of requiring that the political party running for a variety of government positions achieve a majority in the polls, numerous government positions to members of their party. Government functionality is impacted as a result.

f) Damage to National Interest:

Without considering the country's greater interests in order to win elections, the ruling party makes decisions and passes laws. These are designed to catch people off guard. It accomplishes its goal of winning support from the public, but at the expense of the country's overall interests.

Political party systems and democratic government are intricately interwoven. It is impossible to manage representative governance effectively without a party structure. Currently, party rule has replaced democratic rule. In the contemporary state structure, political parties serve a wide range of purposes. The need of the party system's existence may be found in each of these roles. All the functions that political parties perform can be expressed as follows.

There are so many functions of the political parties

a) The governing function:

This complex modern society would be impossible to operate without political parties. Government formation is facilitated by political parties. Additionally, they provide stability to the government, especially if some of the officials are party members. Political parties often work together in the legislative and administrative branches of government. Parties offer crucial internal and external opposition and criticism to the administration.

b) The electoral function:

Political parties are essential to elections in democracies. Candidates are often chosen by political parties during elections. They provide resources and assistance for political campaigns. According to a new electoral research, voters are confused by the complexity of the issues and the variety of options, which makes it difficult for the average person to make the best decision during elections. Because of this, one of the odd roles played by political parties is to make politics more accessible to the general public. To secure votes and safeguard the election of their candidate to the legislature or other public office, political parties must organize their vote bank. However, all political parties work to convince voters that their candidates are more trustworthy than those of their opponents. They establish policies which the electorate must support. With the ability to hold them accountable for policy successes or failures, parties provide a tag with one that the electorate can recognize and accept.

c) The representative

Function Political parties ensure that problems of social importance are included in the political system and help individuals to establish their own beliefs. They are the primary input systems that ensure that societal demands and aspirations are met. One of the fundamental and necessary parts of a party is a function of this nature.

d) The recruitment and participation

In modern, democratic nations, the majority of political activists are party members. Political parties serve the primary purpose of inspiring individuals to become political activists in these nations. They are responsible for providing the states with their political philosophies. High-profile individuals are elected to positions of authority, and candidates for president are frequently the members of political parties. In a parliamentary system, the prime minister is often the leader of the majority party in parliament, and the most significant party members typically hold the other positions of responsibility. Political parties occasionally provide policymakers with information and skills training sessions. Otherwise, traditional leaders like those of military organizations or royal families typically hold power in nations when political parties are impotent. Because they aim to remain in power for a long period, political parties select their candidates from within their own families.

e) Organization and Modernization of Traditional Societies

Political parties play a significant role in the organization and modernization of varied and fragmented societies. A society transits from the traditional to the contemporary stage of development through the process of modernization. A traditional civilization attempts to imbue the distinguishing economic, social, and political characteristics of contemporary society through this process. Organization of a disorganized society into an organized polity is the first step in political parties' modernization role. They cross the gaps between individuals and social groupings to do this. In a society that is disorganized or fractured, this role begins when a party begins the process of nation-building. The political parties have a crucial role in choosing the model of modernization and political growth after the polity is established. Political parties determine the course or model of economic, social, and political growth that a newly formed state will follow. One well-known example is the Indian National Congress (INC). Since its founding in 1885, the INC has been instrumental in uniting India's bitterly divided populace in opposition to the British colonizers. India's course towards modernization during the post-independent era was decided by the INC. But it's not just the post-colonial states that are affected. In the 17th and 18th centuries, parties in Europe and America created and controlled their modernization.

f) Political Socialization

Political socialization is said to be facilitated by political parties. Political socialization is the process through which individuals become familiar with the political tradition, customs, and principles of their nation and pass these values down from one generation to the next. Political parties serve as a conduit via which political culture is transmitted from one generation to the next. People are educated in a variety of methods. First, during election time, political parties and their representatives approach people to tell them of their ideas and programmes in an effort to sway their votes. Second, ruling parties inform the public about the government's initiatives and stances on a variety of subjects. Social media has become an essential instrument for political socialization in recent years. Thirdly, the opposition parties use agitation to highlight the faults of the government's projects and policies and to provide alternatives. People can learn about the government and its policies as a result. Fourth, through organizing and taking part in discussions on television, radio, and in print and electronic ads, the political socialization role is also carried out. Fifth, political parties inform the public of their plans for the future by releasing election manifestos ahead of time. People learn about their political system, its institutions, and its procedures for representation and political participation through these practices.

g) The Formation and Running of Government

The ultimate objective of a political party is the establishment of government. Political parties are distinguished from other social groupings by this feature, such as interest groups or civil society organizations. Political parties participate in the electoral process and run in elections in an effort to seize political power. They choose candidates and run campaigns on their behalf during this process. They work to win widespread popular support in order to establish a government. If they are unable to secure a majority on their own, they attempt to create a government by establishing alliances with other parties who share their views. In countries like India, Australia, and Brazil, this coalition-forming function is quite prevalent. It is now challenging for any party to win the necessary majority due to the societal variety, complex election system, and multi-party system in these countries. Political parties work to build governments after they have the necessary electoral majority. In the ministries and agencies, they appoint elected officials. In this approach, political parties' elected representatives control the administration and actively contribute to the formulation of its policies and plans.

h) Making and Shaping Government's Policies

At first look, it appears that the government's job is to make policies. But a closer inspection reveals that members of the ruling party hold political posts in the administration. The government can be referred to as a "party-government" in this sense. The government's programmes and policies on important subjects are determined in accordance with the party's larger consensus, which reflects the party's philosophy and policy consensus. Political parties' "the formulation of policy" is a crucial task, as Alan R. Ball correctly noted. Making policies and influencing them are two different tasks. Political parties have a direct role in the process of establishing policies, even though they carry out this duty behind the scenes. Parties have an impact on the policymaking process when creating policies. The role of creating policies is only carried out by the ruling party, however the role of influencing policies is shared by the two parties. Generally speaking, the ideology of the ruling party has a significant impact on how policies are developed, with the majority of Left and Centre parties favoring aggressive involvement in the economy and social welfare while the Right and Far-Right parties favor liberalization and privatization.

i) Coordination

Coordination between ministries and organs of government is realized through bodies like Political parties that perform coordination or mediating function between government and society. Political parties stabilize the political system and create and uphold social and governmental cohesion through their coordinating role. At least three layers are involved in the coordination function: coordination between the government and society, coordination within the government, and coordination within society. Governmental coordination takes place at two different levels: between the national, regional, and local levels of government, as well as between the three branches of the legislative, executive branch, and judiciary. While coordination between various levels of government takes place through inter-governmental entities like India's National Development Council and party meetings organized at various levels in the party, try meetings, parliament and its committees, and policy committees. Interest groups and non-governmental organizations are only two examples of the many civil society organizations that regulate society. Parties serve as a vehicle for societal cooperation together with other civil society organizations. Modern political parties have several occupational wings that participate in this process, including the labour unions, farmers, women, and youth wings. These specific occupational wings allow cooperation between party members and voters in that particular occupation.

j) Representation

People in contemporary states lack the time, education, and skills that are necessary to effectively represent themselves in various facets of political and social life. Political parties thus serve as the people's representatives and agents. They speak on behalf of their followers and party members in a variety of settings and forums, including the media, legislatures, assemblies, and election campaigns. The "interest integration function" outlined by Almond and Powel is similar to the representational role of political parties. Political parties unite a variety of interest groups through shared programs. The ability of political parties to successfully integrate votes from various interest groups depends greatly on the success of the government formation process; otherwise, they will not be able to muster the necessary number of votes to create a majority. Political parties perform a wide range of representational duties since representation may take many different forms, including ideology representation, geographical representation, identity representation, and interest representation. Many political parties represent the shared ideologies of their base followers and voters. Some political parties' priorities regional representation. The primary constituency of these parties is located in a specific geographic area, and they choose to identify with and represent that region's culture, language, and religion. Parties that advocate for the needs of their area include the Telangana Rastra Samiti in India, which promoted the idea of Telangana having its own state, and the National Conference, which fought for the autonomy of Jammu and Kashmir. Some gatherings serve to reflect specific identities. Examples of groups that advocate for the interests of Marathis and Dalits, respectively, are the Shiv Sena in Maharashtra and the Bahujan Samaj Party in Uttar Pradesh. Although these parties are successful in winning over people with different identities, a sizable portion of their votes come from their core identity-based supporters. A few political parties also serve as special interest representatives. Issues like climate change, nuclear disarmament, etc. may be of interest.

k) Control over Government

Political parties play a role that goes beyond that of the ruling party. They serve as the opposition as well. In democratic political systems, this position only exists. The political party fights against the tyranny of the government in its capacity as an opposition party. The government's programs and policies are criticized because, in their opinion, they are not in the best interests of the people and the state. They plan demonstrations, marches, and door-to-door canvassing to raise awareness of the governments' flawed objectives and policies. Governments, in turn, take the opposition party's role seriously and provide their ministers and other party members the opportunity to refute the accusations. In other democracies, the opposition parties attempt to overthrow and replace the incumbent party. They submit a motion of no confidence to the Parliament to achieve this. The opposition seizes the chance to establish the government when the ruling party is unable to demonstrate its majority.

l) Making Public Opinion

Political parties primarily perform the democratic function of molding public opinion. Through electoral, public opinion-making, and political socialization activities, political parties have direct relationships with citizens. Political parties serve as influencers of public opinion. They make an effort to mobilize and persuade people to support their stance on a particular subject. Consider the 123 Agreement, commonly known as the India-US Civil Nuclear Agreement, which received significant coverage in Indian media. The political parties were divided, but so was the rest of Indian society. The arrangement was opposed by the main opposition party, the Bharatiya Janata Party, as well as Marxist parties, who also influenced public opinion in their favor. The Indo-US Civil Nuclear Agreement is thought to be one of the few topics that Indians were aware of and shaping foreign policy since Independence. Parties do influence public opinion, but they do it most actively during elections because that is when voters are most likely to turn that view into votes.

Political parties occupy an ambiguous position in modern democracies. It is a product of the tension between the centrality of political parties as key institutions of modern democracy and their increasing inability to perform many of the functions as seen to be essential for the healthy performance of democracy. All the political parties play a pivotal role in the modern democracy. Without the existence of political parties, it is impossible to establish democracy. In Indian parliamentary democracy, there is an existence of the multiple party system. The functions of the political parties increased in the present democratic scenario. The common people are trusted more by political party for the fulfilment of their demand. Coalition government has emerged now in modern democracy as a form of parliamentary democracy. Political party helps to increase political consciousness of the common public. Making crucial decisions on the policies becomes difficult in multiparty political system. Many regional parties have emerged in the current context. This political parties are trying to influence the national politics. Social media and electronic media are making the political party more responsible towards the people.

References

1. Apter, D. E. (1969). "The Political party as a Modernizing Instrument", in Jean Blondel (ed.), *Comparative Government: A Reader,* London: Palgrave, pp. 86-95.
2. Ball, Alan R. *British Political Parties: The Emergence of a Modern Party System.* Macmillan, London, 1987
3. Ball, Alan R. *Modern Government and Politics*, Chatham House, Chatham, 1993
4. Duverger, Maurice. *Political Parties: Their Origin and Activity in Modern State*, University Printing House, Cambridge, 1967

5. Hague, Rod, Martin Harrop and John McCormick. *Comparative Government and Politics: An Introduction,* Red Globe Press, London, 2019
6. Katz, Richard S. "Political Parties" in Daniele Caramani (ed.), *Comparative Politics*, Oxford University Press, New York, 2020
7. Lapalombara, Joseph and Myron Weiner. "The Origin and Development of Political Parties", in Joseph Lapalombara and Myron Weiner (eds.), *Political Parties and Political Development.* Princeton University Press, Princeton, 1969
8. Neumann, S. "Toward a Comparative Study of Political Parties", in Jean Blondel (ed.), *Comparative Government: A Reader*. Palgrave, London, 1969
9. Pettitt, Robin T. *Contemporary Party Politics,* Palgrave, New York, 2014
10. Mondal, S., "Role of Political Parties in Indian Democracy", in *Journal of Advances and Scholarly Researches in Allied Education*, VOL-11, Issue 21, 2006
11. Michels, Robert, Political Parties: A Sociological Study of the Oligarchical Tendencies of Modern Democracy, Martino Fine Books, 2016
12. Chokoborthy, Bidyut, Coalition Politics in India, Oxford University Press, New Delhi, 2014
13. Kumar, Anil. Political Parties in India, Educreation Publishing, Delhi, 2018
14. Tiwari, R K, *Political Parties Party Manifestos and Elections in India 1909-2014*, Taylor & Francis, 2018

Indigenous Scientist and the Struggle for Identity in Colonial India

Mohiuddin Shaikh

Colonial rule introduced the western science in India. However, there is a debate about the spread of modern science in India. the British government started to culture science in this country to establish their imperial interests on a solid basis.[1] Robert Clive established the 'Indian Survey Organization' in 1767 AD.[2] They aimed to practice science in India in a way that would make their empire stronger. It was very difficult for Indian scientists to work in such a situation. The behaviour of the British towards Indians was discriminatory. There was no exception in the field of scientific practice also. The evidence of discriminatory scientific policy could be found in the statements of British officials. This was obvious in colonial science structure which was hostile to the natives.[3] They never looked favourably upon the scientific knowledge and skill of the Indians. In this case, reference can be made to Lansdowne's letter to Cross, in which he questioned the Indian's mental and physical ability to practice science.[4] There are several examples where they tried to keep the natives away from modern knowledge. Robert Orme, in 1872, did not hesitate to give the title 'feminine race'.[5] They tried to close the door for the natives to practice science by various negative arguments.[6] They set up several scientific institutions to use the financial resources of India for the benefit of their empire. GTSI was established (1818 AD) to carry out surveys on various subjects.[7] The Zoological Survey of India, Trigonometrical Survey of India (1802), Botanical Survey of India, Archaeological Survey of India were also established.[8]

Moreover, the main burden of controlling or managing these institutions was handle out of Indian capital by the capital London. As a result, Indian scientists as well as the vast public of India have to suffer since all activities are carried out under their fingers. Despite having suitable talents, skills and qualifications, the country's scientists were denied the rightful positions just because they were 'Indians'. They were not allowed to work independently.[9] Subsequently, Indian scientists raised a protest against it. Indigenous scientific pursuits started due to the indifference and humiliation of the British government towards the scientific practice of Indians. Although the struggle against the British Science Policy started privately, it gradually merged with national-level politics. Several institutions were established focusing on indigenous scientific practice. The Mahendralal established the 'Indian Association for the Cultivation of Science',[10] Prafulla Chandra Roy 'Bengal Chemical and Pharmaceutical Works,[11] Jagdish Chandra Bose 'Vasu Vigyan Mandir' etc.[12] Many scientists came forward in such work, Bholanath Bose, Upendranath Brakshachari, Shishir Kumar MI, Neelaratan Dhar and other famous people.[13] They joined this struggle. People like Rammohan Roy, Derozio, Vidyasagar, Bankim Chandra Chattopadhyay, Syed Ahmed Khan, native Raja-Maharajas, zamindars and others extended their financial support.[14] Several national-level institutions were formed, PA-PAICA.[15] 'Indian Chemical Society', 'National Institute of Science',[16] 'Mahomedan Literary Society' 1863,[17]'Scientific Society',[18] 'Bengal Technical Institute',[19] Indian Science Congress', 'Tata Institute of Fundamental Research' etc.[20] The science movement further moved forward with the trend of India's freedom movement. It was intensified by the Swadeshi movement. Indian scientists ignored all the adversities, and continued their struggle with hard work, self-sacrifice and patriotism and made own identity and glory before the world.[21]

During the English period, there was a debate about the expansion of education in India as well as the spread of Western science. In the debate orientalist group were reluctant to educate Indians on modern knowledge. However, due to Anglicism the western education in India got priority to make low wages clerk and started scientific practice in the hope of financial gain.[22] There have been several studies on the purpose or character of colonial science in India, viz., Deepak Kumar (ed.) 'Science and the Raj' (1857-1905), Irfan Habib 'Domesticating Modern Science', Prateek Chakraborty 'Western Science in Modern India' etc. analysed. British mainly tended to search for those subjects of science that could satisfy their colonial needs. The British rulers formed several scientific organizations keeping in mind the interests of their empire. In this case, the first can be mentioned Robert Clive, who formed the 'Survey of India' (1767) to conduct survey work in Bengal under the direction of the company. Although the history of surveys in India is older.[23] However. One of the objectives of their survey was to determine land revenue in the newly conquered territories. The second need was the military.[24] Later, along with the expansion of British rule in India, they started research in the fields of botany, geology, agriculture, mineralogy, etc. to strengthen and legitimize the empire by using the country's financial resources.

The scientific policy which was conducted in India to exploit and plunder India was controlled by England. The local government had no role in this matter, they had to look to London for the final decision. Dyer wrote to J.R. A look at Royall's letters gives an idea of the matter. Ronald Ross (1898) compares the scientific practice conducted by the British government in India to a stallion.[25] Such an irresponsible and one-sided policy of the colonial ruler did not escape the notice of India's wonder Acharya Prafulla Chandra Roy. He shed light on this in his book 'India Before and After the Mutiny'. Indian scientists as well as the Indian public are the victims of this one-sided policy of the British government.[26] They (the British) denied the 'merit' and 'talent' of Indians besides adopting discriminatory policies towards the natives to maintain dominance in the country. They had an 'inferior' attitude towards the talents and 'skills' of Indian scientists and natives. They never gave 'equality' to Indians. Not only that, they have tried to lower the dignity of the Indian nation as much as possible. The matter can be easily understood by citing some of the sayings and statements of English officials. In a letter to Crush, Lansdowne wrote - 'The kind of advanced mental and physical quality which fundamental scientific research demands is as much to be found among the lively races of our latitudes as among those raised in temperate climates. Not directly. As Lansdowne dismisses the capabilities of the native people, he also reminds them that they (the English) are superior as a nation.[27] The extreme casteism, superiority and discriminatory treatment of the colonial rulers can be found in Lushington's and Colonel D. Pree's statements. Lushington's opinion is - 'The English are indeed a superior race to the Hindus; they know better than that race what is useful to this inferior race.'[28] And Colonel D. Pree said beyond all limits - 'It would be suicidal for Europeans to accept that natives can do a job better than them. They should claim excellence in all matters. The native may be given subordinate and subordinate work. In my old survey team, I never let the natives touch the theodolites, never even do basic calculations because in principle only highly paid Europeans were allowed to do triangulation or other scientific work. However, there are countless examples of colonial rulers' thinking. - Tried to prove the thought correct.[29]

The Indian people did not silently tolerate this sense of racial superiority of the British rule. The first protest against British science policy came through Raja Rammohan. His famous letter to Lord Armhurst in 1823, in which he advocated science education. Derozio, Vidyasagar, Bankimchandra Chattopadhyay and others took this trend forward.[30] Syed Ahmed Khan founded the Scientific Society in 1864. Sometime later, Mahendralal Sarkar gave a real shape to this trend which is still flowing today. Not in the country, but in the World Congress.[31]Dr. Mahendralal Sarkar, the father of modern science in India, is the most memorable among those who contributed to the propagation and institutionalization of modern science in subjugated India.[32] He did not immerse himself only in medical work. He acquired origins in various branches of science. Social reformers, patriots and organizational talents were born in him.[33] A multifaceted genius, Dr. Sarkar's greatest work in life was the establishment of a scientific institution called the 'Association for the Cultivation of Science' in 1876. Though the association was established with noble intentions, however, he had to face various problems. His goals and objectives of this organization are revealed in his speech. He said, "We want an organization in which the mission and objectives of the Royal Institution of London and the British Association for the Advancement of Science will be brought together. The institution we want is one of public education, where tests for lectures on scientific subjects are regularly given and the audience is invited to perform those tests themselves. We want the institution to be entirely under the management and control of the natives".[34] As he had to deal with the financial crisis in supporting this institution, he also had to face the extreme opposition of the then Lt. General Temple Sahib of Bengal. The British rulers never accepted that the natives should become their equals. Even the Indian League opposed Dr. Puradastu's government. Although his indomitable willpower, self-sacrifice and above all deep patriotism brought him success. In addition to the opposition, many people extended their support to him namely

Ishwarchandra Vidyasagar, Gurudas Bandopadhyay, Maharaja of Vijiana village, Rajendralal MI, Father Laphon, Abdul Latif, Meghnad Saha, Chandrasekhar Bhankat Raman and many more.[35] He proves that the poor physique or poor diet of the English-speaking Indians did not prevent their familiarity or competence. Today the institution is a renowned university under the Government of India.[36] Arun Kumar Biswas told the government that "Dr Mahendralal must be considered the first apostle who promoted the cultivation of popular science and scientific research in India, conducted, controlled and funded by only Indian".[37] Jawaharlal Nehru said about him - "In my opinion he is one of our first eminent scientists and a great geologist".[38]

Pramathnath Bose, another prominent scientist was born on 12th May 1855 in the village of Gaipur in the 24 Parganas district. Acharya P.N. Bose, a renowned scientist carried out geological research in vast areas of India and Brahmadesh. Besides, he was a politician, writer and social reformer. Nationalist ideology can be found in him. As he has to fight against the social restrictions of his country. Again, he was vocal in fighting and protesting against British caste discrimination and established the self-respect, dignity, and self-respect of his country.[39] In 1879, after passing the examination of the Royal School of Mines in the geology department he had joined the geology department under the foreign government.[40] During his working life, he searched for mineral resources in India and Brahmadesh (Myanmar) for a long time. He has recorded this researched knowledge in various books and articles. He was the first Indian who got a high position in the British administration. At first, he had to face obstacles from the native society. Seafaring was considered inauspicious in the conservative society of that time. But he did not compromise with it. His protest against British discrimination was evident in Chari. Despite his long service, he resigned in 1903 in protest when his younger and less experienced Thomas Henry Holland was promoted to him.[41] He was highly inspired by Swadeshi thought. While in London, he joined the 'India Society'. In 1884, he established a domestic soap factory in Calcutta. In 1891, he was elected president of the Industrial Conference in Calcutta.[42] About the industry in the country, he wrote in the 'Upay Ki'-article - "Cotton to cloth... industry is the way to increase the country's wealth." During the nationalist Swadeshi movement, he wrote a letter to Jamshedji Naserwanji Tata on February 24, 1904 — "As you are interested in the development of the iron industry of this country, I have to bring to your notice an exceedingly rich and extensive deposit of iron ore which I have just explored in this State".[43] As a result of his research, India's first iron and steel factory 'Tata Iron and Steel Company' was established in 1908. When in 1906, 'Bengal Technical Institute' was formed he served there as Principal for one year and Inspector for about eleven years (1909-20). This institution evolved into 'Jadavpur University' (1955) in independent India.[44] He pointed the way for the development of the country by writing articles and books on scientific education in India, science education in the Bengali language, industrialization, the antiquity of Indian civilization etc. The author started his career by composing the poem 'Okash Kushum'.[45] How to develop indigenous art, he has indicated in his essay 'Upay Ki' and other books.[46]

Acharya Jagdishchandra Bose, one of the greatest scientists of all time in India.[47] He was born on November 24, 1858 AD in Munshiganj village of Mymensingh district of undivided Bengal.[48] He acquired degree in Science from Christ's College, Cambridge and a B.S. from the University of London. Then he returned to the country in 1885 and joined the work of teaching at the Presidency College as a physics teacher. However, he had to suffer discrimination in getting the job. And this is where his rebellious character can be seen.[49] While teaching, he started research work. He overcame various obstacles and gained fame in the world. He worked simultaneously as a scientist, teacher, writer and above all a tireless warrior in the service of the country. He devoted his life to the institutionalization of science in the country. Famous scientist Einstein said about him - "Jagdish Chandra Bose should be erected a victory pillar for any of the invaluable information he has gifted to the world".[50]

Jagdish Chandra Bose was the first Indian scientist who overcame obstacles and adversities to introduce India to the world of science. By his pursuit and struggle the fundamental research of science began in India.[51] The first work for which he gained recognition was the article on the determination of electric wavelength. He penetrated many mysteries in the fields of science such as physics, and biology. For this, he showed hard work, self-sacrifice, and mental fortitude. In the difficult pursuit of establishing India's glory in the world, he had to face repeated obstacles, on behalf of the English authorities and a group of scientific groups in the West.[52] He wrote - "Though the perishable body sinks to the ground, the national hopes and aspirations do not perish. The destruction of mental energy is the real death".[53] On November 30, 1917, Jagadish Chandra Bose said in his speech during the establishment of 'Bose Science Temple' - "For the glory of India and the welfare of the world, I have dedicated this science temple to Devacharan". While in England, he was associated with the 'Royal Society',[54] and then subsequently with the Swadeshi movement against the partition of Bengal in 1905. From his letter written to Rabindranath Tagore from America, is also known about the thought of establishing a Swadeshi laboratory.[55] The matter is clearer if the statement of Professor Rams is presented in this context. He said - "Who may think that a new age of knowledge has begun in India from now on; but the arrival of spring at the sound of a cuckoo is not reasonable". In reply to this, Jagadish Chandra Bose said proudly - "You have no reason to fear, I am sure, soon a hundred cuckoos will announce the advent of spring in the field of science in India". The 'London Times' newspaper praised his laboratory and his contribution to modern science. "Atheneum" magazine wrote about this institution, "The establishment of this science-temple is a memorable event not only in the history of India but also in the history of science. The report containing the results of the research is its identity".[56] Reminding the countrymen of his ancient heritage, he said - "There is no place for a beggar in the world. How long will you endure this humiliation? Will you be forever in debt? Will you never have the strength to give? Besides, he founded all the famous educational institutions of ancient India, Nalanda, Taxila etc. Noting that, "But where are the laboratories, where are the students. Is it so impossible to establish a temple of knowledge? He wanted, "People will gather in Bharat-Tirtha to gather knowledge from different countries."[57] Besides fundamental research in science and the institutionalization of science in his country, he became known as a writer. 'Response in the Living and Non-Living' (1902),[58] 'Plant Response as a Means of Physiological Investigation' (1906), 'Comparative Electro-Physiology (1907) etc.' He is first to be seen in the book 'Abapta' (1921) in the composition 'In Search of the Heritage of India'.[59]

When the country is thriving in the climate of national movement against colonial rule-exploitation, injustice-tyranny. Scientist Prafulla Chandra Roy is one of those people who went beyond their respective fields and devoted their lives to the service of the country. Acharya Roy was a contemporary of the famous scientist Jagadish Chandra Bose. However, despite being known as a scientist in international circles, his identity in his homeland was not just a scientist. Prafullachandra simultaneously work in scientific practice, economic, social and political ideas, public works, literary love, artistic initiatives etc. awakened a sense of wonder and pride. At the root of these works was deep patriotism and love for the motherland which gave him recognition as a hero of the era.[60] Prafulla Chandra Roy was born in 1861 in the village of Raduli in present-day Bangladesh. Father Harishchandra Roy.[61] After researching in chemistry, he obtained the title of D.Sc. After that, he joined Presidency College as a professor in the chemistry department. After joining teaching work, his multifaceted career began. Finding solutions to various problems. In 1895, he discovered a mysterious compound called 'Mercurous Nitrate'. As a result, his fame spread in the world of basic science practice.[62] From 1897-1902, he published 14 articles on nitrate and hyponitrite and 5 articles on the reaction of nitric acid between 1903 and 1911. Researched physical chemistry with student Neel Ratan Dhar and published 5 research papers. The practice of physical chemistry in this country started with his hands. He published a total of 145 research articles on various subjects in his long twenty-year teaching career. As a teacher, he gifted the country with a bunch of scientific scholars. Dr. Rasiklal Ghosh, Dr. Gyanendrachandra, Dr. Gyanendranath Mukherjee etc. gained great fame in science.[63] Along with his insight into the various problems of subjugated India, he understood the solution. He understood very well that the youth of the country is the main tool for national development. Therefore, he pointed out the way for the countrymen to become self-reliant by utilizing their abilities and said - "Do business, take up industry, give up the illusion of jobs". He said, "we are a nation which is not slow and dull......man's ability can reach any point".[64]

He founded 'Bengal Chemical' in 1893. In 1902 it became known as a 'Limited Company'. It was the first chemical factory in sub-continental India.[65] In 1905 AD 'Bengal Chemical' became one of the symbols of indigenous industries centred on the anti-partition Swadeshi movement. In 1912, the Director of Education in Bihar said - "I believe you are the main reason for the establishment of the Chemical Society". Nature Poika wrote in 1916, "In the fundamental chemical research which is now going on in Bangladesh, it can certainly be said that a new spirit has awakened and it is to be hoped that this spirit will Gradually this fundamental research interest will spread to other parts of India and will arise in other branches of science as well".[66] Later, Pulinbehari Sarkar, Shantiswaroop Bhatnagar, Satyendranath Bose, Meghnath Saha, Nobel-winning scientist C. in chemistry, physics, mathematics etc. V. Raman, Srinivasa Ramanujam etc. scientists brightened the face of India in the practice of science. Besides 'Bengal Chemical', Prafulla Chandra Roy has left outstanding contributions in industrial establishments and business sectors such as Bengal Pottery, Bengal Enamel, Bengal Salt, Shipping etc. He is also known for his philanthropic work. He was found as a leader during the country's crises such as famine in Khulna in 1921, Upper Bengal in 1922, North Bengal and East Bengal in 1931, etc. Although he did not agree with Mahatma Gandhi's Charka and Khaddar idea at first, he later participated in its promotion. His generous spirit is also found in philanthropy. Drawing attention to the weak aspects of nation-building, he said, "India must wake up and uplift women and the depressed classes, remove all social inequalities".[67] His native thoughts and national consciousness are more clearly seen in the articles and books written by him. He 'self-consciously' blamed colonial policies for the plight of India. In his essay 'India Before and After the Newton', he criticized British rule and exploitation. The result of his 14 years of hard work is the book 'History of Hindu Chemistry'. In this book, he introduced the glorious past of India in the practice of science. Rich in material on various problems and their solutions.[68]

With the spread of Western education in colonial India, modern science was introduced in this country. The British rulers never thought of improving the people of India through the practice of science by sacrificing their interests. As a protest against this neglect and humiliation of the English ruler, Dr. M. L. Sarkar, J. C. Bose, P. C. Roy etc. started the fight for indigenous identity in scientific practice. Subsequently, this trend of protest and movement of scientific practice did not stop.[69] Meghnath Saha, Satyendranath Bose, KS, Krishnan, C.V. Raman move forward with the hand of others. However, the British scientific community was not alone in its struggle against unfair science. Rammohan Roy, Vidyasagar, Rajendralal MIA, Bankim Chandra Chattopadhyay, Vivekananda, Rabindranath Tagore etc. have left a significant contribution in the promotion and spread of modern knowledge and science in the country and institutionalizing it. With the anti-British movement, national leaders focused on protesting British science policies and expanding scientific practice in the country. 'Indian National Congress', 'Dawn Society' etc. adopted the policy of science promotion. Many national newspapers publicized the need for modern science in nation-building and the selfish British science policy. At the same time, anti-British independence movements, protests and struggles against British science policy continued.[70] The Indian Chemical Society (1928), 'National Institute of Science', 'Indian Science Congress' (1914) and other organizations were formed as a domestic initiative, which showed India's pride and self-identity in the practice of science. In the adverse conditions of subjugated India, through the struggle and protest of scientists in the field of science, Familiarity developed, still flowing in independent India.[71]

References

1. Kochhar, R., "Cultivation of Science in Nineteenth Century Bengal", *Indian JPHYS*, 2008, p.1007
2. Kumar, Deepak (ed.), *Science and Umpire Essay in Indian Context (1700-1947)*, Anamika Publications, 1991, pp. 6-12
3. Sarkar, S., Lahiri, A., (Translation), *Modern Times: India 1880s to 1950s Environment, Finance, Culture*, KP Bagchi and Company, 2019, pp.66-73
4. Kumar, D., Chattopadhyay, M., (trans. Science in British India), *British Bharote Biggan*, Sujan Publications, January, 2007, p.232
5. Ibid., p.231
6. For details see: Sarkar, S., Lahiri, A., Op. cit., p.66
7. Kumar, D., Chattopadhyay, M., Op. cit., p.88
8. Chattopadhyay, S. & Rajvanshi, S., *A Brief History of Science in Colonial India*, Setu Publications, 2021, p.7
9. Kumar, D., Chattopadhyay, M., Op. cit., pp. 115-26
10. Ibid., pp.239-41
11. Ghosh, Devabrata (Ed.), *Partition of Bengal in the Light of the Century*, Setu Publications, 2005, p.103
12. Ray, S., & Bhattacharya, S., *Acharya Jagadishchandra Bose*, Vol. 1, Basu Vigyan Mandir, July, 1936, p.134
13. See for more information: Paa, S., *Vigyansadhak of India*, Vani Shilpa, November, 1986
14. Maiti, Nandalal, *Jeevanveda of Acharya Prafullachandra*, Jnana Vichitra Prakashani, February 2002, pp.9-10
15. Kumar, D., Chattopadhyay, M., Op. cit., pp.232-233
16. Sen, S., & Ghosh, A., *Political Economic Social and Cultural History of Modern India 1885-64*, MM, August, 2008, p.123
17. Ahmed, W., *Thoughts of Bengali Muslims in the Nineteenth Century*, Part-I, Sahitya Akademi, 1983, pp. 137-224
18. Kumar, D., Chattopadhyay, M., Op. cit., p.23
19. Palit, C., *Colonial Bengal in the Light of Science*, Day's Publishing, August, 2018, p.56-62
20. Sen, S., & Ghosh, A., *Op. cit.*, pp.139-141
21. Ghosh, Devabrata, Op. cit., pp.97-105
22. Sen, S., & Ghosh, A., *Op. cit.*, pp. 116-119
23. Howell, Arthur, *Education in British India*, Calcutta, 1872, p.5

24. Chattopadhyay, Partha, *Bangla Newspaper and Bengali Renaissance (1818-1878),* Varbi, January, 2000, p.152
25. Kumar, D., Chattopadhyay, M., Op. cit., pp.115-181
26. Maiti, Nandalal, Op. cit., p.10
27. Kumar, D., Chattopadhyay, M., Op. cit., pp.131-132
28. Ibid., p.61
29. Ibid., p.263
30. Maiti, Nandalal, Op. cit., pp.9-10
31. Kumar, D., Chattopadhyay, M., Op. cit., p.236
32. Palit, C., Op. cit., pp. 37-41
33. He was born on November 2, 1833, at the house of Tarakanath Sarkar in Paikpara village of Howrah district; Paa, S., Op. cit., pp.184-90
34. Roy, Aniruddha (Ed.), *History Research* 18, Pharma KLM Private Limited, January, 2004, p.301
35. Ghosh, Anil Chandra, *Bengali in Science*, Presidency Library, Third Edition, September, 1938, p.21
36. Tripathi, Manorama, Das, Anup Kumar, 'Growth of Scholarly Societies and Their Activities in Pre-Independent India: A Reconnaissance', *Journal of Scientific Temper*, Volume 10(1&2), January-June, 2022, p.116
37. Roy, Aniruddha (ed.), Op. cit., p.300
38. Daw, Abhan, Bose, Pramatnath, *Anandbazar Patrika,* March 15, 2020
39. Gupta, Manoranjan, *Acharya Pramathanath Bose,* Bengal Science Council, 1955, pp.3-31
40. Paa, Sudhanshu, Op. cit., p.148
41. Gupta, Manoranjan, Op. cit., pp.13-29
42. Ibid., pp.11-29
43. Daw, A., Bose, Pramathanath, Op. cit.,
44. Ibid., pp. 32-39
45. Gupta, Manoranjan, Op. cit., pp.63-73
46. Daw, A., Bose, Pramathanath, Op. cit.,
47. Majumdar, Amiyakumar, *Vivekananda's Science-Consciousness,* Rupa & Company, July, 1960, p.169
48. Geddes, Patrick, *An Indian Pioneer of Science, The Life and Work of Sir Jagdish C. Bose*, Longmans, Green, & Co., 1920, p.1
49. Ray, Srimanoj and Bhattacharya Srigopalachandra, Op. cit., pp. 22-27

50. Ghosh, Anil Chandra, op. cit., pp.35-85
51. Rashid, Harun-Or AM (Ed.), Bangla Academy Dhaka, 1971, p.7
52. PA, Sudhanshu, Op. cit., pp.70-75
53. Ghosh, Anil Chandra, op. cit., p.30
54. Ray, Srimanoj and Bhattacharya Srigopalachandra, Op. cit., pp. 28-37
55. Ghosh, Devabrata, Op. cit., pp.100-01
56. Ray, Srimanoj and Bhattacharya Srigopalachandra, Op. cit., pp. 138-39
57. Ghosh, Anil Chandra, op. cit., p.78
58. Geddes, Patrick, Op. cit., p.107
59. Basu, Jagdishchandra Acharya, *Abyapta,* Bengali Vigyan Parishad, Ashin, 1328 Bangabdo, p.1
60. Maiti, Nandalal, Op. cit., p. 14
61. Karr, Sri Jamini Mohan, *Science of Navbharata*, Gurudas Chattopadhyay & Sons, Baishakh, 1362 Bangabd, pp. 18-20
62. Roy, Prafullachandra, *Atmacharit,* Chakraborty, Chatterjee, & Co. Ltd., pp.53-76
63. Maiti, Nandalal, Op. cit., pp.94-114
64. Ghosh, Anil Chandra, Op. cit., pp.107-136
65. "Thirty-Eight Annual, Report", *Bengal Chemical and Pharmaceuticals Limited*, Kolkata, 2018-2019
66. Ghosh, Devabrata, Op. cit., p.103
67. Maiti, Nandalal, Op. cit., pp. 93-149
68. Ibid., pp. 30-57
69. Ibid., pp. 241-267
70. National Education Council in Historical Perspective, *Bengal National Education Council*, Annual, March 11, 1975, pp.5-19
71. https://bn.m.wikipedia.org/wiki, 24th May, 2023

Western Sciences in Colonial India: An identity of Modernity

Ersad Ali

Western science refers to science developed in Western Europe. Science is the method by which one can gain knowledge about something through experiment, observation, conclusion, repetition and universality. These universal characteristics of science were one of the foundations of Western science. Western science essentially progressed through the development of capitalism and was linked to the preservation of imperial interests. When the British, rich in science, expanded their empire in India, their only aim was to make immediate gains. Various survey organizations, botanical research, commercial grain, tea, geological research, science teachers, scientific institutions and above all the Asiatic Society—helped fulfil these interests. As a result, it became possible to take the wealth of India to their own country. Only imperialism-imposed science functioned differently at different times and progressed according to a very clear and definite schedule. In this case, western science became colonial science. Colonial scientists were completely influenced by colonialism. Deepak Kumar in his book 'Science and the Raj' says that "authority, dominance, and rule is the essence of imperialism. "This incongruous equation of dominance of one means the subjugation of the other was the basis of colonialism.[1]

Nature of colonial science: Michael Orbeus in his book 'Science and the British Colonial Imperialism' sees colonial science as a science belonging to imperialist history. He says that apart from astronomy and a few subjects, colonial science was largely applied sciences.[2] The science which creates an integrated knowledge for the realization of practical opportunities and solution of practical problems is called applied science. He did not ignore, however, that colonial scientists enjoyed relative freedom in some areas, which they sometimes protested against political economy. As a result, scientists proposed far-reaching environmental policies in land reform and management.[3] On the other hand, McLeod's main subject is not the science of imperialist history,[4] but he saw science as imperialist history. He divided the course of the evolution of British science into five categories:

1. City-centric (metropolitan) science – its speciality is exploration and its application. As a result, maritime trade progressed, raw materials and new markets were discovered.

2. Colonial science – characterized by urban dominance, primitive societies, purely private research and scientific pursuits – with emphasis on primary production technologies and local markets.

3. Federated science – characterized by cooperative commercial research, higher education and professional competence. This results in improved technology and greater participation in global markets.

4. The science of functional empire — its speciality is the specialized practice of formal science, the predominance of experienced and skilled people, and the prudent management of land, wealth, and industry.

5. Imperial or allied political science – characterized by city-centric systems, integrated basic research, and state patronage of applied science. Linked to all of the above categories is city-centric or system-centric imperial science. Although Orbeus argues that there was no such thing as an imperial science. Science has followed the broad political and administrative division which introduced separate policies and activities in the

case of India and other colonies or autonomous colonies. The aim or objective was certainly there but its nature or intensity varied from place to time. Correspondingly, the structure also changed. However, he never described colonial science as a low-intellectual science. Rather, he shows how colonial science, by collecting various data, came to occupy a very important place in the institutions of the colonizing country.[5]

Application of Western Science in Colonial India:

Survey activities: A certain phase of colonial science began only after the end of the rule of the East India Company. The Company soon realized that the geographical, geological and botanical knowledge of the territories they conquered would be the real basis for their rule. Although scientific thinking had a limited beginning its stride was quite firm. For every ship bound for Asia carried a sergeant naturalist or some medical man. Most of them were natives of either Scotland or Denmark. They were among the earliest botanists and biologists in India. A second group of scientists was drawn from the military and out of these came the early geologists, meteorologists and astronomers. Of course, surveyors were the pioneers of scientific inquiry. James Rennell was foremost among the early surveyors. Began land surveys in 1746 under the orders of the ruler (governor) of Fort William.[6] His surveys were important for revenue needs and in many litigations. Colonel Kelly surveyed the Karnataka region in South India and his maps aided General Iyer Coote's military activities.[7] After the defeat of Tipu Sultan in 1799, Major Lambert led a survey of military and administrative facilities from Koromandal to the Malabar coast. Thus the 'Great Trigonometrical Survey of India' was prepared.[8] The directors of the company then showed enthusiasm for the improvement of navigation and nautical charts in the Indian Ocean. As a result, in 1770 Ritchie was appointed as the first company hydrographical surveyor.[9] In 1839, the first marine survey department (Marine Survey Department) was opened in Bengal and Captain Wallace was its first survey officer.[10]

Botanical Exploration: One of the best uses of science for colonial purposes was found in botanical exploration. European tourists were amazed to see the vast flora and fauna of India. After the Company's rule over Bengal and Madras was consolidated, the military and commercial importance of plant research was realized.[11] In Bengal, Robert Kidd informed the Company's fleet of the region's supply of teak wood, with which ships could be built. In 1786 Kidd proposed to establish a 'Garden of Acclimatization' near Calcutta and it was accepted.[12] The proposal included plans to cultivate carpus, tobacco, coffee, and tea. Later in another account, he writes about the use of coconut shells. Somewhere he says how the cultivation of teak trees will meet the needs of the fleet during the war.[13] Sponsoring Kidd's plan, the company said, 'We are fully aware of the far-reaching consequences of your proposal and are not at all inclined to make any cuts to the proposal on the pretext of expense.'[14] Kidd was succeeded by Roxburgh in 1793. He had previously worked at Samalkota, Madras, and in Lanka, cardamom, and experimented with indigo cultivation.[15] Roxburgh imported about 800 varieties of trees and about 2,200 vines to the Calcutta 'Botanical Gardens'. For his work on botany, he received the gold medal from the 'Royal Society of Arts' three times.[16] Another worker named Forbes explored the appropriate uses of Himalayan plants. He researched the fibres of the ria tree of Assam and the hemp of the Himalayas and approached the 'Royal Society of Arts' and the 'Commercial Association of Manchester' for their appropriate use. On the other hand, JD Hooker visited Bengal, Sikkim, Nepal and Khasia Hills and wrote two famous books in 1855 named 'Flora Indic' and 'Himalayan Journal'.[17]

Geological Explorations: After botanical explorations attention was paid to mycology. In 1808, Abraham Hume, a shipowner of the company, argued that all subjects of mineralogy and geology could be explored with various samples and their chemical analysis.[18] The Royal Institution prepared a plan that stated that 'in India, all the precious minerals of the world can be found.[19] The Company's experience, expertise and assistance can be expected to determine the essential value of these assets and bring them to practical use'. For this purpose, 'Geological Survey of London' was established in 1807. The Raniganj coal mine was ordered to be explored the following year.[20] In 1836 the Company appointed a committee for the investigation of the coal and mineral resources of India. The purpose of this committee was to ascertain the existence, extent and location of coal beds in different parts of India and to determine how quickly these coals can be made practically suitable if necessary.[21] This committee first prepared an inventory of various classes of coal and minerals in India and made a map of all those mineral areas.

Science Education: In the field of science, education is the next step. The Education 'Charter Act' of 1813 is particularly important in the history of science education in colonial India. Section 43 of the Act provides for a grant of one lakh rupees for the science education of residents of British India. However, some ambiguity is observed in this case. However, the debate between Orientalists and Westerners as to what teaching was referred to here lasted for a long time. Finally, in 1835, through the 'Meckley Minutes', the Western method of government was adopted as the policy.[22] In this context, Travellian was quoted as saying 'Our aim should never be through conversion. We should not tie the branch of the tree of knowledge to a trunk which is afflicted with various diseases since no branch can ever prosper upon it. By presenting our literature and educating the native youth through it, we should create a plantation which will branch out towards the support of the government power and thus the ancient stem will go from neglect to natural destruction'. Nothing better exemplifies the attitude of the colonists at that time towards education.[23]

Scientific Institutions: There was no such thing as scientific institution in pre-British India. In 1784, William Jones founded the 'Asiatic Society'. The Society soon became the centre of scientific activity in India. In 1808 the Society decided to set up a committee, whose aim was to make the necessary plans for the spread of the teaching of natural history within India and to make communications to suitable places.[24] Calcutta Medical and Physical Society was established in 1823. This society alleviated much of the loneliness of the latter-day physicians.[25] The Literary and Scientific Society was founded in 1818 at Madras and the 'Literary Society' was founded in Bombay in 1804. These two societies later became branches of the 'Royal Asiatic Society' founded in London in 1825 and later the Bombay Society became a branch of the London Society in 1829.[26]

The activities of colonial science in India which we see in the above discussion were mainly aimed at accumulating knowledge about the resources of the colony and making use of the knowledge to extract these resources. The nature of scientific research was indeed an extension of Western scientific practice. Indeed, institutions like the 'Trigonometric Survey', the 'Agricultural and Botanical Survey', the 'Mining Federation', the 'Geological Survey', the Planters' Association etc. were particularly active in the field of scientific practice.[27] But the people of this country had no opportunity to take advantage of the benefits of their work.[28] Thus, such scientific practice was strictly colonial. Swadeshi science was born as a protest.[29] With the establishment of the 'Indian Association for the Cultivation of Science' in 1876, the practice of indigenous science began in what Roma Rolland described as 'a silent freedom struggle'.[30]

References

1. Kumar D., Chhottopadhaya, M., (Anubad), *British Bharate Biggan [Science in British India]*, Sujon Publication, Kolkata, 2007, pp. 37-38
2. Michael, W., *Science and British Colonial Imperialism*, 1890-1940, Univ. of Sussex, 1979
3. Kumar D., Chhottopadhaya, M., Op. cit., pp.1-5
4. MacLeod, R., 'On Visiting the 'Moving Metropolis': Reflections on the Architecture of Imperial Science', *Historical Records of Australian Science*, vol. 5(3), 1980, pp.1 – 16
5. Ibid.,
6. Kumar D., Chhottopadhaya, M., Op. cit., pp. 37-38
7. Ascoli, F. D., "The Legal Value of Rennails Maps", in F. C. Hirst, *A Memoir upon the Map of Bengal*, Calcutta, 1914
8. *Calcutta Review*, No. IV, 7, 1845, p.77
9. Ibid., p.80
10. *Calcutta Review*, No. 67,133,1878, p.576
11. Kumar D., Chhottopadhaya, M., Op. cit., pp.40-41
12. Home, Public, nos.13-14,16 June, 1786
13. Kumar D., Chhottopadhaya, M., Op. cit., p.41
14. Major-Gen. *Hardwick Collection*, B.M. Add.Mass,12615
15. Kumar D., Chhottopadhaya, M., Op. cit., pp.41-42
16. *Annals of the Royal Botanic Garden of Calcutta*, Vol-V. 1895, p.6
17. Elton-Dyer to Haldane,1907, *Campbell Bannerman Papers*, B.M.Add.Mass.41218, f.188.
18. Dictionary of National Biography, Vol. X, London, 1908, pp.208-9
19. Kumar D., Chhottopadhaya, M., Op. cit., p. 47
20. For details, see Woodward, H.B., *The History of Geological Society of London*, London, 1907
21. Report of the Committee for Investigating the Coal and Mineral Resources of India, calcutta,1838, p. 1
22. Kumar D., Chhottopadhaya, M., Op. cit., p.52
23. Trevelyan, C. E., *Kolkata note, American Philosophical Society Papers*, Philadelphia, Mss. 954, T725, 21 May, 1830
24. *Asiatic Researches*, Vol. XVIII,1, 1929, p.1
25. Medical Selections, No. I, Calcutta, 1833, pp. III-IV
26. See for details: *Journal of the Bombay Branch of Royal Asiatic Society*, Centenary Volume,1905, p.20

27. Basalla, G., "The Spread of Western Science", *Science*, No-156, 1976, p.611
28. Kumar D., Chhottopadhaya, M., Op. cit., p.38
29. Palit, Chittabrata, *Bijnaer Aaloke Oupanibesik Bangla*, Day's Publishing, Kolkata, 2018, p.38; Palit, Chittabrata, 'A Century', *Indian Association for the Cultivation of Science*, Calcutta, 1976
30. Sannal, Abantikumar, Anubad-Roma Rolla, *Bharatborso: Dinponji* (1925-1943), Radical Book Club, 1976, p. 213

Sir Mohammad Azizul Huque: A Charismatic Muslim Man of Bengal

Dr. Kutubuddin Biswas

Sir Mohammad Azizul Huque was an exemplary man of sophistication, talent and dedication. When the Muslim society in the post-Plassey colonial Bengal reached in a state of social, political, economic and cultural stagnation, the rise of Azizul Huque was a startling event in the history of Bengal. His lifelong efforts and activities greatly advanced the society, culture, politics and education of Bengal. His way of thinking was ahead of the times and inspires us today with new thoughts and research. Sir Mohammad Azizul Huque has mentioned Nadia district as a 'poor and afflicted' district in various speeches at the Legislative Assembly. Yet Nadia played an important role in his career. Shantipur of Nadia is a centre of culture of West Bengal. Sir Mohammad Azizul Huque was born in Shantipur town of Nadia district on 27th November 1892 in a noble Muslim family. His father was Munshi Mohammad Moniruddin and the famous poet Mohammad Mozammel Haque was his uncle. After completing primary education at Shantipur Jubilee Madrasa, he passed the 'Entrance Examination' in 1907 from Shantipur Municipality High English School, and passed FA and BA from Calcutta Presidency College in 1909 and 1911 respectively. Later, in 1914, he obtained a B.L. degree from University Law College.[1]

After the introduction of permanent settlement in 1793 AD, the status of Bengal's elite drastically declined. As a result, the education, literature and culture of the Muslim society of Bengal were stuck in a state of chaos. After the war of Plassey, the Muslim society of Bengal lost its aristocracy and glamour.

However, a few Muslim elite families re-emerged with pride in Bengal in the 19th century and contributed significantly to the education, literature and culture of Bengal. Some examples of such prominent elite families are the Fazlul Haque family of Barisal, the Suhrawardy family of Medinipur, Nawab Ali Choudhury family of Mymensingh, Shamsul Huda family of Comilla, Nawab Rani Faizunnessa Choudhury family of Tripura, Abul Kashem family of Burdwan and Haque family of Shantipur (Mozammel).[2] Prominent members of the Haque family of Shantipur include Mohammad Mozammel Haque, Sir Mohammad Azizul Huque, Afzalul Haque and Mohammad Kayem. Their ancestors once lived in Sonar Gaon, the Masnad-i-Ali of Isha Khan, one of the famous Barobhuiynas of Bengal. They fled Sonar Gaon due to Bargi attacks and settled in Shantipur.[3] When Mozammel Haque was born (1860 AD), Shantipur was a prosperous municipal town in Bengal in terms of education, civilization and culture. Shantipur city once occupied the fifth and sixth place in Bengal.[4] It should be noted that Shantipur Municipality was established in 1853 AD and it was the second municipality of undivided Bengal. The first municipality was formed in Darjeeling.[5]

Mohammad Mozammel Haque (1860-1933) was the central figure of the Haque family of Shantipur. He was born in Bauigachi, Shantipur, Nadia just one year earlier than Rabindranath Tagore. Being contemporary to Rabindranath, he was popularly known as "Poet Mozammel Haque of Shantipur".[6] He produced many books like Kusumanjali (1881), Apurba Darshan (1885), Premahar (1898), Jatiya Foara (1912), Hazrat Mohammad (PBUH) (1903), Maharshi Mansoor (1894), Firdausi Charit (1898), Tapas Kahini (1900), Shahnama (1909), Maulana Parichoy (1914), Daraf Khan Ghazi (1919), etc. Some of his novels are - Zohra (1927) and Rangeela Bai. When he started writing, Muslims were in dire straits politically and socially. Muslims were by no means advanced. As a result, a large part of his literary pursuits was spent expressing a sense of compassion for the Muslims. He extolled the past glory of Bengali Muslims in his poetry book 'Jatiya Foara' and urged them to rise again. Not only that, Sir Ashutosh Mukhopadhyay, the then Vice-Chancellor of Calcutta University, being attracted by his literary qualities, appointed him as an Examiner of Bengali Language in 1919 AD and he held this position till his death. He was the Commissioner of Nadia Municipality for 40 years, was a member of the Education Committee of Nadia District Board for 30 years and was an unpaid Magistrate of Nadia for 20 years. He had a deep connection with Bangiya Sahitya Parishad, Calcutta, which awarded him the title of 'Kavyakantha'.[7] He edited and published monthly literary periodicals 'Lahari' (1899), 'Moslem Bharat' (1920) and 'Shantipur'. His 'Firdousi Charit' was selected as a 'text book' in the matriculation examination syllabus.[8] Impressed by his poetic talent; Nawab Ali Chowdhury bestowed upon him the title of "Bulbul-e-Bangla".[9]

Mohammad Afzalul Haque was the son of poet Mozammel Haque. He continued the cultural legacy of the Haque family of Shantipur. He was the owner and manager of Muslim Publishing House at No. 3 College Square, Calcutta. From 1927, Afzalul Haque used to edit 'Nowroz' magazine. He developed a deep relationship with Kazi Nazrul Islam who used to call Afzalul Haque 'Dabjal'. The Haque family of Shantipur had an influential role in the development of Nazrul's life and his literary career. Sunil Kumar Mukhopadhyay said in his research book 'Mozammel Haq', "In fact, Rabindranath's role was at the root of the prosperity of the then best monthly "Pravasi", Nazrul's role was for 'Moslem Bharat'.[10] Nazrul was truly the lifeblood of the magazine. ... We cannot imagine 'Moslem Bharat' without Nazrul or Nazrul without 'Moslem

Bharat'".[11] Afzalul Haque promised the poet Nazrul a reward of Rs. 100/- per month in exchange for sending his writings. He was also a prolific writer and like his father, he was once an examiner of Bengali language at Calcutta University.[12] He served as the first Muslim Chairman of Shantipur Municipality. Mohammad Qayem, the cousin of Mozammel Haque, was another prominent member of the Haq family. He received his education from Shantipur Jubilee Madrasa and lived in Khulna for business. Later, he served as Commissioner of Shantipur Municipality.[13] Sir Mohammad Azizul Haque, nephew of Mozammel Haque, was the beacon of the Haque family of Shantipur town of united Bengal. Azizul Huque (1892 to 1947) was a popular political figure of extraordinary talent in colonial Bengal. He held many important positions and honours throughout his life. In short, he was a successful lawyer, efficient administrator, prolific writer, efficient parliamentarian, skilled diplomat, polyglot, liberal educationist, humanitarian, and social thinker. He was the Minister of Education of undivided Bengal (1934–1937), first elected Speaker of the Legislative Assembly of Bengal (1937–1942), Vice Chancellor of Calcutta University (1938–1942), High Commissioner to the United Province (1942–43), and secretary to the Indian High Commission (1943-46).[14] Some of his research papers are - The Man Behind the Plough, History and Problems of Moslem Education in Bengal, Education and Retrenchment in Bengal, The Sword of the Crescent Moon, Cultural Contribution of Islam to Indian History and Hazrat Muhammad's biography (unpublished). He received a knighthood in 1939 and Calcutta University awarded him D. Lit. The British Government awarded him the title of 'Khan Bahadur', CEI (1937), K, CII (1943).[15]

Azizul Huque's own identity cannot be fulfilled without the identity of his family. His wife's name is Kaniz Khatun. They have five sons and five daughters. They all were well educated and posted at various governmental and non-governmental department. His first son Asadul Haque (1917-1991) graduated in economics, employed in Bungi & Company trading firm.[16] He was a well-known poet. As Sir Azizul Huque was closely involved in government work, he could not write the two chapters of "The Man behind the Plow" in time, Rural Indebtness and Problem of Population. His son wrote the above two chapters on behalf of the father.[17] His second son's Ahsanul Haque was a diplomat. He served as Minister of Commerce in the Union Cabinet of Pakistan and Ambassador of Pakistan to Indonesia and Romania.[18] His third son's Anisul Haque was learned person who obtained Senior Cambridge Degree from Saint Xavier College of Calcutta. He translated Rabindranath Tagore's Gitanjali from Bengali into English. The fourth son Aminul Haque (1931-1973) was working in ISKCON in Durgapur. The fifth son Ansarul Haque was a graduated in commerce and highest degree in shipping. He was Honorary Consul of Greece in Chittagong. His eldest daughter Shahana is a graduate in Economics from Calcutta University. Second daughter Roshan Ara wife of retired Deputy Governor of Bangladesh Bank Mr. M. Golam Dastgir. Azizul Huque's third daughter, Husne Haque, was a professor at Dhaka University of Education and the wife of Agriculture Minister of Bangladesh Government. The fourth daughter, Shaukat Ara, graduated from Calcutta University, used to teach in a Hindi school in Calcutta. The fifth daughter, Haas Mat Ara, is a retired professor at Princess Amrita Kaur College of Nursing, Delhi, with a master's degree in nursing.[19] Shahnara Alam and Husna Haque were calligraphers. Two books on father have been written under their editorship. The names of the two books are *Ajijul Huque: A Biographical Account of his Life and Works* and *M Ajijul Huque: Life Sketch and Selected Writings*.[20]

Sir Mohammad Azizul Huque had profound knowledge of literature, the history of literature, the relation between society and literature, the place of society in literature etc. He believed that society is linked to literature as the soul is linked to the body. Though the Muslims were the majority in colonial Bengal their contribution to Bengali literature was negligible. He once said in a literary meeting that in political and social life, nothing else can affect as much as religious and devotional literature. Bengali literature has had a considerable influence on the motivation that inspired the Bengalis in the past century. However, the contribution of Muslim writers is negligible. They have been ignoring the Bengali language and literature for the past century, but they failed to understand that despite their neglect, Bengali literature has flourished by leaps and bounds. Bengali literature has inspired, enlivened and united the Bengali community and Muslims have failed to reap its fruits.[21] He also lamented that contemporary Bengali literature failed to capture and represent the sentiments and influence of the Muslim community. Bengali language is the mother tongue of Bengalis irrespective of their caste and religion. So, without the contribution from the Bengali Islamic culture and perspective, Bengali literature will remain incomplete.[22] The ultimate culmination of Bengali literature as the mirror of Bengali culture and tradition cannot be achieved without equal contribution from the Hindus and Muslims.

Society, religion and nation have a deep connection with literature. Literature is the beauty as well as the backbone of a nation. He said in this context that, it is true that we have our respective religious histories and ideals, and we cannot give up our respective sects. Yet, it is very much possible to create a glorious future for Bengali as one community being true to our respective beliefs.[23] The creation of a great nation is possible only through national literature and that national literature will have to be built by us. That literature will combine the great ideals of the Buddha, Chaitanya, Shankar, Sita, Savitri, Kanishka, Ashoka, Puru, Pratap Singh, with that of Abu Bakr, Omar, Ali, Khaled, Khadeja, Rabeya, Salahuddin, Mustafa Kamal, etc. It will inspire and uplift us, and will shine like a beacon in the darkness.[24] Actually, Azizul Huque realised the great power of literature. A German writer said, "It is literature which commands the whole nation." The stronger the presence of a community in literature, the stronger its position is in the country. If the presence of a community is weak in literature, it becomes like a bird without nest. Literature reflects the change in custom, tradition and reform of a community.

There is no dearth of poets and writers in the post-independence Muslim society of West Bengal. But the situation of writing on the ideals of their society and religion is very delicate. Nourishment of natural talent in Bengali Muslims is necessary to manifest themself and their community's self-glory. Why do they still refer to the rainbow as Ram Dhanu not as Omar Dhanu, or Vidya Mandir and not Vidya Masjid? Because they failed to exert such in the literature written by them. Ajijul Haque pleaded to the Muslim writers to establish the ideology and true history of the Muslims through literature in front of the nation. It is their burden to spread knowledge about the contribution, sacrifice, bravery, culture and teachings of Islam and Muslims to every Bengali, let all know that in the making of modern Bengal, the Muslims have equal contribution.[25] There are several similarities between both Sir Mohammad Azizul Huque and Rabindra Nath Tagore. Both are Bengalis and both renounced their Knighthood. Rabindranath renounced his British knighthood in protest against the Jallianwala Bagh massacre in 1933 AD and Sir Azizul Huque renounced the knighthood on 16 August 1946 as a protest against the brutality of the British. They exchanged letters on the question of the spread and development of education among common people. Sir Mohammad Azizul Huque first met Rabindra Nath in 1930 at Santiniketan when Azizul Haque was serving as Public Prosecutor of the Krishnanagar Judges Court.[26] 'Bengal Education Week' was celebrated in 1936 at the initiative of Education Minister Sir Azizul Huque and at his request in its valedictory session, Rabindranath delivered the closing speech praising Sir Haque.[27]

'The Man Behind the Plough' written by Sir Mohammad Azizul Huque is a highly acclaimed book. When Rabindra Nath got hold of the book, he wrote a letter to Azizul Huque on July 2, 1939, urging him to translate the book into Bengali. He praised him for upholding the plights of farmers in such a lucid manner and opined that this book should be considered as a text of Economics at the University.[28] Rabindranath Tagore and the British administrator Mr. Leo Amri described this book as "Life Philosophy of Village".[29] Rabindranath Tagore recommended Amiya Chakraborty for appointment to Calcutta University when Azizul uaque was the Vice Chancellor of Calcutta University. Referring to Azizul Huque, Rabindranath wrote on 3rd October 1939 in his letter "My Dear Khan Bahadur Azizul Huque", he wrote, "...I presume you had also met him last time when he was delivering his extension lectures in the University. Amiya came out with fellowship from Bresnose, being the first Indian to attain this distinction. ...I write this to inquire if it would be possible for University of Calcutta to retain his services in a permanent manner. I have known him many long years. As my secretary I had every opportunity to judge his worth from many different angles and I have no hesitation in saying the University would be richer by having him as one of its teachers."[30] Not only that, Sir Azizul Huque came to Santiniketan on February 6, 1940 AD as chief guest at the annual convocation of Sriniketan at the invitation of the poet.

Sir Mohammad Azizul Huque inaugurated the exhibition organized as part of the program.[31] As Vice-Chancellor, Sir Azizul Huque in his convocation address on 28 February 1942 expressed deep grief over Rabindranath's death and mentioned the university's relationship with Rabindra Nath. he said "He was a 'Special University Reader' in 1923 and the Kamala Lecturer in 1930. For two years from the 1st August 1932, he was the 'University Professor of Bengali'' for delivering a course of special lectures on selected topic connected with the Bengali language and literature for the benefit and guidance of post- graduate students and to promote the study and research in Bengali in this University. He addressed in the convocation in 1937. We mourn to his death and amidst the mournful memory, let us remember his message to us in reverence and humility in this dark hour of human peril."[32]

Azizul Huque also said, mourning Rabindra's death "India mourns today the loss of her most illustrious son Rabindranath Tagore. He was one of the greatest savants the world has ever seen. He was known throughout the world as the ambassador of Indian's culture. His contribution to the enrichment of the Bengali language will for ever remain written in indelible character of gold in the national history of the country. His poetry inspired the nation for nearly half century and will continue to do so for all time to come. On the behalf of the University of Calcutta, I convey my profound sense of sorrow at his sad death. His death is the end of an age but his memory will linger in the heart of every Indians for centuries to come."[33] Despite having a deep sense of compassion for his religion, Sir Mohammad Azizul Huque was above all sectarianism and parochialism. He was deeply influenced by his family upbringing and by the ideals and philosophies of Prophet Muhammad (PBUH) and Hazrat Umar Farooq (RA) in his real life. Naturally, his loyalty and compassion towards his religion were strong. He served as the Minister in charge of the Wakf and Registration Department of undivided Bengal while he was the education minister. His compassion for Islam can be understood from a speech he gave in the Legislative Assembly of Bengal on February 19, 1934, "Nobody has any right to interfere with the law of the Shariat; and this law does not interfere with the law of the land."[34]

He was not only well-versed in worldly knowledge but deeply knowledgeable about Islam. He wrote the book 'The Sword of the Crescent Moon' to show respect and honour to the last Prophet Hazrat Muhammad (PBUH). It is a biographical work on the Prophet (PBUH). A highly researched work on the history and culture of Islam. The publisher of the book said about the evaluation of the book, "After Syed Ameer Ali's works, Sir Azizul Huque's present book is perhaps the second most important English work on the only Holy Prophet (SM) by a Benglee Muslim author."[35] He was the first Bengali who was appointed as the High Commissioner of India by the British Government in London in 1942 and held the post for one year. When he arrived in London on 16 May 1942, he was welcomed by the chairman of the "Muslim Society" of Great Britain and other dignitaries. At the same time, another 150 members were present to welcome him. Besides, a large group of government officials, one of whom was Lt. Mohammad Ashraf Khan, Mr. D York (Chairman of the Muslim Society of Great Britain), Assistant Imam of the Working Mosque in London Mr. De Quan met in London to welcome Sir Mohammad Azizul Haque. He was welcomed by reciting Surah Fatiha in the opening ceremony of the meeting. De Quan. After seeing this multi-talented person with his own eyes, Mr. D. York. Expressing deep satisfaction, he was described as "A Distinguished Son of Islam."[36] During his stay in London, he visited various industrial areas in Manchester, Liverpool and London and talked about the training workers there to return to India and be employed in Indian factories.

The length of his work is much greater than the length of his life. He was an influential member of the Bengal Legislative Assembly and was considered to be the best speaker among all the Legislative Assemblies of British India.[37] Sir John Herbert described him as the 'Maker of History'.[38] Regarding his constitutional functions and contribution to the Legislative Assembly, Nurul Amin said, "As a Speaker of the Bengal Legislative Assembly, he gave some very important rulings on the interpretation of the Government of India Act, 1935 and has laid down the lines on which this Assembly is still working. As he rose from one high office to another, honours and distinctions were conferred on him. ... He was a scholar and has written several books but above all he was a gentleman and only those who knew him personally could have any estimation of the sterling qualities of his head and heart. He was truly a people's man."[39] On the other hand Mr. W.C Wordsworth said, "We have admired him (Sir Azizul), his energy, ability, fairness in controversy as a member of the House, as a Minister under the old conditions and as a speaker who set a firm and admirable basis on which this Assembly could build up its traditions."[40] Although he is almost forgotten in the history, he is still alive and present in the breadth of his life work and poetry. Kazi Nazrul Islam, Karunanidhan Bandhopadhyay, Shahadat Hossain, Kutubuddin Biswas wrote poems on his character. Above all, his character, personality, fame and influence have been perfectly depicted in poetry by Mohammad Sultan.[41]

References

1. Kalam, Sheikh Abul and Rage, Sujit. (ed.), *Education Progress, Durgati*, Kolkata, 2013, p.70
2. Biswas, Kutubuddin. (unpublished research book) *Life and Times of Mohammad Azizul Huque (1892-1947)*, Calcutta University, 2021, p. xi
3. Islam, Azhar. *Mozammel Haque*, Dhaka, 1993, p. 9
4. Ibid., p. 9
5. Mitra, Amitabh. *Shantipur – Sekal and Ekal*, Kolkata, 2016, p. 60
6. Ali, Mohammad Amir. *Shantipur and Contemporary Muslim Society*, Dhaka, 1973, p. 83
7. Islam, Aminul. *Vivekananda Islam and Contemporary Nationalism*, Kolkata, 2016, p. 148
8. Biswas, Kutubuddin, Op. cit., p.17
9. Haque, Mohammad Mozammel. *Jatiya Foara*, Calcutta, Second Edition, 1319 Bangabd, p. 41
10. Mukhopadhyay, Sunilkumar. *Mozammel Haque (1860-1933)*, Dhaka, 1970, pp. 85-86
11. Qayyum, Mohammad Abdul. *Nazrul in various contexts*, Dhaka, 2002, p. 163
12. Ali, Mohammad Amir, Op. cit., p.109
13. Kalam, Sheikh Abul and Rage, Sujit, Op. cit., p.70
14. Bhuiya, Iqbal, *Sir Azizul Haque*, Dhaka, 1994, p. 22
15. Ibid., p. 15
16. Ibid.
17. Huque, Mohammad Azizul. *The Man behind the Plow*, Kolkata, 2009, p.120
18. Bhuiya, Iqbal, Op. cit., p.15
19. Ibid., p. 15-17
20. Islam, Sirajul. (Editor) *Banglapedia*, Dhaka, 2003, p.196
21. Hakim, Lokman (editor), *Satyar Dishari*, Ninth Year, Third Issue, 15 October 2007, Kolkata, p. 23
22. Ibid., p. 23
23. Ibid., p. 24
24. Ibid., p. 24
25. Ibid., p. 25
26. Bhuiya, Iqbal, Op. cit., p. 31

27. Ibid., p.35
28. Ibid., pp. 35-36
29. Biswas, Kutubuddin, Op. cit., p. xxi
30. Bhuiya, Iqbal, Op. cit., p. 36
31. Ibid., p. 36
32. *The Calcutta Review*, Feb 1942, p. ii, vol-LXXXII, No.1-3, Jan-March 1942
33. *Star of India*, Friday, 8th August 1941, p.5, Reel No -43
34. *Proceedings of Bengal Legislative Assembly*, 19th February 1934, Vol. XLIII, No.4, p.50
35. Bhuiya, Iqbal, Op. cit., p. 29
36. *Islamic Review*, October 1942, Vol. XXX, Pp. 331–332
37. Ali, Mohammad Amir, Op. cit., p. 104
38. *The Calcutta Review*, Feb 1942, p. xxix, vol-LXXXII, No.1-3, Jan-March 1942
39. Proceedings of Bengal Legislative Assembly, 24th March 1947, pp.459-460
40. Ibid., p. 458
41. Sultan, Mohammad. *Shekwa O Jawabe Shekwa* (Translated Bengali Poetry), Calcutta, 1946, Introduction

Islam and the Quest for National Identity: A Critical Study

Kamal Hasan

This writing attempts to capture the contemporary consciousness of the identity of the Muslim citizens of India and highlights its cultural, instrumental, religious and political identity based on historical sources. Understanding the National Identity of any nation is required to study the ambit of multiple social groups. Narratives, real or imaginary, have to be construed to give these various social groups, direct stakes into the nation. These narratives could be drawn historically, culturally, linguistically, religiously, ethnographically, etc. aiding the construction of the National Identity. As far as the Indian side of identity is concerned, one has to consider that Indian identity is simply a heterogeneous mixture of various regional identities of India. The concept of Indian Islam reveals two contradictory tendencies. The first is to see Islam keeping India at the centre, and the second is to find the meaning of India in the background of Islam. It is these two conflicting trends that have established Indian Islam as an academic and political discourse. The first tendency is to fit the universality of Islam into a specific context and give it a cultural basis. This reveals a distinctly Indian face of Islam which together with other geo-cultural faces of Islam presents a colourful picture of Global Islam. On the contrary, under the second trend, it seems as if the universality of Islam is rising above categories like context and time, creating an area in which the element named 'India' has completely merged. This trend shows that Islam is such a totality in which differences like culture, caste and class are completely absorbed without context.

India is home to a diverse range of religious beliefs, with Hinduism, Islam, Christianity, Sikhism, Buddhism, and Jainism among the most widely practised religions in the country. The religious diversity in India is a result of the country's long history and the influence of various civilizations and cultures that have inhabited the region over the centuries. Religious diversity in India has played a significant role in shaping the country's social fabric and identity.[1] For example, the diversity of religious beliefs has contributed to a rich tradition of tolerance and pluralism, where people of different religious backgrounds coexist peacefully. Cultural, linguistic, and religious diversity in India has a profound impact on the social fabric of the country and shapes its identity in several ways.

Hindustan is one of the historically popular names of the present Indian Subcontinent. The name means "Land of the River Indus". The name Hindustan is quite ancient, derived from the early Persian word "Hindu". The Indus River was called Hindu in the Persian language. Added to it is the popular suffix "stan" (in Persian meaning "place"). Earlier, Hindustan meant the entire subcontinent. Historically, "Hindu" was not the name of any religion but the people living along the banks of the river Indus, regardless of the religion they followed. It was used then and for thousands of years or more later by the peoples of western and central Asia to denote India or rather for the people living on the other side of the Indus River. The word is derived from Sindhu, an Indian name of the Indus from which came the words Hindu and Hindustan, as well as Indus and India.[2]

Most historians now agree that India's introduction to Islam was through Arab traders and not Muslim invaders, as is generally believed. The Arabs had been coming to the Malabar coast in southern India as traders for a long time, well before Islam had been introduced in Arabia. Hundreds of years before the prophethood of Muhammad (PBUH), Arab traders had active commercial relations with the Indians, particularly those inhabiting its coastal areas.[3] These traders used to carry Indian goods, such as spices, to Europe via Syria and Egypt and carried goods from European markets back to India, the East Indies (present Indonesia), China and Japan.[4] According to Tara Chand, in that era, Arab traders had not only established their settlements in many coastal towns and cities of India, but under their influence, the local people of Malabar Coast had also adopted the Arab cognitive doctrine (probably Sabaean).[5] H.G. Rawlinson writes, "The first Arab Muslims began settling in the towns on the Indian coast in the last part of the 7th century." They married Indian women and were treated with respect and allowed to propagate their faith.[6]

According to Tara Chand the minds of the people were perturbed and they were prone to accept new ideas from whatever quarter they came. Islam appeared upon the scene with a simple formula of faith, well-defined dogmas and rites, and democratic theories of social organization. It produced a tremendous effect and before the first quarter of the ninth century was over, the last of the Cheraman Perumal Kings named Cheraman Perumal Vhaskara Ravi Varma of Malabar who reigned at Kodungallur had become a convert to the new religion.[7] Through continued trade between Arab Muslims and Indians, Islam continued to spread in coastal Indian cities and towns, both through immigration and conversion, thus highlighting the presence of Islam in India long before the so-called Muslim invaders arrived.

Ample evidence exists showing that numerous Muslim communities were already leading a prosperous and peaceful life in southern India well before the advent of Muslim rule in Sind, under the protection of the local rulers. However, according to *Chach-Namah*, this was not the case along the coast of Sind, because of the particular hostility of its rulers towards such settlements.[8] There is no evidence of Muslim traders settling in Sind before the Muslim conquest, perhaps except for the rebellious Illafi tribe, which joined the service of Raja Dahir sometime before 704 CE. Though there was hardly any incentive for the Muslim traders to penetrate the land of Sind, they nevertheless may have been exposed through their activities in other parts of the Subcontinent to the populace of Sind even before the Muslim conquest. The Muslim conquest of Sind certainly opened the way for the propagation of Islam on a large scale in the region. We are told by *Chach-Namah* that several chieftains and tribes accepted Islam at the invitation of Muhammad ibn Qasim. The converts were mostly Buddhists or recent Buddhist converts to Hinduism. Some of them might have been motivated by matrimonial considerations, but the majority seemed to have changed their faith under the impact of the kind and just treatment of the Muslims.[9]

Based on the above discussion, it was the Arabs who first brought Islam to the Indian subcontinent, then the Turks completed the mission. Stanley Poole's viewpoint is that: "the real Mohammedan conquerors of India were not Arabs, but Turks. When the armies of the Saracens spread out over the ancient world in the seventh century, they overcame most human obstacles."[10] Though a prominent Indian historian and journalist, Dr. Khuswant Singh, in his *'A History of the Sikhs'*, has discussed the early days of Islam in India. He clearly states that Islam was spread in India not by the Muslim rulers but by the Muslim spiritual masters and missionaries although we cannot deny that some Muslim rulers contributed to this mission whether by military invasion or in other ways.[11] Arab rule was fairly tolerant of Hinduism. They even preserved the temple of a Hindu sun god in Multan[12] which also prevented Hindu attacks on the city that might damage this holy spot. Although the Arabs only conquered the north-western part of India, their tolerant rule won many converts to Islam in that region which remains Muslim to this day. This provided a solid base for further Muslim expansion into India.

The caste system, which originated from Hindu belief, divided society into very strictly controlled social classes. Buddhists were generally oppressed by the Hindu princes throughout the country. Many Buddhists and lower castes welcomed the Muslim armies, who carried the promise of an equal society. The first Muslims of Indian origin was probably from the lower castes, as Islam offered them an escape from the oppressive social system, they were accustomed to. With the conquest of Sindh, Muhammad bin Qasim showed that Islamic law's protection of religious minorities was for the Christians, Jews, Buddhists and Hindus in the subcontinent. They were given religious freedom and were not forced to convert. It is seen as a clear and indisputable fact that the religion of Islam was not spread through violence, coercion, fear, or bloodshed.[13]

The Arab expansion during the eighth century CE was halted owing to certain developments within the Umayyad Empire. In the subsequent centuries, however, the Arabs were replaced by the Turks, who then took the lead in the expansion of the 'Abbasid Empire (c.750- 1258 CE), which had replaced the Umayyads (c. 661- 750 CE). The Turkish tribes played a major role among the Muslim conquerors and rulers who came and made India their home. The Turkic attacks began in the first half of the 11th century starting with Sabuktkin. The process of the establishment of their kingdoms in the North and West of Hindustan started in the late 12th century. Although Sindh was occupied by the Arabs, since the establishment of the Abbasside Caliphate in the 8th Century AD, the Arabs played only a marginal role in influencing the culture and civilisation of Hindustan.[14] The Turkish presence started in the Indian subcontinent in the first half of the 11th century and lasted over 700 years. The Ghaznavid sovereignty was followed by the rule of Ghoris. After this, the Slave dynasty was founded by the Turkish slave Quṭb al-Dīn Aibak, a favourite slave of the sultan Muhammad of Ghor and his most trusted officers. Later another Turkish tribe, the Khilji dynasty ruled India from 1292 A.D. to 1320 A.D. The Khiljis were replaced by the Tughluqs. The Tughluqs ruled from 1320 A.D. to 1414 A.D., from Delhi. Eventually, the Mughals seized power over the whole of the Indian subcontinent until British colonisation.[15]

The Mughal Empire ruled most of India and Pakistan in the 16th and 17th centuries. It consolidated Islam in South Asia and spread Muslim, and particularly Persian arts and culture as well as the faith. The Mughals were Muslims who ruled a country with a large Hindu majority. However, for much of their empire, they allowed Hindus to reach senior government or military positions. Mughal entered the Indian subcontinent not to spread Islam but to political & economic interest.[16] The Mughal rulers provided political unity to India. Several parts of the country came under one administration. A major Mughal contribution to the Indian Subcontinent was their unique architecture. The Muslim Mughal Dynasty built splendid palaces, tombs, minars and forts that still stand today in Delhi, Agra, Jaipur, Lahore, Sheikhupura and many other cities in India and Pakistan.

The most emphatic claim Muslims make in India is that it brought egalitarianism. In Islam, everybody is equal: no high or low, no high caste or outcaste. Seeing this liberty and equality, large numbers of low-caste Hindus eagerly converted to Islam; this saved them from the oppressed and ignominious life offered by the Brahmanical society. The culture was significantly impacted. Cooking was heavily influenced by the Turks and the Persians. Paneer was introduced to Indians by the Turks. Architecture was influenced heavily as existing structures were destroyed in battles and new structures did not live long unless they looked like Muslim architecture. The language was significantly changed. Hindustani evolved from the combination of Hindi which was Sanskrit-focused and Urdu which has Persian influence.[17] Persian words still echo in the courts of India today. Islam came to India by the Arab traders and was established by the Turks. This advent changed the history and civilization of India. From the above discussion, it is clear that both Arab and Turk Muslims' advent to the regions and their principles for spreading Islam were based on religious orders generally. By which they had been able to convince the people to accept Islam and to ensure peace and justice at the same time.

The contribution of Muslim revolutionaries, poets and writers is documented in the history of India's struggle for independence. Titumir raised a revolt against the British Raj. Abul Kalam Azad, Hakim Ajmal Khan and Rafi Ahmed Kidwai are other Muslims who engaged in this endeavour to expel the British. Ashfaqulla Khan of Shahjahanpur conspired to loot the British treasury at Kakori (Lucknow). Khan Abdul Gaffar Khan (popularly known as "Frontier Gandhi") was a noted nationalist who spent 45 years of his 95 years of life in jail.[18] Barakatullah of Bhopal was one of the founders of the Ghadar Party, which created a network of anti-British organisations; Syed Rahmat Shah of the Ghadar Party worked as an underground revolutionary in France and was hanged for his part in the unsuccessful Ghadar Mutiny in 1915; Ali Ahmad Siddiqui of Faizabad (UP) planned the Indian Mutiny in Malaya and Burma, along with Syed Mujtaba Hussain of Jaunpur, and was hanged in 1917; Vakkom Abdul Khadir of Kerala participated in the "Quit India" struggle in 1942 and was hanged; Umar Subhani, an industrialist and millionaire from Bombay, provided Mahatma Gandhi and the Congress party with expenses and ultimately died for the cause of independence. Among Muslim women, Hazrat Mahal, Asghari Begum, and B Amma contributed to the struggle for independence from the British.[19]

It would, however, be incorrect to imagine that the problem of identity among the Indian Muslims is the creation of the process of political development and modernization which started after independence. The contemporary Muslim society of India is essentially a legacy of the pre-independence Muslim community, and as such had inherited most of its problems from its earlier existence. However, a greater awareness of this identity crisis among them has emerged due to an interaction of several factors. The contemporary Muslim society of India suffers from a sense of defeat and humiliation incurred during the partition and the ultimate transfer of powers. In the context of a new secular constitution, Muslim society needed a new orientation, both on the political and social levels. Thus, from the above discussion, it is clear that Islam is an integral part of India and its history. As the Indian subcontinent remains today a multiethnic and multireligious place, it is important to understand the position Islam has in the region. The political claims that some make regarding Islam as if it is an invading religion and foreign to the people of India need to be defied with the truth of Islam's peaceful spread throughout India. Lastly, a more positive approach towards resolving the identity crisis could be the development of an abiding sense of nationalism in all the Indian communities - a sense of nationalism not defined in terms of race, religion or language but in terms of national interest.

References

1. See for details: Gore, M. S., *Unity in Diversity: The Indian Experience in Nation-building*, Rawat Publication, New Delhi, 2002
2. Nehru, J., *Discovery of India*, Penguin Random House India Private Limited, New Delhi, 2008, pp.69-70
3. Hourani, George F., *Arab Seafaring in the Indian Ocean in Ancient and Medieval Times*, Princeton University Press, 1951
4. Nadvi, Sayyid S., *Arab our Hind ka Ta'lluqa*, Karim Sons Publishers, Karachi 1976
5. Chand, T., *Influence of Islam on Indian Culture*, Book Traders, Lahore, 1979, p.30
6. Rawlinson, H.G., *Ancient and Medieval History of India*, Bharattiya Kala Prakashan, 2003
7. Op. cit., p.32
8. Ibid., pp.30-36 & 43
9. Baladhuri, Al, Futuh -al – Buldan, A.Y., R. Muhammad Raawan, (ed.) *Cairo- al-Maktabah -al-Tijariyah-al - Kubra*, 1932, pp.423-24; Chach- Namah - 64
10. Lane-Poole, S., *History of India, Trinity College, Dublin, in History of India*, Edited by A. V. Williams Jackson, 1906, part 1: 3
11. Sing, Khushwant., *A History of the Sikhs*, Princeton University Press, 1N.J., 1963, 1, pp.20-28
12. Singh, Y.P., *Islam in India and Pakistan - a religious history*, Alpha Edition, India, 2015
13. Aboul-Enein, H. Yousuf and Zuhur, Sherifa, *Islamic Rulings on Warfare*, p. 22
14. Chandra, S., *Medieval India: From Sultanat to the Mughals Delhi Sultanat (1206-1526)*, Part-1, Har-Anand Publication Pvt Ltd, Delhi, Sixth Edition, 2019, Chapter 1
15. For more information see: Jackson, V. W., *History of India*, Vol. IX, 9006, pp.34-35
16. See for details: Bhargava, M., *Understanding Mughal India Sixteenth to Eighteenth Centuries*, Orient Blackswan, 2019
17. Dehkan, Abul Hassan. "The Influence of Persian Culture in The Sub-Continent of India And Vice Versa, after the Advent of Islam," *Proceedings of the Indian History Congress*, vol. 32, 1970, pp. 269–80
18. Zakaria, Rafiq, *Indian Muslims: Where Have They Gone Wrong?* Popular Prakashan, 2004, pp. 281–286
19. Ali, Asghar & Roy, Shantimoy, *They Too Fought for India's Freedom: The Role of Minorities*, Hope India Publications, 2006, pp.103–116

Bodo Language: A Case of Fading Identity

Anusree Kundu

Linguistics is the scientific study of human language and it describes and analyses language events to identify with how it behaves. Most of our thoughts and identities are language-mediated and depend directly on our language. The fundamental perception of understanding the world is through our native language and our mother tongue is our mind's conceptual homeland. Language plays a pivotal role in shaping and sustaining the community and is extremely important to the community's identity. The Bodo community and its language are no exception, as both are facing an existential crisis due to myriad reasons. Bodos are primarily an agriculturist community and they cultivate rice, jute, betel nuts, etc. and domesticate pigs and other bovine animals. Though they are the largest ethnolinguistic group in Assam, they are sparsely situated in scattered settlements in West Bengal. The Indian Constitution recognizes them as Scheduled Tribe (1950) and they are bilingual by nature. They are proficient in the Assamese language besides their mother tongue Bodo. About 90% of the community is Hindu while 10% are Christian.[1] The ancient Bodo religion is 'Bathou' and their supreme deity is 'Obonglaore'. In the Bodo language 'Ba' means five and 'thou' means deep. The number five is significant in Bodo culture as they believe that five elements -water, earth, air, fire and sky constitute their deities. The 'Sijou' tree is believed to be the symbol of this deity. Apart from Obonglaore or 'Aham Guru', they worship Mainao, Mairong, Agrang, and some Hindu deities like Shiva, Kali, Durga and Krishna. The Bodo community is divided into Aroi or gotra, like, Swargiyari,

Basumatari, Narjari, Musahari, Goyari, Owari, Doimari, etc. The traditional dance of the Bodos is known as 'Bagudumba' and 'Kherai' and their main festival is 'Bisagu' which is celebrated during the Spring. The traditional dress of the Bodo men and women is 'Aronai' and the 'Dokhona' can only be worn by the Bodo women. So, like other long-standing traditions among the indigenous communities, the Bodos also have their unique language, culture, tradition, dress, festivals, dance, music, food habits and way of life. Under the influence of Western education and globalisation, the Bodo community is gradually losing their unique heritage of language and culture.[2]

Bodo/ Boro is one of the 22 languages recognised in the 8th schedule of the Indian Constitution and appeared as a scheduled language in the 2001 Census of India. According to Sir George Abraham Grierson and Robert Shafer's grouping of the Sino-Tibetan family of languages,[3] Bodo belongs to the Tibeto-Burmese group of Sino-Tibetan language and is spoken by the Bodos of Northeast India, Nepal and Bangladesh.[4] The word 'Bodo' was first derived from the Tibetan word 'Bod' which means 'Homeland' and the 'Bodo' community is mainly from the Mongoloid race.[5] The consciousness of the linguistic identity among the Bodos became more vocal and prominent in the light of Assamese linguistic supremacy in the post-independence period. Despite being the largest tribe of Assam, the Bodos faced concerted and systematic efforts by the dominant Assamese language of the state and its linguistic hegemony. The Bodo language faced multiple issues and challenges and the Bodos have been seriously experiencing not only an identity and linguistic crisis but also economic exploitation, social, cultural and political oppression and above all linguistic dissimilation. As a result, Bodos had gathered the strength to assert because they had begun their search for a distinct identity from the Assamese.

In search of an identity, the Bodo tribe has been agitating for a separate state since the 1980s. Land alienation, marginalisation faced by the mainstream and dominant community, and prolonged economic backwardness are believed to be the driving factors for the Bodo identity movement. While the movement itself began to gain momentum only in the 1960s, the Bodo people's insistence on a distinctive identity against the mainstream Assamese community can be traced to pre-independent India. The Bodo people's consciousness of distinctness may have been a result of the onset of colonisation. Since the colonial period, the Bodos have lived in fear of assimilation and extinction while also being acutely conscious of their "glorious past" now lost. Both the fear of assimilation and the awareness of a lost glory are colonial legacies and may be a result of the Hindu/Assamese cultural hegemony and inspired by colonial writings about the Bodos or Bodo-Kacharis. The Bodo community has repeatedly been subjected to epistemic ignorance. They have been a topic of discussion in the media only during protests and riots, and their history, culture, traditions, and music are rarely used to explain their true identity and nature. The whole community has slowly come to be perceived as 'terrorists.'[6] The Bodo people were categorised as 'Scheduled Tribes' under the Indian Constitution (1950) and it divided the Bodo people into separate groups Hill-tribes or Plain-tribes, and those who converted into Hinduism as Scheduled Caste. Many Bodo leaders saw it as a divisive policy and appealed to the people to enlist themselves as 'tribal' irrespective of their religion in the 1941 census.

The Bodo Sahitya Sabha (BSS) of Assam planned to develop the Bodo language by the 1950s. A plan to introduce the Assam Official Language Act in 1960 recognizing Assamese as an official language in the state and the medium of instruction in educational institutions, triggered a wave of protests. The political parties representing tribes from Khasi, Jaintia, Garo, Lushai, Mikir, and North Kachar hills formed the All-Party Hill Leaders Conference, or APHLC, and their central demand was against the declaration of Assamese as an official language which was intended to assimilate the tribals into Assamese. The Bodo language had not inherited any written script, however, Bishnu Prasad Rabha collected specimens of an ancient Bodo script called 'Deodhai' from the Naga tribes. The inscriptions on stone pillars of the Kachari ruins in Dimapur, Nagaland, are said to be written in the same script.[7] The Bodo writers who had been using the Assamese script began to contemplate the adoption of a Roman script after the declaration of the Assam Language Act. The Bodo language used 'Latin' and 'Eastern Nagari' script and in 1843 Latin script was first used to write the Bodo language. From 1884 to 1904 Latin script was used to teach Bodo children, then Assamese/Bengali script was first introduced in 1915, and in 1952 Bodo Sahitya Sabha decided to use Assamese script. A formal proposal for a Roman script was introduced at the sixth annual conference of Bodo Sahitya Sabha on February 22, 1964. In 1971 BSS again unanimously demanded for the Latin to the Assam Government, which was rejected due to its foreign origin. This rejection led to a movement for the Latin script which later on became a part of the movement for the separate state 'UDAYACHAL'. After a long agitation in 1974 fifteen people of the movement died in police firing and many volunteers were injured, the Assam Government referred the matter to the Union Government. The Central Government intervened and proposed an alternative in the *Devanagari* script. On April 9, 1975, the Bodo Sahitya Sabha, Bodo Liberation Tigers and All Bodo Students Union (ABSU) accepted the *Devanagari* script for the Bodo language, but this did not mean that the desire for political independence within the Bodo had subsided.[8]

In 1967, the Plains Tribal Council of Assam (PTCA) and the ABSU were formed and submitted a memorandum to the President of India, demanding an 'Autonomous Region' for tribals living in the plains of Assam. When this proposal for an 'Autonomous Region' gained significant support from the public, by 1972 the PTCA upgraded their demand from the 'autonomous region' to that of a Union Territory under the name 'Udayachal.' In 1986, Upendra Nath Brahma, known as *Bodofa* (Father of the Bodos) among his people, sent a charter of ninety-two demands to both Assam's chief minister and governor mainly concerning socio-economic and educational issues. The last demand was for the creation of a separate state. At the same time, the Bodoland Security Force (BSF), the first Bodo insurgent group, arose due to the consecutive failures of the ABSU and PTCA in grabbing the central government's attention. The corresponding decade was a phase of extensive violence and ethnic clashes in the history of Assam.[9] On February 20, 1993, the Bodoland Accord was signed to create the Bodoland Autonomous Council (BAC), but the geographical boundaries were left undecided and no earnest attempts were made to address it. Seeing the failure in the implementation of the Bodoland Accord, another insurgent group, the Bodo Liberation Tigers (BLT), was formed on June 18, 1996. The ABSU also restarted their rallies and a third phase of protests for a separate Bodoland began. This phase subsided only with the signing of a Memorandum of Settlement between the BLT and the governments of Assam and India on February 10, 2003, to create the Bodoland Territorial Council (BTC). The districts under its jurisdiction were called the Bodoland Territorial Area District (BTAD).[10]

When Telangana state was created in 2014, a demand for a separate Bodoland state resurfaced. Although Bodoland as a state was never formed, a new peace accord was signed in

January 2020 between the government of India, Assam and Bodo associations. The BTAD was renamed the BTR (Bodoland Territorial Region), an autonomous new territory including the areas contiguous to the BTAD with a majority of the tribal population. The major changes were: an increase in the number of constituencies in the BTR from the earlier forty to sixty, provisions for Bodos living outside of the BTAD, and those living in Karbi Anglong and Dima Hasao to be recognized as 'Scheduled Tribes', and promises to establish several educational institutions like a central university and medical college. The government of India also earmarked a sum of Rs. 250 crore per year for three years for the development of the area, and Bodo youth were to be considered for recruitment into the Indian army. The executive functions were to be exercised by a chief executive. Now, a state of uncomfortable peace prevails across the hills and valleys, but the Bodo community carries the burden of memories of what might have been.[11]

The location of BTR is 26° 7 '12"N to 26° 47' 50"N and 89° 47 '40"E to 92° 18' 30"E. It covers over 9000 sq. km area with 5 districts of the north bank of River Brahmaputra. According to the 2011 census, 31.5% of Bodo speakers live in BTR. From 1963 Bodo language became a medium of instruction at primary school of Bodo dominating areas and now it has become a medium of instruction at secondary level also. Bodo language is a compulsory subject at CBSE and KVS schools in Bodo-dominated areas. From 1996 University of Guwahati started a PG course on Bodo language and literature. Even after efforts to preserve the Bodo language, under the influence of other dominating languages, the Bodo language is losing its identity in Assam, West Bengal and simultaneously all over India.[12] This study has three main objectives, viz.,

I. To make a comparative study on the decreasing rate of the monolingual population of Bodo language speakers in

West Bengal and Assam through the following census years 1991, 2001 and 2011.

II. To identify the causes of the reduction of Bodo speaking population in West Bengal and Assam as well as in India.

III. To forecast the probable number of Bodo-speaking bilingual and trilingual populations of West Bengal and Assam in 2021 and 2031 based on previous census data.

Study Area: Most of the Bodo speakers live in Assam, West Bengal, Nagaland, Arunachal Pradesh, and Meghalaya. I have chosen West Bengal and Assam as my areas of study as these two States have the maximum number of Bodo-speaking populations. West Bengal is located at 22°57' N, 88°37'E and Assam is located at 26°14'N, 91°77'E. According to the 2011 census, total Bodo speakers of West Bengal and Assam are 37654 and 1296162 respectively.[13]

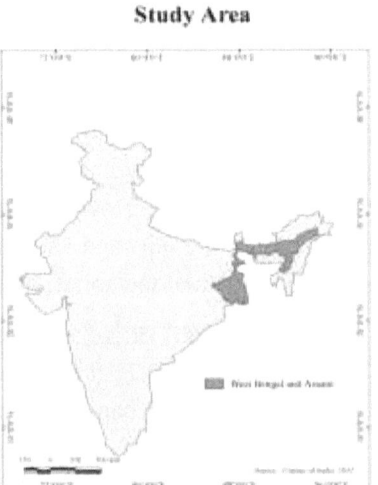

Fig.1: Location Map

Methodology and Data Source: Census data (secondary data) has been collected from the Census of India website (www.censusindia.gov.in). QGIS software is used to prepare the maps. A linguistic survey of India's 2011 report is used. Relevant journals, magazines and websites were used to prepare the report and different cartograms, statistical techniques are used here to represent the data. The location quotient method and Choropleth Map are used to represent the distribution of Bodo speaking population of West Bengal and Assam. A short-term population projection technique (Geometric Increase Method) is used to forecast the probable number of Bodo speakers in West Bengal and Assam in 2021 and 2031.

Result and discussion: Bodo language is mainly spoken by the tribes Rabha, Lalung, Dimasa, Garo, Tripura and Chutiya of Assam, West Bengal, Nagaland, Arunachal Pradesh and Meghalaya. Among the above-mentioned States, the maximum number of Bodo-speaking population live in Assam and West Bengal.

Table No.1: DISTRIBUTION OF BODO SPEAKERS IN INDIA[14]

INDIA/STATE/UNION TERRITORY	ASSAM	WEST BENGAL	OTHER STATES	INDIA
PERCENTAGE (%) OF BODO SPEAKER	95.49	2.89	1.62	100
NO. OF BODO SPEAKERS	1416125	42739	24065	1482929

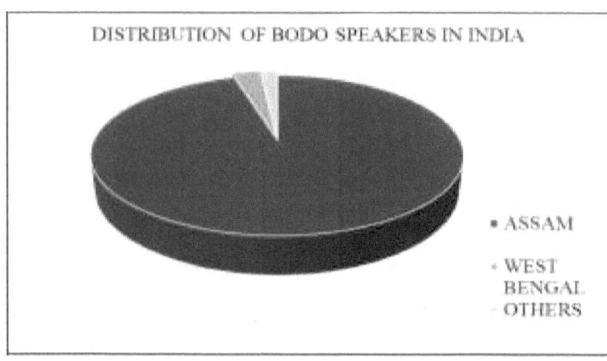

Fig.2: Distribution of Bodo Speakers in India, 2011

According to 2011 census data, 95.49% and 2.89% of Bodo speakers live in Assam and West Bengal respectively. Only 1.62% of Bodo speakers live in the other states of India. In Assam maximum Bodo speakers are inhabited in the districts of Chirang, Baksa, Kokrajhar, Udalguri, Sonitpur, Dhemaji, and Karbi Anglong.[15]

Table No.2: DISTRIBUTION OF BODO SPEAKERS IN ASSAM[16]

District	Total population	Bodo Speaker	Location Quotient
Kokrajhar	843243	251889	5.622
Dhubri	1566396	1407	0.016
Goalpara	822035	35651	0.816
Barpeta	1394755	25722	0.347
Morigaon	776256	11596	0.281

Nagaon	2314629	22506	0.183
Sonitpur	1665125	161447	1.825
Lakhimpur	889010	6950	0.147
Dhemaji	571944	47670	1.568
Tinsukia	1150 062	1187	0.019
Dibrugarh	1185072	391	0.006
Sivasagar	1051736	291	0.005
Jorhat	999221	201	0.003
Golaghat	946279	19876	0.395
Karbi Anglong	813311	43709	1.011
Dima Hasao	188079	1604	0.160
Cachar	1444921	177	0.002
Karimganj	1007976	102	0.001
Hailakandi	542872	277	0.009
Bongaigaon	612665	8351	0.256
Chirang	433061	182382	7.927
Kamrup	1311698	21869	0.313

Kamrup Metropolitan	1059578	20823	0.369
Nalbari	689053	19491	0.532
Baksa	857947	302613	6.639
Darrang	759858	4229	0.104
Udalguri	758746	223714	5.549
	∑Total Population= 26655528	∑Bodo Speaker= 1416125	

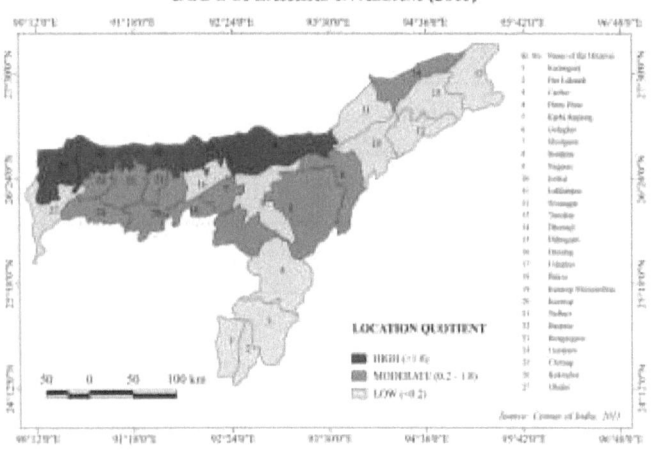

Fig.3: Distribution of Bodo Speakers in Assam (2011)

In West Bengal Bodo speakers live mostly in Jalpaiguri and Darjeeling districts.

Table No.3: DISTRIBUTION OF BODO SPEAKERS IN WEST BENGAL [17]

District	Total population	Bodo Speaker	Location Quotient
Darjeeling	1842034	3607	4.185
Jalpaiguri	3869675	38634	21.33
Coachbihar	2822780	220	0.166
North Dinajpur	3000849	16	0.011
South Dinajpur	1670931	6	0.007
Malda	3997970	9	0.004
Murshidabad	7102430	4	0.001
Birbhum	3502387	0	0
Burdwan	7723663	12	0.003
Nadia	5168488	27	0.011
North 24 Pargana	10082852	61	0.012
Hooghly	5520389	16	0.006
Bankura	3596292	0	0

District	Total population	Bodo Speaker	Location Quotient
Purulia	2927965	6	0.004
Howrah	4841638	5	0.002
Kolkata	4486679	43	0.020
South 24 Pargana	8153176	3	0.0007
West Medinipur	5943300	70	0.025
East Medinipur	5094238	0	0
	∑Total Population= 91347736	∑Bodo Speaker= 42739	

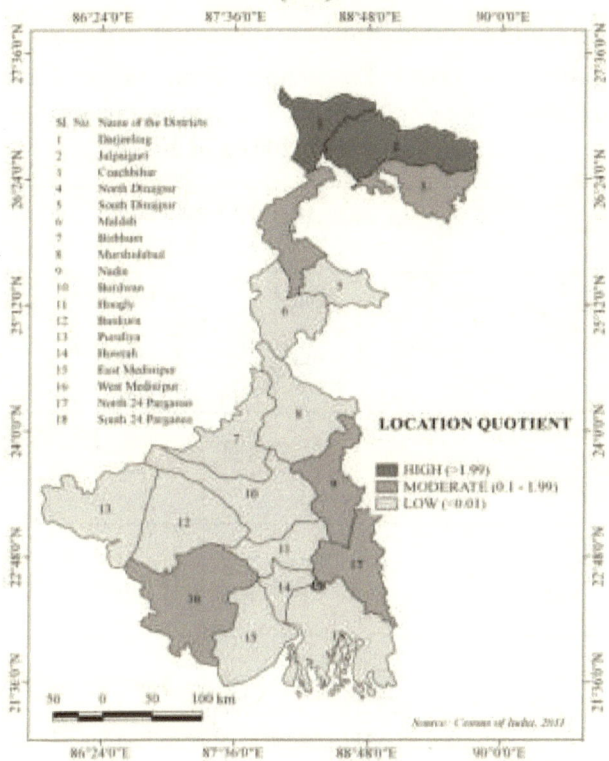

Fig.4: Distribution of Bodo Speakers in West Bengal (2011)

The Trend of monolingualism, bilingualism and trilingualism of Bodo speakers in Assam and West Bengal through the census years 1991, 2001 and 2011 could be seen as: In Assam in the year 1991, 62.44% of Bodo people could speak only in Bodo language whereas in 2011 monolingual population of the Bodo language reached 32.97%. Almost 70% of the Bodo-speaking population has decreased in Assam throughout the census year 1991 to 2011. From the census year 1991 to 2011 in West Bengal approx. 80% of the Bodo-speaking monolingual population has decreased. They are inclined to various languages like Assamese, Bengali, English, Hindi, Nepali, Rabha, Koch, Deori, Lalung, Garo, Santali etc.[18]

Table No.4: Trend of monolingualism, bilingualism and trilingualism of Bodo speakers in Assam through the census years 1991, 2001 and 2011:[19]

CENSUS YEAR	MONOLINGUALS		BILINGUALS		TRILINGUALS		TOTAL SPEAKER	
	NO. OF SPEAKERS	PERCENTAGE (%)	NO. OF SPEAKERS	PERCENTAGE (%)	NO. OF SPEAKERS	PERCENTAGE (%)	NO. OF SPEAKERS	PERCENTAGE (%)
1991	739693	62.44	290149	24.5	154727	13.06	1184569	100
2001	559858	43.2	500308	38.6	235996	18.2	1296162	100
2011	466937	32.97	687927	48.58	261261	18.45	1416125	100

Table No.5: Trend of monolingualism, bilingualism and trilingualism of Bodo speakers in West Bengal through the census years 1991, 2001 and 2011:[20]

CENSUS YEAR	MONOLINGUALS		BILINGUALS		TRILINGUALS		TOTAL SPEAKER	
	NO. OF SPEAKERS	PERCENTAGE (%)	NO. OF SPEAKERS	PERCENTAGE (%)	NO. OF SPEAKERS	PERCENTAGE (%)	NO. OF SPEAKERS	PERCENTAGE (%)
1991	13197	52.44	7918	31.46	4053	16.1	25168	100
2001	10918	29	17691	46.98	9045	24.02	37654	100
2011	7947	18.59	23304	54.53	11488	26.88	42739	100

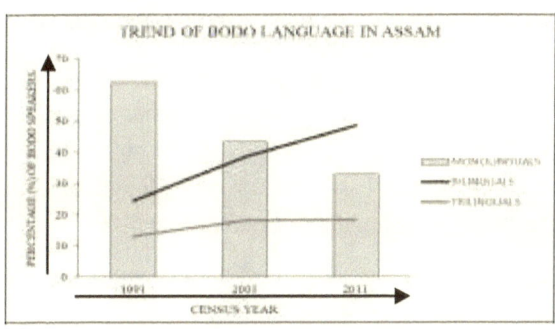

Fig.5: Trend of Bodo Language in Assam

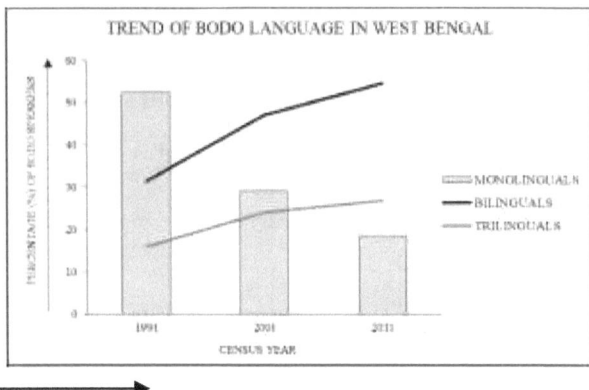

Fig.6: Trend of Bodo

Causes of reduction of monolingualism among the Bodo-speakers:

- Geographical location and various communities: There are many communities like Assamese, Bengali, Rabha, Rajbongshi, and Nepali who live together with Bodos in the geographical location of Assam and West Bengal and communicate with each other in their languages. Thus, multilingualism is increasing in the Bodo community and monolingualism is reduced.[15]

- Higher Education: In the case of higher education there is a lack of books in Bodo language. For higher education and research, Bodos have to learn other languages, leading to the decreasing situation of monolingualism.

- Migration: Inter-district, Intra-state, Inter-state, and Inter-country migration occurs among the Bodo speakers due to better opportunities for higher education, occupation, marriage etc. Migrated Bodos adopt various cultures, and languages of different communities and places and have to speak other languages reducing monolingualism among them. In the time of vacation when they come home, the family members and neighbours also learn different languages from them and multilingualism occurs.

- Globalisation: globalisation is a process by which different cultures and languages spread out all over the world. Under the influence of globalisation, Bodo speakers are inclined to other languages like Assamese, Bengali, Hindi, Nepali, English, Koch, Lalung, Rabha, Deori, Garo, Santali etc. Thus, multilingualism increases, reducing the percentage of monolingualism.

Projection of Bodo-speaking population for the years 2021 and 2031: Population Projection is a method of predicting the population of succeeding years based on the population of the preceding years. The short-term population projection technique includes the Geometric Increase Method, in which it is assumed that the Growth Rate from decade to decade remains constant.

$$P_n = P_o \left(1 + \frac{r}{100}\right)^n \text{ Where,}$$

P_n = Projected Population

P_o = Initial Population

r = Growth Rate

n = No. of Decades

Based on the previous census data, the amount of bilingual and trilingual Bodo-speaking population of Assam and West Bengal has been projected which shows that the bilingual and trilingual Bodo-speaking population is increasing day by day. It can be said that in the wave of multilingualism, the Bodo-speaking monolingual population will gradually vanish.

Table No.6: Projected Population of Assam for 2021 and 2031[21]

Year	1991	2001	2011	2021 (projected)	2031 (projected)
Bilingual Population	290149	500308	687927	1046456	1591841
Trilingual Population	154727	235996	261261	323214	399857

Table No.7: Projected Population of West Bengal for 2021 and 2031[22]

Year	1991	2001	2011	2021 (projected)	2031 (projected)
Bilingual Population	7918	17691	23304	37887	61597
Trilingual Population	4053	9045	11488	18114	28562

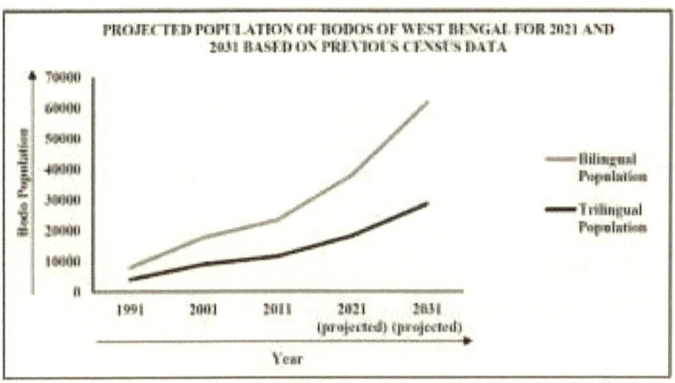

Fig.7: Projected population of West Bengal for 2021 and 2031 based on previous census data

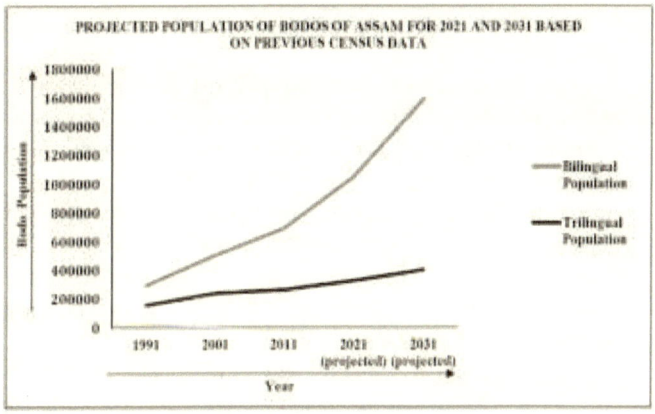

Fig.8: Projected population of Assam for 2021, 2031 based on previous census data

In recent census years, as the population and linguistic data show, the number of Bodo language speakers is decreasing quickly and Bodos are losing their identity. If necessary, measures are not taken soon Bodo language and culture will reach a point of no return. We need to take more positive measures to preserve the identity of the Bodos and their language. On the basis of conclusion, I have some suggestion, such as:

- The government has to make some rules and regulations to preserve the Bodo language.
- Need higher education books in the Bodo language.
- Need to allow them to pursue higher education and research works in the Bodo language.

References

1. "Population by religion community – 2011", Census of India, 2011. The Registrar General & Census Commissioner, Government of India.
2. Kachary, G. B., *Material Culture of the Bodos: A descriptive analysis,* (PhD Thesis, Gauhati University, 2017
3. Grierson, G. A., *Linguistic Survey of India,* Motilal Banarsidass, 1903
4. *Linguistic Survey of India*, West Bengal Part-I, 2011. pp.496, 498
5. Sharma, Manabendra. "Role of Language as an instrument of identity assertion of Bodos", *International journal of multidisciplinary educational research*", vol.10, April 2021, p. 93
6. Narzary, Milan. "An Aversion to 'Savage' Culture: Rectifying Popular Misinterpretations of the Bodoland Movement", *Rising Asia Journal*, Vol. 1, Issue. 1, 2021
7. Boro, Madhu Ram. *The Historical Development of Bodo Language*, NL Publication, Kokrajhar, p. 40
8. Sarmah, Satyendra K., "Script Movement Among the Bodo of Assam", *Proceedings of the Indian History Congress,* V.75, New Delhi, Indian History Congress, pp. 1336, 1336
9. For details see: Dash, Jitendra Narayan. "Udayachal Movement in Assam - Case of Socio-Political Identity for the Bodos," *The Indian Journal of Political Science*, vol. 50, no. 3, 1989, pp. 335–42
10. Desk, Sentinel Digital (28 February 2023). "'Bodoland People's Front to go solo in 2024 Lok Sabha polls' - Sentinelassam". www.sentinelassam.com., taken on May 2023
11. Narzary, M., Op. cit.
12. Basumatary, Birhas G., Bodo Dialects of Brahmaputra Valley: A Linguistic Study, 2006

13. National Commission on Population, Census of India (2006). "Population Projections for India and States 2001–2026", taken on 14 May 2007
14. Census Report of India 1991, 2001, 2011, Government of India.
15. "Census 2011 data rekindles 'demographic invasion' fear in Assam". 26 August 2015, taken on 4 January 2016
16. Census Report of India 1991, 2001, 2011, Government of India.
17. Ibid
18. Ibid.
19. Ibid
20. Ibid
21. Goyary, Nerswn. Baro, Bhowmik C., "A study of multilingualism in Bodo", *Journal of Emerging Technologies and Innovative Research (JETIR)*, Vol.9, March 2022, pp. a341-a342
22. Census of India 1991, 2001, 2011, Government of India.

The Local Dialects of Murshidabad: A Study of Distinct Linguistic Identities

Tawsif Ahmed

As all we know that Language is the only medium through which a person can expresses his thoughts and ideas. The language of expressing his or her thoughts gives that person a unique identity. Language is always and everywhere act as one of the standards means of identity. For example, the Bengali language of West Bengal has given the state a distinct identity and that is distinct from other states within the country. Bengali generally known by its endonym *Bangla* is native language to the West Bengal and Bangladesh. With approximately 234 million native speakers and around 39 million as second language speakers, Bengali became the sixth most spoken native language and the seventh most spoken language by the total number of speakers in the world.[1] More than 80 percent of the people of West Bengal use their mother tongue Bengali language as a spoken language. It is known as one of the widely spoken language to the whole world. Moreover, Bengali language as *Bangla* has given again multiple regional identities based on the local dialects used regionally in the 23 districts of West Bengal and 64 districts of Bangladesh. Majority of the people of more or less all the districts speak Bengali, but various phonetical variations can be observed within this spoken language. Morphological diversity observed in the Bengali language of West Bengal, the morphological diversity of the Bengali language can be divided into five dialects. Those dialects are – *Rahri* dialect, *Barendri* dialect, *Jharkhand* dialect, Bengali dialect and *Kamarupi* or *Rajvanshi* dialect. Out of these five dialects in terms of the spoken language used in Bengal, most of the people speak *Rahri* dialect, the percentage of which is about 98.49.[2]

Regional variation in spoken Bengali constitutes a dialect continuum. Linguist Suniti Kumar Chatterji grouped the dialects of Bengali language into four large clusters- Rarhi, Vangiya, Kamrupi and Varendri,[3] but many alternative grouping schemes have also been proposed. The south-western dialects (Rarhi or Nadia dialect) form the basis of modern standard colloquial Bengali. In the dialects prevalent in much of eastern and south-eastern Bangladesh(Barisal, Chittagong, Dhaka and Sylhet Divisions of Bangladesh), many of the stops and affricates heard in West Bengal and western Bangladesh are pronounced as fricatives. During the standardization of Bengali in the 19th century and early 20th century, the cultural centre of Bengal was in Kolkata, a city founded by the British. What is accepted as the standard form today in both West Bengal and Bangladesh is based on the West-Central dialect of Nadia and Kushtia District.[4] There are cases where speakers of Standard Bengali in West Bengal will use a different word from a speaker of Standard Bengali in Bangladesh, even though both words are of native Bengali descent. For example, the word salt is (salt) lôbôṇ in the east which corresponds to nun (salt) in the west.[5]

The differences in language that can be observed in each district of West Bengal are due to different regions based on education, religion, socio-economic system and personal taste. Murshidabad district also could not cross the boundaries of this variation and variety. Most of the people of Murshidabad district use Bengali as their daily expression language i.e., spoken language. The Bengali language spoken by the people of Murshidabad district belongs to the 'Radhi dialect'.[6] The Radhi dialect of Murshidabad district has given a distinct identity to the Bengali language of Murshidabad as compared to other districts. Just as the whole of Bengal has acquired a distinct identity for the Bengali language in different parts of India, the spoken language used in different parts of Murshidabad district has given a distinct identity to the people of different parts of Murshidabad.

Murshidabad district itself carries a diverse distinct identity from its Nawabi historical context. People of different religions, different races and different languages have been living in this historical district for centuries. For example, the historic town of Lalbagh in Murshidabad district, where Iranian people live since the Nawab period, and in the northern part of the district, there are some Bihari Hindi-speaking people living in the adjoining areas of Dhulian and Malda districts. On the other hand, in the eastern edge of the district of Murshidabad district, Domkal sub-division near Bangladesh and neighboring areas of Nadia district are inhabited by Bengalis coming from Bangladesh. Murshidabad District The residence of this diverse population from different parts of Murshidabad district has given a unique identity to the Bengali language spoken in Murshidabad district.

The Bengali language spoken by most of the people of Murshidabad district belongs to the Rahri dialect. Although the majority of the people in Murshidabad district speak the Rahri dialect, there is regional variation in the use of the Radhi dialect in Murshidabad. River Ganga runs through the middle of Murshidabad district from Malda district in the north to Nadia district in the south. There is a huge diversity in the vast number of people who live on the eastern and western side of this river Ganga and whose everyday communication language is Bengali. All the people of the western part of the river Ganges speak the same dialect as the people of the eastern part also speak. However, although Rahi dialect is used as a spoken language in the entire Murshidabad district, this information language can be observed separately in different regions. Due to regional variations in language, different linguistic forms can be observed even within a dialect, which is known as sub-dialect. Among the Rhari dialects of Murshidabad, different forms of the spoken language can be observed region-wise, sub-division wise in the table below.

Variation on Local dialects of Murshidabad Sub-divisions[7]

মহকুমার নাম Sub-Division	ইংরেজি ভাষায় Sentences in English	স্ট্যান্ডার্ড ভাষায় Standard Bengali language	মহকুমা ভিত্তিক প্রচলিত কথ্য ভাষা Local Dialects
জঙ্গিপুর মহকুমা (বিহার ও ঝাড়খন্ড সংলগ্ন) Jangipur	• what are you doing? • where are you going? • how are you? • where will you go?	• কি করেছো তুমি? • কোথায় থেকে আসছো? • কেমন আছো তুমি? • কোথায় যাবে তুমি?	• কি করেছো তুমি? • কোথায় থেকে আসছো? • কেমন আছো তুমি? • কোথায় যাবে তুমি?
কান্দি মহকুমা Kandhi	• what are you doing? • where are you going? • how are you? • where will you go?	• কি করেছো তুমি? • কোথায় থেকে আসছো? • কেমন আছো তুমি? • কোথায় যাবে তুমি?	• কি করেছো গো? • কতি থেকে আসছো? • ক্যামন আছো গো তুমি? • কতি যাবা তুমিই?
বহরমপুর মহকুমা Berhampore	• what are you doing?	• কি করেছো তুমি?	• কি কচ্ছো তুমি?

	• where are you going? • how are you? • where will you go?	• কোথায় থেকে আসছো? • কেমন আছো তুমি? • কোথায় যাবে তুমি?	• কুত্ থেকে আসছো? • তুমি ক্যামুন আছো? • কুথায় যাবি?
লালবাগ মহকুম Lalbagh	• what are you doing? • where are you going? • how are you? • where will you go?	• কি করছো তুমি? • কোথায় থেকে আসছো? • কেমন আছো তুমি? • কোথায় যাবে তুমি?	• কি করছো তুমি? • কুঠে থাইক্যা আল্যা? • ক্যামন আছো তুমি? • কুঠে থেকে আসছো?
ডোমকল মহকুমা Domkal	• what are you doing? • where are you going? • how are you? • where will you go?	• কি করছো তুমি? • কোথায় থেকে আসছো? • কেমন আছো তুমি? • কোথায় যাবে তুমি?	• কি করছো তুমি? • কুঠে থেকে আসছো? • কেমন আছো তুমি? • কুথে যাবা তুমি?

Looking at the above table, we can see that Murshidabad district is divided into five sub-divisions. Although the spoken languages of these five sub-divisions are theoretically Rahi dialects, there are variations in the languages spoken by the people of the sub-divisions. The reason for this variation is the diverse population living in Murshidabad district. Dhulian,

Suti-1 and Suti-2 of Jangipur sub-divisions adjacent to Malda on the western side of river Ganga i.e., Murshidabad district under Radha region and several areas of Murshidabad district of Jharkhand who speak their regional language known as "Khotta" language. On the other hand, a different type of spoken language is used in Kandi sub-divisions such as Dak-Banglo, Kandi, Kuli, Nagar and Sherpur in the western and southwestern parts of the district, adjoining Birbhum and Burdwan districts. The region has a large number of Rahi dialects. Most of the people in this region use Rahi dialect as information language.

On the other hand, three sub-divisions of Murshidabad district are located on the eastern side of the Ganges, i.e., Bagri region. Among these three sub-divisions, except Baharampur, the center of Baharampur sub-division, the people of Beldanga, Rezinagar, Amtala, Patikabari regions speak a different language which is a mixture of Rahi dialect and Bengali dialect. Apart from this, the information language of this region is Saotali language due to the indigenous people in Palsonda, Chanakya and Morgram regions in the east of this subdivision. Although the population of tribals in this region is small. Another subdivision of the district is Lalbagh. Apart from Lalbagh and Jiyaganj areas of this Lalbagh subdivision, the influence of Bengali dialect can be seen in the spoken language spoken by the people in areas like Bhagbangola, Lalgola Kharibona Nasipur and Akhriganj. The main reason is that these areas are adjacent to the border of Bangladesh. Again, in Lalbagh town of Lalbagh sub-division there are people of Iranian community living since Nawab period who use Urdu as their mother tongue. Due to this the historic city of Lalbagh in Murshidabad has acquired a distinct linguistic identity. Due to the presence of Sikh community in the city of Lalbagh as well as the city of Jiaganj, the prevalence of Punjabi language in the region can be observed as a diverse matter. On the other hand, this last sub-division is Domkal sub-division, which is adjacent to Bangladesh on both sides, so the influence of Bengali dialect can be observed here, especially Nirmalchar, Sheikhpara, Sagarpara, Nabipur and Jalangi etc.[8]

In theory, the spoken Bengali language of Murshidabad district is included in the Radhi dialect. Due to the presence of different ethnic groups in the region of this district, diversity can be observed in the spoken language. Whatever the spoken language of this district, a mixed dialect has developed due to culture, religion, education and social customs. In this district, on the one hand, we observe the influence of Bihari Khotta language, Iranian language, Urdu language, Punjabi language, Bengali language, and Rajvanshi language influence. All in all, we aim for a mixed and varied dialect like the mixed culture of the people of this district. So, we cannot say singularly that the Bengali language spoken in Murshidabad bears only the identity of Rahi dialect. The languages spoken in each region of this diverse Murshidabad district carry a distinct identity.

Last, in the case of writings (official) in Bengali language, although all the people of Murshidabad uniformly followed the same pattern however some minor variation can be seen as it is common throughout the state of West Bengal. Bengali exhibits diglossia, though some scholars have proposed triglossia or even n-glossia or heteroglossia between the written and spoken forms of the language.[9] However, mainly wo styles of writing have emerged, involving somewhat different vocabularies and syntax. One is Shadhu-Bhasa (সাধু ভাষা "upright language") and another is Cholito (চলিত ভাষা "running language"). Shadhu-bhasha is the written language, with longer verb inflections and more of a Pali and Sanskrit-derived Tatsama vocabulary. Songs such as India's national anthem Jana Gana Mana (by Rabindranath

Tagore) were composed in this style. People of Murshidabad are not used to with this type of writing language. Cholito-bhasha, known by linguists as Standard Colloquial Bengali, is a written Bengali style exhibiting a preponderance of colloquial idiom and shortened verb forms and is the standard for written Bengali now. This form came into vogue towards the turn of the 19th century, promoted by the writings of Peary Chand Mitra,[10] Pramatha Chaudhuri and in the later writings of Rabindranath Tagore. This form of Bengali is often referred to as the "Kushtia standard"(Bangladesh), "Nadia dialect" (West Bengal).[11] As the Murshidabad is the neighbor district of Nadia, some of the people of the adjacent border areas like Reginagar, Jalangi, Nawda follow this type of writing language.

References

1. "The World Factbook". www.cia.gov. Central Intelligence Agency, February 2018; "Summary by language size", *Ethnologue,* 24 April 2019
2. Census of India: Murshidabad". www.censusindia.gov.in., 20 November 2019
3. Chatterjee, Suniti Kumar. *The Origin and Development of the Bengali language,* Vol- 1, George Allen and Unwin London, New Edition,1970, pp. 130-141
4. Islam, Sirajul Miah, Sajahan; Khanam, Mahfuza; Ahmed, Sabbir, eds. (2012); *Banglapedia: The National Encyclopedia of Bangladesh* (Online ed.). Dhaka, Bangladesh: Banglapedia Trust, Asiatic Society of Bangladesh, October 2023
5. "History of Bengali (Banglar itihash)", Bengal Telecommunication and Electric Company, 7 July 2011.
6. "52nd Report of the Commissioner for Linguistic Minorities in India", Nclm.nic.in. Ministry of Minority Affairs, 25 May 2017, p. 85,
7. Personal interviews with local peoples and subsequent observation, dated 12th April 2023 to 23rd June 2023.
8. Murshidabad – "Banglapedia", Bangladesh, 26 August 2019
9. "Bengali Language at Cornell", *Department of Asian Studies*, Cornell University, 15 November 2012

10. Huq, Mohammad Daniul. "Alaler Gharer Dulal", In Sirajul Islam; Miah, Sajahan; Khanam, Mahfuza; Ahmed, Sabbir (eds.). *Banglapedia: The National Encyclopedia of Bangladesh (Online ed.),* Dhaka, Bangladesh, Banglapedia Trust, Asiatic Society of Bangladesh, 2012
11. Morshed, Abul Kalam Manjoor. "Dialect", in Sirajul Islam; Miah, Sajahan; Khanam, Mahfuza; Ahmed, Sabbir (eds.). *Banglapedia: The National Encyclopedia of Bangladesh (Online ed.),* Dhaka, Bangladesh: Banglapedia Trust, Asiatic Society of Bangladesh, 2012

Queer Liberation and Assimilation in India: Navigating Historical Contexts and Contemporary Challenges

Swakshadip Sarkar

As the Supreme Court hearing on marriage equality is going on with claims about the LGBTQIAHKK+ (Lesbian, Gay, Bisexual, Transgender, Queer, Intersex, Asexual/Aromantic, *Hijra*, *Kinnar*, *Kothi/Koti* (*Hijras*, *Kinnars* and *Kothis* are individuals who are generally assigned male at birth and identify themselves under the transfeminine spectrum with some unique rituals and culture) and other sexual and gender diverse identities) community being 'urban elitist' made by the Central government is widely being criticised, one might think whether there are rural representations of LGBTQIAHKK+ communities. Being born and brought up in a small town, I had the exact same notion a decade back. The representations that people see in the media are mostly based in cities. I was blessed to find a community around me much later who I can look forward to as a *Koti* individual. What does the queer movement lack then? Why was it unable to represent individuals like me and others who face marginalisation due to multiple intersectional identities? The answer to these questions can be attributed to the approach that the dominant forms of queer movement has taken since it began. This article will look at the assimilationist and liberation approaches within the queer movement in India placing them in a historical context and how the dominance of assimilationist approaches privileges only a few sections of LGBTQIAHKK+ population and further marginalises others.

The Indian queer movement formally started way later than it started in the West. While, in countries like the USA, the UK and other countries in the West, queer movement roughly began in the late 60s and early 70s with Pride walks being organised during that time, the queer movement in India was fuelled by the HIV and AIDS endemic. The earliest records of queer movement in India were mostly fuelled by diasporic organisations like Anamika and Trikone. The latter published a magazine which was widely circulated in India and carried contributions from Indians.[1] The inception of Bombay Dost and Humsafar Trust, its sister organisation in 1990 formally marked a shift in the queer activism in India. The AIDS Bhedbhav Virodhi Andolan (ABVA hereinafter) raised awareness of Section 377's high prevalence of HIV/AIDS among LGBTQIAHKK+ persons as well as the stigma and discrimination encountered by those who had the disease. The first piece to openly support homosexual rights in India was released by ABVA in 1991 under the title Less Than homosexual: A Citizens' Report on the Status of Homosexuality in India.[2] One of the first rallies against police abuse of queer men in India was held after police searches targeted homosexual cruising in Central Park and Connaught Place in New Delhi. On August 11, 1992, the ABVA gathered at the Delhi police headquarters to express their discontent with the force's operations. An important turning point in Indian lesbian activism and discourse was the 1996 Deepa Mehta film Fire. The movie's plot centred on Radha and Sita's forbidden sexual inclinations. When it was launched in 1998, right-wing activists from the Shiv Sena and Bajrang Dal invaded theatres all throughout the country in an effort to stop people from watching it. Thus, the release of this movie sparked a national conversation about lesbian and homosexual rights.[3] India witnessed its first Pride Walk in Kolkata known as 'Friendship Walk' at that time in 1999.

The NAZ Foundation filed a writ suit with the Delhi High Court in 2001, claiming that Section 377 of the Indian Constitution's prohibition on private sexual activity between consenting adults violates basic rights. In 2004, the High Court denied the petition, saying that it contained only intellectual inquiries that the court was unable to consider. The NAZ Foundation filed a petition in 2006 asking India to decriminalise consensual same-sex relationships. The constitutional protections against discrimination and equality were cited by the High Court in its 2009 decision in favour of decriminalisation. The Supreme Court reversed this ruling in 2013, keeping Section 377 in place and making same-sex activity illegal.[4] In 2016, four Indian celebrities contested the verdict that criminalised same-sex relationships. In 2018, the Supreme Court removed Section 377, recognizing privacy as a fundamental right.[5] On the other hand, after years of protest, some gender variant groups were accepted as a third gender in 2014 by the National Legal Services Authority vs. Union of India verdict (hereafter, NALSA judgement). The group has been asked to participate in various social welfare initiatives and be labelled as a socially and economically deprived class by the federal and state governments. Additionally, hiring in government and admission to educational institutions has been subject to requests for reservations. In 2019, India's Parliament passed the Transgender Person's (Protection of Rights) Act, which excluded gender non-conforming individuals and conflated gender with sex. The Act also required medical treatments to legally identify as male or female and lacked penalties for violations.[6]

Queerness has been central to modern politics in many countries across the globe over the last decade. LGBTQ+ people have gained some major rights including the decriminalisation of homosexuality and legalisation of same sex marriage in many countries. This major shift has been possible due to the queer assimilationist approaches within the queer movement. The LGBTQ+ movement has a strategy called queer assimilation that aims to blend into society at large and win legal equality. Instead of opposing and altering those systems, it focuses on attaining acceptance and integration of LGBTQ+ people into current society structures.[7] This can be attributed to embracing modernity in Western nations as demonstrated by Gerhards (2010) in the European Union. Instead of attempting to fundamentally alter cultural norms and values, queer assimilation tries to achieve equality by progressive reforms like the decriminalisation of same-sex relationships and the acknowledgment of the third gender. While this strategy has been useful for securing some legal rights in India and across the globe, it is challenged for having a narrow focus and failing to address the fundamental issues that LGBTQIAHKK+ people confront, such as persecution and marginalisation as is also evident in the Indian context.

For a number of reasons, the queer assimilation movement has drawn criticism. First, it has been criticised for placing a narrow emphasis on legislative and regulatory improvements rather than tackling the underlying causes of marginalisation and oppression i.e. patriarchy, heteronormativity, and cisnormativity.[8] The movement has also come under fire for failing to address intersectionality, as it frequently gives preference to the experiences of white, middle-class, cisgender, and homosexual people (dominant caste upper class cisgender gay men in case of India) while disregarding the experiences of those who identify as being at the intersection of several marginalised identities. Thirdly, rather than attacking oppressive structures, the movement has been accused of upholding the status quo and doing nothing to end them.[9] The distinctive cultural and social representations of

LGBTQIAHKK+ identities might as a result be overlooked. The movement has also come under fire for failing to acknowledge the range of queer experiences and identities, which can lead to ignoring the needs and concerns of those who do not fit into traditional gender and sexuality norms.[10]

In the Indian context, the NALSA judgement that recognised certain transgender identities as a 'third gender' in 2014 and the decriminalisation of homosexuality by partial removal of Section 377 in 2018 have been the legal judgements with regards to the LGBTQIAHKK+ community. These judgements have been criticised to be lacking intersectionality. The NALSA verdict highlighted regional differences in trans* identities such as *Hijras, Aravanis, Shiv Shaktis, Jogappas*, and others, transmen and other transmasculine identities are only twice mentioned.[11] Furthermore, other identities on the transfeminine spectrum like *nupa-manabi*, *kothi* were not mentioned. Therefore, while NALSA recognised some gender-variant identities, it excluded others.[12] In addition, the NALSA judgement promised vertical reservations for the gender variant communities thereby ignoring the intersectional marginalisation faced by gender variant persons belonging to the Dalit, Bahujan and Adivasi (DBA) communities and those with disabilities. Therefore, while it ensured some gender variant communities get access to their basic human rights, it did not take into account the question of caste and disability and how it leads to intersectional marginalisation.

Similarly, the abrogation of Section 377 was considered as a major step in the LGBTQIAHKK+ movement. The court had "decriminalised" homosexuality or overturned a ban on "gay sex," according to headlines in Indian and foreign media.[13] According to some media accounts, the verdict widely signified "legal acceptance" for the "LGBTQ community" as a whole.[14] However, Rastogi (2018) highlighted the experiences of Hijra and Kinnar individuals in Delhi after the partial removal of Section 377. Police abuse of *Kinnara* and *Hijra* individuals appears to have "escalated ever since the Supreme Court judgement against 377. Rastogi (2018) reported that the brutality started the very day of the judgement."[15] One of the survivors mentioned that two to three police officers picked them up and put them into custody and after abusing them, they were hanged up against walls. For a long time, they were verbally abused before being raped. The report also highlighted the ordeal of *Hijra* and *Kinnar* individuals as it highlighted one of the *Kinnara* women asking, "Is it a crime to exist?" Another survivor was quoted "We beg for a living since nobody wants to hire us because we are *kinnaras*. However, if the police see us talking to other individuals, they beat us or chase us away, accusing us of being a public nuisance and prostitution." The use of public order and sex work laws to prosecute, extrajudicially harass, and persecute hijras and other gender non-conforming people dates back a long way, and it appears to be doing so even in the wake of the verdict.[16] Inspite of the judgements, Dalit transgender people continue to face struggles. According to a report by Bansal (2022), in their interactions with police officers, Dalit transgender people also experienced harassment: 23% of Dalit transgender people were forcibly stripped or denuded by the police, and 19% were sexually assaulted when they went to the police for help. Access to public transport and places like parks (50%) and police stations (46%) and government hospitals (43%) was particularly difficult for Dalit transgender people. 56% of Dalit transgender respondents reported having to participate in sexual behaviour to obtain a place to live, food, or a job. Therefore, although the assimilationist approach has brought legal gains for the LGBTQIAHKK+ community in India, it failed to account for the experiences of intersectionality marginalised people along class, caste and disability divide and breaking the structural exclusion and violence faced by them. The LGBTQIAHKK+ individuals who are intersectionality marginalised continue to face violence and marginalisation despite the judgements.

In a society where everyone can live freely and authentically without fear of discrimination or violence based on their gender identity or sexual orientation, queer liberation is a social movement that calls for the total dismantling of oppressive systems that uphold heteronormativity, cisnormativity, and patriarchy. The foundation of queer liberation is the idea that everyone has the right to express themselves in ways that are authentic to who they are and what they want, especially in terms of their sexual orientation and gender identity. Queer liberation opposes the social and cultural standards that now marginalise and stigmatise LGBTQ+ people and works to build a society that is accepting of people with a variety of gender and sexual identities.[17] The movement places a strong emphasis on intersectionality and acknowledges that lesbian, gay, bisexual, transgender, and queer identities do not exist in a vacuum but rather connect with other identities such as racial, ethnic, socioeconomic, and religious ones. In addition to valuing individual expression and freedom, queer liberation seeks to build a society that not only accepts but also celebrates and embraces LGBTQ+ identities. This can entail questioning cultural expectations regarding sexuality and relationships, challenging traditional gender roles and conventions, and fighting for laws and practices that safeguard and support LGBTQ+ people.[18]

Queer liberation is perceived as being too extreme in India because it challenges and aims to fundamentally alter current societal conventions and values surrounding gender and sexuality. It places a strong focus on individual expression, including that of one's sexual orientation and gender identity, and works to destroy oppressive structures that support heteronormativity and cisnormativity.[19] The LGBTQ+ community has experienced tremendous discrimination and marginalisation in India because of the deeply embedded and entrenched conventional social norms and values surrounding gender and sexuality. It is now challenging to promote radical change in a conservative social and political environment as a result of this. It is also difficult to promote sexual emancipation and freedom in India because of the culture's long history of conservatism around sex and sexuality. In addition, substantial societal transformation is required by queer liberation, which is perceived as impossible by those who stand to gain from the current power structures. As a result, there is opposition to accepting the queer liberation idea since it is thought to be too out of the ordinary and dangerous to social order.

There has been significant opposition to the liberationist approaches especially by those who hold more power i.e. dominant caste upper-class cis-gender gay men within the queer movement. For example, in Pune Pride in 2022, there was opposition to an intersectional representation. The theme of the Pride Movement was announced to be 'traditional' with only Indian and Pride flag being allowed in the march. The transgender or Dalit flags were supposedly banned from the Pride March with the Dalit people being asked to keep their "Dalit identity at home."[20] The liberationist approach and its solidarity with other social movements are also oppressed by the assimilationists using the law. The Mumbai Pride in 2020 organised by Queer Azadi Mumbai, a collaboration of different NGOs provides an example of the same. The Pride Walk was cancelled due to the ongoing protests against the implementation of Citizenship Amendment Act (CAA) and National Register for Citizens (NRC). However, a social gathering was organised with slogans being raised from the stage. The community's strong belief that Prides has always been a place for dissent and that the Trans Bill, the CAA, the NRC, and other laws passed by the current administration all affect marginalised people, including LGBTQIAHKK+ people, was at the centre of the gathering. People attended the pride event with posters and signs that said "CAA Sashay Away" and "*Hum Dekhenge*" (We will see). On the bodies of some, the phrase "Pride is a protest" was written. There were anti-CAA slogans which the organisers intended to suppress through sloganeering on stage. However, a prominent BJP leader named Kirit Somaiya received a video of the event, which showed a group of people chanting in favour of anti-CAA protestors. Kirit Somaiya then filed a complaint about the "anti-national" slogans accusing fifty-one people who were seen in the video. A queer activist identified activist Kris Chudawala in a public Facebook post accusing them of sloganeering and "overtaking community proceedings." Kris, a 21-year-old student at the Tata Institute of Social Sciences, was outed in this post, which also unleashed the machinery of the state, the police, the media, and the legal system on a young, defenceless transgender person who had not even come out to their family. The QAM distanced itself from the people who were charged with sedition.[21]

Queer liberationists suffer at the hands of those who subscribe to the politics of respectability as well. The slogans raised at Kolkata Pride in 2022 and the responses towards those slogans point towards the same. During Kolkata Pride 2022, a renowned Dalit queer researcher and activist Saptarshi Bairagi raised slogans from the stage such as "*ami koti ami dhurai, dhuriye dhuriye bhaat khai*" (I am *Koti* and I earn my livelihood through sex work) and "*tulsi tolai diye baati koti bole ami soti, tor ki khoti tor ki khoti?*" (A *Koti* lights the lamp under a Tulsi plant (a religious practice to be performed after being pure) and calls herself a celibate, how is that harming you?) which represented the subaltern LGBTQIAHKK+ cultures representing especially those who engage in *khajra* (sex work). There was opposition by the organisers on stage who wanted the Pride Walk to be a neoliberal capitalist celebration of queer identities scaring the sloganeers of police action. The Facebook posts afterwards criticised these slogans and pointed out how LGBTQIAHKK+ people are being painted as "sluts". This points out towards the dominance of queer assimilationist approaches and how the dominant queer organisations and movements uphold the hetero and cis-normative norms and oppose the liberationist approaches of destroying oppressive structures that push intersectionally marginalised LGBTQIAHKK+ people to the margins. The most glaring example is the hearing of marriage equality in the Supreme Court and the media attention towards it while completely being silent on the protest of Dalit transgender activists for horizontal reservations. The Trans Rights Now Collective organised a peaceful protest demanding horizontal reservation in Chennai and seventeen activists including Grace Banu who has been at the forefront for demanding horizontal reservation were detained.[22] The Supreme Court which is currently hearing the case of marriage equality refused to entertain the plea to clarify whether NALSA judgement which promised reservations for the transgender community indeed promises horizontal reservation.[23] Therefore, the assimilationist idea of upholding heteronormative norms got precedence over the idea of breaking down caste hierarchies within the transgender community. However, in spite of the opposition to the queer liberation approaches, some smaller organisations catering to intersectionally marginalised LGBTQIAHKK+ population such as The Queer Muslim Project and The Dalit Queer Project have been set up in India to highlight their intersectional struggles and marginalisation.

The ongoing argument in India between emancipation and assimilation strategies for LGBTQIAHKK+ people have numerous ramifications for the country's queer movement. First, a sophisticated grasp of the connection between assimilation and liberation approaches is necessary for the Indian queer movement. To accomplish its goals, the movement must strike a balance between the two ways, as each has advantages and disadvantages. In order to be inclusive and reflect the variety of experiences within the community, the queer movement in India must prioritise the perspectives and experiences of marginalised queer people. In order to guarantee the protection and recognition of all LGBTQIAHKK+ people in India, the queer movement must continue to advocate for political and legal action. This involves promoting anti-discrimination laws, marriage equality, and safeguards for both the workplace and one's health. In addition, the queer movement in India has to acknowledge how diverse forms of oppression interact with queerness and confront these interactions. This covers issues pertaining to ability, caste, class, and religion. The LGBTQIAHKK+ movement in India needs to understand the value of working in alliance with other social justice movements to address shared struggles, dismantle social hierarchies, and fight against laws that could negatively impact a sizable portion of the LGBTQIAHKK+ population. Overall, the continual conflict between liberation and assimilation strategies for LGBTQIAHKK+ people in India emphasises the necessity of ongoing discussion and action to build a more just and equitable society for all Indians. While acknowledging the depth and diversity of queer experiences and identities, the movement must continue to push for positive changes for all LGBTQIAHKK+ individuals including those who are intersectionally marginalised.

References

1. Adur, Shweta. "Memories and Apprehensions: Temporalities of Queer South Asian" in *Belonging and Activism in the Diaspora*, Edited by Radha Hegde and Ajay Sahoo, 2017, pp. 304–314; Ratti, Rakesh. *A Lotus of Another Color: An Unfolding of the South Asian Gay and Lesbian Experience*, Alyson Publications, 1993; Karnik, Niranjan. 'Locating HIV/AIDS and India: Cautionary Notes on the Globalization of Categories', *Science, Technology & Human Values*, vol. 26, no. 3, SAGE Publications, July 2001, pp. 322–348
   Gerhards, Jürgen. "Non-discrimination towards homosexuality: The European Union's
2. policy and citizens' attitudes towards homosexuality in 27 European countries", *International Sociology*, 25.1, 2010, pp. 5-28
3. Turner, Elen. 'Indian Feminist Publishing and the Sexual Subaltern', *Rupkatha Journal*, vol. 1, 2014, pp. 131–141
4. Chandrika. 'Suresh Kumar Koushal & Another v. Naz Foundation Others", *International Journal of Law Management & Humanities*, vol. 1, no. 2, 2018, pp. 192–196; Rao, T. S. Sathyanarayana, and K. S. Jacob. 'The Reversal on Gay Rights in India", *Indian Journal of Psychiatry*, vol. 56, No. 1, Medknow, 2014, p. 1
5. Paul, N., 'When Love Wins: Framing Analysis of the Indian Media's Coverage of Section 377, Decriminalization of Same-Sex Relationships', *Newspaper Research Journal*, vol. 43, no. 1, SAGE Publications, Mar. 2022, pp. 7–28
6. Sarkar, Swakshadip. 2022, *Transgender People and Employment in The Era of Diversity and Inclusion*, https://hdevri.com/2022/05/10/transgender-people-and-employment-in-the-era-of-diversity-and-inclusion/. Accessed 8 Jan. 2023.
7. Shepard, Benjamin H. "The queer/gay assimilationist split: The suits vs. the sluts", *Monthly Review*, 53.1, 2001, p. 49
8. Mendez, Laura. 'Queer Assimilation', *Locus: The Seton Hall Journal of Undergraduate Research*, vol. 1, 2018
9. Adam, Erin M. "Intersectional coalitions: The paradoxes of rights-based movement building in LGBTQ and immigrant communities," *Law & Society Review*, 51.1, 2017, pp.132-167.
10. Greensmith, Cameron. "Desiring diversity: The limits of white settler multiculturalism in queer organizations." *Studies in Ethnicity and Nationalism*, 18.1, 2018, pp. 57-77
11. Semmalar, Gee Imaan. "Unpacking Solidarities of the Oppressed: Notes on Trans Struggles in India." *WSQ: Women's Studies Quarterly*, vol. 42, no. 3-4, 2014, pp. 286–291; Bhattacharya, Sayan. "The Transgender Nation and Its Margins: The Many Lives of the Law." *South Asia Multidisciplinary Academic Journal*, No. 20, 2019

12. Sarkar, 2022, op. cit.
13. Gettleman, Jeffrey, Kai Schultz, and Suhasini Raj. "India gay sex ban is struck down 'Indefensible, 'court says." *New York Times*, 6 Sept. 2018; Sinha, Bhadra. "Gay Sex No Longer a Crime in India, Rules Supreme Court in Historic Verdict," *Hindustan Times*, 6 Sept. 2018
14. Bhanj, Jaideep Deo. "'We Are Not Criminals Any More,'" *The Hindu*, 7 Sept. 2018
15. Rastogi, Vartika. "Independent Journalism, Indian News", *The Citizen*, Sept. 2018, (Online Access 23rd April 2023)
16. Human Rights Watch. "India: Enforce Ruling Protecting Transgender People," *Human Rights Watch*, 28 Oct. 2020
17. Ashley, Colin P. "Gay liberation: How a once radical movement got married and settled down," *New Labor Forum*, Vol. 24. No. 3., SAGE Publications, Los Angeles, 2015.
18. Rosenblum, D. "Queer intersectionality and the failure of recent lesbian and gay victories. *Law & Sexuality: Rev"*, Lesbian & Gay Legal Issues, *4*, 83, 1994; Mulé, 2019, Op. cit.,
19. Mulé, Nick J. "Evolving Sexual Citizenry: Developing Queer Liberation Theory," *Erotic Subjects and Outlaws,* Brill, 2019, pp. 19–37
20. Bansal, Shreya. "'Leave Your Caste Identity at Home': Queer Dalits Lack Space in Indian 'Pride.'" https://www.outlookindia.com/, 2 Aug. 2022
21. Nooreyezdan, Nadia. "How Indian Pride Festivals Have Become Political Battlegrounds." *Vice,* 9 Mar. 2020
22. *The Hindu Bureau.* "Transpersons Protest at Kalaignar Memorial, Demand Horizontal Reservation", 17 Apr. 2023
23. *Livelaw News Network.* "Horizontal Reservation for Transgender Persons: Supreme Court Refuses to Entertain Plea to Clarify NALSA Judgment," Www.livelaw.in, 28 Mar. 2023

Forest and Tribal Life of Central India: Interpreting Manoranjan Byapari's Novel Annya Bhuban

Ismail Sarkar

At present Manoranjan Byapari is a towering figure in Bengal's Dalit literature. He has given voice to that voiceless marginal community that has suffered the unfathomable racial discrimination, physical pain and mental trauma. He himself is the life-like exam of that suffering. All of his writings, for instance "Itibritte Chandal Jibon" (Interrogating My Chandal Life: An Autobiography of a Dalit), "Chenra Chenra Jibon", "The Runaway Boy", to name a few, are very brilliantly creative expression of people who were silent for a long time. Protest or resistance is, however, one of the significant themes of his writings, and due to unavoidable urge to establish social justice he in his course of life has harboured a soft corner for Naxalite and eventually he joined it and got arrested. His "Batashe Baruder Gondho"(There's Gunpowder in the Air) highlight how young people in1970s had picked up arms to free lands from the clutches of feudal land lords and states. From this much known gharana of his writing, Byapari has made us experience something new in his very smartly written novel "Annya Bhuban". He, as if, has assimilated his entire life with a totally unknown and marginal section of forest. As a result, many unknown facts we happen to know. Tribal people as we know completely depend upon the forest. So very significantly the forest to the tribal people is the life giver, the preserver. But the coin has other side too. The forest, its damp unhygienic atmosphere, light less life in it, uncertain weather, unexpected frequent attack of fearful animals, all dismay their life. So, the forest to the Tribal people is not always romantically preserver, it is most of the time destroyer too. My paper entitled "Forest and Tribal Life of Central India: Interpreting Manoranjan Byapari's Novel Annya Bhuban" aims at highlighting the chequered life of Tribal people in Forest. The paper also tries to illuminate basic difference between the so-called civilized and that of tribal with their culture means of entertainment, rites and rituals, faith and practice. The prime focus of the paper is to interpret the picture that Manoranjan Byapari has canvassed in this short novel "Annya Bhuban". That is fine. But before doing that we need to focus on what Dalit life is or what the Dalit literature is and who this Byapari is or how far this "Annya Bhuban" differs from his other writings.

Basically, what chronicles the Dalit life as a whole is Dalit literature in general. It is always inclusive documenting their suppression, oppression, struggle, anger, sorrows, and their right. Dalits are struggling hard to reclaim their human dignity, identity and self-respect.[1] "Dalits have produced wide ranges of the literary writings based on their own life experiences. Their experiences as Dalit have led them to depict their inhuman condition which is made by infamous caste system prevailed in India since ages".[2] And this social division is backed by numbers of Hindu religious scriptures collectively known as Dharma Sastra.

Some important Dalit writers and their writings of Bengali Language are: Jatin Bala's poem 'name of life is pain', 'nobody has kept request', and novel "Life of Elixir"; Manohar Mouli Biswas' "Surviving in my world: Growing up Dalit in Bengal",[3] Kalyani Thakur Charal's poetry collection "Charalini",[4] and the list goes on. With these, another name, Manoranjan Byapari, is very much significant. He is a self-taught writer. He has a quite inspiring background before he came to be known as a writer. That life of Byapari is no less than a cinema. He rocks in his life from a Naxalite convict to a rickshaw puller, and at present he serves doubly as a Member of West Bengal Legislative Assembly and the Chairperson of West Bengal Dalit Sahitya Academy.[5] But from the core of his heart, he is a genuine writer of the oppressed class and he still is fighting for that class and here lies his novelty. "He came to prominence with the publication of his influential essay- Is there a Dalit writing in Bengal? Translated by Meenakshi Mukharjee; in the journal of 'Economic and Political Weekly'. While working as a rickshaw puller, he had chance meeting with Mahasweta Devi, and she asked he to write for 'Bartika' Journal".[6] His memoir "Itibritte Chandal Jibon" translated by Shipra Mukherjee as Interrogating My Chandal Life: Autobiography of a Dalit records the experience of oppression and marginalization that Dalits face in Bengal.[7] This book won the Hindu prize. Now it is time to shift our focus to his "Annya Bhuban" as my article is basically centered on this short, but interesting and pertinent to its name, novella. Surprising enough, though Byapari is a Dalit writer, the content of this novel sounds more like a novel that belongs to the genre of Tribal Literature. Now, if we are to spend few words on tribal literature then we must have to say that tribal literature basically "shows how tribal community reacts against the state that exploits the tribal and their property and even civil society what has a lack of good wishes to save the tribal life".[8] For instance, we can mention "Mother Forest" written by tribal activist C.K Janu. Sowvendra Shekhar Hansda also writes on Santali life. In terms of content, "Annya Bhuban", to some extent, touches the border line of texts that are considered under tribal literature.

Very often, when we hear the word 'nature' immediately we remember some names of romantic poets and subsequently our mind sketches a natural scenario often mentioned in their poems. They tried to heal the sorrows of human being by writing their verses about nature. They believe that 'Nature' is source of revelation and sometimes it is preserver. But this is not the case all time. In accordance with mood, time, space, nature plays numerous roles which are sometimes shocking, sometimes heart rendering, sometimes beyond imagination. The narrator of the story categorically mentions all the impediments which an Adivasi always faces in the forest in order to sustain their livelihood. These sufferings would not, perhaps, become plausible if Rajendra, the central character, does not miss his path onwards his destination. The narrator mentions in this region the outbreak of dysentery, Diarrhea, Malaria is very common. Many people die.[9] Besides this, the ferocious animals often take away loves of those people who live in the forests. Nabin, a forest officer says whenever I cast my glance, I find nothing but many black junglee...immediately Nehru was attacked by the Bear. About this ferocity of such Bear, it is said that tigers, for getting sufficient food, do not harm human. But the Bears are very ferociously dangerous.[10] And in the night things become more fearful. No lights but visible darkness engulfs the while forest.

Culture and life style is the indicator to define any race, caste, tribe in a society. In this novel, the people living in the forest are divided into different tribes such 'Gondo'[11], 'Mudiga'[12]. The writer here especially talks about the Adivasi of the Baster district of Chhattisgarh. Among the Adivasi, exchange system has great value. Here people do not use coin paper for transaction for any commodity. Here any goods or commodities are exchanged in exchange of other commodities. The narrator says in one side of Balance is sand on the other side is salt. There is no exchange of cash fere. Exchange system works here. The salt is here more costly than gold.[13] When Rajendra given punishment in the form of depositing a cock and five bottles wine. we see him facing great difficulty. The narrator mentions: in the village Drugkondol or even in the village of Nehru, Rajendra could easily buy these things (cock and wine) for seventy. But here thousand rupees can't buy them because money here is futile like soil, no even more futile than soil.[14]

Most interesting cultural trait is here 'Ghotul'[15] culture. The narrator explains: in the remotest part of the village, far from the habitats of people, the youth of the village voluntarily make such houses in which they assemble for their entertainment. Each night of 'sukla paksa',[16] all unmarried young boys and girls of the village reunite here. They spend the time by gossiping, singing, laughing, till the moon remains in the sky. When the moon disappears, some of them go back to their home, some of them remain there".[17] In this 'Ghotul', the married women are not allowed to enter. Married men can enter the 'Ghotul' but they have to go back at the end of singing and dancing. They are not permitted to spend the night there. This 'Ghotul' is completely their own world of the unmarried youths and they have their separate rules for themselves. Here they are free to do whatever they want but they can't force anyone. Because everyone is here free. Whatever they do it must be upon the mutual consent. Thus, we see that such type of 'Ghotul' really becomes the abode of their entertainment. It plays the role of making each other familiar and subsequently a strong bond is created. It is really interesting.

Among the tribal, women are highly esteemed, and get reverence. They never want any woman to be insulted by any means. But the sense or meaning of respect, in the forest among the tribal, is completely different from what we generally understand in our so-called educated society. For instance, in our civilised society, touching a woman illegally is punishable offence, and Rajendra harbours this societal norm from his early childhood. But in the forest, not touching a woman or not doing physical relation if the girl wants, is a punishable crime and it is insulting to women. For instance, in the story, we observe that Rajendra is very much hungry and moves door to door but none responds providing with shelter or food. Then Ramabati's family comes forward to provide him fooding and lodging and subsequently leads him to 'Ghotul'. Here in the 'Ghotul' Rambati wants Rajendra to be physical with her but Rajendra does not take the advantage. He thinks, preoccupied with former notion of crime and punishment, that touching a woman illegally would also be a punishable crime here in the jungle. And for this act of insulting to a young lady and depriving her of her sexual intention, Rajendra now has to suffer a trial. Here senior members of the tribal community gather under a big tree and seek the reason behind such insult. They say:

Rambati is the most beautiful lady. Forest peacocks cease their dance once they heard the approaching sounds of Rambati's leg... if she once looks at any young lad, he immediately melts into clay. If she wants the eyes of tigers, they young lads will go to forest to please her. And this Rambati of such importance gets insulted by a stranger and how will she tolerate such pain?[18] So, she has made a complaint.

There is a great difference between what the so-called aristocratic society's women think handsome and what these women of forest think. These Adivasi women think men should be muscular with a body like pitch black berry. Surprisingly, women in general think 'white is the colour of beauty' but this notion is completely broken here as these women crave for black. Byapari very artistically has slapped our society where people sometimes become hyena for female body. The narrator says the world of jungle is not like the civilised world where single adult woman is attacked by hungry man. In the kingdom forest women means mother and if somebody, against her consent, advances towards her, the society would punish him hard.[19] And in their society of forest there is no beggar, no prostitute, no rapist. A single young woman alone can go to the deepest forest to collect Mohua. No one dares to tease her.[20]

Byaapari does not stop here criticising the distorted mentality of civilised msn. In the story we see Rajendra very passionately urges Indra a tribal girl for taking a photo of her while she was having her bath. Even he offers her rupees twenty when Indra refuses to be clicked. Her refusal to be clicked shows the moral values that these 'janglee' women harbour there. On the other hand, the narrator scathingly criticises the moral value of the civilised society. In some cases, the narrator opines, some models in the name of art, shows their naked body which is similar to selling their body. Even the show casing of short dressed heroine in movie screens is a prostitution disguised in art. These things are done in exchange of huge of money. But on the contrary Indra's denial to Rajendra's offer is great instance of decency and moral values which the civilised women, in a way, have already sold.

In Adivasi lives, they hold high esteem for women in general. They are the wealth of their society. They provide food and shelter, wine to Adivasi men. They produce happiness and give birth babies. They prosper their domestic life. On the other hand, "men are mere moving toys who only drink and have sex".[21] Here in this Adivasi society, patriarchy does not hold its phallic power in the that much extent which we generally happen to see in our society. Nor do they confine women within the suppressive boundary of male domination. Here young unmarried women are free to do what they wish to do. But exception is everywhere. In some cases, married women face some restrictions. For instance, they are not generally allowed to enter the 'Ghotul' with other men except their husbands. The unmarried women can take the liberty of spending the night with whoever they want. But the married woman by chance spends the night in 'Ghotul' with other man then she must have to face death as punishment. So, we see their culture, law, life style etc. are strange and foreign to us.

We see the narrator to mentions that the Adivasi people pray female body using different parts of tree, animal, river and rare sound that generally forest produces. For instance, the eyes of beautiful Shukuri are compared with calm and cool shadow of woods. In her smile, it seems to the narrator, lies the sound of running dear and running water of spring mixed together, and body is just like the Papaya tree full of fruits. Time and again, the narrator unfurls the importance of forest. The forest to the Adivasi is like mother. From the forest they collect neat, honey, fruits, fuels. They also collect medicine and life's elixir. As water is indispensable to fish so the forest is to the Adivasi… but the selfish civilisation in the name of progress is destroying the entire forest of Adivasi…what civilization gives us, it takes back more in return.[22] Nehru once says that "Sahab, we are junglee and let us remain junglee. See, in our society on one is thief, no one is prostituted, no one is beggar, and on one lies nor betrays anybody. We don't want to leave our forest".[23] Perhaps, Nohru is the mouthpiece of the tribal community and he speaks the mind of their community that don't want the culprit civilization that gives nothing, instead snatches everything.

In every community, in every culture, some specific means of entertainments are there. The Adivasi people also entertain themselves through various means. Singing and dancing are some of the important means of entertainments they generally perform. Dancing and singing are accompanied by the sound of Nagara a musical instrument. In Adivasi lives, wine plays a vital role while they are in the mood of celebration. It is not only in the time of celebration but wine have its presence in each and every aspect of their mood. It is said "to wine, they are very much weak. They don't hesitate to shed blood for a drop of wine. At the time of birth or death, mourning or merriment, in any festival of pooja or general meeting, hosting a guest, marriage or in divorce- in everything, they seek wine at the first place. Without wine, everything, seems to them, tasteless".[24]

Though no one can call Adivasi selfish, but there no is kinder person than one who offers wine to Adivasi. Such is the importance of wine, quite interesting.

Simplicity, honesty and love they epitomize:

This article would be incomplete if their simplicity and honesty are not mentioned. There are unnumbered incidents that epitomize their intrinsic nature of simplicity and honesty. For instance, once incident occurs at the end when a young boy unintentionally kills his uncle accidentally. He does not run away. Rather he himself guards the dead body and sends his elder brother to call the police. They police come but next day and he still guards the body for two days. And finally, he himself help the police carrying their gun and goes to the police station. He thinks that he should be punished for his crime- intentional or unintentional does not matter. Such kind of simplicity is really hard enough to find in our self- centred world. With simplicity and honesty, love of heart deserves especial mention. Love is that powerful emotion that does not require any verbal communication. Rambati does not know the language that Rajendra speaks, yet She has established an inseverable bonding which for Rajendra quite impossible to break and leave her. The narrator draws an emotional picture in which Rambati is sketched as un utmost epitome of frail, tragic and painful at the departure of Rajendra. The narrator says: "…if she had courage enough to express the truth, she could then express that 'in my mind, to my soul, to every pore of my body, to the flow of my blood, to the marrow of my bone– you, O the stranger, has secretly smeared the colour of love'.[25] So, his departure, leaving Rambati at shock and in pain, engraves her unnamed, un recognized, unrequited love. It is really pathetic.

The way Byapari has used the Bengali language deserves tones of acclamation and huge accolades. For instance, the narrator uses periphrasis to mention Rambati's age by saying "twenty-one times, the colourful spring has touched her".[26] Besides this, the portraying an unknown world of forest with unknown people and unfamiliar customs, life styles, attitudes and feeling, Byapari really has shown the readers an "Annya (Other) Bhuban" (World). And to read it is to feel it and to feel it is to fall in the love of those innocent character who knows nothing except 'Jol', 'Jangol', 'Jomi' that is water, forest and land.

References

1. Pramanick, Mrinmoy. "Dalit and Tribal Literature in English Translation", *MHRD UGC EPG Pathsala Module*, No.25, Online access date: December 24, 2021, p.2
2. Hasanujjan, M., "Dalit Writings and New Literatures", *MHRD UGC EPG Pathsala Module*, No. 22. Online access date: December 26, 2021, p.2
3. Manohar Mouli Biswas has written four volumes of poems, one collection of short story, seven books of essays and an autobiography entitled *Amar Bhubaney Ami Benche Thaki* (2013) which is later translated by Angana Dutta and Jaydeep Sarangi and published as *Surviving in My World: Growing Up Dalit in Bengal*.
4. Kalyani Thakur Charal has published four volumes of poetry: *Dhorlei Juddho Sunischit, Je Meye Adhar Gone, Chandalinir Kabita,* and *Chandalini Bhone*. In addition to these, she has published a volume of critical essays titled *Chandalinir Bibriti*, and a collection of short stories, and an autobiography, *Ami Keno Charal Likhi (Why I Write Charal)*. Her autobiography, as well as her essay and poetry collections titled 'Chandalini' (tr: 'the untouchable woman') are widely popular, containing accounts of the discrimination that she faced for reasons of caste, while working in government service.
5. Kuma, Raj. *Dalit Literature and Criticism*, Orient Blackswan Private Limited, Hyderabad, 2019
6. "A Rickshaw Puller's Journey from Prison to Books" in NDTV, Delhi, Nov 08, 2013.
7. Griffin, Peter, "Names, audiences, trolls: The Hindu Lit for Life 2019 had it all", *The Hindu*, 19 January 2019

8. Pramanick, Op. cit., pp.9-10
9. Byapari, Manoranjan, *Anno Bhuban*, Priyasilpa Prakashani, Kolkata, 2006, p. 29 Self-Translation
10. Ibid., p.29
11. The Gondu are the Dravidian ethno-linguistic group. They are one of the largest groups in India.
12. The are the indigenous people live in south India.
13. Byapari, Op. cit., p.8
14. Ibid., p.29
15. Ghotul is tribal youth dormitory in form of a spacious hut surrounded by earthen or wooden wall.
16. The first fortnight between New Moon Day and Full Moon Day is called Shukhla Pakhsha.
17. Byapari, Op. cit., p.18
18. Ibid., pp. 23-24
19. Ibid., p.55
20. Ibid., p.44
21. Ibid., p.70
22. Ibid., p.67
23. Ibid., p.67
24. Ibid., p.28
25. Ibid., p.78
26. Ibid., p.78

Social Philosophy of Indigenous Kurmi (Kudmi) Community of India

Dr. Dhananjoy Mahato

One of the oldest communities in India is the indigenous Kurmi community. Based on the information found in Vedas, Upanishads, Puranas, scriptures, literature, reminiscences of foreign tourists, history books, archeology, researches, it can be said without doubt that Kurmi tribe is purely a tribal community. Original habitant of this community is across the vast area of the Genetic plains of Northeast India. Over time, due to foreign invasions and unfavorable conditions, these people spread to different provinces. Currently, most of the states of the country such as Andhra Pradesh, Madhya Pradesh, Assam, Bihar, Chhattisgarh, Delhi, Uttar Pradesh, Rajasthan, Maharashtra, Himachal Pradesh, Haryana, Jharkhand, Odisha, West Bengal are the habitant place of Kurmi people. The word "Kurmi" is derived from the word "karma", which means agriculture or agricultural work. The word "Kurmi"-- Ku-means the earth and 'Rami' means attachment. That is, the people who are connected with the earth are called Kurmi. In Rikveda Kurmi means pure, skilled, Karma-yogi, great and brave people.[1] Historically, the main source of life of the Kurmi is based on agriculture. Their festivals, ceremonies and customs were centered on agriculture. So, the thoughts, rituals, beliefs and ideas etc. related to agriculture are rooted in their primitive history. The primitive people who started farming in India since the Indian civilization and have kept the agricultural culture alive till date are the Kurmi caste or community.[2] They were the Bhumidhar or land lord from the historic times. Even today they continue to play an important role in the development and livelihood of the rural economy depending on their agricultural resources.

The people of this community mainly live in groups in the forest region to survive from various ferocious animals, diseases, attacks of external enemies and natural disasters. They form distinct identical society with their own traditional rules and principles. They fostered their own manners and judgments, and have some philosophy to maintain the eternal characteristics and traditions of the society. Philosophy is the essence of civilization and culture. The philosophy of a country depends on the social environment, created by surrounding culture of the civilization. As the philosophy of a country is the greatest part of its culture and civilization, they do have own philosophy of culture. Kudmali or Kurmi philosophy based on ancient Indian civilization and culture. Various kinds of good, bad, holy, impure, and wrong actions of people have been analyzed and determined the purpose and goal of their life. Naturally *Kudmali Samaj Darshan* like other Indian philosophies is holistic 'philosophy' where people's life has been directed in a certain direction.[3] Hence, in the article, an attempt has been made to discuss Kudmali of Kurmi Samaj Darshan along with their societal norms, cultural adhesiveness and traditional rituals and customs etc.

Being one of the oldest societies in the world Kurmi has its own social customs and philosophy. The continuity of Kurmi society, since ancient age, has been reflecting their philosophy of life. Kurmi society is basically an agrarian society. They love to live in groups and call each other as *Kutumb* and giving birth to the concept of universal kinship "Vasudhaiva Kutumbkam".[4] Kurmi society formed by Kurmi religious groups. When this society was formed in the beginning, they did not call people as people, people were called "har". The leader and guardian of this "Har" or human Society is Maha-hara or Burha-baba or

Shiva. They consider he is Ish + Har = Ishwar (God).[5] He is the first God of the world, Maheshwar. Burha-baba (Shiva) is the first religion Guru of Hara or Men. He is the exponent of Satya or Sari, modern Sarna religion. At present, the people of the Har community are the indigenous Kurmi community of India. The indigenous Kurmi people are followers and devotees of Lord Shiva. Over time the "hard" people proliferated and split into different groups for livelihood needs and spread to different parts of India. The scattered groups of people of 'Kurram Pahar' Hihiri Pihiri, and Chai-Champa were known as Kherowal.[6] Later this 'Kherowal' group, from Chai Champa province called as Kol, Kurmi, Kara, Santal, Bhumij, Bedia, Mahali, Shabar, Birhar, Munda, Gond, Bhil etc. This group of people has been spread over different provinces. By the passing of time, the 'Kherowal' population was further divided into many sects and sub-groups, but the basic structure of that early society, sociability and religion has remained the same. According to the many ancient folklore it is believed that the Champagarh is the earliest place of living of these people, which is known to be a province of Harappan Indus Civilization.[7] Kurmi or Kurmali community is a part of the Kherowal community. The sociality of this community has been changed and reformed over the time. But the basic structure or roots remain the same. For this reason, Kurmali society is similar to the society of other tribal groups of Kherowal community and some other tribal communities of India. That is why discussing the philosophy of Kurmali society can also understand the philosophy of other tribal societies. Kudmali society is not only of Kudmali race. Even though Kurmi is a cast, Kudmali society is formed by groups of Kurmi-minded groups. One of the characteristics of this society is that the parents, relatives, families, and their member are very united and live each other. They are interrelated with their good, bad, name, reputation etc. Mutual friendship, compassion, cooperation expresses their social unity. They believed that aim and purpose of life is to serve humanity by devoting oneself to the society, keeping the society alive, peaceful and happy.

The Kurmi community follows the philosophy of Communism. It means that all the people of the society can freely and equally consume the crops and other goods produced by them. Although we see the extensive discussion of communism in Marxian philosophy, but the seeds of communism are rooted in Kudmali social philosophy thousands of years ago. Kudmali social philosophy believed in the principle of "Sama-Aj".[8] The word 'Sam Aj' means equal share. Not only in the wealth produced, but equally in happiness, sorrow, joy, pain, dignity, responsibilities, even *kutum kutmali*,[9] everything is said to have an equal 'share'. The Stronger and wiser will not receive more, but the weaker will have an equal share. Kudmali Social Philosophy has adopted this rule. All (produce agricultural materials) are distributed equally, they don't make any difference. Who is small, who is big, who is good, who is bad, who is righteous, who is unrighteous, who is weak, nothing judges them. According to the principle of giving equal share to all, Kudmali society also believes in the principle of getting equal share/opportunities for everyone, be it wealth or any other things. In promoting this principle some practices are mentioned in Kudmali philosophy such as Bhag, Bhog, Veza, Bhoj etc.[10]

Bhag refers to the division. We see the principle of "Samaaj" in Kurmali social philosophy in various aspects such as family, group work, hunting, fishing, dance-song, social management etc. Kurmi community makes an arrangement so that everyone can live in peace and happiness. They distribute equally produced crops, wealth, happiness, peace and prosperity. Bhog means 'Prasad' in Kurmali society. Bhog or prasad is the collection of fruits, sweets, etc. offered to the deity at the place of worship. Laya is a priest in the worship of any Goddess/God in Kurmali. Laya will distribute the Bhog among the devotees. There is no difference in this regard. In Kurmali society, the festival, rituals, ceremonies and the common people work are done by the collection of money and goods. All the families in the village have to bear this cost equally. The principle of equal distribution of these costs is called Veja. Veja is determined by consulting the 'Mahato' and ten people of the village. Every family in the society has to obey this rule. Veza is determined in two ways 1) Chulha Veza and 2) Hal Veza. Everyone participates equally in this Veza, keeping the social unity of the society intact and organizes various types of fun events and festivals. A special custom in Kurmali society is 'Bhoj'. Eating together in a social gathering of one or more families is called 'Bhoj'. According to the ability, the family arrange a Bhoj (Party) for the whole day's food and that day every house of the village keeps Hadi-Band (Stop Cooking). Then five members of the society are called and given responsibility of cooking. When the cooking is done, must be called for food. Everyone sits down to eat together and starts eating only after the food is served equally. Do not get up until everyone has finished eating. Due to the observance of all these rules and principles, all kinds of Bhoj and works are completed in an orderly, peaceful and smooth manner.[11]

In the ancient Indian civilization and culture, through the concept of "Vasudhaiva Kutambakam" world humanity and world brotherhood were established. In the same way, humanistic tone was embedded in the 'Kudmali' social philosophy. Which is still being managed by the people of India. Initially people of Kurmali society used to call people as "Har". The main point of this philosophy is that Har/ Men are born for the people of the society.[12] Human beings cannot be born only to fulfill their own petty interests. According to this philosophy, humans are born to give up their own petty interests, work for the benefit of ten people, and work with self-sacrifice; actions that will harm others can never be done under any circumstances. One should always do for others from the righteous path. No one can ever be cheated or exploited. One cannot accumulate wealth and money alone; a percent of the earnings must be donated to social development work. If someone is in trouble or wants help or not, if he knows, then he should take initiative and help. Don't avoid it, don't run away from people's danger, understand your own difficulties and extend your helping hand as much as possible. Weak, poor, blind, lame, eager should not be ignored or neglected. They should be likeminded fellows in happiness and sorrow. They should not be treated in any way that would hurt their feelings. One must do words and deeds that make everyone happy. Relatives, friends, neighbors, should stand by the side of people with the possible responsibility in social work. You should always be truthful, always brave and a protester of injustice throughout your life.[13] Moreover, when humanism is concerned with the well-being of the entire human race instead of just thinking about the well-being of oneself or the group, it will be called humanism.

Kurmali have their own religious philosophy. According to this, it is said to respect and obey whatever is true and religious. It has been said to be inappropriate and unjust to think about unreal, miraculous and unreal things. Everything that is beneficial to the society should be done. Supernatural things should be avoided by giving priority to mundane things. Heaven, hell, sin, virtue, fate, these are unreal and confusing. In reality it does not exist anywhere. These are just a hypocritical attempt of the cheaters to weaken the minds of the people. Humans are born naturally as a result of the union of a man and a woman. And when we born, death is certain. There is no process that can avoid death. It is an infallible moral law of universal nature. In the process of creation, the five 'Bhutas'[14] combinedly lead to the origin as well as the destruction. There is nothing beyond it, everything is dependent on reality and materiality.

A unique feature in human life is its social connectedness. Since the beginning of civilization, man can never live alone. He has to live within the social environment. Because people are born in a society through the environment. Man cannot move outside the society, whatever improvement, he has to do it through the society. And when all the activities and rituals that he has to do in the society, when he analyzes and makes philosophical inquiries about all the activities and rituals, then it is considered as social philosophy. Judging from this point of view, it can be seen that Kurmali social philosophy is also a complete social philosophy. To this philosophy, society is said to be like a 'mother's lap' while explaining the scope of society. Just as children can be safe in their mother's arms, they can live in extreme, absolute peace and happiness, in the same way, in the Kurmali society, the society is the motherly shelter of the people. In a Jhumur Geet (Song) of eminent poet Upen Mahato has said, *Samajei Janam Dada - Samajei Moron ree - Samaj Hekeik Dada - Suraj Saman ree.*[15] Here he compares society to the sun, saying that just as the sun radiates light to increase us in strength. Similarly, the society provides various opportunities for human development and prosperity. Kurmali social philosophy never sees the individual as big without the society. The place and importance of the society is much higher than the individual. Similarly, it is said to obey all the rules and policies and reforms and culture that exist in the society, leaving the family, killing oneself, stealing, taking drugs, having illicit sex with another woman, disrespecting parents, and neglecting other elders are called anti-social acts. All these antisocial activities are punishable. The five-man rule punishes fines, solitary confinement, or ostracism. In Kurmali society, people are asked to live together and work together. To live with order, honesty, generosity, decency, to protect the family, to provide happiness and prosperity, to maintain social standards and dignity, to be happy in sorrow, in danger in wealth, in happiness in sickness. Being with the people of the society is called social 'Karam'.[16] In the same way that the society helps the man, he has to participate in the social works to benefit of the society. Kurmali social Philosophy clearly states that there will be few positions to run the society. The social administration will select those posts. Those posts will be re-selected in every 12 years. The village will be managed by the village headman who will be called 'Mahato' or Modal or Majhi'.[17] Apart from the welfare of the village, He will look after the Puja Parban and other social functions and his opinion should be given importance to all. In the same way, 'Laya' would be selected for conducting religious ceremonies. In the same way, Kurmali social philosophy, through the management of the work of the country through Chatadars, Parganaits, Mulukdars, and Desh-Morals, commits itself to peace, order, happiness and prosperity in the society by delegating the responsibilities of the society to various authorities.[18]

Kurmali social philosophy is a complete social philosophy. Society is made up of individuals and families and it can be said that a family is a unit of society. It also says about how can the family achieve happiness, peace, prosperity and the individual enjoyment. A family can live a long and healthy life in harmony with family and friends, if he follows the guidance of social philosophy tribal kurmali. How to react during Happiness, suffering, illness, disease, famine, grief, regret, repentance, premature death, etc. has also been found in Kurmali social Philosophy. All the vows and cultural rituals observed in

Kurmali social Philosophy are very significant. The form of vow and rituals observed in every 'Puja/ Parva' festival of Kurmali society indicates social responsibility, duty, order and prosperity of peace. According to them God Lord Shiva and his wife godess Maa-Durga has possess the sixteenth qualities. Such as kindness, mercy, compassion, non-violence, patience, tolerance, moderation, good deeds, righteous thoughts, etc. 'Jita Maa's devotees pray to Jita Maa for the strength of the above qualities so that she can make her children have good character in the society. To them ultimate goal or purpose of human life is to serve the responsibilities and duties of the society, country as well as humanity. It is said in Kurmali social philosophy, people are born for the needs of society and for the society. The goal of life should be to establish oneself as a dignified person of the society by forming a good character through good education, doing the best possible work through moderation and yoga-sadhana. The desire is to enjoy a long healthy life with family and dignity. The purpose of life is to wish for a happy death by maintaining one's religion and culture, giving the children the ability to become a person of good character, meritorious, like a man of the society and become like a common man in old age and leave a happy family.[19]

India, the oldest civilization of the world, has been infiltrated by many social philosophies at different times. All of them became the governors of India by their cunning power and captures the political power of India. By spreading the influence of that power, it attacked the country's own indigenous social customs, culture and philosophy. Eventually this led to the extinction of Indigenous tribal social philosophy. Besides, the modernity and the development of technology gave the final blow to wipe out indigenous cultural philosophy from mainstream Indian culture. But we have to remember that without the own ethnic, social and culture identity no race or nation can survive or progress. Under the pressure of globalization, men have turned himself into a machine, forgetting about his or her family, brothers, sisters, parents, relatives and overall society. We all gradually becoming very nuclear and separate part of our society, forgetting the larger interests of society and humanity. Currently, the trend of war, violence, conflict and communal problems, complexity and chaos are increasing in the society. People are leaning more towards the interests of small individuals. Trusts, faith, gratitude tolerance, patience, forgiveness, are decreasing day by day. Fortunately, social philosophy and subsequent reforms Kurmali tribal people still nurturing its social rules and principles of mutual friendship and collaboration. We all need to learn from them and maybe the peace and order in every society will be restored.

References

1. *Rikveda samhita*:3.10.3 (jankaritoday.com)
2. Yogacharya Saraswati Shrimat Ramananda, *Akhand Veda Gyan*, Kolkata,
3. Mahato, Kiriti and Mahato, Vishwanath. *Kudmali Language and Culture*, Dwitiya Khanda, p.197
4. *Maha-Upanishad*, Chepter-6, page-71
5. Mahato, Kiriti and Mahato, Vishwanath, Op. cit., p.5
6. Mahato, Bhupen. *Chandra:Garam Than,* (kurmik Katha), p.66
7. Mahato Sripoda. *Kurmali Sanskriti o Tantra Dharma*, p.13
8. Mahato, Kiriti and Mahato, Vishwanath, Op. cit., p.196
9. It means maintaining the relationship with the relatives
10. Bhag means division, bhog means consumption, veza means giving share and bhoj means have together
11. Mahato, Sanat Kumar. "Kurmali Language Literature", *Past, Present & future,* Sidho-kanho-Birsha university, 19-01-2023
12. Mahato, Sristidhar. *Kurmali Krishi Sanskriti*, p.123
13. Bagchi, Deepak Kumar. *Indian Philosophy,* Progressive Publishers, Kolkata, 2022, p.11
14. These are *kshiti, ap, tej, marut* and *bom*

15. Mahato, Upen, *Jhumur Kabi Gita*
16. Mahato, Shambhunath. *Kurmali Charik Khadinadi* (Analysis of Kurmali Culture), p.29
17. Mahato, Kiriti and Mahato, Vishwanath, Op. cit., p.210
18. Mahato, Bhupen Chandra. "Garam Than, Kudmi and Kudmali", *Writers' Association*, Satyaban Pally, Raghunathpur, Jhargram 721507, 30 July 2023
19. Siripoda, Bansriyar. *Kudmali Sanskriti O Tantra Dharma,* Mulki Kudmali Vakhi Vaisi, Ramkrishnapur, Kaluhar, Purulia, 2021

Status of Women and The Women's Liberation Movement in Nineteenth Century India: A Historical Analysis

Manas Kumar Das

Feminism has become an important topic in the study of modern history. The wave of feminism that started in Europe in the late 18th century also hit India.[1] Under its influence, the wave of women's liberation movement came in India at the end of the eighteenth century and the beginning of the nineteenth century. Surprisingly the movement was started by the menfolk. In this context the names of Keshav Chandra Sen, Raja Radhakanta Dev, Rammohan Roy, Ishwarchandra Vidyasagar, etc. deserve to be mentioned. Gradually, few Indian women emerged as the torch bearer of this movement. Pandita Ramabai and Tarabai Sinde, Begum Rokeya Sakhawat Hossain, Begum Sharifa Hamid Ali, Sabitribai and others have made important contributions in establishing women's education and dignity during 19th century.[2] As a result of their long movement, today women have been able to gain their rights to a large extent.

In order to review the position of women in India in the 19th century, it is necessary to have a clear understanding of one thing that all the social evils prevailing in the society made the life of the women miserable.[3] They were closely related to each other and bound in the minds of the people in such a way that they were not possible to remove from the society. The ending was not easy. Because in the 11th century, according to the Kaulinya tradition, introduced by the Sena king Ballal Sen,[4] the daughter of a noble Brahmin family had to be married to a noble Brahmin to protect their lineage or prestige. Otherwise, he would have been exiled. So, to protect the kalpita clan, the fathers of marriageable daughters were forced to marry more than one daughter to the same noble man if they did not find a suitable husband. Even with the dying noble Brahmin, the marriage of a child daughter protected their own clan.[5] Poet Satyendanath Dutta in his poem 'Sahmaran' satirizes this system and wrote, "The noble father threw the old man into the neck of the clan." In many cases, the 'noble pot' did not even have the ability to put a piece of vermilion on the daughter's forehead. Naturally, the marriage of this 80–85-year-old man with his 8–10-year-old daughter would soon bring a curse to her life. As a result, on the one hand, as the number of child widows continues to increase in the society, the practice of polygamy grows like an evil wound in the society. Even at that time some noble brahmins had more than 40, 50 or 60 marriages. In 1298 (Bongabdo) Sanjeevani newspaper published the marriage list of aristocratic people in connection with the sad story of Bengali girls. It can be seen there that 1013 aristocrats from 276 villages married 4323 aristocratic daughters. Vidyasagar Mahashay disclosed the data of Hooghly district, where it can be seen that 197 elites of 86 villages have married 1288 girls and made them perpetual dukhini.[6] The socialists were afraid that these child widows could become clans and corrupt the society by giving up their dignity. Therefore, with the aim of 'protecting' the society, these child widows were first eradicated. Their 'chastity' was preserved by burning the dead husband's pyre amidst the beating of drums and bells. In this way, in the name of protecting chastity, another evil practice of sati-immolation or co-death was born in the society.[7] So, if we review in this way, it will be seen that Kaulinya system, child marriage, polygamy and cohabitation were closely related and each system was a curse in the life of women.

The role of Raja Rammohan Roy and his Brahmo Samaj was very important among all the individuals and institutions who have made a significant contribution in protecting the dignity of women in Indian society by freeing them from all these social evils. In terms of women's liberation, the main goal of Raja Rammohan and his Brahmo Samaj was to end the inhumane practices of child marriage, polygamy, caste system, untouchability, child abandonment in the Ganges, etc. which were prevalent in Hindu society.[8] Along with this, improving the social status of Indian women by popularizing education among women. However, in the 19th century, among all these evil practices, the practice of sati-immolation became the most heinous. A survey in 1804 showed that 115 satis were cremated within thirty miles of Calcutta in six months. According to the reports submitted by the local magistrates, from 1815 to 1826 there were 7,154 cases of sati-burning in the Bengal Presidency, 287 in the Madras Presidency, 284 in the Bombay Presidency and an estimated 100 more. In order to stop this unjust practice, Ram Mohan tried to form a strong public opinion by protesting against sati through various newspapers including Sangbad Kaumudi since 1818.[9] He wrote a pamphlet titled 'Sahmaran Abhiy Pravartak va Vivarttak Sambad' in the latter half of 1818 AD and later published its English translation. Citing various Hindu scriptures, he argues that sati-immolation is not sanctioned by ancient scriptures and is nothing but wife-killing. In this context, he actively collected letters and finally, with his own efforts and active cooperation, Lord William Bentinck issued Regulation No.17 on 4th December 1829, prohibiting the practice of sati legally. However, this practice has not completely disappeared from society. In 1987, there was an incident of sati burning in Rupkanwar of Shikarpur district of Rajasthan.[10] Of course, this case should be seen as an exceptional case. However, not only protecting the lives of women from the hands of this prevailing evil practice, but also establishing them in the society with dignity became one of the goals of his life. Besides, the Brahmo Samaj under the leadership of Rammohan Roy also played an important role in establishing the economic rights of women and establishing equal rights for men and women.

After the death of Rammohan Roy, Devendranath Tagore and Keshavchandra Sen expanded the Brahmo Samaj movement. Brahmananda Keshavchandra Sen and his associates played an important role in the defence of women's rights. He founded a social service organization called 'Indian Reform Society'. Among the programs of this organization was education and women's advancement. Besides, in 1864, Keshavachandra Sen established a meeting called 'Brahmika Samaj' for the upliftment of the wives of members of the Brahmo Samaj. In 1866, women were allowed to sit behind the veil in places of worship. This was the first time in the history of Brahmo Samaj that woman also got a place in places of worship along with men. It was an important step in establishing equality between men and women. Keshav Chandra Sen's contribution was also very important in the promotion of women's education. Mary Carpenter came to India in 1866 at the invitation of Keshav Chandra Sen and noticed that one of the major obstacles to female education was the lack of qualified teachers. Therefore, in 1872, Carpenter along with Keshavchandra and another Englishwoman named Annette Akroyd established a 'Normal School' for the training of teachers. Which is one of the initial steps in the field of women education in Bengal. Keshav Chandra Sen had another significant role in the women's liberation movement. In 1872, the Brahma Swamaj Marriage Act or Act III of 1872 adopted by his dedicated efforts to stop child marriage, the followers of the Brahma Samaj accepted the age of 14 as a marriageable bride. But the Brahma Marriage Act did not apply to non-Brahmins. However, in 1929, the Child Marriage Restraint Act, 1929, fixed the minimum age of 14 for all marriageable brides.

This Act is also known as 'Sarda Act'. Apart from this, the Special Marriage Act which was followed in 1955 to prevent child marriage was inspired by these 'three laws' of 1872.[11]

Another pioneer of the women's liberation movement in India in the nineteenth century was Pandit Ishwarchandra Vidyasagar. He continuously fought for the introduction of widow marriage, the abolition of child marriage and male polygamy, the end of Kaulinya system, the expansion of women's education, etc. In fact, on his initiative, the *Widow Marriage Act* was passed on July 26, 1856. Vidyasagar's role against child marriage was also very important. Because he realized that one of the reasons for the plight of girls in that era was child marriage. So, he stood against early marriage of child girls. He gave a scientific explanation about the evils of early marriage and said - "due to marriage at an early age, couples never get to enjoy the mutual love that is the sweet result of marriage, so the child who originates from a very unpleasant relationship with each other, is also likely to be spoiled." ... Physical health, which is the root of all happiness, also suffers from the effects of childhood. ... Child marriage is the main cause of widowhood at a young age, so child marriage is extremely cruel and cruel."[12] The British government enacted a law in 1860 setting the minimum age of marriage for girls at 10 years. Vidyasagar spoke out against it. Finally, with his efforts, the government passed the 'Age of Consent Bill' in 1891. As a result, the minimum age of marriage for girls was increased to 12 years. Even after so many years of independence, the prevalence of child marriage problem is still not less. At present, marriage of girls below the age of 18 is prohibited by various laws. But girls are being married off before the age of 18 in many places, especially in rural areas, ignoring this law. Only in Murshidabad this number is 72 percent.[13] But there is hope now that in many cases girls are going against their families and not agreeing to marry at an early age and are instead looking to study and stand on their own feet. To prepare them for this mindset, they need to be made more aware of the evils of child marriage. Only then can we bring these baby girls back from the face of certain death. Apart from this, Vidyasagar, the awakened icon of modernity, realized that it was not possible to free women from social deprivation without the spread of female education. So, he established thirty-five girls' schools in the rural areas of Bengal. With his help, Drinking Water Bethune established a high school. Which is known as Bethune School.[14] Vidyasagar established the Metropolitan Institution in Calcutta in 1870 AD for the promotion of general higher education. Which is now known as Vidyasagar College. The contribution of this educational institution in the expansion of higher education in Bengal as well as in the expansion of women's education is outstanding. Also, during his tenure as school inspector, he built several girls' schools at his own expense in Burdwan, Hooghly, Nadia districts from 1857 to 1858. After all, in 1890 Nijgram established Bhagwati Vidyalaya in the memory of Bhagwati Devi at Virsingh. Which was his last attempt to promote women's education.[15]

The role of Derozio and his Young Bengal group was also significant in the women's liberation movement in India. They strongly protested against caste system, untouchability, paganism, oppression of women and other social oppression by creating a movement against Hinduism and social prejudices. They showed progressiveness by supporting the abolition of sati-dharma, the introduction of widow marriage and the expansion of women's education. In 'Gnananbeshan' and 'Bengal Spectator' they tried to shape public opinion in favor of women's education, women's emancipation and widow marriage. A letter in support of widow marriage was published in the first issue of the Bengal Spectator in April 1842 and an article entitled 'The Marriage of Hindu Widows' was published in its July issue. Besides, Radhanath Shikdar, one of the prominent representatives of New Bengal and a favorite student of Derozio, helped Vidyasagar in the practice of widow marriage.[16]

The role of several progressive Indian women in India's women's liberation movement was also highly commendable. Pandit Rama Bai of Mysore fought for the advancement of women's education throughout his life and established an institution called 'Arya Mahila Samaj' (1881 AD) in Pune. One of the objectives of this institution was to emancipate women by ending religious bigotry and social prejudices in the society. She builds this Arya Mahila Samaj as an organization to break the hegemony of patriarchy.[17] Besides, she built 'Sarda Bhavan' in Pune and set up Mukti Sadan, Anath Sadan for the emancipation of widows. Besides, Ramabai Ranade of Maharashtra started a movement demanding unpaid and compulsory education for women. Another noble woman Sarojini Naidu presented a 'Demand' to the Government of India in 1917 to establish women's education and women's status, demanding education, health and happiness for the women of India. She was the first Indian lady who campaign for women's suffrage in elections for women's autonomy.[18] Besides, in this episode, Begum Sharifa Hamid Ali and Begum Rokeya Sakhawat Hossain came forward to shine the light of knowledge in the lives of Muslim women who were immersed in the darkness of ignorance.[19] Begum Sharifa advocated for Indian women at a round table meeting held in London as president of the All-India Women's Association. She even represented Indian women in UN human rights talks. On the other hand, Begum Rokeya has tried hard all her life for the spread of women's education. She felt that without education it was not possible to end the degradation of women.[20]

However, even though various laws were enacted to ban the practice of sati-immolation and child marriage or to introduce widow marriage, it was not possible to bring about the reforms that had been ingrained in people's minds for a long time so easily. Even in a patriarchal society, not only men were responsible for the plight of women, but due to long-term reforms, in most cases, they accept it as their fate and bear all the hardships with their faces closed. Due to this, the present society could not be completely free from all these curses. So, to eradicate these superstitions first of all a change of mentality is required. And writers such as Bankimchandra, Rabindranath, Saratchandra, Nazrul played an important role in this work. Through their literary works, they promoted the establishment of women's dignity by ending the discrimination between men and women in the society.[21] None of them were social reformers, so they may not have directly joined the women's liberation movement like a social reformer, but the contribution they left behind in forming a strong public opinion in favor of women's liberation by showing women's problems as social problems is undeniable. Apart from this, various newspapers and magazines like *Vidyadarshan*, *Tattvabodhini*, *Bengal Spectator* etc.[22] also played an important role in shaping public opinion by campaigning against the absurdity of Kaulinya practice, child marriage and polygamy.

Despite this, even though more than seventy years of India's independence have passed, inequality between men and women is noticeable everywhere. They are victims of exploitation and deprivation both at home and abroad.[23] The position of women may have improved a lot in modern times but it is very little compared to the entire population of India. Especially in the case of rural women, still about eighty percent of women are backward in terms of education and economics.

References

1. See for details: Wollstonecraft, M., *Vindication of the Rights of Woman (1792)*, Edited by M. Brody, Penguin, London, 1988
2. Pranakar, *Women in Literature and History in the wake of Women's Day,* Nandnik Publications, Calcutta, 2008
3. Mill, John S., *The Subjection of Women,* J. M. Dent & Sons Ltd., London, 1977
4. Bhattacharya, Sukumari. *Women and Society in Ancient India*, National Book Agency Pvt Ltd, Kolkata, 2006
5. There were five classes of Brahmins – Kulina, Shrotriya, Vanjaja, Gaunakulin and Saptasati. Nandy, Ashok. *Caste and Varna in the Novels of Saratchandra and Tarashankar,* Sahitya Sangeet, Calcutta, 2005, p. 8
6. Vidyasagar, I. *Vidyasagar Rachnavali* (Volume IV), Ananda, Calcutta, 1376 Bangabda, pp. 42-49
7. Chatterjee, Saratchandra. *Value of Women*, Roy M. C. Sarkar Bahadur and Sons, Calcutta, 1924
8. Dubey, S. C., *Indian Society, (Translation: Rajat Roy),* National Book Trust, Calcutta, 1996, p. 102
9. Vidyasagar, I., Op. cit.
10. See for details: Vozzola, Elizabeth C. *Moral Development: Theory and Applications*, Routledge, 23 January 2014
11. Basu, Rajashri. & Chakraborty, Vasavi. (ed.) *Contextual Humanities*, Urbi Publications, Kolkata, 2014
12. Vidyasagar, I., Op. cit., Volume II, p. 3
13. Banu, Khadija (ed.), *Srijani,* Shanmasik Sahitya Patrika, Murshidabad, October 2014, p. 15
14. Acharya, Poromesh. "Education in Old Calcutta" in Chaudhuri, Sukanta (ed.) *Calcutta: The Living City,* Vol. I, Oxford University Press, 1990, p. 87
15. Gupta, Suparna (ed.), *Women in History: Education*, West Bengal History Society, Progressive Publishers, Kolkata, 2001
16. Reddy, Sheshalatha "Henry Derozio and the Romance of Rebellion (1809-1831)", *DQR Studies in Literature*, Vol. 53, 2014, pp. 27–42; Roy, Samaren. *The Bengalees: glimpses of history and culture,* Allied Publishers, New Delhi, 1999, p. 119
17. Chakravarti, Uma. *'Rewriting History: The Life and Times of Pandita Ramabai',* Zubaan Publishers, New Delhi, 1998
18. Banerjee, Kalyani. "Women Class and Caste, Socio-Economic Status of Lower Caste Women", *Women in Politics,* Manuscript, Howrah, 2000.

19. Azad, Humayun. *Women, Bangladesh*, Next Publication, February 1992.
20. Begum, Maleka. *Women's Movement of Bengal*, The University Press Limited, Dhaka, Reprint 2010
21. Banerjee, Ranjit. *Women's Emancipation Movement and Bengali Literature in the Nineteenth Century (1850-1900)*, Pustak Bipani, Calcutta, 1998.
22. Vidyadarshan, Tattvabodhini, Sambad Bhaswar. Ghosh. Vinay (ed.), *Sociology of Bengal in Periodicals* (Volume III), Papyrus, Calcutta, 1981 AD, p. 292.
23. Beauvoir, Simone de. *The Second Sex,* Translated and edited by H. M. Parshley, Picador, London, 1988.

Sir Syed Ahmed: Plural Identity of India with its Relevance in Modern Times

Md Sohel Mondal

During the time of mid-19th century, when the beauty of India was at stake under the shackles of communal hatred, social cacophony and bound of ignorance, Sir Syed Ahmed Khan – the protagonist of cultural cohesion and pioneer of interfaith dialogue – hailed as a renaissance man and effectively uniting factor. How much he undertook, the latter coming seminal scenarios can be advanced to explain. As a result, the most explicit example is that of Aligarh Muslim University, his ever-enduring endeavor for Indian religious unison, which made out a Hindu student Mr. Ishwari Prasad its first graduate. Souls of India, ranging from Kabir to Tulsidas or Tagore to Najrul, extend a hale and hearty approach for togetherness crossing the illusory dogma-made boundaries of separation between expounded cultural diversities in India. With alluring oeuvre, Syed Ahmed Khan stepped ahead with his versatility in bureaucracy, politics, fieldwork, education, lecture, literature, character and expediency to keep their principles pragmatically alive by bringing all communities of different cultures in an inclusive concert. Although, it was not like sipping a tea-cup, he had to go in the rain and sun behind this purpose. Along with, broad visionaries with such visions, that kind of Kabir or Tuslidas, come out with love and peace to unite the country under one umbrella. Though, how much hardship is required, when the current atmosphere of the country is under strain of growing separation, inter-religious disengagement and communal hatred, it's high time to revisit the teachings of Sir

Syed Ahmed and make India the world's largest democracy in true sense.

"As a matter of fact, Hindus and Muslims are the eyes of a beautiful bride that is Hindustan..." - Desperately, very few Hindustanis know the expounded meaning of this saying and the person who said so. Therefore, outwardly the 'beauty of bride' is waning gradually from the land of the golden bird. Actually, this is what makes the essence of India. Historically, India has a long and rich legacy for the birth and growth of different world cultures, philosophies and religions here. As well as the country welcomed and accepted the coming-from-outside cultural hues and dyed herself with them in integration. The legacy poised India as a unique and universal epitome of cultural pluralism and interfaith integration. Whenever this traditional cultural identity tended to be haunted, a pioneer was born. They became epitomized reminders, directors and revivers of this priceless unity among the masses irrespective of caste, creed, language, religion, colour and border.

Definitely, Sir Sayed Ahmed Khan was one of these exemplified personalities who stood strong during his time as a pacificator of indigenous animosity and unificator of different cultures. He put no stone unturned for the mission to preserve the treasure of India - unity in diversity. He worked hard to make a mass conscience of mutual brotherhood among inter and intra-cultural fractions. He tried to bind all rampant religions and their cultures like Hindu, Muslim, Budhists, Jain and even foreign Christian with a rope of national unity as Indians. It was as he conceived: "All Hindu, Mulsim, Christian and Sikhs inhabit this country as one nation." At the same time, as a Muslim Sir Khan was so worried seeing the intra-fragmentation of Muslim community based on meager differences of thoughts and actions which caused them lag behind in every stage of standardless. He undertook giant courage to bring them together and pushed the community other way towards intellectual development through awakening and reformation.

However, the society overwhelmed by hegemony of luring dividers was not in alacrity to accept his call. He was maligned, dishearten, deserted and harassed for his unconventionally courageous voice of unison with all religious and cultural groups, but he never compromised. He was a visionary architect of future India that any such effort of cultural separation could lead the country to destruction. His values and legacies are to be epitomized even after a century to enliven the very spirit of India especially at a time when religious integration and cultural diversity are at stake due to politicalized and poisoned communism. His practical teachings have become as consolidated as that the aim is now not limited to national boundaries but, a broader unity. Sir Syed Ahmad is typically a universal icon for the path showing of cultural pluralism.

The epoch Sir Syed (1817-1898) lived in was a crossing course; one of power and other of period. Provincial dynasties including Muslim giants exerted no influence. The British got control even over nationwide policy formation and administration. One collapsed and another emerged. Meanwhile, with the robust transformation of renaissance the new world order started to roll forward modernity.

[1] The war of Independence in 1857 ended with a roar of fear in British authority and a crack in the national unity. It became harder for Syed to make a balanced decision for all people. Scattered with fright, a large number of community people underwent starvation of food, wealth, education, decision and so on. On the other hand, with the implementation of some British policies, people of India merged into two sectors. Especially, in the case of education and religious practices, all national intellectuals stood as two-party opposition inclining separately to flexibility and orthodoxy. Indian communities

broke into inter and intra-differences. Contrasting ideologies came out in animosity. The own community of Sir Sayed Ahmed, Muslims, became poor prey of this. *Fatwas* spelt against him. In this nick point of time, Sir Syed Ahmed being a legal middleman stepped forward with a manifestation of national representation.

He served as a civil servant in different regions. He sincerely utilized his possession for the sake of the nation and its people. He tried to unite Muslims themselves and befriend other communities and vice versa. For the upliftment of a community, as he perceived, utilization of opportunities was primarily necessary. "In fact," as Allama Iqbal said, "he was the first Indian Muslim who felt the need for a fresh orientation of Islam and worked for it – his sensitive nature was the first to react to the modern age."[2] As a remedy of time when India is labeled under 'Country of Particular Concern' in terms of religious freedom by international watchdogs,[3] it is indispensable to turn back to *Sayed Effects* and take the country ahead. It's required to remember the lions hare of Sir Syed Ahmed in consolidating the democratic edifice of India and the secular attitude of its citizens while transmitting this spirit to the rest of the world. "The panacea for prevailing ills in the Indian canvas of secularism can be achieved in reviving our values along with the corresponding imputation and instilling them in the veins of all nationals. Ultra-nationalism, violent religiosity and political contention were not part of our India. These over-spirited emotions spoil the pluralistic and multi-ethnic culture of a civilization."[4] In the contrasting time of what Sir Syed expected, each person should be remembered 'religion doesn't teach animosity' and incited with the elixir of 'peace is the way'. Then the citizens can proclaim 'better than the entire world, is our India.' There would be no paradox with India.

As Sir Syed Ahmed is revered for his heroic acts in different spectrums of pluralism, he's appallingly criticized for his inquiry of transformation. His reconciliation with the British government was severely objected by contemporary national intellectuals including Muslims. Even today, it's tried to present him as anti-national by linking the theoretical inception of Pakistan.[5] At the same time, when the Congress emerged as a national political unity against the British, Sir Syed Ahmed didn't come down this track too. Apparently, assessing it seems so. Indeed, Sir Ahmed articulated different strategies behind these scenes of allegations at a prospect of progressive India. He tried to preach the system of cross-cultural environment in Indian society. He measured every step-in accordance with the need of time.

In a country as diverse as India, it is very hard to instill the philosophy of unity in each community individually. For an effective result, it is necessary to make a rope inclusive of all. That's why, in all actions, Sir Syed gave priority to the collective consciousness of national unity. 'My nation' was his imperative slogan. To him, the theory of nation was like a *qaum* or community. As closer one is addressed, it's more closely regarded and treated. He perceived and conveyed the understanding of one being all. Thus, all people in the land of a large diverse country like India with due respect to their caste, creed, tenet, faith and religion can come closer and merge in one. By this way, all issues of polarization, as far as they are counted, can be turned out as pluralistic factors. He said, "By the word 'Nation', I mean both the Hindus and Mohammadans."[6]

In addition, he allowed no reason to topple this process of multicultural and intra-religious unity. He ardently opposed the politics of separation which blatantly destroy the nature of diverse India till this day. "The business can't be done by force," he pointed out in a speech at Meerut, "And the greater the enmity and animosity, the greater will be their loss." He added also, "...it is my duty to show clearly what this unwarrantable interference has been, and to protect my nation from the evils they may arise from it."[7]

A pluralistic society means the unanimous and amicable coexistence of different cultures, unless it is to be adversely labeled. This is possible when the culture or custom of a community is exposed openly to another community with a general subjective and objective sense. There should not be barriers like over-imposition and conservatism. They should be respectful and rightful to each other. Sir Syed Ahmed approached with this attitude in all his activities including education, politics and even in religious matters.[8] Obviously, it accepts all. Similarly, Sir Syed Ahmed made giant endeavors to bring all together in their thoughts, activities, education and belief. Without difference of culture and faith, they are bound with a sense of oneness. This helped the society to grow collectively with a pace of prosperity and development.

As a man of creativity, Sir Syed urged each community for self-conscience to create their distinctive identity. What the matter of concern was mutual animosity raised from misunderstandings. With this prospect, he pushed for true knowledge about the teachings of a culture or religions. He tried to disseminate the correct form of a faith which is free from all vested inclusions of man. He taught Muslims as well as Hindus and Christains about their religious principles supporting the unity of humanity. He espoused this *religious pluralism* in his works, though nor completed, like *The Mohammedan Commentary on the Holy Quran, Life of Muhammed* and *The Mohammedan Commentary on Holy Bible, etc.*[9] Sir opted for the option of being own but for others. Sir Syed himself, as a foremost example, participated in events of different titles and spoke only for religious harmony and communal unity. He tried to transmit this message from core sources of various religions including Hindu Scriptures and Bible. He also had an inclusive circle of friends from all sects of society. Thus, the pioneer has shown the ways of national unity.

Sir Syed Ahmed, being the advocate of cultural unity in the paradoxical period of the 19th century, was well equipped with different dimensions of knowledge. He perceived that only the actual realization of human essence can eradicate the prevailing illness of division between people of multicultural countries like India. Broad knowledge of a reality was requisitely required for this enlightenment. In all his commitments for inter and intra-faith unity, he put education and proper knowledge at the utmost priority. It helps to create mutual understanding which was very lacking in the society. As a consequence, all fell against each other unconsciously ignoring their own religious principles and social ethics. His visionary steps made him lead some unprecedented breakthroughs in his upcoming days. This success effectively instilled the values of democratic feeling into the veins of Indian nationals irrespective of any religion and culture.

As a visionary of modern human breakthrough, he was a staunch promoter of reconciliation of scientific knowledge with religious revelation. Blind imitation is worthless unless it's observed and analyzed. 'Practical morality' is the true essence of all religions. A unity of humanity should be followed among Hindu, Muslims and all. Sir Syed toiled hard to give an impetus among people of different strata for mutual coexistence under the bond of brotherhood. After his visit to the UK in 1969, Sir Syed was totally attuned about factors which catapulted the West to the ladder of development. As well as he discovered some other elements that prevented his own community and the whole nation from growing further.[10] After he returned, his observations made the foundation of the Scientific Society which compromised Muslims, Hindus and Christians to evaluate perfectly the measures for a pluralistic India. He was targeted by separatists, ultra-communal people. However, he was as stubborn as a mountain with an intention of harmonization of Indian societies.

Another milestone was when he turned his Madrasatul-Uloom into Mohammedan Anglo-Oriental College (1875), dreaming of the Cambridge and Cordova of India. Then he proclaimed, "This college may expand into a university, whose sons shall go through the length and breadth of the land to preach the gospel of free enquiry, of large heartened toleration and pure morality."[11] Initiating a policy of real nationalism, the MAO welcomed all knowledge seekers with no restriction of caste or creed. Still, the nationalism flourishes in the garb of gear of Aligarh Muslim University (AMU). More than that it started as a movement - the Aligarh Movement that catapulted the spirit of scientific education with religious obligation across the country as well as beyond the Indian subcontinent. By this, he advocated Oxbridge-like education which teaches to accept the modern ideas, accept reformation and avoid rigidity.

Abundance of knowledge with lack of precise presentation is a kind of blunder. The true form of communication can put out different barriers of get-together between different cultures. Sir Syed Ahmed felt this very illusive cause behind the cultural participation of his people. As a linguist, the educationalist Sir Syed gave a widely accepted and down-to-people pathway of communication. Instead of a hindrance, language should be a bridge between people and their cultures. When the Language of the Courts (*Adaliya Zuban*) Urdu was only confined to rhetoric complexities, romantic speculation and academic purposes, Sir Syed stood for making it more smooth as well as easily accessible to common people. In this track, his efforts brought forth the Urdu Defense Association in 1900.[12]

The localization of Urdu gifted with many favours in the movement spearheaded by the pragmatist Sir Syed Ahmed Khan. The community people deprived for years started to fathom out the hidden sources of texts and literature. Subsequently, people tended to rational thinking and object and blind imitation of an idea or practice when the proliferated amount of knowledge espoused to them. At the same time, mutual interaction between different classes and exchange of ideas became more comfortable. They started to share their vested ideas to the whole world in their writings and conversations. Thus, the visionary Sir Syed can be labeled as a figurehead behind the inception of mother tongue media in the process of knowledge acquisition.[13]

Sir Syed, as a writer, himself exhaustively used the language of commons to make people aware of mutual understanding and forewarn them the consequences of separation, communal clash and violence. In all works like *Tahzeeb-al-Akhlaque* and *Khutbat-e-Ahmadiyya* he tried to extract the good morals of other religions and put them before the people as universal attributions of a human. Along with, he wrote at a prospect to educate people about the building process of a civilized and modern society keeping aside any kind of preconceptions and misunderstandings.[14]

It is useless to urge a child to write something without giving in his hand a piece of chalk. Likewise, national unity with such a huge diversity of cultures and faiths is an illusory imagination in a country like India. This is something that can't be indoctrinated in people's minds and behaviors till it is so cherished. With this vision, Sir Syed decided to make some platforms which will make this movement of unity to upcoming periods. He organized intellectuals of different cultures and bound them together in institutions like the British India Association (1886), MAO College (1875) and Scientific Society.[15] On the other hand, when some political elements of power-hunger always dissuade the common people from unity and peace and try to drive them back to separation and animosity. The pragmatist Sir Syed went forward with the United Patriotic Association (1888) as a counter-maneuver. He opposed the policy of separation in political parties like Congress, League and Arya Samaj. Instead, he advocated for a platform combining all Hindu, Muslims and Christian Missionaries in a political mode of only-for-people.

When India was engulfed in mutual abhorrence, ignorance, animosity, social superstition and cultural conservatism, Sir Syed wielded the weapon of *tahzib* or refinement to reform Indian communities into a society of progress, modernity and unity. He tried to make the countrymen reconcile with education, science, rational philosophy and mutual understanding. He was one the luminous torchbearers of reformation and pluralistic culture in 19th century Indian society. For the panacea of contemporary menace prevailing over the atmosphere of pluralism in India, his values and principles are to be shored up and patiently applied.[16] The movement is to be followed to push forward the future of interfaith dialogue to further steps from where the pioneer Sir Syeed Ahmed has accomplished.

Reference

1. Jalbani, Junaid Ali., *Great Struggles of Sir Syed Ahmed Khan in Uplifting the Muslims in the Field of Education after the 1857 Revolt*, Shaheed Benazir Bhutto University, 2021
2. "The Founder." *Aligarh Muslim University*, http://amu.ac.in. Accessed 29 Mar. 2023
3. G, Sampath., "India's Designation by the USCIRF," *The Hindu*, 28 Apr. 2022

4. Mondal, Md Sohel., "Restoring the Historic Glory in Contemporary India," *Reflections*. Live, 2020
5. Paracha, Nadeem F., "The Forgotten Past: Sir Syed and the Birth of Muslim Nationalism in South Asia", *The Scroll*, Aug. 2016
6. Kidwai, Shafey., *Sir Syed Ahmad Khan*. Taylor & Francis, 2020
7. Sir Syed Ahmed on *the Present State of Indian Politics, Consisting of Speeches and Letters*, The Pioneer Press, 1888
8. Malik, Hafeez., "The Religious Liberalism of Sir Sayyid Ahmad Khan," *The Muslim World*, no. 3, Wiley, July 1964, pp. 160–69
9. Ramsey, Charles M., "Sir Sayyid Ahmed and the Religious Foundations for a Pluralist Society," Baylor Institute for Studies of Religion, Baylor University, 2019
10. Khan, Sir Syed Ahmed, and Moulvi Samiullah Khan, *Musafiran-i-London*, 1961
11. Noorani, A. G., "History of Aligarh Muslim University", *Frontline*, 27 Apr. 2016
12. Kidwai A. R. (Ed.) *Sir Syed Ahmad Khan: Muslim Renaissance Man of India: A Bicentenary Commemorative Volume*, Viva Books Originals, 2020
13. Mohammad, Aslam., "Vision of Sir Syed Ahmad Khan," *Academia.Edu*, 1 Jan. 2018
14. Troll, Christian W., *Sayyid Ahmad Khan,* Vikas Publishing House, New Delhi, 1978
15. Sing, M. K., *Encyclopedia of India's War of Independence (1857-1947)*, 1st ed., Anmol Publication, 2009
16. Graham, G F I., *The life and work of Syed Ahmed Khan, C.S.I.*, Alpha Edition, New Delhi, 2020

Hindutva in the Post-Truth Era: Electoral and Non-Electoral Narratives

Reshmi Biswas & Suranjana Mitra

The foremost significance of today's political scenario is very sensitive. People have become result oriented. Lifestyle concerns are at prominence, and this takes us to the two most significant trends that are dominant in today's politics:

i. Post-truth era

ii. Hindutva in the post-truth politics era

Post-truth era is an era where public opinions are shaped based on particular personal emotions or beliefs rather than scientific or factual analysis. India is a place where emotions have their unique colour. In Indian culture as considered in most occidental civilizations, emotion matters a lot be it a simple thread ceremony of a child, the win of the city team or the national team in a cricket match or be it related to the diverse foods we enjoy all around the country. This feature of the Indian culture has made a mark on the global stage and has provided a unique identity to Indians globally. Though at times becoming stereotypical it has never lost its sense of being an effervescent feature of the country. The same feature has made a considerable impact on Indian society as well as politics in both a positive and negative manner. The positive side has been the cherished ideal of unity within diversity that has been a reminiscent strength of the Indian population, while the negative side has been the communalisation of politics, casteism, racism and other forms of structural violence that have plagued our great civilization. This negativity stems from the very same emotion that cherishes diversity in our culture. Elections have been a polarising facet of Indian democracy for a long time. Electoral successes determine not only policy formulation but societal changes that can be induced with the power bestowed through the election, the same is applicable for both central as well as state politics considering the quasi-federal structure of the Indian state. The new century though provided India with a new form of politics – Coalition blocs did not stay strong for a long time.

After Narendra Modi became chief minister of Gujarat for the second time, in 2007. There was bickering within the BJP. BJP leader Gordhan Zadafiya, the junior home minister in Modi's first cabinet rebelled against the party and floated a new outfit- Maha Gujarat Janata Party (MJP) just ahead of the elections. Modi's close friend a corporate executive wrote a letter to the chief (Sarsangchalak) Mohan Bhagwat complaining about how some within the BJP were trying to barrack Modi and his efforts to run the state government. RSS commonly known as the fulcrum peace of the RSS family (the Sangh Parivar) is a conglomerate of three dozen socio-political organizations built up for a common Hindu nationalist cause. At that point in time, RSS was struggling with shrinking membership and units. Its affiliates were pulling in different directions and the political arm of BJP was beset with infighting and intrigue. The then Sarsangchalak, K. S Sudarshan, was not ready to accept the contributions of BJP's prime minister, Atal Behari Vajpayee and deputy PM L. K Advani in nation building. Instead, Sudarshan was very vocal in announcing that Congress party's former PM Indira Gandhi was the best PM the country had ever had. At a public function, he even snubbed Modi who was seated in the front row at a function organised, he walked past Modi, totally ignoring him while the Gujarat Chief minister stood up with folded hands before Sudarshan.

RSS had decided to change its face. Mohan Bhagwat who succeeded Sudarshan had read the executive's missive with concern. The letter written by Modi's corporate friend hinted at the rising star of Hindutva. i.e., Modi and the RSS leadership. He wanted to say that some within the Sangh were trying to create this rift. Bhagwat had invited the executive to Nagpur for a detailed convo. A meeting that took place for hours, helped Bhagwat understand the misunderstandings that were being created between the RSS leadership and Modi. Bhagwat was hesitant to receive an invitation to launch a book written by Modi. The book profiled a collection of people who had influenced Modi starting from the 2nd Sarsanghchalak to Madhukar Rao Bhagwat, Mohan Bhagwat's father. The name of the book was "Jyotipunj". Years later, Bhagwat remarked to a friend that the corporate executive was partly responsible for Modi becoming the PM of India. Bhagwat had travelled to Ahmedabad to launch Modi's book.

The major change that came to Indian politics was in 2014 when the BJP-led National Democratic Alliance came to power after a gap of 10 years with the biggest mandate provided to the Bharatiya Janta Party since the 1990s, the charismatic leadership of Narendra Modi combined with the ruthless campaigning against the mismanagement of the UPA2 government and its policy paralysis led to a wave that was unprecedented in Indian politics since the beginning of the coalition era. What came after it was in the same manner unprecedented. A vehement push to change narratives ensued with the government. Truth, historical as well as contemporary came to be challenged and the means of providing these challenges were of the most surprising character as Hindutva supporting right-wing political (BJP, Shiv Sena) and social groups (RSS, VHP, Hindu Mahasabha) and more so the fringe groups (Shree Ram Sene, Karni Sena, Bajrang Dal) linked with the ideology took up the job to expand the electoral victory to other aspects such as culture, education even food and daily practices. Not only attacks on the opposite ideologies increased, but neutral agencies were also slowly influenced to become extensions of the Hindutva supporting right-wing ideology. The felling of a statue of Lenin inside a public park by BJP workers after their win in the state of Tripura, the attacks on couples on Valentine's Day by Bajrang Dal, deletion of courses on Mughal India in text books, petitions to rename Taj Mahal as Tejo Mahaley are some of the many examples in which the right wing has tried to assert its understanding of the world upon the populace. The narrative has slowly paved way for questioning realities, blatant misrepresentation, misinformation, provocation, misdirection of facts and counter-narratives without rationality and logic and instead dependence on emotive values that are considered true rather than facts which can be verified.

What can be surmised from this is a reflection of a global trend that is becoming a potent trick in the playbook of majoritarian political parties all throughout the globe is the phenomenon of post-truth where truth is not a fact but an interpretation, a situation where selective emphasis on certain facts is taken as sacrosanct and others are dismissed as opposite narratives. Post-truth is a terminology used popularly in news media to address the process of spreading and repeating false or fake news so that in long run it becomes a dominant discourse. India as the land of emotion is witnessing a diverse notion of the post-truth era where public opinion is being shaped by personal belief or emotion related to it, not by scientific or logical reasoning. Now the question arises from when this narrative of the 'death of truth' or post-truth entered Indian politics dominantly and how it has been playing/ being played in the Indian political discourse. The answer comes from 2014 and the right wing that got its launching pad with the election to become a part of the mainstream narrative after being in the opposition for more than a decade. The liberal welfarist ideology of the Congress-led centre-left and the leftist ideas of other regional parties started to wane in face of the Hindutva supporting right-wing conservative neo-liberal onslaught which took the country by storm.

The year is 2014 and the banner is NDA2, with the landmark victory in the election, the Hindutva-supporting right-wing BJP-led NDA2 starts making space for the post-truth narrative to operate. It starts employing both the mainstream and the fringe of the right wing to amass votes as well as public opinion in favour of its rule. Therefore, the phenomenon can be analysed from two very different perspectives. One is the traditional expansion of the electoral footprint to gather as much legislative power as possible to make changes in the political realm as well as the social realm.

Eight decades after the RSS was founded, circumstances and people had come together to bring the levers of power that controlled the destiny of the country within its reach. RSS still believes that with or without power, steering India's destiny is its founding mission. The RSS considers itself the committed agent of high Hindu thought, that would ultimately baptise the world. Golwalkar said the world stayed of our conception will evolve out of a federation of an autonomous and self-contained nations under a common centre linking them. It is a grand world unifying thought of Hindus alone, that can supply the abiding basis for human brotherhood and that knowledge of the inner spirit will charge the human mind with the sublime urge to toil for the happiness of mankind. While opening out full and free scope for every small life specialty. RSS was formed on Vijaya Dashami Day by a Maharashtrian Brahmin in 1925. It was built on the unshakeable belief that India is a Hindu nation, that belongs only to the Hindus. Anyone may become its citizen but the Hindus have a civilisational claim on the geographical entity called India or Bharat, the name preferred by Sangh Parivar. RSS staunchly believes in the cultural unity of not just India but also the subcontinent, including Afghanistan, Pakistan, Bangladesh, and Myanmar. It envisions its large geographical swathe extending from Gandhar (Kandahar) to Brahmadesh (Myanmar). Coalescing into a single nation or Akhanda Bharat at some point in the future, even if it is centuries from now. This shows that the concept of Akhanda Bharat as propagated by RSS is more an object of faith and belief and is not only a matter of reality and actuality. This drive is propagated by RSS to culturally unite the people of this country as Hindus, anyone living in Bharat or India is a Hindu, it is, therefore, a cultural concept not a religious concept to RSS as is wrongly understood. To RSS, Muslims in India are as much Hindus as Christians and other communities. The modern-day RSS propagates that Christians and Muslims living in India are just not religious entities. They are Indians and Hindus only that their ways of religious worship are different.

The Sangh has two questions- the first is a Bismarkian dream of creating an Akhanda Bharat and the second is becoming the Vishwa Guru, a concept strongly floated by the Modi government since 2014. While it seems that Akhanda Bharat is a near-impossible proposition from the present vantage, the RSS it is within its grasp. RSS is one of the pioneer propagators of Indian yoga across the globe. Incidentally, what RSS claimed has now been accepted by the United Nations as it celebrated the 21st of June each year as the International Day of Yoga. RSS feels it is proof of validity to their claim where Indian values and way of life are globally accepted. Golwalkar, the second Sarsanghchalak, envisioned that the world state will evolve out of a federation of autonomous and self-contained nations linked to a common centre. The warp and weft of this global fabric will emerge from Hindu thought. The first step is to convert India into a muscular Hindu nation. RSS is organised like a military, and much of its ideological idea is derived from 19th-century European ideas of nationhood filtering Indian history and culture through them by Hindu leaders such as Swami Vivekananda, Bal Gangadhar Tilak, and V. D Savarkar. It however rejects the notion of a nation-state and instead believes in a cultural nation separate from the state. In this way the modern-day RSS has discarded RSS literature of the early 1930s, where Russian, German and Japanese nationalism was admired.

The primary goal of any political party is to secure political power and to hold it either singly or in cooperation with other political parties namely in a coalition. What distinguishes the BJP from other political parties post-2014 is the sheer ruthlessness in its approach to expanding its power. The swathes of power the party holds over certain sections have been no less than tremendous, to say the least. The coming to power paved the way for it to cater to other sections that haven't been traditionally part of the Hindutva supporting right-wing bandwagon. Power acts as a great gravitational pull to people as well groups who seek more power and therefore alignment to the powerful is a very common feature in Indian politics as this ensures less victimisation and more electoral as well as social gain, not to mention economic gain. This phenomenon can be exemplified by various Indian parties aligning with the ruling coalition at the centre whenever there was a need to get benefits. The examples vary from the Trinamool Congress, Lok Janshakti Party, National Conference and even very recently Shiv Sena (Uddhav Thackeray faction). In the post-truth era, ideological coalitions are immaterial, what matters is creating beneficial electoral alliances and staying in power. To ensure this some old and some new tricks started to emerge. The power of the Governor was used blatantly to get parties favourable to the BJP to form governments which though an old trick in the arsenal of the Old Congress was reintroduced by the BJP with success in Manipur, Goa and Karnataka. Horse trading to lure in legislators has been the trick that has been often repeated whose example was Madhya Pradesh and Maharashtra.

Often a party seeks to attain the political goal of getting into power corridors of states and the centre against the background of a common ideological belief shared by its members and in such a case this ideological perspective becomes another salient feature of the party that distinguishes it from other social groups. BJP's Hindutva-supporting right-wing ideologically driven power-seeking electoral manoeuvres went beyond the defined roles of a political party as it went on to create a new base for its new kind of post-truth politics. But the real effects of the post-truth playbook on the emotions of the people began during the campaigning period just before 2014, which in actuality created the image that the BJP-led NDA 2 and its fringe elements needed to carry which was the main game card for the party. BJP in these campaigns was been to attract the belief, emotion, and confidence of both the conservative population as well as liberal (centre liberal?). The conservative side was already leaning towards the BJP and its allies because of the long-implemented liberal policies of the UPA1 and UPA2 governments which according to the Hindutva-supporting right wing created a society which was more modern and less aligned with the traditional values of what the right considered was the Indian culture that required expansion. This approach was the traditional political expansion based on ideological accreditation. The liberals were brought onto the BJP bandwagon through a continued campaign of falsifying the success of the earlier regime as failures, and policies implemented as either unnecessary or having a negative impact. Through a series of online and offline campaigns a dystopian future was predicted as well as portrayed if the UPA was given another lease of life and the only way to stop was to join the bandwagon of the BJP, the liberal section enamoured by the technocrats joining the party along with support from business class combined with cataclysmic India against Corruption movement out of which the Aam Admi Party was born agreed to put faith in the moderate face of the NDA. This was one of the trump cards of the post-truth movement in Indian politics when the liberal class apprehensive of the failures of the liberal political parties joined hands with the conservative right wing in the expectation that ideology will not be playing a major role and rather policy formulation will be the driving force of the government.

Thus, a sizeable chunk of the Indian population through various promises related to their emotions, be it creating employment which was a rational demand of the liberal sections, or promise to build the ram mandir which was a demand of the Hindutva supporting right wing (pointing out the Gujarat model), or be it bring back 'kala Dhan', black money from the Swiss bank and even the near nonsensical promise of depositing 15 lakhs to every citizen's account. Thus, what was done during the campaign trail was a careful overlapping of two contradictory sections of people to get a majority in the Indian Lok Sabha and control the levers of power, which was the first part of what is the post-truth narrative of successful hegemonic dominance. The process of channelling mass emotion and building up a dominant notion through it which in long run becomes a discourse of truth, which is nothing but a process to not only hold onto power but create a system where no opposition exists because every narrative is corruptible, every fact is questionable and there is no true target as the target of goal accomplishment keeps on moving.

The process was a massive success. BJP and its allies infiltrated newer electoral areas which were never on the radar of the older Hindutva supporting right wing mentality. Northeastern states came into the ambit of the BJP which was a success in bringing the non-ideological strategy. The states in the northeast of India are mostly Christian-dominated (except Assam and Tripura), which is considered a minority in the rest of India and accused by the traditional right wing of indulging in anti-national activities of religious conversion through its various charities. The BJP not only overcame this stigma but registered big wins in the states by appealing to the Christian as well as the tribal identities of the northeastern populace with the additional promise of a Delhi-driven double-engine government in the state. The only exception to this phenomenon has been the state of Kerala where the Left Front government not only came to power riding high on electoral welfarist policies but won an unprecedented second term based on its success in dealing with natural catastrophes that lashed the state in the last part of the 2020s.

The success of this strategy was also repeated in the traditional conservative BJP-supporting areas of North India where 2 big states- Uttar Pradesh which the BJP won twice in the decade and in Madhya Pradesh where it took back power from the Congress despite getting lesser seats through the defection of a chunk of Congress legislators. This attitude successfully worked again in the 2019 election. The 2019 election was again a success on this two-pronged strategy of joining liberal and conservative sentiments to get back to power where the party harped the tunes of the national sentiment of nationalism and patriotism to assert their role as the sole conservator of the traditional ideas, and at the same time asserted its role as a neutral pro-people governance driven institution to get the liberals on their side who couldn't get a replacement from the devastated Congress party. The PM was spotted in multiple campaigns that voting for the party will be considered as voting for the soldiers to get traditional on the side of the party whereas he was also seen with the entrepreneurs, industrialists, and social networking CEOs to drive home the idea that the traditional part is to be combined with progressive modern policies to create a new India. The party also managed to attract the attention of conservatives through issues of ram mandir, and the issue of love jihad.

Hindutva has been the long-standing yet unofficial ideology of the BJP. The failure of the BJP to resonate the same ideology with the masses in earlier elections led it to devise the post-truth strategy of a two-pronged approach to increase its base. The idea of Hindutva though has not been dumped by the right wing rather it has been sent to a section where it is spreading and engulfing newer additions and yet not harming the liberal narrative of the BJP. The BJP with the help of RSS has been able to establish a linkage between Hindutva and the notion of post-truth which in the long run is helping in vote bank politics as well as non-electoral politics.

One cannot deny the fact that a huge number of BJP voters are primarily Hindus who believe in the principles of age-old Hinduism as well as the need to revive it by contradicting the ideas that existed between the old Hinduism and the subsequent revivalism. This in turn seeks to obliterate and invisiblize the periods of both Islamic rule (sultanate) as well as colonial rule (British Rule). The Hindutva revivalism that the right-wing Hindutva fringe along with the BJP and the RSS seeks to harness with its post-truth strategy has somehow sought to obliterate the post-independent history as well by claiming that the 70-odd years before the NDA2 was all gloom and doom with the Nehru Gandhi family dominating the country without any development. Conveniently trying to erase its earlier participation in the very same where in 1977-99 its predecessors were part of the Morarji Desai government which ran for 3- odd years, the minor stints in governments in the 1990s and finally the Vajpayee government by holistically clubbing them into the same dark phase of pre-NDA2 years.

The main agent behind the aforementioned phenomenon hasn't been the BJP but rather the right-wing fringe with whom the BJP and NDA as a whole seek to distance themselves to keep the electoral unity of liberals and conservatives together, but at the same time patronise and support at a local level. The fringe elements of the Hindu right-wing such as the Bajrang dal, Karni Sena, Hindu Sena, Hindu Jagruti Sena etc. Parallelly this is also a fact that Hindutva the core ideology of RSS is the backbone of these fringe outfits in today's time has shown a modern rendition which is helping to catch the attention of people who have their roots in their rich culture and religion but have adopted a modern thought process with contemporary realities. The inclusion of more woman-centric attitudes, acceptance attitudes towards the LGBTQ community, and reforms for lower caste all are an indication of the modernisation narrative.

Through the post-truth apparatus, the right-wing Hindutva brigade (both the mainstream and the fringe) are trying to impose a dominant narrative which has been, decimating all the existing political agendas that stand against it and thus the established discourse is automatically being treated as the truth which can be moulded, changed and mis/reinterpreted for the sake of the powerholders. They are trying to establish hegemonic control over dominant discourses of the society which shapes public opinion for not only the present but the future as well. What is evident is that the Hindutva juggernaut is here to stay in Indian politics as both the mainstream and the fringe are leading it in two opposite paths which end in the same destination- hegemonic dominance of insular Hindutva based on electoral overlapping successes as well as cultural control of the socio-political sphere. No democracy is perfect and India being one of the largest is no exception to this fact. But it is also a fact that the democratic corridors are shrinking, the right-wing Hindutva ideology is expanding itself and the opposition in its vein attempt to hold onto votes is falling into the trap of answering with soft Hindutva which is no competition to the NDA and the RSS which has expertise in Hindutva politics both at the electoral and non-electoral level. Instead, there is a need to harness the democratic ideals enshrined in the constitution and strengthen dissenting voices instead of labelling them as antithetical to India's growth story to lead India to a better future in the new century.

References

1. Ambekar, S., *The RSS: Roadmaps for the 21st Century*, Rupa Publications, 2019
2. Anand, A., *Know About RSS*. Prabhat Prakashan, 2016
3. Anand, A., *RSS roadmap for 21st century India — rewrite history, 'Indianise' education, museum revamp*, The Print (Online Platform) September 30, 2019
4. Anderson, E. A., & Jaffrelot, C., "Hindu nationalism and the 'saffronisation of the public sphere': an interview with Christophe Jaffrelot", *Contemporary South Asia*, 26 (4), 2018, pp. 468–482,
5. Anderson, E. A., & Longkumer, A., 'Neo-Hindutva: evolving forms, spaces, and expressions of Hindu nationalism', *Contemporary South Asia, 26* (4), 2018, pp. 371–377
6. Bhadrakumar, M., 'Modi's post-truth politics', *The Week*, April 12, 2019
7. Brahms, Y., *"Philosophy of Post-Truth"*, *The Institute of National Security Studies*, March 19, 2023
8. Farkas, J., & Schou, J., *Post-Truth, Fake News and Democracy: Mapping the Politics of Falsehood*, Routledge, 2019
9. Fuller, S., *Post-Truth: Knowledge as A Power Game*. Anthem Press, Delhi, 2018

10. Jaffrelot, C., "The Modi-centric BJP 2014 election campaign: new techniques and old tactics", *Contemporary South Asia*, *23* (2), 2015, pp. 151–166
11. Jaffrelot, C., "Narendra Modi between Hindutva and sub-nationalism: The Gujarati *Asmita* of a Hindu Hriday Samrat", *India Review*, *15* (2), 2016, pp. 196–217
12. Kaul, N., "Rise of the Political Right in India: Hindutva-Development Mix, Modi Myth, and Dualities", *Journal of Labor and Society*, *20* (4), 2017, pp. 523–548
13. Narayan, D., *The RSS: And the making of the deep nation.* Penguin Random House India Private Limited, 2019, See the Introduction.
14. Noorani, A. G. *The RSS*, Leftword Books, 2020
15. Andersen, Walter. "The Rashtriya Swayamsevak Sangh: III: Participation in Politics," *Economic and Political Weekly*, vol. 7, no. 13, 1972, pp. 673–82

Negative Identity of Indian Party Politics: A Study

Biplab Mondal

In 1947, India emerged as an independent state. A decade before this, the British ruling group on the one hand and the Indian National Congress on the other hand continued to conduct themselves as the main backbone of the country's governance through the policy of parallel governance to manage the administration of India. The Muslim League made its debut in the meantime, but due to a lack of mutual understanding, the country was divided by the wildfire of communalism. India's two main religious groups have achieved their own goals to fulfil their narrow interests and eventually, the country was bifurcated into two distinct geographical entities by barbed wire. Indian governance was handed over to the then National Congress and the grand scheme of making the world's largest democracy gradually started. On January 26, 1950, the world's largest statutory written constitution was dedicated to the people of India and from there the outline of India's party system was determined.

India currently bears the hallmarks of a multi-party state structure. Parties that emerge based on language and regions in the arena of politics gave birth to multi-party politics. Satisfying narrow interests has been the main outline of this multi-party state system. Due to the multi-party system, the major political parties of the country lost their importance and prestige in the cut-throat competition to gain political power to come to the forefront of Indian Politics. Smaller, regional and other interest-based parties continued to sacrifice domestic and foreign policies to satisfy their interests. The larger parties are forced to seek the support of these small interest groups for vote bank politics. Interestingly, the parties belonging to this multi-party state system are not aware of anything other than their self-interests. For the most part, they are not driven by any principles or ideals. Much can be said in Nachiketa's voice as:

"Today who is on the right, tomorrow he will be on the left,

He who is in tricolour today, tomorrow will be a devotee of Ram."

This party system of India is not allowing the foreign policy of this country or any internal policy to be effective whose outcome is terrible. The neglected people of large section of society are remaining neglected for a long time, their socio-economic progress is not noticeable. The regional party system is enough to break the fundamental integrity of India. Religious antagonism is increasing in society due to communal support groups. The main cause of social degradation is the Indian multi-party system. Even the democratic, unicentric or small states with two-party systems are currently setting high standards in all aspects, the multi-party system is the main reason behind India's backwardness in many areas even after 75 years of independence.

India is the flag-bearer of great principles, idealism and humanism and is praised as one of the largest democracies. The world's economic powerhouses are today consulting and following the footprints of India in many spheres. Indians within and outside the country are striving to make India great again. The country is poised to make leaps and bounds of development in the economy, military and polity. The recent strong stand of India in World Politics in international affairs screams the success of India's post-independence foreign policy. In 1947, after the 190-year-long chain of subjugation was finally loosened, a wave of strong enthusiasm for the nationalist ideology swept over the country. The sacrifice of hundreds of brave freedom fighters created the context of the country's independence. In response to the growing opposition to the tyrannical ruling class since the post-42 movement, the Constitution of India began to contemplate the inclusion of autonomous rule. Perhaps somewhat frightened by the naval mutiny or the advancement of the Azad Hind Force, they ventured to start a process of parallel governance within the country. India was simultaneously being ruled by the British ruling class, the National Congress and the Muslim League.

Independent India has been committed to upholding the country's traditions along with the ambition to present itself as a model of democracy. It became necessary to critically evaluate the actions and policies of the government in everyday life to keep alive the spirit of democracy. To impose checks and balances on the ruling party, several opposition parties emerged in India. In an endeavour of uniting themselves, Indians of varied cultural, communal and regional backgrounds found themselves under different ideological groups instead of one. India's successive party systems continued to evolve from unicentric or bi-party to multi-party systems. New political parties began to emerge out of small interest groups as India felt the need to consolidate its internal organizational processes. While reviewing the policies, and ideals of these multi-divisive political parties, we find the following issues.

Since 1952, political parties in India have faced competition in electoral battles. Since then, multi-party existence has become central to Indian politics. Until 1967, the Congress party remained unchallenged at the centre and in the states but later Congress's dominance declined in several states. After 1995, Congress' attempts to seize power at the Centre began to reveal several weaknesses. At that time Bhartiya Janata Party formed a coalition government with the support of its regional allies. This trend of forming alliances of Indian political parties has crippled the progress of the country. The coalition government formed by BJP before 2000 failed to show any achievement apart from only the 'Pradhan Mantri Gramin Jatiya Sadak Yojna' due to the narrow interests of the allied parties within the coalition. Later, Congress again wanted to advance the process of fulfilling its own interests with the support of the successful democratic parties, but the alliance called UPA did not get a suitable platform for determining a strong foreign policy or domestic policy. When the power was again transferred to the hands of the Bhartiya Janata Party, that government again failed to properly advance the nation due to the lack of a single leadership. It was only when the Bhartiya Janata Party came to power with a strong majority, that the scenario somewhat changed. Although the two progressive parties, Congress and BJP, emerged as the major popular parties in India today, the selfish designs of smaller parties, be they right-wing or left-wing, still fail to provide a positive and stable environment to meet the overall interests of Indian political parties or the country.

One of the aspects of the Indian party system is unicentric whereas the Indian state structure should be federated. Due to this tendency of centralization, most of the parties who rose to the top of power are always ready to assert their dominance. Congress, UPA, and BJP each have been able to gradually create hegemony to fulfil their party interests. Once they came to power, they started doing everything possible to remain in that position of power. These political parties for their interests keep the same person as the prime minister and also the supreme leader of the party. The top-level leaders from the centre control party workers down to the district level. Due to this central interference, proper development across all regional, linguistic, and financial levels remains neglected. Various regional demands and public interests rarely are conveyed to the centre and are often neglected. This tendency of centralization is by no means positive enough for the overall development of a country as diverse as India. However, the political parties in desperate attempts to gain selfish party interests, even misuse their power to neglect the national interest. All ruling parties at the zenith of power since the independence have fulfilled their interests in this way and staggered the development of India's national progress.

One of the essential features of democratic governance is the presence of opposition parties. A strong opposition party in any democratic state can create an environment for the progress of the state to move forward at full speed. But if the existence of that opposition party becomes almost non-existent, then the state system becomes non-benevolent, and that democracy becomes an autocratic dictatorship. Today in India's party system, the presence of opposition parties is very weak. To sustain the country's democracy the opposition parties failed to protect their own as well as national interests by putting pressure on the government. Soon after the seizure of power, the defeated parties were forced to forego their existence. The main reason is the petty self-interest of the smaller parties and individual leaders. They are determined to maintain only their power and influence without following the moral ideals of the party. Although the Indian Constitution passed the Anti-Secession Act (1955) in this regard, its existence is still on paper only. As the leadership of the defeated party left the party to join the other side, the existence of the opposition gradually weakened, and the opposition faced a big question mark in terms of stabilizing its identity.

There is no universality in the ideological form of India's party system. Most of the political parties in the advanced democracies of the world are not guided by the ideals of individualism or narrow party principles or individual ideals. Rather, the fundamental principles or ideals of most parties remain almost the same. As a result, their policy in the administration of the state is in no way completely different. However, in India, the basic structural arrangement, ideology and policies of the parties are different fundamentally which is largely responsible for the fragmentation of India's party system. Socialist democracy can be the strongest weapon of Congress for the development and progress of the nation. For it is this ideal that will establish the strongest forms of social order or will reveal the creative aspects of human well-being. On the other hand, the Communist Party with the ideologies of Marx and Engels, can offer communism as the mainstay for the progress of India. They believe in the dictatorship of the proletariat, social distribution and social ownership of wealth tend to be regarded as its main objectives. The BJP shows the dream of building the nation with the help of capitalism and individualism and progress through strong nationalism. It is the ideological differences within the party system, that handicap the nation and as a developing country, it faces considerable obstacles in obtaining special assistance and important membership in international forums.

We shall see the Indian political parties making fun of the great words like freedom, democracy and secularism etched in the preamble of the Indian Constitution. The two major communities of India, Hindu and Muslim, failed to put an example of brotherhood and peaceful coexistence. Ideological differences between Hindus and Muslims have created communal antagonism in many cases. Many parties and leaders are still committed to running the state and winning elections with divisive policies in the name of religion. It is the duty of every Indian to create and maintain the integrity of the nation, but a faction of them is creating a poisonous climate of communal hatred by indulging in communal politics. The root of this nuisance can be found in the creation of the Hindu Mahasabha on one side and the Muslim League on the other. Apart from this, major political parties often patronise and give special incentives to a particular religious group to disturb the religious integrity of the country. The time has come for us to think about the fact that the unity of the country will be destroyed if the politics of religious division is not stopped.

An important part of the Indian party system is the presence of regional parties. Major political parties are engaged in the pursuit of the greater interests of the elites and continue to neglect the interests of the smaller sections of society. As a result, it has been seen that the interests of the common people of the society are being largely undermined. In such a situation many regional parties with regional interests are emerging. Parties that get 3 per cent of the vote in any election are known as regional parties, as decided by the Constitution of India or the Election Commission. All these regional groups like DMK, Akali Dal, Muslim League, and Telugu Desam have never attained the status of major political parties. These groups continue to thrive by supporting major parties to fulfil their regional interests. As a result, that territorial division is often giving rise to small states and fuelling demands for separate geographical territories for newer interest groups. Although the role of these parties in regional interests is undisputed, on the other hand, it is giving birth to a small regional mentality.

The trend of changing parties can be identified as a significant corruption of the Indian party system. In many cases, a person after winning the election on behalf of a political party tries to exert his individual influence, but in case the party is defeated in the election, he may not hesitate to jump to the winning party to retain his socio-political-economic power. This trend betrays the benefits of a democracy and plays with the sentiments of the voters. An Act was passed in 1985 to stop this tendency of switching parties like child's play, but still, it continues to corrupt Indian politics. Note that in 1967, a member of the Haryana Legislative Assembly changed parties 3 times on the same day. It is time for stricter implementation of the party change policy.

Critical analysis of the Indian party system reveals the existence of various pressure groups in the opposition and within a party, like farmers, labourers, workers, students, teachers, youth etc. They put pressure on the government at different times on various issues to fulfil their interests. Some of their activities undoubtedly produce positive results for that particular group, but sometimes they pressurise a stable and smooth-running government with ill intention to destabilise it. Overlooking the greater interest of the nation, these pressure groups often disrupt national progress, mislead people and hamper its prestige in the international sphere. These pressure groups act as special-purpose organizations whose activities and ideologies are largely tools for fulfilling self-interest rather than national. As a consequence, these pressure groups in several states of India turned into regional political parties that succeeded in usurping major powers and managed to take over the governance of the state.

The Indian party system in the political sphere is flowing along many channels and producing mixed results. In many cases, a very conducive atmosphere has been created for the flourishment of democracy, while in some the result is not at all a sign of real progress in the world. As the largest democracy with a multitude of cultures and communities, India could not be governed by any strict moral code in many respects. Religious tensions, casteism, caste-discriminatory lifestyles, regionalism, and ideological diversity have reflected the destructive nature of the Indian party system. Coalition politics is a major divisive aspect of the Indian party system. Many times, the public service manifestoes that political parties float in election campaigns have never become a reality after taking power. In the context of evaluating the outlines of the Indian party system, it can be said in the words of Sri Ramakrishna Dev', - "Jato Mot Tato Path (As many opinions, as many ways)". Maybe the Indian party system has played an active role in politics in fulfilling the interests of small and large political parties in this country, but it can be said, that the "Party system in India has failed to provide a solid base for parliamentary democracy."

References

1. Debnath, Arnav. and Naskar, Govinda. *Political Theory; Concepts*, Kalyani Publications, Kalyani, 2022, pp. 32 & 226
2. Chakrabarti, Radharaman. *Aspects of political thinking in India*, Pragatishil Prokashak. 2008, pp. 27 & 202
3. Das, Deepak Kumar. *Theory of Politics,* Ekushey Publications, Kolkata 2015, pp. 49, 56, 82
4. Ghosh, Krityapriya. *Political Science (Rashtra tatva)*, P.B.R.P., 2006, p. 78
5. Pramanik, N., *Outline of Modern State Theory*, Chhaya Prakashani, Kolkata, 2019, p.75
6. Mukhopadhyay, Gautam. *Political theory; Perspectives and Controversies,* Setu Prakashani, Kolkata, 2019, pp.42 & 55
7. Ghosh, Soma, Gupta, Atanu. *Political Theory (Rjnoitik tatva)*, Mitram Prakashani, Kolkata, 2023, pp. 57 & 98
8. DeSouza, Peter Ronald. *India's Political Parties: 6 (Readings in Indian Government and Politics),* Sage India, 2006
9. Zoya, Hasan. *Parties & Party Politics in India*, Oxford University Press, New Delhi, 2004
10. Jaffrelot, C., "A new party system or a new political system?", *Contemporary South Asia*, Volume 28, Issue-2, 2020
11. Malji, Andrea. "The Rise of Hindu Nationalism and Its Regional and Global Ramifications", *Asian Politics,* Volume 23:1, Spring 2018
12. Dalal, Rajbir Singh. "Recent Trends in Indian Politics: An Introspection," *The Indian Journal of Political Science*, vol. 73, no. 2, 2012, pp. 375–84.

13. Chakrabarty, Bidyut. "Coalition Politics in India: A Cultural Synergy or Political Expediency?", *Oxford Academic (Online),* January 2006, pp.19-63
14. Rather, Tariq. "Coalition Politics in India", In book *Futuristic Trends in Social Science,* Selfypage Developers Pvt. Ltd (IIP), January 2023, pp.1-17
15. Kumar, Manoj. "Coalition Politics in India: History and Analysis of Political Alliances", *SSRN (Online)*, 22 Apr 2017

Amavati Ritual: A Mass Cultural Identity of Chotonagpur Region

Santosh Mahato

This chapter discuss about the *Amavati* ritual and its distinct observing methods. This ritual is also known by other names such as *Ambubachi, Amavati, Ambavarti, Aangbavati*, etc. Different names have been mentioned in different places in this writing. This chapter first highlights the practices of *Amavati* ritual in initial period of and then briefly discusses its several features. I have also tried to sketch that how this culture is different from others cultural aspects of Bengali people, and how it bears the distinct identity. This cultural has been fostered by the mainly Kurmi people Manbhum since time immemorial. The place is located at the South-Western part of West Bengal mainly Purulia district & and eastern part of Jharkhan (Chotonagpur Plateau). Today, in Jharkhand the people form the parts of the Dhanbad, Bokaro, Ranchi, Saraikela Kharsawan and East Singhbhum observed this cultural festive.[1] This is a kind of whole month festivals observe by them. This writing also discussed about the Rajasalha which is attached to this culture. Besides various negs or customs of Rajasalha, the rituals of eating mangoes, prohibition of ploughing have also been discussed. In short, all the rituals and customs that have to be observed on Amavati Culture Day have been discussed thoroughly. Finally, I have mentioned the significance and consequences of observing these negachar or customs. on Amavati Culture Day was also discussed.

Basically, the seventh day of Ashad month is called Amavati. Houses and courtyards are cleaned with cow dung in the morning on the day of Amavati. There is a neg or custom of eating mangoes on Amavati day.² People of Kurmali observe the 7ᵗʰ day of Ashad as the day of Amavati or Ambubachi. This culture is associated with agriculture. Earth is considered as mother and this day is regarded as the first day of the menstrual cycle of Mother Earth or Basumata. Some people believe that this day is the birthday of the world. On the day of Ambubachi, ploughing the soil or even scratching the soil is not allowed. Sowing of seeds is also prohibited. All agricultural activities remain suspended and agricultural tools are kept on wood or stone.³ All the farming families eat mangoes together with milk and chira (flatted rice). It is believed that by observing these customs, people will be free from stomach disease, and snake or insect bites will not harm the body for the next year. By the end of Ambubachi, paddy can be planted and the seedbed can be prepared.⁴ Before planting paddy, village deities are worshipped on that day and their grace is sought and permission is sought before the beginning of cultivation.⁵ As mother nature becomes full of newly grown leaves and greenery, the glorification of the beauty of mother nature or Herihar is called 'Angbabati' in Kurmali.⁶

The first day of Ashad month is observed as Rajasalha by the Kurmis. According to the Kurmi belief, in primitive times, people started farming by cutting down bushes, trees and forests, levelling the land and making cultivable lands. In those days there was no concept of private property and one could plant paddy wherever he could. And when Ashad month came, the work of planting paddy started quickly. As time passed problems started over who would plant which field. The Kurmis were tribals and originally lived in Bastis and Di (small Basti). They were vastly experienced and knowledgeable in all matters. One of them was chosen as the Mahat or the leader of the village. As cultivation was essential for their livelihood, everyone consulted the Mahat in case any problem arose in matters of cultivation in a gathering (locally known as Mir). This was known as Rajasalha as the Kurmis consulted (salha) their leader (raja) and then only started cultivation. Once a year the Kurmis gather in a Mir to receive counsel/ salha from their leader/ raja to solve problems and start farming. On that day they did not engage in farming and till today they observe the first day of Ashad month as Rajasalha and stay away from ploughing or digging.[7]

Ambubachi Tithi is the day of Ambavati Puja in the public consciousness of Manbhum. Rural deities are worshipped on this day in every village. From early morning, all the women of every household get busy cleaning the house, entrance, and courtyard with cow dung dissolved in water. However, preparations for Ambubachi Puja start days before among the men of the village. The Kurmis believe that for the well-being of the village and its residents, village deities should be worshipped on this day. One such collective thought operates among the masses, and vigour and enthusiasm fills them.[8] On the day of Ambavati, village deities can be worshipped by the village 'sholoana' (all the families of the village together) or by an individual family. Almost every village deity of Manbhum is worshipped by different indigenous people on this day.[9] In the context of Amavati culture, it can be noted that this culture has been continuously practised by the people of the Kurmi community in the Chotanagpur Plateau since ancient times. Other Hitmitan/Harmitan (Friends), or the communities that are allies or friendly to the Kurmis, also practice this culture. In Kurmali this culture is called Amavati/Aambavati because of the importance of the mango tree and mango fruit. The tradition of eating mango on this day is old. Ripe mangos can only be eaten after the 7th day of Ashad or Ambubachi probably to increase the benefits of mango in the summer heat of Chotonagpur plateau and to propagate mango tree plantation.

Mango is used as a medicine to cure many ailments such as burns (jhala) in the body during the sun, sunstroke, dryness, etc.[10] Therefore, the elders at that time decided when to eat mango fruit, how to use mango fruit medicinally and how to maintain the mango tree's lineage. If they can keep mangoes in the tree till the 7th day of Ashad, the mangoes will be fully ripe, the mango seeds will start germinating and the mango fruits will be used as medicine. This neg or custom shows how much nature was loved by the Kurmi people. Because not only to taste ripe mangoes but also to meditate on how the mango tree will survive in nature is the main point of this neg or custom.[11]

During this festival so many rituals or negachar are to be observed viz., Keeping plough, spade, tiller above the ground, placing other implements on wood or stone, stop farming, worshiping village deities, eating ripe mango with milk, eating meat or meat pita, sending mangoes, and jackfruits to the new Behai (father-in-law's house). The people of this localities believe that eating mangoes with milk prevents poisonous insects - spiders and snakes. Stomach diseases are destroyed during the rainy season. They also believe that eating burnt meat with skin does not cause other stomach diseases like monsoon dysentery. And finally, they have faith that, worshiping rural deities increases courage in the mind and strength in the body. Helplessness is removed. It would seem that some power is always there as a protector in case of danger. No one shall spoil the crops of the field or take them away secretly.[12]

Folk beliefs regarding the prohibition of ploughing on Ambubachi day: Ambubachi is an important Parban (festival or custom) in the life of rural Bengal farmers. Popularly known as Amavati in the farming community of Purulia district and adjoining areas, it is celebrated on 7th Ashad each year. On that day farmers eat mangoes, chira, milk etc. and farming activities are stopped, especially ploughing or digging. The folk belief in the farming community is that on the day of Ambubachi, is the day of the world's menstrual cycle.[13] Most of the farmers of Purulia keep various farming implements like ploughs, yokes, ladders etc. on a big stone or wood so that they can avoid contact with the soil and worship the farming implements with rice powder (pituli) and vermilion. Farmers believe that eating mangoes and milk on that day increases the body's resistance to poisons and increases life expectancy.[14]

The day of 'Ambavati' is very sacred in the consciousness of the people of Manbhum. After the scorching heat of Baisakh and Jaishtha, monsoon rains drench the earth on Ashad. Bosom of Basumata (Earth) will produce crops. Farmers' farms will be filled with ripe crops. Happiness and prosperity will descend in the life of farming families of the village. That is why on this Ambati day there is worship to appease the village deities on the one hand and to honour Vasumata on the other. Taking the blessings of both, various agricultural communities of Manbhum start toiling in the fields.[15] Finally, it can be said that Amabati culture is one of the agricultural rituals of the Kurmi people. The above discussion proves that. Amavati culture is inextricably linked with nature. In the discussion of Amavati culture, one thing is clear there is no doubt that the people of the Kurmi community are closely related to agriculture. Judging from all aspects, it can be said that Amabati culture is one of the agricultural cultures of the Kurmi people.

References

1. Chisholm, Hugh, ed. "Manbhum" . *Encyclopædia Britannica*, Vol. 17 (11th ed.), Cambridge University Press, 1911, p. 542
2. Mahat, Shambhunath and Mahat, Shaktipada, *Kurmali Chari*, West Bengal Kurmali Academy Publication, Purulia, 2021, p- 26
3. Ibid.,
4. Mahat, Kiriti and Mahat, Vishwanath, *Kurmali Language and Culture* (Eds.), Mulki Kurmali Bakhi Baisi Publication, Purulia, 2021, pp- 132-133

5. Mahat, Srishtihar, *Kurmali Neg-Niti-Negachar*, Manbhum Dalit Literary Publications, Purulia, 2021, Page- 161
6. Bansari, Siripad, *Kurmali Culture and Tantra Patience*, Mulki Kurmali Bakhi Baisi Publication, Purulia, 2021, pp-22-23
7. Mahat, Shambhunath, *Kurmali Charik Khadindi*, West Bengal Kurmali Academy Publication, Purulia, 2021, pp-23-24
8. Mahat, Kshirod Chandra, *Manbhum Sanskriti*, Bengali Sahitya Sangsad, Kolkata, 2016, page-34
9. Ibid., p. 35
10. Interview: Pradeep Kumar Mahat, Jaipur, Purulia, West Bengal 15/03/2023
11. Mahat, Shambhunath, 2021, Op. cit., pp. 24-25
12. Mahat, Srishtihar, 2021, Op. cit., p. 161
13. Mahat, Nimaikrishna, *Agriculture of Manbhum*, Knowledge Bank Publishers and Distributors, Kolkata, 2017, pg-58
14. Ibid., p. 58
15. Mahat, Kshirodchandra, *Manbhum Sanskriti*, Bangiya Sahitya Sangsad, Kolkata, 2016, page-35

Exploring the Role of Women's Print Media in the Indian Nationalist Movement: A Study of Select Women's Magazines in Colonial India

Obaidul Hoque

The Indian Nationalist Movement was a significant period in Indian history, characterized by various social, cultural, and political transformations. During this period, though, the participation of women in the freedom struggle has been well documented, their contribution through print media has received less attention. Women's print media emerged as a powerful tool for expressing their opinions, mobilizing public support, and creating a sense of collective identity among women. This chapter aims to explore the role of women's print media in the Indian Nationalist Movement through a focused analysis of select women's magazines in colonial India. The late 19th and early 20th centuries saw the emergence of a vibrant print culture in India, with women's magazines playing a significant role in shaping public opinion. These magazines were not just a platform for literary expression but also served as vehicles for political activism, social reform, and nationalist sentiment. The editors and contributors of these magazines were women who were deeply committed to the cause of India's freedom from British rule.

The study will focus on select women's magazines that were published in colonial India, including *Stri Dharma, Bharati, and Kadambari*. These magazines were widely circulated and had a significant impact on their readers, particularly women who were otherwise excluded from mainstream political discourse. The research will examine the content of these magazines, including their editorial policy, articles, stories, and poems, to understand how they contributed to the nationalist movement. The study adopts a qualitative research approach and draws on primary sources such as women's magazines, editorials, and articles, as well as secondary sources such as historical accounts and academic literature. The primary sources will include the magazines themselves, which will be analysed using content analysis techniques. The secondary sources will include historical texts, biographies, and other scholarly works on the nationalist movement and women's participation in it. This paper tried to find the answers of following research questions:

a) What was the historical and cultural significance of women's magazines in colonial India, and how did those shape their contribution to the nationalist movement?

b) What themes and issues did women's magazines in colonial India focus on, and how did they contribute to the nationalist discourse?

c) How did women's magazines in colonial India address the issue of women's participation in the nationalist movement, and what impact did this have on women's empowerment?

The study is organized into four segments. The first segments provide an overview of the historical and cultural context in which women's magazines emerged in India. The second chapter focuses on the role of three women's magazines in the nationalist movement, examining their contribution to the development of a feminist and nationalist discourse. The third chapter analyses the representation of women's experiences of colonialism, their struggles for independence, and their efforts towards social reform in women's magazines. The fourth and final chapter examines the role of famous women writers in shaping the content of these magazines and their impact on the broader feminist and nationalist movements in India.

In conclusion, this research will contribute to our understanding of the role of women in the nationalist movement in colonial India and highlight the significant contributions of women's print media to the cause of Indian independence. By examining the content of select women's magazines, the study will provide insights into the editorial policy, themes, and issues that shaped their contribution to the nationalist discourse. The study is significant not only for its historical value but also for its contemporary relevance, as it sheds light on the ways in which women's magazines can serve as a platform for political activism and women's empowerment. This study seeks to provide a nuanced understanding of the role of women's print media in the Indian Nationalist Movement and its impact on the lives of Indian women during the colonial period. By exploring the contributions of women's magazines to the nationalist discourse and the broader feminist and nationalist movements in India, this study sheds light on an important but often neglected aspect of Indian history.

Women's magazines in India have played a significant role in shaping women's identity, social roles, and cultural practices. These magazines emerged in the late 19th century and have since then become an integral part of Indian media culture. This chapter aims to explore the historical and cultural context in which women's magazines emerged in India and how they evolved over time. The research draws upon primary and secondary sources, including historical archives, magazines, and scholarly articles, to provide a comprehensive overview of the emergence and development of women's magazines in India.

Early Magazines and Their Cultural Significance:

The first women's magazine in India was published in 1880 under the title of "Ladies' Magazine." This magazine was primarily aimed at the urban middle-class women and covered topics such as fashion, beauty, health, and cooking. The magazine's content was largely influenced by Western ideas of femininity and domesticity, and it sought to promote the virtues of Victorian womanhood. According to Singh (2012), the emergence of women's magazines in India was linked to the changing social and cultural landscape of colonial India. The spread of Western education and modernity had challenged traditional gender roles and norms, and women's magazines emerged as a response to these changes.[1] These magazines provided a platform for women to participate in public discourse and express their views on various social and cultural issues.

Emergence of Nationalism and Its Impact on Women's Magazines:

The emergence of Indian nationalism in the early 20th century had a significant impact on women's magazines. Women's magazines became an important tool for nationalist leaders to mobilize women in the struggle for independence. Magazines such as "Stri Dharma" and "Bharati" published articles on the importance of women's education, women's rights, and the role of women in the nationalist movement. According to Chakraborty (2015), women's magazines played a significant role in shaping the image of the Indian woman in the nationalist discourse. These magazines emphasized the virtues of Indian womanhood, such as piety, self-sacrifice, and devotion to the family and the nation. They also celebrated the role of women in the nationalist struggle, highlighting their contributions as political activists, writers, and artists.[2]

Impact of Globalization and Liberalization on Women's Magazines:

The liberalization of the Indian economy in the 1990s had a significant impact on women's magazines. The opening up of the Indian market to global media and consumer culture led to the emergence of a new generation of women's magazines that catered to the aspirations of urban, educated women. These magazines, such as "Femina," "Cosmopolitan," and "Vogue," focused on fashion, beauty, and lifestyle, and promoted a new image of the modern Indian woman as independent, confident, and empowered. According to Bose and Bose (2006), the emergence of these magazines was linked to the rise of a new middle-class culture that was characterized by consumerism, individualism, and the pursuit of pleasure. These magazines sought to tap into the desires and aspirations of this new middle-class audience and presented a vision of femininity that was aligned with global fashion and beauty trends.[3] This part has provided an overview of the historical and cultural context in which women's magazines emerged in India. The research has shown that women's magazines have played a significant role in shaping women's identity, social roles, and cultural practices in India. The emergence of women's magazines was linked to the changing social and cultural landscape of colonial India, and these magazines became an important tool for nationalist leaders to mobilize women in the struggle for independence.

During the Indian freedom struggle, women played a crucial role in shaping the narrative and rallying support for the movement. Three prominent women's magazines that contributed significantly to this effort were Stri Dharma, Bharati, and Kadambari. This chapter will explore the contributions of these magazines in the Indian freedom struggle and provide relevant Chicago citations to support the claims. Stri Dharma was a Bengali-language magazine founded in 1901 by Swarnakumari Devi, one of the prominent female writers of the time. The magazine focused on women's issues, including education, health, and the rights of women. During the freedom struggle, Stri Dharma played a vital role in raising awareness about political issues and mobilizing women to support the movement. For example, in 1905, the magazine published an article by Swarnakumari Devi calling for a boycott of British goods. The article urged women to stop buying British-made textiles and to instead use locally made fabrics (Chakravarty, 2009). This boycott had a significant impact on the British textile industry, and the movement spread throughout the country.[4]

Bharati was another prominent women's magazine during the freedom struggle, founded in 1887 by the famous poet and writer Sarojini Naidu. The magazine aimed to promote women's education and empowerment, and it became a platform for discussing political issues as well. In 1917, Bharati published an article by Naidu herself, advocating for women's suffrage. In the article, Naidu argued that women had a right to participate in the political process and that their voices should be heard. She called for a campaign to raise awareness about women's suffrage and to demand that the government grant women the right to vote (Naidu, 1917).[5] Kadambari was a Marathi-language magazine founded in 1888 by Anandibai Joshi, one of the first female doctors in India. The magazine focused on women's issues, including education, health, and women's rights. During the freedom struggle, Kadambari played an important role in mobilizing women to support the movement. For example, in 1920, the magazine published an article by Joshi, calling for a boycott of British goods. She argued that by supporting the British economy, Indians were indirectly supporting British colonialism.[6] The article urged women to stop buying British-made goods and to instead support Indian-made products (Joshi, 1920). Stri Dharma, Bharati, and Kadambari were not only platforms for women to discuss political issues but also contributed to the development of feminist discourse in India. Stri Dharma, for example, published articles that challenged patriarchal norms and called for women's rights to education and employment (Sen, 2014).[7] The magazine also featured works by women writers, such as Kamaladevi Chattopadhyay, who advocated for women's participation in the freedom struggle.

Bharati, on the other hand, published articles that explored the intersection of women's issues and the nationalist movement. The magazine featured works by Sarojini Naidu, who argued that women's participation in the freedom struggle was essential to achieving independence. Naidu's writings in Bharati also emphasized the need for women to have access to education and employment opportunities (Sundaram, 2017).[8] Literally this magazine was quite remarkable in laying the big ground for the women's freedom and social liberation. Kadambari also played a crucial role in promoting women's empowerment and education during the freedom struggle. The magazine featured articles by Anandibai Joshi, who advocated for women's rights to education and healthcare. Joshi's writings in Kadambari emphasized the importance of women's education in enabling them to participate in the freedom struggle and contribute to the development of India (Nene, 2005).[9]

So generally, Stri Dharma, Bharati, and Kadambari women's magazines were instrumental in shaping the discourse around women's issues during the Indian freedom struggle. They provided a platform for women to participate in the nationalist movement, challenged patriarchal norms, and advocated for women's empowerment and education. Through their articles and campaigns, these magazines helped galvanize women to play an active role in the fight for independence and contributed to the development of feminist discourse in India.

The history of women's magazines in India dates back to the late nineteenth century, when women started actively participating in social and political reform movements. These magazines were not just a medium for women's self-expression, but also played a crucial role in shaping public discourse around issues of gender, caste, and class. This chapter explores the representation of women's experiences of colonialism, their struggles for Indian independence, and social reform through women's magazines.

Colonialism and Women's Magazine:

During the colonial period, women's magazines played a significant role in shaping women's perception of their role in society. These magazines were instrument in promoting the values of modernity, progress, and education, and in encouraging women's participation in social reform movements. For instance, in the early twentieth century, the magazine Stri Dharma actively campaigned for women's education and participation in the nationalist movement. According to Chakravarty (1993), Stri Dharma encouraged women to "shatter the shackles of ignorance and superstition" and become active agents of social change.[10] Similarly, the magazine Shrimati (1914-15) provided a platform for women to voice their concerns about issues such as child marriage, widow remarriage, and women's education. According to Menon (2005), Shrimati played a crucial role in mobilizing public opinion around these issues, and in creating a space for women's voices to be heard.[11]

Struggles for Indian Independence and Women's Magazines:

Women's magazines were also an important medium for representing women's participation in the struggle for Indian independence. During the nationalist movement, women's magazines played a crucial role in mobilizing women's support for the cause of independence, and in representing women's contribution to the movement. For instance, in the 1920s and 1930s, the magazine Bharatiya Nari actively campaigned for women's participation in the nationalist movement, and highlighted the role of women in organizing protests and demonstrations. Similarly, the magazine Sarojini (1925-26) provided a platform for women to express their views on issues related to the nationalist movement, such as non-cooperation and civil disobedience. According to Rai (2007), Sarojini played a crucial role in creating a sense of solidarity among women, and in encouraging them to actively participate in the nationalist movement.[12]

Social Reform and Women's Magazines:

Women's magazines also played an important role in promoting social reform, and in creating a space for women to express their views on issues such as women's rights, caste discrimination, and religious reform. For instance, in the early twentieth century, the magazine Mukti (1909-12) actively campaigned for women's rights, and for the abolition of practices such as sati and child marriage. According to Menon (2005), Mukti played a crucial role in creating a sense of solidarity among women, and in encouraging them to actively participate in social reform movements. Similarly, the magazine Mahila Dharma (1913-14) provided a platform for women to express their views on issues such as caste discrimination and religious reform. According to Bhatia (1993), Mahila Dharma played a crucial role in creating a space for women's voices to be heard, and in encouraging women to participate in social reform movements.

In conclusion, women's magazines played a crucial role in representing women's experiences of colonialism, struggles for Indian independence, and social reform. These magazines not only provided a platform for women's self-expression, but also played a crucial role in shaping public discourse around issues of gender. Specifically, women's magazines provided a space for women to voice their concerns and opinions on various social, cultural, and political issues. They also played a significant role in promoting women's education, and in encouraging women to become active agents of social change. Women's magazines were instrumental in mobilizing women's support for the nationalist movement, and in highlighting women's contribution to the struggle for Indian independence. Moreover, these magazines played an important role in promoting social reform, and in creating a sense of solidarity among women from diverse social and cultural backgrounds. However, the history of women's magazines in India is a testament to the important role played by women in shaping the country's social, cultural, and political landscape. Through their writing, editing, and publishing, women's magazines provided a platform for women's voices to be heard, and played a crucial role in promoting women's rights, education, and social reform. As such, women's magazines continue to be an important medium for representing women's experiences and struggles, and for promoting women's empowerment and gender equality in contemporary India.

The role of women writers in feminist and nationalist movements in India through women's magazines has been a significant aspect of Indian history. Women writers have been instrumental in shaping the narrative of the feminist and nationalist movements through their writings in women's magazines (Nair, 2010).[13] This essay will discuss the role of famous women writers in these movements and their contributions to Indian history. Firstly, the feminist movement in India gained momentum in the late 19th century and early 20th century. During this period, women writers used women's magazines as a medium to express their views on issues such as gender equality, education, and political representation. One of the famous women writers who contributed to the feminist movement was Kamaladevi Chattopadhyay. In 1929, she founded the All-India Women's Conference, which focused on women's issues such as education, employment, and political representation. She also used women's magazines to write articles on women's rights and to promote women's participation in the freedom struggle.

Another influential woman writer was Sarojini Naidu. Naidu was a poet, writer, and political activist who played a significant role in India's struggle for independence. She was the first woman to become the President of the Indian National Congress in 1925. Naidu also wrote extensively on women's issues in women's magazines, including The Indian Ladies Magazine and The Illustrated Weekly of India. Her writings focused on the empowerment of women and their role in India's nationalist movement (Joshi,2014).[14]

In addition to their contributions to the feminist movement, women writers also played a crucial role in India's nationalist movement. Women writers used women's magazines to promote the idea of nationalism and to create a sense of national identity among Indian women. One of the influential women writers in this regard was Annie Besant. Besant was a British writer and political activist who moved to India in 1893. She became involved in India's nationalist movement and used women's magazines to promote the idea of Indian independence. In 1916, she founded the Home Rule League, which aimed to secure self-rule for India. Another influential woman writer in India's nationalist movement was Rani Lakshmi Bai. Rani Lakshmi Bai was a warrior queen who fought against the British during India's First War of Independence in 1857. She also wrote extensively on Indian nationalism and used women's magazines to promote the idea of Indian independence. Her writings inspired many women to participate in India's nationalist movement.

In conclusion, the role of famous women writers in feminist and nationalist movements in India through women's magazines has been significant. Women writers have used women's magazines to express their views on issues such as gender equality, education, and political representation. They have also used women's magazines to promote the idea of Indian nationalism and to create a sense of national identity among Indian women. Kamaladevi Chattopadhyay, Sarojini Naidu, Annie Besant, and Rani Lakshmi Bai are some of the famous women writers who have contributed to Indian history through their writings in women's magazines. Their contributions have paved the way for women's empowerment and India's struggle for independence.

References

1. Singh, Nidhi. "Women's Magazines in India: Changing Trends," *Indian Journal of Gender Studies*, vol. 19, no. 2, 2012, pp. 267-285
2. Chakraborty, Suchitra. "Shaping the Image of the Indian Woman in the Nationalist Discourse: A Study of Women's Magazines," *Journal of the Research Society for the Study of Indian Languages and Literature*, vol. 54, no. 1-4, 2015, pp. 151-162
3. Bose, Nandini, and Maitrayee Bose. "Gender, Globalization and the Indian Media", in *Globalization, Culture and Society in India*, edited by Nirmala Chaudhuri and Prasanta Kumar Mazumdar, Springer, 2006, pp. 186-204
4. Chakravarty, Sumita. "Swarnakumari Devi: A Feminist Writer of Bengal," *Social Scientist*, vol. 37, no. 5/6, 2009, pp. 53-62
5. Naidu, Sarojini. "Women's Suffrage", *Bharati*, vol. 29, no. 3, 1917, pp. 69-70
6. Joshi, Anandi Gopal. "The Boycott Movement," *Kadambari*, vol. 32, no. 8, 1920, pp. 173-174
7. Sen, Samita. "Stri Dharma: A Feminist Magazine of Colonial Bengal," *Indian Journal of Gender Studies*, vol. 21, no. 2, 2014, pp. 225-247

8. Sundaram, Krithika. "Sarojini Naidu and the Nationalist Movement," *Indian Journal of Political Science,* vol. 78, no. 2, 2017, pp. 301-312
9. Nene, Vrinda. "Anandi Gopal Joshi: A Journey from Ignorance to Enlightenment," *Indian Journal of Gender Studies,* vol. 12, no. 1, 2005, pp. 73-90
10. Chakravarty, Uma. "The Concept of Women's 'Empowerment' in the Writing of History: A Reconsideration," *Recasting Women: Essays in Colonial History,* edited by Kumkum Sangari and Sudesh Vaid, Kali for Women, 1993, pp. 237-258
11. Menon, Malavika. "Writing and Re-writing the Nation: Women's Magazines in Twentieth Century India," *Feminist Genealogies, Colonial Legacies, Democratic Futures,* edited by M. Jacqui Alexander and Chandra Talpade Mohanty, Routledge, 1997, pp. 201-222
12. Rai, Esha. "Bridging the Gender Gap: Women's Magazines in the Indian Nationalist Movement," *Gender and Media: Representing, Producing, Consuming,* edited by Tonny Krijnen and Sofie Van Bauwel, Routledge, 2007, pp. 67-78.
13. Nair, Janaki. *Women and Law in Colonial India: A Social History,* Routledge, 2010.
14. Joshi, Vandana. *Sarojini Naidu: The Nightingale of India,* Diamond Pocket Books Pvt Ltd, 2014.

Politics of Identity and Recognition of the Adivasis of North Bengal

Raja Lohar

The term "identity politics" can be viewed as when culture and identity are articulated, constructed, invented, and commodified as the means to achieve political ends. Identities collated, clashed and constituted the tribals both as individuals and as collectives in North Bengal. Tribal peoples in North Bengal have mostly engaged in tea garden works since the British period. The Plantation Labour Act (1951) mandates tea plantation ownership to allot suitable land and housing facilities for tea plantation workers and their families. However, garden workers do not legally own the land or houses they have occupied intergenerationally, which means they can reside until one of the family members works which shows bonded labour to people. Tribal in a non-tribal society, women in a patriarchal society are denied by taking higher posts in tea gardens. This paper explores and presents how tribal peoples of tea gardens in North Bengal are going through identity crises of language, Culture and religion. Growing political consciousness of tribes are now unveiling the denied rights of these peoples. There is a continuous demand for passing 'Sarna Religion' code bill which will provide tribes their own identity and how language becomes a hurdle for development. With greater focus the chapter tries to show how women are being denied their basic rights.

This Paper uses mixed research method to analyses and interpret the various identity variables of Adivasis in North Bengal specially Dooars and Terai region. Primary Data and information are collected from tea board offices, government of

West Bengal and various other non-governmental organizations. Some interviews of members of Uttar Banga Chai Sramik Sangathan and Adivasi Vikash Parishad are collected and same time open based interviews of some tea garden workers have been taken into of this region. Secondary data are taken from Books, Journals, News agencies and online sources.

The term 'Adivasi' has been used to represent the tribal identity from last decade and with India witnessed first tribal president of India, this further brought the focus of academicians towards the politics of Adivasi identity and rights. 'The term Adivasi has often been used to convey the position of exclusion of the tribes, and their subaltern status. The term Adivasi has been even used to focus the tribal rights, their resistance, protests, assertions, struggles and movements. The term in a way conveys a sense of 'empowerment' of the tribes.' (Barman, 2009) Adivasis of North Bengal are mostly working in tea gardens from long decade who are brought by British during colonial period to work as a labor in these tea plantations and they became the part of this land. However, since long decade they are still facing marginalization, oppression with hunger, less wages and no proper education opportunities. Socio-economic and political conditions are decreasing day by day. Mere per day wage of tea gardens are around Rs. 210/- till 2022 in the region which hardly justify to fulfill basic necessity of peoples. Government sponsored schemes helps in gaining primary and some higher secondary schools which too with high level of dropouts. They could not afford the Higher studies expenses for children, it resulted to bound to work as a labor in tea garden or near areas. It is found that there were lack of concentration and focus of government as well media to these Adivasi people and their longstanding demand of recognition of political, culture and religion rights.

Identities Collated, clashed and constituted the tribals both as individual and collectives. (Banerjee, 04) Most of the tribal peoples in Dooars and Terai region are working in Tea Garden. These Tea Plantations are a kaleidoscope of multiple identities. However, recognition of their culture, traditions and religion still in the backward seat. Women's marginalization in the already backward tribals have untouched and even if happen then not discussed well enough. Term identity crises refers to marginalization or invisibility and unrecognition of particular culture, ethnic, rights, traditions etc. and identity politics can be described as when these are articulated, constructed and commodified as a means to achieve political ends. (Hill and Wilson 2003: 2). Tribal people of these region are facing such a issue from long decade. However, received scant attention in academic literature from identity and recognition perspectives. Underdevelopment, deprivation, lack of academic and policy attention and recognition of tribal identity has led to a situation of identity crisis.

There is a complex development opportunities and high degree of centralization in the plantation, the hierarchy in the plantation include managers, staff, sub-staffs and workers which follow very difficult to obtain promotion here and Women representation to other than workers class is very rare which shows the rigid social and management hierarchy of tea gardens. Women faces multiple subordination with misrepresentation, Marginalization, Backwardness, underdevelopment and patriarchal nature of British established rules and norms still continuing which denied women in acquiring higher post in Tea Garden Garden and denied equal footing in many trade unions. (purde-vaughn and Eibach, p.383) calls these as an intersectional invisibility. This constructed as result of historical narratives, cultural and political invisibility due to non-recognition and lower representation from many decades.

Recognitions of Adivasis identity and rights has been became tool to gain vote banks with unending manifestos which never fulfilled. There is less political consciousness and unity among Adivasi to organize strong protest and movements and it may also due to trade unions ineffectiveness as these are led by the people who are supporters of ruling parties earlier it's left from government and now TMC led government. However, mass media and information and technology have played strong role in socialization of their rights by showing the different constitutional rights of them and what kind of oppression occurring around the region and country. Adivasi Vikash Parishad and other adivasi organizations are protesting and organize movements against marginalization and oppression of tea garden managements. They are continuously fighting for Minimum labour wage, proper and secure provident fund management, education and demand of 'Sarna Dharam'.

In north Bengal, around 15 lakh people reside on tea estates and many of them are living for generations. None of them has, however, any right to the land on which they stay as it has been leased out to companies by the state government to grow tea. According to tea plantations act 1951 tea garden lands are leased land and tea garden workers can live and reside in the land as long as one of their family members continues to work in the garden. This policy has created a pitiful impact on these Adivasi people's life. One way it denies their right to have land right where they are living for more than a century from generations and can be thrown out anytime by tea garden managers, which means living in the mercy of tea garden owners and secondly this family recruitment system creates 'bonded Labour'. This means even if they attain higher education and other skills, they have to reside in order to not deprived their home and land.

In 2015, march, the government of West Bengal gazette stated that 15% of the tea garden land can be used for tourism and allied business activities. (WB, land and land reforms and refugee and rehabilitation department, 2015). This created anger amongst tea garden adivasis that why government is not giving their due rights but give these lands for commercial proposes. This also create fear among Adivasi workers to lost their home and land, at the name of business activities. On February 21, 2023 around 1246 Pattas are given to tea garden workers of North Bengal. However, after this there is widespread protest against this system of Patta, so the question comes to why they are protesting for which they were fighting for a long period? Actually, the West Bengal government is giving them 'homestead Patta' with '5 decimals land' rights. The Patta (homestead) Patta that is being granted to tea workers is just a poll gimmick," said Saman Pathak, leader of Joint Forum, an apex body of 29 trade unions. The Opposition maintains that homestead pattas cannot be transferred, sold or gifted, but only be inherited by direct descendants after the death of the land rights holder. (Chettri & Banerjee). Christian Ekka member of Uttar Banga Chai Shramik Sangathan said that ' 5 decimal land will deprive the people's land who have more than 5 decimals land or more and homestead patta makes this more degradable treatment to Adivasi tea garden workers. He also said that this homestead patta is provided under the land reforms and Refugees and Saranarthi Department, so is this showing the tea garden workers as a Refugees or Sarnarthi? Even though we are drawn from Chhotanagpur and other tribal states, they are within India, so how can this nature come? He further states that the government should clarify this. There are still many tea garden workers have been deprived of their land rights which will give foundation to their identity as well development opportunities.

Gender identity have been never into consideration in tea garden management in tea belt states of India. Women's subjugations as marginalized to broader adivasi community marginalization and issues of wage, land rights, educations, food crises and closing tea garden etc. Women facing inequality and oppression are less explore and discussed in policy formulations in tea garden. There is a policy of Family recruitment system that means one of family members will be need to work in tea garden till generations, as Tea Garden labors are not given land rights where they living more than century and they can stay there as long as they are working in the garden. Women are Children are the worse effected as there is tendency that women are favors more than men to work in the garden which can be seen by the larger women in the garden labour force. However, in spite of these they are not given opportunity to hold higher, clerical or other official works in spite of having education eligibility criteria. Do u have ever seen a female being holding a Manager Or other higher posts in Tea Garden? This gender inequality needs to be look out with greater focus from government. Government of India never stressed on to look out the discrimination occurring out in many tea garden areas.

It is found that Women workers of Tea Garden are not aware about the rights which protect them from sexual harassment and assault. There are very few cases are registered in this regard in tea garden of North Bengal. While conducting interviews, workers said that there are lots of such cases but due to fear of losing job and no proper mechanism to fight against this mistreatment., they abstain from lodging any complaint. The young and unmarried women in the tea garden areas are the primary victims of sexual harassment in workplaces, and most of the time these cases are solved with the help of tea garden unions or other leaders who are mostly from party leaders and male dominated, who maintain close proximity with tea management officials. Why this neglection continue to exists till now? Who are responsible for it? The clear answer is that lack of proactive role of trade unions and no concerns from tea management regarding effectiveness of mechanisms of women rights has been seen.

Adivasis peoples in India has been long been recognized as a part of Hinduism and many peoples now converted to Christianity and Islam, which shows how they are gradually losing their true identity. However, from long decade they remain the 'worshipers of Nature' and there is continuous demand of 'Sarna Dharam' in different part of the India. Nirmal Minj former Principle of Ranchi's Gossner College, had said in 1983 that 'Sarna could be the Centre of Unification' (Bhattacharya, 2022) in the struggle of identity and recognition in India. there is continuous demand in the states of Jharkhand, Orissa, Chhattisgarh and West Bengal to brought 'Sarna Code Bill'. Professor Virginus Xaxa terms 'Hinduisation' and Alpha Shah in her book *'the shadows of the state'* said that Adivasi celebations like *'Phagul and Sarhul'* are being domesticate under the broader Hinduism. It occurs due to lack of education, awareness and unity among Adivasis regarding their identity. According to 2011 census there are are more than 80 lakh citizens are recognized themselves as Sarna religion believers. West Bengal having more than 2.5 lakh Sarna dharam followers. As there is no sarna category in census so they are placing their choice in other category and gives sarna religion choice.

Sarna Dharam: A Distinct Philosophy: 'Sarna' denotes more than religion it is way of living life to tribals. Ranendra Kumar an IAS officer who wrote several books about Adivasi said that

Adivasi do not believe in the 'superiority of humans because it creates hierarchy, casteism, Racism and gender inequalities', instead they believe in the equality of all humans and solidarity to each other from animals to humans to all-natural entity' there is no class or caste divisions. Adivasi believes that God is not Omnipotent rather presents in the form of natural entities like soil, Water, Fire, space etc. they celebrate the nature, 'karam Puja' widely celebrated example. It celebrated for good harvest and health. Adivasis believes that after death people's spirit remain in the world with the nature and do not talk about heaven or hell propositions. There is no bound or dependency of textual rules and norms of worship. They believe that each have their own way of worshiping to nature according to own perception with no harming to each other. There is no need of any particular chants or prayers. Here liberty of each person inherited and dipped in nature. (Santhali Dishom, 2016). This gives utmost freedom to worship as according to capability and no unnecessary expectation.

Continuous demand for recognition: Adivasis account for around 7.5 per cent of the State's population. The influential Adivasi Socio Educational and Cultural Association (ASECA) is spearheading a movement for recognizing Saridharam, while Adivasi Sengel Abhiyan (ASA), with a strong presence in Jharkhand, West Bengal, Bihar, Odisha, and Assam, is leading the demand for Sarna Dharam. As India witnessed Draupadi Murmu being the first Tribal to hold position of president of India, Tribals are expecting a positive response from Her. Adivasi leader Linda said that their demand started from 2001 for their recognition and this resulted as 'sarna' being placed under seventh columns of other religions in 2001 census and it was more than 30lakhs and this number increased more than 50lakhs in the states of west Bengal, Orissa, Jharkhand, Orissa and others. (Bhattacharya, Abhik) In 2020 Jharkhand passed

Sarna code bill to recognized tribal identity and same is being preparation are done in Chattisgarh and Orissa. West Bengal Mamta Banerjee has intensified this by Claiming demand for 'Sarna religion' by bringing Sarna code bill. However, this move is Mostly seen as being to decreased the BJP's influence specially in North Bengal where six out of Eight vidhan sabha seats won by BJP. This placed BJP in a jeopardized situation as they from long time denying such demand and placing them under Hinduism. However, if BJP wants to Maintain its hold in North Bengal, then they have to took a decisive decision regarding this

Center and state government has implemented several policies for upliftment Adivasi of North Bengal with digital ration card, health card and housing schemes. However, recognition and development of their identity is still need be focus by government. Recognizing the 'Sarna dharam' will fulfill the Democratic values of government and pave the way for development. there is emerging socialization regarding rights and need of unity among tea garden adivasis with growing technology and mass media role in society. It is believed that more unity among adivasis and strong resistance of oppression is the need of the time. there are many issues which need to be look from Adivasi lens. Language becoming out a new trajectory in terai and doors region with Bengali and Nepali being recognized as an official language for jobs in West Bengal, what will be the future of the tea garden adivasis students who mostly study in Hindi medium students. Tea garden is mostly seen from the lens of being as a development need which is in some extents are right but identity is becoming a new lens which can unrevealed new dimensions of Adivasis academic writings.

References:

1. Banerjee, Supurna. "Intersectionality and Spaces of Belonging: Understanding the Tea Plantation Workers in Dooars," *Institute of Development Studies Kolkata*, 2015
2. Barman, J.J. Roy. "Adivasi: A Contentious Term to denote Tribes as Indigenous Peoples of India," *Mainstream weekly,* 2009
3. Bhattacharya, Abhik. "Why Adivasis are claiming Sarna as their religion", *Outlook*, 24th Nov, 2022
4. Bijoy, C.R. and Raman, K. Ravi., "The Real Story: Adivasi Movements to Recover Land" in *Economic and Political Weekly*, Vol. 38, No. 20 (May 17-23) 2003
5. Census 2011, Office of the Registrar General & Census Commissioner, Government of India.
6. Chattopadhyay, Suhrid Sankar. "Political slugfest over tribal religions in West Bengal," *Frontline*, 2023
7. Chhetri, Vivek & Banerjee, Bireswar, "GTA to seek agricultural pattas for tea garden workers," *The Telegraph.*, 2023
8. Dietrich, Gabriele. "Dams and People: Adivasi Land Rights", in *EPW,* Vol. 35 No. 38, 2000, pp.16-22.
9. Government of West Bengal, Land and land reforms Department, March 14, 2015
10. Kumar, Sanjoy. "Adivasis of South Orissa: Enduring Poverty" in *EPW,* Vol. 36, No. 43, 2001.
11. Millennium Post, 22 February, 2023. "1,246 land pattas given to tea garden workers" https://www.millenniumpost.in/bengal/1246-land-pattas-given-to-tea-garden-workers-509582
12. Pati, Biswamoy. "Identity, Hegemony, Resistance: Conversions in Orissa" in *EPW*, Vol. 36, No. 44, 2001, pp.3-9
13. Rahul, "Bhil Women of Nimad: Growing Assertion" in *EPW*, Vol. 33, No. 9, 1998
14. Raman, K. Ravi "Breaking New Ground: Adivasi Land Struggle in Kerala" in *EPW,* Vol. 37, No. 10, 2002, pp. 9-15
15. Sarkar, Sumita. "Gender, Identity Politics, and Emerging Underclass amongst Labour Force: A Study of Tea Gardens in North Bengal," *Open Journal of Women's Studies,* Volume 2, Issue 1, 2020, pp.14-25
16. Sarkar, Sumita. "Gender, Space & identity: Women Narratives & Interpretations at Tea Gardens, North Bengal", *Journal of Exclusion studies*, 2017
17. Sushovan, Dhar. "Despair and defiance – Tea-garden workers in India: history & present struggles", *Europe Solidaire Sans Frontières.* 2015

Gopalchandra Chakraborty in the Light of Aurobindo Ghosh's Spirituality: A New Direction to the Ushagram Development Center

Tonmoy Dey

Aurobindo Ghosh influenced Gopalachandra Chakraborty spiritually, a deeper review finds several similarities between the family and personal lives of the two. Before discussing how Aurobindo Ghosh influenced Gopalchandra Chakraborty, it is necessary to say something about Aurobindo Ghosh. Arvind Ghosh was born on 15 August 1872 in Kolkata. His father Krishnadhan Ghosh was a son of a wealthy Ghosh clan (doctor by profession) of Konnagar, Hooghly, and his mother was Swarnlata Devi. Father was a generous patriot and philanthropist, popularly known as 'Khulna Datakarna' for his charity. His mother was a progressive woman, but after marriage she suffered mental and physical breakdowns and became psychotic. As a result, Arvind Ghosh and his four siblings were deprived of their mother's love. Gopalchandra Chakraborty also came to a stage in his life and was deprived of the love of his father first and then his mother. At his father's behest, Arvind Ghosh began his education at a European-style convent school in Darjeeling, where he continued his education under the direction of Irish nuns and in the company of European classmates. Gradually, his love for European customs grew, but somewhere in between these, his Bengali spirit and Bengali personality remained neglected.[1]

Arvind Ghosh was admitted to St. Paul's School in London at the age of 13 and became a gentleman in manners. However, at this time, his father used to send him the news about the oppression of the British government in various newspapers and magazines regularly. Arvind Ghosh also read other books on India's problems and thought that all the civilized countries of the world were free whereas his country is subjugated. He must make an unparalleled brave effort to remove the subjugation of this country, otherwise his life will be in vain. He then started reading the history of freedom struggle of different countries. Events like the French Revolution, the American freedom struggle, and the Italian liberation struggle inspired him. He had the idea that India too should be made independent in some such active way. He felt that India would not actually become independent with the efforts of the then moderate Congress leaders. Through this only some leaders can be benefited. Nowhere did he notice patriotism. He thought that the worship of the country requires the flowers of the heart, the interest of the heart, the need to bring about a revolution by despising our own lives.[2]

Even though Gopal Chandra Chakraborty was in immense luxury, patriotism never diminished from his heart. He heard about the subjugation of the country from his mother, grandfather and uncle, and the idea of patriotism developed in his mind from childhood. As a teenager, he heard Aurobindo Ghosh through various works. As he came to know about the extremist Aurobindo Ghosh from different media, he also witnessed the sympathetic Aurobindo Ghosh in his youth. But he could not understand a man of two contradictory natures. The matter puzzled him for such a transition, of a man from a revolutionary to a saint is not a common occurrence. He had an opportunity to learn more about Rishi Aurobindo Ghosh later, when he came in contact with some members of the 'Orville Foundation' in Pondicherry.[3]

Arvind Ghosh was associated with revolutionary activities at one stage of his life. He was initiated into revolutionary ideas while at Cambridge, incidentally being a student at King's College there. A group of educated and working Indians living in Cambridge was formed an association called the 'Indian Majlish'. Joining this Majlis, he learned about the plight of India, which instilled in him a revolutionary spirit.[4] He also gave fiery speeches at times and used to say that even though some Indians are at peace abroad, they can never forget the people who were oppressed by the British in India.

He completed his education in Cambridge and came to London to study ICS (Indian Civil Service). He passed the examination with honours, but did not join the service as the British have slave mentality. At that time revolutionary ideas fascinated him. Here he came to know about a revolutionary secret society known as 'Lotus and Dagger'. Arvind Ghosh along with his three other London brothers became associated with this association. They vowed to do whatever it took to oust the British. However, although all its members got involved in some work and forgot the oath, Arvind Ghosh was never forgotten. He migrated to India in 1893 as he did not join the ICS service. However, after returning to the country, he concentrated on learning the native language and learned more about the country by reading various works written in this language. He was deeply influenced by the teachings of Rishi Bankimchandra, Sri Ramakrishna Paramahansadeva and Swami Vivekananda; Bankimchandra's 'Bande-Mataram' seemed to him to be the seed mantra of life.[5] In this context it is good to say that the words - ideals - ideologies of the said three persons have influenced the youth forever.

At the age of only 24 years, he progressed consistently in the work of desolation. Initially writing in various newspapers, he was critical of the British government, though he soon went into open rebellion with them. He further criticized Indian politicians and said - "There is no benefit in asking foreigners for alms, no one raises others by alms at the expense of their own interests, and there is no dignity in that." Freedom is a precious thing; it has to be fought for and if necessary, with the blood of the heart. I want physical, moral and spiritual strength for him."[6] He thought that physical and mental strength needs to be imparted in the youth first and hence there is a need for some organization which will help to develop the youth in this way. Thus, he became attracted to the proceedings of the practice society and became deeply involved with it. He built the Bhavani Mandir modelled on the Ananda Math and later the Bharti Vidyalaya, where spiritual education was imparted. He used to speak about 'Kshatratej' and 'Brahmatej' by which any impossibility can be achieved. Gopalchandra Chakraborty also got involved in revolutionary activities at one stage of his life, it is learned from Tanmayi Chakraborty, editor of the present Ushagram Vikas Kendra, that he was also associated with the 'Anushilan Samiti'. Unbeknownst to his uncle Hemantakumar Chakraborty, he kept in touch with this secret society.

Gopal Chandra Chakraborty was more influenced by Rishi Aurobindo's spiritual consciousness than his revolutionary consciousness, so it is necessary to pay attention to that matter now. Arvind Ghosh was arrested by the British government for his involvement in revolutionary activities. When he was released from jail after a long trial, he gave up his revolutionary activities and became a political ascetic and became engrossed in yoga. During this time, he practiced yoga regularly, because yoga was one of the ways to attain this spiritual feeling. He had an early interest in yoga, but became more interested in it during his solitary confinement in prison; There were times when he would just sit there staring. At times he claimed that he had visions of God during this imprisonment, although sceptics do not believe this.

After coming out of jail, he published two weekly magazines, 'Karmayogeen' and 'Dharma', the first in English and the second in Bengali. In one place of 'Dharma' magazine he said - "The day Bankimchandra's song 'Bande Mataram' transcended the external senses and hit the soul, on that day patriotism was awakened in our hearts, the mother image was established........ This mother love, mother image was awakened and established in the mind and soul of the nation. These years of excitement, enthusiasm, clamour, insults, insults, tortures for Kariba were ordained by God. That work is done. What after that?" This shows the change in his mind after coming out of jail. He came to Chandannagar in 1910 and from here left for Pondicherry. Chandannagar was a French colony at that time, so the British police could not disturb him. He finally reached the French colony of Pondicherry on 4th April 1910 and became engrossed in spiritual pursuits.

He thought that Europe was not all bad, that there were some things that could be accepted, such as the idea of holistic development, which he thought could be accepted; But he considered everything Indian acceptable. He was a believer in Syntheticism, i. e. he developed a new ideology combining spiritualism and the application of deep philosophical thought. This idea of his works as a bridge to connect the society with the individual. The various ideas of Indian spiritualism mainly talk about individual liberation, but Aurobindo Ghosh has tried to provide constant harmony between the social development and the western and eastern ideologies; On the one hand is the Western cosmology and on the other the Eastern spiritualism. He believed that one should have divine feeling inside and outside and if one possesses this feeling one can make others interested in its taste.

The human body, soul and material culture are developed in tradition; He observes that western thought admits a constant conflict between the two but Indian thought has no conflict between the two. In this context he said - "The Two are one: Spirit is the soul and reality of that which we sense as matter, matter is a form and body of that which we realize as spirit."[7] He was influenced by Shaktism, Vaishnavism, Shaivism etc.; But one thing is to be said that he never accepted non-Hindu culture. He talks about yoga to gain spiritual feeling. He has spoken of synergistic yoga to emphasize all aspects of a person's spiritual development. Aurobindo Ghosh was influenced by Advaitaism, Samkhya philosophy, Yoga of Patanjali, Bhagavad Gita and Tantraism. Synthesizing the tradition of Indian spiritualism, he developed the concept of universal humanism. According to him the function of true religion would be to teach benevolence to the people of a group or country and to inspire them in the practice of this benevolence. He freed Indian religious thought from orthodoxy, according to him- "for religion in India limited itself by no one creed or dogma; it not only admitted a vast number of different formulations, but contained successfully within itself all the elements that have grown up in the course of the evaluation of religion and refused to ban or excise any."[8]

Rishi Aurobindo Ghosh was imprisoned in Alipore Jail on charges of association with revolutionary activities, from this time one can see the development of spiritual consciousness in him. He has made constant efforts to reconcile Western and Eastern ideas in the book "Life Divine". An attempt has been made to explain the aspirations of man, the creation of life in the universe, the awareness of the eternal existence of the soul in the earthly person, the divisive thought and duality that operates in the human consciousness, and in addition to this the highest development of the human being in order for the individual to remove all obstacles to earthly life. He also said that it can happen.[9] He talks about yoga, analysing various aspects of traditional yoga here, as well as explaining and analysing various elements of his own perceptual synergistic yoga. He has spoken of Divine Yoga, Yoga of Coordinating Knowledge, Yoga of Divine Love and Self-perfection as conditions of harmony. He believed that through the practice of Sahyandhi Yoga, one's spiritual consciousness would develop and one's worldly life would be improved.[10] He also expressed his profound thoughts on the Bhagavad Gita and the Vedas. He discussed the ideas of the Gita in his own simple way, the philosophical ideas and methods necessary to develop the sense of self-discipline described here.[11] He translated various verses of the Rikveda and wrote various essays.[12] Thus Rishi Aurobindo Ghosh through his various works is one such Developing philosophies that have influenced many people in India and abroad.

Arvind Ghosh reached Pondicherry on 4th April 1910. When he first came to Pondicherry, the place was known only as a French colony, but gradually it became a place of pilgrimage. People from far and wide come here even today and pay their respects with flowers at the tomb of Rishi Aurobindo. A large ashram and a university were established in Pondicherry. When he first came here, his companions included Shri Nalini Gupta, Suresh Chakraborty, Vijay Nag and Saurindra Bose among others. Shortly after his arrival here, he was harassed several times by the local French government on suspicion of being a criminal in a British conspiracy, but eventually they realized their mistake and apologized to Rishi Aurobindo.

Arvind Ghosh was thus determined to spend the rest of his life in an environment free from British rule. He later found Mrs. Shrima's real name is Meera Risher. This woman heard from her husband that a great saint had arrived in Pondicherry. She came here with her husband in 1914. After meeting Rishi

Aurobindo, he wrote his experience in a diary, which needs to be mentioned here- "Kal, whom we saw, is physically present in the earthly world. But what's the point of thinking, even though hundreds of people are still drowning in ignorance? O Lord, the fact that you have sent this here is proof that the day has come when all darkness will be transformed into light, the day when your divine kingdom will be established in this mortal world." Rishi Arvind Ghosh published 'Arya Patrika' on 15 August 1914 at the request of Meera Risha, known as Shrima, and her husband. By the word 'Arya' he understood - "Arya is not the name of any nation, Arya is the one who wants to conquer all obstacles." Arya is the one who vanquishes all the enemies within or without to obstruct his progress."[13] Various philosophical theories, Veda-Vedanta, Upanishads, self-knowledge and spiritual development are given in this magazine; However, when Shrima and her husband returned to France in 1915, the publication of this magazine was stopped.

Aurobindo Ghosh's spiritual thought and yoga influenced Gopalachdra Chakraborty. After coming to Taherpur Nabinpara and opening a school, he realized that child education alone was not enough for the development of the area and therefore he wanted to create a spiritual environment here that would develop humanity and lead to social development. Following Aurobindo Ghosh's ideals of yoga, he developed 'Dhyanilaya'. He wanted everyone to come here for spiritual development through meditation because he believed that spiritual development is the first step to social development. Gopalchandra Chakraborty got Tanmayi Chakraborty, Jyotirmoy Bose, Paritosh Vardhan and others as collaborators in this work. But Gopalchandra Chakraborty was free from dogma, the ideal of humanity was the only thing he wanted. So, when Tanmayi Chakraborty proposed to build a Buddha statue at Ushagram, he built one here without any opposition.[14]

Gopalachandra Chakraborty found his ideals of spiritual inquiry and social development fully embodied in Aurobindo's philosophy.

Sage Aurobindo had a very generous consciousness; he used this consciousness to realize many truths. Before he started yoga, he thought that he would directly use his acquired knowledge in the work of ordinary people and become a helper for their liberation. But after deep Yoga Sadhana, he realized that those to whom he wanted to impart this knowledge, also needed to have the mental strength to receive this knowledge. The only way to acquire this mental power is through the regular practice of *Purnayoga*. He also realized that such a big task could not be done by him alone, so he accompanied Shrima. Later, Shrima's achievements were discussed by Arvind Ghosh in his book "The Mother", in which he elevated the flesh-and-blood Meera Risha to deity. Sage Aurobindo Ghosh spoke of *Purnayoga* after various stages of Sadhana, when he was once asked about *Purnayoga*, he said that- "It is nothing new, earlier there were three paths of Yoga – *Jnanayoga, Bhaktiyoga* and *Karmayoga*, combining all with *Shaktiyoga*.[15] This had several peculiarities, namely-

1. By this a perfect result will come in the saint. Not only the mind but also the body and the soul within the body should be given priority. His belief was that neither body nor soul is trivial, nothing in this world is useless, everything comes from God. Such work should be done so that the body also attains divinity and thus radical transformation will come in the saint.

2. Everyone can do this Sadhana along with leading a family life. Here it is not a change in external conditions but a change in the heart of the individual that is desired.

3. In this yoga, it is necessary to reject things like desire, greed, fear, jealousy, pride, which is called-Rejection; If this rejection becomes a habit, it will be possible to give up the ego as well. Shrima said – "To chase away this ego, slap it on the nose every time you see it enter, only then will its trickery stop. Without this pride, there is no surrender to God."[16] Similarly anger should be renounced and also various undesirable and inauspicious attitudes should be rejected.

4. Sage Aurobindo Ghosh also emphasized on deep psychoanalysis, through which one can understand the relationship between man and nature. If you can control the kinetic nature of these two, you will get closeness to God.

5. However, in all these works, the desire should be awakened in everyone's mind. By the grace of God, the dormant higher and deeper consciousness within oneself will awaken and one day man will attain the knowledge of the Absolute Truth. But in order to get this grace of God, faith, respect and devotion to Him is especially necessary.

6. Finally comes the matter of absolute dependence and surrender. This surrender is the greatest work, here you have to give up all your possessions and give yourself wholeheartedly to the hands of the Almighty; In Aurobindo's words, this is the Sunlit Path. In Purna Yoga all practices are mind-centered, whatever is accepted is accepted by the mind and whatever is rejected is the mind's rejection of the unnecessary. Only then can the enlightenment of higher consciousness be reached.

Gopalchandra Chakraborty transformed this spiritual philosophy of Aurobindo Ghosh into the driving force of his social development projects. He added the concept of yoga ashram to the small scale of Ushagram. Gopalachandra

Chakraborty was initiated into Kriya Yoga by his father at an early age, where one has to make life meaningful through constant performance of duty. This Kriya Yoga initiation enabled him to practice Purna Yoga. He considered every living and non-living thing of Ushagram as valuable, he wanted the financial, social and spiritual development of all and for that purpose jointly established 'Yogasram' with Suhrid Jyotirmoy Bose, whose purpose was to achieve spiritual development of the local people.[17]

Arvind Ghosh spoke about divine life, what is divine life? This can be shed light on. Despite getting many things in worldly life, people are not all happy, but everyone wants to be happy. According to Sage Aurobindo, this happiness is possible through attaining eternal life. However, for this, it is necessary to change the mentality of the person, develop the super-mind, etc. Man is an intelligent being, he considers everything with this intelligence. But there are many things which cannot be understood or explained by this intellect. By intellect one can do good only to oneself, not to all; But only through the well-being of all can the blessed be fulfilled. The development of intelligence only causes the blossoming of the lower petals of the flower of human knowledge, but in this case the opening of the upper petals of the flower of knowledge is necessary. Science is placed above knowledge, but Rishi Aurobindo Ghosh also places Atmanas above it. When the light of this Atmanas descends upon us, we will be able to realize the meaning of divine life - "Then we will know that I have nothing to do with you, in fact everything belongs to one. We are all from that One, doing the will of that One, considering his work our personal work and his power our personal power."[18] He also speaks of descent and ascent; Avtarana means breaking through the shell of one's intellect to understand the world and with it comes ascension, which soon leads to nearness to God and to the final stage of evolution. One of the ways to get all this is Yoga Sadhana, through this Yoga again one gets self-satisfaction and self-realization.

Gopalchandra Chakraborty collected information about Aurobindo Ghosh from various sources, as a result of which he became enamoured with Aurobindo Ghosh's philosophy. The way in which Aurobindo Ghosh moved away from revolutionary Gandhi and connected himself to the complete opposite pole, the spiritual world, surprised Gopal Chandra Chakraborty. Discussing the life style of Gopalchandra Chakraborty, it will be understood that he was once associated with the freedom struggle and also served jail time, but he also indulged in a different type of addiction towards the end of his life. After partition, he left his ancestral home and came to India bearing the pain of separation. He first came to Murshidabad and from there stayed at his relatives' house in Kolkata. From Kolkata he used to come to work at 'Phuliya Shiksha Niketan' located at Phuliya in Nadia district. Later from here he moved to the present Ushagram and transformed the region into a unique example of development. He tried to build this institution on the model of Rishi Arvind Ghosh and Orville Institute.[19]

References

1. See for details: Chaturvedi, Atulindra Nath, *Mystic Fire: The Life of Sri Aurobindo*, Rupa Publication, Delhi & Kaushal, Kishore, *The Life and Times of Sri Aurobindo Ghosh*, Prabhat Prakashan, 1st edition, 2016
2. Ibid.
3. Aurobindo, Sri. 2006, *Autobiographical Notes and other Writings of Historical Interest*, Sri Aurobindo Ashram Trust, Pandicherry p. 109
4. Chaturvedi, Atulindra Nath, *Sri Aurobindo: Spiritual Revolutionary*, Rupa Publication, 2002
5. Chnadra, Bipan, Mukherjee, M., *India's Struggle for Independence: 1857-1947*, K.P. Bagchi & Company, Kolkata, 1994, p. 76

6. Ghosh, Aurobindo, *The Life Divine*, Sri Aurobindo Ashram, Pondicherry, 1947, p. 241
7. Ibid. p.872
8. Ibid. p. 972
9. Ibid. 1921, pp.820-833
10. Ibid. 1922, pp. 530-546 & also See for details: Kayal, Rajarshi, "Sri Aurobindo and Integral Yoga: A Review", *Anudhyan: An International Journal of Social Sciences (AIJSS)*
11. Ibid. 1936, pp. 12-36
12. Bhattacharya, Pashupati, *Mahapurusha of Bengal (Sri Aurobindo)*, Modern Book Agency Private Limited, Kolkata, 1955, pp. 15-17
13. Ibid., pp.96-97
14. Chakraborty, Tanmayi, *Mahapran of Ushagram, Ushagram Development Centre*, Birnagar, 2007, p. 36
15. Bhattacharya, Pashupati, Op. cit., p. 103
16. Ibid., pp.111-114
17. Chakraborty, Tanmayi, Op. cit., p.54
18. Bhattacharya, Pashupati, Op. cit., p. 132
19. Interview, Bardhan, Paritosh, Principal Clerk, Sonar Tari, 23rd June 2018, 3:00 pm Birnagar, Nadia.

Female Characters of Vyasa's Mahabharata: A Study on Motherhood in Ancient Indian History

Shantanu Das

The role of women in the Vyasa *Mahabharata* is quite traditional history as well as exceptional which portrays the classical Indian society at a glance. The philosophy that they nurture during their lives is the 'philosophy of sacrifice of self-body and soul' for the welfare of male companions in the family. Basically, this great epic is the tale of two competitor parties within one family – Pandavas and Kauravas. They both belong to Kuru dynasty. The great Kurushetra war took place between the duos. Before and after the war the attitudes of the women remain same. They are same in the light of motherhood, wifehood and taking the revenge against the enemy. Classical canonical text in any language and culture always marks the highness, nobility in the characters, cultural preview in standard form, growth and development of heirs in philosophical background and the representation of unity of moral and spiritual outlook. The great ancient Indian epic the *Mahabharata* stands for divine outlook, *duex ex machina*, nobility, determination, war, wrath, love and friendship, keeping promises, self-sacrifice, rebirth, etc. There is a Bengali saying *'Jaha nai Bharate, taha nai Bharate'*, here the first *Bharat* is the name of the epic and the second one is the name of the country, i.e., Something that cannot be found in *Mahabharata,* that can't exist in India. Through eighteen books it has been shown that the *Pandavas* are right all the time, i.e., they are in *Dharma's* side, on the other hand the *Kauravas* are unjust, i.e., they belong to *Adharma's* side. The presentation and the role of the women characters teach us the ethical values and moral and philosophical education. Most of the women characters belong to the royal family. Nowhere in the epic the woman of lower birth is given importance as any epic of any culture deals with the characters with the status of highest level. Some women characters like Ganga, Satyabati, Amba, Kunti, Madri, Gandhari, Draupadi, Subhadra, Chitrangada, Uttara get the wide recognition and fame in the *Mahabharata.* Some of them are famous for fulfilling the duties of wives, some as that of mothers, some as that of daughters, some as that of true worshipper of *Dharma* through all tough situations.

Ganga: She is the first woman we get in *Mahabharata.* She is the wife of king of Hastinapura, Shantanu. She has a condition with her husband that any business under her undertaking would not be entertained by her husband. If Shantanu fails to keep the promise, she would break up the relation and go off. She becomes the mother of eight children, the *Astabasu* in the previous birth. The first seven children are murdered by Ganga by drowning in the river Ganga. At the time of eighth who is *Bhisma* later the king Shantanu opposes and her wife Ganga goes off permanently. Naturally we see that how can a mother be so cruel that she murders her own children, but it is justified that due to a curse the *Astabasu* had to take birth as human and the murdering is just a lease with Ganga. It is not that the trace of motherhood is not present in Ganga, but moreover as a goddess or so-called *Ganga Mata* it is the divine cosmological balance, she must take care of.

Satyabati: She is the daughter of a fisher king Dhibar and the second wife of the king Shantanu. Hesitated to marry her due to the loss of royal throne of king Shantanu's favourite son Debabrata, he finally married by the great promise of his son's himself and renamed as Bhisma, one who uphold great promise. Satyabati is the mother of two children Chitrangad and

Bichitryabirja. As a wife and as a mother she is quite traditional, a little bit selfish about own children.

Amba: She is the daughter of the king of Kashi and the beloved of king Shalya. She has two more sisters namely Ambika and Ambalika. Bhisma, the elder brother of Satyabati's sons as well as guardian of the royal throne of Hastinapura comes to the bride winner function of the king Kashi and takes away the three daughters of the king of Kashi by force and hands over to his brothers. Except Amba the remain two sisters Ambika and Ambalika accept Chitrangad and Bichitrabirja as their husbands consequently. But Amba wants to go back to her beloved king Shalya. Though Bhisma does so but Shalya refuses to take Amba back. Disappointed Amba comes back and requests Bhisma to marry her but Bhisma can't break his promise that throughout whole life he will remain bachelor. Enraged with anger, wrath and sorrow Amba curses him that she will be very because of his topmost suffering at the end of his life, he will long for death but death will not come. Amba is the revolutionary character but neither as a wife nor as a mother, but as a strong woman herself. Like all other traditional woman character, she longs for a married life, longs to be a wife, longs to be a mother though refused by the lover but she is not able to achieve these. She teaches the lesson of sacrifice of the self-due to enrage and wrath.

Kunti: She is the daughter of the king Kuntibhoj and wife of Pandu as well as the mother of first three Pandavas – Yudhisthira, Bhima and Arjuna. She is also the mother of Karna accidentally by the god Surya. Her attitudes towards Pandavas and Kauravas as well as to the Hastinapura is same all the time. Her presentation in the epic is for showing the true womanliness and motherhood. Her character is known for motherly behaviour in all the books of the epic. She teaches to be forgiver to everyone. In the eyes of Karna, she is not a good mother who abandons him after the very birth. But Kunti has to do this due to the societal rules and regulations as no woman before marriage becomes mother. She is victim of society that she remains silent in the bad situations of Karna.

Madri: She is the daughter of the king Madra and the second wife of Pandu as well as the mother of last two Pandavas – Nakula and Sahadeva. She has not played any crucial or vital role in the epic. Again, she is the traditional mother in its true sense.

Gandhari: She is the daughter of Subal, the king of Gandhar and the wife of Dhritarastra, the king of Hastinapur. Mother of Duryodhan and remaining ninety-nine sons and a daughter, Gandhari has some realistic approaches towards the kingdom, the royal throne, the great Kurushetra war and the hypocritical attitudes of her sons especially Duryodhan. She has covered her eyes with a bit of cloth to show the dedication level towards her husband as her husband is the born blind. She always rebukes her sons for their treachery and conspiracy against the Pandavas. Before the war she tries to make out Duryodhan and all others not to involve in the war as it will be the destruction of the whole Kuru dynasty, but in vain. Her character gives us the moral and spiritual education over the understanding of life. She is unable to teach her sons the ethical values in life as they are beyond that.

Darupadi: She is the central woman character of this epic. If war is the predominant feature in any epic and it happens due to a woman, then she can be compared to Sita in *Ramayana* or Helen in the *Iliad.* She is the daughter of Drupad, the king of Panchal. She has a brother named Dhristyadumnya who is the commander-in-chief of Pandavas in the great war. Many consider that she is the very cause of the war, the destruction of the whole Kuru dynasty. Wife of all the Pandavas, she accompanies them in the life exiled in forest. She is the victim in the cunningness of Sakuni, stated as stake by *Dharmaraj* Yudhisthir and consequent loss to them. In the Book of the Assembly Hall Dusshasana by the order of his elder brother tries to undress her in front of each and every elder of Kuru dynasty. Her appearance in this epic can't be ignored as she remains behind the destruction of Kurus. She accompanies the Pandavas in their last great journey towards heaven and dies first as she has some different feelings for Arjun, the third Pandavas. Sri Krishna adores her as his lovable sister. Her character can be analysed in terms of some of those women in any classical text who is responsible for everything. The character of Darupadi shows the philosophy of social education and reflections towards life. She never leaves the Pandavas in any situation. Like her husbands she has the wrath in her heart that it is only the war which can satisfy her anguishes.

Subhadra: She is the sister of Sri Krishna and the wife of the third Pandava Arjun. She is a traditional woman, a wife and a mother. Her son Abhimunya exhibits one of the best artillery skills in the great war with the seven opponent warriors calked Saptarathi. The character of Subhadra remains the 'Angel in the House' in the epic. At the death of Abhimunya in the war Subhadra's motherly affections and enrage with grief forces Arjun to take the oath to kill Jayadrath in the next day before the sunset. She is a lovable mother in its true sense.

Chitrangada: She is another wife of Arjun according to the *Gandharva* rule. Her only son Babrubahan is considered as one of the revolutionary characters in the epic. It is Babrubahan who catches the sacred horse of Pandavas in their Ashwamedhika Jagjna after their victory in the great war. For this he has to fight with Arjun without knowing their relation to each other. After the appearance of Chitrangada both the warriors draw peace. The character of Chitrangada is not at all significant except the particular book *Ashwamedika Prava*. She is called the holy woman 'Sati' and her son Babrubahan is considered as 'Satiputra'. Her role in the epic is quite passive. She bears a good moral character by not interfering in the life at the court of Hastinapura.

Uttara: She is the wife of Abhimunya, the son of Arjun. Daughter of king Virata Uttara is got married to Abhimunya at the end of the book *Virata Parva.* Like other woman character her role in the epic is also small except the time when Ashwathhama, the son of Dronacharya wants to kill the baby in Uttara's womb by attacking with the *Brahmashir Astra.* By the magical appearance of Vyasdeb and Sri Krishna the baby is saved. Her role is quite traditional and she presents herself as the lovable mother who loves her child before the birth.

Concept of Motherhood: A mother is not only someone who simply gives birth a child but also, she has been nourishing her child or children throughout the lives with love and sacrificing care. From the very ancient time especially from the Rig-vedic time the mother and motherhood has been universally acknowledging the most sacred rites and rituals of all in the world. There were some educated women in that time namely Gargi, Apala, Maitreyi who showed their virtues and regards towards mankind and made history. The women are considered as deity or goddesses. In some mythological scripts some goddesses are described like Devi Laxmi (the goddess of wealth), Devi Saraswati (the goddess of knowledge and learning), Devi Durga (the goddess of power and strength) and so on. All are considered as supernatural mothers and worshipped by all especially Hindu families to gain prosperous living and peace of mind. In Indian great epics the Ramayana and the Mahabharata there is the justification and worshipping of those motherly powers. In Ramayana the hero Sri Ram Chandra worships the goddess Durga to gain more power and blessings to kill Ravana, the king of Lanka. In Mahabharata the great war has been taken place for a woman. Each and every mythological literary text celebrates the motherhood and it has some qualitative and ethical value over human lives. From the ancient time till now this concept of motherhood has been remaining unchanged. This is the root of all philosophical education and learning.

From being mother to a hero in any sacred text to being mother of any state we have been moving on. It was Smt. Indira Gandi who became the prime minister of India once, like her it was Smt. Sirimavo Bandarnayek who became the prime minister of Sri Lanka once, it was Smt. Sarojini Naidu who became the Governor of the state West Bengal once and now the West Bengal has been ruled by Miss Mamata Banerjee since 2011. All have represented the ethical and motherly powers to propitiate the demonic forces through their ruling authorities in India. A Nigerian born novelist Buchi Emecheta wrote a novel named '*The Joys of Motherhood*' in 1979. The basis of the novel is the necessity for a woman to be fertile, and above all to give birth to sons. Here in this novel the joys of motherhood is shown above all anything in the world.

The above mentioned ten women characters and their ethical and moral values over the epic have been reflecting in the modern women in India. They are the models of being traditional motherhood and the root of philosophical education. We see in modern women the revolutionary nature as that of in Amba, the strict mother as that of in Ganga, the lovable and sacrificing nature as that of in Kunti and Madri, the traditional wife as that of in Darupadi, the unsupportive nature towards sons in their wicked games as that of in Gandhari. The Indian culture and civilization from the dawn of its true sense has been bearing the moral and ethical education of the characters in Mahabharata. They all teach us how to be strict, how to be strong in any situation, how to become a sacrifice for the welfare of the societal rules, how not to be supporter in sons' sinful deeds and so on.

Niskama Karma is that type of work which does not bear any fruit, that is totally free from any type of wishes and desires. Basically, the mentioned women characters of the epic are the epitome of that fruitless work or so called *Niskama Karma* through their lives. What the primal God Sri Krishna teaches Arjuna before the great war about the work, the women characters have showed this *karma* throughout their lives and philosophy. In *Srimadbhagbat Geeta* it has been described that someone who nourishes this *karma* in his or her life, he or she surely gain the universal and eternal peace, or so-called *Moksha*. Everyone should learn this for the purification of the soul as after death only the physical body made of blood and flesh dies, not the soul. Soul cannot die because it has no birth value. This is the highest type of quality education that we get from the epic *Mahabharata*. The study of motherhood in those characters remains evergreen throughout the centuries if we become able to apprehend the lesson of *Niskama karma*.

The mythological and sacred literary texts of any culture and religion teach us to live our lives morally correct. The lives, roles and characters of *Mahabharata* exhibit the lesson of everything that are needful to live a prosperous life full of self-satisfaction and self-estimation. Any branch of knowledge maybe its philosophy, maybe its education, maybe its literature, maybe its science all deal with the possible new findings in that particular field and to input the ethical value over the human life. The concept of motherhood should be considered as the main branch of all philosophical preachings and educational outfields. The reflections of that education are clearly visible at any point of view. Decades after decades many critics and researchers come and create some new viewpoints in any literary field and justify their approaches. To conclude the discussed topic, I would like to simplify the idea of the root of moral and philosophical education should be the views of the writers of the canonical sacred text and they definitely emphasised and celebrated the concept of motherhood which is the epitome of all moral being of a man. There is no any branch of knowledge and learning in the world which can provide the qualitative education that an ancient sacred topic can covering everything that a human being longs for throughout the life.

References:

1. Vyasa, Krishnadaipayana, *The Mahabharata*, translated and edited by J.A.B. van Buitenen, Brill, Chicago, 1975
2. Bhattacharya, Samarendra, *Bhagbatgeeta*, Book Syndicate Private limited, Kolkata, edition 2013
3. Bagchi, Dipak Kumar, *Bharatiya Nity Vidya*, Pragatishil Prakashak, Kolkata, 2008, pp.23-27
4. Swami Prabhupada, A.C. Bhaktivedanta, Shreel, *Bhagavad-Gita as It is*, The Bhaktivedanta Book Trust, Hare Krishna Land, Mumbai, 1986
5. Vivekananda Swami, *Udbhodhan Karyalaya*, Kolkata, 58th edition 2020.
6. Gupta Kalyan Chandra & Bandapadhyaya Amitabh, *The Philosophy of religion*, West Bengal state book Board, 3rd edition 1990, pp. 262
7. Das Swami Ramsukh, *Geetasarstsar*, Geeta Press, Gorakhpur.
8. Emecheta, Buchi, *The Joys of Motherhood*, Afriacan Writers' Series, Heinemann Educational Publisher, Halley Court, Jordan Hill, Oxford OE2 8EJ, 1979
9. Swami Prabhupada A.C. Bhaktivedanta Shreel, *Krisna: The Supreme Personality of Godhead*, The Bhaktivedanta Book Trust, Hare Krishna Land, Mumbai, 2010
10. Basu Rajshekhar, *Krishnadaipayana Vyas Krita Mahabharata*, Patitpaban Publishers, Hooghly, January 2021

Contemporary Communal and Identity Politics in India: An Evaluation from Historical Perspective

Nandita Das

Historically, India has been plagued by the communal problems since the British colonial rules. Although the pre-existing socio-economic complexities helped the British communal policy makers, quite a number of factors in the rise of communal politics with the exposure of communal identity have shaped 'nationalism' in defective manner in contemporary India. From 1870s, the Hindu and Muslim landlords and Government servants had tried to develop the common conservative politics for promoting their socio-economic interests of which the extreme reaction was the emergence of Muslim league and Hindu Mahasabha in Indian. They had inevitably supplemented the British ruler for protecting the existing colonial and political structure. It is a pertinent fact that India's societal class identity was overwhelmed in communal religious identity in contemporary India. Hence, the origin of communal politics and in India was solidly grounded by the British communal hidden agenda. Notwithstanding, the British policy of Divide and Rule could succeed because of Indian internal socio-economic, cultural and political conditions which favored towards its effectiveness. This chapter aims to evaluate the causes of the gradual expansion of identity politics in the Post Independence period which is presumably rooted in rooted in British communal policy.

Communal and identity issue enormously amplified in contemporary Indian politics, that is a major factor of intellectual's discussions. Because of this issue entirely affected

Indian socio-political-economic and also cultural perspective. Even the emergence of this issue is not a new matter. In general sense the term 'communal' specifically related with religion that is the basis of society and a primary source of social division, which applies to political, cultural and socio-economic interest. Communalism is a belief in India that Hindus, Muslims, Christians and Sikhs from different communities which are separately consolidated. It is a sense of identity based on religion and the determinant of their basic social relationship; they possess the inherent tendency to act as a separate entity in these fields. On the other side identity politics demonstrates to a tendency of people sharing a particular racial, linguistic, ethnic, social, religious or cultural identity to form exclusive political alliances to promote their particular interest. Its aim is to reclaim greater self-determination and political freedom for marginalized groups or entities in these fields. In the perspective of democratic India's multifarious identity for presenting overall outline, this historical analysis is significant. We are focusing on the roots of contemporary communal and identity politics in India. Apart from this, searching the causes of gradual vast manifestation of identity issues in the post-independence period, which factors are effective behind it is another purpose of this research article. Indian ancient civilization of the world reflects its multicultural character with a broad variety of regions, languages, religions, casts and classes entered into recent 21st century with conflicting debates for multitudinous identities.

So, for various research works accomplished on the historically burning communal issue that immensely enlarged in the post-colonial period as a demand of multi-identity. From the viewpoint of historian Bipan Chandra, communalism was not a fragmented relic of the past heritage or a continuation of medieval ideology. Even this communal antagonism not existed in our tradition or not an inevitable product of our history. It is emerged as a consequence of the emergence of modern politics that identified a sharp break around 1857 with the politics of medieval or ancient. This newly emerged modern politics is based on popular sovereignty, participation and mobilization of public opinion, since this phase the term 'people' started to be defined narrowly. So, it is exposed that communalism was a modern phenomenon that emerged as a consequence of British colonial impact and the response of various Indian social classes and groups. Actually, the basis of communal politics in India is that the notion of religion serving as the foundation of new political process regarding popular participation[1]. After all the social roots of communalism as also its socio-economic and political objectives were modern in the present[2]. Primarily it can be said that, communalism was one of the byproducts of colonialism, of colonial under development and in recent period due to failure of capitalism to develop socio economic perspective. During the Second World War, history witnessed lack of development of modern industries and socio-cultural services, also massive rise in prices, increasing unemployment specially educated middle and lower-middle classes underwent a serious crisis of disappointment, insecurity and anxiety. Thus, in a position of economic misery increasingly disruption of their class position, social status and value systems, which created an atmosphere of violence and brutality that led to communal riots. The notable fact is that nepotism and corruption were used on a large scale and the deficiency of a vigorous struggle to transform society[3]. In 1931 report of the Kanpur Riots Enquiry Committee mentions that the social, religious and political factors are mainly responsible for the birth of communal problems.

The term 'communalism' was first used by British colonialist to describe colonies like India, where substantial religious minorities existed beside a religious a religious majority. Uses of the term express a negative appellation of orthodoxy antagonism and parochialism that is helping to justify its civilizing mission. In the age of modern mass politics religious politics has a greater potency qualitatively and more dangerous than in the pre modern era. Thus, communalism becomes a genre of manipulation where appreciation of religious identity is historically and socially variable. Whereas formation and expansion of religious identity takes place hugely is civil society and also secular emphasis concerning state and civil society needs to be imposed.[4]

In the broad historical point of view, communalism was an extravagant form of reaction that also exposed the role of Muslim League and Hindu Mahasabha in politics. This eminently led them to join hands with British rulers who were excessively interested to keep up the existing colonial, political and economic structure, where class identity was submerged in communal identity. After all, since 1885 communalism served as the second line of defense of both imperialism and the reactionary social forces, such as the Jaigirdari elements as the Hindu and Muslim landlords and government servants had tried to grow up common conservative politics to promote their socio-economic interest. The basic communal arguments initiated by Syed Ahammed Khan, that Hindus and Muslims had separate economic, political and social interest, which assumption led against democracy that it would induce the majority community's domination over the minority[5].

A major factor existed in the sphere of expansion of communal consciousness that anti-imperialism, national liberation spirit developed as uneven manner. Many extremists identified nationalism as related with the revival of Hinduism and ever talked in terms of ancient Indian culture, where manifested the exclusion of medieval Indian culture. In this way distorted unscientific view of Indian history act as a prominent fact for the spread of communal consciousness[6]. During post-independence phase 'identity' became a political instrument of self-actualization and thus spread the sub-nationalistic developments that led the Indian democracy to the challenging cross roads[7].

Scholars analyzed the framework of identity politics on the basis of Charles Taylor's argumentation that to such developments – the demand for dignity and compulsion to find one's authenticity are reproving for understanding the identity politics of individuals and groups[8]. In the pre-modern era people accepted the pre-existing ascriptive hierarchies i.e., the concepts of birth-based superiority and inferiority. Modernity has transformed human life by giving anteriority to equal dignity which is intrinsic to all human beings. So, it is manifested that even hierarchies can exist in today's society but they are gradually achievement-based but not birth-based[9]. Since the last decade of 20th century, Eriksen observes that worldwide effective unified forces of globalization and the fragmenting forces of identity politics are two sides of the same coin[10]. In the recent conflicting perspective of identity politics, Castells argues that at the same time economics, societies and institutions are being globally structured and also different cultural identities are being reaffirmed[11]. In the 21st century society entrapped in the complex process of globalization and sometimes problematical issues of identity.

India's neo liberal arrangement has intensified the gap among various important human groups, where a small circle of technological educated professionals' verses the huge number of working poor remained in informal sector who mostly fill excluded from post liberalization economic progress. This is the specific fault lines about India's contested identity problem[12]. In the perspective of globalization period identity politics became macro, although from the stand point of political process revealed that many propelled economic reforms were big concern in India's elite politics but identity conflict directed nation's popular politics was subordinate[13].

In the light of 75years of Indian Independence from an in-depth historical insight we will try to focus on roots of contemporary communal and identity politics in India. Although since pre independent period India's land infiltrated by conflictus communal problem that obstructed to grow up properly nationalistic consciousness. Even in this area various research works has been done but, in this approach, hardly evaluated. So, it can be said that our proposed analysis of causes regarding contemporary communal and identity politics which is presumably rooted in British communal policy. This research evaluation from historical perspective is very relevant. As in recent period the struggles for identities became burning issues in India. The study conducted on the basis of following two research questions- first, what are the causes of the gradual expansion of identity politics in the post-independence period? Second, is it (contemporary communal and identity politics) rooted historical communal policy of British raj? The objective of this paper is to analyze the causes regarding the gradual expansion of identity politics since India's independent phase. It is an effect of historical communal politics of British Empire –to analyze this issue is also the purpose of study.

Contemporary India faces various challenges, such as economic divides based on class, caste and the more threatening fundamentalist communal drives. In the recent past it has been manifested that religious loyalties and social structures are emerging as alternative focal point that is more political in nature. This politicization applies as much to religion and caste as to the highly personalized domains of families, friendship, neighborhoods and peer groups. With the distortion of

Hinduism, there is an atmosphere of growing alienation and intolerance between majority and minority communities. From his view point nation inherent dynamic imbalances and institutional erosions its basic thrust towards empowering under privilege people leading the prospect of a real challenge of change.[14] A. Koholi expressed regarding this issue that centralization and powerlessness tendencies in Indian democracy are generated through the nearby absence of systematic authority links between state apex and vast social periphery. Since 1950s Indian nationalist Congress party disguised auspice links with regional and local influences, in this way creating a chain of authority. From his view point over the last two decades these links authority structure decade due to the spread of democratic politics and enfeeble influence of regional forces. Thus, India's plural diversities and the erosion of traditional social authority, also the motive of national party originated and enormously fragmented political society[15]. This issue raised previously concerns of Samuel Huntington view about third world developing society to that extent the problem of centralization and powerlessness is an intrinsic prospect of the disequilibrium within Institutional development and mobilized demand.[16]

Since Independent period the majority of Indian population was not still actively mobilized as political actors. As a result, members of the dominant castes were thus mostly able to influence the middle and lower rural class. Such as in case of kheda district in the western state of Gujrat during 1960s politics and society were controlled by the dominant landowning caste of the patidars, although they were minority near 20% of local population with time deliberately awaken diverse middle group, like the khatriyas who constituted almost 40% of local. Thus, their number translated into political power. In this way backward castes were assembled as an electoral block, which co-operate the issue of gradual expansion of identity politics. In case of West Bengal state onwards 1916s confronted quite a few radical movements organized by tribal peasants, because of confiscation of land against the landowning elite class. In this perspective various communist parties achieved relevant, as national leadership of the Congress faced growing political power challenges. Notwithstanding it was manifested that nearly all-over Indian politics incorporated backward castes on a new basis. Furthermore, power oriented national leaders in India destroyed institutional rebuilding and failed to assured public good even they viewed as the agents of people's representatives[17].

S. Kakar shows his study that conventionalize authoritarian proposing and massive use of ego shielding projection also dogmatism pronounced political process that endorse ethnic violence and narrowly divided religious community. These are turn out gradually one of the psychological levels of those are involved in communal riot[18]. From A. Nandy's observation it is manifested that a new form of complicated religious violence has entered the Asian scene, in which the state, ideologies of national security, the media, development and modernity propagated by the modern intelligentsia and the middle classes play crucial role. According to his view point the foremost recent trends is that every religion has been split into two; faith and ideology. By faith religion as a way of life, tradition that operationally plural. On the other side ideology religion as a sub national, national or cross-national identifier of population contesting for political or socio-economic interests. The modern state always prefers to deal with religious ideology rather than with faiths. The imported western ideology of secularism has become gradually in compatible. Specifically, to the problem of religion as intertwined with the political process of the country. He expressed as such of example at that time of writing, two minister of central cabinet in India and numbers of individuals in the higher strata of ruling party have been accused communalism not only encouraging but also supporting the vicious activities and publicly threatening civil right workers[19].

Indian political scientist A. Varshney explained that a fundamental political question in India has been about how democracy and diversity should be combined. Because of their geographical concentration, language and tribe became the basis of federalism in India[20]. In a cumulative spirit of enquiry, a step toward the investigation of links between civil society and ethnic conflict. Although networks of community can be built nationally, internationally and an electronic age also virtually. From his point of view ethnic conflicts are a regular feature of plural democracy and they organized for achieving resources, identity, patronage and policies[21]. The major engrossment of India's politics has on the whole been with the issue of group identity, not with question of economic development. From their point of view the resurgence of religious and ethnic identity movements has two related yet distinct implication. First, religious and ethnic movement occurred in various parts of the world by religious and ethnic nationalism, if such nationalism is majoritarian and it has even threatened implication for religious and ethnic minorities. Second, such movements have tended to undermine the rights of vulnerable members of their own community[22]. After all, besides the various overall historically significant socio-political effective tendencies, recently observes a major factor regarding media propagated distorted information mostly exposed negative site of identity issue in India.

From Bipan Chandra's historical analysis, it is manifested that British rule and policy hold a notable liability for the growth of communalism in modern India. The British rulers encouraged it and helped its expansion among community[23].

Nationalist point of view was communalism definitely a product of British policy. They steadily applied division in Indian society for their own imperial purpose[24]. In this perspective explicated the British policy of divide and rule succeeded only because something in the internal socio-economic, cultural and political society favored its success. Even it grows up not only because served the political needs of British colonial power but also social needs of some reactionary section of Indian society[25]. Accordingly, J. Nehru apparently shows that, there was an implicit propensity towards division in India, the British ruler adopted the communal policy and induced in every fissiparous tendency in the country[26]. At that time regarding this worrying fact Rabindranath Tagore expressed for the purpose of Indian political leaders in 1907 that Muslims could be used against Hindus perilously, who used then is not so important. He also pointed that pre-independent 'great ocean' i.e., masses separated from the educated few, who were mainly Hindus. Actually, urgent necessary to set up a bridge for powerful national movement[27]. The British imperial administration did not grow up communalism for the devotion of that community. The main objective of the British policy of divide and rule was to obstruct the politicalization of Indian people, to make obstacle in their way of consolidation and also disrupt the process of Indian nation building. At one time anti-imperialist nationalist movement arrows, the communal policy was also directed onwards inhibiting its expansion, through dividing its actual supporters[28]. After analyzing the socio-economic conflicting situation within the rising middle classes historian R. Palme Dutt expressed that, Indian soil was adequately easy for applying divided rule policy on the latent antagonism[29]. Beni Prasad also expressed a similar view that internal various factors of the Indian situation British Govt. did strike on policies calculated to sustained the differences between two communities[30]. B. Chandra comments that, in fact apart from the socio-economic situation British policy was determining of the communal issues.

After all, discussing the various historical analytical expression we can say that British rulers did play a crucial role in the promotion and spread of communalism in modern India. Finally, we can draw concluding remarks that, communal seeds were hidden in the Indian socio-economic levels, but keep it proper political sphere Britishers narrowly capable its enlargement of roots with tree, which long-term reaction seen even today.

References

1. Chandra, Bipan. *Communalism in Modern India*. Vani Educational Books, 1984, pp. 1-18.
2. *Selected Works*, Vol 7, 1936, p. 69.
3. Chandra, Bipan. *Communalism in Modern India*. Vani Educational Books, 1984, pp. 34-48.
4. Vanaik, Achin. *Communalism Contested: Religion, Modernity and Secularization*. Vistaar Publiation, 1997, pp. 30-55
5. Chandra, Bipan. *Communalism in Modern India*. Vani Educational Books, 1984, pp. 78-91
6. *Ibid*, pp. 209-226
7. Dam, Srimayee. "The Myth of Identity Politics in India: Identity Constructs over Political Realities". *Indian Journal of Political Science*, vol. LXXII no. 4, Oct-Dec 2011, pp. 913-926.
8. Taylor, Charles. *Multiculturalism and the Politics of Recognition*. Princeton UP, 1995.
9. Vibha Pingle, et al. *India's Identity Politics: Then and Now*. www.worldscientific.com
   https://doi.org /10.1142/9789812774729_0013
10. Eriksen, H. Thomas. *Globalization: The Key Concepts*. Routledge, 2014. p. 159.
11. Castells, Manuel. "*Globalization and Identity: A Comparative Perspective*". https://docs.llull.cat > transfer
12. Chadha, Kalyani. "*From Cast to Faith; Contemporary Identity Politics in a Globalized India*"2018, vol.20(I)84-87 https://journals.sagepub.com/home/jmo

13. Vibha Pingle, et al. *India's Identity Politics: Then and Now.* www.worldscientific.com
    https://doi.org /10.1142/9789812774729_0013
14. Kothari, Rajni. "*Rethinking Democracy*" Orient Longman pvt. Ltd. 2005
15. Kohli, Atul "*Democracy and Development in India: From Socialism to Pro Business*" Oxford University Press 2009.
16. Huntington, Samuel "*Political order in Changing Societies*" New Haven: Yale University Press 1968
17. Kohli, Atul. "*Democracy and Development in India: From Socialism to Pro Business*" Oxford University Press 2009.
18. Kakar, Sdhir. "Some Unconscious Aspects of Ethnic Violence in India" *Mirrors of Violence* edited by Das, pp135-145.
19. Nandy, Ashis. "The Politics of Secularism and the Recovery of Religious Tolerance", *Secularism and its Critics* edited by Bhargava Rajeev, oxford India paperbacks, 1998.
20. Varshney, Ashutosh. "On Dealing with Regional Identity" 17th Jan,2013 asiasociety.org
21. Varshney, A. *Ethnic Conflict and Civic Life; Hindus and Muslims in India.* Yale University Press, 2002
22. Vibha Pingle, et al. *India's Identity Politics: Then and Now.* www.worldscientific.com
    https://doi.org /10.1142/9789812774729_0013
23. Chandra, Bipan. "*Communalism in Modern India*" Vani Educational Books,1984 pp237-253.
24. Robinson, Francis. *Separatism among Indian Muslim,* p.2. Also see Krishna Gopal, Hindu-Muslim relation in British India, p.173,
25. Chandra, Bipan. "*Communalism in Modern India*" Vani Educational Books,1984 pp237-253.
26. Nehru, Jahar Lal. SW, vol.7, pp.69-70
27. Quoted in Sarkar, Sumit. The Swadeshi Movement in Bengal 1903-1908, p.83
28. Chandra, B. Ibid.
29. Dutt, P.R., *India Today* p.425
30. Prasad, Beni, *The Hindu-Muslim Question*, p.163

Exploring the Secularism of India: A Historical and Contemporary Analysis

Md Hashim Saikh & Ibrahim Sk

India is a land of rich diverse cultures, traditions, religions, and languages that have coexisted for centuries. The concept of secularism, which entails the separation of religion from the state, has been enshrined in the Indian Constitution after its amendment in 1976. In a secular state, citizens are free to practice, profess, and propagate any religion of their choice without state interference. However, the concept of secularism has changed in recent times and it has been a subject of much debate in Indian society. This chapter aims to investigate the secularism of India, including its historical roots and contemporary significance. It explores the concept of secularism in India, including its historical roots, contemporary significance, challenges, and opportunities. Using the available literature, the study investigates the perceptions of Indian citizens, scholars, experts, and community leaders on the topic of secularism in India. The study finds that India's secularism has been evident throughout history, from the ancient Harappan civilization to the medieval and modern eras. The Harappan society was renowned for its secular ethos, as evidenced by the absence of any evidence of religious dominance in their ruins. The analysis reveals key themes related to the historical evolution of secularism in India, including the role of leaders such as Asoka, Akbar, Nehru, Gandhi, and Ambedkar in promoting religious diversity and pluralism. The analysis also highlighted the current challenges to secularism in India, including the rise of religious extremism, communal violence, and political polarization. The paper argues that despite the challenges, secularism remains a vital principle for Indian society and that policymakers, scholars, and community leaders need to work together to promote religious diversity, tolerance, and pluralism in India.

India is the largest functioning democracy in the world. Besides, it is the largest secular nation where multiple religions have coexisted since the early history of civilization. However, there has been debate and discourse about the secular identity of this country, especially after the current government, the National Democratic Alliance (NDA), headed by the Bharatiya Janata Party, came to power in 2014. Although the concept of secularism existed in the Indian subcontinent from the early history of the Indus Valley Civilization (3000 BC), it was not until 1976 that the Indian Constitution adopted the term secularism in its Preamble and formally declared itself a secular country.[1] India has always been famous for its diversity. Here, multiple religions, including some of the largest religions like Hinduism, Islam, Christianity, and Buddhism, have co-existed for centuries. Yet the country has retained its secular nature. These people, known as secularists, want the country to remain secular. On the other hand, the anti-secularist, right-wing Hindu Nationalists discard the secular ethos and demand that the country be identified as a Hindu Rashtra, a nation of Hindu religion, as Hinduism is the most practiced majoritarian religion in the country. Moreover, they argued that there are countries identified by majoritarian religion, for example, Pakistan and countries in the Middle East that are identified as Islamic countries because Islam is the major religion in these countries. But there is no country identified as a Hindu country except the small Asian Himalayan country of Bhutan. Therefore, they strongly demand a Hindu Rashtra and want to abolish the secular identity of the country. This paper aims to explore the notion of secularism and put some light on the debate over whether India should be recognized as a secular country.

The term 'secularism' was first used by a British reformer, George Jacob Holyoake, in the 19th century, in his writings such as 'Principle of Secularism' and The Origin and Nature of Secularism".[2] The word secularism denotes the separation of religion from the state, where all citizens can freely profess, practice, and propagate any religion of their choice without any interference of the state. The word "secular" is mentioned in the preamble of the Indian Constitution, which glorifies the nation's secular identity to the rest of the world. The fundamental rights of the Indian Constitution guarantee freedom of religion to all its citizens.[3]

Dr. B.R. Ambedkar explained secularism as "it (secular state) does not mean that we shall not take into consideration the religious sentiment of the people. All that a secular state means is that this parliament shall not be competent to impose any particular religion upon rest of the people. This is the only limitation that the constitution recognizes."[4] Dr. S. Radhakrishnan, former president of India, philosopher, and scholar, said that "when India is said to be a secular state, it does not mean that we rejected the reality of the unseen spirit or the relevance of religion to life or that we exalt irreligion. It does not mean that secularism itself becomes a positive religion or that the state assumes divine prerogatives. We hold that not one religion should be given preferential status.[5] Mahatma Gandhi argued that "I do not expect India of my dreams to develop one religion, i.e., to be wholly Hindu or wholly Christian, or wholly Mussalman, but I want it to be wholly tolerant, with its religious working side by side with one another".[6]

Secularism, by its very nature, is a dynamic concept. It has variable meanings across different cultures. The western concept of secularism is different from that of its Indian counterpart. In the West, secularism is completely detached from religion. In contrast, Indian secularism recognizes the existence of religions in the state. Although the Indian Constitution emphasizes the separation of religion from the state administration, in reality, it has been perceived that the state has often indulged in religious matters. For instance, the state has interfered in the funding of Hindu festivals, provided Hajj subsidies for Muslims, and so on. As Rajeev Bhargava has mentioned, a "principled distance" is maintained. This discourse on the maintenance of equal distance parameters is often questioned. It has been very often alleged that the Indian state administration is slightly partial to the majoritarian religion of the country.

The history of India witnessed the tradition of secularism through the diversified cultures, traditions, languages, religions, and social movements that glorify the secular identity of India across the world. In the Harappan civilization, there has not been a single structure that can be termed a temple. In the Vedic age, people used to worship the natural forces. There was no temple where people could worship these natural gods. The Mauryan Emperor Asoka was the first ruler to declare that the state would not prosecute any religious sect. He appealed to his subjects for the tolerance amongst sects. He also requested that people honor the dhamma (religion) of others.[7] The sixth century BCE was a period of great religious upheaval. In India, the scenario was no different. India witnessed the growth of two great alternative religions: Buddhism and Jainism. These two religions were the reaction against the caste system and the discrimination caused by the Hindu religion. These two religions emphasized that true happiness does not lie in material prosperity or the performance of rituals. These two were not only religions but also doctrines that challenged Brahminical dominance. But the emergence of these two religions did not affect the secular nature of the sub-continent. The people of ancient India had freedom of religion, and the state granted citizenship to each individual regardless of whether someone's religion was Hinduism, Buddhism, Jainism, or any other. Even after the arrival of Islam and Christianity in India, the exploration of religious tolerance and the coexistence of different faiths continued.[8]

In medieval India, the Sufi and Bhakti movements strengthened the people of different communities with the message of love and peace. The chief proponents of these movements were Khawaja Moinuddin Chisti, Baba Farid, Sant Kabir Das, Saint Tukaram, Guru Nanak, and Mira Bai. They were bestowed for constructing a secular community from various religious sects. This was reflected in the remarks of Guru Nanak, "There is no Hindu and no Mussalman, as there is no distinction between man and man" as it has strengthened the root of secularism in India.[9] The great Mughal emperor Akbar also exalted the policy of tolerance for various religions. He was well known in the pages of history for his religious policies for different religions. After marrying Jodha Bai of Amber, he abolished the pilgrim tax for Hindus. He also abolished the jijiya tax for Muslims. He allowed his Hindu wives to worship their own gods. In 1575 CE, he built Ibadat Khana (Hall of Prayer) at his capital city, Fatehpur Sikri, wherein he invited different intellectuals and scholars from all religions, like Hinduism, Jainism, Christianity, and Zoroastrianism, for religious discussions. Some of the scholars were Pursottam Das (Hindu), Dastur Maharji Rana (Parsi), Hira Bijaya Suri (Jain), Aquabiva, and Monserrate (Christians). In 1582 CE, he proclaimed a new religion called *Din-i-Ilahi* (Divide Monotheism), which believes in one God and in *Sul-i-Kul* (peace to all). It comprises all the good points of all religions.[10] These policies of Akbar strengthened and smoothed the spirit of secularism in medieval India. Besides that, the commander of Akbar's Army was a Hindu named Mansingh, and among the forty thousand Rajput soldiers, more than five hundred were Hindu sardar. Akbar's Prime Minister was also a Hindu named Raghunath Das. On the other hand, Maharana Pratap Singh appointed Hakim Suri, a Muslim, as the commander of his army. In the regime of Chattrapati Shivaji, Siddhi Halal and Nur Khan were appointed as Sardar of his army.[11]

All these examples from medieval Indian history point to the fact that the rulers of the various states were not rigid in their religious beliefs and preferred to maintain a middle path, which is basically known as the secular path. In other words, they did not give preference to any religion over others and kept religions away from the state administration. In the history of modern India, we see the development of religious political organizations and the clash of religions over the dominance of the country. It was mainly due to the policy of the British that there was a clash between religions in India. For their own good, the then-British Government of India divided the people of India according to their religions and tried to divide them based on their religions. Yet, there were several Indian political leaders who tried to maintain the secular nature of the country in that situation.

The chief defenders of the secular ideology were Motilal Nehru, Jawahar Lal Nehru, and M.K. Gandhi. The constitution was drafted by Motilal Nehru, who was the chairman of the historic Nehru Committee in 1928. He had the following provisions on secularism: "There shall be no state religion for the commonwealth of India or for any province in the commonwealth, nor shall the state, either directly or indirectly, endow any religion with any preference or impose any disability on account of religious beliefs or religious status."[12] Gandhi's secularism was based on a commitment to the brotherhood of religious communities based on their respect for and pursuit of truth. Pandit J. L. Nehru's secularism was based on a commitment to scientific humanism tinged with a progressive view of historical change. Jawaharlal Nehru has been a leading champion of the concept of the secular state. The creation of India as a secular state has been accepted as one of his greatest achievements. He was especially concerned with the transformation of India from a 'caste-ridden' society in which communalism constitutes a major threat to all the values that he cherished to a 'national state," which includes people of all religions and shades of opinion and is essentially secular as a state.

The doctrine of secularism came much later in the discussion, but the idea of secularism was deeply rooted in ancient Indian society. The concept of "Sarva Dharma Samvaba" is a great example of this from the very beginning. Secularism also has to undergo different terrain and difficulties of its own from time to time.[13] The framers of the constitution rightly pointed out the problems at the very initial stage and hence incorporated the ideas of mutual tolerance and pluralism. India is a multi-religious country that appears to be its own when it comes to religious tolerance, but in contemporary times, the doctrine of secularism is at stake. The presence of a huge diversity of religions in Indian society that used to live peacefully has changed now towards a majority-minority debate. As Hindu followers constitute 80% of the country's population, they proclaim a majoritarian system, whereas other religions like Muslims, Jains, Christians, Sikhs, and Buddhists are being targeted due to their minority share in the population. For various reasons, harmony and peace between the majority and minorities have been greatly disrupted in the current scenario. Many critics have argued that the secular ethos of the country has been threatened since the Modi government came to power at the centre in 2014. There is a huge shift in the political debate regarding the idea of secularism. The Bharatiya Janata Party (BJP), the ruling party in the government, has been promoting Hindu nationalism since the early days of its political existence. The examples that the ruling party ideology targets minorities and emphasizes Hindu nationalist ideology include the abrogation of Article 370, the Triple Talaq bill, and the CAA. These policies created outrage among the minority groups as well as among liberals and secularists, which is a much broader debate altogether. There are many instances of lynching and communal violence that have occurred and created fear among the minority community of the country. Besides that, the much-debated Citizenship Amendment Bill has created havoc among a single community, i.e., Muslims in India. The call for 'Hindu Rashtra' and the Uniform Civil Code similarly put the idea of secularism in danger, as many politicians in the country have done very often. Even school textbooks sometimes contain communal literature that creates a sense of discrimination on the basis of religion in children's minds. The Indian Constitution is highly known for its large accommodation of different diversity, be it religions, languages, cultures, interests, etc.

Communal violence is one of the biggest threats to Indian secularism. There are many events of communal violence that led to a large disturbance to the harmony and peace of society. The government's non-response to communal violence shows its biases towards the majority group. One of the most recent instances of communal violence occurred in February 2020 in North East Delhi between two groups of pro- and anti-Citizenship Amendment Act (CAA) protestors. To investigate the violence, a five-member committee comprised of Justice Madan B. Lokur, Justice A.P. Shah, Justice R.S. Sodhi, Justice Anjana Prakash, and G.K. Pillai, IAS (Retd.), was formed, titled

"Uncertain Justice: A Citizens Committee Report on the North East Delhi Violence 2020," which clearly stated that BJP leader Kapil Mishra's communal hate speech triggered the violence. Even Delhi police are involved in acts of violence, and the Committee holds its view that "Delhi police failed to prevent the violence and expresses serious concern at the instances of police complicity of varying degrees in the violence."[14]

The problem of communal violence has been a threat to the unity of India since its independence. There is a series of communal violence that occurred in different cities in India. Of course, the partition of India and the creation of Pakistan as a separate state have led to the division of the people of India, followed by huge communal tension. After the partition, the very first riot occurred in Jabalpur, Madhya Pradesh, in 1961 between Hindus and Muslims, and then the list goes on to Ahmedabad riots (1969), Anti-Sikh riots (1984), Meerut riots (1987), Bhagalpur riots (1989), Mumbai riots (1992), Gujarat riots (2002), and so on.[15] The change in political power has brought a plethora of dynamism to the debate in civil society after the coming of the Bharatiya Janata Party (BJP) in the centre. The notion of nationalism has been elevated above any other by various organizations that have an affiliation with the party, directly or indirectly. The term "Love Jihad" has become popular in recent times with accusations of Muslim men trying to seduce and marry Hindu women to proselytize them. In reaction to it, the Hindu organizations brought "Ghar Wapsi" (homecoming) to proselytize Muslim and Christian women.[16] In several states, a new variation of "Bulldozer Justice" has developed to destroy people's homes, focusing in particular on Muslims who have recently taken part in any protests. The demolition of the house of activist Javed Mohammad in Uttar Pradesh is one examples of this, where the constitutionality of the action is questioned.[17] In the case of Faizal Usman Khan, a

25-year-old Muslim taxi driver was assaulted by a group of men late night near to Mumbai, India's Economic capital. When he cried for mercy, they instructed Faizal to chant "Jai Shri Ram" (Glory to Lord Ram) which has become a catchphrase for the nation's Hindu supremacists.[18]

The imposition of one's beliefs on others is a big problem in any secular country, unlike India, and it is against the law of the land. For instance, the cow is considered to be a sacred animal in Hinduism, but very often we see mob lynching and the killing of many innocent Muslims and other minorities in the name of the protection of the holy cow. Many scholars have also argued that these activities are done with the support of the state apparatus. The cases related to cow protection violence based on rumor have increased in mostly BJP-ruled states where the Hindu vigilante groups are most active. When the majoritarian-led government responded late, the hope of India's minorities was jeopardized. Jaffrelot opines that "In the state of Haryana, Gau Raksha Dal–affiliated groups—armed with field hockey sticks—patrol the highway linking Chandigarh and New Delhi, where they inspect trucks (often with the blessing of the state police) likely to be transporting cows."[19]

The rising intolerance in the country caused fear among minority communities in India. The alleged suppression of minorities in the country has brought a different image of India to the world stage despite having a centuries-old religious plural society. The cultural policing of the majority group towards the minority have led to a panic situation. Meanwhile, some of them think that India is the land of Hindus, so a kind of special privilege must be ensured. Hence, the unification or enactment of a uniform civil code is almost impossible. The fate of secularism is being questioned at present because of the partiality for hate speech shown by top leaders of the BJP party and various radical Hindu organizations. One example is the rise in hate crimes and the growing intolerance among people. In a study, the data shows that "Christians comprise 2% of India's population (but face 11.55% of all hate crimes in the period 2014–18) and Muslims comprise 14% of India's population (but face 64.54% of all hate crimes in the period 2014–18), can we put these numbers in proper perspective. Even as we witness a rise in hate crimes against all communities, the overwhelming majority of hate crimes target religious minorities."[20]

In this era of information technology (IT), the flow of information is very fast, which has a greater impact on election campaigning and other socialization processes. The use of social media has significantly increased among Indian citizens recently. It has become difficult to choose the correct information in the sea of misinformation, especially for people from rural areas who lack the knowledge of fact-checking. The issue of Ram-Janam Bhoomi, or the Babri Masjid demolition case, is one of them and plays a vital role in polarizing society on religious lines. The trust between the majority and the minority has greatly been affected because of this flow of misinformation, which ultimately created chaos. Similar concern has been pointed out by Indian Nobel Laureate in Economics, Amartya Sen, who says, "As an Indian citizen, I don't want Modi as my PM.... He has not done enough to make minorities feel safe.... There is a problem in understanding the issues of education, especially school education, and healthcare. But I don't see this understanding in Mr. Modi's program."[21] Through social media, the majoritarian tendency and polarization were evident immediately before the election. The press is considered the fourth pillar of democracy, and its independence is equally important. The freedom of the press in India is extensively criticized by many national and international organizations at present, and it has been ranked 150th among the 180 countries in the World Press Freedom Index (2022), published by Reporters

Without Borders (RSF). The biased narratives of TV news often add fuel to the communal clash in India because the news media is alleged to spread religious hatred among the citizens through their controversial shows and debates. Hence, the contemporary doctrine of secularism has faced so many criticisms from civil society groups, national and international media houses.

The power politics of India have undergone a paradigm shift in every sphere under the BJP-led NDA government. The majoritarian Hindu nationalists still aspire to make India a "one-culture country". However, the Constitution of India largely accommodates the diversity of the country. The multicultural character of the country is not a weakness; rather, it is a strength that makes our country beautiful on the international stage. The ideals of various leaders, thinkers, and academicians of the country, like Mahatma Gandhi, Jawaharlal Nehru, Dr. BR Ambedkar, Ram Mohan Roy, Rabindranath Tagore, and Patel, have taught us the strength of unity. The Guardian of the Constitution, the Supreme Court, has so far successfully performed its duty in protecting the constitution. The people of the country, especially the majority population, should show fraternity and tolerance towards one another by respecting the values of reciprocity. The centuries-old civilization of Indian society has an indigenous system of mutual tolerance all its own that should be promoted. The independence of the judiciary must be ensured in order to protect the secular values of the Indian constitution. The credibility of TV news must be protected to bring real issues to the citizens. The education system is to be kept before anything else to strive towards scientific advancement. **Secularism is very essential for the smooth functioning of a democratic country. Regardless of multiple threats, the nation and its people must maintain a secular identity in order to thrive in the world and accommodate diversity among us.**

References

1. Singh, Gurmukh Nihal, *Land Marks in Indian Constitutional and National Development,* Atma Ram & Sons, Delhi, 1952, p.175
2. Holyoke, George Jacob., *English Secularism: A Confession of Belief,* Library of Alexandria. 1896
3. Article 12-35 of Indian Constitution deals with fundamental rights of the citizen; Gauba, O.P, *Indian Political Thought,* Mayur Publishers, Delhi, 2019
4. Pylee, M.V., *India's Constitution,* S. Chand Publication, Delhi, 2007, p.14
5. Radhakrishnan, S., *Recovery of Faith,* Hind Pocket Book Pvt. Ltd. Publication, 1955, p.184
6. Gandhi, M. K., *India of My Dreams*: *Religious Tolerance in India,* 1947, Chapter 62
7. Dahiya Punam Dalal, *Ancient and Medieval India,* McGraw Hill Education Pvt. Ltd. Publication, Delhi, 2017
8. Ibid.
9. Rizvi, M. M. A., "Secularism in India: Retrospect and Prospects", *The Indian Journal of Political Science*, No. 66, 4, 2005
10. Dahiya, 2017, Op. cit.,
11. Tara, S., *Secular India,* Anmol Publication, New Delhi, 1991
12. Nehru Report, 1928
13. Yerankar, S., *Secularism in India: Theory and Practice.* Adhyayan Publisher & Distributors, Delhi, 2006
14. *Uncertain Justice: A Citizens Committee Report on the North East Delhi Violence 2020, 2022,* Constitutional Conduct Group (CCG), *p. 163*
15. PTI. "Chronology of communal violence in India", *Hindustan Time,* 2011
16. Jaffrelot, C., *The BJP in Power: Indian Democracy and Religious Nationalism,* Carnegie Endowment for International Peace, 2019, p. 55
17. Lokur, M. B., 'Bulldozer injustice to 'teach a lesson', *The Hindu* (Online Platform), 17 June, 2022
18. Ayyub, R., "What a Rising Tide of Violence Against Muslims in India Says About Modi's Second Term", *Twitter,* 2019, June 28
19. Jaffrelot, C., *The BJP in Power: Indian Democracy and Religious Nationalism,* Carnegie Endowment for International Peace, 2019, p. 55
20. Basu, D., "Dominance of Majoritarian Politics and Hate Crimes Against Religious Minorities in India, 2009–2018", *UMass Amherst Economics Working Papers,* 2019, p. 29
21. "A Clear and Present Danger to India's Secularism", *The Diplomat,* 2014, June 10

The Pioneer of Duars' Education System Sri Satyendra Prasad Roy: A Review

Soumyadipta Sinha

The district of Jalpaiguri of West Bengal has unique natural beauty, surrounded by tea plantations and green mountains. This is one of the most visited districts of the state. However, since long time, this region was deprived of the touch of education. Initially, because of the outbreak of malaria and black fever this region remained aloof from the other regions. Later tea-industrialists came here for mass trading and business and gradually schools started to be built one by one with their initiative for the benefit of workers family. The Satyendra Prasad Roy was one of them who not only started the construction of schools, but also many schools got financial support due to his initiatives. One of the prominent personalities of the district, he earned considerable reputation not only as a scholar but also as a sports lover.

Among the districts of North Bengal, Jalpaiguri has a unique geographical feature. This diverse district has several forests, reserve forests, tea gardens. Naturally that creates attraction for the outside visitors. According to the geographical environment and the nature of the production system, the district can be divided into three parts,[1] namely:

a) Northern Highlands

b) Interspersed with tea plantations and forests

c) Plains Agricultural Zone

The touch of education came much later in this district. While the process of education started slowly in the eastern part after independence, the western part of the Duars was practically in darkness. However, I think a few things need to be discussed before discussing the issues related to education. After the arrival of the British Government in this country they associated themselves with tea and jute trade. Those associated with these businesses, known as tea-planters, originally came from Scotland. Meanwhile, when the tea industry was established in Dooars from 1874 AD, the British hunted the tribals from Manbhum (Purulia), Singhbhum, Ranchi, Hazaribagh, Chotanagpur, Santal Parganas in a net of incitement, temptation and conspiracy. The Bengalis also came to this region for employment or as part of the coconut business.[2] This is how the dominance of the Bengalis was established throughout the Dooars region. on the basis of Bengali dominancy, various tea gardens started to be established one by one. As an example, the name of Mughalkata tea garden can be mentioned. Among those who came forward in the first phase were Gopalchandra Ghosh, Jayachandra Sanyal, Yadav Chakraborty, Munshi Ahiruddin, Bhavanicharan Ghatak, Keshavachandra Ghatak and others. Under the patronage of these tea industrialists, Jalpaiguri witnessed remarkable progress in education, culture and sports during this period.[3]

Due to the progress of tea industry, many elite personalities emerged. These individuals played a significant role in the expansion of education in Duars. Among them Amuligopal Sengupta, Birendra Khasanbish, Satyendranath Bhattacharya, Birendra Chandra Ghosh, Dr. Nanigopal Chakraborty, SK Majumder, Dr. Chinmoy Lahiri and others. Metelli Secondary School, Banarhat High School, Birpara High School, Kalchini Union Academy, Madarihat High School were established under their initiative. During this episode, Satyendra Prasad Roy emerged as one of the prominent personalities of Duars as well as whole Jalpaiguri. Who is better known as SP Roy. He is a bright personality in the world of education, culture and sports. It can be said that a new chapter was introduced in the world of education and sports in the district mainly by his hands.

Before discussing about Satyendra Prasad Roy, I feel the need to mention a few things in this context. It should be mentioned that Muslims also came forward to lead in the contemporary period. Among which the names of Rahim Bux Sahib and his son-in-law Mosharraf Hossain have to be mentioned. Later Rahim started some gardens with the help of Bux Saheb's brother's son Walier Rahman Mosharraf Hossain. according to the research of Dr. Shiv Shankar Mukherjee's, it is known that 126 influential Bengalis were present at this time, of whom 90 were Hindus and 36 were Muslims.[4]

Now let's dive into the main topic of discussion. After the city of Jalpaiguri became famous, several families became popular, among which the names of Roy family, Ghosh family, Chatterjee family have to be mentioned. Among them Satyendra Prasad Roy was the prominent person of Roy family. He was the son of famous tea industrialist Tarini Roy. After completing his education, he joined the tea garden established by his father. That is, he carried forward the family business in a hereditary manner. It can be seen that in 1952, the Chairman of I.I.P.A and later the Government of India formed the T-Board, and he was elected as its member, and later appointed as Vice-Chairman.[5] Construction of school, town club, stadium was completed under his initiative. A number of elites came forward for the expansion of education in Jalpaiguri district. We can see both the individual as well as collective initiatives. Before independence, the image of the district education system was very poor. In the next phase, there was some momentum, based on which many schools were built in the district. Satyendra Prasad Roy's personal initiative and role in this episode is undoubtedly considered as a significant issue. A list of the schools he supported financially will make the point much clearer –

Chart No. 1[6]

List of school constructed by S Prasad Roy

Sl No.	Name of the School	Year of establishment
1	Central Girls High School,	1954
2	Shishumahal Primary School,	1944
3	Mainaguri High School,	1948
4	Nagarakata High School	1958
5	Sonali Girls High School	1954
6	Mathura T-Estate Senior Basic School	1963
7	Deshbandhunagar High School	1964
8	Jalpaiguri High School	1959
9	Mohitnagar High School	1953
10	Belacoba High School	1954
11	Dhupguri High School	1945
12	Bairatiguri High School	1960
13	Falakata High School	1886
14	Falakata Girls High School	1948

15	Kalchini High School	1963
16	Kumargram High School	1934
17	Bannerhat High School	1949
18	Basirhat High School	1952

That is, it appears that the above list is quite long. There was a time when only a handful of schools were established in the district and schools in other parts of the district were virtually non-existent. At that time these tea farmers not only attached themselves to trade, but felt the urge to expand education, which resulted in the initiative of Satyendra Prasad Roy. He realized that the extension of education to the remote areas of the Duars was particularly important. Already the incidence of black fever and malaria was very high in the Dooars, naturally the region did not show much progress during the colonial period. Later, when the city began to expand, the population began to increase gradually, many people started arriving for the sake of jobs and business. Due to their arrival, when the need to build a school was felt, then Satyendra Prasad Roy, BC Ghosh, Niyogi family and others came forward.

However, two things need to be mentioned in this context, that is that the late Satyendra Prasad Roy, who came as an educationist, associated himself with sports. It is true that at a time various clubs such as Victoria Club, Star Club, Diamond Jubilee Club etc. were formed under the patronage of the English tea tax collectors. Meanwhile, after the rise of the city of Jalpaiguri, the practice of sports was not the same for a long time, although the Jalpaiguri Town Club was formed in 1898 with the aim of giving priority to the practice of sports. In the first phase, Swargiya Rai Bahadur Harimohan Chandra, Rai Bahadur Priyanath Bandyopadhyay etc. came forward, but later

Nalinikant Rahut, Kaminikant Rahut etc. became active. Of course, Satyendra Prasad Roy's name is eagerly mentioned. Because his love for playing football was always passionable. Not only that, he was also known as Khyada Babu in the sports world. In this case, it must be said that he used to appear on the field wearing boots and jersey. The original intention was to boost the morale of the players. Based on this, many football players got jobs in Mathura tea garden, Sarada tea garden, Atiyabari tea garden, Kamala tea garden. That is, its great role in creating employment cannot be denied. However, the over-employment of workers subsequently hampered the management of the plantations. Anyway, that's out of the question. As the game of football became popular in Jalpaiguri district, various tournaments were organized. Including Kumudini Cup, Sonullah Shield, Syed Shield, Faizunnessa Shield etc. At the same time, various clubs started to be formed, among which the name of Young Bengal Club has to be mentioned.[7]

After the establishment of the Mathura Tea Gardens by the father of the famous Mr. Satyendra Prasad Roy, Tarini Prasad Roy, later Satyendra Prasad acquired the Atiyabari Kathalaguri, Ramjhora and Raipur tea gardens respectively. It is said that he was associated with the game of football at the town club for about forty (40) years. Apart from helping various clubs, he also helped with the grounds of Milan Sangh and Jalpaiguri Cultural Club. It can be said that he was a sports lover from the beginning. On the other hand, the name of the Roy family has come up in the discussion in the field of education. It has already been said that he was quite enthusiastic about the spread of education and many schools were built under his patronage. He helped the poor and needy students financially. In this case, the students of Prasandev Mahila College were helped by setting up a mortuary fund, which was formed in the name of her mother. Along with this, he organized a fund in Anandachandra College in the name of Tariniprasad Roy to buy books for poor students. Not just the beginning, his contribution in establishing Anandachandra Education-Teachers College, Cooch Behar Polytechnic, Alipurduar College was outstanding.[8] So it is seen that his role in the development of sports and education was undoubtedly important.

Satyendra Prasad Roy, a tea industrialist and an education enthusiast, came forward to build many school buildings on his own initiative. Among which mention must be made of Shishumahal Primary Schools in the district city. On the other hand, he was instrumental in the development of Central Girls School. Subsequently, the grant received from the Government for the construction of the Banarhat Girls' School was due to the role of Mr. Satyendra Prasad Roy, a prominent industrialist of Jalpaiguri.[9] Satyendra Prasad Roy's initiative went beyond the city His contribution was also significant in building the Senior Basic School at Belakoba under his initiative At a time when the Duars region was known as the 'Dwari of Yam', where teachers were difficult to find, schools were established for the children of tea plantation workers and other workers. By virtue of education, their self-awareness has increased, association has come.[10] All these were made possible by the brutality of Satyendra Prasad Ray. If the tea-industrial community not come forward at that time, the vast areas of the Dooars might have remained backward even today. Finally, it has to be said that this personality of the great worker died on September 7, 1987 in Kolkata Basically, many refugees and youths got jobs and business opportunities through his hands. On the other hand, his contribution in the form of education expansion and sports lover was considerable in a word, it can be said that there was an overall momentum in Jalpaiguri district due to his arrival.

References

1. Ghosh, Vasudev, "Rivers and Folklore of Jalpaiguri District" (translated from Bengali), *Jalpaiguri District Compendium*, Vol. 2, Kirat Bhumi, (Editor: Arvind Ghosh), p.81
2. Ghosh, Anandagopal, 'Satkahan on Development and Affairs of Bengali tribal Societies in the 19th century' (translated from Bengali), in Kar, Arvind, *Kirat Bhoomi* 24th Year 1916, pp.7-8
3. Chakraborty, Kamakhya Prasad, "Role of Bengali Entrepreneurs in the Establishment of Tea Industry" (translated from Bengali), in Kar, Arvind, edit. *Jalpaiguri District Collection (1859-1998), Kirat Bhumi*, pp. 235-239
4. Biswas, Supam, *"Growth of Bengali Entrepreneurs in the Tea Industry of Jalpaiguri District"* (translated from Bengali), *Readers Service*, 2015, p. 61
5. Kar, Arvind., (ed.) "Some Prominent Families of Jalpaiguri District" (translated from Bengali), *Kirat Bhumi*, Jalpaiguri District Collection, 1869-1994, p. 557
6. Biswas, Supam, "North Bengal Education and Bengali Tea-Planters", *Changing Scenario of Education in Bengal*, Editor-Kalikrishana Sutradhar, Abhijit Roy, Abhijeet Publication, New Delhi, 2022, p.192
7. Biswas, Supam., "The Broad Almost Football Game of Dooars-Terai Tea-Band: Development and Dissolution of Bengali Tea-Entrepreneurs in North Bengal" (translated from Bengali), *Readers Service*, Calcutta, 2015 pp.124-125
8. Bhattacharya, Ajitesh. (ed.) "Oral interview conducted by Anandagopal Ghosh, addressed to Satyendra Prasad Roy" (translated from Bengali), Date – 23.08.1987, Madhuparni, Special Jalpaiguri District Issue, 1987
9. Dutta, Pratibha, *Twenty-Five Years Memoir of Banarhat Girls' School* (translated from Bengali), Banarhat Secondary Girls' School, Jalpaiguri, Memoir 2011, p.17
10. Suniti Bala, Chanda, *One Hundred Years of Women's Education Progress in Jalpaiguri District* in edited book of Charuchandra Sanyal, Jalpaiguri District Centenary Commemorative Book, 1970, p.157

Democratic Decentralization & Good Governance in India: A Comparative Study

Prasanta Adhikary

In recent days, there are movements towards decentralization throughout the world. At the same time, however, the meaning, essence, and strategies of decentralization are still subjects of lively debate. Decentralization is sometimes regarded as an alternative to centralization. However, when viewed from the policy angle, decentralization is a complement and not an alternative to centralization. Sometimes decentralization is considered as falling exclusively within public sector reform, yet it is much more than public sector, civil service or administrative reform. It involves the relationship of all societal actors, whether governmental, private sector or civil society. There is no doubt that a clear understanding of the concept will lead to proper design and effective implementation of decentralization policies and strategies. The aim of this paper is to trace the relationship between decentralization and good governance in India and other countries, particularly how the latter influences the design of decentralization polices and legal frameworks. An additional aim is to highlight factors that need to be taken into account when formulating strategies for the implementation of decentralization policies in India. The first part of the paper deals with the concept of decentralization and outlines the relationship between decentralization and good governance in general. At the second part, the study will also take into consideration the problems faced and the challenges met by the local bodies of India. The article basically is supposed to be a theoretical one. However, some empirical findings have also been taken into consideration to prove the point as mentioned in the proposed study.

The concept of 'Governance' is not new. It is as government itself. Both the terms are derived respectively, from the old French words *governance* and *government*. Initially their meanings were very close, referring to acts or manner of government. By the mid-16th century, however, government denoted a "system by which something is governed" and by the early 18th century it further evolved to acquire the meaning of a "governing authority." In this process the term governance gradually became marginalized, and by the 19th century it was deemed to reflect an incipient archaism. For the next 100 years, it would hardly be used as a political term.[1] Dictionaries would define government in terms of a governing authority, including the political order and its institutional framework, while governance was treated as the agency and process of governing, and was often viewed as archaic. However, during 1980s under economic reforms, especially under globalization the use of term governance became popular with its emphasis on the process and manner of governing to the notion of sustainable development. Meanwhile, organizations such as the IMF, NGOs, the UN and its agencies, the World Bank and international media were quick to pick up the term and use it in a variety of ways. The concept of Good Governance has gained prominence around the world in recent times. It has become a buzzword in the vocabulary of polity and administrative reform in the developing countries, mainly due to the importance given to it by international community. Actually, the term governance has become synonymous to sound development management. In recent times the concept of Good Governance first emerged in the mid-1980s as governability with the emphasis on adherence to the rule of law. Following the collapse of the Soviet Union and the end of the cold war, the term governance came to be used to define the reinventing of public administration, particularly in the developing countries, to make it more receptive to the needs of globalization.[2]

Definitions and descriptions of decentralization used in the papers include as first "Decentralization is usually referred to as the transfer of powers from central government to lower levels in a political-administrative and territorial hierarchy.[3] This official power transfer can take two main forms. Administrative decentralization, also known as de-concentration, refers to a transfer to lower-level central government authorities, or to other local authorities who are upwardly accountable to the central government.[4] In contrast, political, or democratic, decentralization refers to the transfer of authority to representative and downwardly accountable actors, such as elected local governments."[5] Secondly, "The term decentralization is used to cover a broad range of transfers of the "locus of decision making" from central governments to regional, municipal or local governments".[6] Third, Decentralization reform refers to "transforming the local institutional infrastructure for natural resource management on which local forest management is based".[7] Finally, "Decentralization is "the means to allow for the participation of people and local governments".[8]

There are four types of decentralization such as:[9]

Political decentralization: groups at different levels of government–central, meso and local–are empowered to make decisions related to what affects them.

Administrative decentralization: different levels of government administer resources and matters that have been delegated to them, generally through a constitution. In terms of decentralization as a process of change, and according to the level of transfer of responsibilities, it is useful to distinguish between de-concentration, delegation and devolution.

Fiscal decentralization: in this case, previously concentrated powers to tax and generate revenues are dispersed to other levels of government, e.g., local governments are given the power to raise and retain financial resources to fulfill their responsibilities.

Market decentralization: government privatizes or deregulates private functions, such as occurred in the case of New Zealand Forest sector".

Local governments and off-center administrative units in many developing countries have limited opportunities to produce services. A local management approach that is powerless and dependent on central government subsidies has been identified as the root of the problem in these countries. Local public services extensively controlled by the central authority, and the desire of the center to be active in local management, also has a negative impact on citizen participation. In this context, developing countries have put a power increase formula into practice for local authorities by reducing the power of the central government. While some have decentralized the management structure politically, others have chosen to decentralize their systems in administrative aspects, especially when their population has a variety of ethnicities. Political decentralization refers to a federal-state system where a state government has greater power between the national government and the local people.[10] It has been observed that prior to decentralization most of the activities of the state government were carried out by the federal government. Political thinkers who advocate decentralization state that making decisions relevant to the local unit with the participation of the broader society will be more effective, conscious and optimal than the policies of national government will in determining the interests of the public. Federal structures emerging within political decentralization recognize a certain degree of autonomy to communities that differ based on religion, language and ethnicity. States with complex cultural aspects and an increase in identity politics may encounter separation problems from time to time. This situation suggests that a political decentralized system, while having the advantage of a formula for various local problems and needs, will lead to geographical separation. One of the possible crises is the ethnic conflict phenomenon. Ethnic conflict encompasses all forms of small and large-scale violence acts. An ethnic group is a group of people who belong to a certain ascriptive category, such as race, ethnicity, language, tribe, religion, and so forth. Secessionism is distinct from ethnic conflict. It refers to the desire of groups for an independent state. Secessionism is usually associated with violence and often accompanied by ethnic conflict, but it may not be right to associate it with either violence or ethnic conflict.[11]

However, the realization of political decentralization in regions where ethnic divisions are present can lead to the idea of establishing new statelets by threatening national peace. Administrative decentralization, however, does not carry a similar risk. It is a fact that developing countries have centralized for political, economic, administrative and social reasons. A major portion of public services are planned in the capitals of these countries and by conducting them from there, there is a strong centralism in administrative and financial areas. In this context, the functions carried out by the central administration become increasingly complex. The increase in workload, and the difficulty in adapting the general policy to local needs may lead to transferring decision-making responsibility to subordinate units.[12] This situation, expressed as administrative decentralization, emerges in the form of policies that transfer municipal services, education, social welfare, housing, the administration and delivery of social services to subnational governments.[13] Civil service reform is usually a supporting strategy for more general decentralization in government operations or service delivery. One does not decentralize the civil service as an end in itself -- one does so in order to provide services better, manage resources more efficiently, or support other general outcome goals. The civil service as a whole can be seen as one of the main instruments with which the government fulfills its obligations. In the context of decentralization, this tool must often be reshaped in order to perform a new set of duties efficiently, equitably, and effectively. Reform of the civil service, therefore, is the process of modifying rules and incentives to obtain a more efficient, dedicated and performing government labor-force in newly decentralized environment.[14] It is observed that administrative decentralization, which is the distributing of responsibility for decision-making and administration to local communities, has recently become widespread in the developing world.[9] This has especially drawn attention as a mechanism in which responsibilities of tender, the selection of local projects and identification of beneficiaries are devolved from the central ministries to local governments or community representatives. Such trials were initially implemented in the 1980s in various countries including: Armenia, Albania, Bosnia and Herzegovina, Brazil, China, El Salvador, Georgia, India, Mexico, South Africa, Uganda and Uzbekistan.[15] Administrative decentralization is intended to eliminate the drawbacks of excessive centralization, to ensure public participation in management, to establish a balance between local services and local needs and to improve productivity or effectiveness in public services.[16] It has been observed that freedom of status such as self –decision making, implementation, and financial autonomy have expanded local units 'influence areas. However, this authorization is not the same thing as constitutional sovereignty in federalism but is a partial autonomy. In this context, the benefit from active participation in decisions is that administration units maximize their functional qualities such as decision - making, implementation, spending their own resources, and being elected to serve, while being enabled to establish an effective service management with administrative decentralization in the unitary structures.[17]

If we talk about the Fiscal Decentralization, it aims at providing the necessary financial resources for local governments to exercise the functions defined in the law. This reform aims to create more revenue for local government to provide local support in improving the quantity and quality of local services. This can be achieved with the use of transfers that are income transfers to the central government at the local level. Sharing their conditional grants and unconditional grants are mechanisms by which central government operates. Fiscal decentralization reform, aims at strengthening the unconditional transfers as grants that bring local autonomy and accountability of local-level bodies.[13] Since the late 90s, Albania has made great pass on drafting a legal basis and institutional framework for implementation of a general structure of fiscal decentralization. The Albanian government has formulated and ratified a decentralization strategy, which is in line with the European Charter of local autonomy and the Constitution of the country. These served as a starting point for drafting the 8652 law "On Organization and Functioning of Local Government" which laid the foundation for fiscal decentralization.[18] Government made significant the transition of functions and funds (especially unconditional grants) from central government to local government units, providing to them a legal fiscal autonomy, so they can make their own decisions in the interest of local community.[19]

Now if we observe the process of decentralization of local government in India, we will be surprised that the spirit of democratic decentralization that evolved over the years is being practiced only in a limited way. It is realized that development efforts in India did not address the issues of equity and to the development of the mass, though it is an important process in the democratic development of the country. It is defined as the process of political devolution, fiscal and decision-making from the central government at the local level so as to facilitate greater direct participation of citizens in governance. As one of the most important reforms, decentralization of power has several objectives. It aims to make sustainable the democratic system, making challenge to the monopoly of decision-making. As a result of this process, we have separation of functions between central and local government, this increases the efficiency and the transparency in government.[20] Finally, in 1992, by the 73rd[21] and 74th[22] constitutional amendment Acts a major step in this direction was taken. 73rd amendment act introduces the reform in the rural local bodies, whereas 74th amendment act introduce reform in the urban local bodies. These amendments have accorded constitutional recognition to rural and urban local bodies. It implies that precisely defined governance functions are formally assigned by law to local governments, backed by adequate transfer of a basket of financial grants and tax handles, and they are given staff so that they have the necessary wherewithal to carry out their responsibilities.

The structure of the Indian Local Government

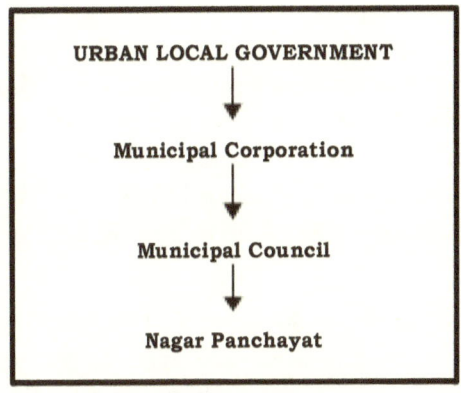

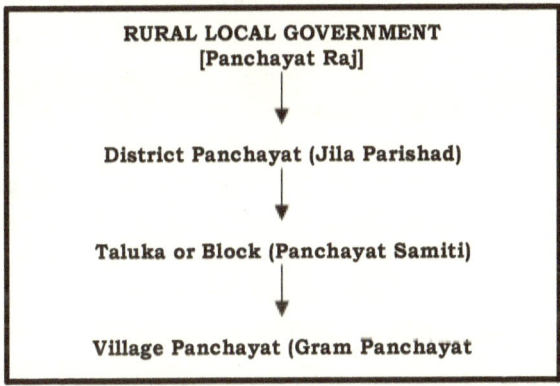

Due to these initiatives two major achievements of the local bodies found throughout the period. First is the Rising of Women Representation: The proportion of elected women representatives has been steadily rising since the enactment of the 73rd Amendment Act. Currently, India has 260,512 Panchayats with 3.1 million elected representatives, of which a record 1.3 million are women. While there is merely 7–8% representation in Parliament and State Assemblies for women, an astounding 49% of elected local representatives (in states like Odisha it has crossed 50%) are women. Second is the Creating Healthy Competition among Various States: The passage of the 73rd and 74th Amendments has created healthy competition among various states regarding devolution (the 3Fs: funds, functions, and functionaries). For instance: Kerala has devolved 29 of its functions to Panchayats. Rajasthan took the inspiration from Kerala to devolve many key departments such as health, education, women, and agriculture to PRIs. Similarly, Bihar came out with the idea of "Panchayat Sarkar" and states such as Odisha have increased 50% seats for women.[23]

Since the passing of 30 years of 73rd and 74th amendment Acts, still there are some important issues with Local Governments in India. First, the insufficient funding which is inadequate to meet their basic requirements of the local bodies, including inflexibility in spending the allocated budget. Second the absence of proper Infrastructure of Garm Panchayats, third is the lack of sufficient staff or skilled manpower, fourth is the untimely and delayed election that hampered the smooth functioning of the local bodies. Fifth is the downgraded role of local government. Local governments are merely acting as an implementation machinery rather than a policy-making body for local development. Technology-enabled schemes have further downgraded their role. And the last one is the rampant corruption.[24] Criminal elements and contractors are attracted to local government elections, tempted by the large sums of money now flowing to them. Thus, forming a market chain of corruption operates, involving a partnership between elected representatives and officials at all levels.[25]

It is certain that the structure of Indian local self-government, that is functioning in the states, is one of the best methods of decentralization of democratic power and good governance. Though there are some constraints in functioning the local governments in an absolute manner, however, there are much possibilities in near future. This needs some reform policies, viz.,

a) revitalizing Gram Sabha in Gram Panchayat and Wards Committees in Municipal areas to achieve the objective of the peoples' participation in real terms. b) Local organizational structure to be strengthen with the sufficient manpower, specially, serious efforts should be made towards recruitment and appointment of support and technical staff to ensure the smooth functioning of panchayats. c) A new method or a comprehensive mechanism to be devised for taxation at the local level. d) government should sufficiently fund the local bodies with proper monitoring of release, expenditure, utilization and audit process. Last but not the least, Government should develop such mechanism which eliminate or minimise the rate of corruptions which is the most vulnerable part of Indian governance.

References

1. Arora, Dinesh, "Good Governance: A Study of the Concept in Indian Context", *Studocu*; Mikhail Ilyin, "Governance: What is Behind the Word?", *IPSA*, Participation, Vol. 37, No.1, May 2013, p. 4
2. Tripathi, R., "Good Governance: Origin, Importance and Development in India", *International Journal of Development Research*, Vol. 07, Issue, 11, pp.16968-16970, November, 2017, pp. 16969-16970
3. Agrawal, Arun, and Jesse Ribot. "Accountability in Decentralization: A Framework with South Asian and West African Cases," *The Journal of Developing Areas*, vol. 33, no. 4, 1999, pp. 473–502.
4. Ribot, J. *Democratic Decentralization of Natural Resources in Beyond Structural Adjustment*, 2003, pp.159-182
5. Litvack, J., Junaid A., & Bird R., *Rethinking Decentralization in Developing Countries*, World Bank Books, 1998; Rondinelli, D. A., 1981, "Government Decentralization in Comparative Perspective: Theory and Practice in Developing Countries", *International Review of Administrative Sciences*, Vol. XLVII, No.2, p.137.
6. Rondinelli, D. A. and Nellis, J., 1986, "Assessing Decentralization Policies: A Case for Cautious Optimism", *Development Policy Review*, Vol. IV, No. 1
7. Ribot, J. Op. cit.
8. Morell, M., "FAO Experience in Decentralization in the Forest Sector Interlaken Workshop", *FONP*, Agricultural Organization UN, Rome, March 2014

9. Yuliani, Elizabeth Linda, presented paper *Decentralization, deconcentration and devolution: what do they mean?* at the Interlaken Workshop on Decentralization, Interlaken, Switzerland, 27-30 April 2004.

10. Falleti, Tulia G. "A Sequential Theory of Decentralization: Latin American Cases in Comparative Perspective," *The American Political Science Review*, vol. 99, no. 3, 2005, pp. 327–46.

11. Brancati, Dawn., *Decentralization: Fueling the Fire or Dampening the Flames of Ethnic Conflict and Secessionism,* Institute of Qualitative Political Science, Cambridge, 2005

12. Ozmen, A., "Notes to the Concept of Decentralization", *European Scientific Journal*, vol.10, No.10 April 2014

13. Falleti, Tulia G. Op. cit.,

14. See for details: worldbank.org, 2014

15. Bashaasha, B., Najjingo M., Mangheni, Nkonya E., *Decentralization and rural service delivery in Uganda,* DIIS, 2013

16. Eryılmaz, B., *Public Administration-Kamu Yönetimi, Okutman Publishing-Okutman Yayıncılık,* Ankara, 2011, p.97

17. Ozmen, A., Op. cit.

18. Effective Public Policy Institute, "*Decentralization and Eastern European Countries*" Friedrich Ebert Stiftung Schroeder. L, "Fiscal Decentralization Policy Study", Albania 2000

19. Burki, S., Perry. G, Dillinger. *World Bank document,* "*Albania: Decentralization in Transition*", "Beyond the Center: Decentralizing the State", 2002

20. Swedish Institute for Public Administration, "*Strengthening Decentralization and Local Governance*", Final Rapport, 2002

21. Article 243I of the 73rd Constitutional Amendment Act, 1992 says that at the expiration of every fifth year; the Governor shall constitute a State Finance Commission to review the financial position of the Panchayats. It will make recommendations to the Governor in matters of distribution and possible allocation/ appropriation of the net proceeds of the taxes, duties, tolls and fees between the State and the Panchayats and the grants-in-aid to the Panchayats from the Consolidated Fund of the State.

22. Article 243ZD of the 74th Constitutional Amendment Act, 1992 related to municipalities provides that every State at the district level shall constitute a District Planning Committee, which would be responsible for consolidation of development plans prepared by the Panchayats and the Municipalities through proposing a development plan for the district as a whole.

23. https://www.drishtiias.com/daily-updates/daily-news-analysis/democratic-decentralisation-in-india-1, Access date 28th October 2023
24. Bardhan, Pranab and Dilip Mookherjee. "Corruption and Decentralization of Infrastructure Delivery in Developing Countries." *Working Paper*, University of California, Berkeley, 2000
25. Dristhi, Ibid.

India-Myanmar Bilateral Relations: A Historical Analysis and Future Prospects

Md Rajibul Islam

India and Myanmar (formerly known as Burma) both achieved independence from the British Empire in the years 1947 and 1948, respectively.[1] After independence, India and Myanmar established formal diplomatic relations in 1948, and both nations signed the treaty of friendship in 1951, a historical milestone in India-Myanmar bilateral relations that emphasized cooperation in various areas, such as economic, political, and cultural.[2] The historical connections between India and Myanmar started in the ancient period when trade, the spread of Buddhism, and cultural exchanges flourished along the Bay of Bengal maritime routes.[3] India-Myanmar relations have deep-rooted historical, ethnic, cultural, and religious ties, which have significantly shaped the bilateral relationship between the two nations. India and Myanmar share a 1643 km land border with Arunachal Pradesh, Nagaland, Manipur, and Mizoram as well as a maritime boundary in the Bay of Bengal and the Andaman Sea. Due to Myanmar's geopolitical and geostrategic significance for India, it has a multi-dimensional purpose. This has led to multi-dimensional relations and makes Myanmar an essential land bridge for India's access to the Southeast Asia region. Their relationship is integral to India's Look East Policy, aiming for a more influential Asia and stronger connectivity, which forms the foundation of India's strategic interests in this region.[4]

In the 1950s, India and Myanmar enjoyed a period of stable bilateral diplomatic relations and shared common interests within the Non-Aligned Movement (NAM). The NAM comprised a coalition of countries dedicated to maintaining a stance of neutrality and independence amid the geopolitical rivalries of the Cold War era, abstaining from aligning themselves with either the Western bloc, led by the United States, or the Eastern bloc, led by the Soviet Union. But in 1962, the political landscape changed in Myanmar with a military coup. Myanmar's foreign policy under the military regime leaned toward isolationism which had significant effects on the country's interactions with other nations as well as neighbouring country India also affected. The strong bilateral relations between India and Myanmar were initially established after independence but gradually weakened due to changing political dynamics in Myanmar.[5] The 1962 military coup in Myanmar significantly impacted the bilateral relationship between India and Myanmar. The military coup, led by General Ne Win, implemented an isolationist policy known as the 'Burmese Road to Socialism' which aimed to nationalize industries and create a strong state. The introduction of isolationist policies and the authoritarian turn in Myanmar's governance created a rift that lasted for several decades between India and Myanmar.[6]

General Ne Win's period of leadership in Myanmar (1962-1988) witnessed fluctuating bilateral relations between India and Myanmar. These ups and downs can be attributed to various political, strategic, and economic areas. The period between 1988 and 1990 marked a low point in India-Myanmar relations due to the transition period and India's stance against human rights violations. However, India's adoption of the 'Look East' policy in 1991 and subsequent developments led to a gradual thaw in relations, resulting in increased cooperation in various sectors.[7]

Between 1994 and 1996, the period witnessed a notable enhancement of economic cooperation between India and Myanmar. Both countries recognized the mutual benefits of closer economic ties and took concrete steps to facilitate trade, investment, and infrastructure development. The period between 1997 and 1999 witnessed efforts by India and Myanmar to address security challenges and improve cooperation in areas like counter-terrorism and anti-narcotics efforts. The first decade of the 21st century witnessed strategic engagement between India and Myanmar with the multifaceted nature of their relations such as infrastructure, energy, telecommunications, and information technology.[8]

India's approach to its bilateral relations with Myanmar is characterized by a strategic and multifaceted engagement encompassing economic, strategic, security, cultural, connectivity, trade, energy, and regional influence in the southeast region. Due to national interest, India tried to build good relations with Myanmar's current government. This study has some specific objectives and purposes viz. To study a comprehensive and detailed examination of the historical analysis of India-Myanmar bilateral relations since their independence from the British Empire. To identify and analyze the challenges that India and Myanmar have faced in their bilateral relations. To explore potential opportunities and prospects for cooperation between India and Myanmar. The methodology of this study is based on historical, descriptive, and analytical. This paper analyzes the evolution of India-Myanmar relations since independence from the British Empire. This study was carried out with the help of secondary data sources, including research articles, journals, books, official documents, bilateral agreements, and joint statements between India and Myanmar.

India and Burma (Now Myanmar) have shared historical connections since the ancient period. The spread of Buddhism from India profoundly influenced Burmese culture, shaping their way of life and societal norms. This cultural bond nurtured a feeling of closeness and mutual comprehension between India and Burma (Myanmar). The historical connections between India and Myanmar are deeply rooted in shared cultural, religious, and historical experiences. These ties serve as a strong foundation for their modern-day relations, fostering mutual understanding, cooperation, and a sense of shared history that continues to shape their diplomatic, cultural, and economic interactions. After the Third Anglo-Burmese War ended in 1886, the British Empire took control of Burma and integrated with British India. But in 1937, Burma province was formally separated from British India.[9]

India and Myanmar are deeply rooted in history, culture, trade, connectivity, and proximity. They span the realms of religion, culture, ethnicity, and political history and continue to play a vital role in shaping the relationship between nations. These connections are not just historical artifacts but remain vibrant and relevant in contemporary interactions and cooperation between India and Myanmar.[10] India and Myanmar share close geographical proximity and historical linkage, with mutual contact in trade, culture, and religion. During the colonial era, both countries were under British India.[11] Finally, Burma gained independence from the British ruler in 1948.

After independence from the British Empire, both India and Myanmar formally established diplomatic relations in 1948. Myanmar's post-independence politics can be categorized into different phases based on governance's function such as;

1. U Nu Era (1948-1962)
2. Ne Win Era (1962-1988)
3. Transition Period (1988-1990)

4. State Peace and Development Council (SPDC) Era (1991-2010)
5. Period 2011-2021
6. Period 2021- to present time: Military coup

However, over the years, the relationship between India and Myanmar witnessed some ups and downs due to changes in political scenarios in Myanmar.[12]

In 1951, India and Myanmar signed a Treaty of Friendship. This treaty aimed to strengthen their bilateral relations and promote mutual cooperation in various economic, political, and cultural areas. Both nations continue to play a significant role in shaping the relationship between India and Myanmar.[13] India's evolving foreign policy toward Myanmar highlights the changing priorities and challenges it has faced from time to time. Due to the geopolitical interest, India's comprehensive and patient approach focuses on peace, conflict resolution, and building positive relations with Myanmar.[14] Therefore, India and Myanmar's bilateral relationship is characterized by both cooperation and challenges since independence. Their shared history, geographical proximity, and geopolitical considerations have all shaped their bilateral ties. Despite the occasional ups and downs, both nations have shown a commitment to maintaining good relations and have engaged in various dimensions of economic, political, trade, diplomatic, and security initiatives to strengthen their ties over the years.

India-Myanmar bilateral relations have evolved through different distinct phases. The first phase (1948-1962) was characterized by good bilateral relations, where the two nations established diplomatic ties and signed the Treaty of Friendship. In the second phase (1962-1988) of India-Myanmar relations, during this period, the relationship between India and Myanmar faced challenges due to Myanmar's isolationist policies and political changes. But the bilateral relationship improved during the 1970s and 1980s because of high-level official visits from both sides, such as Indira Gandhi's visit to Rangoon in 1969, A. B. Vajpayee's visit to Myanmar in 1977, Ne Win's visit to India in 1980, Narasimha Rao's visit in 1981, Rajiv Gandhi's visit in 1987. The Third Phase (1988-1992) of India-Myanmar bilateral relations, was marked by India's principled stand in support of democracy and human rights in Myanmar, which led to a deterioration in bilateral ties between India and Myanmar. The fourth phase (1993-2010) of India-Myanmar relations was characterized by a proactive India's engagement with Myanmar through strategic, economic, and geopolitical considerations. India sought to build a more constructive and cooperative relationship with Myanmar. India initiated a policy of engagement with Myanmar, and India adopted its 'Look East' policy, improving bilateral relations and increasing cooperation with Myanmar. The fifth phase (2011-2021) of India-Myanmar relations commenced after the historic November 2010 general elections in Myanmar, which marked the end of decades of military rule. The transition to democracy in Myanmar brought about significant changes and encouraged India to adopt a more proactive and optimistic approach to its Myanmar policy.[15]

The current phase (2021- present time): In November 2020, Myanmar held a general election in which the National League for Democracy (NLD) secured a landslide victory in the parliament. On February 1, 2021, the military, led by Commander-in-Chief Min Aung Hlaing, staged a coup. They alleged voter fraud and irregularities in the November 2020 election. In 2021, Myanmar experienced a significant political upheaval as the military, known as the Tatmadaw, once again assumed control of the country, effectively ending a brief period of civilian rule.

Myanmar holds significant geopolitical and geostrategic importance for India. The country's strategic location makes it an essential connecting hub between South Asia, East Asia, and

Southeast Asia, and it also has access to vital maritime routes through the Bay of Bengal and the Andaman Sea.[16] Indo-Myanmar relations are deeply rooted in history and civilizational ties, with a long-standing history of socio-economic, commercial, political, and cultural connections dating back to ancient and medieval times. Beyond historical connections, there are ethnic links between the people of Myanmar and certain Indian states that border Myanmar, namely Arunachal Pradesh, Manipur, Nagaland, and Mizoram. In the contemporary era, India and Myanmar continue to enjoy warm and friendly relations. Myanmar is strategically important for India as it is the only gateway connecting India by land to Southeast Asia.[17] Myanmar is an essential neighbour country for India sharing extensive land and maritime boundaries. During Myanmar's military rule, India pursued a policy of non-involvement, but the introduction of the 'Look East Policy' marked a shift toward greater engagement of India with Myanmar. Because of Myanmar's close economic and military ties with China are a concern for India, as China's presence in Myanmar's ports and naval facilities raises strategic issues in the Indian Ocean region. Myanmar also acts as a buffer nation between India's North-Eastern region and Chinese provinces.[18]

India-Myanmar relations evolved from friendly and close ties between (1948 and 1962) to reduced and strained relations from (1962 to 1991) due to the military coup led by General Ne Win in 1962. During General Ne Win's rule in Myanmar from (1962 to 1988), India adopted a neutral stance in its bilateral relations with Myanmar. China seized this opportunity to deepen its ties with Myanmar. This geopolitical shift and Myanmar's growing closeness with China prompted India to reassess its foreign policy towards Myanmar. India recognized the importance of engaging more proactively with Myanmar to safeguard its regional strategic interests and counterbalance

China's influence. India's foreign policy towards Myanmar evolved, focusing on pragmatic engagement, economic cooperation, and diplomatic efforts to improve relations.[19] However, since the early 1990s, India's stance towards Myanmar has undergone a significant transformation, influenced by three major factors; the rise of China as a Regional Power, Geostrategic Considerations, and Active and Pragmatic Engagement. This shift marked a transition from a values-centric approach to a more balanced and pragmatic engagement, underlining the importance of mutual benefits and strategic imperatives in shaping India's policy towards Myanmar.[20] India's approach to Myanmar since 1992 reflects a sophisticated and multifaceted strategy that combines the pursuit of economic and strategic interests with a principled stand on democratic values and human rights.[21]

After independence in 1948, it shared cordial political relations with India under leaders like Jawaharlal Nehru and U Nu. However, a shift occurred with the rise of military rule in Myanmar under Ne Win, leading to a period of cold relations marked by mistrust and political suppression, and the nationalization of petty trade, causing mass alienation among the Indian community in Myanmar.[22] The political relations between India and Myanmar have evolved from time to time guided by shared historical ties, mutual strategic interests, and a commitment to regional stability. This dynamic partnership has seen both countries collaborating on a wide range of diplomatic, security, and regional issues, strengthening their bilateral ties and contributing to the broader stability of the Indo-Pacific region. Their multifaceted engagement holds great promise for the future, as they continue to work together on common goals while addressing challenges.

The economic relationship between India and Myanmar has been growing rapidly. Both countries have recognized the potential for mutually beneficial trade and investment opportunities. As a result, trade between the two nations has been increasing steadily. This growth in bilateral economic ties promises to foster closer economic cooperation in the future.[23] Both countries recognize the potential for mutually beneficial economic engagement. India seeks to leverage Myanmar's resources, such as natural gas, while also contributing to Myanmar's development through investment, infrastructure projects, and trade. Initiatives like the Kaladan Multi-Modal Transit Transport Project and the India-Myanmar-Thailand Trilateral Highway exemplify this collaborative approach. The economic relations between India and Myanmar have grown significantly over the years, driven by shared geographical advantages, economic complementarity, and a mutual commitment to fostering development and trade.

India and Myanmar share strong cultural and historical ties rooted in their common heritage, with cultural exchanges dating back to ancient times. Both nations have maintained a close bond, evident through frequent cultural performances and exchanges since 1997, including visits by Burmese bands to India and Myanmar, and an annual Indian Film Festival in Yangon. Additionally, initiatives like yoga and Bharatnatyam classes and events celebrating Rabindranath Tagore's 150th birthday have further strengthened their cultural connections.[24] This cultural affinity has created a strong bond between the two nations, fostering a sense of camaraderie and contributing to the enhancement of diplomatic, economic, and people-to-people ties. As they celebrate each other's cultures, India and Myanmar pave the way for a future of greater collaboration, understanding, and friendship that transcends borders, languages, and differences, enriching the cultural tapestry of the entire region.

The India-Myanmar border presents a series of complex challenges due to its porous characteristics. The border is highly porous, inadequately guarded, and stretches across a remote and underdeveloped region known for insurgency activities. To address these challenges, India must allocate adequate resources, implement robust security measures, and collaborate with Myanmar to effectively manage and secure the border.[25] China has been actively reducing India's influence in Myanmar by implementing the 'String of Pearls strategy' in which China builds a network of military and commercial surrounding the Indian Ocean Region (IOR). China's political support activities for Myanmar, including using its veto power at the United Nations, have further strengthened their relations. In response, India has adopted a more realistic foreign policy approach, striving to build trust and improve relations with Myanmar since 1992.[26]

India faces several challenges in its relationship with Myanmar, a neighbouring country with which it shares a long border. These challenges encompass the bilateral relationship's political, economic, security, and humanitarian aspects. Balancing political, economic, security, and humanitarian concerns while engaging with Myanmar is essential for strengthening bilateral relations and promoting regional stability. India must continue to employ diplomatic skills, economic cooperation, and strategic thinking to navigate these challenges effectively.

Apart from porous border challenges, India-Myanmar relations are currently experiencing significant development opportunities, particularly due to the frequent exchanges of high-level official visits from both countries. These mutual visits provide a platform to enhance bilateral cooperation in various areas, including the economy, trade, security, and culture. India-Myanmar relations are witnessing significant opportunities for development across multiple sectors. The frequent exchanges of high-level officials have paved the way for enhanced cooperation in economy, trade, security, and culture. As both countries continue to explore avenues of collaboration and engagement, the future looks promising for further strengthening their bilateral ties.[27] For both India and Myanmar, the relationship is seen as mutually beneficial, offering opportunities for economic growth, regional cooperation, and cultural exchange. The strong historical, geographical, and strategic ties between the two nations continue to shape their diplomatic and economic relations, making Indo-Myanmar relations a significant pillar of India's regional and global engagement.[28] Efforts aimed at bolstering connectivity and fostering economic integration between India and Southeast and East Asia via Myanmar have encouraged the initiation and planning of various significant ongoing and proposed road, rail, and maritime connectivity projects[29] such as;

1. The India-Myanmar-Thailand Trilateral Highway (IMTTH)
2. The New India-Myanmar-Laos-Vietnam-Cambodia Highway
3. The Mekong–India Economic Corridor
4. The Delhi–Hanoi Railway Link
5. The Kaladan Multimodal Transit Transport Project

Myanmar holds immense significance for India across a spectrum of dimensions, encompassing economic, political, cultural, security, geopolitical, geostrategic, and connectivity aspects. The attainment of these multifaceted objectives depends on fostering strong and amicable relations between the two nations.[30]

India and Myanmar share a unique and historically significant relationship that encompasses political, economic, cultural, and strategic dimensions. This multifaceted partnership is grounded in their shared geographical proximity, historical ties, and a mutual understanding of the importance of regional stability and development. Over the years, both nations have worked to deepen their cooperation, leading to a relationship with great promise for the future. The India-Myanmar bilateral relationship is a dynamic and evolving partnership that holds immense potential. By capitalizing on their geographical proximity, historical ties, and shared interests, India and Myanmar can work together to create a more interconnected, prosperous. India-Myanmar bilateral relations have traversed a complex historical trajectory, marked by shared cultural ties, political challenges, economic opportunities, and security concerns. As both nations look to the future, the prospects for enhanced cooperation and partnership remain promising, particularly in the context of India's 'Act East Policy' and Myanmar's increasing engagement with the global community. The India-Myanmar bilateral relationship is poised for significant growth and collaboration in various domains. As both nations adapt to changing geopolitical dynamics, they can build a strategic partnership that benefits their respective citizens and contributes to peace, stability, and prosperity in the region.

The bilateral relations between India and Myanmar have characteristics of shared history, geographical proximity, cultural ties, and contemporary geopolitical complexities. Over the years, both nations have navigated a dynamic landscape characterized by evolving political contexts, economic aspirations, security challenges, and the influence of regional and global actors. The bilateral relations between India and Myanmar have indeed witnessed a mix of ups and downs over the years, but overall, they can be characterized as having a generally positive and friendly. Both countries continue to work together to address challenges and strengthen their ties for mutual benefit. In the 21st century, the global landscape has become increasingly interconnected, and nations worldwide have recognized the importance of interdependence and cooperation. This interconnectedness extends to political, economic, social, and environmental dimensions. In this context, it is essential for nations to maintain good relations with one another to address shared challenges and seize opportunities for mutual benefit. India's relationship with Myanmar holds immense potential for economic, security, and cultural cooperation. Policymakers in India should indeed adopt a pragmatic approach towards Myanmar.

References

1. Singh, Langpoklakpam Suraj. "India and the Quest for Democracy in Myanmar: Rethinking India's Myanmar Policy." *The Indian Journal of Political Science* vol. 71, no. 3,2010, pp. 1003-1016.
2. Hiep, Tran Xuan, Nguyen Tuan Binh, and Tran Thai Bao. "Chinese Factors in India Relationship with Myanmar in the Period 1992–2014." *Journal of Educational and Social Research* vol.11, no.1, 2021, pp.92-100.
3. Gottschlich, Pierre. "New developments in India–Myanmar bilateral relations?" *Journal Current Southeast Asian Affairs* vol. 34, no.2, 2015, pp.139-163.
4. Kumar, Ashok. "India-Myanmar Relations: A Strategic Analysis." *Himachal Pradesh University Journal* vol. 8, no.1, 2020, pp.71-87.
5. Lall, Marie. "Indo-Myanmar relations in the era of pipeline diplomacy." *Contemporary Southeast Asia* vol. 28, no. 3,2006, pp. 424-446.
6. Routray, Bibhu. "India-Myanmar relations: Triumph of pragmatism." *Jindal Journal of International Affairs* vol. 1, Issue 1, 2011, pp. 299-321.
7. Yhome, Khriezo. "India-Myanmar Relations (1998-2008): A Decade of Redefining Bilateral Relations." ORF occasional paper, 2009.
8. Routray, loc.cit., p.306.
9. Singh, Amit. "Emerging Trends in India–Myanmar Relations." *Maritime Affairs: Journal of the National Maritime Foundation of India* vol. 8, no. 2, 2012, pp. 25-47.

10. Bhatia, Rajiv Kumar. "Myanmar-India Relations: The Way Forward." *Indian Foreign Affairs Journal* vol. 6, no. 3, 2011, pp. 315-326.
11. Choudhary, L. K. "Indo-Myanmar Relations: Retrospect and Prospect." *India Quarterly: A Journal of International Affairs* vol. 61, no. 4, 2005, pp. 143–168.
12. Bhatia, op. cit., p.317.
13. Singh, op., cit., p.29.
14. Egreteau, Renaud. "A passage to Burma? India, development, and democratization in Myanmar." *Contemporary Politics* vol.17, no.4, 2011, pp.467-486.
15. Singh, op. cit., p.30.
16. Ahamed, Akkas, Md Sayedur Rahman, and Nur Hossain. "China-Myanmar Bilateral Relations: An Analytical Study of Some Geostrategic and Economic Issues." *Journal of Public Administration and Governance* vol. 10, no.3, 2020, pp.321-343.
17. Janesar, Mohammad, and Rajesh Sahu. "The Role of Indian Diaspora: A Look at India-Myanmar Relations." *IUP Journal of International Relations* vol.13, Issue 3, 2019, pp. 53-67.
18. Singh, Amit. "Diaspora as a Factor in India–Myanmar Relations." *Maritime Affairs: Journal of the National Maritime Foundation of India* vol. 9, no. 2, 2013, pp. 82-96.
19. Hiep, op., cit., p.94.
20. Sidhu, Jatswan S. "India's Myanmar Policy since 1988: Between Democratic Ideals and Geostrategic Imperatives." *Journal of International Studies* vol. 5, 2009, pp.93-108.
21. Jha, Gaurav Kumar, and Amrita Banerjee. "India–Myanmar Relations: Coming off the Circle." *South Asian Survey* vol.19, no.1, 2012, pp.79-99.
22. Ibid., p.85.
23. Wu, Zhaoli. "India-Myanmar Bilateral Relations: Cooperate Actively and Progress Significantly." *Annual Report on the Development of International Relations in the Indian Ocean Region (2014)*, 2015, pp.155-169.
24. Mir, Ishfaq Ahmad. "India's cultural relationship with Asian nations." *International Journal of Economic, Business, Accounting, Agriculture Management and Sharia Administration (IJEBAS)* vol.3, no.2, 2023, pp.361-368
25. Das, Pushpita. "Security challenges and the management of the India–Myanmar border." *Strategic Analysis* vol.42, no.6, 2018, pp. 578-594.

26. Hiep, op., cit., p.98.
27. Wu, op., cit., p.157.
28. Janesar, op. cit., p.56.
29. Yhome, Khriezo. "The Burma Roads: India's Search for Connectivity through Myanmar." *Asian Survey* vol.55, no.6, 2015, pp.1217-1240.
30. Dixit, Jyotindra Nath. *India's Foreign Policy and Its Neighbours*. Gyan Publishing House, 2001.

The Role of Internet and Mass-Media in the Transformation of Bengali Culture: An Overview

Papia Biswas

The cultural heritage of the Bengali people is very old. The activities of every human being living in a society is one of the elements of their culture. Internet and mass media influence the entire world today. It can be said that internet and mass media are controlling the world. However, its impact is not less on the culture of Bengal. Bengali society, politics, knowledge and science, food, clothing, language, folklore, art architecture have the influences of Mass media everywhere. Mass media has played a very positive role in eradicating ignorance, superstition, imparting education, dealing with disasters, preventing various diseases (such as Polio, HIV) while the negative role of internet and mass media in society cannot be ignored. These are killing the unique indicators of Bengali culture. Indicating aspects of Bengali culture has slowly been destroyed by the invasion of globalization and by the hands of the Internet. What is the role of internet and mass media on Bengali society and culture?, is it possible for the media to destroy Bengali cultural diversity?, and how much Bengali culture is being damaged by the impact of globalization and net culture? - are the main questions that has been discussed in this paper.

The history of the Bengali people is very rich. The history of the Bengal can be found in places like Mainamati, Mahasthangarh, Chandraketugarh, Karnasuvarna, Tamralipta, Vikramshila,[1] Murshidabad etc. in undivided Bengal. Culture cannot develop without tradition. A nation's identity defines its people, history, politics, economy, society and culture. From society, social values, religion, morals, folk beliefs, food habits, clothing, language-literature, music to acting, painting, art-architecture and all the accessories of human life, collectively formed the cultural landscape. Every activity of people living in society is one of the elements of their culture. Every society in the world has its own culture. Society acquires its own cultural characteristics mainly because of the variation in the natural environment and the different strategies and tools used to adapt to it.[2] The arrival of foreign forces, invasion, colonial rule, exploitation and various cultural elements have created the culture of Bengal. Bengali's own style has been added to it.

Mass media plays a huge role in our culture and mind. Proper use of mass media plays a positive role in the field of entertainment, improvement of knowledge, removal of prejudices, development of women. Media has played a significant role in increasing preventive awareness of Polio, HIV. Nowadays various web pages are being used through TV, radio and internet to spread awareness about various natural calamities. An internet connection exposes a vast wealth of information to any individual. The media also has the power to control and change public consumption.[3] Direct satellite broadcasting, Internet, TV, newspapers, mobiles are all changing traditional maps. The rapid production and distribution of digital technology is taking society into a new world.[4]

The media and internet have had some positive effects as well as huge negative effects on our culture and mind. Excessive internet use is destroying our thinking. There is an aversion to critical and analytical topics and discussion among the current generation, behind which the influence of internet culture cannot be denied. As a result, a popular culture has emerged in addition to our traditional culture. One of the mediums of promoting this culture is the internet and mass media. For this reason, it is also called media culture, which is currently influencing Bengali culture as well as the whole world. Due to media culture, folk culture is also very weak today. Folk culture was very popular among the masses in the pre-media era. The reason was that there was no purpose behind the development of this culture. It was created at the whim of the mind, just for the joy of creation. Folk culture is the customs, folk customs, traditional rules and regulations which are spread by the common people from their forefathers. Folk culture is based on tradition.[5] The originality and individuality of a nation can be preserved only through folk culture. But this kind of creation and untimely death of the creator happened due to internet and mass media. Nowadays people are spending hours behind television, mobile, laptop, tab. Due to excessive misuse of media, elements of present Bengali culture are getting weaker and weaker. As a result of the culture based on mass entertainment, Bengali culture today is a victim of the imperialism of world culture, which is also influencing the taste of the people. This bad culture stunts the cultural development of people and gives birth to luxury and extravagance in life.

Due to the global process called globalization, the whole world is now part of the global village. Although the primary basis of globalization was economy but globalization did not stop only with economic globalization. Globalization has affected society, politics, religion, knowledge and science through the media. The impact of globalization has not fallen evenly on Indian society. The people at the very bottom of the society have suffered the most.[6] World culture has a perverse influence on the Bengali people. Bengali society is being made accustomed to violent pornographic films, low-cut clothes, food habits. Economy, culture and climate play an important role in choosing clothes. Only because of the advertisements of foreign brands of clothes on TV, the new Bengali generation is getting used to jeans, t-shirts, gowns, leaving traditional clothes. In our humid summer weather, jeans are not only uncomfortable but also unhealthy. The impact of globalization through the media is also present on the Bengali marriage institution. Apart from Bengali folklore, pre-wedding ceremonies like mehndi, music, pre-wedding photo shoot are also taking place in Bengali culture. Along with Bengali language, English translation is getting place in the wedding invitation letter. In some cases, the entire card is written in English. There has been a big change in the food menu. The book Prakriti Paingalam describes the diet of Bengalis. It is said there as:

"ওগগরা ভত্তা রন্তঅ পত্তা গাইক ঘিত্তা দুগ্ধ সযুক্তা

মোইলি মচ্ছা নালিত গচ্ছা ...."

That is, there is a description of hot rice, Gawa Ghee (Clarified Butter), Mourala Fish / Carplate Fish, and Nalita Shak (Leafy Vegetable) in Kalapata.[7] However, deer, goat, fowl, fish, curd, pitha were served at the wedding feast. Today, wedding feasts are also the effect of globalization. Tandoori chicken, butter naan, chole-batora, fried rice, mutton rezala, ice cream has taken place there instead of Bengali food. The food list of the special page of Bengali first-class newspaper is filled with recipes of various foreign cuisines. Young people are getting attracted to fast food and junk food only by watching advertisements on television channels without judging the nutritional quality. As a result, restaurants after restaurants are being built in small and big villages and towns of Bengal. The first restaurant in Bengal was opened keeping in mind the English customers. In the 1830s, English-educated Bengali youth also started going there, mainly to taste the taste of forbidden and unconventional food in the society at that time. In the 1840s, many educated Bengali youths including Rajnarayan Basu, Michael Madhusudan Dutt tasted forbidden food in such restaurants.[8] Besides English restaurants, Muslim cooks also open restaurants. Various Mughlai dishes such as Kebab, Korma, Biryani are becoming popular there. Although the food habits of the Bengali society remain the same.

Currently, under the influence of various media culture, the culture of drinking has been added along with eating habits. Alcohol is mentioned in various poems from the Charya-pada onwards. Vaishnava scriptures also refer to women's drinking.[9] But that drinking was not common among all or openly. At present there are pubs in almost every neighbourhood which are spreading the culture of drinking among the common people. The negative role of TV serials, web series, advertisements in spreading the culture of Madhyapan (Hard-Drinking) among common Bengali families cannot be denied. Addiction to alcohol, fast food, junk food, cold drinks is causing adverse reactions in the body. Obesity is now becoming a social disease.

The attitudes towards leisure activities have also changed. Sports were one of the means of entertainment. Sports is one of the parts of life and education. Physical, mental, moral and social development is possible through this. *Kho-Kho, Hadudu, Danguli, hide and seek, thief-police* games started to become popular among children and teenagers at the end of the 20th century.[10] Cricket dominance killed popular games in Bengal. Currently, the media has exploited the popularity of cricket with IPL, T-20 tournaments and advertisements to confuse the public. Along with this is the boom of mobile phones. Childhood is now Android oriented. By playing they mean online games or watching cut channels for hours. Along with this, families are attracted to mega serials. As many new technologies are being used in entertainment by the hand of globalization, the distorted form of Hollywood genre is distorting our entertainment industry. Violence, sex, suspicion, mistrust are now the staples of mega serials, web series, movies.

Which is increasing crime tendency in the society. Directors and producers know very well that pleasing a handful of audiences will not raise their production costs. As a result, these serials and web series are running on the same formula by sacrificing subtlety and artistry. On the other hand, TV channels are becoming pay channels one after another. As a result, free telecasting is replaced by monthly cable fees for the middle class. The business of pornography is growing and spreading to the masses through accessible means like mobile phones. Our youth is affected by a kind of digital cocaine. Social interaction and friendship are losing to Facebook, Instagram, WhatsApp friendship. Facebook, Twitter, Instagram etc. has become the means of social communication and interaction. We are becoming alone among all.

In the interim there was a hope that the cultural order would be streamlined through the internet. But the misuse of media is pushing us to create social conflict, extreme nationalism, extreme bigotry in Bengal as well as in the whole world. Communal riots are now gaining momentum based on false news spread on the internet. Which has created obstacles in the way of communal unity of Bengal. In many cases, the administration has to deal with the situation by shutting down the internet connection. It can be said that due to the abundance of internet and mass media, Bengali honest middle class is declining.

Despite regional distinctiveness, what is known as Bengali culture is mainly language dependent. Bengali culture is basically developed depending on Bengali language. Bengali culture can be said to have started from the emergence of Bengali language. The Bengali language of the twenty-first century has undergone many changes from the Bengali of chary-pada, the oldest form of the Bengali language.[11] The difference is also noticeable in the practical application of the language. Many foreign words have infiltrated the Bengali language, Arabic, Persian, Portuguese, Chinese, English predominate. As a result, Bengali language has been enriched. The original Bengali language was never in crisis. But through the internet, Bengalis are now global citizens and as a result, the crisis in the Bengali language is approaching. Bengali language is losing its sweetness due to the use of additional Hindi and English language in the sentence formation in Bengali. Children of the present generation are learning to use bi-language and tri-language (mostly Bengali Hindi and English) in sentence formation due to more mobile and TV addiction. The present generation takes a special pride in speaking Hindi and English to each other which is degrading the Bengali language culture. Children are being taught basic words in English from a very young age and parents feel a sense of pride in that which is a form of cultural degradation.

Media had an importance as one of the means of education. In Bengal, internet, TV, radio, newspaper was the popular medium of education. In the corona period, the importance of online education and internet as a medium increase. West Bengal Government brought Taruner Swapno Scheme in 2021 to solve the problem of school students.[12] Through this project government, govt aided, govt. 12th class students of sponsored schools are given 10,000 rupees to buy tabs. The objective was to enable all students of class 12th to take online classes. But in most cases the students did not utilize this opportunity but most of them increased their interest towards the world of entertainment. In many cases the lower-class families could not accumulate the money to recharge the tab. On the other hand, students from wealthy families have been able to improve their education by investing money through apps like Byju's, Unacademy etc.[13] In this case, it will not be an exaggeration to say that the Internet has created social differences. As a result of promoting the importance of English and Hindi education in mass media, private English medium schools have sprung up like Mushrooms. In 19th century Bengal, there was a tendency in Bengali society to adopt the positive aspects of Western culture. During this time, along with some social reforms, English education was also promoted and spread. The real beginning of English education in India was through the Charter Act of 1813 AD.[14] Although this English education was restricted to the upper classes of the society. The culture stream of the lower strata of society was continuous. But nowadays, due to the interest in English education, a kind of neglect is being observed in Bengali language education. The number of students in government schools through Bengali is decreasing. Aswini Datta Memorial Girls High School, Poddar Nagar High School, Hindu Academy, Baghbazar Bani Girls High School are going to be closed in Kolkata.[15] Besides Kolkata, the number of students in Bengali medium schools in the district is decreasing, which is a matter of real concern.

Bengali's attempt to become international in the 21st century is destroying its own cultural heritage. It is natural that there will be a change in culture. But today, courtesy of the internet and mass media, culture has become one-sided, which is highly detrimental to cultural diversity. Media culture is increasingly serving the current generation with an image of a false culture instead of the typical Bengali culture, making the media the most powerful tool of cultural aggression.

References

1. Roy, N., *Bangalir itihas: Aadi parba*, Dey's publishing, Kolkata, 1412, p. 15
2. For details of culture see: Murshid, G., *Bengali Culture Over a Thousand Years*, Sarbari Sinha (Translator), Niyogi Books Private Limited; First Edition, 2018

3. Narula, U., *Handbook of communication: models, perspective, strategies*, Atlantic, New Delhi, 2006, p. 38
4. Herbert, J., *Practicing Global Journalism*, Focal Press, 2003, p.10
5. Ahmed, W., *BanglarLok-Sanskriti*, Bangla Academy, Dhaka, 1965, p.13
6. Bagchi, A. K., *Biswayan: Bhabna- Durbhavna,* National Book Agency Private Limited, Kolkata, 2002, p. 135
7. Roy, N., Op. cit., p. 444
8. Murshid, G., *Hajar Bachorer Bangla Sanskriti*, Abosar Prakashana sangha, Dhaka, 2016, p. 495
9. Ibid., p. 490
10. Barkar, Edward B., *Sport in Bengal: And How, When, and Where to Seek It*, Wentworth Press, 2016
11. Roy, N., Op. cit., p. 216
12. https://govtschemes.in/ west-bengal-taruner-swapna-scheme#gsc.tab
13. These are online education platforms that provides learning opportunities to the students of all streams and particularly to the aspirants who are preparing for the competitive exams.
14. Bandopadhyay, Shekhar., *Palashi theke partition*, Orient Longman, 2004, p. 174
15. *Anandabazar Patrika*, 5th March, 2018

Women from the Pit of Subjugation to the Sunrise of Freedom: Rokeya Begum Shakhawat Hossain, B. Amma and Khairunnesha

Arindam Mandal

The development of Western modern education began to change the social landscape of India mainly from the nineteenth century. The passing of the charter in 1813 AD opened some revolutionary aspects in the Indian education system. Along with the teaching of Indian languages and ethics, philosophy, logic, English education and scientific thought penetrated. Although the Muslim community in India did not receive English education in the early stages, the Hindu community welcomed philosophy, logic and English education and was increasingly vocal against old-fashion and superstition. However, although the patriarchy of Hindu society prevented women from English education and modernity in the first stage, gradually women entered the field of education. However, the main subject of the social reform work done by the colonial government and the educated Indians was the Indian women's society. How is the place of women in any civilization? -This gives that civilization a specific place. In the eyes of the Europeans, however, the place of Indian women was not very good. James Mill in his book 'The History of British India' condemned the Indian civilization by demeaning the status of Indian women.[1] This is the reason why the Indian intellectual society responded to this criticism of India and spoke about reforms in various aspects of the society. However, only some notable male intellectuals and freedom fighters should not be discussed in the pursuit of society's progress, freedom movement and social reform. In India gradually the Muslim women community also came forward in this work and became brilliant astrologers. Zebunnesa, Begum Hazrat Mahal, Khayarunnessa, Abadi Banu Begum (B. Amma), Rokeya Shakhayat Hossain, Jobeda Khatun, Fulbahar Bibi and others are particularly notable among them.

Rokeya Shakhawat Hossain emerged as exceptional in thinking and action ahead of time in the 20th century work-oriented social system. The role she played as a woman in the women's liberation movement in Bangladesh is rare in the history of India. Rokeya Shakhawat Hussain was born in 1880 AD in present day Rangpur district of Bangladesh. As the son of a zamindar family of Pariaband, Rokeya Shawkhayat Hossain never had to fall into economic poverty. Muslim society in contemporary Bengal was basically divided into two groups; Namely – Ashraf and Atraf.[2] Their family belonged to Ashraf class. As a result, they strictly followed the Purdah system. Although Rokeya's father Muhammad Abu Ali Haider was educated in Urdu and Persian, he thought that Bengali could not be the mother tongue of Ashraf Muslims. Therefore, he prohibited the entry of Bengali language in the family and also did not make any provision for the education of the women in the family. However, Rokeya Shakhawat Hussain's indomitable desire and genuine attraction towards education made him learn Urdu and Persian as well as Bengali and English. She was helped by his elder brother Ibrahim. She did not have the fortune of studying in any school, Pathshala, Maktab or Madrasah in Pariaband. Contemporary society and extraterrestrials had many influences on the life of the young Rokey. At the age of 16, she was married to Syed Shakhayat Hussain, an official of Bhagalpur.[3] However, Rokeya lost her husband within a short time in 1909 AD and due to the pressure of some family members, she had to leave Bhagalpur and move to Calcutta. She changed her lifestyle drastically by settling permanently in Calcutta. Her new chapter began with education, reforms and writing.

The Bengali works published by Rokeya prove that his Bengali foundation was strong enough. Her sultana's dream' and his letters written in English suggest that he also learned English well. sultana's dream' is not translated from Bengali to English.[4] The extreme strictures and restrictions of veiling blocked the lives of millions of contemporary women. She dreamed of breaking this blockade and liberating the women's society. Instead of religious education, modernizing the education of Muslim women, eliminating veiling, achieving better status of women like men, breaking the bonds of the male-dominated society and declaring Jihad against the orthodox conservative society and superstitious mullahs and clerics, he became involved in the struggle for Muslim society and women's society. Rokeya thought of Bengalis, Bengali Muslims, women's education and women's awakening. In the 20th century, Rokeya made great efforts to spread education among the Muslim women. Rokeya accomplished was the establishment of Shakhawat Memorial Girls School which played a very important role in spreading modern education among Muslim women. Another notable program was her establishment of Anjuman-e-Khaitan-e-Islam to extend a helping hand to distressed women. But Shakhawat Memorial Girls School in Kolkata is not the first school for women. In 1909 AD Surwabardi's mother Khujasta Aftar Banu established a second school for Muslim women. Rokeya had clean ideas about school administration. He believed that quality development of teachers should also be maintained in order to provide good education. Gradually this Shakhawat Memorial School was upgraded to High School in 1930 AD.[5] At that time most of the teachers were Hindus. So, she drew the attention of the British Raj to fill the vacancy. She advocated teaching training for teachers. As a result, the British government started the Muslim Training School in 1919 AD.[6] wanted to empower women in Muslim society, as he understood that excessive conservatism had left Muslim women behind and Muslim society had progressed at a snail's pace. But she wanted to bring about a radical change in the social system that would lead to the emancipation of women. That is why he emphasized on conventional practical matters.

Rokeya Shakhawat took up the pen for women's liberation. Her two volume 'Motichur' created a stir in contemporary Bangladesh. The first part consists mainly of seven essays. Among these three famous essays are *'Degradation of Womanhood'*, *Ardhangini* and *Burkha* - in which Muslim women were subjected to coercion, tyranny and siege.[7] Therefore, in the book 'Avarodh Vasini', she has beautifully depicted the miseries of the women's society. She believed that women's emancipation would only be achieved if the blockade of Antapur, but the blockade of reformism and stupidity was broken. She said she had to remain veiled in front of her relatives since she was 5 years old. Blockade system was in operation in the name of screen. The more veiled a woman is, the more she can hide like a screw in the corner of the house, the purer she is.[8] Rokeya visited different parts of the Indian subcontinent and noticed that the Muslim women community in all of India is extremely neglected, oppressed and suffering in the social system. So, she said to the women - Have you ever thought about your plight? What are we in the civilized world of the twentieth century? maid? I hear that slavery is gone from the world, but is our slavery gone?[9]

Although Rokeya Shakhawat Hussain did not directly participate in the independence movement, she promoted women's nationalism through her writings. Rokeya's Swadeshi thought is reflected in her poem 'Nirupambir' where Kanailal is highly praised.[10] Joining the Swadeshi Movement, she told the countrymen to use native materials. During the 1905 A. H. Bengal partition movement, when she said that women should come forward to serve the country along with men in the Swadeshi and boycott movements. So, the British should not be blamed unnecessarily. Those who betray the country are heinous criminals. She, however, spoke of men playing a more important role while talking about the freedom struggle. Because he thought that women are emotional and caring by nature. They take care of children and help them grow up to be ideal people. But she did not support communal politics and Muslim League politics. Rokeya in her fable 'Muktiphal' criticized the politics of moderate Congress petitions and flattery. *Kangalini, Kangalini's* disease- recovery etc., has beautifully highlighted the subjugation, independence and nationalism in allegorical writings. In her essays 'Peasant's Misery' and 'Enfield', she spoke about British imperialism and exploitation and blamed English rule for the plight of peasant society.[11] As she talked about reviving the Enfield industry in Rangpur, again like Gandhiji, she advocated for the strong economy of the society and the state by appealing to make yarn in spinning wheels. She said Hindus, Muslims, Sikhs, Christians, Buddhists, Jains, Bengalis, Marathi, Madras are all Indians. Her conviction, awareness, thoughts of women's liberation and the spirit of national service behind direct politics drew many Muslim women to the stage of the national movement.[12]

B. Amma's real name is Abadi Banu Begum. She was born in 1852 AD in a middle-class Muslim family in United Pradesh. Although she was only 5 years old at the time of the Mutiny, the wave of sepoy mutiny swept over her family. B. Amma married Abdul Ali Khan, a high official working in Rampur,

Uttar Pradesh, at the age of eighteen. They had five sons including one daughter. As the mother of the famous Ali brothers and a freedom fighter, she played a significant role in India's freedom struggle.[13] On June 1-2, 1920, the Allahabad Conference of the Central Khilafat Committee decided to embark on a four-stage non-cooperation movement – abdication of titles, relinquishment of all government jobs including the police and army, and non-payment of all taxes.[14] When the Khilafat and non-violent non-cooperation movement began in 1920, women leaders The most prominent among them was B. Amma who joined this movement. Linking the Khilafat movement with the non-violent non-cooperation movement, Gandhiji preached Hindu-Muslim unity by addressing meetings held in various parts of the country and called upon women to participate in the movement. She urged to abandon foreign goods and adopt indigenous khadi cloth.[15] In order to involve Muslim women in this movement, Mahatma Gandhi, while giving a speech in Pabna district of East Bengal, compared the British rule as 'Satan's rule' and called upon Muslim women to shun foreign clothing to save Islam from Satan. Responding to Gandhiji's call, Muslim women participated in the Khilafat movement. B. Amma initially inspired the women's society to join the freedom struggle by addressing various meetings. B. Amma was joined by many generous Muslim women in promoting awareness and patriotism. He went from door to door to the common people to build Swadeshi Money Bank. B. Amma and his two sons Maulana Mohammad Ali and Shaukat Ali traveled to different parts of Bangladesh during the Non-Cooperation Movement with Gandhiji in 1921 AD. Bengali Muslim women were inspired by B. Amma's eloquent speech and joined the non-cooperation Khilafat movement. B. Amma said in a meeting on 28th September 1921 AD 'Today I have opened my veil. I think all those present in the meeting are like sons to my son (Mahammad Ali, Shaukat Ali). I want my children to fear none but God alone. Imprisonment and hanging are insignificant. Two sons are imprisoned, but my crores of sons are around me.'[16]

Addressing a gathering of about 600 people from different parts of the country in Ahmedabad, B. Amma urged women to join the Swadeshi programme. Women were asked to volunteer. Encouraged picketing, boycott, hoisting of national flag. During the annual session of the Congress in Calcutta in 1917 AD, Jailbandi attended as a representative of his two sons. Annie Besant was the president on the occasion. Sarojini Naidu was present. *Bandemataram* and *Allah Akbar* were chanted in this meeting. In this meeting, B. Amma addressed the political meeting of the traditional men. She said in Urdu speech - "If necessary for the liberation of the motherland, husbands and sons should be sent to jail and themselves should be taken to jail without fear." My children are imprisoned for the freedom of the country. That's why I feel proud as a mother'.[17] B. Amma used khaddar all her life and preached about Hindu Muslim unity. When he wanted to hold a meeting for national service and freedom in the frontier provinces, the British government banned it.[18] However, she traveled widely in Bihar to spread political consciousness and tried to meet the prisoners. Her campaign program created a stir in Bihar. As a result, the common people of Bihar handed over twenty thousand rupees to B. Amma. Gandhiji advised B. Amma to serve the country slowly but steadily. In 1880 B. Amma's husband Maulvi Abdul Ali Khan died after a long illness. B. Amma's age was 28 at that time. In this situation, B. Amma encouraged her two sons to study English to make them employable. As a widowed Muslim woman, the courage with which she followed Gandhiji and joined the non-violent non-cooperation and Khilafat movement after the death of her husband and encouraged the Indian women's society under the umbrella of Congress politics is rare and unique in Indian Muslim women's history.

In India's independence struggle, B. Amma told in a meeting, held in Lahore, that for the past 150 years Indians had helped the British rule at various times. Even during the Great Mutiny, the British government received a large share of aid. So, she said that a lot of help was given to the British government, now we would give no more. Now freedom will come only through struggle. She not only spoke of political freedom but also dreamed of economic freedom. She wanted to stimulate indigenous industry through the use of indigenous products. Throughout his life, he tried to use and expand the customer base. 1922 AD A meeting in Shimla urged women to use khaddar. At a meeting in Punjab, she called on women to achieve swaraj. The people of Dwarbhanga in Bihar were impressed by B. Amma's campaign and gave him 60 thousand rupees and the people of Munger gave twenty thousand rupees.[19] But when the country needed her the most, she died in November 1924 AD. After the death of this noble woman, Gandhiji said - 'It is as if B. Amma realized in this country that India's independence is impossible without Hindu-Muslim unity and Khedar.[20] Freedom heroes like Balgangadhar also said - 'There should be no shortage of heroines like B Amma in this country. Thousands of brave women like B. Amma are needed to make the country free.'[21]

Khairunnessa is one of the main characters in Muslim women's history of consciousness and freedom movement. Although many thinkers appeared on the educational map of Bengal in the 19th century, the Bengali Muslim society was far behind the Hindu society. Although efforts were made to spread education widely in the social system, women's education was somewhat difficult and a result of social prejudices. The Addams Report showed that women were destined to sink into the depths of illiteracy and superstition. The man of Rangpur, Dinajpur districts did not want to marry an educated girl.[22] The women in the society had to obey various restrictions including patriarchy. However, Khairunnessa advised and urged the Muslim women to take education and move towards progress in the last phase of the nineteenth century and the beginning of the twentieth century. She was born in 1873 AD in a middle-class family in Sirajganj, Bangladesh.[23] She ran a night school to educate Muslim girls. Khairunnessa wrote a women's book called 'Satir Patibhakti'. In this book, she shed light on husband-wife relationship and upbringing and education of sons. This book provides the logistics of thinking about the environment. She also gave a clear opinion about what the housework should be. According to her, the degradation of women in the society is the reason for the degradation of the society. Khairunnessa says that the family in which the women of the family suffer is quickly disintegrated.[24] When the people of Bangladesh were struggling in the background of the Swadeshi movement and freedom struggle, the women's society did not sit quietly. Khairunnessa joined Sarala Devi Chaudhurani Lakshmir Bhandar to launch indigenous industries when the boycott of foreign industries began and called for Muslim women to come forward. During the Swadeshi Movement, Khairunnessa through her Swadeshi writings called upon the women of Bengal to be initiated into the mantra of Swadeshi. In 1905 AD, she wrote under the title 'Swadesanurag' that Muslim women should be more attracted to Swadeshi goods, hand in hand with all Indian men. Muslim women should abstain from foreign products.

The women's society should strive to revive the native industry of Bengal. For this, the Muslim women society must receive real education. She further emphasizes the education of women and says that women are not only the mothers of children, but they are the mothers of all good deeds.[25] Khairunnessa appealed to the women of the Muslim community to spread the Swadeshi spirit, saying, "we must commit ourselves to shun foreign goods, shun foreign cloths and perfumes, and buy and use Indian products produced in different parts of India that are fine, durable and soft. our country's money will stay in the country, the tide will come in the domestic industry and the brothers and sisters of the working country will be able to earn something."[26] She was actually a patriot. She knew very well that if men and children are not developed for the betterment of the country, our country will fall behind. In the newspaper "Nabnoor" she said that if there is no education for girls, there will be no overall development of the society. She compared a life without education to a sunless world i.e., a dark life. Emphasizing on women's education, he said - 'If a woman of character is educated, she should be more beautiful like Manikanchan Yoga. Susila If a woman is wise, the family becomes much happier. Learning education should be a duty for both men and women which is also mentioned in Hindu scriptures and Hadith Sharif. So, education is our duty and imperative – no doubt about it.'[27]

The progress of individual, society and state depends on what kind of education is there in the society and state. Education brings the progress. In subjugated India, on the one hand, society and state formation had to be done. On the other hand, British imperialism had to be tried to get rid of it. In this situation, Khairunnessa has tried to make the society aware of the various barriers to women's education in our country. She observed that during those times Hindu girls could go out as much as Muslim girls but could not go out in the same way. As a result, it was almost impossible for Muslim women to get school education, madrasa education. If not of age, it was forbidden to go to another house without preserving the dignity of the siege custom. So, it can be said that the lack of schools in proper places is responsible for the lack of education of Muslim women. Moreover, the financial condition of the Muslim community was very poor since the time of the Permanent Settlement. Keeping food in the stomachs of all the family members was quite a challenge. Hence, there is very little interest in Muslim society in learning about the boundless poverty. Khairunnessa observed that the Hindu society gradually adopted modern science education and led their society towards progress. However, the country's wealthy landlords, rich Muslim society at that time could not facilitate the education of women. She thought that society needs Sumata to have good children. So, first of all, we have to think about women's education and women's progress.

In the 19th and 20th centuries, society was quite illiterate orthodox. When reformation and renaissance took place in Hindu society, Islamic society was still shrouded in fanaticism. Under the cover of this bigotry, Rokeya Shakhayat Hossain, B Amma, Khairunnessa broke the mold of the Muslim society and came out of the traditional norms and joined the social consciousness and reform, women's liberation, education, progress and freedom movement and set a bright example in the history of contemporary India. Independent-minded, like Tejaswini, Mahayasi, Dripta, women are star daughters of Mother India. Through her writings, Rokeya has taken the society forward through the expansion of education by hitting the roots of the siege system of the Muslim society of Bengal through well-thought-out ideas and programs. Convincing women like B. Amma jumped directly into the freedom struggle and mobilized the women's society all over India. The women of the country slowly participated in the national politics, non-violent, violent, national politics. The scale and intensity of the freedom movement grew exponentially. And the emergence of modern-minded women like Khairunnessa in Bangladesh plays one of the most important roles in the education and respect of women in Bengali women's society. Not only the political freedom of India, but only through the liberation of women in the social system, it is possible to get true consciousness and freedom, the life stories of the three women in question prove that.

References

1. See for details: Mill, J., *History of British India*, Vol. 3 Wealth of Nation, 2014
2. Basu, R., "Rokeya Shakhawat Hossain, A feminist voice of early 20th century
Bengal", in Amal Kumar Mukhopadhyay (ed.), *The Bengal intellectual tradition*, Kolkata,
K.P. Bagchi and Cong, 1998, p-209
3. Ibid, p-212
4. Murshed, G., *Rassundari to Rokeya*, Dhaka, Retirement Publishing House, 1993, p-172
5. Banerjee, S., *March Towards Modernity, Bengali Women*, Dhaka, Dolphin, p-114
6. Basu, R., Op. cit., p-216
7. Hussain, Rokey S., *"Degradation of Women"*, *Motichur*, Vol. 1, (Ed.) Dhaka, Bangla Academy, 1999, pp. 446-447
8. Ibid., p. 447
9. Navnoor, Bhadra, 1311 p. 208
10. Nirupama, Veer. *Rokeya Rachnabali*, p-526
11. Hossain, A., *Muslim Women's Struggle for Freedom in Colonial Bengal* (1873-1940), Progressive Publishers, Kolkata, 2003, p. 192
12. Rokeya Rachnaballi. *Sorrows and Enfield's of Cultivation*, Op. cit., pp. 207-209; Quayum, M. A., "The Essential Rokeya, Selected Works of Rokeya Sakhawat Hossain (1880-1932)", in *Women and Gender: The Middle East and the Islamic World*, Volume: 13, Brill, 2013
13. Hossain, A., Op. cit., p.192
14. Chandra, B, Tripathi, A, (trans.), *Freedom Struggle*, National Book Trust, Kolkata, p-175
15. Hossain, A., p-192

16. Biswas, K., *Indian Women on the Stage of Freedom Struggle*, Kolkata, Pharma, KLM, 1987, Page 164
17. Rahman, M. A. *Heroism in India's Freedom Struggle, Kolkata*, Provincial Book Agency, 1987, Page 31
18. *Amritbazar Patrika*, September 2, 1922
19. Ibid., February 5, 1922
20. Ibid., 23rd September, 1922
21. Rahman, M A., Op. cit., p-13
22. Gupta, S., (ed.) *Women in History*, Progressive Publishers, Kolkata, p-49
23. "Educator Khairunnessa, Zhanan Mohfil, Selected Works of Bengali Muslim Writers, 1904-1938", in Sharin Akhtar and Mousumi Bhowmik (eds.) *Stri*, Calcutta, 1998, pp. 36–39
24. Hossain, A., Op. cit., p.115
25. Ibid., p.115
26. Khairunnessa, "Swadesanurag, Navnur: Third Year", Issue – 6, 1312 (Bangabd), pp. 277-287
27. Educator Khairunnessa, said Mohfil, Op. cit., pp. 36-39

Post-Modern Feminist Authors of Indian and Their Feminism Conscience of Composing: A Study

Md Manzar Reza

Feminist authors of post-modern India mainly address the designation of women in society and their marginalized position. Early postmodern feminist literature exhibits innovative and diverse approaches concerning women. Some post-modern feminist authors are cited to exemplify their feminist perspectives. Over the last three decades, Indo-Anglian literature has received significant contributions from women writers, including Kamala Das, Kamala Markandaya, Ruth Prawer Jhabvala, Anita Desai, Arundhati Roy, Shashi Deshpande, Jhumpa Lahiri, Shobha De, Nayanata Shagal, Meena Alexraander, and others. Each of these writers possesses a distinct writing style, but they share common themes in their portrayal and analysis of women. The stories crafted by these women writers may have had limited recognition in the past. Hence, the goal of this writing is to demonstrate how post-modern feminist authors depict women in their literature. Moreover, it also highlights the approaches of women authors whose presentations reflect a significant shift in their feminist consciousness. In addition, I have also tried to present the brief sketches of various social activities of these authors who took the basic inspirations of writings from the practical ground.

The woman writers of post-independence Indian, has remarkable contributed to the school of Indian novel, poetry, short stories etc. However, many of them are artistic and exceptional woman authors. They all have a mark of new consciousness about the feeble dilemma of the Indian women.

English novels of these women authors hold the most important part of the modern Indian writings. Through their writings the reader can see the existing world very clearly. In the modern Indian English literary fiction, these woman novelists are getting succeeded by leaps and bounds, and the woman characters in their novels usually stand substance to their feminist approach, outlook as well as perception. They are utmost in watching the life of the Indian women and their interests in the study of their inner mind. The women in their novels have depicted on the verge of existential dilemma. They also travail of the life of subservient women in a male subjugated society governed by the austere traditions and restrictions. As Patricia Meyer remarks: "There seems to be something that we call in a woman's point of view on outlook sufficiently distinct to be recognizable through the countries."

Kamala Markandaya, as an expatriate writer, has been living in England for few years, observed the state of freedom of women. According to her the Indian women are only busy with the domestic work's and stay whole life as home maker. Her fiction evinces woman characters in different life-roles, and encounters the theme of the East-West relationships. The modern city and the town culture, brought in by the British rule on traditional Indian life, has impacted on her fiction. She is able to create living characters in meaningful dilemmas. She is a feminist to create a character, Rukhmani, a rustic woman in her first novel 'Nectar I am Sieve' the story of which illustrates the truth of Coleridge's line- 'work without hope draws nectar in a sieve'. Nayantara Sahgal, another post-modernist, is usually regarded as an exponent of the political novel. However, her fiction is also preoccupied with the modern Indian woman's approaches for sexual relation. It means the women's freedom and self-realization about physical relation. Her woman characters Maya, Uma, Saroja and Mara represent women grind against the marriage code. One of her novels 'The Day in Shadow' is about the domestic plot. Anita Desai, is another youngest of the major Indian English woman novelists. Unlike Shehgal, her fiction conveys the true significance of things. Desai's protagonists are mostly women from school girl to grandmother who has all breakable introverts trapped in their own abilities. Her women characters are emotional, several, endearing and rebel by nature. Like Kamala Das Suraya, Jhumpa Lahiri, Anita Desai's fiction is also a reflection of social, social activities and political precedence takes over probing of the mind. It also illustrations the East-West discord as expressed in the lives of Indian emigrants to Britain. Desai's women characters; Maya from 'Cry, The Peacock', Monisha and Amala from 'Voices in the City', Sita from 'Where Shall We Go This Summer' Raka from 'Fire on the Mountain' etc. represent the feministic features of her composing. The practical narratives written by these women writers has given a chance to the readers to investigate deep into the heart of Indian women from various strata of society. These narratives would also arise a question in readers minds that- is feminism really in search of identity?

Meena Alexander is another post-modern Indian writer whose fictions reflects the multi-cultural life of women who belong to diverse ethnic and religious communities. Her works examine the disparate elements of her heritage and cultural displacements concentrating particularly on her status as educated woman. She is a feminist in the perspective of literary and cultural issues. She remarked herself as "while I'm writing, I didn't think I consciously write as a woman, I have little doubt that some of my deepest emotions and insights spring from having been born into a female body learning to grow up as a woman in both a traditional Indian culture". Alexander's verse generally favors Indian themes. Majority of her works deals with feminist issues. Her fictions dominate with female characters. For instance, her work, 'I Root My Name' intimates the painful experiences of women. Her 'Storm' contemplates the feminist ideal of recreating and rewriting a pure female self-identity. Her poetry of "River and Bridge" explores similar personal and feminist themes. Her fiction also relates with women's roles as a healer of communal ills.

Shashi Deshpande has earnestly been accepted as a significant literary figure on the contemporary literary scene. Shashi Deshpande's novels represent the contemporary modern women's struggle to define and attain an autonomous selfhood. Her female protagonists are at great pains to free themselves from stultifying, traditional constraints. The social and cultural change in the post- Independence India has made women conscious of the need to define themselves, their place in society, and their surroundings. Female quest for identity has been at pet theme for many a woman's novelist. Shashi Deshpande has also been one of such writers and she makes an earnest effort to understand the inner dimension of the female characters. For the portrayal of the predicament of middleclass educated Indian women, their inner conflict and quest for identity, issues pertaining to parent-child relationship, marriage and sex, and their exploitation. As, Shashi Deshpande in one of her interviews expressed her inner thinking about feminist movement as, "if others see something feminist in my writing, I must say that it is not consciously done, it is because the world for women is like that and I am mirroring the world." Shobhaa De, a supermodel, celebrity journalist and the well-known author stands as a pioneer in the field of popular fiction and ranks among the first to explore the world of the urban woman in India. With her extraordinary ability, she presents very sensitive aspect of human life. Her way of narrating every aspect of human relationships is wonderful. Really, she is frank in narrating the incidents and situations with a touch of open heartedness. She has given importance to women's issues and they are dealt with psychology in her style of intimate understanding. Her novels indicate the arrival of a new Indian woman, who eager to defy the well-entrenched moral orthodoxy of the patriarchal social system. Her female characters break all shackles of customs and traditions that tie them in the predicaments and rein in their freedoms and rights. They are not against the entire social system and values but are not ready to accept them as they are.

Manju Kapur, is an English professor, wrote several fictions. Her first novel, 'Difficult Daughters' received the 'Common Wealth Award' for the Eurasian region. Her novel 'A Married Woman' which is a seductive story of a love at a time of political and religious upheaval, told with sympathy and intelligence. It is the story of an artist whose canvas challenges constrains of middle-class existence. Manju Kapur describes through her protagonist, Astha as "a woman should be aware, self-control, strong will, self-reliant and rational, having faith in the inner strength of womanhood. A meaningful change can be brought only from within by being free in the deeper psychic sense." Astha wants to break her dependence on others and proceed on the path of full human status that poses a threat to Hemant and his male superiority. She finds herself trapped between the pressure of modern developing society and shackles of ancient biases. She sets out on her quest for a more meaningful life in her lesbian relationship. She canonizes and comments on her feminine sensibility, by raising the social issues related to women. In her writings, Manju Kapur has emphasized on the issues of patriarchy, inter-religious marriage, and family bond, and male-female bond, co-existence of past and present.

Feminism in its literary sense is the physical and psychic liberation of women from the mean traditional rule of man. Since time immemorial in the world, particularly in Asian countries and in India the social practice and creeds have by and large control of man. Amazingly compress the whole debate of feminism by highlighting how the cultural machinery operative within any society imposes idea of performativity on the gender present the society. A society that privileges the male gender over female gender believes in ritual repetition of certain task activities that relegate female gender to a subordinate status. Thus, 'woman' becomes category which is socially, politically, economically and in various other ways exploited and these exploitations could be both visible as well as invisible. Feminisms are number of movements, ideologies and social activism that seeks to attain social equity for women. To challenge this preoccupied thoughts of minds, women writers like Mahasweta Devi, Sara Joseph and Arundhati Roy, Jhumpa Lahore's emerged in Indian land. Their writings consider as a major source of inspiration for the marginalized women of India. Besides writings, they paved the way to activism to reach at the nook and corner of society. They all socially devoted to serve the humanity and expand their helping hand to the poorest of the poor.

Arundhati Roy is a renowned Indian author and activist known for her literary works and social activism. She gained international fame when her debut novel, "The God of Small Things," received the prestigious Booker Prize in 1997. This stands out in the realm of modern narrative fiction. Roy's novel "The Ministry of Utmost Happiness" explores the lives of diverse characters, including Muslim women, in contemporary India. In addition to her novels, Roy has written numerous essays and non-fiction works on topics such as politics, human rights, and the environment. Her writing often challenges established systems and advocates for justice and social change. Roy has been a vocal advocate for environmental causes, particularly in her opposition to large-scale dam projects in India and their impact on local communities and ecosystems. She has spoken out against issues like corporate globalization, caste-based discrimination, and the rights of marginalized communities, rights of the widows. Her activism is often associated with her strong critique of economic and political power structures. Arundhati Roy's literary works and social activism are deeply intertwined, as her writing often reflects her commitment to social justice and her critique of the status quo. She is known for her eloquent and thought-provoking prose, which has had a significant impact on both the literary and activist communities. Kamala Das, was another renowned Indian poet, novelist, and short story writer from Kerala. Her literary journey is characterized by a bold and candid exploration of themes like love, sexuality, and gender roles. Her notable works include "The Descendants," "Summer in Calcutta," and "My Story," which is an autobiographical account of her life. Kamala Das's writing style is marked by its confessional and introspective nature, often breaking societal norms and challenging the traditional roles assigned to women. "The Sirens": This collection of poems is one of her early works and established her as a feminist poet who challenged societal norms. Her poetry and prose have had a profound impact on Indian literature, as she gave voice to the innermost thoughts and desires of women, making her a significant figure in the feminist literary movement.

Anita Desai's works, like "Clear Light of Day" and "In Custody," incorporate postmodern elements and explore themes of identity and alienation of women. Kiran Desai, another feminist writer popularly known for her "The Inheritance of Loss". It won the Man Booker Prize and is celebrated for its intricate storytelling and exploration of the Indian diaspora. These writers have contributed to the diversity and complexity of contemporary Indian literature with their postmodern styles and unique perspectives. "An Introduction" and "The Looking Glass": These are some of her famous poems that are often studied for their feminist themes and her distinctive poetic style. Attia Hossain, an aristocrat from Lucknow, and a graduate from Cambridge University was associated with a group of socialist writers and was a member of All-India Women's Conference. Participant in the First All-India Progressive Writers' Conference, Lucknow, 1936. Besides her social activities she was involved in literary creation and performances. Her works included 'Of Meals and Memories', Phoenix Fled, Sunlight on a Broken Column.

References

1. Shiner, M., *Feminism: The Essential writings*, Vintage Books, 1994, p. xiv
2. Uma, N., *Indian Women writer's at the Cross Roads*, Pen crafts, New Delhi,1996
3. Nahal, C., 'Feminism in English fiction-forms and Variants,' in *Feminism and Recent fiction in English*, edited by Sushila Singh, Prestige books, New Delhi, 1991, p 17
4. Deshpande, S., "Roots and Shadows- A Feminist Study" Ed. Amaranth Prasad, Swroop Book, New Delhi,2009, p129
5. Dinesh, S. K., *Feminism and Post Feminism*, Swarup and Sons, New Delhi, 2004, p.3.
6. Krishnaswamy, N., et al. *Contemporary Literary Theory*, Macmillan, New York, 2001, p. 73.
7. Alice, A., "Is Queer a Post Feminist Fashion?", *Abstract for M/NILA*, November, 2002
8. Singh, S., "Feminism and Recent Fiction in English, Prestige Books, New Delhi, 1991
9. Spacks", in Patricia Ann M., *The female imagination*, distributed by Random House, Knopf, First Edition, 1975
10. Mayne's P., *West End play The Bird of Time*, London, 1961
11. Hossain, A., *Phoenix Fled Chatto & Windus*, London, 1953

12. Hossain, A., *Sunlight on a Broken Column Chatto & Windus*, London 1961
13. Alexander, Meena, *The Storm: A Poem in Five Parts*, Red Dust, New York, 1989
14. Alexander, Meena, *River and Bridge*. TSAR Publications, 1996
15. Alexander, Meena, *I Root My Name,* United Writers, Calcutta, 1977
16. Manju, Kapur, *A Married Woman*, Penguin Publishers., New Delhi, 2002
17. Specks, Patricia M., *Feminist Sensuality,* Tops One, Antwerp, 2002
18. Janet, R., *Women writer's Talking*, Cambridge, London, 1981
19. Pathak, K., *Feminism,* https://www.academia.edu/7032161/Feminism
20. Desai, A., *Clear Light of Day,* Random House India, 1980
21. De, S., *Surviving Men*, Penguin Publishers, New Delhi, 1998
22. Qureshi, B., "Arundhati Roy — beloved for her fiction, derided for her politics — won't be silenced", *The Washington Post*, Democracy Dies in Darkness, August 2019

The Covid-19 Pandemic: Impact on Accredited Social Health Activist (Asha) Workers in Darjeeling District

Yangji Tamang

The COVID -19 pandemic has caused a catastropic loss of human lives globally and has emerged as a significant threat to food security, workplace safety, and public health. Healthcare professionals have been relentlessly providing their services across the world, including in the Darjeeling district of West Bengal. The doctors in this region encounter numerous challenges as they treat COVID-19 patients while also working towards preventing further infections and educating the public about relevant policies. Despite these daunting challenges, healthcare workers continue to work tirelessly at the forefront of this unprecedented crisis, demonstrating exceptional courage and commitment., ASHA volunteers went door-to-door and engaged with residents, but unfortunately, they faced at of challenging working conditions due to insufficient protective gear during the pandemic. One of the key obstacles they encountered was the risk to their families. Accredited social health activists, play a crucial role in the rural health infrastructure of India by going door to door to vaccinate individuals and encourage them to receive the vaccine. Despite their importance, these workers lack proper rights and are considered voluntary workers. This paper aims to analyze the significant contribution of the ASHA community in combatting the pandemic. Furthermore, an additional paper will examine the pandemic's impact on ASHA workers' socio-economic conditions.

Community health workers who are certified as social health activists work for the Indian government's National Rural Health Mission {NHRM}. They are among India's frontline health personnel auxiliary nurse midwives and Anganwadi workers. ASHA staff members are community volunteers with training in providing information and assisting people in obtaining benefits from the many healthcare programs offered by the government. They act as a conduit between underserved populations and facilities including district hospitals, sub-centers, and primary health centers. The ASHA workers and auxiliary nurse midwives are members of the National Rural Health Mission launched by the Ministry of Health and Family Welfare in 2005. These workers are selected from the local community and receive training to become health educators. They create awareness about various health issues, mobilize the community for local health planning, and improve the utilization and accountability of existing health services. ASHAs have played a significant role in reducing maternal and infant mortality rates in India. The community shall select and oversee the ASHA who will provide reports to it. They will receive training to serve as a bridge between society and the public health system. India's rural health infrastructure is supported by ASHA workers. They have been actively involved in informing the public and assisting those affected by COVID-19 since the pandemic started. In remote hamlets and villages where poverty and illiteracy are ingrained, ASHA is designated by the Indian government as the primary health care information distribution. ASHA staff are among the community's lowest-paid laborers. They serve as the community's and public health interaction. ASHA staff are the primary point of contact for any health-relatedness of underprivileged people in both rural and urban areas. They receive a pitiful honorarium and are not viewed as employees but rather as volunteers. The ASHA volunteers are hindered by poor honorarium earnings and frequently face food insecurity.

I have been tried to highlights two objectives of through this writing.

- To analyze the role of the accredited social health activist (ASHA) community in the fight against the pandemic situation in the Darjeeling district.
- To highlight the issues and challenges encountered by ASHA staff in the Darjeeling district.

Darjeeling district is the northernmost district of the state of West Bengal in eastern India in the foothills of the Himalayas. In the Darjeeling district, more than 1440 workers are working. Randomly 60 ASHA workers have been taken in the Darjeeling district for the study from both public health centers and sub-centers. To conduct this study both primary and secondary data were used. The respondents belonged to different rural and urban areas, castes, and classes. A semi-structured questionnaire has been used for this investigation with an emphasis on the following: - a)demographic details (age, education, marital status, household size); b)information on work; c)remuneration (payment structure, pending months of payment, health insurance, etc.); d)safety at work (provision of safety gear, self-isolation possibilities, precautions taken to deal with infections); e)household socio-economic conditions(intensifications of housework, employment and earnings of other members, etc.)

During the COVID-19 pandemic, ASHA workers played a crucial role in various activities such as contact tracing. With the imposition of the lockdown, ASHA workers were responsible for tracking people who had returned from other states and countries. This included NRIs, migrants, and students who returned home (khadeeja Vayalil, 2021) necessary information out these and submitted reports to relevant authorities. They also ensured that these individuals were quarantined and followed up with them regularly, providing necessary instructions. ASHA workers acted as a bridge between the quarantine individuals, society, and the health department. Their efforts were essential in curbing the spread of the virus.

The doctors in the region of Darjeeling district encounter numerous challenges as they treat COVID-19 patients while also working towards preventing further infections and educating the public about relevant policies. Despite these daunting challenges, healthcare workers continue to work tirelessly at the forefront of this unprecedented crisis, demonstrating exceptional courage and commitment., ASHA volunteers went door-to-door and engaged with residents, but unfortunately, Due to insufficient protective gear during the pandemic, they encountered obstacles in delivering information about vaccines. One of the key obstacles they encountered was the risk to their families. Accredited social health activists, play a crucial role in the rural health infrastructure of India by going door to door to vaccinate individuals and encourage them to receive the vaccine. Despite their importance, these workers lack proper rights and are considered voluntary workers.

The epidemic and lockdown have resulted in increased work for ASHA. Before the pandemic, an ASHA worked on average six to seven hours per day to perform the responsibilities assigned to her, such as driving for vaccinations, awareness campaigns, helping expectant mothers attend awareness campaigns, and participating in vaccination efforts. Consultation with health officials, however, most of these tasks were suspended during the lockdown except for the care of pregnant women (Niyati and S. Nelson 2020). Despite the suspension regular for most ASHAs increased by two to three hours per day due to the new tasks assigned to them to contain the spread of the infection. The additional responsibilities include polling 30-50 households every day to learn about the travel history and the health status of household members, giving advice on quarantine, observing people in quarantine, and examining the preparation and submission of reports to the medical officer at the primary care facility (PHC).

Due to the COVID-19 pandemic, many patients have faced difficulties accessing essential medicines and services because of lockdowns and travel restrictions. During this time, ASHA workers have been compiling a list of patients in need of such services, collecting the necessary medicines, and ensuring their availability to those who require them. ASHA workers are also providing these services to those in quarantine. Additionally, they provide various other services, including food facilities to those in quarantine. According to my research, I found that the ASHAs (Accredited Social Health Activists) have not been fairly compensated for their loss of income due to COVID-19-related tasks. These workers receive a fixed honorarium from the State Government, along with task-based incentives shared by both the State and Central Governments. The fixed amount varies across States, ranging from Rs 4500 in West Bengal to Rs 10,000 in Andhra Pradesh. However, the incentive amount for specific tasks remains the same. My research indicates that many ASHAs have experienced irregularity in payments, with some payments pending for up to four or five months. I have included a list in my report, which provides further details regarding payments and irregularities. of essential services. Remuneration of ASHA members in Darjeeling district in the state of West Bengal monthly fixed salary-4500/- and allowance

- Each pregnant woman deliveredl:300/ (only for government hospitals)

- pulse polio programme:75/- (per day)
- Measles-Rubella vaccines 2 (below two-year child);75/-
- Measles-Rubella Vaccines 2 (below two- year child): 75/-
- For T.V patients medicine deliver:1000/- (per patient)
- For survey: 300/-etc.

The efforts of the community health workers i.e., ASHA in combating the COVID-19 pandemic gained widespread recognition. They played a crucial role in controlling the spread of the virus by conducting contact tracing of infected individuals, screening returning migrant workers for the coronavirus, and educating rural communities about the disease and ways to prevent its transmission. ASHA volunteers are not considered employees and are typically compensated through incentives instead of wages. although states are allowed to provide a small, fixed monthly salary to Accredited Social Health Activists (ASHA), campaigners argue that the typical monthly income of an ASHA falls far below the minimum wage. despite honorary ASHA members struggling to make ends meet. Their salary is simply not enough to meet their basic needs and support their families, educate their children, and manage their household tasks. The government needs to recognize the challenges faced by ASHA workers, such as the lack of safety measures like health insurance, pensions, and maternity leave, and take preventive measures to address this issue.

References

1. Niyati, S., & Nelson Mandela, S. "Impact of the pandemic on accredited social health activists (ASHA) in India", in *Review of Agrarian Studies*, Vol. 10 (2369-2020-1851), 2020.
2. Shrivastava, R., Singh, A., Khan, A., Choubey, S., Haney, J. R., Karyotaki, E., & Naslund, J. A. "Stress alleviation methods for community-based health Activists (SAMBHAV): Development of a digital program for stress reduction for community health workers in rural India," *SSM-Mental Health*, 100230, 2023

3. Saprii, L., Richards, E., Kokho, P., & Theobald, S. "Community health workers in rural India: analyzing the opportunities and challenges Accredited Social Health Activists (ASHAs) face in realizing their multiple roles", *Human Resources for Health*, Vol. 13(1), 2015, pp.1-13
4. Gopalan, S. S., Mohanty, S., & Das, A. "Assessing community health workers' performance motivation: a mixed-methods approach on India's Accredited Social Health Activists (ASHA) Programme", *BMJ open*, Vol. 2(5), 2012
5. Shrivastava, S. R., & Shrivastava, P. S. "Evaluation of trained Accredited Social Health Activist (ASHA) workers regarding their knowledge, attitude, and practices about child health", *Rural and Remote Health*, Vo. 12(4), 2012, pp. 1-7
6. Agarwal, S., Curtis, S. L., Angeles, G., Speizer, I. S., Singh, K., & Thomas, J. C. "The impact of India's accredited social health activist (ASHA) program on the utilization of maternity services: a nationally representative longitudinal modeling study", *Human Resources for Health*, Vol. 17, 2019, pp. 1-13
7. Vayalil, Khadeeja. "Role of accredited social health activists (ASHAs) in pandemic era of covid-19", Journal of Emerging Technologies and Innovative Research, Vol-8, 2021
8. Shukla, Aayushi., "Corona Warriors: The Asha workers of Uttar Pradesh", *Vaccineswork*, online post, 28 January 2022
9. Giri, Pramod. "ASHA workers in Bengal's Darjeeling threaten to stop work if not paid on time", *Hindustan Times*, Jul 29, 2021
10. David, Rohit. "State ASHA workers battle abuse, poor salary and lack of proper training", *Hindustan Times*, May 11, 2020

Physical Features and Settlement of Coochbehar: A Distinct Geographical Identity of West Bengal

Md Ajijur Rahaman

One of the biggest obstacles to sustainability is urbanization. It is an intricate transformational process that impacts both people and environments. As a result, the size and number of urban areas worldwide are constantly growing. In recent days due to rapid urbanization, it is largely affecting the live of west Bengal. Urbanization is the process of becoming urban, or to say it another way, urbanization is a cycle that a country goes through as it transitions from rural to industrial society. People move from rural to urban regions, which are referred to as the concentration of people linked with the non-agricultural sector and changes in land usage and rural suffering. It is a geographical phenomenon that affects people, places, and infrastructure. It is transforming population concentration, structural change, and socio-cultural change. While a sign of growth, the quantity and expansion of urban areas have negative effects on individuals and society as well as the long-term viability of the environment. Because tomorrow's bigger cities will be smaller communities today. With planned or unplanned expansion throughout time, towns have more environmental issues than their rural environs do from their inception to their maturity. So, in this situation, it is critical to examine the growth pattern of urban areas. Since the majority of environmental issues have their origins in a town's development or expansion, which has a negative impact on the town's natural stability. The unfortunate situation of numerous first-order towns and cities, as well as metropolitan and agglomeration cities, suffering from numerous environmental tribulations frequently makes headlines. However, the towns of lower order of sequence or smaller in size are not properly highlighted, even though they will face the same problems in the future. Hence the primary emphasis of this paper is to know the Coochbehar physical features and its settlement patterns, and also to see how this area is distinct from other districts of Bengal.[1]

Cooch Behar town is the administrative center for the Cooch Behar district in West Bengal, India. At 26°22′n 89°29′e, it is positioned in the eastern Himalayan foothills. In the area of north Bengal, Coochbehar is a planned town. There are several uses for the municipality's territory. Residential usage makes up the largest portion of the overall area. Good land cover is also needed for transportation and communication. 64.78% of the total area is made up of public and semi-public residential zones. The green belt barely makes approximately 0.36% of the entire area of Coochbehar Municipality due to deforestation. 0.46 square kilometers are utilized for a variety of purposes. The area used for commerce and industry was 0.07 km2 and 0.13 km2, respectively. 0.3 square kilometers of underdeveloped land are utilized for agriculture. A board of councilors chosen from each of Cooch Behar's 20 wards makes up the municipality, along with a few others selected by the state government.[2] A chairman is chosen by the board of councilors from among its elected members; the chairman serves as the municipality's executive leader. In the municipality, the All-India Trinamool Congress is in charge. The town's tourism, health, and education are all managed by the state government.

A prince who practiced feudalism governed Koch Bihar up till the 28th day of August 1949. It was on August 28, 1949, when the Maharaja of Koch Bihar ceded control of the area to the Government of India. On September 12, 1949, the administration was turned over to the Indian government. On January 30, 1950, Koch Bihar was then moved and became a district by joining West Bengal[3]. According to its physiography, the district is a part of the Lower Ganga Plain's Barind tract, location between the southern peninsula and the northern Mountains. The northern side of Koch Bihar is mostly covered with terai (marshy) vegetation. The district of Koch Bihar is situated within the latitudinal ranges of 25°57'47" to 26°36'20" N and 88°47'44" to 89°54'35" E.[4] Major crops including rice, wheat, lentils, tobacco, and jute are cultivated in Koch Bihar, where agriculture dominates the economy. There are 2,819,086 districts, and around 89.70% of the population lives in rural areas. The district's gender ratio is 942 females for every 1,000 men, which is lower than the state's, which is 950 females for every 1,000 males.[5] The population under the age of six makes up 11.77% of the whole population, and there are 963 people between the ages of 0 and six who are male.[6] According to the 2011 Indian census, Koch Bihar is the district in West Bengal with the highest percentage of people who belong to the Scheduled Caste.[7] The population of the Schedule Caste (SC) is mostly involved in agriculture, although overall and regional food security is still less than in other districts of West Bengal. According to statistics, 90 percent of the district's land is rural, where inadequate irrigation infrastructure, a lack of basic agricultural tools, and a lack of agricultural expertise impede all agricultural activities. Infrastructural advancements in the area are also behind schedule. Around 650 km of the district's roads are unmetalled, whereas 545 km are, according to research, showing a sad state of the transport infrastructure.[8] Despite still, there are just 102 kilometers of rails in existence. According to the 2011 census, the district has a health index score of 16, which is rather low when compared to other districts. The districts' income index and education index show the same pattern. The overall situation represents how behind the district is. According to M Ray & Rahman,[9] Koch Bihar is divided into 12 blocks: Haldibari, Mekhliganj, Mathabhanga-I, Mathabhanga-II, Sitalkuchi, Cooch Behar-I, Cooch Behar II, Tufanganj-I, Tufanganj-II, Dinhata-I, Dinhata-II, and Sitai (Figure 1).

Figure 1 : Geography of Cooch Behar district

Koch Bihar has several different geographical features; however, no researcher has yet conducted a thorough analysis of any of these features. The present study was focused on the physical features of Cooch Behar and its settlements patterns. While poorly recorded, the history of the whole region of North Bengal reveals continuous changes in authority and corresponding changes in the territorial position of that power. It is acknowledged that only the undivided Dinajpur and Malda regions of what is now North Bengal have a strong historical foundation, whereas Cooch Behar, Jalpaiguri, and Darjeeling lack systematic historical backing for their origins.[10] Before to 1200 AD, Bengal did not exist.[11] The Pragjyotishpur region included all of modern-day North Bengal and the northern half of modern-day Bangladesh. Ancient Indian mythical scriptures make reference to Pragjyotishpur by name. The region of

Pragjyotishpur was afterwards split into Poundra (Poundrabardhana) and Kamrup. Poundravardhan was the region that stretched along the western bank of the Koratoya. Popularly known as Kamrupa, the eastern bank of the river Korotoya extended up to the powerful River Bramhaputara. Early in history, the district Cooch Behar was created to be a part of Kamrupa's western boundary. Harendra Narayan Choudhuri (1903) observed that 'at no point maybe did the nation Kamrupa recognize dominion of one entity totally.[12] Prior to the separation of that nation between the Koch ruler Naranarayan and his brother Shukladhvaja (Chila Ray), in the middle of the sixteenth century, Cooch Behar had no independent existence as a distinct principality.[13]

Mahiranga Danava, who is said to have been the first king of Kamarup and was followed by three kings, is the first known ruler of the kingdom. After them, Pragjyotishpura seems to have been inhabited by a Kirata race. Bhaskar Barman became Kamarup's significant king in 639 AD. The Koch, Mech, Garo, and Bhot tribes took control of the nation after the Gupta and Pala dynasties. The name of the kingdom Kamrupa was altered in the 13th century when Kamtapur became its new capital (Presently, Gosanimari located fifteen miles south to the present Cooch Behar town). The state was renamed Kamta as a result, and from that point until the end of the 19th century, Kamta served as the political and cultural hub of eastern India.[14]

Native rulers consecutively controlled the Kamta kingdom, starting with Sandhya Roy in 1255 AD and ending with Nilamber in 1482 AD. Hunter (1876) claimed that the Khen dynasty succeeded the Pal dynasty. Hossasin Sah, the Muslim Chief, took Kamta in 1493, but he was unable to rule the area for more than 12 years. The Muslim had been expelled, and the Kamta Kingdom had descended into chaos.[15] In the meanwhile, the Koch leaders were gradually gaining control. Vishva Singha invaded the kingdom in 1515 AD and overthrew the Muslim monarch. From Darrang in the upper valley of the Brahmaputra to the boundaries of the Purnea District, Vishva Sinha established an empire.[16]

Just once, in conjunction with the State's first settlement, was the whole of Cooch Behar surveyed for settlement reasons. There doesn't seem to have ever been a comprehensive measurement of lands done until the Khas Tehsil system was established in 1872. Until the year 1790, or in the pre-Ijardari era, the settlement was made annually, and the jotedars were usually always permitted to extend their contracts based on the jama paid the year before. With the implementation of the Ijardari system, it was the responsibility of the farmers to determine the value of their land, and the State paid little attention to the agreements these individuals reached with the rayats. Measurement of lauds was sometimes used in the Khas mehals and in the case of new settlements, and this was done using the primitive khashrah or ancient native method. This is still the case in the majority of Bengal's rural areas today, this method seems to have been popular in the nation from very ancient times. The measurement was done without the aid of a compass and using a rope or rod that was fixedly measured in linear increments of 2 feet. The length was varied for debutants and criminals. Using this rod or rope, both the boundary survey and the interior fitting were previously conducted, and, like everything else from the past, needed a great deal of the surveyor's own talent and training.

The main rivers in the Koch Bihar district run slantedly from north to south. Except for one, who arrives from the Gumma Duars, all of them rise from the Himalayas and enter the district via the Western Duars of the Jalpaiguri district. The study region has a well-developed river system. The area is traversed by six river systems that travel south-easterly. The Tista

System, The Jaldhaka System, The Torsha System, The Kaljani System, The Raidak System, and The Gadadhar System are those that share the role as the principal source of water supply in order from west to east.[17] The rivers are calm throughout the dry season, and because of the Tista's proximity, they continue to be shallow. But, owing to the regular rainfall on the hills, there is a rapid surge in the rivers, which causes them to overrun their banks and gushes water that destroys houses and fields of crops.[18] One of the most important production variables is the land. All individual activities are fundamentally based on the land resource. Throughout the years, there have been several modifications to the land use pattern. The net sown area was 260.2, 252.5, and 250.6 thousand hectares during 1981–1982, 2001–2002, and 2010–2011, respectively, which amounted to an average of 76% of the district's 331.57 thousand hectares of total geographic area. The information on the district of Koch in Bihar's land use pattern is provided below.

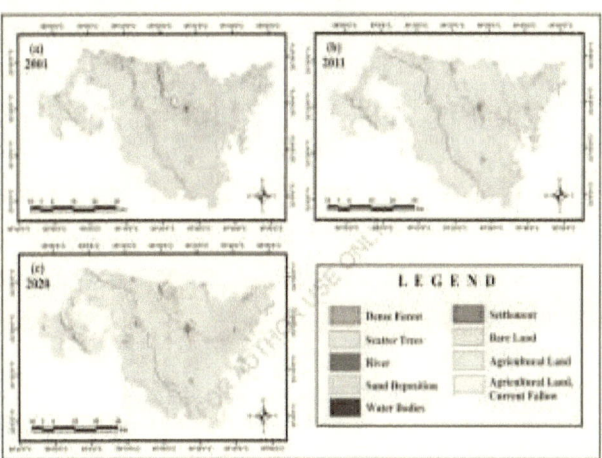

Figure 2 : Land use map of Koch Bihar district (2001-2020)

Figures 2 and 3 show that the LULC has nine primary classifications, which are shown on the map as dense forest, scatter trees, rivers, sand deposits, water bodies, settlements, barren land, and agricultural land for the years 2001, 2010, and 2020. According to results from classified maps, in 2001, different classes occupied different amounts of space: agricultural land accounted for approximately 41.49 percent of the total, bare land for 0.64 percent, settlement areas for 2.90 percent, dense forest for 13.93 percent, and rivers and water bodies for approximately 2.12 and 0.20 total percent. To the contrary, compared to 41.49 percent of the area in 2001, roughly 55.29 percent of the area was covered by agricultural land in 2011. This indicates that the amount of agricultural land is growing, and by 2020, there will only be 56.44 percent of it left. Just 7.60 percent of the land was covered in deep forest, with 8.61 percent of it being covered with scattered trees.

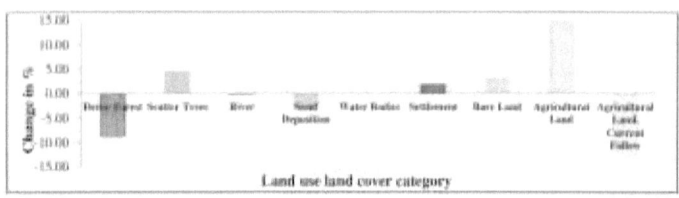

Figure 3 : Change detection of different land use and land cover classes in Cooch Behar district (2001-2020)

The 2020 picture shows a drop from 13.39 percent to 5.09 percent thick woodland. It reveals a big alteration around -8.84 percent decline of thick forest, 9.52% fear trees, 4.82 settlement, and 2.66% barren land and dehydrogenate monoxide bodies. In 2011, thick terrain, sparse trees, and settlement expanded. From 2001 to 2011, agriculture on present fellow land changed by -12.65%, a substantial shift in a defined year. From 2001 to 2020, agricultural land increased significantly on the mainland. Agricultural land increased 351.76km2 from 2001 to 2020. These river and water features are under modest forestry. Dense forest class loss declined throughout the previous three decades. Population pressure caused the conversion of thick forest regions to habitation and agricultural land.

The germination of crops relies on a variety of variables, including crop acreage, input control, and yield.[19] The fertility of the soil, monsoon behavior, rainfall, irrigation, the availability of agricultural laborers, climate changes, pricing, etc., determine the cultivated area and production. More than 80% of the district's gross cultivated land was used for the main crops of rice, wheat, maize, jute, potato, tobacco, legumes, and vegetables. The following are the district's primary crops:[20]

- Paddy of three kinds, the aus, aman and boro.
- Jute: the capsularis and the oliotaris.
- Tobacco
- Rape and mustard seeds.
- Pulses: mug, masur, khesari, thakri, kulti, arahar etc.
- Barleyand Wheat.
- China and kaon, Millets.
- Indian corn (Makai).
- Roots and bulbs: mainly potato but also onion, garlic, ginger and turmeric.
- Mutha or matting grass

Towards the end of the colonial period, a differentiated peasantry, an expanding number of intermediaries, and an army of landless sharecroppers who lived on landlords' land were the hallmarks of agricultural relations in the princely state of Cooch Behar. The lowest classes of the peasants, who were becoming more and more in debt, were under growing pressure from rising rents. The jotedars of princely Cooch Behar were the greatest landowners after Independence. They had significant landholdings. In Kalmandasguri, one jotedar owned the vast bulk of the land. There were just four landowning families in the whole village, and they were all related. The jotedar owned the land on which all other houses in Kalmandasguri were landless and resided. The jotedars regularly forcibly removed these families from their homes and exacted various forms of criminal payment. The Cooch Behar Krishak Sabha started organizing sharecroppers and farmers from the low end of the economic spectrum banding together in the 1950s to seek control of unused jotedar land and to oppose the forceful removal of adhiars from their homes. The drive in Kalmandasguri to find and seize benami land became stronger after the United Front Government took power. After the Left Front took office in 1977, ongoing mobilization helped to establish the circumstances for the execution of land reform. The first and striking result of land reform was the creation of a far fairer system of land ownership in Kalmandasguri. According to the village surveys that WIDER did in Kalmandasguri in the 1980s, land reform significantly and favorably impacted the earnings of the village's landless families. 28% of the total revenues of the formerly landless families who benefited from this initiative were derived from allotted land. In Kalmandasguri, before land reform, all but four households did not own any land. After the land reform, 78% of households had access to farmland. About majority of the cropland in the village was farmed by sharecroppers prior to land reform. Just 8 families rented property in 2005; they together farmed 7.99 acres.

References

1. For details see: Raha. Bipasha & Chattopadhyay, Subhayu. *Mapping The Path to Maturity: A Connected History of Bengal and the North-East,* Manohar Publishers & Distributors, Delhi, 2018; Bose and Prosad, Shesadri. *Some Snippets About North Bengal Studies in Historical Perspectives,* Om Publications, 2021
2. The Portal of North Bengal Development Department". Government of West Bengal. Retrieved 27 July 2023
3. Choudhury, Namita. *Urbanization in North Bengal in the Post - Independence Period*, University of North Bengal, 1988

4. Rukhsana, and Ashraful Alam. "A Study of Availability and Sustainability in India", *Agriculture, Food and Nutrition Security*, Online publication, January 2021
5. Ray, M. & Rahaman, M. "Disparity of Socio-Economic Development in Cooch Behar District, West Bengal, India: A CD Block Level Appraisal." *Indian Journal of Spatial Science*, vol. 8(2), 2017, pp. 45-51
6. Bhattacharjee, S. "Child Health Situation in Cooch Behar District: An Analysis in Respect of Protein-Energy Malnutrition", P. E. M., 2012
7. A Case Study of Nature and Characteristics of Rural Labour Out-Migration: A Case Study of Sitalkuchi Block in Koch Bihar District, *West Bengal*. No. May, 2021
8. Sarkar, Aditi, "Natural Resource Mapping Using Hybrid Classification Approach: Case Study of Cooch Behar District", *West Bengal*. No. 3, 2014, pp. 499–507
9. Ray M & Rahman, Op. cit.
10. Chaudhuri, Harendra Narayan. "The Cooch Behar State and Its Land Revenue Settlements." Cooch Behar State Press, Cooch Behar, 1903 pp. 54-76
11. Sarkar, Dulon, and Abdul Hannan. "Transport System in Pre-Independent Cooch Behar: A Historical Geography Transport System in Pre – Independent Cooch Behar", *A Historical Geography Perspective*, No. June, 2022
12. Choudhuri, Op. cit. pp.1-667
13. Das, M. "The Pattern of Demographic Changes in Darjeeling Hill Areas: Implications for Future Generations", Doctoral Dissertation, University of North Bengal, 2008.
14. Pal, Nripendra Nath. *Itikathai Cooch Behar (A brief history of Cooch Behar)*, Anima Prakashani, Kolkata, 2000, pp.1–32
15. Ahmed, K. C. *A History of Cooch Behar (in Bengali)*, Part I. Cooch Behar State. 1936
16. Pal, Nripendra Nath., Op. cit.
17. *District Gazetteers*, Koch Bihar, 1977
18. Ahmad, Ausaf. "Regional Pattern of Industrial Licensing," *Social Scientist*, Vol. 2, No. 9, 1974, p. 3
19. Rukhsana, "Impact of Microclimate on Agriculture in India: Transformation and Adaptation," in *Agriculture, Food and Nutrition Security*, No. June, 2021, pp. 41–59
20. Ahmed, A, Op. cit. pp. 41-59

Identity Formation of Women in Ancient India: A Review

Pipasa Kundu

"Under the father in childhood, under the husband in youth, under the son in old age - women will never be free."[1] This Brahmanical interpretation of the question of women's rights has influenced the epics and even contemporary historiography. But the oppressed of the society have come forward to demand their rights. Their history is not of surrender, but of struggle. The familiar myths of caste, civilization, slaves, devdasis, chastity, and happy family come into question with the participation of women, Dalits and lower-class people. Women are therefore not silent participants but highly active in this interpretation of history. India is a diverse country and home to diverse cultures since the dawn of history. While evidence of the matriarchal social structure of non-Aryan cultures in early Indian society is numerous, the Aryan culture showed disagreements about the status of women. In the ancient history of India, society has deprived women of everything essential for human dignity and declared that women do not deserve freedom. She should follow her husband's footsteps like a shadow. Women have been deprived of all the rights that can give freedom to them - education, right to choose a partner, independent occupation, right to property, right to her own body, right to maintain the decision to have children, participate in the governance of society or state or the right to express her opinion.

Orientalist historians in the nineteenth century glorified the status of women in ancient India. Again, nationalist historians have shown that the position of women in ancient India was respectable and egalitarian. They were the equals of men in all spheres of life; in learning, intelligence, knowledge of scriptures, in politics, in raising and maintaining family, in law, in inheritance of property, etc. But if we look at the position of women in ancient India, we will see that it was not very noble. We shall find the status of women through the following examples: "The wife's place in the house is below the husband, she will always follow the husband, give the leftovers to the wife after the meal."[2] The Atharvaveda mentions mantras for the birth of a son. The Taittiriya Aranyak mentions, 'Wife is companion, daughter is a curse, son is the light of heaven.'[3] A Vedanga source mentions atonement for killing blackbirds, vultures, weasels, hawks, dogs, Shudras and women.[4] Women could be mortgaged, bought, sold, given away as dowry or as gifts to guests. As mentioned in the scriptures, women bring physical pleasure. Manu said, "The wife could be beaten and subdued if necessary." Manu also said, "All courtesans are thieves and cheats". "Killing a prostitute is not a punishable offence," says Gautam.[5] In the epic Ramayana, we see Sita being suspected and having to prove her chastity, and women are held hostage in Mahabharata. Draupadi was molested in front of everyone. In Ramayana, when Surpanaka proposes love, Rama advises to immediately punish her. Also, in various Sanskrit literature written in ancient times, women were primarily seen as housewives and mothers, especially the mother of a son. Her social status depended on her genealogy and serviceability. Personal worth was determined by her looks and youth. What is not expected of her but what is blameworthy in the eyes of society is her academic intelligence, independent thinking ability and personality. This stereotype is prevalent in the epics and Puranas from the Vedic age except for a few.

Despite this position of women in ancient times, some women took the initiative in the question of their status. Maybe not always consciously, nor even successfully, but we shall find a pattern of mixed responses in the various Sanskrit literature written from the Vedic period to the Gupta period. Written evidence has not yet been corroborated with archaeological data in the Harappan civilization, so we do not have definite proof of the status of women. Apart from erotic references to women in the Vedic sources, we find some female characters that are significant in other ways. The Rigveda has evidence of women fighting on the battlefield, there is the account of the victory of Mud-Galini. Again, Vispala lost a leg and Badhrimati lost an arm in the battle. Badhrimati and Shashiyasi are mentioned for their bravery. Hence it is clear that at least some women participated in warfare. Although girls did not have the right to get an education, some women received an education and they participated in various debates and also got rebuked from male sages. The conservative nature of the society was reflected when Gargi argued rationally and successfully cornered the learned sage in the argument, and Yajnavalkya's unwarrantedly rebuked her saying, 'Don't ask any more questions else your head will fall off.'[6] Ghosha composed a hymn to Sutra No. 27 of the Rig Veda. Although Lopamudra was the wife of sage Agastya, she reasoned with her husband and raised questions about the duties of a husband by scolding him. Again, in the second epilogue of the Brihadaranyakopanishad, we find dialogues between Yajnavalkya and his wife Maitreyi, it mentions that before going to the forest for penance, Yajnavalkya wanted to divide his properties between his two wives Katyayani and Maitreyi. While Katyayani agreed, Maitreyi asked, 'Will I become immortal with what you are offering? What shall I do with something that doesn't make me immortal?' - In other words, we can see that some women in the society were aware of their educational and intellectual qualities.

Buddhist and Jain texts mention the Brahmavadini who practised lifelong celibacy and were engaged in scriptures. Most of the songs written by the bhikkhunis recorded in the 'Therigatha' were daughters of rich families before renouncing home. According to Jain texts, Jayanti, daughter of the King of Kausambi, vowed to practice lifelong celibacy and study religion and philosophy. The story of Ganika Amrapali in Vinaya Pitaka of the Mulasarvastivadins mentions that she donated bamboo groves to Buddhism. King Bimbisara of Magadha went to Vaishali to meet Amrapali. In the Buddhist literature, we see that Sirima took 1000 kahapanas for her daughter Courtesan Salavati in one night.[7] We read in Shyama Jatak that the courtesan Shyama of Kashi had 500 concubines.[8] That is, among the few women who fall into the category of brahmavadini and courtesans, they live based on their own taste, and independent ideology. If we look at the epics, we will see many female characters are questioning their sense of entitlement, and status and expressing anger from time to time.

Let us first take the words of Ramayana. As its composition begins later, some of the mythic elements have intruded into its core. However, we see that Kaikeyi dared to bind King Dasharatha to his past promise, Urmila did not go with Laxman to Vanavas and stayed in the palace, and none of the queens of Dasharatha became Sati after his death. Mandodari slanders her husband Ravana while lamenting: Sita is not superior to me in lineage, qualification or beauty, nor even my equal, you do not understand that in lust.[9] She praised Ravana yet also blamed him: You have orphaned this entire family of demons; You do not listen to benevolent friends.[10] Not only Mandodari could scold her husband as she was a demon, but after Ramachandra refused to accept Sita, she also said, "You have my heart which is in my own control, what can I do about my body which is not under my control?".[11] When Sita was proving her chastity by going through fire, she said: If I do not think of anyone other than Raghava, then Madhavi Devi (Earth) shelter me within you. If I have worshipped Ram in heart, deed and word, then Madhavi Devi takes me in your shelter. I don't know anyone except Ram. If I have spoken the truth, let Madhavi Devi shelter me.[12] This is the last act of Sita. What is noteworthy here is what Sita is asking for in return for proof of her purity. Not once did she say that if I kept the trust of Rama, he and the subjects should leave their doubts about me; let me once again be the beloved bride of Rama; let me sit next to him on the throne. Therefore, she proved her purity by taking an oath of extreme truth to protect her dignity. But she has no more prayers or expectations from Rama, from society, from life. Despite being devoted to Rama, Sita let out her anger towards her husband and society.

If we look at the Mahabharata, we can see many references to the humiliation of women. But in some cases, we shall also find the identity of women's bravery. Gandhari repeatedly reprimanded Dhritarashtra, reminding him to tame unruly Duryodhana and to leave him if he refused to obey; Dhritarashtra was not following the path he himself considered just out of cowardice and blind filial piety.[13] She even insulted her husband in open court and blamed him for the entire Kurukshetra war, unlike the conventional ideals of a devoted wife. She publicly cursed Krishna as he could have prevented the Kurukshetra war and bloodshed.[14] Draupadi had heated arguments with her husband, the righteous Yudhisthira, about the solution to the moral, political and philosophical problems of life.[15] This was not the proper conduct of a devoted wife. Kunti, decided to live in the forest for the rest of her life along with Dhritarashtra and Gandhari, she did not listen to the requests of her sons.[16] This shows that in old age, she could make decisions of her own. After a few years Dushyanta left

Shakuntala in the ashram, Shakuntala brought her children to the royal court and reprimanded the king.[17] In the Mahabharata, women could drink soma (wine?);[18] walk publicly and make decisions about themselves. Women like Shakuntala and Satyavati could marry men of their choice without their father's permission and if necessary, women like Savitri could argue with their fathers in public to establish their decision to marry their desired persons. When Bhishma abducted the 3 sisters Amba, Ambika, and Ambalika, Amba told him that she loved Shalvaraj. Damayanti, mother of two children, could tell her mother without hesitation to arrange for her remarriage (swayambar) as she could not live without her previous husband Nala, who abandoned her without any trace.[19] Hidimba forced Bhimsen to accept her love and marriage proposal. Similarly, Ulupi and Chitrangada also fell in love with Arjuna and offered to marry him. Satyavati, Ganga and Shakuntala could set conditions to uphold their power and rights before accepting love proposals from men. Ganga agreed to marry Shantanu on condition that he could never ask her any questions else she would leave. Draupadi could kick the lustful king Kichak without waiting for justice.[20] Amba and Ambalika conceived children through the practice of Niyog. These are the praiseworthy success stories of brave women of a time when women were thought to be evil, cause of all evil and sorrow,[21] when Bhishma told Yudhisthira in Shantiparva that there was nothing eviler than a woman as like a snake and untrustworthy[22] and therefore woman did not deserve freedom.[23] Yudhishthira condemned women, saying that women were the root of all sorrow.[24] Krishna said that when tainted women begot varnashankaras and ultimately bring doom.[25]

Prostitutes received nothing but contempt, hatred and ignorance from the society. Prostitutes and courtesans had some status in the Maurya era as the Arthasastra mentions the appointment of 'Ganikadhyaksha' who worked for the government as spies and informers. Manu mentioned that all prostitutes were thieves and cheats[26] and Gautama said that killing a prostitute was not a punishable offence.[27] However, courtesans and prostitutes paid taxes to the state and raping a prostitute was punishable. Manu's law was prevalent in the post-Maurya era. During this time the Puranas began to be composed and they showed growing evidence of oppression of women. Various Puranas have been composed for centuries by many scholars, but irrespective of their religious and philosophical doctrines, they all agreed to oppress women. The Sanskrit literature also depicted the image of women in a stereotypical fashion. Kalidasa depicted Shakuntala as a typical housewife in his play 'Abhigyan-Shakuntalam', while marrying her off her father Kanva advised her to take care of the elderly, be friendly with the wives of her husband's brothers and not to disobey her husband in anger.[28] When Shakuntala came to know that Dushyanta denied their love, the Gandharva marriage and his promise, she said, 'When that love ends like this, what will happen by reminding (the king)? However, I have to come clean of this taint.' Without addressing him as 'Aryaputra', she said 'As you are a king of the Puru dynasty, I expect matching behaviour and action of dignity from you.' In Bhavabhuti's 'Malatimadhava', when Malati's father wanted to arrange her marriage with a groom unworthy of her to appease the king, Malati said, 'Is the king's appeasement of greater importance to my father rather than Malati?'.

Though not a standard norm, examples of women rulers were there in ancient India. Nayanika/ Naganika, the queen of King Satakarni of the Satavahana dynasty, ruled the kingdom as the guardian of her two infant sons. Again, Prabhavatigupta, daughter of Chandragupta-II, ruled the Vakataka kingdom as the guardian of her minor son after the death of King Rudrasen.

Apart from such exceptions, the status of women was inferior in the eyes of the law. There was no citizenship law for women and no political-legal status as social entities in ancient India. Physical and mental oppression of women thus became easier for the upper class of society. The period from the Vedic age up to the 6th century AD only presents a fragmented and partial picture of women. Most of the sources point to the elite and ruling-class women of the society who could sometimes ignore the precepts of the scriptures under economic and social influence and power. Moreover, the influence of Buddhism and Jainism temporarily violated the precepts of Brahmanical laws and gave way to progressive thought. But that effect did not last long. Therefore, an almost real picture of society is reflected in the Smrtiti and Dharmashastras, which has forever governed the society of India.

However, an underlying stream of independent thought has been flowing whose expansion was thoughtful if not powerful. The Smriti writers wanted to keep patriarchy alive by introducing various rules and restrictions, deep in heart they were afraid of the matriarchal spirit. We find many protestant or brilliant female characters in various literatures written in the long background of ancient India. Even in contemporary times many matriarchal societies coexist with women-dominated groups motivated by Brahminical religious thought. Aryavarta was invaded by foreign nations from the north-west of India after the Mauryan era. As a result, assimilation and mixing of cultures began, and at the same time, a kind of conservative values arose among the law makers who made women as the main target. Lawmakers then became anxious to preserve women's chastity, with dire social consequences. Women were blinded by superstitions fostered by the theories of reincarnation and karma, coupled with fatalism, and beliefs in sraddha, supernatural actions and atonement. In other words, the attempt to narrow women's rights as a whole began in the Gupta period - the detailed practice of which can be seen in the Puranas, Smritis and Dharmashastras. As a result, it is not an exaggeration to say that even though the next five long centuries have passed, significant protesting female characters are almost rare.

References:

1. Bhattacharya, Sukumari. *Anthology*, Gangchil, Third Edition, Kolkata, October 2014.
2. Chakraborty, Uma (trans. Amlan Bhattacharya), *A History of Ancient India: Through the Eyes of the People*, Setu Prakasani, Calcutta, 2017.
3. Singh, Kankar. *Religion and Women: Ancient India*, Radical Impressions, Kolkata, Third Edition, 2017
4. Chattopadhyay, Bhaskar. *Aryan Social and State System of India (Ancient Period)*, Progressive Publishers, Calcutta, 2nd edition, December, 2005
5. Bhattacharya, B., *Outline of Sanskrit Literature*, Book World, Kolkata, 29th Edition, September 2006
6. *Maitrayani Samhita* 1:10:11, 3:6:3; *Shatapatha Brahmana* 13:2:24
7. *Taittiriya Samhita* 6:5:8:7
8. *Dhammapadatika,* Pali Text Society, London, 1906-14, pp. 308-9
9. *Ramayana*, 6:111:28
10. Ibid., 6:111:76
11. Ibid., 6:116:9
12. Ibid., 7:98:7, pp. 8, 9
13. *Mahabharata*, 2:75:8-10 & 5:122:9
14. Ibid., 11:25:42
15. Ibid., 3:37, pp. 30, 32, 37
16. Ibid., 15:16-17
17. Ibid., 1:69 1-27
18. Ibid., 15:17:17
19. Ibid., 3:53-78
20. Ibid., 4:16:19-20
21. Ibid., 1:159:11
22. Ibid., 5:37:29
23. Ibid, 12:10:20

24. Ibid., 12:6
25. Ibid., 6:23:41
26. *Arthasastra*, 9:259-60
27. *Gautam Dharmasutra*, 22:2
28. *Abhigyan-Shakuntalam*, 4/18.

Bengal to the Outside World: The Role of Sultan Ghiyas Uddin Azam Shah

Md Sk Maruf Azam

Undivided Bengal was one of the most an important province in medieval India. Its eastern boundary was Chittagong and the western limit was Tiliagaddi (near Rajmahal). The estimated length from east to west is 400 hundred krosh. With the Himalayas in the north and the Sundarbans in the south, the estimated width from north to south was 200 hundred krosh.[1] This area was more than 400 hundred years under the Turkish rule (Hussain Sahi and Illiyas Sahi dynasty). Although Turkish rule was established in Bengal, as an auxiliary political centre, its rulers often denied the supremacy of Delhi. It can be said that Bengal was truly independent during the reign of Delhi Sultanate.[2] It has a long history that how the Bengal play very crucial role in the political, economic and cultural aspects during this time. I am not going to discuss that aspects here, rather I have tried to focus on how the Bengal made considerable impact to outside world, both politically and economically, during this phase. Specially, I have highlighted the role of Azam Shah of the Ilyas Shahi dynasty in making the Bengal well-known state to the other states of India and outside world.

Azam Shah ascended the throne of Bengal in 1390-91 AD with the title of 'Ghiyas-ud-din Azam Shah'.[3] Among all the independent Sultans of Bengal, there was no one with such an interesting character as him. There are few incidents happened in his life as strange and fantastical way that his life seems like a fairytale.[4] Ghiyas-ud-din Azam Shah became famous as a very accomplished statesman, a just judge, and a good ruler. He was distinguished for his character traits, patronage of scholars and poets, devotion to Sufi saints, establishment of madrasas at the heart of Islamic civilization and exchange of ambassadors with the Emperor of China.[5] Bengal not only became known to the outside world during his reign, but also influenced the people of other lands. The honour and prestige of Bengal increased in abroad due to his multidimensional initiatives. Several Arab, Chinese and Indian historical records mention the same with the name of Azam Shah.[6]

His first initiative was the establishing relationship with Jaunpur state. For the first time, he sent an ambassador to the ruler of Jaunpur, Khwaja Malik Sarwar, also known as Khawaja-e-Jahan, who founded the independent and mighty Jaunpur kingdom. The authoritative book Tarikh-e-Mubarakshahi mentions, "The ruler of Lakhnauti presented elephants to Khawaja-e-Jahan".[7] By this gesture Azam Shah established an alliance with the kingdom of Jaunpur. It is not known whether any other Sultan of Bengal exchanged ambassadors with foreign countries before him.[8]

Azam Shah himself was a great scholar and advocate of learning. He used to write poetry in the Persian language. He was fascinated with the Persian art of literature. Therefore, once he invited the famous Iranian poet Hafez to Bengal. The Riaz-us-Salatin records an interesting incident of Sultan Ghiyas-ud-Din Azam Shah falling fatally ill and selecting three harem girls named Sar, Gul and Lala to wash his body after his death. However, the Sultan recovered and started showing more favour to the three girls making other girls in the harem jealous of them. The Three girls complained to the Sultan that they were being teased by the jealous ladies.[9] Listening to their complaints the emotional Sultan instantly composed the first stanza of a poem in Persian and said; "Saki Hadim-i-Sarv, Gul and Lala

Mirawad".[10] But the Sultan could not compose a fitting second part of the poem and wrote it to the poet Hafiz in the city of Shiraz in Iran through an emissary. Hafiz immediately completed the poem, added a few of his own verses and wrote back to the Sultan.[11] Ghiyas-ud-Din, having received the poem, was pleased and appropriately rewarded Hafez. First stanza of the poem is like-

> *O (love) bestower of nectar! The subjects of Sar, Gul and Lala have appeared.*

This topic indeed has appeared for three proud beauties.[12] The 'Aini-e-Akbari' mentions that Khawajah Hafiz of Shiraz sent Ghiyas-ud-din an ode in the form of a Ghazal which occurs in the following verse: 'O paraquets of Hindustan, taste its sweetness, sweets are being sent from Persia to Bengal. Hafez, you do not refrain from sending poems to Ghiyas-ud-din's court. Because when your lament reaches there, hope will be fulfilled.'[13] A few stanzas of this ghazal are quoted in Riaz and Ain, the complete ghazal (compiled by Hafis's close friend Muhammad Gul-Andam shortly after his death) is available in Diwan-i-Hafiz.[14] He mentions the name of the Sultan, the names of the three maidservants, the name of Bengal in the ghazal, and laments (perhaps due to age) not being able to cross the route to Bengal in one year.[15]

Making relationship with Sufi Sadhaka Balkhi of Bihar was his next initiative. Ghiyas-ud-Din Azam Shah was a great admirer of the Sufi saint Muzaffar Shams Balkhi and they used to exchange letters among them. He also advised on religion and governance.[16] Balkhi's letter reveals that Ghiyas-ud-Din was at first preoccupied with pleasure and enjoyment, but during his correspondence with Balkhi he lived a holy and pious life. Ghiyas-ud-Din was endowed with learning, magnanimity, generosity, fearlessness etc. and thus he became popular as a king. Ghiyas-uddin as a poet used to write beautiful ghazals and send them to Muzaffar Shams Balkhi.[17] Balkhi's twelve letters were recently discovered by Professor Syed Hasan Askari who introduced them in the article 'Correspondence of the 14th century two Sufi saints of Bihar with the contemporary sovereigns of Delhi and Bengal'.[18] A few letters reveal that Muzaffar Shams Balkhi sailed from Chittagong port on his last visit to Makkah. A few years later, he passed away in 803 Hijri. He intended to go to Mecca and be buried there.[19]

Establishing relations with Arab countries was one of the great generous initiatives. Sultan Ghiyas-ud-Din Azam Shah established madrasas in Mecca and Medina Sharif at a great expense and sent large sums of money to be distributed among the inhabitants of these two cities. Evidence of this can be found in the books written by some contemporary Arab and Indo-Pak historians. These books are Ibn-e-Hajar's Inba-ul-Ghumr, Taqi-al Farsi's Iqduth-Thamin; Qutb-ud-Din Hanfi's Tarikh-i-Makkah and Al-Sakhawir's Al-Jaw-Lami.[20] At the instigation of one of Azam Shah's vizier Khan Jahan, he established madrasas in Mecca and Medina and sent extensive gifts to the inhabitants. The Sultan sent money and gifts via his personal Habsi servant Yakut.[21] Azam Shah's madrasa in Mecca was built near the Harem Sharif called Bab-e-Ummehani and Madrasa near Masjid-e-Nabvi in Madinah was built at Hosan-ul-Atik. Both madrasas are known as Bengali madrasas or Gyasiyan madrasas.[22] Apart from this, two tracts of land and four water bodies near the Mecca-Madrasah were purchased and donated to the Madrasah. The income from this property was spent on teachers, students, staff and necessities of the madrasa. A house situated in front of the madrasa building was also purchased for five hundred gold coins and waqf for the madrasa.[23] So much money was sent from Bengal that everyone in Makkah and Madinah got a share of it. The Sultan also sent money through Yakut to dig the canal at Arafat. Maulana Hasan

(Sharif of Makkah) accepted this money and said, "we will make the necessary arrangements." This money was amounted to thirty thousand gold coins.[24]

Another important achievement of Azam Shah was that he revived China's ancient cultural contact with India. The Emperor of China also sent envoys to Bengal with gifts for the Sultan and his consort. Even, the Emperor of China requested the Sultan of Bengal to send Buddhist monks to China. A Buddhist monk named Maharatna Dharmaraja visited China in 1410-1411 AD to fulfil that request.[25] The sending of this envoy by Ghiyas-ud-Din is known from various historical records of China such as *Si-yong-chao-kung-tien-lu*, *Shu-yu-chou-t seu-lu* and *Ming-she*, the official record of the Ming dynasty etc. In the book *Shu-yu-chou-t seu-lu,* it is written that in the third year of the reign of Yang-lo (1405) the king of Bengal sent an envoy to the royal court of China. In the sixth year of Yong-lo's reign (1408 AD), the king of that country (Bengal) again sent envoys. This envoy arrived at the port of Tai-t-sang with gifts and the emperor (of China) sent the Minister of Foreign Affairs there to receive him.[26] Another royal delegation of Bengal sent to China in 1408 and 1409 consisted of 230 members, and this number suggests that commercial interest was also at play apart from diplomatic reasons.[27] The exchange of ambassadors between Bengal and China is further known from Ma-Huan book *Ying-Zai-Sheng-Lan* and by the interpreter of the Chinese delegation.[28] Ma-Huan reached Chittagong in 1406 AD after a twenty-day voyage from Nicobar via the island of Sumatra. From Chittagong by small ship, he arrived at Sunudakong (Sonargaon) town by river. According to him, the distance of Sonargaon from the sea mouth is more or less 150 miles From Sonargaon. Ma-Huan travelled northwest and reached the capital of 'Pangkola' crossing 25 settlements. He did not mention the name of the capital. Then the capital of Bengal was

Gaur.[29] He described that the Bengalis were honest and made a lot of money from business, even if they lost, they never lied or tried to cheat anyone. Chinese accounts also laud about the condition of peasants of Bengal as who ploughed, sowed, weeded, irrigated and laboured throughout the year to produce crops.[30] There is also a special mention of the cotton textiles of Bengal in the Chines accounts. The muslin industry of Bengal attracted foreigners, because in no other country could such fine clothes be found.[31] Tea was not produced here, so people here do not entertain guests with tea, instead, they entertain guests with betel leaves.[32] Therefore, the Chinese accounts present a picture of the beautiful and abundant country of Bengal at that time.

Chittagong Port was the main corridor in connection with the outside world. The fact that Chittagong Port became an international hub during the reign of Azam Shah is available in various accounts. According to the accounts of Arab geographers, Sandwip in Chittagong was a busy commercial port at that time. Arab merchant ships used to come here and over time Arabs settled in this area of Chittagong.[33] Chittagong Port saw great growth during his tenure due to the successful expansion of trade and commerce with the Far East.[34] After starting the journey from Sumatra, the Chinese delegation reached Cheh-ti-gan (Chatgaon) port in Bangladesh after twenty-one days by sea.[35] Muzaffar Shams Balkhi went to Mecca for Hajj for the last time from Chittagong port. He stayed in Chittagong for a month. From Chittagong, Balkhi wrote a letter to Sultan Ghiyasuddin requesting him to send a Farman to the clerks of Chittagong, so that they accommodate the dervishes travelling for Makkah on the first ship.[36] There is evidence that Bengal pilgrims used to go to Arabia with the help of Chittagong port. Bengalis were active in international trade. Gold and silver coins of Bengal were minted. The currency was called tanka and was used in international trade.[37] Many of the rich men of the capital had ships and they did trade with foreign countries. Ma-Huan saw boats being built by sea in this country and very likely Chittagong was the centre of boat building.[38] It is clear from the Chinese accounts that Azam Shah had complete authority over Sonargaon and the port of Chittagong.[39]

Building relationship with Arakan King was one of the best initiatives of Azam Saha. The exiled king of Arakan took refuge in Azam Shah's court and Azam Shah tried to install him on the throne of Arakan but failed.[40] When Arakan became a rival centre of power in the 15th century, Raja Rajathu's son Raja Naramekhala (1397 – 1401) was forced to flee to Gauda, the capital of Bengal, in the first year of his reign.[41]

Through the above discussion, we can conclude that Ghiyas-ud-din Azam Shah was one of the most prominent Sultans of Bengal in the Middle Ages. How he established relations in the international field at that time bears witness to his great skill. He gained fame by establishing relations with neighbouring states, practising literature, respecting Sufi saints, building madrasa, and inns in Arab countries, establishing relations with China, assisting in international trade and establishing relations with the state of Arakan. Hence, the historian Sukhmoy Banerjee has rightly said that among all the independent Sultans of Bengal, no one has an interesting character like him. Some incidents in his life are so strange that he is considered to be the equivalent of a fairy tale prince.

References

1. Salim, Ghulam Hussain; *Riaz-us-Salatin*, Sriramprana Gupta (ed.), Divya Prakash, Dhaka, 2007 p.28
2. Chowdhury, Teslim, *History of India from the Early Middle Ages to the Medieval Transition 600-1556,* Progressive Publisher, Kolkata, 2015 p. 522
3. Ibid., p.533

4. Mukhopadhyay, Sukhmoy; *Two Hundred Years of Bengal History: The Period of the Independent Sultans (1338-1538)*, Bharti Book Stall, Calcutta, July 1960, p.82
5. Karim, Abdul. *History of Bengal, Society and Politics*, Jatiya Sahitya Prakash, Dhaka, February 2022, p.207
6. Karim, Abdul. *History of Bengal from Muslim Conquest to Sepoy Revolution (1200-1858 AD)*, Jatiya Sahitya Prakash, Dhaka, 2021, p.80
7. Mukhopadhyay, Sukhmoy, Op. cit., p.98
8. Karim, Abdul, 2022, Op. cit., p.216
9. Ibid., p. 210
10. Khan, Saheb Abid Ali, *Smriti of Gaur and Pandua*, Chowdhury Shamsur Rahman (s.) Sopan Publishers, Kolkata, 2011, p.35
11. Mukhopadhyay, Sukhmoy, Op. cit., p.84
12. Salim, Ghulam Hussain, Op. cit., p.88
13. Allami, Abul Fazl, *The Ain-i Akbari*, vol.2, (T.) Colonel H.S. Jarrett, The Asiatic Society, Kolkata, Second reprint in March 2010, p.161
14. Majumdar, Sriramesh Chandra (ed.) *History of Bangladesh*, Volume II, General Printers and Publishers Private Limited, Kolkata, Falgun 1373, p. 42
15. Ahmad, Wakil, *Roots and self-identity of Muslims of Bengal (Middle Ages)*, Books, Dhaka 2022, p. 89
16. Karim, Abdul, 2022, Op. cit., p.215
17. Majumdar, Sriramesh Chandra (S.), Op. cit., p.43
18. Mukhopadhyay, Sukhmoy, Op. cit., p.91
19. Ibid., p. 98
20. Karim, Abdul, 2022, Op. cit., p.212
21. Ibid., p. 213
22. Karim, Abdul, 2021, Op. cit., p.74
23. Karim, Abdul, 2022, Op. cit., p.213
24. Ibid., p. 214
25. Chowdhury, Teslim, Op. cit., p.533
26. Mukhopadhyay, Sukhmoy, Op. cit., p.99
27. Ahmad, Wakil, Op. cit., p. 89
28. Mukhopadhyay, Sukhmoy, Op. cit., p.106
29. Ahmad, Wakil, *Foreign Tourists of Bengal*, Gatidhara, Dhaka, May 2014, p. 30
30. Karim, Abdul, 2021, Op. cit., p.75
31. Ibid., p. 76
32. Rahim, M., Chowdhury, A. Momin, Abdul, Mahmud AB, Mohiuddin, Islam, Sirajul, *History of Bangladesh*, Nowroz Kitabistan, Dhaka 1971, p. 190
33. Rahman, M., *Social Cultural and Economic History of Bengal*, Merit Fair Publications, September 2013, Dhaka, p. 50

34. Rizvi, S. A., *The Bright India of the Past,* (ed.) Anshupati Dasgupta, Progressive Publishers, Kolkata 2015, p. 134
35. Rahim, M., Chowdhury, A., 1971, Op. cit., p.189
36. Mukhopadhyay, Sukhmoy, Op. cit., p.98
37. Karim, Abdul, 2021, Op. cit., p.76
38. Ahmad, Wakil, 2014, Op. cit., p.31
39. Karim, Abdul, 2022, Op. cit., p.220
40. Chowdhury, Teslim, Op. cit., p.533
41. www.britinnica.com/biography/Narameikhla, 10.03.2023, 06:04pm.

Basanti Devi: A Woman Activist of Manbhum's Quit India Movement

Tapas Mahato

Quit India Movement was the last nationwide platform for Indian women to exhibit the feminine strength and aspiration. It was the time when the women from nook and corner of India arrived at the street to direct action with imperial British.[1] Gandhiji's slogan of Do-or-Die enthralled the heart and mind of the women.[2] Women, whether the rich or the poor, from cities, towns, kosba, villages fight with mighty British government at per their male counterpart. In this context, Bengal was leading the country. Basanti Devi was one of the prominent women of this phase who not only participated in the Quit India Movement but also led the women folk of her localities as like Matong Gini Hazra.[3] Hence, here, in this writing I have concentrate to focus on the courage, strength, strategy and sacrifices of Basanti Devi who have actively played in the Quit India Movement in Manbhum region of Bengal.

On the call of Gandhiji, the Quit India movement started all over India on 9th August 1942. On the night of August 9 in the town of Purulia, the headquarters of Manbhum district, news came over the radio that members of the Congress Committee, including Mahatma Gandhi, had been arrested.[4] Like the rest of India, the Purulia Shilpashram was surrounded by the police before sunrise on 10th August. They had a warrant in the name of Bibhuti Bhushan Dasgupta, Kabichariya and Purnendu Mukhopadhyay, as Purnendu Mukhopadhyay was not in Purulia that day, the police arrested the two. Immediately, the police seized the ashram and ordered the ashram residents to leave. As the ashram residents did not agree, the police arrested Labanya Prabha Ghosh, Shashi Chandra Bandopadhyay, Arun Chandra Ghosh, Baidyanath Dutta, Ramkinkar Mahato and Kamala Ghosh. When Atul Chandra Ghosh returned to Purulia on 11th August from the Bombay session of the National Congress, he too was arrested on August 13th.[5] But before his arrest, he made a list of actions for Manbhoomi workers. According to his instructions, the Congress workers of the district got together and distributed picketing leaflets, formed various meeting societies by communicating among themselves and engaged in future programs, and the police arrested them too. All of them were sentenced to three to nine months in prison. On 10th August, the government confiscated the following institutions in its brutal crackdown, among them were -Majhihira Ashram and Basic School, Bhutam Ashram, Atal Ashram of Jahanabad, Congress Office of Chasha Thana, Purulia Shilpashram and Congress Office, Mukti Press, Tulin and Hutumra Ashram. On the same day, along with the hartal in Katrash and Dhanbad, the student and labour strike began.[6] Several Congress workers from Katrash including Congress leader Subhash Chandra Bose were arrested. It can be seen that all the leaders of the Manbhum Congress were arrested and detained in Hazaribagh and Dwarbhanga jails before this movement could even take shape. Despite Gandhiji's call for a movement on August 9, Manbhoomi's Quit India Movement of 1942 began on September 30 as all the leaders of Manbhum were arrested and party workers were disoriented at first.[7] Even though there was a call for non-violent movements all over India, the movements turned violent. The Congress workers of Manabhoomi at first assumed that the movement would be non-violent since their party leaders were true non-violent.[8] At that time, the Congress in Manbhum was led by second-tier leaders of relatively young age. Among them were Krishna Prasad Chowdhury of Laxmanpur, Baidyanath Mahato of Hura, Chitra

Bhushan Dasgupta, Amal Chandra Ghosh, Jugal Prasad Sengupta, Girish Chandra Majumdar, Bhajahari Mahato of Nirami Store, Girish Mahato, Hemchandra Mahato, Satyakinkar Mahato, Labanya Prabha Ghosh and many other men and women.[9]

Rishi Nibaran Chandra's youngest daughter Basanti Devi took an active part in the 1942 movement. She was then married, and the mother of a son. The leaders and workers of Manbhum decided that the movement would be non-violent and no workers could bring any weapons. However, the work of destroying road bridges and railway bridges, cutting telephone lines, and uprooting railway lines will continue to paralyze the administration and government machinery and lines of communication. Preparations for the movement of 42 had been going on for some time. At that time in a secret hideout at a resort in Girigiri, 5 miles away from Purulia city, Ramlal Saraogi, one of the leaders of the Swadeshi movement, used to come. He drew the outlines and plans of the movement there; Chitra Bhushan Dasgupta and Basanti Devi used to deliver them to the party workers secretly avoiding the police. Once Basanti Devi took the responsibility of delivering some manifestos to Manbazar, one of the workers drove Basanti Devi to Kenda on a bicycle. By the time they reached, the evening had passed and Chunaram was present there as preplanned. They took cover in the forest of Kenda in darkness to spend the night and avoid the police. A little before dawn they set foot on the way to Manbazar.[10] Apart from these dare-devil works, Basanti Devi travelled throughout villages and towns of Manbhum on foot to communicate and gather workers for the Congress, to increase public relations, and to motivate village women to join the country's freedom struggle. Never did she heed the threats of the police or the supporters of the British; from her teenage, she fought for the freedom of the country.[11]

Before the movement was fully launched, Prafulla Sen and Annada Chowdhury discussed the supply of machinery for uprooting railway lines and for cutting the telegraph lines from a secret hideout in Calcutta. But the problem was that the machines had to be delivered secretly to the workers in Manbhum from the hideout in Calcutta. Basanti Devi immediately agreed to this difficult task. But those heavy machines can't be transported easily by her in a traditional khaddar sari. She came to Purulia for preparation and went to the house of Jugal Kishore Sengupta to ask his wife to lend a modern-looking sari. The next day Basanti Devi left for Kolkata with that saree and went to an old house in Chorbagan, Kolkata. Just before evening, Praful Sen gave her a small trunk containing the tools for the operation and asked her to deliver that to the revolutionaries as soon as she reached Purulia.[12] After the evening, she reached Howrah railway station with the trunk in a taxi. A man was waiting for her with a first-class ticket. She boarded the first-class compartment with the trunk and other passengers thought she was a Punjabi woman due to her dress and tall figure. Indeed, Basanti Devi was tall, chubby and had long hair. The train reached Adra early in the morning, and she took the trunk to the house of Dr Tarak Roy at Beniyasol with the help of a coolie. Dr Roy was a respected name in the area, his wife Devi was the niece of revolutionary Bhupati Majumder and sister of Mrs. Rekha Mallick of Purulia. The house of Dr Roy in Adra was called Mughal Sarai Junction by the freedom fighters of Manbhum as it was one of the hideouts for them. Many revolutionaries took food and shelter at the house of Devi and Swadeshi workers called it Barwari kitchen. Similarly, another barwari kitchen was the family of Chapa Devi, wife of Hemchandra Mahato of Agra village of Manbazar thana. The third was the barwari kitchen of the wife of Krishna Prasad Chowdhury of Ura, Laxmanpur. Basanti Devi used to deliver food prepared from these three kitchens to the undercover Swadeshi agitators.[13] Another important role of Basanti Devi was to raise the logistics and funds for running the kitchens by begging.

Apart from these, Basanti Devi took part in the Language movement and the Calcutta Satyagraha even after India's independence, she also fought against the barbaric attitude of the Bihar government since the inception of the Lok Sevak Sangha. Later she tirelessly worked for social service, especially for the welfare of women till her death. Such an example of a woman freedom fighter and social worker is very rare not only in Manbhum but in the whole West Bengal.[14] In the Quit India movement of 1942, Basanti Devi acted fearlessly from the frontline. After independence, Basanti Devi acted as the Superintendent of 'Wardha Marwari Mahila Samaj Kalyan Samiti' for a long time, and later returned to Manbhum with the desire to serve rural areas on the instructions of Gandhiji. When Basanti Devi and her husband were looking for ways of Gram Seva (rural service), her elder brother Bibhuti Bhushan Dasgupta arranged a few bighas of barren land in Nimri from the zamindar of Chandil, Amulya Jana.[15] They started living a very simple life in a mud house and set an example of honesty and sacrifice to the people of Manbhum. They toiled to make the barren land fertile with the help of the villagers and set up a centre of rural service Lok Sebayatan. Many of the renowned social workers and Gandhian leaders of India visited the Lok Sebayatan and praised her efforts. This centre inspired many rural gentries and became one of the best rural service centres in the country. As a recognition of her efforts in social service, she received the Bajaj Award with one lakh rupees of award money. She donated the entire sum of the award to repay the loan she took to build the Lok Sebayatan. Her tireless and dedicated life ended at the age of 88 in 2001.[16]

Her contribution to the Manbhum is unparalleled. Yet, she has not received her due recognition. The news of her receiving the Bajaj Award was proudly printed in the newspapers in Bihar, but not in any Bengali newspaper. Even her own Mukti magazine, which she started during the fight for independence, did not cover the news. None from Manbhum came forward to preserve the memory of the firebrand daughter of Manbhum. Snehalata Ghosh, a longtime resident of the Lok Sebayatan ashram, recently published a book "*Basudi O Tar Lok Sebayatan*" which immensely helped revive the memory of Basanti Devi.[17] The book describes the activities of Basanti Devi at the Lok Sebayatan Centre and affectionately remembers her contributions. I intend to publish a biography of Basanti Devi in the near future.

References

1. Green, Jen, *Gandhi and the Quit India Movement.* Capstone Global Library, 2013, see the introduction
2. Douglas, Allen, *The Philosophy of Mahatma Gandhi for the Twenty-First Century*, Lexington Books, 2008 p. 228
3. For details see: Maity, Pradyot Kumar, *Quit India Movement in Bengal and the Tamralipta Jatiya Sarkar*, Punthi Pustak, 2002; Thakur, Bharti, *Women in Gandhi's Mass Movements,* Deep and Deep Publications, 2006
4. Kumar, Raj, *Essays on Indian Freedom Movement*, (History and culture series), Discovery Publishing House, 2003, p. 108
5. Bose, Asit & Mondal, Pradip Kumar, *Manbhum is the Identity of Puruliya*, (Manbhum Purulia Parichay) p. 209
6. Mahato, Alaka. 'Role Of Labanya Prabha Ghosh in Freedom Movement of Manbhum District', *IJCRT*, Volume 10, Issue 12 December 2022
7. Bose, Asit & Mondal, Pradip Kumar, Op. cit.
8. Verma, Jawahar Lal, *The Quit India Movement in Bihar & Jharkhand*, Janaki Prakashan, Bihar, 2012
9. Shukla, V., *Rebellion of 1942: Quit India Movement*, H.K. Publishers & Distributors, 1989
10. Mukhopadhyay, Subhash Chandra, *Freedom Struggle of Manbhum District 1857-1947*, p.228

11. Bose Asit & Mondal Pradip Kumar, Op. cit., p. 12-56
12. Kumari, Saroj. *Role of women in the freedom movement in Bihar, 1912-1947.* Janaki Prakashan, Patna, 2005, pp. 138-179
13. Bose Asit & Mondal Pradip Kumar, Op. cit.,
14. Saxena, K. S. "Women in Freedom Movement in India", in Tripathi, R. S. Tiwari, R. P. (ed.) *Perspectives on Indian Women*, APH Publishing, 1999
15. Verma, H. N, *Eminent Indian Women*, Great Indian Publishers, New Delhi, 1998
16. Mukhopadhyay, Subhash Chandra, Op. cit.
17. See for details: Ghosh, S. *Basudi O Tar Lok Sebayatan*

Challenges Towards Muslims Political Identity in India in 21st Century

Dr. Md Zaharul Hoque

The politics of Muslims in India has been a contentious issue for decades. The Muslim community, which comprises a significant proportion of the Indian population, has faced challenges in terms of political representation and equal opportunities. This chapter aims to analyse the current state of Muslim politics in India and the challenges faced by the Muslim community in the country. The paper discusses the historical context of Muslim politics in India, the current state of Muslim representation in politics, and the challenges faced by the community in terms of discrimination, exclusion, and marginalization. The chapter also concludes possible suggestions that are in need for greater political representation and inclusivity for Muslims in India.

Muslims in India have been a significant political force for decades. However, the community has faced significant challenges in terms of political representation, social and economic opportunities, and inclusion. Muslims constitute around 14% of the Indian population, making them the largest minority group in the country. Despite this, their political representation has been limited, and they have often been subjected to discrimination and exclusion. However, there are only 5 percent Muslim representatives in the 17th Lok Sabha after the 2019 parliamentary election, same as the average Muslim representation in the Lok Sabha since Independence. In 2019 there were 25 Muslim representatives elected to the Lok Sabha compared to 22 in the previous one. Hence, political underrepresentation of Indian Muslims is hardly a recent development, and historically the community representation has remained far below its share in the population. The community also lags behind on almost all socio-economic indicators. It becomes important to engage with the question of Muslim representation in contemporary India in the light of the BJP in power, and what it means for Indian Muslims. The paper is an attempt to analyse Muslim representation against the backdrop of 2019 parliamentary elections, and how it is the culmination of long-term shifts in Indian politics resulting in a decisively majoritarian turn of democracy in India.

The historical context of Muslim political identity in India is complex and spans over a millennium. Islam first arrived in the Indian subcontinent in the 7th century with the Arab traders and later with the conquests of Islamic empires. The Delhi Sultanate, established in the early 13th century, marked the first significant political entity ruled by Muslims in India. The Mughal Empire was one of the most powerful and influential Muslim empires in India. It reached its zenith under Emperor Akbar, known for his policy of religious tolerance. However, subsequent emperors faced challenges from regional powers, leading to a decline in centralized Mughal authority. Thereafter, various independent Muslim sultanates emerged in the Deccan and other regions of India. These sultanates, such as the Bahmani Sultanate and the Sultanate of Bijapur, played a crucial role in shaping the political landscape. As the Mughal Empire weakened, regional powers like the Marathas, Sikhs, and various Muslim states in the Deccan and Awadh gained prominence. This period witnessed the emergence of diverse political identities, including Muslim ones. The British East India Company's conquest of India in the mid-19th century marked a significant shift in the political landscape. During this period, Muslims, along with other communities, were drawn into early forms of organized political movements against colonial rule. The partition of India in 1947 led to the creation of Pakistan as a separate state for Muslims. This event, driven by religious and political considerations, profoundly influenced the political identity of Muslims in the subcontinent.

After partition, India became home to one of the world's largest Muslim minorities. The Indian Constitution guaranteed religious freedom and equal rights to all citizens, including Muslims. The community played a significant role in shaping the political and cultural fabric of independent India. Muslim political identity in post-independence India has been shaped by various movements and political parties. The All-India Muslim Personal Law Board, for instance, advocates for the protection of Muslim personal laws. Additionally, political parties like the Indian Union Muslim League and others have represented the interests of Muslims in the political sphere. Muslims in India have grappled with questions of identity, representation, and participation in the political process. Debates over issues like reservation, uniform civil code, and socio-economic development have been central to discussions on Muslim political identity. In the wake of the Partition of 1947, Muslims in India found themselves stripped of their politics. For the first time they were unable even to make any constitutional claims about their cause representing the needs of minority or caste groups more generally. Reduced to a purely self-interested group, they came to focus on issues limited to defending their religion and protecting its Personal Law. These included several famous controversies: the Hazratbal incident of 1963, the Shahbano case of 1985, the Babri Masjid dispute, and latest the Citizenship Amendment Act & NRC issues. Muslim politics after Independence, however, was reduced to a purely defensive practice of making claims in the name of culture and religion that had to be mediated at the national level by old élites. But this way of doing things itself came to an end with the destruction of the Babri Masjid. The nearly three subsequent decades of India's economic liberalisation and political fragmentation allowed for the dissolution of Muslim politics as well. This meant breaking the monopoly of north India and its élites both internally, through low-caste politics, and externally by the emergence of new élites in other parts of the country.

Despite the significant role that Muslims have played in India's political history, their representation in current Indian politics is very limited. Muslims have traditionally been associated with the Indian National Congress, but in recent years, there has been a shift towards the Bharatiya Janata Party (BJP), a right-wing Hindu nationalist party. The BJP has been accused of promoting anti-Muslim sentiments and policies, which has led to the marginalization of the Muslim community. The lack of political representation for Muslims in India has led to a sense of alienation and disillusionment. Muslims feel that their voices are not being heard and that their concerns are not being addressed. This has led to a rise in communal tensions and violence, particularly in states with a significant Muslim population such as Uttar Pradesh and Bihar. Political underrepresentation by itself may not necessarily be linked to majoritarianism. Muslims have been consistently underrepresented in the legislative arena even in the past.

Table: 1. Muslim representation in Lok Sabha and Rajya Sabha (1952–2019)

Phase	Muslim Percentage in Lok Sabha	Phase	Muslim Percentage in Rajya Sabha
1952–1971	5%	1952–1977	10%

1977–1984	8%	1978–1989	10%
1989–2019	6%	1990–2019	12%
2019	5%	2019	7%

However, what is distinct is a decidedly majoritarian understanding of democracy in contemporary India. The lower representation of Muslims is likely to further embolden this majoritarian impulse and strengthen the culture of impunity in relation to minorities. For instance, the onward March of BJP has coincided with the rise in incidence of cow-related hate crimes, and the number of states where they have been committed.

The Muslim community in India faces significant challenges, including discrimination, exclusion, and marginalization. Muslims are often subjected to religious profiling and discrimination in employment, education, and housing. They are also disproportionately affected by poverty and unemployment, which further exacerbates their exclusion from mainstream society. The rise of Hindutva, a right-wing Hindu nationalist ideology, has further marginalized the Muslim community in India. The BJP has been accused of promoting Hindutva and pursuing policies that discriminate against Muslims. The BJP's policies, such as the Citizenship Amendment Act (CAA) and the National Register of Citizens (NRC), have been criticized for being discriminatory towards Muslims. Muslims in India face several challenges concerning their political identity. These challenges include:

1. Marginalization and Underrepresentation: Muslims often experience marginalization in the political arena, with limited

representation in legislative bodies, political parties, and decision-making processes. This underrepresentation diminishes their influence and hinders their ability to effectively advocate for their community's concerns and interests.

2. Communal Polarization: Muslims frequently face the challenge of communal polarization, where their political identity is exploited for political gains. They are often portrayed as a homogeneous and monolithic group, leading to the perpetuation of stereotypes and prejudices. This polarization can result in the marginalization of Muslim voices and contribute to a divisive political atmosphere.

3. Stereotyping and Stigmatization: Muslims are sometimes subject to negative stereotyping and stigmatization based on their political identity. They may be labelled as "anti-national" or "extremist," leading to their exclusion from mainstream political processes and public discourse. Such stereotypes undermine their political agency and hinder their ability to engage meaningfully in the political sphere.

4. Discriminatory Practices: Muslims face discriminatory practices in politics, such as religious profiling, which can limit their access to political participation and representation. They may encounter barriers in obtaining political positions, party nominations, and electoral constituencies due to their religious background, further exacerbating their underrepresentation.

5. Hindutva Politics: The rise of Hindutva ideology and right-wing Hindu nationalist parties in India has created additional challenges for Muslim political identity. Hindutva politics promotes a majoritarian narrative, which can marginalize and exclude Muslims from political power. Policies and rhetoric associated with Hindutva politics can further deepen divisions and perpetuate discrimination against the Muslim community.

6. Threats to Secularism: Muslims in India have historically identified with the idea of a secular and pluralistic state. However, the challenges to secularism in the country can impact their political identity. Instances of religious favouritism or exclusionary policies can erode the sense of equal citizenship and hinder the full participation of Muslims in the political process.

Addressing these challenges requires efforts to promote inclusive and equitable political systems that recognize and value the political identity of Muslims. It is crucial to ensure fair representation, combat communal polarization, challenge stereotypes, and uphold the principles of secularism and equal citizenship for all. By addressing these challenges, India can strive towards a more inclusive and representative political landscape that embraces the diversity of its population. In conclusion, the politics of Muslims in India is a complex and contentious issue. The lack of political representation for Muslims in India has led to a sense of alienation and disillusionment. Muslims face significant challenges in terms of discrimination, exclusion, and marginalization. The rise of Hindutva and the BJP's policies have further exacerbated these challenges. There is a need for greater political representation and inclusivity for Muslims in India. The government and civil society must work towards creating an environment that promotes equality and inclusivity for all communities

References:

1. Ahmad, H. "Muslim Politics in India: Historical Trajectories and Contemporary Challenges", *South Asian Politics*, 7(3), 2019, pp.1-14
2. Ahmed, I., "The Politics of Muslim Identity in India", *Journal of Muslim Minority Affairs*, 29(3), 2009, pp. 325-338
3. Kumar, S., & Palshikar, S., "Muslim Representation in Indian Politics: Emerging Trends and Challenges", *Economic and Political Weekly*, 53(42-43), 2018, pp. 29-36

4. Hasan, Z., "The Politics of Muslim Alienation in India", *Economic and Political Weekly,* 42(43), 2007, pp. 4377-4382
5. Ahmed, H., "BJP is Emerging as Second-most Preferred Political Choice for Muslim Voters in India," *The Print,* May 13, 2019
6. Roy, P., & Sopariwala, Dorab R., *The Verdict: Decoding India's Elections, Gurugram,* Penguin Random House, 2019, p. 227
7. Matta, A., "Anti-NRC-CAA Protests Have Left Women More Empowered, Confident at Home", *The swaddle*, 15, 2020
8. Engineer, Asghar Ali. "Islam And Muslims in India. Problems of Identity and Existence," *Oriente Moderno*, Vol. 23 (84), No. 1, 2004, pp. 71–82.
9. Mehta, Pratap B., "Hindu Nationalism: From Ethnic Identity to Authoritarian Repression", *Studies in Indian Politics*, Volume 10, Issue 1, Online published June 2022
10. Sahoo, N., "Mounting Majoritarianism and Political Polarization in India," *Carnegie: Endowment for International Peace*, (online published) August 18, 2020
11. Ahmed, Hilal. "Researching India's Muslims Identities, methods, politics", *HAU: Journal of Ethnographic Theory*, Volume 10, Number 3, 2020
12. Puri, Balraj. "Autonomy and Participation: Dimensions of Indian Muslim Identity," *Economic and Political Weekly*, vol. 13, no. 40, 1978, pp. 1706–12
13. Devji, Faisal, "The fate of Muslim Politics in India", *LSE,* Online Published June 19, 2023,
14. Engineer, Asghar Ali. "Remaking Indian Muslim Identity," *Economic and Political Weekly*, vol. 26, no. 16, 1991, pp. 1036–38

The Story of Anurupa Devi: Woman's Struggle for Self-Identity Through the Idea of Creation

Mousumi Singha

Anurupa Devi's debut in the literary world was in the early 20th century. She gained popularity in Bengali literature by writing the novel like 'Poshyaputra' (1911), appeared serially in Bharti, and marked the beginning of her emergence as literary icon. Sukumar Sen said about her- " that she made name before the male writers of Bhagalpur's. Anurupa Devi (1882-1958) was quite popular before the story was published in Bharti (1914) as her work *Kuntlin* was awarded earlier."[1] Her works ranged into novels, stories, plays and essays. Her literature depicts the position of women in the contemporary social, political and cultural environment. In the nineteenth century, under the influence of Western meditation, the Bengali society was disrupted. Bengali women wanted to say from the hard oppression of the patriarchal society-"My liberation is in light of light in this sky".[2] She said-"I consider literature to be inextricably linked with society, I believe its main function is to entertain and guide society."[3] She considered literature to guide society and education. For this reason, she wanted to understand literature in the context of the era and established women in the ideals of that era. At this time, the story of Anurupa Devi shows the diversity and magnificence of female characters and women have made their own place in every field of society with their own merits.

Her family and surrounding environment helped to develop this mindset and mindset of the writer. She was born on 9 September 1882 at Bagbazar, Calcutta at her maternal uncle

Nagendranath Banerjee's home. Her father Mukundadev Mukhopadhyay was a Deputy Magistrate and her mother was a Dhara Sundori. Grandfather was prominent writer Bhudev Mukhopadhyay. She was adhered to the conservative Hindu society. However, she is characterized as a progressive minded woman and supporter of women education. Bhudev Mukhopadhyay was in need of a grandson before the birth of Anurupa Devi. But when a daughter was born, everyone was dismayed. About that, Anurupa Devi has said in her autobiography of life that even though she was born on earth, she was not able to bring joy to anyone, but instead brought despair and joy to the hearts of all who were inspired by hope. But later, noticing the great interest of Anurupa Devi in her education, her grandfather Bhudev Mukhopadhyay arranged for her to learn Sanskrit and Bengali at home. On the other hand, maternal grandfather Nagendranath Banerjee was a theatre personality. He was the "initiator of Calcutta's modern theatre society".[4]Daughters of such families are usually married at the age of ten (February 23, 1893). Her husband's name was Shikarnath Banerjee. He was a resident of Uttarpara. Due to work he has to stay in Majhafarpur in Bihar, Anurupa Devi also had to live there with her husband. Her husband inspired her to teach English and write literature to keep her abreast of the times.

Anurupa Devi was not educated through the so-called school and college education. But the encouragement of her grandfather and husband helped her to be home-educated and lead an ideal life. She maintained the ideal of home life even in her creative life. On the one hand, she wrote stories in 'Bharati' magazine. In all those stories there is as much faith in country and religion as there is an attempt to violate unbridled bigotry. She was involved as a woman in social service, many women's schools, several women's welfare ashrams, establishment of women's cooperative societies, and campaign against polygamy and usury and the Hindu Code Bill movement. On the other hand, she was opposed to the discussion of women's rights in the progressive movement of contemporary women's awakening. She considered this women's right to be a blind imitation of the West. In a book written by her, she said- "...Women can never grow up by raising jealousy and hatred by protesting against men, she must grow up by the greatness of her character, by showing her ability. Independence has to be earned."[5] Her life experience fuelled her literary creation.

Needless to say, Anurupa Devi developed a strong bond with the Tagore family. In her memoirs published in 'Pravasi' magazine (Poush, 1348), she described her friendship with Bela or Madhurilata and their family's long relationship with her father. She said - "Her eldest daughter Madhuri or Bela lived among us for a few years in Majahfarpur. At that time, we were bound by an unbreakable or deep bond of love, the people of Majahfarpur and our relatives on both sides know very well. The closeness of my father's house with their house had been going on since the time of my father Mahadev."[6] Even when Swarnkumari Devi was the editor of 'Bharti' magazine, Anurupa Devi first started literary practice in 'Anamika' in that magazine. Swarnakumari and the inspiration of her magazine helped her to expand her popularity in the literary world. About her acquaintance with these two women of Thakurbari and her literary inspiration, Anurupa Devi said-"...Svarnakumari Devi was not the main help in my progress in the literary world and her sister's intervention in my public service work would have been independent today. I don't know, as a result of which these two women of the same family (both of them had a strange resemblance in appearance) had come forward to remove the obstacles in the journey of my life from both sides."[7]

The contemporary socio-religious climate also influenced her literary career. In the nineteenth century, due to the influence of western education and culture, the time came to reevaluate the traditional social ideology of Bengal. At that time, Derozio's *Young Bengal* group was formed around Hindu College. They attack conservative Hinduism. His students soon began to ridicule the traditional practices, disrespect for Hindu gods and goddesses, disrespect for the Brahmin priest, renunciation of Upvits, conversion to Christianity and Hinduism. This religious upheaval shakes the society. The rational thinkers began to talk about against the ritual of burning sati, child marriage, women's education. Ram Mohan Roy abolished the practice of sati immolation. At that time many orthodox Hindus protested against his breaking of tradition and even many had to stay in solitary confinement. Conservative thinking in Hindu society was one of the obstacles in accepting men and women as equal human beings. So far, the society felt the need to reestablish the neglected women.[8] Gradually, the schools, colleges and the system of teaching English was introduced. Various methods are adopted to spread the education among women. As a result, behind almost all the movements of the 19th century, the denigration of femininity and the desire for women's emancipation became active. The manifestation of which can be seen in the suppression of sati, widow marriage law, the movement against Kaulinya system and the expansion of women's education. There were also limitations in this women's liberation movement. It did not touch the women of all strata of the society, only thought of the upper caste women.

In a male dominated society, women were seen as mere servants, taints, slaves of desire, incarnations of falsehood. After the death of the husband, they were abandoned in the cremation ground like the waste of the society. Against such slander, this conservative society was forced to give importance to women's rights, her equality with men, voting rights, social status and human appeals of women. Protested against the practice of marrying young women, depriving them of education etc. Established girls' schools, colleges of that time took a particularly active role. Vidyasagar's contribution in this matter is foremost. But many conservative people came forward in favor of this woman education. Radhakantadev, Baidyanath Roy, Prasannakumar Tagore, Dakshinaranjan Mukhopadhyay etc. are memorable among them.[9] Even many women were directly or indirectly associated with political agitation. In history, the Queen Lakshmibai and Mataji Maharani Tapaswini of Jhansi were involved in the struggle against the British in the Sepoy Mutiny. In the wake of the 19th century Swadesh Bhavna, Bahunari was initiated into the mantra of freedom in the liberation of Mother India. Along with men, women are also involved in politics. Congress leader Janakinath Ghosal's wife Swarnakumari Devi is notable in this regard. Many of his songs inspired men and women in the swadeshi movement with the mantra of patriotism. The noble form and self-sacrifice of women can be seen in the bloody struggle of patriotism. Prakshatha Devi's entry into the world of literature (1912) was at the time of realizing one of the greatest truths of this renaissance of the nineteenth century. Contemporary social thought, religious atmosphere, conflict between conservative and liberal Hindu society, women's awakening all these aspects will influence the literary creation of Anurupa Devi.[10]

Anurupa Devi entered the world of literature with the hand of novel. The number of her novels is about 33. Besides she wrote a number of short stories, about 28 stories. These stories were successively published in four books of stories namely 'Praner Porosh' (1914), 'Chitradeep' (1915), 'Rangashankha' (1915), 'Madhumalli' (1917). But after her death, another book of stories was published namely 'Tronch Mithuner Milon Setu'. These stories were printed in magazines like 'Bharathi', 'Jhanvi', 'Bharatvarsh', 'Bangashri', 'Bharatamhila', 'Yamuna', 'Basumati', 'Suprabhat' etc. before being published in the library. Among her stories, 'Praner Porosh' is dedicated to Nirupama Devi. The dedication part is as follows- 'To the poetess Shrimati Nirupma Devi who established the achievements of Bangasahitya'. 'Chitradeep' is dedicated to Indira Devi. There she writes - 'The Chitradeep was given to Sricharankamal of Srimati Indira Devi Pujaniya Didi, a well-known writer in the literary world, who is a constant companion of literary pursuits.' And it is surprising that 'Rangashankha' says in the dedicatory part of the story - 'Janani Banga... in this life I don't want meaning, I don't want value, if you give me a place on your lotus feet and two amals.'[11] The author's dedication to her stories foreshadows her deep fascination with women writers and women. Her stories are quite dedicated in depicting the position of women but not so literary artistic as compared to others writings of the time.

The three notable stories of his 'Praner Porosh' are 'Chirodiner Sur', 'Urochithi' and 'Mrinmayi'. The story 'Chirodiner Sur' was published in the year of 1334 in the annual 'Basumati' Patika. The story is huge. Its subject is Mohant's religion. Its context is centered around Adityapur village in Burdwan district. Narrator Aditya Pura's history of Sivabhakti brings in contexts from the Ramayana that seem to stem from his personal life. The story begins in such a religious atmosphere. The main character is Maheshanand. One day a young handsome boy appeared in his ashram. Mahesananda, a believer in Shaktism, at first avoided him but when he heard his name Bhaveshananda, he was awakened to the idea of a Shivanurupa portrait. Mahesananda thinks Bhavesh is his God-sent messenger. The writer described his thoughts as follows-

"The boy whom Mohantji gave shelter to him that evening, his name is Bhavesh!" Hearing the name, Mahesananda did not say anything, his words became strong in his mind that God had definitely prepared this boy for me. If not, why did he, whose name could have been Karthik, Vinod, or Sukumar, become Bhavesh? Once he thought, if this was his child."[12] After Bhavesh's arrival at the ashram, Mahesananda devoted himself to various human welfare. Even taught Bhavesh about varna, poetry of Kalidasa, grammar and English. Until then, Mahesananda taught him as an angel of God. But Mahesananda's disciples recognized Bhavesh first as the son of a Baiji of Calcutta. One said - "He is the son of a famous Baiji, I have caught him by seeing his face and hearing his voice." I saw her mother in a royal palace in Calcutta, so I recognized her. The writer put this spiritual fantasy of Mahesananda in front of reality. The story is no longer spiritual. Became the story of the relationship between Baiji and the zamindar of Calcutta. The story revolves around Mahesanand's drowning. Then Mahesananda realizes that Bhavesh is not a boy, she is a girl. He is his abandoned daughter Archana - whose mother betrayed Maheshanand and left him. The author has revealed this treacherous form of woman through Maheshananda. Mahesananda tells his daughter Archana about her mother - "But you are the daughter of that treacherous Kiran - whom I loved more than the blood of my own breast, and who poisoned that blood of mine with her fierce roar!"[13] But next to this treacherous woman, another loving woman has drawn the child. The author who disguised as a man at the beginning of the story is because of the father's reluctance towards the treacherous mother. Her husband takes the only three-month-old child away from his mother's arms. His mother also died after a month of grief. This homeless proletarian woman takes refuge with her father in disguise. When her father also learns her identity and refuses to accept her, the form of helplessness of women becomes clear in Archana's face. There was no way to express his rights in that situation except by crying. He said to his father about his rights – "But did you leave me in crime? And want to do today? Am I guilty of my mother's sin? And if it is here or why I come? Want to say, I have no claim on you? I am not one of you?"[14] But the storyteller Anurupa Devi could not finally establish this child of a tainted woman as a woman in the society. Mahesananda accepted Archana as a premonition. Mahashananda says - "You will be my Bhavesha from today forever."[15] He surrenders himself to that Bhavesha. The author here depicts Archana as a holy woman. His father had to take refuge with him. In the story 'Chirodiner Sur', the writer Archana performed the last pooja for the purity of a woman under the guise of Bhavesh.

Anurupa Devi's story 'Urochithi' was published in 'Bharat Varsha' magazine. The writer has highlighted that the family is the first area of women's oppression through the story 'Urochithi'. On one side of this story is shown how society becomes an active partner in family-based women's oppression. On the other hand, it is shown that women's path to education was not smooth. In the Ancient and Middle Ages, women's education by sending girls to public schools was not widely practiced. As a result of the renaissance of the nineteenth century, the practice of women's education began in Bengal, but its number is very small. In the story of 'Urochithi' it is said first- "Amibala Roy Indranath Roy's eldest daughter got the first place in the university in this year's IA examination, so there was quite a bit of movement in the student community."[16] The writer has indicated through Amiya the expansion of women's education in Bengal - which has not happened so widely so far. Again, it has been said that the expansion of women's education is not easily accepted by the male society and has been ridiculed. The writer introduced her in this way-"The girl is not a school student, she has defeated hundreds of thousands of students twice or twice by taking private exams, many insulted-chitra used to flatter herself by saying that if they were taught privately, they would also get first rank by seven times".[17] Again, the woman who is partly responsible for the tragic fate of women has also been portrayed by the writer Yogen Mallick's wife Shailabala. Because she did not oppose her husband's torture on her. Evidence of society's activeness in women abuse can be found in the description of Devi: "When a husband beats his wife, the other neighbours have no right to stop them, but if they forcefully enter the house, trespass is declared."[18] Hence no protest was made against the unjust torture of Yogen Mallick's wife. Again, the writer wants to show how helpless and subject to the situation the woman is through Shailabala. Because-"The husband sometimes lifts the jewel on his head and dances, sometimes he breaks it by trampling it with his feet!"[19] In other words, she had become a puppet in her husband's hand. It is known through Amiya that even in the 19th century women had a keenness of thought or intelligence. Therefore, she did all the housework and all the responsibilities of her siblings but learned arithmetic from her father within a few days. Although Bab first said- "What will I do after learning numbers? You are a girl! "Girls don't have brains."[20] The allusions to the suppression of women are noteworthy. As a result of the expansion of women's education in the nineteenth century, a revolution took place in the psyche of women. A sense of individuality arises. This sense of individuality can also be seen in Amiya, the heroine of the story. She makes her own decisions about her life. Hence his statement-"Is it incongruous to have such a provision for women as men are to abstain from adultery? In my opinion, for the society, the responsibility of both is no less." I have no desire to die at all. Rather than that, I am willing to die only once."[21] Although at the end of the story, it is revealed that

Amiya's husband wanted to test Amiya's personality through the letter. We find evidence that only men and women helped to change the status of women. A picture of the agitation that was going on in the contemporary society around the problem of defining the position of women. There is also an indication that the woman had an opinion of her own. The Amiya character created by Anurupa is glorious in individuality.

A little different from the form of female education that is revealed in the story 'Urichithi', the position of women in the society is introduced in the story 'Mrinmayi'. The setting of the story is chosen in Taltala Street of Kolkata and the climax of the story is built around the heroine's visit to the theatre. The author has named the story woman-centric. That woman is the heroine of this story Mrinmayi. Swami Khitishchandra is his life. Khitishchandra is a thoughtful and well-established young professor. Mrinmayi wants to switch from a domestic life to a life of outdoor hobbies to meet manly hobbies. Mrinmayi used to call his girlfriend Surbala as 'Miner Katha'. 'Miner Katha' was as if his girlfriend was Mrinmayi's own mind. Because when Surbala proposed to Mrinmoyi to go to see 'Madhavi Kankan' performance at Minerva Theatre, then his heart's desire was united with Surbala's resignation. At that time, the writer said about Mrinmoyi - "Shunya Mrinmoyi's face became excited." He eagerly said, 'I will go brother, I had a great desire to see this until I heard it from didi's (elder sister) mouth."[22] Moner Kotha talks about watching theater in their house. But Kshitish, a representative of the educated society, stops her. However, due to her husband's actions, Mrinmayi does not allow Mrinmayi to step into the outside world. In this situation, Mrinmayi goes out from the theater with her maid and slaves to protect her honour.

Women going to the theater and watching movies were against the norms of the society. Women who were associated with the theater were considered untouchable prostitutes. That woman was considered as a prostitute in the society. This story is based on star theater actress Saramkumari Natty Binodini. Although they are prostitutes, they are not inhuman. Sarmai heals the sick Mrinmayi with good care. Sarma's envy at the beauty of Mrinmayi brings out the eternal truth of femininity. It is not erased by the untouchability of his actions. On the other hand, even in the 19th century, women could not get away from the idea of worldly meditation imposed on them. So, when Mrinmayi spends the night with Sarma, her husband Kshitishchandra does not take her home. She has to return home after a chastity test. It is done. Sarma's satire on this society is an expression of the author's hidden thoughts. Sarma said- "Don't you even think about the fact that the mother came to the girl's house saying that she would show her chastity?"[23] This question is put directly to the society of that time. Anurupa Devi could not actually place the woman in society, but through love the woman could be placed out of the brothel as a human being.

Some of the notable stories in the 'Chitradeep' are 'Porajay', 'Devadasi', 'Aangthi', 'On the day of sacrifice' and 'Dhumketu' etc. The story of 'Defeat' echoes the protest against the orthodoxy of Hinduism and ultimately the victory of truth against this society. The story contains both of the two divisions of Hindu society that were observed in the 19th century renaissance. The representative of the conservative society is Vibhuti's mother. They are Hindus. A Marathi Brahmin girl falls in love with Vibhuti, the child of that family. Both of them are determined to be bound by Parinaya Sutra. The conservative Hindu society does not accept their love. Here is the defeat of Bibhuti and Reba's love. But The story doesn't end with defeat. The story turns with women's awakening and victory. Reba is the female character. Reba is seen as a photo model in the beginning of the story. But in the second stage of the story, the distressed, frustrated and humiliated model Reba is transformed into a trinity in the knowledge of Hindu scriptures. He excels in scriptures and arguments. The society paid tribute to the virtues of women in this threefold nature. To the reawakened Hindu-Christian Reverend Mukherjee, Rebbe is not just a woman but the ideal of the whole woman. The woman who made the wrong ideas of the conservative Hindu society visible to everyone through arguments. Reverend Mukherjee's thoughts on Reba are expressed as follows – "She looked with a tearful gaze once upon the unchanging face of her rival and accepted silent defeat."[24] The triumph of real truth against the orthodoxies of Hindu society and the protest of their failed love is proclaimed through the female character named Reba. Even though the name of the story is 'defeat', victory is the end of this story.

The story of 'Devdasi' by Prastha Devi is a unique story. The title of the story suggests that Devadasi is about women. At the very beginning of the story, it is said - "When Appe Chidambaram, the old priest of the famous Pingleshwar temple in Trinaveni, took all the burdens of the child Bishoka and left his restless mother to die in peace, everyone understood that the number of Devadasis in this temple had increased."[25] The writer first wants to indicate the situation of that time. In the nineteenth century and early twentieth century too, many people used to donate their daughters to the goddess temple either intentionally or out of necessity. The author weaves the story of the famous Pingleshwar temple in Trinabeli, the old priest Appe Chidambaram and some Devadasis. In this story, the storyteller has shown on the one hand the humiliation and humiliation of women in the patriarchal social system, as well as the image of the oppression of the respected worshipers of the Hindu society. The chief acharya of the temple, Sadashiva Deshpante, therefore said to Devdasi Bishoka effortlessly, "You go to Devdasi-dhari, you are my wife as a deva-representation". The writer Devdasi Champa character wants to show the motherly form of women through drawing. The mother's love and emotional aspect for the child is also clear although the story says "The duty of the Devdasi is to keep the mind calm.... Devdasi's love for the family members is not adorned."[26] In Hinduism Devdasi Champa Couldn't crush the anxiety of motherhood. Her motherly spark can be seen in this story. The character of Bishoka is also governed by the Devadasi tradition of Hindu society. He believed that - "Devdasi is devoted to God"[27] The author made a dramatic change to the traditional Hindu Sanskar. The king character entered the story. He awakened the real truth in Bishoka. Consumables of priests. Hearing this, the human form is awakened in Bishoka. Therefore, the mother of a housewife calls the mother of her child, and the maternal essence awakens in her. After the kiss he embarrassed the child."[28] Even though Bishoka has motherhood in her, she is just a neglected devadasi to the society. They have no place in the society. Marriage, home and family reform etc. Being a devadasi as a girl, Bishoka is deprived and untouchable. Bishoka ultimately does not surrender herself to the neglected society and the priest. Here the character of Bishoka brightening as in individuality.

The story of 'Angthi" is a different kind of story. Through this story of different flavours, the storyteller has presented a beautiful picture of women's existence in the world. At the beginning of the story, the sound of a healthy relationship and the breakup of that relationship is heard. It can be said that the author presents the story through symbols. The female role is depicted through the husband-wife relationship. The narrator of the story Sri Annadacharan Sarkar goes for a sea trip and finds a diamond ring. As a result, he places an advertisement in the newspaper to return the precious ring to its rightful owner. Later in the story, the true owner of the ring writes a letter to the storyteller-" This is her ring. Finally, she had such a ring on her finger, I remember it well."[29] His wife is not alive so he asks to send the ring to Ramakrishna Mission Sevashram. Only his wife is as precious to him as the diamond ring.

The background of the story "On the Day of Renunciation" is Japan. The main theme of the story is the war between Japan and Russia. The narrator of the story, Shirish and Nepal meet a Japanese girl while they are in Japan. The radical change in their thinking about women with that Japanese girl Minami is the significant indication of this story. Nepali Bengali women compared to Japanese women in this story foreshadows the true form of women. Bengali women cannot send their husbands and sons to war with a smile. Because Bengali women are very emotional. But the Japanese girl Minami seems to them to be a pashani and compared to Bengali women, the narrator says - "Ha, Pashani Minami! Such a scene would never have been seen in India. People there are not fanatics devoid of anything else, affection, love, kindness."[30] Because Minami lost her only brother in the war. However, her kindness and affection for her brother was not revealed in front of everyone. But the radical change of the narrator's thoughts about women gives the story another dimension. One day and four days when he was sleepy, the narrator heard a woman crying in a free voice. Going forward, the narrator is surprised to see Minami. Then Minami says - "When the people of the world wake up, I will have to join the celebration of my homeland, my heaven on earth, my beloved homeland more than my brother. But if I don't get this rest, my chest is bursting."[31] On the one hand, a woman can sacrifice her love for her motherland and shed tears for that love. The author has very skillfully presented the universal form of women through the story of war. A woman's love, love, and religion of sacrifice are one in all countries, all the time.[32]

Therefore, it can be said that Anurupa Devi's stories are written in the context of unfavourable social and family environment. Even though women did not have the opportunity to study and practice literature, many women writers like Anurupa Devi did not hesitate to advance in literary pursuits. The use of language and mannerisms are not so visible. Although her short stories are of high literary quality, the historical value of the times or the importance of the stories in identifying the social position of women cannot be denied. In her short stories, various aspects of women's identity in social, religious and political conditions have emerged. In his short stories, except for Reba and Minami, all are married women. Some are mothers, some are daughters. They wanted to embrace the cultural and social changes of the 19th century. Sometimes their will was hindered by the contemporary conservative society. Somewhere women received Bengali and Sanskrit education as well as English education. The educated female characters in her stories felt the urge to break out of traditional social bonds. Religion Knowledge, science, logic and argument overcome her despite obstacles in their lives. Her female characters are characterized by changing social status. In her stories, women are universal in affection, love, jealousy, passion, motherhood. Above all, the female characters depicted by her have become a symbol of humanity in the contemporary social context.

References

1. Sen, Sukumar, *History of Bengali Literature (Bengla Sahitter Itihas)*, Vol. V, (1891-1914), Ananda Publisher, 5th Edition, 2009, p.232
2. Tagore, Rabindranath, *Gitbithan*, No. 339, Biswabharati Library Section, New Edition (1419 B), p. 141
3. Debi, Anurupa, *Women in Literature and Creation (Sristi O Sahitaya Nari)*, Calcutta University, 1st Edition, 1949, introductory chapters
4. Sen, Abhijit & Bhaduri, Anindita. *Selected Stories of Anurupa Devi*, De's Publishing, First Release, 2002, p.8.
5. Debi, Anurupa, Op. cit, see: introductory Chapters
6. Sen, Abhijit & Bhaduri, Anindita, Op. cit., p. 185

7. Ibid., p.196
8. See for details: Basu, Swapan, *History of Bengal New Consciousness (1826-1856)*, Book Trade, Calcutta, third Edition, 2002
9. Ibid.
10. See for details: Das, Sunil. *Bharati: History and Composition*, Literary Folk, Calcutta, First Release,1984
11. Chowdhury, Shribhudev, *Bengali Literature Short Story and Storyteller*, Modern Book Agency Pvt. Ltd., Kolkata, 5th ed. 2003, reprint 2006-2007.
12. Sen, Abhijit & Bhaduri, Anindita, Op. cit., p. 196
13. Ibid. p. 40
14. Ibid. p. 42
15. Ibid. p. 58
16. Ibid. pp. 58-60
17. Ibid. pp. 61-63
18. Ibid. p. 88
19. Ibid. p. 84
20. Ibid. pp.126-131
21. Ibid. p. 130
22. Ibid. p. 130
23. Ibid. p. 130
24. Ibid. p. 130
25. Ibid. p. 130
26. Ibid. p. 134
27. Ibid. p. 25
28. Ibid. p. 31
29. Ibid. p. 32
30. Ibid. p. 97
31. Ibid. p. 105
32. For more about women depiction in literature see: Ghosh, Sudakshina, *Women's Tales in women' Novels* (From Kahake to Subarnalata), Dej. Publishing, Kolkata, First Edition, January, 2008.

Murshidabad During Anti-Partition & Swadeshi Movement: A Study

Prosenjit Das

As all we know that Bengal remained always in the forefront of the Indian nationalist movement. Bengal not only provided the leaders of the movements but also the people form each and every corner participated in different time in different anti-imperialist movement. The anti-partition of Bengal and subsequent Swadeshi movement was the first upheavals in which the common people of Bengal emerged altogether to protest against the British. Each district and talukas organised mass level movements under the local leaders to withdraw the British decision of division of Bengal. In this juncture, specially, the people of Murshidabad actively took part in the protest, procession and rallies along with the mainstream movement organised by the leaders of Kolkata & Dhaka. However, the role and contribution of Murshidabad has yet been written thoroughly in the history of National Movement. Hence, this article made an effort to highlights the role of Murshidabad during anti-partition and swadeshi movement.

At the beginning of the 20th century, Lord Curzon wanted to divide Bengal and weaken Bengali nationalist movement. In the words of Home Secretary Risley: "United Bengal is a strength, if Bengal is divided, the strength will spread in different directions." In December 1903, the Risley Paper was published with the approval of the Secretary of India.[1] The people of Bengal came to know about the proposal of partition of Bengal. Spontaneous protests and agitations started against this proposal. Within the first two months of the announcement of the proposal for the partition of Bengal, 500 protest meetings were held only in East Bengal, especially in Dhaka, Mymensingh, and Chittagong.[2] Surendranath Banerjee, Krishna Kumar Mitra, Prithvish Roy and other leaders campaigned vigorously against the proposal of partition by writing articles in various newspapers and magazines. Despite the protests, the decision to divide Bengal was announced on 19th July 1905 and became effective on 16th October. With the sound of 'Bande Mataram' and Rabindranath's Swadeshi songs, the people of undivided Bengal started the anti-separation movement through Arandhan and Rakhi Bandhan activities.[3] Subsequently, Swadeshi movement spread in various districts of undivided Bengal including Murshidabad district in turn to boycott the foreign (British) product. This was a kind of nonviolent protest to week the imperial power economically rather politically.[4]

The Indian national movement got a new dimension with the beginning of the Swadeshi movement at the beginning of the 20th century. In Bengal and other parts of India, women, students, and a large part of the people of towns and villages were actively involved in politics for the first time. Almost all major political movements of the Indian national movement emerged during this period. From conservative soft approach to political extremism, from revolutionary terrorism to existing socialism, application-appeal policy. Swadeshi movement is the source of all political movements from public speaking to indirect resistance and boycott.[5] This time Bengal became the centre of the Indian nationalist movement. The British government wanted to divide Bengal and weaken the nationalist movement.

The political history of Murshidabad district is quite vibrant and it dates back to the establishment of Shashanka's second capital, Karnasubarna, in the seventh century,[6] but the continuous history of the region dates back to the Mughal period. There was a long struggle against the establishment of Muslim rule in Bengal. Murshidabad always played important role during the Mughal rule. Since the people of Murshidabad remained active in struggle to prove the self-dependency.[7] In 1757 AD, the sun of India's independence set in the desert of Palashi on the soil of Murshidabad. Siraj, the independent Nawab of Bengal, Bihar and Orissa, was killed on the ground. Lord Clive laid the foundations of the British Empire with the deadly arsenal of Hindu and Muslim treachery.[8] Again, 100 years after the Battle of Palashi, Indian sepoys from Murshidabad Barack Square took up arms against the British in 1857.[9] Then in 1905, on October 16, when Lord Curzon announced the division Bengal into two arms. Like other districts of undivided Bengal, the wave of the anti-partition and Swadeshi movement engulfed the whole area of Murshidabad.

With the spread of movement, the citizens of Murshidabad gathered in a meeting against the partition of Bengal under the auspices of the Baharampur Association in the Grand Hall of Baharampur. Maharaja Manindra Chandra Nandi of Kashim Bazar was elected as the representative of the district in this meeting.[10] On August 7, 1905, Maharaja Manindra Chandra Nandi presided over an anti-partition meeting in the Town Hall of Calcutta. In this meeting, it was decided to boycott foreign goods. Such an incident against the British Raj was undoubtedly an adventurous move. For the promotion of indigenous textiles and other industries, Manindra Chandra installed sixteen looms in Kashim Bazar and made every effort to encourage his subjects to use Swadeshi cloth in his zamindari. He donated to the National Education Council which was formed to help students in the Swadeshi movement.[11] He praised the two English newspapers 'Englishman' and 'The Statesman' for opposing the plan of partition of Bengal. In his speech, he urged the people of the entire country to continue strong agitation against the plan of partition of Bengal until it was withdrawn. British official CR Cleveland wrote in a report that Manindra Chandra was one of the main agitators against the partition of Bengal. He also donated money during the establishment of Bangalaxmi Cotton Mill.[12] Students of the Nawab Bahadur High School of Lalbagh in Murshidabad district and Hindu and Muslim residents of the locals protested and mourned against the partition of Bengal. Students left their shoes, clothes and umbrellas and attended school barefoot in dhoti and chadar. Kolkata's English daily Amritbazar Patrika urged the country to follow Murshidabad's example.[13] In November 1905, Bhavani Kishore Chakraborty presided over a meeting at Behrampur where the students were ordered to disobey the Carlyle circular and continue the Swadeshi movement.[14]

The Swadeshi and Boycott movement had a profound impact on the Kandi sub-division. Ramendra Sundar Trivedi, the Principal of Ripon College and Secretary of Bangiya Sahitya Parishad, organized a powerful Swadeshi movement in Kandi and surrounding areas. He planned to observe the day of the Bengal partition as a day of national mourning.[15] He also wrote a patriotic booklet called 'Banga Laxmir Brata Katha' and his daughter Girija recited the book publicly. He wrote in the book 'O Mother Lakshmi bless us. We shall not take glass in exchange for gold. We shall not wear bangles when we have shankhas. We shall not beg door to door. We shall rather eat uncut rice.' It was a wonderful composition full of compassion for the country written to awaken the sense of nationalism among the girls. The booklet had such an influence on Bengali women that the British government banned the book.[16] By the passing of time, Swadeshi and boycott movements continued get momentum in Murshidabad district. In May 1906, a women's meeting was held at Baharampur under the chairmanship of Mohini Mohan Roy. On that day another large gathering was held under the chairmanship of the famous writer Nikhilnath Roy. All those gathered in the meetings took an oath of boycott. Swadeshi and boycott movement became stronger when Surendranath Bandopadhyay came to Murshidabad district that year to address a large gathering.[17] At Kasimbabazar station, a crowd of 1,000 people greeted Surendranath Bandopadhyay with Vande Mataram. In 1907, the Bengal Provincial Conference was held at Baharampur and the first Bengal Literary Conference was held at Kashim Bazar to add a new dimension to the Swadeshi movement in Murshidabad. Previously, the Bengal Provincial Conference at Barisal in 1906 was disrupted due to baton charges and other repressive policies by the British police. However, the people of Murshidabad made the Bengal Provincial Conference of 1907 a success, about 1500 delegates from different districts of Bengal participated in this conference. Krishnakumar Mitra, editor of 'Sanjibani' newspaper, Motilal Ghosh, editor of 'Amrito Bazar' newspaper, extremist leader Bipin Chandra Pal, Deen Mohammad, Abul Ghafoor and other national leaders attended this conference.[18]

Krishnanath College of Murshidabad played a noteworthy role in the promotion of the Swadeshi and Boycott movement. Professor Hiralal of Krishnanath College conducted the Swadeshi campaign among the students. The British government issued the Carlyle Circular prohibiting students from participating in any kind of patriotic or political movement and threatened to withhold grants to educational institutions that failed to prevent students from participating in patriotic movements.[19] However, the students of Krishnanath College ignored this circular and intensified their anti-British movement. The District Magistrate sent a copy of the circular to Baikunth Nath Sen, a member of the board of management of Krishnanath College, and directed him to take action against the students participating in the Swadeshi movement. Baikunth Nath Sen sternly reminded the District Magistrate that the entire expense of Krishnanath College was met by Maharaja Manindra Chandra Nandi of Kashimbazar. The Carlyle circular said that students' participation in politics was ruining their discipline, in reply Baikunth Nath Sen said that political meetings and associations and meeting processions cannot and should not destroy students' discipline. Later, law-breaking and rebellion continued to increase just as in the poet's word, "The tighter their bond is, the more my bond will break, the more blood there is in their eyes, the more will open my eyes."[20]

Even during such a disaster in the country, the police could not lay hands on the students of Baharampur Krishnanath College. As one of the reasons for this, Yogendra Nath De Sarkar, a famous revolutionary and an alumnus of Krishnanath College, says in his memoirs "The main reason was the amazing influence of the personality of an Anglo-Bengali scholar. Fortunately, Edward Manmohini Wheeler was then the Principal of Krishnanath College".[21] Due to his mild personality, his influence and prestige in the local English circles and the ruling circles of that time were extraordinary. As a result, despite their active participation in the political movement, the students of his college did not feel the slightest impression of government repression. How the students of Krishnanath College learned to love the country with all their heart and soul staying under his shelter, is unparalleled in the history of the educational institutions of the entire country. Not only in the open movement, the college students jumped into the Swadeshi movement by forming secret societies. Bipin Pal refused to testify in the "Vandemataram" case and went to jail. Processions and gatherings were banned with the force of Regulation Acts, and societies like Yugantar, Anushilan Samiti, and Atma Unnati Samiti, became secret societies. Gradually

Baharampur Krishnanath College became a stronghold of the revolutionaries. The teaching reputation of this college then spread all over the country, students from East Bengal and North Bengal were flocking to get admission to this college, many of them carrying the message of other secret societies. At that time Bandemataram Samiti, Shaheed Samiti and especially the Yugantar Samiti came to this college to recruit cadres. Later, Anusheelan Samiti and Yugantar were involved in a competition to strengthen their associations. Several knives and swords were collected by special means from the Murshidabad Imambari. It is heard that some firearms are also tried to be smuggled from the Hazarduari armoury of the Nawab Palace.[22] Revolutionary Yogendra Nath De Sarkar said in his memoirs, "The students of Krishnanath School and College had taken vows like volunteer soldiers of India's revolutionary moral struggle for 40 years. Among them were Nikhil Guha Roy, Avinash Roy, Atul Ghosh, Satish Chakraborty, Rajen Pal, Jogen Sarkar and others." The names of Nalini Bagchi, Surya Sen, and Niranjan Sen, who were students of this college are written in golden letters in the history of Bengal's revolutionary movement. Ramakrishna's disciple Swami Akhandananda established the Ramakrishna Mission at Sargachi near Baharampur a few years before the Swadeshi movement began. At that time, Swami Akhandananda inspired the youth of Baharampur Krishnanath College in patriotism in various ways. Revolutionary Aurobindo Ghosh once said that Ramakrishna Paramahansa was infact running the Swadeshi movement of Bangladesh on real terms. When he was arrested in the bomb case, Dakshineshwar soil was found in his house.[23]

It is unnecessary to elaborate on how the Ramakrishna Mission and Vivekananda were the source of inspiration and strength in revolutionary Bengal during that period. Swami Vivekananda's words echoed among the students, "Freedom o freedom is the cry of life, freedom o freedom is the song of the soul." Students from Baharampur used to go to the Sargachi ashram to Akhandananda to hear Swami Vivekananda's message. They often went and requested Swami Akhandananda to explain Vivekananda's ideals of patriotism and public service and Akhandananda used to passionately recite Swamiji's words. The students used to hear from him about revolutionary Jatin Mukherjee.[24] Akhandananda said "Jatindranath would have been 19 years old and very friendly with me. I used to talk about him sometimes so one day Naren wanted to see Jatin. I arranged a meeting for Jatin and Naren. At that time, the Bengal government did not look favourably at Swamiji, despite that Jatin often came to meet Swamiji" Incidentally, Atul Sen, a student of Krishnanath College in Baharampur, was a friend of Jatindranath. He arranged their journey from there towards Orissa. Later, when it came to light, he had to suffer a lot of abuse at the hands of the police. When the group of spies got the news that Jatindranath, Chitra Priya, Naren, Manoranjan Jatish, four trusted revolutionary companions were travelling to Orissa, a group of armed police forces led by Tarat advanced in that direction. Crossing the border at Baleswar, Jatindranath entered the deep forest region of Mayur Bhanj with his companions. Finally, a fierce battle broke out between the two. Niren and Jyotish were injured when Chitra Priya fell on the ground hit by a bullet.[25]Contemporary local newspapers of Murshidabad also played a significant role in promoting the Swadeshi movement. 'Murshidabad Hitoshi' played an important role in promoting and spreading the Swadeshi movement.[26] The newspaper had very vividly exposed the unspeakable oppression of the British government on the students.

References

1. See for details: Sarkar, Sumit, *Swadeshi Movement in Bengal 1903-1908*, People's Publishing House, New Delhi, reprint 1994
2. Biswas, A. K. "Paradox of Anti-Partition Agitation and Swadeshi Movement in Bengal (1905)," *Social Scientist*, vol. 23, no. 4/6, 1995, pp. 38–57
3. Bhattacharya, Ramkrishna, *Bangabhanga: Swadeshi: Biplabbad* (A Study of the anti-partition movement in Bengal 1905-08), K P Bagchi & Company, Kolkata, 2016
4. Sarkar, Sumit, 1994, Op. cit.
5. Biswas, A. K., Op. cit.
6. Sengupta, Nitish. *Land of Two Rivers: A History of Bengal- From the Mahabharata to Mujib,* Penguin, Delhi, 2011
7. Chaudhury, Sushil. *Profile of a Forgotten Capital: Murshidabad in The Eighteenth Century*, Manohar, Delhi, 2018
8. Bandyopadhyay, Sekhar. *From Plassey to Partition and After: A History of Modern India*, Orient Blackswan, New Delhi, 2016; Dalrymple, W., *The Anarchy: The East India Company, Corporate Violence, and the Pillage of an Empire*. Bloomsbury, USA, 2019
9. Sarkar, Sumit, *Modern India (1885-1947),* K. P Bagchi and Company, Calcutta, 1993, pp. 1-20
10. Gupta, Prafulla Kumar, *Murshidabad in freedom struggle*, B. Kundu Publisher, Calcutta, 1957, pp.3-14
11. Das, Kalyan Kumar, *Murshidabad in Freedom Struggle*, Murshidabad, 2007, pp. 31-32
12. Ibid.
13. *Amritbazar Patrika*, November, 2005
14. Gupta, Prafulla Kumar, *Murshidabad in freedom struggle*, B. Kundu Publisher, Calcutta, 1957, pp.3-14
15. Das, Biswas Prakash, *Manishi of Murshidabad*, Aakash Publishers, Murshidabad, 2001, pp.52-53
16. Ibid.,
17. Gupta, Prafulla Kumar, Op. cit.
18. Chandra, Bipan and others., *India's Freedom Struggle*, K. P. Bagchi & Company, Calcutta, pp. 101-105
19. Das, Biswas Prakash, Op. cit., pp.52-53; Walsh, J H Tull. *A history of Murshidabad District (Bengal): with biographies of some of its noted families,* Alpha Edition, 2019
20. Ibid.
21. Gupta, Prafulla Kumar, Op. cit.; *Murshidabad District Gazetteer,* 2003, pp.130-133

22. Ibid.
23. Gupta, Prafulla Kumar, Op. cit.,
24. Ibid.
25. Tripathi, Amlesh. *Indian National Congress in Freedom Struggle*, (in Bengali) Anand Publishers, Kolkata, (in English Oxford 2014)
26. O'Malley, L.S.S., *Bengal District Gazetteers: Murshidabad*, Logos Press, 2017

Feminism - Voice of 'Others' in Indian Perspectives

Ramkrishna Das

Feminism, a political perception, based on two fundamental premises, it creates gender difference on the foundation of a structural inequality between women and men, by which women suffer systematic social injustice, and that the inequality between the sexes is not the product of biological necessity but is produced by the cultural construction of gender differences. This perception gives feminism with its double agenda to understand the social and psychic mechanism that construct and perpetuate gender inequality and then to change them. The structure of power –which are therefore described as political- operate to re-enforce gender stereotypes is also based on ideology (false belief) teaching to maintain the so called the constructed 'universal', 'infallible', aesthetics that fully/entirely gender biases the ground upon which the proletariat perpetuate the gender stereotype construction. Feminism, here, try to 'take over' the canon and rescue it from patriarchy by helping readers scan texts, genres or movements so as to relentlessly make visible the components of gender and gender bias in the academy which has so far tried to conceal them.

To perpetuate such gender stereotyping the contribution of 'language' and 'text' (not text but paradigm) are nonetheless important, rather, the patriarchy firstly, to maintain such gender construction provides Andro-text(male-based) to promote universal and to adopt these aesthetics values and merits and are constantly trained them to read from the men's point of view. Women's text (Gyno-text) when there are available, are rejected by Male to have nothing to its equal value as virtue. Women readers, following in and trained with-in male defined form of reading, agree with this assessment as women have nothing of their own language to write the text different from the male text, they are forced to use the sexist language, a language that does not capture the 'essence' of value and experience as paradigm is used by patriarchy through dictions, linearity and order everything as 'truth' and 'universal'. Elaine Showalter (1979), a feminist critic, in her essay "Feminist criticism in the wilderness" coined a term 'Gyno-text' as opposed to the Andro-text (Male-based) where she says the Woman as author and producer of text and meanings. Showalter shows and divides the culture between Men's culture and Female's culture, where she emphasizes more and more to write about themselves (whether it is her body or her own personal matter), which is hostile more than unite and besides this they have been restricted themselves by offering a narrative of suffering in which they are seen always and only as victims. In this process gyno-criticism loses the weapon it could have had hijack the agenda of patriarchy, the weapon of laughter. For instances, we take the poem of Kamala Das's 'An Introduction' where we see the same as gyno-critics says. Kamala Das repeatedly told of the inhuman torture and atrocity done by contemporary politically patriarchy power and the humiliation she bears, she constantly objects and raises to the injustices and inequalities in all fields that we find the same in 'A Literature of Their Own' (1977) by Showalter where she divides three phases of feminism;

1. 1840-1880 –Feminine phase.
2. 1880-1920-Feminint phase.
3. 1920-onwards-Female phase.

In third phase i.e., female phase Woman writers draw the same qualities as found in gyno-text where woman writer's search for identity as opposed to the identity imposed by patriarchy and writing on with their own body in French term 'chora' and 'semiotic' as described by Kristeva where Kristeva demonstrates that to avoid such sexist language woman should uses pre-oedipal language. the language before a child acquires to take in them the symbolic language devised by patriarchy. For H. Cixous, woman must celebrate in their writing: "Woman must write through their bodies, they must invent the impregnable language that will wreck partitions, classes, and rhetoric, regulations and codes, they must submerge, cut through, get beyond the ultimate reserve- discourse, including the one that laughs at the very idea of pronouncing the word 'silence…' such is the strength of woman that, sweeping away syntax, breaking that famous thread (just a tiny little thread, they say) which acts for men as a surrogate umbilical chord."

Similarly, 'semiotic' language i.e., the language of imaginary stage where child does not acquire such symbolic language as proposed by Lacan, a post structuralist psychologist. Symbolic and Semiotic are not two different types of language, but two different aspects of language, both of which have their existence in any given sentence. The model, is that of the unconscious and the conscious, here is working. The symbolic is the orderly surface of strict distinctions and through which language works and such language creates binary opposition where symbolic structure is given more prominence in spite of being all signifier but signified is supposed to be the superior and through the post-structuralist view point, we see that all are signifiers even supposing signified is also signifiers that distort the surface/ symbolic/stable meaning supposing rational in accordance with logocentrism. A diagram is given below through which language works:

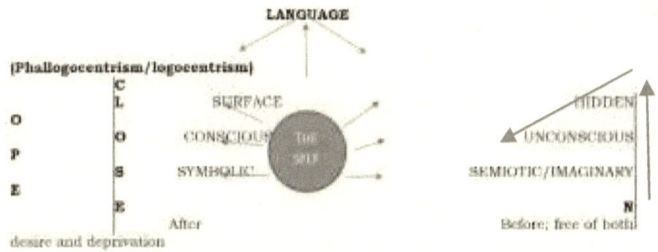

Kristeva's Explanation

Language question is one of the most contentious areas of feminist criticism. Through this diagram, we perceive language is nothing but a proposition by the construction of logocentrism. Such semiotic is seen as inherently subversive politically, and always threatens the closed symbolic order embodied in such conventions as govt. received cultural values, and the grammar of standard language. And at the same time we find Spivak's translation study 'Draupdi' written by Mahasweata Devi, in Ecriture Feminine, Helene Cixous's 'The Laugh of Medeusa' is successful in its creation of writing style that allows woman to claim authority because it was created on the foundation of woman's claim to herself of body, therefore eliminating the oppressive effects of patriarchal control of rhetoric, phallogocentrism, prirotizing the masculine form of reason, gyno-critics do not offer such narratives of laughter by which the agenda of patriarchy could have had hijack ,rather Draupdi ,a regional name, different from Hindu mythology, but same in temperament, could by the abusive laughter neglecting her brutal rape once done had nothing to be covered up and showed and feared the patriarchal.

Simone De Beauvoir in her book 'The Second Sex' she says Woman is always seen as 'Other' not in herself but as relative to him. she is called 'the sex' by which she appeals essentially to the Male as sexual being. Such gender construction brings first alterity; where the superiority of the norms and the inferiority of all departure from the norm i.e., Man is seen as the norm and Woman as the departure. Next, alterity breeds inequality and injustice, where Woman is defined in relation to Man, and then, alterity breeds hostility, where the relationship between Man and Woman should be seen as 'friendship' instead of it is seen as largely oppositional and here, a woman's role is conditioned by the bio-logical fact of sex and they are seen as only sexual entity which is both demeaning and limiting. This myth of 'Woman as Other' naturalizes the discourse where Man and Woman are regarded as subject other relation and Woman is measured by the standard of Man and found 'inferior'. This is the process of othering where the Woman is always seen, not as independent or unique but as variation and flawed version of the Male. The subordination of Woman is not the result of a particular historical event. As a result, their lack of organization as a homogeneous group Woman have been unable to demolish the myth of 'Woman as other' which has crippled them down the ages. the reason is that they thought they have done nothing till Man helps to reach their destination and their lack of concrete organization that make them herded together into a unit which can stand face to face with the co-relative unit. Now we observe from the viewpoint of Beauvoir that what Woman is doing at the charity of Man, next, the relation between Woman and their oppressors Man, has more in its bio-logical fact rather than in a historical process, then Woman have not been able to create a gender-based bonding among themselves than can surmount ethnic or class origins. Woman have acquiesced in this second-class status and have not challenged it.

As an example of feminist criticism, the novel Wuthering Height by Sandra M. Gilbert and Susan Gubar, from their book The Madwoman in the Attic. Gilbert and Gubar's strategy with Bronte's novel are to see it as a female version of the male form known as the Bildungsroman means the 'formation' in which the hero's growth to manhood is perceived, as a 'process of victory of self-discovery' for example, Joyce's A Portrait of the Artist as a 'Young Man, on the contrary the heroine of Wuthering Height Catherine or any girl if taken we see that the growth of a heroine to a womanhood describes a process of 'anxious self-denial'. Catherine leaving all her preferences submits herself to Heathcliff symbolizing 'concealment and doubleness' i.e., education (constructed) that helps her to repress her own impulses and encircle herself with the fetters of "reason" where she reduces her own and at the same time submitting herself to the norms of patriarchy symbolize by Heathcliff. We see saying Catherine that he (Heathcliff) is 'more myself than I am'. Here, Heathcliff too is degrading and powerless and so Catherine has learnt, correctly, that it is degrading to be a woman it is even more degrading to be like a woman. Heathcliff's return at the end of the novel, in accordance with Freud, we can say that, the 'return of the repressed' representing 'the return of her true self's desires without the rebirth of her former powers', inevitably calling into her self-rejection, self-starvation, madness and death, 'a complex of psycho-neurotic symptoms that is almost clearly associated with female feelings of powerlessness and rage' and bears the construction of gender identity.

Judith Butler, a third wave feminist, influenced by deconstructive thought, embody a post-modern view of gender, proposing that gender cannot be treated as essence, but must be taken as a 'performative construct' in her best-known book Gender Trouble: 'there is no gender identity behind the expression of gender; that identity is performatively constituted by the very "expressions" that are said to be its result.' Butler argues in taking of Beauvoir's famous claim that 'one is not born, but rather becomes a woman' that woman is a process, a becoming, from one to another, as we infer from Vivekananda's speech 'be means becoming' i.e., to get an ultimate stage you have to repeatedly act/perform, rather than a fixed identity. Such ongoing process is constituted by discourse. Outside the system of discourse, one cannot acquire identity requires a sequence of acts inevitably and repetitively in Butler's view point identities are, she writes, the effects of institutions, practices, discourses like Foucault, her proposal is that gender is not a natural, but the effect of discourses that power controls. As we can infer from the view point of Butler are as follows:

1. There is no gender identity that precedes language.
2. Gender is thus a performativity that constitute identity.
3. There is no natural or unitary identity rather all identity as the effect of discourse.

References:

1. Ruthven, K.K., *Feminist Literary Studies: an interaction*, 1984, reprint: C.U.P., Cambridge, 1990
2. Morris, Pam, *Literature and Feminism: An Introduction*, Black Well, Oxford, 1993
3. Showalter, Elaine (ed), *The New Feminist Criticism: Essays on Woman, Literature, and theory,* 1994, reprint: London, Virago,1985
4. Marks, Elaine and de Courtivron, Isabelle, (ed) *New French Feminism*, Harvester,1981, p.256
5. Goodman, Lizbeth (ed), *Literature and gender*, Routledge the open university, London, 1996
6. Gilbert, Sandra and Gubar, Susan, *The Madwoman in The Attic: and The Woman writer and the nineteenth century imagination*, Yall university press, 2nd edn,2000
7. Cixous, Hélène, et al. "The Laugh of the Medusa." Signs, vol. 1, no. 4, 1976, pp. 875–93. JSTOR
8. Das, Kamal, (Poem) 'An Introduction,' It was published in her first collection, Summary in Calcutta in 1965
9. Butler, Judith. *Gender Trouble; Feminism and the Subversion of Identity*, Taylor & Francis, 2011

10. The Second Sex (French: Le Deuxième Sexe) is a 1949 book by the French existentialist philosopher Simone de Beauvoir. Beauvoir wrote the book in about 14 months between 1946 and 1949. She published the work in two volumes: Facts and Myths, and Lived Experience.
11. Deka, Kaushik Kr., *Subaltern Voice in Mahasweta Devi's Draupadi*, Ilkogretim Online - Elementary Education Online, 2021; Vol 20 (Issue 2): pp. 2891-2895
12. Oliver, Kelly. "Julia Kristeva's Feminist Revolutions." *Hypatia*, vol. 8, no. 3, 1993, pp. 94–114. *JSTOR*

Indian Public Library: A Gateway Towards Women Empowerment

Chinmoy Ghosh

Library and Information Centre is a vital resource centre. It disseminates knowledge to the masses as a whole. A nation's development is greatly depending on the development of its human resources irrespective of the caste, creed and gender. Human resources are resourceful only when they can access to the knowledge centre viz. library and information centre. Women empowerment will be ensured and enhanced if the women can access and utilize the resources of public libraries. In the developing countries, like India, women and girls are deprived of education, social respect, healthcare etc. Another gap between boys and girls, men and women particularly in the rural areas of developing countries is the 'digital divide' i.e., access to information and communication technologies. Now a days information is available in digital form and the maximum number of women have no or minimum access to digital information. As a result, they cannot know the nascent information. Public libraries are a trusted and traditional information resource at the heart of communities. Without information it is worthless to discuss about development. Like community hub, libraries can be applied in unique ways to improve lives of communities. This paper tries to show how library can play a vital role to empowering girls and women as by-

i) Rethinking the role of public library towards nation's development.

ii) To show how a public library can be a safer place for women empowerment.

Empowerment is the process of obtaining basic opportunities for marginalized people, either directly by those people, or through the help of non-marginalized who share their own access to these opportunities. It also includes actively thwarting attempts to deny those opportunities. Empowerment also includes encouraging, and developing the skills for self-sufficiency with a focus on eliminating the future need for charity or welfare for the individuals (Wikipedia). Women empowerment here means social, legal, economic, political empowerment. Public library is such a place where all type of motivational work can be done. Public libraries are called 'People's University' where a person irrespective of age, cast, creed, colour, gender can access this without any barrier.

Now a days Library is not merely storing house of books, journal and magazine. Now library gives various types of services like career support, computer training, special information dissemination etc. Library always play a vital role for giving information, developing reading habit for education and research purposes. In modern days librarians are giving services according to the need of users via modern technology. Public libraries are more easily accessible to masses. Public library, the Local gateway to knowledge, provides a basic condition for lifelong learning, independent decision- making and cultural development of the individual and social groups. UNESCO defines public Library as the local gateway to knowledge which provides arrangements for lifelong learning. It leads to independent decision making, cultural development and making social group. The UNESCO manifesto also states that it should be an institution established under the clear mandate of law maintained fully from public fund, offering all its service free of cost and open for free and equal use by all members of the community irrespective their age, sex, religion, language structural level of education. UNESCO thinks that public library as a living force for education, culture and information, and as an essential agent for the fostering of peace and spiritual welfare through the minds of men and women.

According to 2011 census in West Bengal literacy among male and female is 81.69 percent and 66.57 percent respectively. Also, female sex ratio is 950 among 1000male. From the above data one can easily understand the situation. Though it is said that male and female are equal in every point of view but in real situation it is not the same. Female in rural areas are spent maximum time in a day for household work either by pressure or having no option to employ herself in self-development. There are many families where elders think females are only for housework and they have no right to education. There are some villages where no basic educational institution is situated. Here public libraries and community library cum information centers can fill up the gap.

Programmes that seek to increase ICT skills among women and girls:

i) The International 'Girls in ICT Day', (i.e., fourth Thursday in April every year) launched in April 2011 by the International Telecommunications Union (ITU), aims to encourage more girls and women to access technology and consider careers in the technology field.

ii) The ITU has initiated other programs including the Digital Literacy for Women & Girls joint program with Telecentre.org, Community ICT Centers for Women's Empowerment, and Girls in ICT, in cooperation with the United Nations Educational, Scientific, and Cultural Organization (UNESCO).

iii) UNESCO has an entire strategy on gender equality that includes ensuring ICT access for girls and women, and training to help girls and women enter technology professions.

Here I am furnishing the list of Government schemes that are meant for women of India. These dedicated schemes targeting women as key beneficiaries.

Health and Empowerment

1. Integrated Child Development Services (ICDS) (http://wcd.nic.in/icds.htm)

2. Janani Suraksha Yojana (JSY) (http://jknrhm.com/PDF/JSR.pdf)

3. Swastha Sathi (https://swasthyasathi.gov.in/)

4. National Food Security Mission (http://nfsm.gov.in/)

5. National Rural Health Mission (http://www.mohfw.nic.in/NRHM.htm)

6. Targeted Public Distribution System (TPDS) (http://fcamin.nic.in/dfpd_html/tpds.htm)

7. Antyodaya Anna Yojana (AAY) (http://fcamin.nic.in/dfpd_html/aay.htm)

Education and Empowerment

8. District Primary Education Programme (DPEP) (http://www.nuepa.org/libdoc/docservices/ds/dpep.pd)

9. Kasturba Gandhi BalikaVidyalaya (http://ssa.nic.in/girls-education/kasturba-gandhi-balika-vidyalaya)

10. Sarva Shiksha Abhiyan (SSA) (http://ssa.nic.in)

11. Kanyashree prakalpa. Financial aid for education to girl student.

(http://wbcdwdsw.gov.in/User/wings_kannyesre)

12. National Programme for Education of Girls at Elementary Level (http://ssa.nic.in/girls-education/npegel)

13. Eklavya Model Residential School (http://tribal.nic.in)

14. Establishment of Ashram Schools in Tribal Sub-Plan Areas (http://tribal.nic.in/)

15. Upgradation of Merit of Sc/St Students (http://socialjustice.nic.in/merit.php)

16. Central Sector Scholarship of Top-Class Education for SC students

(http://socialjustice.nic.in/topclass.php)

17. Rajiv Gandhi National Fellowship Scheme (RGNFS) for SC/ST (http://www.ugc.ac.in/more/RGNF_scst.pdf)

18. Rashtriya Madhyamik Shiksha Abhiyan

(http://planipolis.iiep.unesco.org/upload/India/India_Scheme_secondary_education.pdf)

19. Scheme for construction and running of Girls' Hostel for students of Secondary & Higher Secondary Schools.

(http://mhrd.gov.in/sites/upload_files/mhrd/files)

20. Indira Gandhi Scholarship for Single Girl Child for pursuing Higher and Technical Education (http://www.ugc.ac.in/notices/igsgc_1011.pdf)

21. Scheme of Capacity Building for Women Managers in Higher Education

(http://www.ugcwomenmanagers.org)

22. Development of Women Studies in Colleges and Universities

(http://www.ugc.ac.in/financialsupport/guidelinepdf/women/annexure1.pdf)

23. Rupashree Prakalpa (http://wbcdwdsw.gov.in/User/rupashree_prakalpa)

24. Utkarsha Bangla Prakalpa(https://www.pbssd.gov.in/)

Economic Empowerment

25. Lakshmir Bhandar Prakalpa(https://drive.google.com/file/d/1AlSxyYvI-YIRShRVBdLD5dTWyWgoZl1e/view)

26. Support to Training and Employment Program (STEP) for Women)

(http://wcd.nic.in/schemes/step_scheme.pdf)

27. Self -Employment Scheme for Rehabilitation of Manual Scavengers

(http://socialjustice.nic.in/srms.php)

28. Mahila samakhya(http://mhrd.gov.in/sites/upload_files/mhrd/files/Genesis.pdf)

29. Working Women's Hostel (http://www.wcd.nic.in/schemes/scheme_of_working_women_hostel.pdf)

30. Rajiv Gandhi National Crèche (http://www.iccw.in/creche_scheme.html)

31. Scheme of Marketing Development of Tribal Products/Produce

(http://tribal.nic.in/index2.asp?sublinkid=507&langid=1)

32. Rashtriya Mahila Kosh

33. Sukanya Samriddhi Yoyona.

Legal & Political Empowerment

34. Ujjawala Scheme for Prevention of Trafficking and Rescue, Rehabilitation and Reintegration (http://wcd.nic.in/schemes/ujjawala)

35. Indira Gandhi MatritvaSahyogYojana (IGMSY) - A Conditional Maternity Benefit Scheme. (http://wcd.nic.in/schemes.htm)

36. Rajiv Gandhi Scheme for Empowerment of Adolescent Girls (RGSEAG) SABLA
(http://wcd.nic.in/schemes/sabla.htm)

37. Financial Assistance and Support Services to Victims of Rape: A Scheme For Restorative Justice
(http://wcd.nic.in/schemes/Financialssistancerapevictimscheme.pdf)

38. Leadership Development of Minority Women Scheme (http://www.minorityaffairs.gov.in/leadership_minority)

Other Important Rehabilitative and Development Schemes

39. National Mission for Empowerment of Women (http://nmew.gov.in)

40. Swadhar- A scheme for Women in Difficult Circumstances (http://wcd.nic.in/schemes/swadhar.pdf)

41. Gender Budgeting Scheme (http://wcd.nic.in/schemes/gbscheme.pdf)

42. Panchayat Mahila Evam Yuva Shakti Abhiyan (PMEYSA) (http://panchayat.gov.in/data/File/PMEYSALetter.pdf)

43. Muktir Alo (http://wbcdwdsw.gov.in/User/scheme_muktiralo)

Programmes can be started by Libraries for empowering women and girls:

i) Women, particular in rural areas have lack of choices and opportunities to improve their living standards. They are restricted by poverty, poor access to health care services and education. These problems eternalize gender discriminations and their inferior status long time. women´s rights still need to be recognized so that one can reach the gaps regarding gender equity.

ii) Entrepreneurship development programme can be done in library for women and girls. Many govt. agencies do workshop on new technology, skill development programme, how to create a new venture, Training of Self-help group etc. These can be introduced in libraries because rural libraries are easily accessible to rural women.

iii) At a time of tight development budgets, investing in new infrastructure is risky. Working with libraries offers a better and smarter way of doing development because it is a trusted and easily accessible. Development can be done by doing more than enabling access to information. Libraries have safe and supportive environments that often provide services to different type of people such as youth and women — and that have played an important role in literacy, advancing skills and solving problems for developing nation.

iv) Safety concerns is the primary barrier to accessing ICTs for women and girls. Libraries can play an important role in creating safe spaces. It is noted that female librarians also act as mentors and role models.

v) Mobile phone and mobile internet are forms to bridge 'digital divide'. In rural areas women have less access to mobile and mobile internet due to some social barriers. Here library can play a vital role to offer these women for accessing internet in library and also ICT training.

vi) Public libraries can play a vital role in proving free and compulsory education to all the people. If public libraries can be merged with school education department, then it will fruitful for interior areas where primary school is not easily accessible. Those who are neo literate, illiterate; document should be there specially for them like pictorial representation of a message, graph, pictorial book etc.

vii) Adult education centre can be created within public libraries where adult people can get their elementary education, agricultural information, advantages of many Govt. schemes, economic information etc in their leisure time. For this library should open at the evening.

viii) If Govt. create new Community library cum Information Centers with infrastructural support, then it will be able to provide need-based information on health, nutrition, rural resources management, markets, education, livelihood, agriculture etc. relevant to rural people. The information on different development programmes of government and other agencies provided by CLICs could be of much benefit in order to make Indian rural women empowered.

ix) In library some discussions on great works on literature can be made. This will inspire participants and the classes will be transformed from mere reading and discussion, to include writing and scholarly analysis. This results the creation of a social network of women-readers who have gained knowledge, confidence and support by their intellectual engagement and vocalization with other women.

x) Rural women in India are mainly illiterate and involved in agriculture. As a result, necessary information, knowledge and resources are required to assist them. Mainly they are non-literate and here librarians have duty to repackage the information which will assists them to get this information in a meaningful way.

xi) "Library on wheel" can be introduced to reach the underprivileged interior women for giving latest news, information on agriculture, digital information etc.

xii) In India boosting of income and job creation is done by agricultural productivity. For agricultural productivity farmers need access to agricultural training and information, along with access to markets and financial opportunities. Libraries here can act like information hub where farmers can get appropriate information for their increasing agricultural productivity.

xiii) India has a rich cultural community. Public library can be a historical research point because here many valuable and rare documents are preserved.

xiv) Conduct career guidance program on various competitive examinations, various courses of state and central government.

Public libraries are important because they are public, free, and serve learning, social, civic, and economic needs. Public libraries are called 'people's university'. Though public libraries have power to develop our society in many angles but till now only 19 states of our country have enacted their public library act. We hope that Govt. and other agencies should look into the matter as library can be a part of the women empowerment as well as national development.

References:

1. Department of Women & Child Development and Social Welfare, Government of India. (http://wbcdwdsw.gov.in/User/wcdw_stat)
2. Women Empowerment in India. retrieved from https://en.wikipedia.org/wiki/Empowerment
3. Ministry of Social Justice & Empowerment, Government of India, (https://socialjustice.gov.in/)
4. Ministry of Women & Child Empowerment, Government of India, (https://wcd.nic.in/)
5. Oyelude, A., & Bamigbola, A. "Women Empowerment through access to information (ATI): The strategic roles of non- governmental organizations in Nigeria", 2012, July
6. United Nations Educational Scientific Cultural Organization. http://www.unesco.org/webworld/libraries/manifestos/libraman.html

7. Bhuvaneshwari Ravi, & Gayathri Vivek, Importance of Partnership for development of public library in India, DESIDOC, Journal of Library and Information Technology, 33 (1) 2014
8. UNESCO Manifesto. (2014). Retrieved January 17, 2014 from http://unesco.org.
9. Gutam, J. N., & Sunil Kumar, Community Information and Library service for rural people, Information Communication Library and community development, (1st ed.), B. R. Publishing Corporation, Delhi, 2004 pp.400-412
10. Bhuvaneshwari Ravi, & Gayathri V., "Importance of partnership for development of public libraries in India", in *DESIDOC Journal of Library and Information Technology,* 33(1), 2014, pp.10-20
11. Akhter, Md. Yosuf; Deb, Prasenjit; and Biswas, Jahar, "Role of Public Libraries with special reference to Women Empowerment through Kanyashree Prakalpa in West Bengal of India", *Library Philosophy and Practice* (e-journal), 2021
12. Abdul Kalam, A. P. J & Sivathanu Pillai. *Envisioning an Empowered Nation* (1st ed.) Tata Mc Graw Hill Publishing company, New Delhi, 2004
13. Sharma, Usha, *Women in South Asia Employment Empowerment and Human Development* (1st ed.), Authors Press, Delhi, 2003, pp. 1 – 30
14. Sasi, P. K., "Role of Public Libraries on Women Empowerment: A Study with Special Reference to District Library Malappuram", *IOSR Journal of Humanities and Social Science* (IOSR-JHSS), Volume 19, Issue 10, Ver. VII, Oct. 2014, pp. 25-44
15. Hugar, Jayaprakash G. Faras, A., *Public Library System In India*, Creative Book, Delhi, 2021
16. Hada, Kapil Singh, Bajpai, R. P., *Integrated Indian Public Library System*, Partridge Publishing India, 2014 Gutam, J. N., & Sunil Kumar. (2004). Community Information and Library service for rural people, information communication library and community development (1st ed., pp.410-412) Delhi: B R publishing corporation.

Computer and Teacher of Higher Secondary Education: A Study of New India

Dr. Tafajul Hoque

The advancement of computer technology in the current digital era has gone above and beyond what we could have ever imagined. Computers have many uses in many different industries, but one shouldn't overlook their use in educational Institutions. In the process of teaching and learning, it is highly beneficial and modern concept. Hence, both teachers and students greatly need the computer literacy to cope up the ongoing changes in the intellectual world. The computer is a machine that processes incoming data, produces output, and receives more input and acts with multiple way. The computer is otherwise called as a 'Stupid Genius' even though we have computers with artificial intelligence. The use of computers in education system and the way that people learn has undergone a revolution. It has enormous educational implications and has the power to multiply human intelligence. Our nations have taken the initiative to apply the New Education Policy (both in 1986 and recently in 2020), in teaching and learning process with more emphasize on digital learning. These policies made compulsory for both the teachers and students to learn some basic computer knowledge with application.

The use of a computer by teacher can improve the teaching-learning process. While a teacher's perspective on a concept is typically shaped by their views and knowledge about it. Besides it is also true that their comprehension of a concept can be influenced by the preexisting perspectives on it. Because they are the ones transferring knowledge to students, teachers are crucial to their ability to learn. Furthermore, it is unrealistic to assume that only speaking or writing something will be adequate to teach in a first-developing country like India, where knowledge is expanding at an exponential rate in every field. So, there is a perceived necessity for the teacher to be aware of computer use in the teaching process. However, some teachers have developed computer phobia as the result of the psychological impact of computers. Therefore, the researcher must choose this kind of study to comprehend the school teachers' attitudes towards computers. As there are not so many studies on teachers' attitudes towards computers so far. Hence, this study and the investigation is an honest and modest move on the part of the researcher. This helped me understand the attitudes of the teachers of mainly higher secondary school and the future prospects.

A computer is a multipurpose device that may be configured to automatically perform a series of logical or mathematical processes. Now a days, our educational system has been greatly impacted by computers. The teacher must come to terms with the physicality of the computers and understand how to effectively leverage the instructional potential of the devices. The primary goal of Higher Secondary Education in India is to prepare students as responsible and productive adult. It also passes on the information and wisdom of the society to the younger generation and aid in the intellectual growth of children. So, educators must meet societal needs. The 21st century is the era of information technology. Therefore, it is essential that each and every student should inform accordingly to their standard to compete the world. Everyone who have been impacted by the spread of computer technology feels necessity to use computers and engage with them. The use of computers by higher secondary students affects their awareness. Computer use among higher secondary students can be correlated with computer attitude, computer science achievement, computer self-efficacy, internet attitude, and computer anxiety. The use of computers, computer attitudes, academic achievement in computer science, computer self-efficacy, internet attitudes, and computer anxiety of the higher secondary pupils all have a role in how well this study turns out. Computer education is seen as a crucial component of education in today's age of technological growth. Yet key elements that determine how far a student develops in the field of computer education include his or her use of computer. The students are conversant with computers because computer education is now a prerequisite for many higher secondary levels. There is a chance that the students and teachers in upper secondary levels will have strong computer skills.

The professors' expertise in computers will be highly beneficial to the pupils' future development. Teachers must have computer literacy for this. Knowing about the different fundamental aspects of computers and the basic abilities needed in operating computers is one definition of computer knowledge. It also covers computer applications in the process of teaching and learning. If teachers are used as an example with the aid of the most recent technology, the computer, e-learning enables the learner to get knowledge about the subject they choose to learn. A very key factor in developing a genuine interest in computers is having a positive attitude about them. Without a positive attitude towards computers, teachers might not be interested in them, which would harm their knowledge of computers and make it challenging for them to teach using computers, which would have a negative impact on student learning. Thus, if the teachers have a positive attitude about computers, there may be a chance for them to be inspired to learn about computers as it is obvious that instructors have a great need for computer literacy. The use of PPT presentation,

Google Meet for online classes and Google forms for online examination became the new trends in the educational institutions during covid-19 period.

Computers are everywhere because they have several uses in practically in every sectors. In the current world the presence of computers makes people feel at ease and at home. If a person can read and write that individual is said to be literate. He or she is regarded as illiterate if not. Yet, the definition of literacy in the context of computers is different, and one should be aware of this. Awareness and understanding of the computer, its function in society, and its impact on education is a definition of computer literate. However, the overall definition of computer literacy must be broad in scope therefore it must also cover information retrieval, statistics, and other relevant system applications in addition to programming. In other words, computer literacy covers both using a computer and operating one. Together with the three fundamental skills of reading, writing, and math, or the three we should also be proficient in the fourth which stands for the computer.

A person's attitude is more or less constant, enduring state of mental preparation that causes them to react in a certain way to any topic or circumstance that it is related to. Because attitudes play a significant part in shaping how people respond to a circumstance, they may be used to forecast human behavior. A person's willingness to act is also a result of a complicated combination of sentiments, desires, anxieties, convictions, prejudices, and other emotional dispositions. Many psychologists have different definitions of attitudes. A behavior may be either favorable or negative towards the psychological object or class of objects depending on an attitude. According to Sommer & Sommer (1986), a person's attitudes on a subject are a culmination of their beliefs, emotions, knowledge, and opinions. One of the foremost experts on social psychology, all port (1935), believed that "attitudes" were the most crucial element in deciding how social interactions turned out. Cantril (1934) stated that an individual is more or less predisposed to react in a particular way to every topic or event that it is involved with because attitude is a more or less permanent enduring condition of readiness of mental organization. The statement an attitude is a method of conceptualizing an object" was made by Farris (193, guide 1). According to Morgan (1934), attitudes are essentially mental postures, guides for behavior to which each new experience is referred before a response are formed. Attitudes are a conceptual framework that facilitates in the interpretation and processing of information, according to Baron and Byrne (2004). They go on to add that attitudes allow for self-expression, self-esteem, which heightens feelings of self-worth, and an impression-encouraging role. According to Sarnff (1960), attitude is the disposition to react favorably or unfavorably to a class of object. Attitudes towards Computer may lead in a behavior that may be favorable or unfavorable towards Computer. A positive attitude towards computers is crucial for generating genuine interest in them. If teachers don't have a positive attitude towards computers, they might not be interested in them, which would impair their knowledge of computers. They might also find it challenging to teach using computers, which would impact students' learning.

The goals set forth for the current study are as follows

- To study the teachers' attitude towards computer education.
- To research the significance difference between the instructors, live in rural area and in metropolitan areas in respects of their attitudes towards computer education.
- To investigate the significance of the attitudes towards computer education that differs between teachers of science and arts topics.

- To investigate the significance of the attitude towards computer education that differs between teachers with experience up to 10 years and above 10 years.

Today it seems inevitable that teachers will use computers. The process of teaching is now carried out online or online teaching. E-learning is a form of education that uses the most recent technology a computer to assist learners in learning about the subject they want to study. Yet the teacher's contributions to online instruction are significant. He must be aware of his computer-assisted teaching methodology. Future pedagogy is largely dependent on the three ways: Windows, Web, and Wire or Wireless (internet). A modern professor could be characterized as being wired, windowed, and webbed-even by you. A very key factor in developing a genuine interest in computers is having a positive attitude about them. Without a positive attitude towards computers, teachers might not be interested in them, which would harm their knowledge of computers and make it challenging for them to teach using computers, which would have a negative impact on student learning. Thus, if the teachers have a positive attitude about computers, there may be a chance for them to be inspired to learn about computers as it is obvious that instructors have a great need for computer literacy.

The following are the important findings of the present investigation

- There are no discernible differences in the attitudes of male and female teachers towards computer instruction.
- There is no substantial difference between the instructors residing in rural region and in urban area in respects of their attitude towards computer education.
- Teacher in scientific and artistic subject does not differ considerably in their attitudes about computer education.
- There is no significant difference between the teachers having the teaching experience up to 10 years and above 10

years in respects of their attitude towards computer education.

To keep in view the need of time it is advised that teachers, parents, community members, and other stakeholders in education emphasis and get involved in creating an environment that is conducive to computer education for their children. Regular computer teachers should be involuntarily appointed to every level by the federal and state governments. It is imperative that all Board and university levels have computer education as a required course in their curriculum. Moreover, a brief programme and a mandatory computer introduction should be offered to in-service teachers.

The following suggestions are considered for the further research on attitude of higher secondary school teachers towards computer

i) This investigation was conducted in Dumkal, a block in the district of Murshidabad. More research can therefore be done in other regions of the nation and overseas.

ii) Higher secondary school teachers are the only participants in this study. It may be held for the instructors of other classes, college lecturers, and students as well.

iii) The Bengali-medium professors who were the subject of the current research. The professors who instruct in the English medium may be the subject of additional research.

iv) The current inquiry was done on the instructors working for the WBCHSE board. Further research may be done in the boards of CBSE, ICSE, and other schools board as well.

v) The researcher only uses four variables in the current study. Future research may require more variables, such as marital status, salary, etc.

The present inquiry is a highly unique study undertaken in a developing country like India to explore the teachers' attitude towards computer and consequently this study has contributed to the field of computer education. Besides, the study found that the majority of instructors have a positive attitude towards computers, which helps them prepare for challenges in the classroom of the future.

References

1. Aggarwal, Y.P., *Statistical Methods: Concepts and Application and computation*, Sterling Publishers (P) Ltd., New Delhi, 1986.
2. Best John, W., *Research in Education*, Prentice Hall Inc. Englewood Cliffs, 1977
3. Edwards, L. Allen, *Technique of Attitude Scale Construction,* Vakils Feffer and Simons (P) Ltd, Bombay, 1957
4. Durndell. A. & Thompson. K., "Gender and Computing: A decade of change"?, *Computer and Education, 28 (1), 1.* 1997.
5. Cantril, H., *Attitudes in the making, Understanding the child.* 1934.
6. Guildford, J. P., *Psychometric method* (2nd Edition) Tata McGraw Hill Publishing Company Ltd., Bombay, 1954
7. Koul, Lokesh, *Methodology of Education Research*, (2nd Edition), Bikash Publishing House (P) Ltd, New Delhi, 2002
8. Kulsum, Umme. "Teachers Attitudes Towards Computer", SETRAD, *National Conference on Integrating Technology into Teaching and Learning.*
9. Sidhu, Kulbir Singh. *Methodology of Research in Education,* Sterling Publishers (P) Ltd, New Delhi, 1999
10. S., Rajasekar. "University Students Attitudes Towards Computer", SETRAD, *Recent Research in education and Psychology, Vol.10, No. I-II,1-5.* 2005.
11. Seyal., Afzall H. Rahim Md. Mahbubur, & Rahaman, Md. Noah. "Computer attitudes of non-computing academics: a study of technical colleges in Brunei Darussalam", *Information and Management,* Vol. 37, 169-180, 2000.

Lifelong Learning and Rapid Social Change: A New Identity of India

Saidul Islam & Md Kawsar Hossain

Education liberates from darkness and their knowledge, and attitude is the power to progress forward. Education can lead a nation to its position. Immediately after birth a human being begins learning as a child which leads to life. There is no room for repetition in lifelong learning or cradle-to-grave learning. Reflecting on a more holistic view of lifelong learning, it can be seen that it recognizes learning in different environments and situations. The formal education framework of lifelong learning is related to recurrent training, but it is not the same thing. The opportunities and consequences of lifelong and life-long learning are actually a concept. Education policy, labour market policy, industrial policy, regional policy, industrial policy, social policy and cultural policy, are all influenced by lifelong learning and they all have a common responsibility for lifelong and life-long learning. Lifelong learning can be defined as all purposeful educational activities undertaken on an ongoing basis with the aim of improving knowledge, skills and abilities. It includes various forms of education and training which are formal, non-formal and informal. It is on these frameworks that all education and training depend on working methods to develop the individual's ability to search for information, actively and independently develop knowledge.

The European Commission Memorandum was a new initiative on lifelong learning. The concept of "recurrent training" can be called its invention in the early 1960s. According to the ideas of the time, learning should be self-directed, taking care of one's own needs. However, these ideas remained vague concepts and did not translate into strategies. Repetitive training instead took the form of specific educational training in the 1960s and 1970s. The concept of lifelong learning was re-emerged in the late 1980s and early 1990s when the International Commission on Education for the 21st Century "Learning: the treasure within" report to UNESCO in 1996. According to the commission, education is an ongoing process of developing knowledge and skills; It is also primarily an exceptional means of personal development and relationship building. Following the European Council in Lisbon in March 2000, the European Commission drew up a Memorandum on Lifelong Learning with the aim of developing a coherent strategy for lifelong learning in Europe. The Memorandum was made official in October 2000 under the Swedish EU presidency to achieve its objectives. This was followed by debates in Europe on strategies for implementing lifelong learning at individual and institutional levels, the results of which were used to prepare action plans for the implementation of lifelong learning. These policy objectives, concrete initiatives set the criteria for the implementation of lifelong learning in Europe. According to the memorandum, lifelong learning can bring all forms of education and learning under one umbrella. The implementation of these actions and principles of lifelong learning will be the responsibility of the partnership between the Member States, the European Commission, the social partners, business and training institutions and the various sectors of education and training. These integrated policies and strategies will be developed at the government level. Six key messages are at the heart of the memorandum: ensuring the acquisition of skills necessary for participation in the knowledge society and guaranteeing universal and continuous access that will help to enhance individuals' basic skills. Five new basic skills were mentioned in Lisbon – IT skills, foreign languages, technological environment, entrepreneurship and social skills. Increasing the level of investment in human resources. Ensuring continuity of innovation in lifelong learning and continuing education. Assessment of learning guidance and counselling aimed at improving non-formal and informal ways of learning to ensure everyone has access to good quality information for learning.

Lifelong learning is a concept that emphasizes continuous learning throughout a person's life. Lifelong learning can be a source of personal growth or professional development as a person acquires new skills and masters' new technologies and competencies well into adulthood. Some lifelong learners enroll in adult education programs. Others take non-credit courses at institutes of higher education such as a state university or community college; some simply audit these classes. Distance learning opportunities also exist via online courses. Most of these offerings are geared toward adult learning for people who are no longer in school but interested in continuing education. Lifelong learning activities take three principal forms.

1. Job training: Job training or accreditation may be required for workers seeking employment or a promotion in their current job. The cost of such training typically gets covered by an employer. In other cases, tuition can be offset by financial aid provided by government agencies.

2. Professional development: Some people seek continuing education as a means of learning skills for a future job. They pick up these new skills through universities or trade schools as they prepare to enter a new professional industry. They may also give themselves an informal education via articles, videos, and podcasts.

3. Personal fulfilment: Yet another form of lifelong learning is the informal learning that people use to get greater fulfilment out of their own lives. A person may be happily employed or

happily retired, but they still see the benefit in new forms of personal learning. They might enroll in courses that teach critical thinking skills or tangible skills that can be applied to a hobby.

In the field of education, the need for lifelong education is from the birth of a child to death. Because if there is no comprehensive education, no person can live in harmony with the society. Moreover, the need for this education is immense for the way of life in this changing society, some of the requirements are highlighted here as follows:

Enthusiasm for exploration: Education is of great use in the progress of evolving human civilization. Observing the evolution of human civilization, it is seen that modern civilization has been developed as a result of human struggle for thousands of years. In the spirit of new discoveries and exploration, human beings have advanced human civilization from the ancient stone age to the modern nuclear age. has been able to bring. Man has been able to control the adverse natural environment for the benefit of education. Education is at the root of this rapid progress of human civilization.

Biological and Physical Development: Education is of immense importance in the biological and physical development of a human child. For a few years after birth, the human child is completely helpless and dependent. Compared to other animals, the physical growth of the human child is often slow. It takes at least a year for him to stand upright on two legs. takes Through the imitation and help of elders in the family, the child gradually acquires physical ability and fulfils his biological needs. Not only physical ability, but education is necessary to make the human child possess good health.

Mental Development: Education is no less important in the mental development of a child. A human child is born with certain latent potentials. Education is necessary for the development of these latent potentials. Education is of considerable importance in the proper and normal development of the child's instincts, impulses, needs, interests, intelligence, memory, ideas, thoughts, language etc.

Effective Adaptation: Education is also needed to effectively adapt to the changing environment. People have to adapt or adapt to these three types of environments, natural, social and mental. Education helps the individual to master the behaviour suitable for adapting to the changing environment.

Preservation and transmission of social heritage: The usefulness of education in the preservation and transmission of social heritage is great. It is through the virtue of education that we can get to know the accumulated experience of our ancestors. Again, we leave what is best and necessary in our experience to our posterity. Apart from the above areas, there is a need for education in various areas of individual life such as personality development, formation of ideal character, protection of national unity etc.

Now we should know the importance of lifelong learning. Whether pursuing personal interests and passions or chasing professional ambitions, lifelong learning can help us to achieve personal fulfilment and satisfaction. It recognizes that humans have a natural drive to explore, learn and grow and encourages us to improve our own quality of life and sense of self-worth by paying attention to the ideas and goals that inspire us. We're all lifelong learners. But what does personal fulfilment mean?. The reality is that most of us have goals or interests outside of our formal schooling and jobs. This is part of what it means to be human: we have a natural curiosity and we are natural learners. We develop and grow thanks to our ability to learn. Lifelong learning recognizes that not all of our learning comes from a classroom.

- For example, in childhood, we learn to talk or ride a bike.
- As an adult, we learn how to use a smartphone or learn how to cook a new dish.

These are examples of the everyday lifelong learning we engage in on a daily basis, either through socialization, trial and error, or self-initiated study. Personal fulfilment and development refer to natural interests, curiosity, and motivations that lead us to learn new things. We learn for ourselves, not for someone else.

Key checklist for lifelong learning:

- Voluntary
- Self-motivated or self-initiated
- Doesn't always require a cost
- Often informal
- Self-taught or instruction that is sought
- Motivation is out of personal interest or personal development

Examples of lifelong learning:

Here are some of the types of lifelong learning initiatives that you can engage in:

- Developing a new skill (e.g., sewing, cooking, programming, public speaking, etc)
- Self-taught study (e.g., learning a new language, researching a topic of interest, subscribing to a podcast, etc)
- Learning a new sport or activity (e.g., Joining martial arts, learning to ski, learning to exercise, etc)
- Learning to use a new technology (e.g., smart devices, new software applications, etc)
- Acquiring new knowledge (taking a self-interest course via online education or classroom-based course)

Incorporating lifelong learning in your life can offer many long-term benefits, including:

1. Renewed self-motivation:

Sometimes we get stuck in a rut doing things simply because we have to do them, like going to work or cleaning the house.

Figuring out what inspires you puts you back in the driver's seat and is a reminder that you can really do things in life that you want to do.

2. Recognition of personal interests and goals:

Re-igniting what makes you tick as a person reduces boredom, makes life more interesting, and can even open future opportunities.

You never know where your interests will lead you if you focus on them.

3. Improvement in other personal and professional skills:

While we're busy learning a new skill or acquiring new knowledge, we're also building other valuable skills that can help us in our personal and professional lives. This is because we utilize other skills in order to learn something new. For example, learning to sew requires problem-solving. Learning to draw involves developing creativity. Skill development can include interpersonal skills, creativity, problem-solving, critical thinking, leadership, reflection, adaptability and much more.

4. Improved self-confidence:

Becoming more knowledgeable or skilled in something can increase our self-confidence in both our personal and professional lives. In our personal lives, this confidence can stem from the satisfaction of devoting time and effort to learning and improving, giving us a sense of accomplishment. In our professional lives, this self-confidence can be the feeling of trust we have in our knowledge and the ability to apply what we've learned.

Sometimes lifelong learning is used to describe a type of behaviour that employers are seeking within the organization. Employers are recognizing that formal education credentials are not the only way to recognize and develop talent and that lifelong learning may be the desired trait. Thanks to the fast pace of today's knowledge economy, organizations are seeing lifelong learning as a core component in employee development. The idea is that employees should engage in constant personal learning in order to be adaptable and flexible for the organization to stay competitive and relevant. This type of personal learning is often referred to as continuous learning. You can read more about continuous learning and what it means for both the employee and employer here.

According to some researchers, however, there is criticism that organizations are leveraging the concept of lifelong learning in order to place the responsibility of learning on employees instead of offering the resources, support and training needed to foster this kind of workforce. Do I need to be proactive about lifelong learning? Most people will learn something new at some point in their daily routine just by talking with other people, browsing the internet based on personal interest, reading the newspaper, or engaging in personal interest. However, if making more effort to learn something new is important for either personal, family, or career reasons, or there is a need for a more organized structure, then here are some steps to get started.

There are some ways of how we can adopt lifelong learning in our life. These are as follows:

1. Recognize your own personal interests and goals: Lifelong learning is about you, not other people and what they want. Reflect on what you're passionate about and what you envision for your own future. If progressing your career is your personal

interest, then there are ways to participate in self-directed learning to accomplish this goal.

2. Make a list of what you would like to learn or be able to do: Once you've identified what motivates you, explore what it is about that particular interest or goal that you want to achieve. Returning to our example of someone having a passion for history, perhaps it is desired to simply expand knowledge on the history of Europe. Or perhaps the interest is so strong that going for a Ph.D. is a dream goal. Both of these are different levels of interest that entail different ways of learning.

3. Identify how you would like to get involved and the resources available: Achieving our personal goals begins with figuring out how to get started. Researching and reading about the interest and goal can help to formulate how to go about learning it. With our history example: the person who wants to simply learn more about a particular historical time period could discover books in the library catalogue, blogs, magazines and podcasts dedicated to the subject, or even museums and talks. The individual who wanted to achieve A Ph.D. in history as a personal goal could research university programs that could be done part-time or online, as well as the steps one would need to take to reach the doctorate level.

4. Structure the learning goal into your life: Fitting a new learning goal into your busy life takes consideration and effort. If you don't make time and space for it, it won't happen. It can easily lead to discouragement or quitting the learning initiative altogether. Plan out how the requirements of the new learning initiative can fit into your life or what you need to do to make it fit. For example, if learning a new language is the learning goal, can you make time for one hour a day? Or does 15 minutes a day sound more realistic? Understanding the time and space you can devote to the learning goal can help you to stick with the goal in the long-run.

5. Make a commitment: Committing to your decision to engage in a new learning initiative is the final and most important step. If you've set realistic expectations and have the self-motivation to see it through, commit to it and avoid making excuses.

Advantage of lifelong learning for the younger generations:

The need for lifelong learning:

The last few decades have seen the learner evolve into the current Gen Z or I Gen learner, and the Learning process itself has undergone a lot of change – from a very linear and one-dimensional approach, which was fairly formal and assumed to last us a lifetime, to a very social, informal way of learning. Today, the shelf life of knowledge/information, and therefore our skills, has reduced considerably and so learning has to be continual. Thus developed the concept of lifelong learning.

The talent marketplace today - the future of work:

Traditionally, learning is associated with formal education at school, college, or university. Formal education and the resulting qualifications are important to get a good career start; however, acquiring new skills and reskilling to meet the current market demand and maximizing opportunities, is as important! Businesses today are preparing for jobs that don't exist. The talent needs of an organization is changing. The gig economy and the increasing skills gap have had a severe impact on the talent marketplace. Not only is it hard to attract and source quality talent, it is also difficult to keep them engaged for a reasonable tenure, while controlling costs. Increased digitization and globalization have led to extreme flexibility when it comes to hiring new talent. Having only a set of skills is no longer enough as companies prefer part-time, project-based, independent resources or freelancers more than ever before. The focus is shifting from qualification-based to skills-based jobs. So, what are the traits of the future worker?.

Undoubtedly, the jobs of the future will be defined by new tools, including AI, AR/VR, Big data, IoT, and the likes, which in turn necessitates skilling and reskilling of the workforce on these new and emergent technologies. However, what would also be crucial for people participating in the future of work is to know how to collaborate with these new artificially intelligent and automated systems. Their attitudes, behaviours, and most importantly their mindset and ability to adapt to change will set them apart from the automated systems.

Emotional and Artificial Intelligence will be at duel:

Additionally, a thorough understanding of the domain in which the functional expertise is being applied, through the lens of the emerging trends & technologies, would be incredibly valuable as more and more organizations will look for talent who can understand and solve their business problems. The need would be to build teams with domain expertise – people who can speak the domain language, ask relevant questions, and understand the business goals completely. At Hurix, we look at the future worker to have a T-shaped personality, with deep skilling in the specific area of expertise overlaid with domain expertise on one hand and on the other, the right-brained abilities to think creatively and be emotionally intelligent enough to adapt to an ever-changing world.

Is it only professional though?

Lifelong learning is not just for a professional uplift; it enhances the learners' understanding of the world around, provides more and better opportunities and improves the quality of life.

- Lifelong learning is a process of gaining knowledge and new skills throughout life for personal or professional fulfilment

- Lifelong learning helps create a positive attitude to learning both for personal and professional development
- Lifelong learning can be formal or informal, directed or self-paced
- Lifelong learning can also be indirect – through conversations, unexpected lessons learned, relationships, and even travel

Helps discover new interests:

Learning new skills can open up new opportunities and possibilities. Learners may develop an interest in an area that they never explored before. Continuous learning fuels creativity and innovation, helping the learners use their knowledge and skills in meaningful ways.

Builds confidence through mastery:

Lifelong learning is mostly a voluntary initiative taken by the learner. The willingness to learn something new and excel at it is what makes learning effective. Pursuing a course, a new skill or a hobby willingly encourages them to not only complete the course, but also master it.

Helps learn practical skills:

The mandatory courses and learning programs aside, lifelong learning teaches us practical skills. A school or college does not teach learners about every skill required in life. However, there are online platforms that offer a range of courses across subjects such as business, arts, health, personal development and more. Concepts such as taxes, handling finances, or improving communication skills, computer skills etc., can be learned through such online mediums.

Improves chances for job mobility:

Job mobility is one of the main factors that influence learners to continue learning. Equipping oneself with new technologies and the latest skills sought by the job market improves the chances of getting better job opportunities. Engaging in lifelong learning helps the learners stay competitive in the labor market.

Improves adaptability:

Learning something new might seem like a challenge at first. However, post the academic years, learners will always have to upskill themselves with the latest skills and software. Incorporating a culture of lifelong learning at the educational institutions will acclimate the learners to adapt to new technologies easily. It will increase their confidence to adopt new skills.

Lifelong learning versus book reading:

Taking a look at how much application I have made of the book-acquired knowledge compared to lifelong lessons, I realize the importance of this form of learning. First, lifelong learning helps discover and apply one's natural talents. For instance, it is only through life's experiences stated above that I discovered my business acumen that has ended up becoming an integral part of me. Books only relate to us other people's lives (sometimes fictional characters) rather than mould us into the people we should be. Secondly, lifelong experiences open up our thinking to help us exploit different options available. Having a daughter at an early age and without any source of income forced me to think up alternatives of solving my problems. First, I opened the restaurant and when this failed to kick off, I joined the army where I had a chance to learn numerous lessons. Having undergone various challenging times and emerged victorious does not only make us stronger, but also wiser. Wisdom is being able to discern right or wrong by predicting the possible outcomes of each action. Having a personal experience of a situation equips one with the relevant wisdom to evaluate similar life occurrences and make the best decision. Books cannot equip one with such amazing knowledge.

A personal encounter is not comparable to a simple familiarization though a book. In addition, lifelong learning assists us in finding purpose in our lives. Before my daughter was born, all that mattered to me was attending lavish parties and drinking alcohol with a bunch of friends. However, all that changed when the little bundle of joy came. I had to stay home with the mother and her or go find a reliable source of income. I now had a duty to dedicate myself to rather than waste my life. When at the battle field, I had to ensure I came out alive every time as someone depended on me. She had added meaning to my otherwise meaningless life. No matter how many books I had read on the similar experiences, not a single one moved me enough to change. However, one lifelong experience altered all that.

Optimization of lifelong learning:

The best place to optimize lifelong learning is at the learning institutions. Universities and colleges dedicated to research avail the best platforms for promotion of lifelong learning. Students should be allowed to plan their research, determine the scope of this research and carry it out in informal places. The research topics should involve the integration of several topics so as to emulate life in all aspects. However, if this has to happen, then the teaching format in these institutions has to take a different angle. For instance, students should be taught how to plan and assess their own research (Angelo & Cross, 1993). They should cease from being passive learners and become active learners who are conversant with the proceedings of the research. Peer assessment should also be encouraged greatly. Lifelong learning does not take any definite sequence. It, instead, varies from person to person. Since all people are also different, the dissimilar experiences become the mostly appropriate in bringing out differences in our talents and abilities. This sets apart lifelong learning from ordinary literature studies that only impart the same knowledge and expected different results.

Reference:

1. Use of the term 'Lifelong Learning' can be traced back to 1920s, used by Yeaxlee (1921) and Lindeman (1926) but was popularized by the work of UNESCO (Fauré et al., 1972)
2. Kember, D. "A Reconceptualization of the Research into University Academics Conceptions of Teaching", *Learning and Instruction*, No. 7, 1997, pp. 255-275. (Cited in Scientific Research: An Academic Online Publishers)
3. Deb, Prasenjit, *Lifelong Learning*, Indira Gandhi Open University, New Delhi, September 2022
4. Mandal, S., 'The rise of lifelong learning and fall of adult education in India', *London Review of Education,* Vol. 17 (3), 2019
5. Aggarwal, Vijita Singh, *Lifelong Learning: The Challenge in Context of India, RJSSM*, Volume: 01, Number: 10, Feb-2012, pp.1-9
6. Mauch, Werner. & Narang, Renuka. (Edited) *Lifelong learning and institutions of higher education in the 21st century: report on the preparatory Meeting for the World Conference on Higher Education*, Preparatory Meeting for the World Conference on Higher Education, Mumbai, India, 1998, Published by Director, Department of Adult and Continuing Education and Extension, University of Mumbai . Mumbai, India. g: UNESCO Institute of Education, Hamburg, Germany, Original Edition 1998
7. Mandal, S., "Learning the World? Changing Dimensions of Adult Education and Lifelong Learning in India", in Milana, M., Nesbit, T. (eds) *Global Perspectives on Adult Education and Learning Policy*, Palgrave Studies in Global Citizenship Education and Democracy. Palgrave Macmillan, London, 2015
8. Bordoloi, R., Das, Prasenjit, Das, Kandarpa. "Lifelong learning opportunities through MOOCs" in *India*,16 April 2020
9. MHRD (Ministry of Human Resource Development) (1992) "National Policy on Education 1986" (as modified in 1992), Government of India, New Delhi
10. MHRD (Ministry of Human Resource Development) (2018a) *All India Survey on Higher Education 2017–18*, Government of India, New Delhi
11. CFI Team (December 9, 2022) The Importance of Lifelong Learning,
12. Kris Powers, Eight Benefits of Lifelong Learning, April 29th, 2015
13. Learning Theories: Continuous Learning, VALAMIS, Knowledge Hub, June 17, 2023

14. Ramakrishnan, Manasa. "Lifelong Learning is the New Normal. Here's How You Benefit from It", Emeritus – Online Learning, 15 February 2022
15. https://www.waldenu.edu/programs/resource/the-many-benefits-of-lifelong-learning

Role of Educational Technology in Shaping Indian Society

Binita Bhakat

Teaching and learning have evolved significantly from lecture to role learning to internet-enabled learning to knowledge-based education to technological innovation-centred education. According to Namreen Asif the educational technology has grown exponentially in India. With its large population and diverse educational landscape, India has seen a rise in the use of technology in education throughout the years. Educational Technology, often called EdTech, also has a profound impact on shaping society. Indian society is a versatile society. Many castes, creeds, religions, and categories have formed Indian society and live together peacefully. In India, there exist many religions, customs, and beliefs. The social structure of Indian society is an amalgam of various castes, religions, languages, ethnicities, social classes, etc. Educational technology (EdTech) has had a profound and transformational impact on Indian society, affecting numerous aspects of education, society, and the economy.

Effective use of technology in the classroom necessitates a paradigm shift from teaching to learning, necessitating adequate training and learning styles and technical support, which emphasises learning and gives enough technical support to assist faculty in integrating technology into instruction. Rogers, D.L. (2000). Several trends in educational technology (EdTech) are emerging in India. Because the EdTech landscape moves so quickly, it's important to note that the following trends are based on information available at the time. Significant developments may have occurred since then. Here are some of India's current educational technology trends as of 2021.

Online Learning Platforms: Online learning platforms such as Byju's, Unacademy, Vedantu, and Coursera have grown in popularity. These platforms provided diverse courses, from K-12 education to professional and skill development.

Government projects: The Indian government has emphasised integrating technology into education through projects such as Digital India and the National Education Policy (NEP) 2020. Efforts were being undertaken nationwide to deliver digital infrastructure and content to schools and universities.

E-Learning During the Epidemic: The COVID-19 epidemic spurred online learning uptake in India. To preserve educational continuity, schools and colleges must transition to online classes. This experience increased public acceptance of digital learning technologies.

MOOCs (Massive Open Online Courses): MOOC sites such as Coursera, edX, and SWAYAM provide free and paid courses from Indian and foreign universities. Indian students had boosted their participation on these sites.

Language-Based Learning: To reach a more diversified audience, many EdTech platforms focused on offering information in regional languages.

Skill Development: As the value of employable skills grew, EdTech platforms began to offer courses in coding, data science, digital marketing, and entrepreneurship.

Online Assessment and Certification: Online assessment tools and platforms were becoming more popular for administering tests and certifications. Many educational institutions were experimenting with hybrid learning models that integrated online and offline components, giving students flexibility in their learning journeys.

Gamification and Virtual Reality (VR): Gamified learning experiences and the usage of VR in education have grown in popularity. Gamification makes learning more enjoyable and engaging, whereas virtual reality immerses students in virtual surroundings for greater learning experiences.

Coding and STEM Education: There has been an increase in the demand for coding and STEM (Science, Technology, Engineering, and Mathematics) education. Coding courses were available on many EdTech platforms for students of various ages.

Professional Development for Teachers: EdTech platforms that offer opportunities for professional development for educators, such as training in online teaching methods and digital tools.

Educational technology is essential to social development by contributing to society's growth, progress, and well-being. EdTech has the potential to break down educational barriers by providing people in rural or underserved locations with access to high-quality learning resources and opportunities. This increased access helps to overcome educational attainment gaps, empowering individuals and communities. Technology allows students to communicate with peers and professionals worldwide, promoting cross-cultural understanding and collaboration. In an interconnected society, this global vision is critical for social advancement. EdTech promotes a culture of lifelong learning by promoting the idea that education is not limited to a certain age or stage of life. This promotes personal and professional development throughout the rest of one's life. EdTech can meet a wide range of learning needs and abilities, making education more accessible. It offers tools and resources to students with disabilities and fosters diversity and inclusion in the classroom. Individuals are equipped with essential skills for the current workforce through educational technologies. It helps people stay competitive in the job market by providing courses and tools in areas such as coding, digital literacy, and technical skills. Online communities of learners, educators, and specialists can be facilitated through EdTech. These communities offer assistance, collaboration, and networking, promoting social development and cohesion. EdTech enables people to take charge of their own learning. It supports self-directed learning and pursuing one's interests and passions, which contributes to personal growth and fulfilment.

Thus, Educational technology promotes access to education, skill development, creativity, inclusion, and global connectedness, all of which contribute to social development. It enables individuals, groups, and societies to face problems and grab opportunities for advancement and well-being. However, ensuring fair access to technology and addressing potential difficulties such as the digital divide is critical to maximising technology's positive influence on social development.

EdTech can be used to construct digital archives and repositories for storing and preserving cultural artefacts, papers, images, and recordings. These digital collections assure the preservation of cultural heritage for future generations. Virtual museums and online displays give a venue for displaying cultural artefacts and creative forms to a global audience. This enables people to explore and appreciate cultural treasures without regard for physical limitations. Language preservation is an essential component of cultural heritage. To preserve linguistic diversity, EdTech tools and apps can be developed to educate and promote endangered or minority languages.

Online Courses and Seminars: Educational technology platforms can hold online courses and seminars on various cultural preservation topics. Traditional crafts, storytelling, music, and dance are some of the themes covered in these workshops, which allow participants to study and practice cultural customs.

Collaborative Projects: EdTech can help cultural institutions, scholars, and communities work together on collaborative projects. These collaborations may include the digitisation of historical records, the recording of oral histories, and the conduct of ethnographic research to chronicle and conserve cultural practices. This technology helps to document, safeguard, and promote cultural heritage by employing digital technologies, virtual experiences, and online resources. It spans geographical and generational divides, ensuring that cultural traditions do not perish but continue to enhance society.

Educational technology platforms can offer interactive and engaging materials to teach citizens about their rights, the political system, the electoral process, and how government institutions work. This assists individuals in becoming more knowledgeable and responsible citizens. EdTech tools can provide voter education resources such as voter registration information, candidate profiles, and ballot measure explanations. These materials enable voters to make informed voting decisions during elections. Educational technology can host online courses and webinars on political development, governance, and public policy. These courses can be made available to a global audience, allowing for the exchange of ideas and best practices. Educational technology can host online courses and webinars on political development, governance, and public policy. These courses can be made available to a global audience, allowing for the exchange of ideas and best practices.

Election monitoring efforts can be aided by EdTech platforms that allow citizens to report problems or share information about the electoral process. During elections, this improves transparency and accountability. Online forums, social media, and video conferencing tools can help encourage political debates and conversations. Individuals can use these venues to engage in constructive political dialogue and exchange differing points of view.

Thus, Educational technology is critical to political growth because it provides citizens with knowledge, promotes civic involvement, promotes transparency and accountability, and improves the general functioning of political systems. It contributes to developing and enhancing political institutions and processes by increasing informed and engaged citizenship.

The significance of technology in teaching cannot be overstated. Indeed, the advent of computers in the classroom has made it easier for teachers to convey knowledge and for students to learn that knowledge. As a result of using technology, the enjoyment of the teaching and learning processes has improved. Teachers and students should use knowledge effectively to break down the barriers that impede many children and schools from realising their full potential. As a result, every country must develop a more technologically advanced education system in the future. Raja (2018). Educational technology is transforming Indian society by making education more accessible, personalised, and effective. However, to maximise the benefits of technology for all parts of the population, it is critical to solve difficulties and guarantee that it is utilised appropriately. However, while EdTech provides various benefits, it also brings obstacles, including worries about the digital divide (unequal access to technology), effective digital pedagogy, and data privacy and security concerns. It is critical to address these difficulties and guarantee equitable access to technology to maximise its benefits for Indian society.

Reference:

1. Allahyarova, T. "Search for a New Paradigm in The Educational System in the Era of Artificial Intelligence and Digital Technologies: Challenges, Opportunities", *Actual Problems in the System of Education: General Secondary Education Institution – Pre-University Training – Higher Education Institution*, 2, 2022, pp. 179–190
2. Jaipal, D. A. "Role of Education in Shaping Indian Society". IJARCMSS, July- September, 2019
3. Namreen, Asif V., A. & Niyaz, Panakaje. "Paradigm Shift - The Role of Educational Technology and Internet in Indian Education System", International Journal of Case Studies in Business IT and Education, December 2022
4. Raja, R., & Nagasubramani, P. C. "Impact of modern technology in education", *Journal of Applied and Advanced Research*, 2018, pp. S33–S35
5. Rogers, D.L. (n.d.). "A Paradigm Shift: Technology Integration for Higher Education in the New Millennium", *AACE Review (Formerly AACE Journal)*, 1(13), pp. 19–33
6. Ball, S. J. "Following policy: Networks, network ethnography and education policy mobilities", *Journal of Education Policy*, 31(5), 2016, pp. 549–566
7. Annual Status of Education Report (ASER). (2016). Annual Status of Education Report. New Delhi: Pratham.
8. Miglani, Neha, "Educational Technology in India: The Field and Teacher's Sensemaking", *Sage Journal*, Vol. 16, Issue: 1, November 2018
9. H., Chetana M., "Role of Technology in Indian Education", Volume 6, Issue 3, 2019 JETIR March 2019
10. Raja, R. & Nagasubramani, P. C., "Impact of modern technology in education", *Journal of Applied and Advanced Research,* Vol. 3(S1): 33 May 2018
11. Miglani, Neha & Burch, Patricia. "Educational Technology in India: The Field and Teacher's Sensemaking", *Sage Journals (Online)*, Volume 16, Issue 1, November 2018

Development of Education and Knowledge System in Medieval Bengal: A Survey of 13th to 16th Century

Gopal Singha

The sultans of Bengal encouraged the spread of education and knowledge system to fulfil their religious obligations as Islam attached immense importance to the extension of *ilm* or knowledge. The rulers, the Sufis, Ulama, Nobles, Chieftains and Philanthropists all have contributed to this process of dissemination. In the medieval Bengal the education and knowledge system were closely associated with religious instructions. Both the Hindus and Muslims, as the two dominant religious groups, developed separate educational structures on the basis of their religious traditions. The institutions like Tols and Madrasas were responsible for spreading the education of the intellectual elite, the Brahman Pandits and the Muslims Moulavis. Such Tols and Madrasas could be found in all important centres of cultural life. Nabadwip, Mithila and Benares were famous for their Tols and Madrasa. Islamic Education in Bengal during Muslims rule envisaged several facets such as the traditional systems of education, the Islamic science, curriculum and text books, Institutions of education (Madrasas, Khanqahs), academy or the seminary of teachers and Milad\ Jalsa etc. There were the Maktabs or the elementary schools attached to the mosques. These where the principles center of religion or theological study. Besides there were the Madrasas where instruction in the higher branches of Islamic learning was imparted.

Religious instruction was the basis of primary education in the maktab and masjid. The Imam of the mosque was expected to teach his students the fundamentals of Islam and other rituals. Contemporary Bengali literature substantiates the view that the Muslim children used to performed ablution and prayer in the maktab, mainly to understand the fundamentals of Quran and Hadith. It can therefore, be presumed that the Quran and the Hadith were also included in the courses of education at the primary and higher levels. Besides these subjects, other sciences such as logic, arithmetic, medicine, alchemy, hindasa [geometry], astronomy and others were also taught in the Madrasas. The statement of Abul Fazl, though belonging to a later period, confirms this. He wrote, 'Every boy ought to read books on morals, arithmetic, agriculture, mensuration, geometry, astronomy, physiognomy, household, matters, rules of government, medicine, logic, higher mathematics, sciences and history, all of which may be gradually acquired'. Although the Madrasas had provisions for advanced studies in all these subjects, yet studying all these subjects by each and every student was not mandatory. Anatomy was a branch of medical science that was considered a subject of study in the Madrasas of first grade, again archery which formed an important component in the art of warfare was taught to those interested in it. Beautiful writing on the inscription slabs of the masjid and other monuments of Bengal leads us to infer that penmanship or calligraphy was also introduced as an important subject of study in the Madrasas of higher learning.

Muslim women secluded from outside view by the custom of purdah, or veiling it would seem were even more isolated from social and cultural change than their men were, thus any attempt to trace the history of women's education in Bengal during the period under review becomes considerably handicapped by the paucity of materials. These problems notwithstanding, some examples of the more enlightened and cultured Sultans of Muslims India, whether in the Paramount Empire of Delhi or in its dependencies, who patronized or pioneered female education are not far to seek.

During the medieval period Nabadwip become the principal center of education for the Hindus and attracted students from various parts of Bengal. Nabadwip was famous for the study of Navya Nyaya and the Smritis. Raghunath Shiromani the unrivalled scholar of Navya and Vasudeva Sarvabhauma renowned for his scholarship were teachers at Nabadwip. Sri Chaitanya, the young ascetic and preacher of Bhakti succeeded in convincing Vasudeva that the doctrine of Maya and Vedantic Philosophy had given way to Bhaki and the latter was drawn into the fold of Bhakti cult or vaisnavism. Nabadwip or Nadia became the chief center of Sanskrit studies in the 18th century. The curriculum was based on the culture of the people and was closely related to their religion. It must, however, be pointed out that though religion occupied a large place in the curriculum however the subjects like Astronomy, Medicine and others were also imparted. In these institutions, men who had obtained considerable eminence in such special studies as grammar, logic, law, rhetoric and metaphysics, and their scholarship would compare favorably with that of the best classical scholars of all times, get employed.

During this period, new ideas and values in the religious-social fields. It produced a great intellectual and cultural force as well in the history of man. Islam has attached great importance to enlightenment and culture as well as to decent living and refined manners. It has stressed the need for the development of both mind and body, the progress of the intellectual faculties of man. Qadi Rukn al- Din Samarqandi was one of the distinguished scholars of the early years of the Muslims rule in Bengal. He was the Qadi of Lakhnawti in the reign of 'all Mardan Khanji. It is known from an Arabic version of a Sanskrit mystic work called Amritkand that a Brahmin yogi[ascetic] named Bhojar Brahmin came from Kamrup to Lakhnawti and had religious and philosophical discussions with him. Being convinced of the superior ideals of Islam, the yogi became a Muslim and learnt Islamic science. He acquired so great proficiency in Islamic knowledge that the Muslim divines gave him the right to legal decisions.

The Muslims of his subcontinent brought with them the system of education and courses of studies that obtained in the 'Abbasid Caliphate of Baghdad. They consistently followed this in the madrasah education everywhere with little or no modification. The Bengali Muslim rulers and ulema, who were educated under the same education system, naturally introduced it in Bengal. Maulana Sharf al-Din Abu Tawwamah, who came from Bukhara, taught both religious and secular Sciences. To understand the educational development under the Muslim rule, it's important to understand the educational condition before the advent of the Islam in Bengal. It is indeed difficult to determine the system and nature of education that prevailed in pre-Islam Bengal due to the paucity of the historical sources. The materials give us only a generalized idea about the education in Bengal before Islam. The Buddhist and Brahmanic religious centers practically served as educational centers. Fa-Hien stayed at Tamralipta for two years to study and copy various Buddhist manuscripts, Brahmanic and Buddhist learning had developed appreciably and become widespread when Hiuen – Tsang visited Kajangal, Pundravardhan, Kamarupa, Samatata, Tamralipta, and Karnasuvarna. He noticed more than 300 Buddhist shramanas in 6/7 vihars at Kajangala, more than 3000 shramanas in 20 viharas in Pundravardhan more than 2000 shramanas in 30 viharas in Samatata and more than 2000 shramanas in the 10 viharas both at Tamralipta and

Karnasuvarna, Hiuen Nalanda, where more than 10000 sramanas resided to learn... all the Buddhist learning. The curriculum also included various secular subjects such as grammar, philosophy, medicine, astronomy, music, and arts, Chaturveda, Sankhya, Mahayana shastras, Yoga shastras, etc. thus by the 6th -7th century Aryan language and learning primary based on Brahmanic- jaina – Buddhist religions had reached Bengal.

Immediate decades before the conquest by the Turkish Muslims Bengal was passing with socio-political anarchy, M. N. Roy remarked that, "after the downfall of Buddhism, the country found itself in a wars state of economic ruin political oppression, intellectual, anarchy, and spiritual chaos Practically the entire society was involved in that tragic process of decay and decomposition. Cultivations of knowledge were definitely limited to the upper classes people of the society for example Brahmans, ministers, military officers' members, members of royal families etc. in course of time some socio- religious groups created under the strict caste system in Hindu society such as Brahman, Kshatriya, Vaishya, and Shudra. There were about nearly hundred castes and sub – castes existed in the then Hindu society among which social interactions were prohibited. The lower classes of Hindus had no social rights, even they had no permission to enter into the city. The caste system was strictly observed in educational system and the lower classes of Hindus were extremely out of educational facilities. Different religious shastras were taught in the Hindu temples such as Veda, Agama, Niti, Mimangsa, Vedanta, Shruti, Smriti, and Purana...... it is difficult to know how these shastras were taught." It may be assumed that Brahman Pundits used to establish Chatuspathis in their own houses or in and around the temples and take students as many as they could manage, under their care. Students used to study one or more subjects under one teacher [Acharya] and then move to others for others subjects. Recitation and listening were the methods of education and the Brahman himself was meant by the school. The vedic learning, mythological stories of Hinduism, Mathematics, and Astrological learning were among the main subjects, of education. The site of religious centre like temple houses of Brahmans, guest houses and even sometimes the shadowed space under a big tree used as a place of educational practice. Tol was educational centre only for the sons of Brahman and Pathshala was for Kshatriya and Vaishya, no education for the Shudra. The medium of education was Sanskrit language, which was not the language of common people.

The educational system in Muslim Bengal developed following the tradition of central Islamic lands as most of the rulers and officials were immigrants from the then Muslim world. From the early days of Islam, Masjid was learning centre, where teaching was offered in all branches of Islamic studies, from elementary stage to the highest level to the different aged groups. The most learned personalities of the respective communities were selected as Imams of the Masjids. With the expansion of Islamic territories, Masjid retained the function of education along with its original purpose as place prayers. After the foundation of Muslim rule in Bengal, Masjids developed as the nerve centers of the society. In every administrative center and other important places where there was a sizable Muslim population, the sultans and their officers or wealthy persons constructed Majids. The imams of the Masjids were acknowledged teachers who were considered able to teach inhabitant s of the locality. They sometimes had to instruct the prayer offering people how to perform prayers, or sometimes teach the children about the primary teachings of Islam or the correct recitation of the Holy Qura'n. The education practiced in the Masjids was mainly related to Islamic learning and instructed through informal ways. Thus, Masjids functioned as informal learning centres. There were hundreds of Masjids constructed throughout Bengal. Of some 200 inscriptions so far discovered more than 100 relate to the masjid of Pandua of Maldah district of West Bengal, built by Sultan Sikandar Shah in 1375 having a dimension of 507.5 feet north to south and 285.5 feet east to west with an enclosed open court. Khan Jahan's Masjid at Bagerhat of Bangladesh is another notable example popularly known as Shat Gumbad [sixty tombs] Masjid, one of the most impressive Muslims monuments in Indian subcontinent , built by the Wali Muhammad a high official in the court of Sultan Alauddin Hussian Shah , Boro Sona Masjid in Gaur built by Nusrat Shah, Bagha Masjid, of Rajhahi, built by Sultan Nusrat Shah, Kusumba Masjid, of Rajshahi, Bangladesh etc. educational practice in the Masjids is also evident from its architectural features and technique. In every Masjid, besides having a central prayer room, there were also other attached rooms which were mainly used for educational practice. There were also rooms for the scholars and learners together with ablution and other logistic facilities. Because of these facilities, many scholars used to establish their educational circles around the Masjids. Thus, an educational practice and education friendly environment developed in and around the Masjids in Bengal during the medieval Bengal.

Primary education was an immediate and important concern of the Muslim society as the Muslim children needed education to understand instructions of Islam and observe religious duties. Accordingly, Maqtabs developed in the Muslim society of Bengal as the primary educational centres with the fundamentals of Islamic practices together with some basic education. The Maktabs were primary originated with the

Masjids and sometimes organized either in a house attached to the Masjid, or in a private house of respective locality. These were established either by wealthy individuals of the respective locality. Sufi- Alims or by joint efforts of the inhabitants being supported by the state endowment as well as of individuals. The than historical evidences support the idea of widespread existence of Maktabs throughout the region and their effectiveness in promoting primary education in the society. Mukundaram states "Maktabs were also set up where Muslim children taught by Makhdums wherever the Muslims predominated in numbers. There were 1,00000 primary schools [Maktabs] in Bengal and Bihar, the population of which was estimated at 4000000, so that there would be a village school [Maktab] for more than three hundred school boys between the age of 5 and 12". This number referred us to the fact that how widely primary educational facilities developed in Bengal. A Masjid is seldom found in the village area without a Maktab. Apart from the general Maqtabs, there was another kind of special Maktab for memorizing the Holy Quran known as Hafzkhana. The wealthy persons often used to maintain private teachers in their house for educating their own children in a better domestic environment. Adam states "there are many private Mohammedan schools [Maktabs] begun and conducted by individuals of studious habits who have made the cultivation of letters the chief occupation of their lives, and by whom the profession of learning is followed, not merely as a means of livelihood, but as a meritorious work productive of moral and religious benefit to themselves and their fellow creatures." Thus, primary educational facilities widely expanded in the society during the medieval Bengal rule, which remarkably contributed to remove illiteracy from the society of Bengal.

Besides Masjid and Maktab, the most important educational institution developed in the Muslim society was the Madrasah.

A good number of Madrasahs were set up in the cities and important places by the Muslim rulers, nobles and philanthropic, persons the most notable example is Nizamiya Madrasah of Baghdad founded by Nizam-al-Mulk in 1065A.D. After the Muslim conquest of Bengal Bakhtiyar Khalji and his successor Khalji Maliks established Masjids, Madrasahs and Khanqah [seats conquered territories] in the capital city Lakhnauti and other important administrative centres of their conquered territories. Lakhnauti become the earliest learning centre, which gradually extended throughout the region. Madrasahs were primarily established by an individual scholar-sufi- Alim, and having congenial atmosphere and enthusiastic support from the local inhabitants, ruling elite, official wealthy individuals, philanthropic persons they gradually turned localities of Bengal, but also from other parts of Indian subcontinent and even from different parts of the then Muslim world. Many historical literary and epigraphic evidences provide us the information that there were many Madrasahs in different parts of Bengal, through it is different to identify definitely because of long lapse of time. Ghiyath-al-Din Iwaz Khalji, a lieutenant of Bakhtiyar Khalji, built a superb Masjid. The discovered inscription of the reign of Shams al-Din Yusuf Shah from the debris of Darasbari supports that a Jami Masjid was erected in 1479 A.D. Another inscription discovered from its debris of the time of Sultan Ala al-Din –Husain Shah, which records the constructions of Madrasah in 1502 A.D. It may be presumed that Shams al-Din Yusuf Shah started constructing a Jami Masjid and Madrasha building was finally completed in the reign of Ala al Din Husayn Shah in 1502 A.D. the inscription begins with the well-known hadith search after knowledge even if it be in china and states that the Madrasah was established for the teaching of the sciences of religion and for instruction in the principles which lead to certainly. It indicates it was a higher educational institution. The name

Darasbari [college compound Madrasah] itself testifies that there was a good arrangement for education. Dar al- Khyrat [the house of benevolence] was another Madrasah built at Triveni in Hoogly district of West Bengal. From the discovered inscription, it may be said that the Madrasah was founded by Qadi Nasir Muhammad in 1298 during the reign of Sultan Rukh ai-Din Kay-ka-us, which continued to flourish afterwards. It was rebuilt by Khan Jhahan Zafar Khan in 1313 A.D. during the reign of Shams al- din Firuz Shah. The Navagrama inscriptions support the idea of having an academy of learning together with a Masjid, a Madrasah in the Khittah Simlabad during the reign of Sultan the inscription that the Madrasah was founded by Ullugh Rahim Khan, the head of Khittah Simlabad. Another epigraph discovered in a little Masjids of Englishbazar police station in Malda district of the reign of Ala al Din Hussain Shah dated with 1502 A.D.

Besides Madrasah, another kind of learning centre grew up in different important places of Bengal, which was known as Majlis, Abu al- Fazl said, 'All civilized nation has schools for the education of their youth, but Hindustan is particularly famous for its seminaries.' The Majilises developed around distinguished individual scholars in response to the desire of inquisitive students for higher learning. The learning centre of Shaikh Jalaluddin Tabrizi at Deotala of Pandua was one of the earliest Majilises. The site of his academic centre acquired the designation of Tabrizabad after his name, Shaikh Tabrizi originally came from Tabriz of Persia and settled down at Deotala, most probably in the beginning of 13th century. Another important learning centre was founded at Sonargaon, near to Dhaka city by Shaikh Sharf al-Din Abu Tawama, who travelled from Bukhara to Delhi during the time of Sultan Ghiyath al- Din Balban and then to Bengal accompanying his pupil Sharf al- Din Yahya Maneri from Bihar in the early 80s of 13th century. Shaikh Abu Tawama was a highly learned personality who accomplished in accomplished in diverse branches of education including religious studies, Chemistry, Natural Science etc. He built up an academy at Sonargaon, which soon earned its fame as an excellent centre of higher education. Another seminar together with a hospital organized by Shaikh Ala-al-Haque at Pandua, an important trading and learning centre of medieval Bengal. Shaikh Ala-al-Haque devoted to the promotion of education and cultural pursuits there by establishing seminary, which was extensively supported with the boarding lodging and hospital facilities for the scholars and learners. Shaikh Taqi al-Din Arabi founded a Majilis at Mahisun, identified as Mahisantosh of present Rajshahi district most probably in the mid of 13th century. Yahya Maneri, the father of the renowned scholar Shaikh Sharaf al-Din Maneri is reported to have received education under Mawlana Taqi al-Din Arabi at Mahisun. Considering the importance of its geo-economic location, Sultan Rukn al- Din Barbak Shah established a mint there.

Another important academy was founded at Gangarampur, Dinajpur by Shaikh Ata in the early Sultanate period of Bengal. The centre received patronage and support from several Sultans, Sultan Sikandar Shah built a domed structure there in 1363A.D. Sultan Jalal al- Din Fath Shah reconstructed a stone building there in 1482A.D. Sultan Shams al- din Mazaffar Shah constructed a Masjid there, Sultan Ala al-Din Husain Shah constructed another Masjid in 1512 A.D. Another important learning centre of Husain Shahi period was founded by Shah Muazzam Danishmand known as Shah Daula at Bagha, Rajshahi, Sultan Nasir al-Din Nusrat Shah [1519-1531 A.D] erected a Jami Masjid there in 1523-1531A.D. and centering this Masjid, a learning centre was developed. From the accounts of Abdul Latif, it is known that Hawda Mian ran a learning centre in a mud-built house. Hawda Main is possibly a corrupt form of the original name of Hamid Danishmand son of Shan Muazzam Danishmand. Mughal emperor Shah Jahan made an endowment of 42 village to this centre during his time. William Adam in his report marked that 'that Madrasah at at Kushba, Bagha is an endowed institution of long-standing. Thus, the institution continued to flourish through generations. From the time of the Muslim conquest Satgaon developed into a seat of learning and intellectual life. These are references of the establishment of two madrasahs at Tribeni in Satgaon. These two madrasahs diffused Islamic learning and knowledge in the Satgaon region and contributed to the promotion of intellectual life of the Muslims of that area. Nagor in the Birbhum district was another intellectual centre in West Bengal. According to Riyas-al-Salatin, Sultan Ghiyath al- Din, Zaman Shah and the renowned saint Hadrat Nur Qutb 'Alam in their youth, had their education from Hamid al-Din Kunjnashin of Nagor. Mandaran [Bankura- Vishnupur] developed into a centre of Islamic learning from the time of Sultan Husain Shah, if not earlier. An inscription dated 1502 A. D. records the establishment of a madrasah at Mandaran at the order of Sultan Husain Shah. The inscription commemorating the foundation of the madrasahs been referred earlier. According to Firishta, Rangpur was a centre of Muslim learning from the time of Muslim conquest. 'He built a city in place of Nadia, with the name of Rangpur and made it his capital. No evidence of the construction of Madrasah in Chittagong has been discovered. Its importance as the biggest sea-port of Bengal suggests that it was a cultural centre from the time of Muslim settlement there. Chittagong was also a seat of great military and administrative significance.

It difficult to determine the content and course curricula of education in the institutions developed in Muslim Bengal due to the shortage of the shortage of information rather we can only sketch an outline. The Maktabs were the primary educational centres for the muslim children. The content of primary education included all the basic courses of Islamic studies and practices such as correct recitation of the Holy Quran, principles relating to ablution, five prayers [salat], fasting [Ramadhan], pilgrimage [hajj], zakat, basic teachings from the Holy Quran, Hadith and Fiqh. Along with these subjects, the elements of Arabic, Persian and Bangla languages, some basic education on diverse subjects such as arithmetic, history, mathematics, geography, etc, were also taught to the students in the Maktabs. As the Muslims children are instructed to start observing prayers at the age of seven, it is assumed that they had to start primary education at the age of five. Generally, Imams of Masjids were entitled with the responsibility of teaching the children in the Maktabs. After completing primary education in the Maktabs, the students would proceed to the Madrasah. Yazdan Bakhsh in 1503, writing Nam-i-Haq a work on Fiqh supposed to be written by Sharaf al-Din Abu Tawamah or by some of his disciples, support the idea of incorporating Hadith and Fiqh studies into the courses of study at higher levels. Learning Arabic as the language of the Holy Quran and Persian as the court language had been given importance in the courses of study even from the primary to higher level. They learnt Persian books Panjnama, Gulisthan, Amadnama, Bostan, Yusuf, -Zuleikha, Sikandarnama, Bahar Danish and Arabic books Mizan, Munshaib, Sarf Mir, Miat Amil, Sarh-i-Miat Amil, Sarh-i-Miat Ami and others. The chief aim was to attain such proficiency in the Persian language as might enable them to earn their livelihood. Analytical study of the Holy Quran Hadith Fiqh and Usul –al- Fiqh formed the principal courses of the advanced studies in the Majilises. Besides these diverse subjects such economics, geography, alchemy, geometry, history, and others were also taught in higher educational centers. Thought a later period, Abu al- Fazl statement supports the idea. He writes 'Every boy ought to read books on morals, arithmetic, agriculture, mensuration, geometry astronomy, anatomy, physiognomy, household matters, rules of governmental, medicine, logic, higher mathematics, science and history, all of which may gradually be acquired, work of Euclid on geometry, and of Ptolemy on astronomy in translation and those of Ibn –Sina Ans Ibn Rushd on medicine were used as textbooks. Intensive course on Arabic and Persian language and literature were also taught in these institutions for advanced learners. Observing the beautiful writing on the inscription slabs and transcribing books, we may assume that the penmanship was taught in the higher learning center. Courses were not required to study every subject. Academic activities were informal. The courses of studies and general policies were determined by their respective teachers and heads known as Mudir, Mudarris, Muallim, Ustadh, Shaikhs, Muhadddith, Mufassir, Faqih etc.

The important thing is that the mediaeval education was provided freely and it was free from all kinds of fees. There was no discrimination based on caste and creed in proving educational facility. Lodging boarding medical facilities together with educational materials including books papers and even cloths were also provided freely to the learners. Through there was no separate department of education in the state administration promotion of learning was considered an important duty of the state. The state generously used to assign the income of waqf –endowments, tax- free land, scholarships for the scholars, for the maintenance of educational institutions. Higher learning centres were, in all fairness, financed by the Muslim rulers of Bengal. The rulers, high officials, scholars, wealthy individuals enthusiastically used to contribute in the educational activities by private charity, endowments and other logistic supports.

In Bengal, several institutions were founded by Muslim rulers for the propagation of Islamic culture and learning. They also contributed munificently to the development of vernacular literature. It was under their fostering care that the Ramayana and the Mahabharata were rendered into Bengali verse. Just as the Hindu teachers confined their attention to subjects like theology, philosophy, literature and grammar, so also the Muslim teachers confined themselves to the Quran and Hadis its commentaries, traditions general literature, philosophy and the history of the Muslim world. However, as according to Jadunath Sarkar, towards the close of the medieval era, privately owned town colleges often, functioned without any endowment or permanent source of income and therefore lacked stability. Their life depended entirely upon the capacity of the individual teacher as had been the case with the indigenous Hindu institutions of Navadwip or Bhattapalli. The traditional system of education that had developed in medieval Bengal gradually started to decline with the fall of the Muslim rule in Bengal. On assuming power in Bengal, the pre modern period, continued the study of traditional oriental languages. They adopted Orientalism as an official policy partly out of expediency and caution and partly out of an emergent sense that an efficient administration rested on an understanding of 'Indian knowledge system' but the traditional education of Bengal soon lost grounds and was replaced by the colonial system of English education that was introduced by the middle of the 19th century.

References

1. Jaffar, S. A. *Education in Muslim India [1000-1800 A. C]*, Lahore, 1936, p-121
2. Sarkar, J. N. *History of Bengal,* Patna,1977, Vol-2, p-34

3. Nathan, Mirza. *Baharistan – i-Ghaibi*, vol-1, tr. MI Borah, Gauhati, 1963, p.51
4. Ali, A. K. M. Yaqub. *Education for Muslim under the Bengal Sultanate*, Islamic Studies, vol-24, pp-421-43
5. Tabatabai, Ghulam Hussain. *Siyar-al- Mutakhkhirin*, vol-2, 3, Calcutta, 1999
6. Fazl, Abul. *Ain-i- Akbari*, Tr, by Blockmann, Calcutta, 1878, p-279
7. Adam, William. *Report on Vernacular Education in Bengal and Bihar*, Calcutta, 1868, p-112
8. Basu, A. N. (ed.), *Adam Report on Education 1835-38*, Calcutta, 1941, p-227
9. Salim, Gulam Husain, *Riyas-us- Salatin*, trans, Abdus Salam, Calcutta, 1904, p-108
10. Siraj, Minhaj-I., *Tabaqat-I –Nasiri*, trans, H. G. Kaverty, Calcutta, 1941, p-277
11. Khan, Abid-i-Ali. "Memories of Gaur and Pandua" in H. Stapleton [ed], *Bengal Secretariat*, 1931, pp-157-58
12. Mazumder, R. C. *History of Medieval Bengal*, Calcutta, 1973, pp-229-30
13. Chakrabarti, Rachana. "Education in colonial Bengal" in *Encyclopedia of Women & Islamic Culture*, pp-35
14. Kaumuddin, Md., *Islamic Education and Libraries in Bengal Ch-4*, PhD-thesis, University of Calcutta, 1992, p-88
15. Bagchi, P. C., *Political Relation between- Bengal and Chaina in the Pathan Period*, vol-1, Calcutta, 1945, p-124
16. Ali, Mohar. *History of the Muslim Bengal*, V-1B, Islamic Foundation of Bangladesh, pp-654-56
17. Tarafdar, M. R., *Hussain Shahi Bengal a Socio-Political Study*, Dhaka, 1965, p-11
18. Ray, M. N., *The Historical Role of Islam*, 1981, p-34
19. Sen, Sukumar [ed.], *Viprada's Manasa- Vijaya*, The Asiatic Society, Calcutta, 1953, p-18
20. Quraishi, Mansooruddin A., *Muslim Education and Learning in Gujarat*, 1972, p-131
21. Rahaman, A. R., *Social and Cultural History of Bengal*, Pakistan, pp-234-245

Three Distinguished Women of British Indian: Kadambini Ganguli, Sarala Devi Chowdhury & Matangini Hazra

Namrata Dutta

The status of women in Indian society has changed drastically over the last few decades. In today's society, women are becoming increasingly aware of self-empowerment. Fuelled by that power, they can realize their wishes, and dreams, to protest against various injustices starting from the right to education, right to expression of opinion, right to vote, labour right, equal pay, reproductive right, right to divorce, and right to property. There has been a gathering storm of feminism or the feminist movement. However, the picture of women's position in the social sphere during the British era was completely different. They used to spend their days as someone's daughter, someone's consort, someone's mother, silently digesting curses and abuses hurled at them, being imprisoned in the four walls of the house, fasting daily for the well-being of their husband and children, and worshipping different types of gods and goddesses. In short, women's lives were devoted to religion and the betterment of the household. They had no right to live for themselves, no right to see and understand the outside world with their own eyes. Also, their right to education was taken away under the guise of religious restrictions. Three daughters of Bengal - Kadambini Ganguly (Bose), Sarla Devi Choudhurani, and Matangini Hazra brought a breath of fresh air to this hectic life of women. They set an example that if there is love and devotion towards one's work, one can crush all the hurdles and reach one's desired goal, and at the same time, it is possible to create a favourable environment for those around them who are struggling with the adversities of time.

I should start my writing with an observation that clearly depict the picture of colonial Bengal. As we all know that the social evil practices were everywhere, but can you believe that the three was discriminatory practice in the case of treatment of illness. During that time, besides the Kaviraj (Ayurvedic practitioner) treatment the western medicine was also introduced. Although it gradually spread among the Babu community of the country, it remained confined to men only and not to women. Because at that time, wives and daughters who were suffering from illness, were only allowed to drink blessed water, holy water and herbal medicine prescribed by the kaviraj. They were not allowed to be seen or touched by either Kaviraj or European doctors who were, after all, males from outside of the family.[1] In rare situations, when doctors came to see critically ill patients, women patients were placed behind thick enclosures surrounded by female servants to help the doctor diagnose. During this phase few women of Bengal emerged as the saviour of womenfolk of India.

Kadambini Basu (born on 18th July 1861) was the daughter of Braja Kishore Basu, headmaster of Bhagalpur school and a Brahma reformer, made a milestone in the life of Indian women by ignoring all the rules of society and learning education and entering the professional world of her choice.[2] Their original home was in Chandshi, Barisal, Bangladesh.[3] Professor Brajkishore Basu of Baharampur Krishnanath College strongly encouraged daughter Kadambini to pursue higher education from early childhood. At that time, Bamabodhini magazine edited by Umesh Chandra Dutt published the class-3 student Kadambini's essay 'Coconut Tree' as the best essay.[4] About her writings, Umesh Chandra Dutt said that girls usually write essays related to virtues and God. But in this case, the girl who can write such an experiential work using the intelligent presence of mind, her education and writing skills have to be admired.[5] Indeed, going beyond the familiar territory of the conservative society is not only admirable but a matter of courage. Kadambini later became one of the best students of the Banga Mahila Vidyalaya, started in April 1876 by the liberal progressive Dwarkanath Gangopadhyay. In 1877, Kadambini stood first in the Suburban Student Scholarship Examination at the age of 14. She was the first Indian woman to sit alone at the entrance of Calcutta University and passed with honours with good marks. As a reward, she received a junior scholarship of Rs 15 from the junior Lord and books worth Rs 50 from the government. Meanwhile, Bethune School Committee President Justice Richard Garth said, 'You have already been honoured by the commendations of the lieutenant Governor of Bengal and by the more substantial reward which he has conferred on you and I hope and believe present which you are asked to accept at my hands from a gentleman of high rank and positions of Dacca, is only on additional proof of your career and as showing how much native gentlemen, although they may not yourself, appreciate and good sense and determined energy which have induced you to continue to improve your mind and to prosecute your studies so much longer and more successfully that then the generality.'[6]

It may seem that as the daughter of a liberal father and born in a progressive family, Kadambini did not have to face even the nominal barriers of conservative society in her transition from education to work life. But this pleasant idea is completely false. Keshav Chandra Sen was sternly against even a girl's desire to study, dream, and ambition and made fun of the manner of speaking, mannerisms, food habits, and clothes worn by educated women. The matter is clarified by Satyendranath Tagore's letter to his wife Gyanadanandini where he wrote,

'Bengali women wear such clothes that it is as good as not wearing them.'[7] In response to this, Brahmamohini Devi, wife of Durgamohan Das, and Rukmini, wife of Gurucharan Mahalavish, wove together a new type of dress for girls with a mix of local and foreign - and put a cloth over the gowns of British women. However, the conservative Bengali society termed this dress as non-Hindu and it was published on December 12, 1880, in the pages of Nababibhakar newspaper.[8] Next, there was a huge commotion about girls appearing in the entrance examination. Meanwhile, Kadambini after passing the Entrance exam, started fighting for the right of girls to study medicine and finally, she won. Madras Medical College was the first to open doors for girls to study medicine.[9] Now she decided to study B.A. and got admitted to Bethune School. Kadambini Bose, who passed with honours in 1883, became the first female graduate of British India. That year she tied the knot with Dwarkanath Ganguly and became Kadambini Ganguly.[10] Pandit Ramkumar Vidyaratna officiated at the wedding which was solemnized under Act III of 1872. But many friends of Dwarkanath Ganguly like Shivnath Shastri Anandamohan Bose, and Umesh Chandra Dutta were absent at the wedding possibly because the age difference between the bride and groom was much and the bride and groom were Kayastha and Brahmin respectively.[11] Therefore, many heads of society could not accept this disparate marriage. Amar Dutta said, "Dwarkanath's friends could not approve of his marriage with 20-21-year-old young women at a relatively advanced age."[12] Many again thought that after marriage Dwaraka would abandon his wife's education. However, even after the marriage, with the full support and encouragement of her husband, Dwarkanath Ganguly, Kadambini continued her studies and other activities.[13] In 1875 AD Kadambini got Dwarkanath on her side when she started agitation for admission of women to Madras Medical College.[14] He gave a new impetus to the movement - why only Madras? Girls should be taught medicine at Calcutta Medical College too. It was said in Brahmo public opinion, '...if there be any one another, the want of lady doctors is most keenly felt, it is no doubt, India. The system of Zenana seclusion makes it nearly impossible for male doctors to be very useful in treating female patients, consequently, a very large number of our women came to premature death from want of proper medical attendance. We know of instances, where, with the utmost difficulty female patients could be induced to allow the doctor to feel their pulse only. Besides, their disease is peculiar to them, and it is simply impossible for male doctors to diagnose or treat them. The establishment of medical institutions for the tuition of lady students is a necessity these days in India.'[15] From Prabhat Chandra's writings, it is known that in 1882 AD, if she wanted to study medicine after passing the BA examination, she could get admitted to the medical college without paying fees. The rule was that anyone (any person) who passed the B.A. examination could join the medical college free of charge.[16] This 'anyone' refers to both men and women, as the rules were unchanged even when a woman graduated, the authorities were forced to allow her to be admitted. Meanwhile, the male teachers felt discomfort while explaining the body parts in the anatomy class and the male students started making various vulgar remarks. Pushing away all the obstacles, Kadambini Received the title of 'Graduate of Bengal Medical College (GBMC)' and got an opportunity to study midwifery and surgery.

Now the real fight begins. At this time, the mothers and sisters of rural Bengal, to protect their chastity without seeking treatment from foreigners, to get rid of all the diseases, relied on folk deities like Ateshwar, Jwarasur, Rajvallabhi, Hari Jhi, Basanta Ray, Olabibi, etc.[17] They also relied on blessed water, talisman, charms or fasting for one night. In short, the women especially in rural Bengal were left to luck if ever they got sick. Kadambini devoted herself to their service and found her husband by her side. She started treating children and poor women free of cost. But those for whose service she had fought so hard turned their backs on her. As an example of this, according to his assistant Ngendidi, Kadambini saved the life of a dying woman from a rich family while giving birth. But after taking a bath, she saw that they had arranged their dinner with the servants, and they even had to clean their own dishes. She attended an exhibition organized by the American government in Chicago with hand-made gifts and artworks made by women. By this, she presented the sense of taste and beauty of Indian women to the whole world. Not only that, she was also associated with the Indian National Movement. She was one of the 6 women delegates at the Congress session in Bombay in 1889.[18] Kadambini was also one of the initiators of the women's conference organized by the Maharani of Baroda during the Swadeshi movement. Collected a lot of money for the benefit of Gandhiji. Along with poet Kamini Roy, he monitored the conditions of women and children of coal miners in the Bihar and Orissa regions. It is often said that 'girls are the enemy of girls'. Many women of 19th century Bengal have put into practice the conventional saying - educated girls became widows, the hands of Mlechas fell on the body, did chastity-caste-religion go away, etc. with many real examples. But Kadambini came as a blessing in the lives of helpless women by overcoming all social barriers. On the one hand, the people of India were fighting fiercely to free India from the British in a political struggle, on the other hand, Kadambini fought against the roots of superstition in the Indian society to free women.

Another woman of this decade is Sarala Devi Chaudhurani, daughter of Swarna Kumari Devi and Janakinath Ghosal. Both her parents were patriots, her mother engaged in political activities of Congress and her father was a devoted Congress worker. She had another identity; she was the niece of Rabindranath Tagore. Sarala Devi was a poet, writer and political figure. She passed entrance in 1886 at the age of thirteen and in 1890, at the age of 17, she passed the English Honors BA examination.[19] Her contributions are: despite being a daughter of a conservative society, she arranged physical exercise and training for with the help of wrestlers and body builders, for building a strong foundation of physical strength in Bengalis. In imitation of 'Shivaji festival' she started 'Pratapaditya festival' in 1930. Bipin Chandra writes in his 'Young India' that as necessity is the mother of invention, Sarala Devi is the mother of Pratapaditya to meet the necessity of a hero for Bengal.[20] Then she observed the festival of Udyaditya, the son of Pratyapaditya. In 1904 she started 'Beerashtami Vrata' whose purpose was to make the boys of Bengal physically and mentally strong.[21] She also established Lakshmir Bhandar and Swadeshi Stores to promote selling of indigenous goods. For this 'Lakshmir Bhandar' she collected indigenous products for girls from different districts of Bengal. Again, Sarala Devi and Yogesh Chandra Chowdhury opened 'Swadeshi Stores' together.[22] Not only that, she used to dress herself in full swadeshi clothes when she attended any function.

For her revolutionary mindset, she became known as the Fire Maiden of the Fire Age. She was a prominent intellectual in the first half of the nineteenth century. In 1910, she founded the first women's organization in Allahabad whose name was Bharat Stri Mahamandal. From her 'Jeerna Jharapata', we come to know about the interior of the Thakurbari, her thoughts on Swadeshi, British oppression on tea garden coolies and on indigo farmers, women's education, the work of Brahmo Samaj, etc. Besides, she highlighted women's power in a different perspective through Bharati magazine. Sarla Devi showed that to defeat the enemy and the British power, there can be no argument that one must always embark on the field, take up arms or participate in the war against subjugation -irrespective on gender. She showed that there is no word 'impossible' in the world, if one has willpower and self-confidence, no obstacle can stand in way. She set a unique precedent by participating in breaking the chains of subjugation in India through various constructive programs without taking up arms or being imprisoned.

A woman's life is limited to ups and downs. According to Romila Thapar, in ancient Indian society, women were sometimes respected and sometimes tortured.[23] Even during the colonial period, this image of women's life was not altered much. Rather, this difference is widely visible at this time. Although everyone jumped to liberate the country, no one, even in Congress, was bothered to solve the women's problem. Although it is seen that Indian nationalists have compared the country with 'mother'. Gradually Indian nationalists for their own political interests started connecting the house girls - brides who had been inside the house to the outside world. As a result, they were able to devote themselves to the work of liberating the country along with men. One example of this is Matangini Hazra, a brave Indian girl during British rule. Matangini, the daughter of Thakurdas Maiti and Bhagwati Devi, was born into an ordinary poor peasant family and could not get the so-called education.[24] She was married to Trilochan Hazra in her childhood, but Trilochan died childless when she was only 18 years old. But this is where her life as an average woman does not end, but begins here. Matangini, who was heavily influenced by the saints of Tamluk, who did not eat without worshipping, was arrested by the police during the Civil Disobedience Movement of 1932 for preparing salt at the

Alinan Salt Centre.[25] She again joined movement against the chowkidari tax of Tamluk police station and was imprisoned in Baharampur Jail. She had immense faith in Gandhiji.[26] Like Gandhiji, she also did not hesitate to serve the distressed and helpless for which she is popularly known as 'Gandhiburi'. In 1933 she attended the sub-district congress conference at Srirampur. She used to make her own khadi. When she was about 72, the Congress leadership planned to capture various police stations and other government offices in the Medinipur district. For this purpose, she started the journey with about 6000 Congress supporters and volunteers to fulfil the goal. As they neared the city, the Crown Police broke up their marching bands under Section 144 of the Indian Penal Code. Meanwhile, Matangini was shot by police firing. Along with Matangini, others who were killed that day were Lakshminarayan Das, Purimadhava Pramanik, Nagendranath Samant, Jiban Chandra Bera and others. We must acknowledge that irrespective of the religion and gender, when older persons spend their days waiting for death and remembering the names of God, old Matangini truly served her God by devoting her life to the service of the nation. It can also be said that although she was a political leader, she was not a social thinker at all. Behind his politics was the idea of economic freedom on the one hand and the dream of building an independent India through social development.

However, these three women set a unique precedent by their actions in India as well as in Bengal during the British period. Each of these three gave importance to their will, to the awakening of their minds, by pointing a thumb in the face of the conservative society. They set an ideal example for all the women of Bengal. Not only in contemporary but also in modern times, they give a message to every modern woman that there will be many obstacles in the way of life on the way to achieving the goal. But do not be afraid of it and fall back. Many years ago today, the British power left the country, and the 'Amrit Mahotsav' freedom is celebrated. Starting from the scientific platform, various voluntary organizations and private initiatives are continuing their work to destroy the remnants of superstition in the minds of the countrymen. Women today are determined to become independent not only educationally but also financially. Financial independence means freeing yourself. This freedom does not mean arbitrariness, it does not mean tyranny. To be free means to protect oneself from every moment of humiliation, and to fulfil one's smallest desires. Being free doesn't mean living as a parasite by being someone's glutton. To be free means to transform every moment of the day into silent laughter, a constant stream of silent cries, and unspoken screams. Women often have to face various obstacles in the path of financial independence and liberation from the pre-primary condition. But instead of crushing yourself, you have to defeat all the obstacles, overcome the fear and smile victoriously. You have to reach your goal. These three women of British India teach today's women through their actions that if we can cross all barriers to reach our goals, why can't we? We are there to empower your mind, we have examples of work. Just resolve to make your dreams come true, dreams will come true. This is where Kadambini Basu Ganguly, Sarala Devi Choudhurani, Matangini Hazra became Ananya.

References

1. Samant, Arvind. *The State of the Patient, Nineteenth Century Bengal*, Progressive Publishers, Kolkata, June 2004, p-27
2. *Bangla Ajatak*, 18th July, 2021
3. Ibid.
4. Biswas, Soma. *Four women doctors who pioneered the practice of medicine in Bangladesh in the 19th century,* KP Bagchi & Company, Kolkata, First Edition-2015, p-75
5. Ibid. p-75
6. Ibid. pp. 77-78

7. Ibid. p-78
8. Ibid. p-78
9. *Bangla Ajatak,* Op. cit.
10. Sen, Ishita. *Dwarkanath Ganguly, Kadambini Ganguly and Samakal*, 20 April 2021
11. Ibid.
12. Ibid.
13. Samant, Arvind. Op. cit., pp-24-26
14. Bangla Ajatak, Op. cit.
15. Biswas, Soma. Op. cit., p-78
16. Ibid. p. 87
17. Ibid. p. 45
18. *Bangla Ajatak,* Op. cit.
19. Dasgupta, Kamala. *Women of Bengal in the Freedom Struggle*, Radical Impressions, Kolkata, 2015, p-52
20. Ibid. p-53
21. Sen, Shuchibrata & Sen, Amiya. *Modern India, 1885-1964: Political Economic Social and Cultural History,* Mitram, Kolkata, 2008 p-336
22. Dasgupta, Kamala. Op. cit., p-54
23. Sen, Shuchibrata & Sen, Amiya., Op. cit., p-327
24. Ibid., p-335
25. Dasgupta, Kamala. Op. cit., p.207
26. Ibid., p-208

Limitation of Women's Participation in Indian Politics: A Political Survey

Priya Dutta

In the progress of any country men and women equally play important roles. About half of India's total population (as per the 2011 census - 6,89,608,045 women out of 1,416,459,205) are women. If this half of the population is backward, the overall progress of the country is not possible. One of the way this progress is politics. The term participation in politics has a wider meaning and is not limited to voting but also a political consciousness. It involves political activism and decision-making. In the post-independence era, the Indian constitution has spoken about gender equality between men and women. Women's participation in politics is very important in this gender equality of men and women. So that they can play an important role in making decisions and implementing various programs as public representatives. Draupadi Murmu is a woman President of our country. Once Chief Minister Mayawati of Uttar Pradesh, Jayalalitha of the South, now Mamata Banerjee in West Bengal have demonstrated activism, sharp intelligence, and organizational prowess in political work.[1] Currently Supriya Sule (Representative - Nationalist Congress Party) is campaigning for the education of young girls and against female foeticide. Besides, Bobby Kinnar or Bobby Daling (Representative of Aam Aadmi Party), Chandrani Murmu (Representative of Biju Janata Dal), Anupriya Patil (Representative - Apana Dal Party), Shashi Panja (Representative - Trinamool Congress), Mahua Maitra (Representative - Trinamool Congress), Veena George (Representative - Communist Party of India) etc. have taken exemplary steps in the field of women and child welfare, public health etc. But this is not the full picture of women's empowerment or women's participation in the political sphere. Generally, even today women from lower class and ordinary families are far away from the political arena. The participation of women in various elections in Parliament and State Assemblies is relatively less than that of men. In this case, the constitution says to give adequate representation to women (33%), but in reality, women get fewer opportunities.[2] The survey found that in most cases the families of women who got tickets are clan politicians. Besides aggressive threats, an expensive electoral system, patriarchy, and conventional attitudes make it less likely for women to win elections.[3] Women's work is housework and child-rearing, not politics, etc. are responsible for keeping women behind in politics. This article discusses the various reasons behind women's under-representation in parliament and politics.

The preamble of the Indian Constitution mentions gender equality between men and women. One of the steps in this gender equality is the participation of women in politics and taking an active role in decision-making and implementation of various programs as public representatives in parliament.[4] The main objective of this research article is to discuss how women started actively participating in politics and the various obstacles and limitations faced by women in politics. There is no instance of political expression of women's power in ancient or medieval India without a mass revolution. Examples of women's political participation can be found in some uprisings during the British period, including the Santal Rebellion. But these women belonged to tribal communities who already enjoyed many freedoms.[5] In fact, direct and widespread participation of women in Indian politics began during the Non-Cooperation Movement (1920-1922) under the leadership of Mahatma Gandhi. Against the backdrop of the Indian National

Movement between 1920 and 1940, the first political awakening of women, irrespective of caste, creed, caste, and caste, took place under the leadership of Gandhiji. Inspired by Gandhiji's ideology and ideals of non-violence, many women from middle-class and lower-class families joined the non-cooperation and satyagraha movements.[6]

Gandhiji believed that - "Woman is the companion of man gifted with equal mental capacities. She has the right to participate in the minutest details of the activities of men and she has the right of freedom and liberty as he...".[7] All over the country, women have abandoned their veiled lives in droves to attend meetings, marches and picket shops selling foreign goods and liquor. Many high-class women actively participated in the call to boycott foreign clothes. In the 1930s, ordinary women from middle-class, peasant families also spontaneously joined civil disobedience movements. Besides, in the Quit India movement, many women sacrificed their lives, youth, wealth, dignity and everything for the freedom of the country. All these heroic women were shot dead by the police and jailed with a smile. Dalit Shantabai Valerao and Tarabai Kamble were among these women. These women not only participated in politics but also played an important role in sheltering the revolutionary men in their homes, providing them with food and clothing, gathering information about the enemy by being spies, hiding weapons and explosives and smuggling them to other places.[8] At times many women had to break family ties to shelter revolutionary men. For example, in August 1915, widow Nanibala Mukherjee was forced to sever her family ties by sheltering her distant relative Amarnath Chatterjee and his three friends following a police raid on a working-class cooperative organization in Calcutta.[9] So it can be said that from the Partition of Bengal movement (1905-1911) to the subsequent non-cooperation movement (1920-22) and the revolutionary movement of the 1930s, women had an important contribution. But these women came from educated middle-class families of the society, upper class and women from poor peasant families associated with blue-collar jobs did not join this struggle.

These were the stories of women's participation in various political activities before independence. In the post-independence period, it was the collective efforts of women led by the WIA (Women's Indian Association founded in Madras in 1917 under the presidency of Dorothy Jinarasa) that Indian women got one of their rights under the Rule of India Act of 1919, which came into effect in 1921.[10] But this franchise was very limited. According to the principle of "No taxation without representation" both men and women were given the right to vote based on property.[11] In the 1930s, members of the three women's organizations continued their struggle for the extension of women's suffrage and their representation in the legislature. The Simon Commission in 1927 outlined three conditions for the extension of the franchise. Namely- a) Women should be at least 25 years old. b) Must be educated and c) She should be entitled to the husband's (living or dead) property. Finally, in 1950, women were given the right to vote as part of universal suffrage in India. It is included in Article 326 of the Constitution.[12] One of the notable women politicians of today who have set a significant precedent in politics in 2022 is Supriya Sule, a member of the Nationalist Congress Party who has been elected to the Lok Sabha for the third time. Sule protested against the education of young women and female foeticide. The Nationalist Youth Congress wing she created in 2012 gives young women a platform in politics. In addition, in several gatherings organized, he shed light on the abortion of female foetuses, the end of the dowry system and the empowerment of women.[13] Bobby Kinnar has created history by becoming the first transgender woman member of the

Municipal Corporation of Delhi (MCD). Bobby is currently a member of the Aam Aadmi Party and is particularly known for his contributions to children, women, and disabled people.[14]

Shashi Panja, currently serving as the Cabinet Minister of Women and Child Development and Social Welfare Department of West Bengal, is a physician, politician and representative of the Trinamool Congress. In 2010 he was elected councilor of Kolkata Municipal Corporation. She has made important contributions to various programs related to women's and children's welfare. Anupriya Patel is a representative of the active Apna Dal Party in Uttar Pradesh who is currently serving as the Minister of State for Commerce and Industry of India. Currently, she is actively working for women empowerment as a member of various committees of parliament for women empowerment and the welfare of other backward classes. A member of the Communist Party of India, Veena started her career as a journalist. Currently, she is serving as Minister of Health and Family Welfare.[15] She first contested the 2016 assembly elections. She retained his seat as a cabinet minister from 2016 to 2021 with a margin of 19,003 votes. Mahua Maitra was elected from the Karimpur constituency in the 2016 assembly election. She initially joined the Yuva Bharata Congress but later joined the Trinamool Congress. Mahua is now a member of the Seventeenth Lok Sabha and represents Krishnanagar in West Bengal. Besides, he is associated with many welfares works.[16]

Although the mentioned women come from all backgrounds and levels of society, this is not a complete picture of women's participation in politics. Overall, many women from lower-class and ordinary families are far away from the arena of politics. The participation of women in various elections of Panchayat, Parliament and State Assembly is much less than that of men. In this regard, after solving many problems, the constitution finally recognized the reservation of 33% seats for women (the 73rd and 74th constitutional amendments in 1994 established reservation of 33% seats for women in local governments.)[17] Women do not participate in politics for various reasons. And sometimes even if they want to, they don't get all the opportunities to participate. According to the election records, it is proved that although the constitution says to reserve 33 per cent of seats for women, in reality very few tickets are given to women representatives. And most of the women who are given tickets have families of dynastic politicians.[18] As a result, girls from ordinary families have to work hard to get election tickets. Besides, many political parties still believe that disconnection is one of the main problems in women's participation in politics. That is, most of the women are confined to the house and are not known to the outside world and people. As a result, the chances of women winning elections are very low. Considering this, they are not given election tickets.

The parliamentary election system is expensive. Even today many women are not financially independent. In this case, many of them are dependent on the family. The lack of funds for these expensive elections, in this case, the lack of funding from the party, deters many women from participating in politics. Besides, even today women politicians are victims of insults, ugly comments, and aggressive threats, so they keep themselves away from the arena of politics. Even in recent times, very few women are found as full ministers or ministers of state. In the previous 'National Democratic Alliance' government, out of 30 full ministers, only 3 were women.[19] Even in recent times very few women are found as full ministers or ministers of state. In the previous 'National Democratic Alliance' government, out of 30 full ministers, only 3 were women.[20] One of the reasons for the minority of women in key ministerial posts is attributed to patriarchal mentality. One of the expressions of this prevailing patriarchy is that women's main work is cooking and husband and child-rearing. Even in recent times, very few women are found as full ministers or ministers of state. In the previous 'National Democratic Alliance' government, out of 30 full ministers, only 3 were women.[21] One of the reasons for the minority of women in key ministerial posts is attributed to patriarchal mentality. One of the expressions of this prevailing patriarchy is that women's main work is cooking and husband and child-rearing.

Besides, many women are engaged in housekeeping as well as jobs, in this situation active participation in politics becomes an additional burden for them. Global studies have shown that the patriarchal mentality keeps women confined to the home, and in many families, family relatives including husbands and children support women's political participation, but despite this support, many women politicians feel guilty for not giving enough time to their families, especially children.[22] Education plays an important role among women in the question of political representation. Literacy is not only limited to contesting elections; it also extends to voting.[23] It is generally seen that states with low literacy rates of women also have low representation of women. Public perception of politics acts as a barrier to women's participation in politics. In many societies, women view politics as 'dirty'.[24] They see it as a male domain and view the political arena as full of dishonesty, bribery and corruption. Which is dirty and ugly in terms of female participation. Many women use this as an excuse not to join politics, an attitude that discourages women and makes it difficult for them to enter male-dominated political institutions.

Strong confidence is required to participate in any task and complete it successfully. Participation in politics, public exposure and intense scrutiny require confident action. Being involved in politics requires self-confidence, competence, courage to face various oppositions and the ability to take risks and challenges. Lack of trust is one of the reasons for women's limited participation in politics. Although women have the potential to lead, fear and inferiority sometimes keep them away from participating in politics. In today's era, social media plays an important role in creating public opinion or changing public opinion. The way social media identifies women politicians has important implications for their participation in politics.[25] Many times, people attack women politicians without verifying the truth of ugly pictures, videos or negative comments circulated in the media. As a result, women often distance themselves from politics and mass media.

In addition to all these factors, religion often hinders women's participation in politics.[26] Although there is no such restriction on women's participation in the Muslim scriptures (Quran), in reality, the picture is very different.[27] Even today, women from many conservative families, despite their strong interest, actively participate in the capital for family reasons. can't Also, many religious leaders do not accept women's participation in politics well. In the 20th century, women have been able to gain political, economic and social rights to a greater extent. But overall, it can be understood that even today women are constantly struggling to get their rights in all spheres of life including politics. The country is still governed by a patriarchal mindset regarding the role of women. As a result, they consider it their responsibility to keep women confined to the home instead of bringing them into the larger social sphere. In this case, political parties have to play a more active role for women to participate in politics. Male party members can also provide financial support to women candidates for proper political education, encouragement of participation, cooperation and election process. Apart from the protection of women candidates, specific reservations can also be introduced in the team. Above all, by changing the aggressive nature of politics and making it suitable for women (Hindu, Muslim or other communities) to enter, active and free entry of women members along with men in Indian politics and decision-making on important political issues will be possible. Besides, if women actively participate in politics, various problems of abused and neglected women in society can be solved quickly.

References

1. Banerjee, Kalyani, *Where Women Stand Today*, Granthmitra, Kolkata, 2012
2. Khanna, Manuka. "Political Participation of Women in India," *The Indian Journal of Political Science*, vol. 70, no. 1, 2009, pp. 55–64
3. Praveen, Rai, "Electoral Participation of Women in India: Key Determinants and Barriers", *Economic and Political Weekly*, XVLI (3), January 2011, pp. 47–55
4. Government of India, "The Constitution of India", Ministry of Law and Justice, 22 March 2014
5. Banerjee, Kalyani. *Politics and Feminism*, Progressive Publishers, Kolkata, 2009, p. 24
6. Ibid., p.25
7. Kishwar, Madhu. "Gandhi on Women," *Economic and Political Weekly*, vol. 20, no. 40, 1985, pp. 1691–702.
8. Mondal, Susanta. "Quit India Movement: Rethinking the Role of Women", *History Research Journal*, Vol-5-Issue-4-July-August-2019, pp.1561-1569
9. Banerjee, Kalyani, 2009, Op. cit., p.32
10. Ibid., p.54
11. Ibid., p.58
12. Ibid., p. 61
13. Tuwani, Vedika, "Women Politicians," *Who Made the News* (On Line), 2022, Dec, 2022
14. Ibid.
15. See the site of Ministry of Women & Child Development, https://wcd.nic.in ›

16. Barman, Sourav Roy, Mathew, L., "Mic Testing: Mahua Moitra, the Trinamool MP who pulls no punches", *The Indian Express,* Kolkata, Up dated by February 8, 2023 Thursday, Nov 09, 2023
17. United Nations Development Programme. "Gender Inequality Index". Human Development Indices: A statistical update 2012, March 2014; 17th Lok Sabha to see more women power", *Daily Pioneer*, 25 May 2019.
18. Ibid.
19. Banerjee, Kalyani, 2009, Op. cit., p. 163
20. Ibid. p. 175
21. Ibid.,
22. Ara, Fardaus, "Barriers to the Political Participation of Women: A Global Perspective", *Society & Change*, vol. XIII, No.4, October-December 2019, pp. 8
23. Chaurasia, Kritanjali, "The Link Between Education and Participation of Women in Politics", *Observer Research Foundation*, January 29, 2022
24. Ara, Fardaus, Op. cit.
25. Ibid.
26. Ibid.
27. Haleem, M. A. S. Abdel. *The Qur'an*, Oxford University Press, New York, 2008; Ibn Kathir. "Tafsir Ibn Kathir (English): Surah Al Nisa", *Quran for you.* Tafsir, December, 2019.

Feminism and Intersectionality in India: Challenges and Opportunities

Rajarshi Maity

It has become a staple of feminist activism to ensure that diverse, converging persecutory systems are used to shape women's lives. Antiracist movements are where this understanding that persecution is most definitely not a particular cycle or linked political connection but is instead best seen as constituted of various, unifying, or united frameworks begins. Women's rights activists examine the claim that women's oppression may be discovered by looking solely at their orientation. The lengthy and painful heritage of its rejections is perhaps "the most pressing challenge confronting contemporary feminism," and intersectionality is offered as a speculative and political answer. The "primary commitment that ladies' examinations have made to date" has been praised as the intersectionality theory[1].

Women's activist artistic analysis has existed for around 200 years at this point. This academic analysis is made in light of the perception of women's circumstances in the long run and accomplishment of their unique and helpful activity without assistance from anyone else. Feminism serves as the foundation for scholarly research of women's activist movements. Two waves of feminism have come and gone. In the Primary Wave, women had successfully fought for their social liberties, the opportunity to pursue higher education, and the ability to obtain positions in the relevant business sectors. The fact that this wave served as a prelude to later women's activists' more profound and unpretentious social activism was more significant. The Second Wave, also known as the Ladies' Freedom Movement, focused on the differences between men and women and investigated the origins and current practices of orientation segregation in belief systems, culture, and society. The early development of the women's activist academic analysis aimed to look for an opportunity and manner to deal with the change component of writing between individual and political, which can be inferred from the women's activists' philosophy[2].

Every nation has its own unique combination of ingenuity, creativity, and aesthetic sensibility. Countries' social standards and manner of life can be seen through the viewpoint of a women's activist is perhaps the most active theory used today to interpret any piece of writing. The idea of inequality is used to organize the world by man-centered civilization. Influential people control the weak, the wealthy rule over the less wealthy, and men exercise dominance over women. Globally, the great bulk of societal structures are centered on men. Women have historically been suppressed, persecuted, and treated like consumer objects in societies dominated by men. During the nineteenth and twentieth century's, notable sociopolitical and cultural advancements helped to increase female awareness[3]. Throughout their various books, authors have tried to present a fair representation of social and familial patterns seen throughout the world. Recent abstract art depicts women defying their traditional place as optional members of society and families. These and the earlier works need to be analyzed from the perspectives of feminist activists using various feminism-related theories and speculations. Humans differ in terms of their organic, mental, and social makeup. In particular, there are depictions of male and female that includes sexual allusions, as well as manly and ladylike allusions to orientation. Men are more grounded than women; women experience periods, pregnancy, and labour; men do not. Male and female are something normal, naturally separate. The ladylike and manly socially resolved human brain study, however, isn't thought of "as" male or female but rather "be" people. The neighborhood has been aware of the sex-related accusations for a long time.

Whereas women are perceived as gentle, devoted, and giving animals, men are seen as dominant figures. Language that has specific nouns that seem to be reserved for men only, such as the landowner's expression, but no property manager, executive, or director, demonstrates social disparities. Moreover, you can use the greeting "ace" while greeting married or single guys[4]. Versus the labels "miss" or "courtesan" given to numerous women due to their reliance on men. Routine occurrence is frequently accused for making women feel like peons. Women are frequently seen as weak and dependent on masculine strength. According to Dagun, there is no investigation that demonstrates a connection between organic circumstances and differences in behaviour. Alternatively, it is often discovered that some social traits do not completely determine behaviour[5]. A tool for women to fight for their rights and achieve parity with men in the political, social, and economic spheres is the women's activist hypothesis. Scholarly feminism is a scholarly report using a women's activist hypothesis approach when it comes to academic investigation. Scientists should read as women or read as women while conducting research using this methodology, and there is growing awareness that differences in sexual orientation will affect the scholarly importance of certain findings. The preceding will look at the women's activist theory and the main area of the study of feminism in academic writing.

This section oversees the writing review of the continuing study that addresses feminism as a scholarly hypothesis and it focuses on earlier investigations related to writing orientation[6]. The important theories and scholars are also taken into consideration in this section. The review also considers how sex and orientation have changed in terms of the society that determines what a woman does for a living. They freedom is a crucial topic that was included by many authors and academics in their novels who intended to depict the challenging conditions of women. When that happens, their role changes from being accommodating to playing involved characters.

A prominent hypothesis in Western modern research is feminism. In the 20th century, as it developed, it challenged basic assumptions. A few feminism-related patterns have addressed a variety of themes, including women's standing in families and society, female awareness, how males treat women, and how they are mistreated. Academic history makes references to shifts in a woman's place and status[7]. The limited status of women and their dominance by men have not been uncommon changes in social progression and improvement.

Ordinarily, women are born free, but several widely accepted human traditions bound them. In the sphere of ladies, these chains are evident. Up to the 20th century, male journalists made up a major portion of the English writing, and female characters were depicted from a male perspective. Female researchers and journalists who used pseudonyms, with the exception of men like the Brontë sisters, George Eliot, and others, were few in number. Virginia Wolf found a solution to the problem of male dominance of women immediately after the 20th century:" Female essayists and critics of the 20th century created the model for women's activism composition and writing. Before the 1960s, men would often resolve disputes with women. Because of the women's testimonies, recognition was attained, and they were passionate about resolving the feminist challenges[8]. Despite the fact that women's difficulties have not been addressed, they share men's reality in the same way that they reserve the right to vote.

Several females made valiant attempts to continue reaching the goals that were unmet.

As soon as the new invention was successful, ladies invited the new world. In Canada and the States, the extent of the problems they had to deal with had shifted, and new associations and performances had entered the picture. By advocating equality and parity between women and men, these organizations accepted the defense of women's status in their community. The extraordinary influence of well-known women's rights activists like Germaine Greer, Kate Millet, and others led to resistance against the maltreatment and exploitation of women by men. Women's activist tactics are seen as the best way to draw attention to the injustices done to women throughout the world. Although the foundation of feminism may be traced back to the earlier time in France, the Netherlands, and England in 1872 and 1890, the rise of women's activism began in the 1960s.

Feminism began as a scholastic trend before transitioning into a socio-political movement. These events contributed to the rise of feminism. The 1960s and 1970s saw the westernization of the idea, which is now of global significance. What do women need? was one of feminism's central questions. Who is the real advocate for women? These are the most frequently asked questions within feminism. According to commentator Carmen Vasquez, women's activists have differing opinions about the significance and meaning of feminism[9]. He adds that there are as many definitions of feminism as there are women's activists. The examination of modern feminism addresses a variety of female circumstances, including: a) the language used to describe women; b) the evaluation of women's value; and c) the potential of feminism. Showalter, a prominent somewhat English-speaking American women's rights campaigner, referred to the underlying interests in traditional core concepts like depiction, themes, and subject. Some commentators, including Derrida, agreed that the intellectual messages don't adequately address the current reality.

Perspectives of Feminism in contemporary Indian English literature is vibrant. In contemporary Indian English literature, feminism takes center stage, showcasing diverse perspectives and struggles faced by women. These narratives delve into societal norms, cultural expectations, and the evolving roles of women, offering a vivid portrayal of their experiences. Authors like Arundhati Roy, Anita Desai, and Arundhati Roy have skillfully woven feminist themes into their works, shedding light on the challenges women encounter in a patriarchal society. Through their stories, they depict the complexities of gender inequality, discrimination, and the quest for female empowerment. Indian literature reflects the multifaceted nature of feminism, exploring various facets such as intersectionality, caste, class, and regional differences impacting women's lives. Characters often grapple with societal pressures, familial obligations, and the struggle for identity and independence. These narratives also highlight the resilience and agency of women, showcasing their strength in overcoming adversity. They challenge stereotypes and redefine traditional gender roles, offering a nuanced perspective on feminism that goes beyond a mere binary outlook.

Moreover, contemporary Indian English literature serves as a platform for marginalized voices, amplifying the experiences of LGBTQ+ individuals, women from diverse backgrounds, and those facing multiple forms of oppression. The exploration of feminist themes in Indian literature invites readers to introspect, fostering conversations about gender dynamics, social justice, and the need for inclusive and equitable societies. It encourages readers to critically examine societal norms and advocate for change, promoting a more egalitarian future. In conclusion, contemporary Indian English literature offers a rich tapestry of feminist perspectives, exploring the complexities of women's lives and their ongoing struggle for equality. These narratives not only entertain but also enlighten and provoke thoughts, contributing to the broader discourse on feminism and societal transformation.

Meanwhile, Selden divides the focus of works on abstract feminism into five categories viz. Science, which frequently views women as inferior, feeble, and weak; Experience; difficulties with the menstrual cycle, childbirth, breastfeeding, etc. are generally seen as having only limited insight in women; Men make "firm requests," while women speak with less authority. Due of this, it will induce women to make unfavorable assumptions about men; women will merely wink; By casual interactions, feminist researchers have undermined masculine power. The sexuality of women is developing, disobedient, unique, and open. In any case, males still tend to acknowledge this less; Men's social and financial requirements are regularly made by women's activist founders. Women's activist-positioned academic scientists can select only a few decisions from these several centers as being more important. If the expansive idea of "intersectionality" was enthusiastically adopted in the 1990s and the middle of the 2000s, and furthermore, it appeared that there was a general disregard for the origins, context, and implications of the concept, in more recent years, intersectionality has been the subject of analysis in women's activist theory[10]. I now move to a few of such evaluations, focusing specifically on those that contradict the four scientific benefits I discussed in the previous section.

Alice Ludvig has argued that intersectionality faces challenges because the social world is "unrealistically complicated," despite intersectionality's scientific guarantee to capture core complexity without reducing or splitting contemporaneous encounters with mistreatment. The continuation of contrasts, in Ludvig's opinion, is a weak point in the multidimensional hypothesis. What basis is there for deciding which classes are noteworthy at any given time? Ludvig points out, for instance, that it is frequently impractical for a woman to draw the conclusion that she has been oppressed because of her orientation or for another reason, like an unfamiliar accent, even though she is aware of the specific type of overt bias at play in a separation encounter. Shuddhabrata Sengupta agrees with Ludwig that the phenomenology of abuse finally resists its reduction to "tomahawks," "designs," or even "frameworks"; the "variable based math of our reality" is too unchangeably perplexing and problematic, mocking even a methodology that intends to catch immutability[11]. In any case, Ludwig asserts that the definitional problem facing intersectionality researchers is "who characterizes when, when, which, and why specific contrasts are given attention while others are not"? Additionally, Kathryn Russell maintains that we need 'contentions about when and when we might underline one factor over another' as well as 'investigations concerning how orientation, race, and class are related'. Russell suggests that 'present grant is by all accounts locked in a tight position between exploding social classifications together and isolating them out in a rundown'. Undoubtedly, Crenshaw's initial discussion of intersectionality anticipates this circumstance, whether to straighten or fragment social encounters of various persecutions. What this arrangement of responses reveals is that much 'multifaceted' insightful examination, which accepts the stability and informative force of monistic classifications even as it investigates their changes and mixes, has avoided the strategic and applied challenge that intersectionality presents to categorical essentialism. These categories have been described as having a "verifiable base" in the interactions of typically unique subgroups. Instead of problematical zing the connections between abuse frameworks and personality traits, Russell's "tight spot" and Ludvig's definitional question for intersectionality presuppose their sufficiency[12]. The conflating of "complexity" and "specificity" with more aggressively persecuted groups, such as "ladies with an unfamiliar highlight," and the conflating of "straightforwardness" and "no exclusiveness" with (generally) favored groups, such as "ladies without a complement designated as unfamiliar," reveals that only one pivot system is anticipated.

Challenges and Opportunities in Feminism in India:

1. The Commission on the Situation with Ladies affirms the Beijing Declaration and Action Plan, the minutes of the Twenty-third Special Meeting of the General Gathering, and the statements made by the Commission on the occasion of the Tenth, Fifteenth, and Twenty-First Commemorations of the Fourth World Gathering on Ladies[13].

2. The Commission emphasizes that the Convention on the Elimination of All Forms of Gender-Based Violence Against Women and the Convention on the Rights of the Child, and the Discretionary Conventions Thereto, as well as other relevant conventions and agreements, such as the Global Contract on Financial, Social, and Social Freedoms and the Worldwide Pledge on Common and Political Privileges, provide a global legal system and a comprehensive arrangement of measures for recognizing orientation balance and the strengthening

3. The Commission reaffirms that the Beijing Statement and Stage for Activity, the result reports of its surveys, the outcomes of relevant major Joined Countries meetings and highest points, as well as the progression to those gatherings and culminations, have established a strong starting point for practical turn of events, and that the full, powerful, and accelerated execution of the Beijing Statement and Stage for Activity will make an

essential commitment to the execution of the Beijing Declaration and Stage for Activity

4. The Commission also affirms the commitments made to promoting equity and the empowerment of all women and young women at significant United Nations summits and meetings, keeping in mind the World Gathering for Population and Advancement, its programme of activities, and the survey results that it commissioned. It believes that the Sendai System for Calamity Danger Decrease 2015–2030, the Addis Ababa Activity Plan of the Third World Conference on Financing for Advancement, and the New Metropolitan Plan all help, among other things, to the betterment of the situation of young and rural women[14]. The Commission examines the Paris Agreement, which was adopted as part of the Assembled Nations Framework Convention on Climate Change.

5. The Commission also examines the New York Announcement for Displaced People and Transients and the Declaration on the Right to Advancement.

6. The Commission recognizes the importance of relevant Global Work Association standards related to the recognition that women have a greater than equal right to work and that workplace freedoms are essential for the financial empowerment of women, keeping in mind those for rural areas. The Commission also reviews the respected work plan of the Worldwide Work Association and the Global Work Association Announcement on Central Standards and Privileges at Work and notes the significance of them.

7. The Commission acknowledges the significant pretended contributions made by territorial drives, instruments, and shows in their respective districts and nations, as well as in their follow-up systems, to the achievement of gender equity and the

empowerment of all women and young women, keeping in mind those for provincial regions[15].

8. The Commission emphasizes the relationship that is steadily improving between achieving orientation fairness and the empowerment of all women and young women, keeping in mind those in provincial regions, as well as the full, powerful, and expedited execution of the Beijing Statement and Stage for Activity and the orientation responsive execution of the 2030 Plan for Maintainable Turn of Events. In order to achieve practical outcomes, advance peaceful, just, and comprehensive social orders, improve maintained, comprehensive, and manageable monetary development and efficiency, end neediness in all of its structures and aspects globally, and ensure the public good, it is recognized that orientation fairness and the strengthening of country ladies, young ladies, and women's full and equal support and administration in the economy are essential.

9. The Commission reaffirms that advancing, ensuring, and respecting the fundamental liberties and opportunities of all women and young women, including the right to improvement, which are widely shared, unified, connected, and interconnected, are essential for women's financial strength and should be incorporated into all strategies and projects aimed at eliminating destitution and strengthening women's finances[16]. The Commission also reiterates the need for:

10. The Commission believes that the 2030 Plan can only be successfully implemented if provincial women have the same financial freedoms, financial security, and autonomy as men. It emphasizes the value of making administrative and other changes to recognize the equal freedoms of women and men, as well as young women and young men where appropriate, to access financial and useful assets, including real estate and other natural resources, property rights, and legacy privileges, while also fitting new and existing technology, financial products and services,

including but not limited to microfinance, and women's full and useful business and respectable work.

Because women are tired of being subjected to everything, feminism was developed. Late specialists and pundits have become more aware of feminism and women's issues. It is clear that the Women's activist speculative design is essential for any scholarly study that examines female issues. In order to better understand and analyses any obstacles faced by women's activists, hypothetical discussions on the ideal models for women's freedoms are crucial. The current study focuses on one of the concerns surrounding women's freedom and the progression of the various stages that women's privileges have undergone, as well as the major researchers and their points of view. The core of a woman's privileges is the male transcendence that underpins a society that is dominated by men. Several women's activist pundits have analyzed this power and the issues surrounding the liberation of women from male bonds and socio-familial structures, and they have presented their perspectives in pertinent key articles and books addressing the women's activist hypothesis. Feminist theories would undoubtedly aid experts and commentators in their analysis of current or previous utterances. Although I briefly assessed the overall merits of the aforementioned analyses, it is much more crucial to note that many fundamental commitments with respect to "intersectionality" address the ways in which the concept has penetrated various fields of study, experimental locales, and philosophical spheres, as opposed to Crenshaw's own generative work or the more extensive collection of integrative grants delivered by Dark women's activist.

References

1. Balachandranan, K. *Essays on Canadian Literature*, Prakash Books Depot, Bareilly, 2001
2. Berger, Michele Tracy and Kathleen Guidroz, eds. *The Intersectional Approach: Transforming the Academy Through Race, Class, and Gender*, The University of North Carolina Press, Chapel Hill. 2009
3. Bilge, Sirma. 'Recent Feminist Outlooks on Intersectionality,' *Diogenes* Vol. 57, 2010, pp. 58–72
4. Bowleg, Lisa. 'When Black + Lesbian + Woman ≠ Black Lesbian Woman: The Methodological Challenges of Qualitative and Quantitative Intersectionality Research,' *Sex Roles*, 59, 5–6, 2008, pp. 312–25
5. Chang, Robert S. and Jerome McCristal Culp, Jr. 'After Intersectionality,' *UMKC Law Review* 71, 2002, pp. 485–91
6. Cole, Elizabeth R. 'Coalitions as a Model for Intersectionality: From Practice to Theory,' *Sex Roles* 59, 5–6, 2008, pp. 443–53
7. Davis, Kathy. 'Intersectionality as Buzzword: A Sociology of Science Perspective on What Makes a Feminist Theory Successful,' *Feminist Theory*, vol. 9.1, 2008, pp. 67–85
8. Dhamoon, Rita Kaur. 'Considerations on Mainstreaming Intersectionality,' *Political Research Quarterly*, 64.1, 2011, pp. 230–43
9. Dill, Bonnie Thornton and Ruth Enid Zambrana. 'Critical Thinking About Inequality: An Emerging Lens,' in *Emerging Intersections: Race, Class, and Gender in Theory, Policy and Practice*, edited by Bonnie Thornton Dill and Ruth Enid Zambrana, Rutgers University Press, New Jersey, New Brunswick, 2009, pp. 1–21
10. Pyyhtinen, Olli. *Simmel and "the social"*, Palgrave Macmillan, New York, 2010
11. Quoted by N. Krishnaswamy et.al. *Contemporary Literary Theory*, Macmillan, New Delhi, 2001, p.73
12. Ratna, Nyoman K., *Teori, Metode, dan Teknik Penelitian Sastra*, Pustaka Pelajar, Yogyakarta, 2004
13. Shukla, Bhaskar. *Feminism and Post feminism: the Context of Modern India Women Poets Writing in English*, Sarup and Sons, New Delhi, 2004, p.30
14. Sugihastuti. *Teori dan Apresiasi Sastra*, Pustaka pelajar. Yogyakarta, 2002
15. Suharto, Sugiharti. *Kritik Sastra Feminis, Teori dan Aplikasinya*, Pustaka Jaya, 2002
16. Yasa, I Nyoman. *Teori Sastra dan Penerapannya*, Karya Putra Darwanti, Bandung, 2012

Mahasweta Devi's Draupadi: A Historical Perspective and the Role of the State

Sukanta Barman

When ideology fails, Louis Althusser holds, repressive state apparatuses (RSA)[1] come into force, in order to convince the dominated class that whatever the state is doing, is actually doing for the best interest of its people. The state is more lethal about this towards its marginalised, "unprivileged and underdeveloped" people, the subaltern people, to borrow a phrase from Gramsci, Guha and Spivak.[2] Among the subalterns, there is the dalit subaltern, and within the dalit subaltern, one category that suffers most and gets brutally exploited is the female dalit subaltern. India is a great nation and has a great cultural and spiritual past. It had great leaders and even now seems to have great leaders, if few. Inspite of this, it has not progressed as it was thought to. After independence and till now, the state is shamelessly and blatantly using its 'coercive power'[3] to subdue the female dalit subalterns, regardless of them posing a threat. Mahasweta Devi is a modern Indian writer. Her story "Draupadi" exposes the brutality of the so-called highly cultured and high-heritage nation called India through its antagonist and associates, whereas the identity of the rebel dalits in general and the rebel dalit women in particular is annihilated. The resistance of a naked female body, just like the epical Draupadi, shames us all. It is also seen as a rebuttal to the embedded and towering patriarchy in our society. Dopdi Mejhen's case is not only a slap on the face of patriarchy, it is an irreversible slap on the face of the nation.

In her essay, Radha Chakravarty observes, "Dopdi Mejhen in Draupadi is a tribal woman involved in the Naxalbari insurgency... and Dopdi is an outcaste excluded from the mainstream on account of her tribal descent yet determined to play her part in the political arena."[4] Stories like Mahasweta Devi's "Draupadi" draw material from contemporary history – so the historiography of such stories cannot be dismissed. Devi herself said "I have always people's version of history ... In all my writings I have tried to present the subaltern point of view."[5] Although Mahaweta Devi says that "When I write, I never think of myself as a woman. I look at the class, not at the gender problem."[6] But by the way it has indeed become a gender problem of a tribal woman in particular and tribal women and all women in general, as observed by Radha Chakravarty. Thus, subaltern and subaltern females are two major themes of Devi. By the way, "subaltern" is a term coined by Antonio Gramsci, whereas Ranajit Guha used it extensively and Gayatri Chakravarty Spivak popularised it.[7] Devi also said 'My approach is forensic [...] everywhere, my search is for what lies behind."[8] So history, subaltern, female subaltern, tribal female subaltern – all these things boil down to one figure –Dopdi Mejhen in "Draupadi".

As Chakravarty continues, the "outcasts and the dispossededed"[9] are Devi's main subjects of her subaltern presentation of women. Tribal women like Dopdi Mejhen become her spokespersons. Dopdi is the "underprivileged"[10] woman in the "hierarchy of exclusions."[11] Though gendered representation does not get priority in Devi we see rather a contradiction in the case of Draupadi in the story. Here Dopdi is fighting with her destiny after her rape.

There has not been a single word mentioned about what happened to Draupadi Mejhen after her multiple rapes. We have extensively prided ourselves on the naked resistance that

Draupadi bluntly showed to Senanayak. We are overtly satisfied with that. Have we ever thought beyond that? What could possibly happen to Dopdi Mejhen after that beastly encounter with the police men? The story does not mention it. Let's imagine. Perhaps she was again raped by Senanayak himself, not been able to digest the fierce defiant resistance from Dopdi. It's also possible that the police force presents there also raped her again and again. It's unlikely she was released after that final confrontation with Senanayak. Perhaps she was taken into police custody for some more time. There also perhaps she was again raped. All these *perhapss* are the only reality to the fate of Dopdi. There is little chance that something otherwise could happen to Dopdi, as unfortunate was her destiny. It would not be wrong to say that the answer to Dopdi's question lies with the government and its ideology. Any government's chief objective is to subdue, to dominate, to suppress, to rule, and that is to be done by any "method" suitable to the government. When it fails in ideology, it always switches to its proven method of coercive powers.

The historical background of Devi's story "Draupadi" goes back to Naxalbari Movements of the 1960s. Leftist politics, rather extreme leftist politics ruled the Bengal landscape from 1950s onwards, as opined by Gautam Chattopadhyaya.[12] Leftist intellectualism created a lot of unease to the Central Government led by Congress Party in India. In mid-1960s a farmer's revolution in Naxalbari tried to shake the foundation of Indian State. Marcus Franda observed that "unlike most other areas of West Bengal, where peasant movements are led almost solely by middle-class leadership from Calcutta, Naxalbari has spawned an indigenous agrarian reform leadership led by the lower classes"[13] including the tribals. The combination of poor tribal farmers that included women and the strong leftist gentlemen intellectuals was very deadly and created a strong wave of rebellion – it sent a clear message that Naxalbari Movement did not remain localised to a single place called Naxalbari but it spread itself to some other sensitive parts of India. The Naxalbari Movement revolted against an unethical coalition of government and the landed class, though the nexus was never officially admitted, but as the victims of such coupling suffered first-hand, they took resolutions to take up arms. Government of India was highly alerted by this, as it is reflected in the book "Naxalbari and After: A Frontier Anthology".[14]

At the beginning of 1970s, East Pakistan now Bangladesh had a tough time fighting the atrocities and exploitations of the armed forces of West Pakistan now Pakistan, to snatch away their long-cherished freedom, based on linguistic demands. Government of India was very sensitive on this issue and feared a possible armed uprising if the tribal peasants of West Bengal joined hands with freedom fighters (*muktiyoddhas*) of East Pakistan at the instigation of gentlemen revolutionaries of Bengal who were ideologically extreme Leftists.[15] Government of India thought it to a threat to its sovereignty and strategically employed huge military and police force to ruthlessly subdue the Naxalbari Movements. It treacherously cracked down even the shadow of a revolution. As Lawrence Lifschultz observes, "If a guerrilla-style insurgency had persisted, these forces would undoubtedly have come to dominate the politics of the movement. It was this trend that the Indian authorities were determined to pre-empt by intervention."[16] It is in this context that the case of tribal women such as Dopdi Mejhen is pertinent. Unquestionably the government of India failed in its ideology to convince its tribal population about its so-called good governance and attitude towards equality. Therefore, the State itself had to employ what Althusser calls "Repressive State

Apparatuses", represented by the figures like Captain Arjan Singh and Senanayak in the story.

Antonio Gramsci writes, "The relationship between the intellectuals and the world of production is not as direct as it is with the fundamental social groups but is, in varying degrees, 'mediated' by the whole fabric of society and by the complex superstructures, of which the intellectuals are, precisely, the 'functionaries'. It should be possible both to measure the 'organic quality' of the various intellectual strata and their degree of connection with a fundamental social group, and to establish a gradation of their functions and of the superstructures from the bottom to the top (from the structural base upwards). What we can do, for the moment, is to fix two major superstructural 'levels': the one that can be called 'civil society', that is the ensemble of organisms commonly called 'private', and that of 'political society' or 'the State'. These two levels correspond on the one hand to the function of 'hegemony' which the dominant social group exercises throughout society and on the other hand to that of 'direct domination' or command exercised through the State and 'juridical' government. The functions in question are precisely organisational and connective. The intellectuals are the dominant's group's 'deputies' exercising the subaltern functions of social hegemony and the political government. These comprise: 1. The 'spontaneous' consent given by the great masses of the population to the general direction imposed on social life by the dominant fundamental group; this consent is 'historically' caused by the prestige (and consequent confidence) which the dominant group enjoys because of its position and function in the world of production. 2. The apparatus of state coercive power which 'legally' enforces discipline on those groups who do not 'consent' either actively or passively. This apparatus is, however, constituted for the whole of society in anticipation of moments of crisis of command and direction when spontaneous consent has failed."[17]

It is observable from the story of Devi's "Draupadi" that the consent was not obtained from the poor tribal mass, or the tribal mass did not give their consent or the government felt it below dignity to ask for consent from the tribal mass. In any case the general well-being of the tribal population is not taken into account seriously and sincerely – whatever minimum is done is done for the ruling class or ruling party's or government's vested interest, perhaps for a vote bank politics in a romanticised democracy like ours. So, nothing fruitful happens due to the lack of a proper political will. They are always left in the dark, unnoticed, uncared, and unnourished. The State fails to fulfil its duty towards its marginalised citizens. They rebel and the government comes down heavily on them, failing ideologically. They employ what Gramsci calls the "apparatus of state coercive power". This is when "spontaneous consent has failed." In order to maintain their "direct domination" the government has done so. The government in such act tried to correct a distorted history of the tribal poor.

Louis Althusser observes "...in the *Communist Manifesto* and the *Eighteenth Brumaire*...the State is explicitly conceived as a repressive apparatus. The State is a 'machine' of repression, which enables the ruling classes (in the nineteenth century the bourgeois class and the 'class' of big landowners) to ensure their domination over the working class, thus enabling the former to subject the latter to the process of surplus-value extortion (i.e., to capitalist exploitation). "The State is thus first of all what the Marxist classics have called the State Apparatus. This term means: not only the specialized apparatus (in the narrow sense) whose existence and necessity I have recognised in relation to the requirements of legal practice, i.e., the police, the courts, the prisons; but also the army, which (the proletariat has paid for this experience with its blood)intervenes directly as a supplementary repressive force in the last instance, when the police and its specialized auxiliary corps are "outrun by events"; and above this ensemble, the head of State, the government and the administration. "Presented in this form, the Marxist-Leninist 'theory' of the State has its finger on the essential point, and not for one moment can there be any question of rejecting the fact that this really is the essential point. The State Apparatus, which defines the State as a force of repressive execution and intervention 'in the interests of the ruling classes' in the class struggle conducted by the bourgeoisie and its allies against the proletariat, is quite certainly the State, and quite certainly defines its basic 'function'...Thus, the definition of the State as a class State, existing in the Repressive State Appratus, casts a brilliant light on all the facts observable in the various orders or repression whatever their domains: from the massacres of June 1848 and of the Paris Commune, of Bloody Sunday, May1905 in Petrograd, of the Resistance, of Charone, etc., to the mere (and relatively anodyne) interventions of a 'censorship' which has banned Diderot's La Religieuse or a play by Gatti on Franco; it casts light on all direct or indirect forms of exploitation and extermination of the masses of the people (imperialist wars); it casts light on that subtle everyday domination beneath which can be glimpsed, in the forms of political democracy, for example, what Lenin, following Marx, called the dictatorship of the bourgeoisie..."[18]

We have a similar instance in case of Dopdi Mejhen - the tribal woman trying hard to save the interest of her class, the proletariat class. Her revolt is against people like Surjo Sahu and other figures who have created man-made inequality in society for their own self-interest. So, the point raised by

Althusser is not amiss. Following Gramsci, Louis Althusser holds that the State is obviously a repressive machine, an instrument of torture. As in case of "Draupadi", it helps the landed class or the bourgeois or the rich or the bureaucrats in every way possible at the cost of poor tribal lives. It does not make any distinction between tribal males or tribal females. The atrocities that are shown in the story "Draupadi" show this blatantly. The dead bodies of tribals are found with their hands tied at the backside. Bones are broken. Eyes are plucked. Obviously, every body part is brutally mutilated even after death.[19] The treatment to females is even more horrific. When Dopdi Mejehn is apprehended by Senanayak and Co., she has been ordered by Senanayak, an expert in extreme left politics, to "make" her.[20] To make is the other name to 'rape' her. How could a high government officer like Senanayak deliver such an order? Is he backed up by his superiors in the Cabinet? Obviously, he is, otherwise he could not do this and for this he is not answerable to anybody. Interestingly, all the lower officers and constables comply the order of Senanayak - they have properly "made" her. Multiple rapes on her over a period of time have taken place – nobody's conscience has risen. Is this the method of the state? Obviously, it is. When the State is frightened, even by a poor tribal woman like Dopdi, it deliberately does the most heinous act, most hated thing in the history of mankind, in order to flex its muscle. And the government is shameless in this regard. To show others, to show the possible rebels what could happen to them, Dopdi's case is showcased to the world. The government thinks it is its victory. But victory cannot be done through rape.

Rekha in her essay observes, "Being a tribal, a woman and a naxalite, Dopdi vis-á-vis the patriarchal state bears a brunt of triple deviancy. She is a political, moral and gender deviant. Outside the pale of normative gendered boundaries, as envisioned by the 'other,' she can be 'made up' without compunction. It is ironically at this juncture that she, till now at the receiving end of the "voice of the male authority" finally emerges as an autonomous agent of her own subject. In the process, she in turn 'unmakes' her making and thus reverses the subject-object equation and emerges as the most powerful subject. Like Dhouli, Dopdi's empowerment, at best, remains tentative. The forces of exploitation have received a setback but only temporarily. Nevertheless, a possible space for resistance has been explored."[21]

It is Dopdi's power borne out of perhaps her pure blood theory that she has shown fierce resistance in front of Senanayak. She retains her dignity as a woman- she is unwilling to clothe herself - nobody is able to clothe her and she comes full naked with her mangled breasts and distorted and bleeding vagina to confront Senanayak, to tell him bluntly to "counter"[22] her. Senanayak is morally defeated and frightened perhaps for the first time in his life before a woman, nay, before an unarmed woman, completely devoid of clothing. His shirt is stained, metaphorically, the honour of the government or the government official is stained. Dopdi remains invincible- she uses her raped body as an instrument of resistance and for the time being she comes out victorious. Rekha further observes that in "'Draupadi' Mahasweta Devi moves from socio-cultural to political spaces to problematize the subaltern women's location within these spaces. Both the colonial and the post-colonial spaces are fraught with similar spatial divisions that hierarchies and otherize and thus lead to multiple exploitation of the tribals, especially tribal women…In 'Draupadi' Mahasweta Devi takes up the spatial probe of female existence from multiple angles. Herein a tribal woman, Dopdi, is situated at the intersection of class struggle within the contours of gender and nation. This location is then used as a creative pre-text to explore its repercussions on/for the protagonist."²³

The condition of tribal marginalised dalit subalterns like Dopdi is the moot point of today's debate. She is a woman, she is a tribal, she is poor, she has no formal education, she has not been provided any health facility whatsoever- she kills the mice of her head with kerosene, she has nothing to eat- only occasionally somebody like Mushai Tudu's wife gives her some rice with no curry. Yet the State is afraid of beings like her. The state without fulfilling its duty prefers to "make" her and ultimately to kill her, thus suppressing, subduing and subjugating a voice that needs to be heard. What more pathetic than this could be in a modern state like ours! The country is deriving a sadistic pleasure in crucifying figures like Dopdi and to project her as "the other". Rekha is apt to hold that Draupadi is a case of "subalterization, genderization and marginalization." "In 'Draupadi' Mahasweta Devi takes up the spatial probe of female existence from multiple angles. Herein a tribal woman, Dopdi, is situated at the intersection of class struggle within the contours of gender and nation. This location is then used as a creative pre-text to explore its repercussions on/for the protagonist."²⁴

Then what may be the possible future of Dopdi Mejhen? The "sexual politics" of Dopdi has been made a textual politics by Devi. The story of rape victim is not rare in literature. Rajeswari Sunder Rajan cites several examples of such victims. Samuel Richardson's Clarrissa Harlowe, E. M. Forster's Miss Adela Quested in *"A Passage to India"*, Hardy's Tess in *"Tess of the d'Urbervilles", Galsworthy's* Irene Forsythe in *"The Man of Property"* are some of the examples where "rape serves as an allegory for other political encounters."²⁵ Clarrissa painfully declares: "I am a cipher." As Rajan rightly observes, "All that is really left for the raped woman to do is to fade away: Adela, doing the decent thing, retracts her charge and returns to England; Clarissa, transcending her body's humiliation, falls ill and dies."[26] What other thing may happen to Dopdi Mejhen after her rape multiple in nature? The answer is not given but it is not difficult to assume that her future is a grim and dark one.

Dopdi Mejhen has been named after the Mahabharat protagonist Draupadi. Draupadi had a cause to fight. Here in Devi's story the natural question is whose Mahabharata is she fighting? In a larger sense she is fighting the Mahabharata of her own people, the tribal people, and the tribal women. Her story is not as glorious as Draupadi, the wife of the Pandavas. In fact, her husband Dulna Majhi dies at the hands of police, whereas the husbands of Panchali live and live gloriously. The Draupadi of the Mahbharata has been humiliated through an effort in disrobing her but thanks to Krishna, the Kauravas have not been successful. Here Dopdi has been stripped naked, has been raped, she has nothing but a bare body to hold on. Yet she holds to the last straw, her body, which becomes a unique weapon to resistance. The fight of Dopdi is even more critical than the Draupadi of the Mahabharata. Vrinda Nabar makes a just observation in this regard. "Mahasweta Devi's Draupadi is no royal princess but a tribal woman caught in the crossfire between Naxal rebels and the establishment...In captivity, Dopdi faces a worse fate than her namesake. This is real life, not mythology and no Krishna appears to protect her shame. She is unconscious as she is stripped naked, tortured, mutilated and raped, her breasts bitten raw, the nipples torn. But unlike Draupadi, Dopdi does not seek to conceal her shame. Though tactically defeated and ostensibly a "victim", Mahasweta's Draupadi retains her dignity."[27] At the end Dopdi asks, "Are you a man?... There isn't a man here that I should be ashamed."[28]

And Senanayak is no man just as the State is not manly. The State is challenged by Dopdi. It is the state which is ultimately subdued and humiliated. To Dopdi and to thousands like Dopdi, the state itself has become terrified by a bare woman's body. As Deepti Misri has written: "In "Draupadi" Mahasweta renders the state as a gendered institution that bestows on its male, upper-caste representatives a prosthetic masculinity that stems from official power. The masculinity of the army officers Senanayak and Arjan Singh derives from precisely such an institutional arrangement...But while it is true that the male organ of a gun keeps the law in place by backing up its foundational authority, Mahasweta shows that the power of the state is also contingent on the obedience and docility of its subjects. In the story's conclusion, the multiply-raped Draupadi issues a brazen challenge to the state agents whose masculinity resides in state power."[29] In the book, "Seeing Like a State" James C Scott makes an interesting observation which may be pertinent here. Modern countries have a tendency to impose all its ideologies and principles on their citizens, if need be, forcefully, and do not mind impose them with taxes or lives. Senanayak is such an agent through which the state achieves such feats. Rape or rather custodial rape is weapon in the hands of figures like Senanayak. "Draupadi's raped body is made allegorically representative of the rebel community but also (and specifically) of female rebels who are particularly susceptible to this form of disciplinary violence."[30]

References

1. Althusser, Louis. "Ideology and ideological state apparatuses (notes towards an investigation)," *The anthropology of the state: A reader:* 9.1, 2006, pp.86-98
2. Antonio Gramsci coined the term 'subaltern', whereas Ranajit Guha used it extensively in "Subaltern Studies' and Gayatri Chakravarty Spivak popularised it in "Can the Subaltern Speak?"

3. Gramsci, Antonio. "The intellectuals," - From Prison Notebooks, Contemporary *sociological thought–Themes and theories*, 2005, pp. 49-58
4. Chakravarty, Radha. "Other Histories: Gender and Politics in the Fiction of Mahasweta Devi", *India International Centre*, Winter 2012-Spring 2013, Vol. 39, No. ¾, pp. 122-133.
5. Devi, Mahasweta. *The Queen of Jhansi*, Original Bengali version. Translated by Sagaree and Mandira Sengupta (in 2000), *Seagull*, Kolkata, 1956
6. Chakravarty, Radha. Op. cit., pp. 122-133
7. Spivak, Gayatri Chakravorty. 'Can the Subaltern Speak?', in Patrick Williams and Laura Chrisman (eds.), *Colonial Discourse and Postcolonial Theory*, Columbia University Press, New York, 1994.
8. Devi. Mahasweta. "Personal interview", 8 August 1999. Calcutta
9. Chakravarty, Radha. Op. cit.
10. Ibid.
11. Ibid.
12. Chattopadhyaya, Gautam. Communism and the Freedom Movement in Bengal, Cambridge University Press, New Delhi, 1970
13. Franda, F Marcus. *Radical Politics in West Bengal*, Mass., Cambridge, 1971, p-153.
14. Sen, Samar, Debabrata Panda, and Ashish Lahiri. *Naxalbari and After: A Frontier Anthology*, Kathashilpa Calcutta, *2 Vol*, 1978.
15. In the Introduction to the translation of Devi's "Draupadi" by Gayatri Chakravarty Spivak in Critical Inquiry, The University of Chicago, Winter 1981.
16. Lifschultz, Lawrence. *The Unfinished Revolution, London*, 1979, pp. 25-26
17. Gramsci, Antonio. Op. cit., pp. 49-58.
18. Althusser, Louis. Op. cit., pp.86-98.
19. All references and quotations of "Draupadi" have been taken from Spivak's translation of Devi's "Draupadi" from Critical Inquiry. Op. cit.
20. Ibid.
21. Rekha. "The Poetics and Politics of Space: A Reading of Mahasweta Devi's Subaltern Stories," *Indian Literature*, Vol. 54, No. 6, November/December 2010, Sahitya Akademi, pp. 143-160
22. Spivak. Gayatri Chakravorty. (1981) Op. cit.
23. Rekha. Op. cit., pp. 143-160
24. Ibid.

25. Rajan, Rajeswari Sunder. "Life after Rape: Narrative, Theory, and Feminism," in *Borderwork - Feminist Engagements with Comparative Literature* (ed.) Margaret R. Higonnet. Cornell University Press, New York, 1994

26. Ibid.

27. Nabar, Vrinda. "Whose "Mahabharat"? A Point of View", *Indian Literature*, Vol. 49, No. 1, Jan-Feb 2005, Sahitya Akademi, pp. 176-185.

28. Spivak. Gayatri Chakravorty. (1981) Op. cit.

29. Misri, Deepti. "Are you a man? Performing Naked Protest in India", Signs, Vol. 36, No. 3, Spring 2011, The University of Chicago Press, pp. 603-625.

30. Scott, James C. *Seeing Like a State: How Certain Schemes to Improve the Human Condition Have Failed,* Yale University Press, New Haven, 1998.

Authors' Identity

Professor Alok Kumar Ghosh: HOD, Department of History, University of Kalyani, W.B.

Dr. Indra Kumar Mistri: Principal, Murshidabad Adarsha Mahavidyalaya, (University of Kalyani), Murshidabad, W.B.

Dr. Firoj High Sarwar: Assistant Professor of History, Murshidabad Adarsha Mahavidyalaya, (University of Kalyani) Murshidabad, W.B.

Biswarup Ganguly: Assistant Professor of History, Murshidabad Adarsha Mahavidyalaya, (University of Kalyani) Murshidabad, W.B.

Dr. Md Zaharul Hoque: Assistant Professor, Department of Teacher Education, Baba Saheb Ambedkar Education University.

Dr. Dhananjoy Mahato: Assistant Professor of Philosophy, Murshidabad Adarsha Mahavidyalaya, Murshidabad, W.B.

Dr. Mst. Swapna Khatun: Assistant Professor, Department of Political Science, North-Bengal International University, Rajshahi, Bangladesh

Dr. Bikash Das: Assistant Professor of History, Raja Birendra Chandra College, Murshidabad, W.B.

Dr. Kutubuddin Biswas: Associate Professor, Department of History, J. R. Mahavidyalaya, Murshidabad, W.B.

Dr. Tafajul Hoque: Assistant Professor, Basantapur Education College, Murshidabad, W.B.

Md Ajijur Rahaman: Assistant Professor in History, Gorubathan Govt. College, Kalimpong, W.B.

Arindam Mandal: Assistant Professor, K. N. College, Murshidabad, W.B.

Md Jamirul Islam: Assistant Professor, Department of Political Science, Vijaygarh Jyotish Ray College, Kolkata, W.B.

Md Kawsar Hossain: Assistant Professor, Department of Education, Domkal Girls' College, Murshidabad, W.B.

Milan Chandra Roy: Assistant Professor, Department of History, Syamsundar College, Burdwan, W.B.

Tonmoy Dey: Assistant Professor of History, Krishnagar Government College, Nadia, W.B.

Papia Biswas: Assistant Professor, Department of History, Murshidabad Adarsha Mahavidyalaya, Murshidabad, W.B.

Ersad Ali: Assistant Professor of History, Raja Birendra Chandra College, Murshidabad, W.B.

Mousumi Singha: Assistant Professor, Department of Bengali, Murshidabad Adarsha Mahavidyalaya, Murshidabad, W.B.

Manas Kumar Das: Assistant Professor of History, Dumkal College, Murshidabad, W.B.

Sukanta Barman: Assistant Professor, Department of English, Murshidabad Adarsha Mahavidyalaya, Murshidabad, W.B

Chinmoy Ghosh: Librarian, Birbhum Mahavidyalaya, Birbhum, W.B.

Ismail Sarkar: State aided college teacher, Department of English, Murshidabad Adarsha Mahavidyalaya, Murshidabad, W.B.

Biplab Mondal: State Aided College Teacher, Political Science, Suri Vidyasagar College, Birbhum, W. B.

Benazir Rahaman: State Aided College Teacher, Department of Political Science, Prof. Syed Nurul Hasan College, Murshidabad, W.B.

Sujoy Pal: Guest Lecturer, Department- Political Science, Bimal Chandra College of Law, W.B.

Animesh Chowdhury: State Aided College Teacher, Department of Political Science, Kandi Raj College, Murshidabad, W.B.

Shantanu Das: State Aided College Teacher, Dept. of English, Bardwan Mahavidyalaya, Purulia, W.B.

Ramkrishna Das: State aided college teacher, Department of English, Sagardighi K. K. S. Mahavidyalaya, Murshidabad, W.B.

Rajarshi Maity: State aided college teacher, Department of English, Sagardighi K. K. S. Mahavidyalaya, Murshidabad, W.B.

Tawsif Ahmed: State aided college teacher, Department of Political Science, Murshidabad Adarsha Mahavidyalaya, Murshidabad, W.B.

Anusree Kundu: State aided college teacher, Department of Geography, Murshidabad Adarsha Mahavidyalaya, Murshidabad, W.B.

Soumyadipta Sinha: State Aided College Teacher, Department of History, Ananda Chandra College, Jalpaiguri, W.B.

Prosenjit das: State Aided College Teacher, Department of History, Nagar College, Murshidabad, W.B.

Nandita Das: State Aided College Teacher, Berhampore Girls' College, Murshidabad, West Bengal

Saidul Islam: State aided college teacher, Department of Education, Domkal Girls' College, Murshidabad, W.B.

Alampik Debbarma: Research Scholar, Tripura University, Tripura

Obaidul Hoque: Research Scholar at Darul Huda Islamic University, Kerala.

Prasanta Adhikary: Research Scholar, Department of Political Science, Seacom Skills University, Birbhum, W.B.

Raja Lohar: Research Scholar, Department of Political Science, University of North Bengal, W.B.

Santosh Mahato: Research Scholar, Department of History, Sidho-Kanho- Birsha University, Purulia, West Bengal

Md Sohel Mondal: Research Scholar, Darul Huda Islamic University, Kerala

Swakshadip Sarkar: Doctoral Candidate, Victoria University of Wellington, New Zealand

Tapas Mahato: Research Scholar, Department of History, Sidho- Kanho-Birsha University, Purulia, West Bengal

Jisan Sarowar: Ph. D Scholar, Department of Political Science, Aligarh Muslim University, UP

Md Rajibul Islam: Ph. D Scholar, Department of Political Science, Aligarh Muslim University, UP

Md Manzar Reza: Research scholar (PhD), Department of English. RKDF University, Ranchi.

Binita Bhakat: Research Scholar, Rabindra Bharati University, Kolkata, W.B.

Gopal Singha: PhD Scholar, Department of Islamic History and Culture, University of Calcutta, W.B

Yangji Tamang: Independent Scholar, University of North Bengal, W.B.

Kamal Hasan: Independent Scholar, Department of History, Aligarh Muslim University, UP

Reshmi Biswas: Independent Scholars, Department of Political Science, Calcutta University, Kolkata, W.B.

Suranjana Mitra: Independent Scholars, Department of Political Science, Calcutta University, Kolkata, W.B.

Priya Dutta: Independent Scholar, Murshidabad University, Murshidabad, W.B.

Namrata Dutta: Independent Scholar, Former affiliation to University of Kalyani, W.B.

Mohiuddin Shaikh: Independent Scholar, Former affiliation to University of Kalyani, W.B.

Md. Sk Maruf Azam: Independent Scholar, Former Associated to West Bengal State University, W.B.

Ibrahim Sk: Independent Scholar, Department of Political Science, Aligarh Muslim University, U.P.

Md Hashim Saikh: Independent Scholar, Department of Political Science, Indira Gandhi National Open University, New Delhi

Pipasa Kundu: Assistant Teacher, Murshidabad, W.B.

www.ingramcontent.com/pod-product-compliance
Lightning Source LLC
LaVergne TN
LVHW091651070526
838199LV00050B/2143